Dynamical Systems in Engineering

Dynamical Systems in Engineering

Editor

Ioannis Dassios

MDPI • Basel • Beijing • Wuhan • Barcelona • Belgrade • Manchester • Tokyo • Cluj • Tianjin

Editor
Ioannis Dassios
University College Dublin
Ireland

Editorial Office
MDPI
St. Alban-Anlage 66
4052 Basel, Switzerland

This is a reprint of articles from the Special Issue published online in the open access journal *Mathematics* (ISSN 2227-7390) (available at: https://www.mdpi.com/journal/mathematics/special_issues/Dynamical_Systems_in_Engineering).

For citation purposes, cite each article independently as indicated on the article page online and as indicated below:

LastName, A.A.; LastName, B.B.; LastName, C.C. Article Title. *Journal Name* **Year**, *Volume Number*, Page Range.

ISBN 978-3-0365-7109-6 (Hbk)
ISBN 978-3-0365-7108-9 (PDF)

© 2023 by the authors. Articles in this book are Open Access and distributed under the Creative Commons Attribution (CC BY) license, which allows users to download, copy and build upon published articles, as long as the author and publisher are properly credited, which ensures maximum dissemination and a wider impact of our publications.

The book as a whole is distributed by MDPI under the terms and conditions of the Creative Commons license CC BY-NC-ND.

Contents

About the Editor vii

Nehad Ali Shah, Ioannis Dassios, Essam R. El-Zahar, Jae Dong Chung and Somaye Taherifar
The Variational Iteration Transform Method for Solving the Time-Fractional Fornberg–Whitham Equation and Comparison with Decomposition Transform Method
Reprinted from: *Mathematics* **2021**, *9*, 141, doi:10.3390/math9020141 1

Odysseas Kosmas, Pieter Boom and Andrey P. Jivkov
On the Geometric Description of Nonlinear Elasticity via an Energy Approach Using Barycentric Coordinates
Reprinted from: *Mathematics* **2021**, *9*, 1689, doi:10.3390/math9141689 15

Fátima Cruz, Ricardo Almeida and Natália Martins
Variational Problems with Time Delay and Higher-Order Distributed-Order Fractional Derivatives with Arbitrary Kernels
Reprinted from: *Mathematics* **2021**, *9*, 1665, doi:10.3390/math9141665 31

Antonios Mitsopoulos and Michael Tsamparlis
Quadratic First Integrals of Time-Dependent Dynamical Systems of the Form $\ddot{q}^a = -\Gamma^a_{bc}\dot{q}^b\dot{q}^c - \omega(t)Q^a(q)$
Reprinted from: *Mathematics* **2021**, *9*, 1503, doi:10.3390/math9131503 49

Vasile Drăgan, Ivan Ganchev Ivanov, Ioan-Lucian Popa and Ovidiu Bagdasar
Closed-Loop Nash Equilibrium in the Class of Piecewise Constant Strategies in a Linear State Feedback Form for Stochastic LQ Games
Reprinted from: *Mathematics* **2021**, *9*, 2713, doi:10.3390/math9212713 87

Damir Vrančić and Mikuláš Huba
High-Order Filtered PID Controller Tuning Based on Magnitude Optimum
Reprinted from: *Mathematics* **2021**, *9*, 1340, doi:10.3390/math9121340 103

Javier Rico-Azagra and Montserrat Gil-Martínez
Feedforward of Measurable Disturbances to Improve Multi-Input Feedback Control
Reprinted from: *Mathematics* **2021**, *9*, 2114, doi:10.3390/math9172114 127

Sara I. Abdelsalam and Abdullah Z. Zaher
Leveraging Elasticity to Uncover the Role of Rabinowitsch Suspension through a Wavelike Conduit: Consolidated Blood Suspension Application
Reprinted from: *Mathematics* **2021**, *9*, 2008, doi:10.3390/math9162008 141

Elsayed Badr, Sultan Almotairi and Abdallah El Ghamry
A Comparative Study among New Hybrid Root Finding Algorithms and Traditional Methods
Reprinted from: *Mathematics* **2021**, *9*, 1306, doi:10.3390/math9111306 167

Usman Riaz, Akbar Zada, Zeeshan Ali, Ioan-Lucian Popa, Shahram Rezapour and Sina Etemad
On a Riemann–Liouville Type Implicit Coupled System via Generalized Boundary Conditions [†]
Reprinted from: *Mathematics* **2021**, *9*, 1205, doi:10.3390/math9111205 183

Meghadri Das, Guruprasad Samanta and Manuel De la Sen
Stability Analysis and Optimal Control of a Fractional Order Synthetic Drugs Transmission Model
Reprinted from: *Mathematics* **2021**, *9*, 703, doi:10.3390/math9070703 205

About the Editor

Ioannis Dassios

Ioannis Dassios is currently a UCD Research Fellow/Assistant Professor at University College Dublin, Ireland. His research interests include dynamical and control systems, dynamical networks, differential and difference equations, singular systems, systems of differential equations of fractional order, optimization methods, linear algebra, and mathematical modeling of engineering problems.

He studied Mathematics, completed a two-year M.Sc. in Applied Mathematics, and obtained his Ph.D. degree at University of Athens, Greece with the grade "Excellent" (the highest mark in the Greek system).

He had positions at the University of Edinburgh, U.K; University of Manchester, U.K.; and University of Limerick, Ireland.

He has published more than 110 articles, a book, and two edited books, has served as a reviewer more than 1100 times in more than 100 different in peer reviewed journals, and is also member of editorial boards of peer-reviewed journals (Mathematics and Computers in Simulation Elsevier (MATCOM), Applied Sciences, Mathematics MDPI, Open Physics DeGruyter, and Experimental Results Cambridge University Press, etc.). He has also been the Guest Editor of more than 15 Special Issues, and has been member in committees of international conferences (both organizing and technical).

Finally, he has received several awards (Grants for research results over the period 2016–2023 from the UCD Output-Based Research Support Scheme (OBRSS), the 325 Years of Fractional Calculus Award in testimony of the High Regard of my Achievements in the Area of Fractional Calculus and its Applications, several travel support awards by MDPI Basel Switzerland, "Top 1% peer reviewer in Mathematics and Engineering" award by Web of Science Group, Clarivative Analytics for three consecutive years.

Article

The Variational Iteration Transform Method for Solving the Time-Fractional Fornberg–Whitham Equation and Comparison with Decomposition Transform Method

Nehad Ali Shah [1,2,*], Ioannis Dassios [3], Essam R. El-Zahar [4,5], Jae Dong Chung [6] and Somaye Taherifar [7]

[1] Informetrics Research Group, Ton Duc Thang University, Ho Chi Minh City 58307, Vietnam
[2] Faculty of Mathematics & Statistics, Ton Duc Thang University, Ho Chi Minh City 58307, Vietnam
[3] AMPSAS, University College Dublin, D04 Dublin, Ireland; ioannis.dassios@ucd.ie
[4] Department of Mathematics, College of Science and Humanities in Al-Kharj, Prince Sattam bin Abdulaziz University, P.O. Box 83, Al-Kharj 11942, Saudi Arabia; er.elzahar@psau.edu.sa
[5] Department of Basic Engineering Science, Faculty of Engineering, Menoufia University, Shebin El-Kom 32511, Egypt
[6] Department of Mechanical Engineering, Sejong University, Seoul 05006, Korea; jdchung@sejong.ac.kr
[7] Department of Computer Sciences, Faculty of Mathematics and Computer Sciences, Shahid Chamran University of Ahvaz, Ahvaz 61355-145, Iran; s.taherifar@scu.ac.ir or s.taherifar@gmail.com
* Correspondence: nehad.ali.shah@tdtu.edu.vn

Abstract: In this article, modified techniques, namely the variational iteration transform and Shehu decomposition method, are implemented to achieve an approximate analytical solution for the time-fractional Fornberg–Whitham equation. A comparison is made between the results of the variational iteration transform method and the Shehu decomposition method. The solution procedure reveals that the variational iteration transform method and Shehu decomposition method is effective, reliable and straightforward. The variational iteration transform methods solve non-linear problems without using Adomian's polynomials and He's polynomials, which is a clear advantage over the decomposition technique. The solutions achieved are compared with the corresponding exact result to show the efficiency and accuracy of the existing methods in solving a wide variety of linear and non-linear problems arising in various science areas.

Keywords: Fractional Fornberg–Whitham equation; variational iteration transform method; Shehu decomposition method; partial differential equation; approximate solution; Caputo's operator

Citation: Shah, N.A.; Dassios, I.; El-Zahar, E.R.; Chung, J.D.; Taherifar, S. The Variational Iteration Transform Method for Solving the Time-Fractional Fornberg–Whitham Equation and Comparison with Decomposition Transform Method. *Mathematics* **2021**, *9*, 141. https://doi.org/10.3390/math9020141

Received: 7 December 2020
Accepted: 30 December 2020
Published: 11 January 2021

Publisher's Note: MDPI stays neutral with regard to jurisdictional claims in published maps and institutional affiliations.

Copyright: © 2021 by the authors. Licensee MDPI, Basel, Switzerland. This article is an open access article distributed under the terms and conditions of the Creative Commons Attribution (CC BY) license (https://creativecommons.org/licenses/by/4.0/).

1. Introduction

In recent decades, the fractional calculus (FC) implemented in several phenomena in physics, engineering, fluid mechanics, biology and other applied sciences can be defined very effectively using fractional calculus mathematical tools. Fractional derivatives (FDs) provide an excellent tool for describing the hereditary and memory properties of different processes and materials. The FD has occurred in several engineering and sciences problems such as diffusion and reaction processes, frequency-dependent signal processing and system identification, damping behaviour materials, relaxation and creeping for viscoelastic materials [1–4].

The analysis of nonlinear wave equations and their solutions is of vital significance in several fields of science. Travelling wave ideas are among the most attractive solutions for nonlinear fractional partial differential equations (FPDEs). Nonlinear FPDEs are commonly known as complex physical and mechanical processes. Therefore, it is of great significance to get exact solutions for nonlinear FPDEs, and in general, travelling wave solutions are among the exciting types of solutions for nonlinear FPDEs. On the other hand, other nonlinear FPDEs, such as the Kortewegde-Vries or the Camassa-Holm equations, have been identified to have several moving wave results. These are design equations for nonlinear multi-directional dispersive waves in shallow water [5,6].

The study of the Fornberg–Whitham equation (FWE) is of great importance in many fields of mathematical physics. The Fornberg–Whitham equation [7,8] is given as

$$D_\eta \mu - D_{\xi\xi\eta}\mu + D_\xi \mu = \mu D_{\xi\xi\xi}\mu - \mu D_\xi \mu + 3 D_\xi \mu D_{\xi\xi}\mu. \tag{1}$$

The qualitative behavior of wave breakage, a nonlinear dispersive wave equation, appears in the study. The FWE is shown to allow peakon solutions as a numerical simulation for limiting wave heights and the occurrence of wave breaks. In 1978, Fornberg and Whitham achieve a peaked solution of the form $\mu(\xi,\eta) = C e^{\left(-\frac{\xi}{2} - \frac{4\eta}{3}\right)}$, where C is constant. Tian and Zhou [2] have identified the implicit type of wave propagation solutions called antikink-like wave solutions and kink-like wave solutions. The analysis of FWEs by different numerical and analytical methods, such as Laplace decomposition technique [9], Lie Symmetry [10], variational iteration technique [11], differential transformation technique [12], new iterative technique [13], homotopy-perturbation technique [14] and homotopy analysis transform technique [15].

The variational iteration method was first developed by J.H.He and was successfully applied to autonomous ODEs in [16,17]. This technique has been demonstrated to be an effective method for solving different types of problems. Similarly, this method is modified with the Shehu transform method's help, so the modified technique is called the variational iteration transform method (VITM). Different types of DEs and PDEs have solved VITM. For instance, this technique is used for solving linear fractional differential equations in [18]. This technique is applied in [19] for solving nonlinear oscillator equations. As a benefit of VITM over Adomian's decomposition process, the former approach provides the problem's solution without computing Adomian's polynomials. This system gives a fast solution to the problem while the [20] mesh point methods provide approximation at mesh points. This method is also useful for obtaining an accurate approximation of the exact solution. G. Adomian is the American mathematician who introduced the Adomian decomposition method. It is focused on searching for solutions in the form of a series and on the decomposition of the nonlinear operator into a sequence where the terms are recurrently computed to use Adomian polynomials [21]. This technique is modified with Shehu transformation, so the modified approach is the Shehu decomposition method. This method is applied to the nonhomogeneous fractional differential equations [22–24].

The present manuscript is concerned with the analytical solution of time-fractional Fornberg–Whitham equation. The solution of time-fractional Fornberg–Whitham equation is a topic for the researchers since long. Recently the analytical solution of time-fractional Fornberg–Whitham equation is the main focus of the researchers and mathematicians. This was the challenging work to extend or develop the existing techniques for the solution of fractional-order Fornberg–Whitham equation. Many of them have got success and developed innovative techniques to solve fractional-order Fornberg–Whitham equation. In this regard, the current research work is a novel contribution towards the analytical solution of fractional-order Fornberg–Whitham equations. The present research work is conducted in a very simple and straightforward manner to achieve the analytical solutions of the targeted problems with a small amount of numerical calculations. The convergence of the proposed method is trivial. In conclusion the proposed technique are considered to be the sophisticated contribution towards the analytical solution of fractional-order partial differential equations which are frequently arising in science and engineering.

This article has used the Shehu decomposition method and the variational iteration transform method to solve the fractional-order Fornberg–Whitham equation, including Caputo sense in the fractional derivative. The SDM and VITM obtain semi-analytic solutions in the form of series solutions. It simply improves the original problem lucidly, and so one can test the result with high accuracy and convergence.

The outline of this article is as follows. In Section 2, the basic definition of Shehu transform and fractional calculus are discussed. In Section 3, the variational iteration transform method and Shehu decomposition method are discussed. In Section 4, two test examples of fractional-order Fornberg–Whitham equation are given to elucidate the suggested schemes. In Section 5, conclusions of the work.

2. Preliminaries Concepts

In this section of the article, we represent Caputo's fractional operator to inspect our proposed problem. In addition to this, we will give the basic concept of Shehu transform, inverse Shehu transform and the Shehu transform of nth derivative for further analysis and investigation.

Definition 1. *The Riemann-Liouville fractional integral is given by [25,26]*

$$I_0^\gamma f(\tau) = \frac{1}{\Gamma(\gamma)} \int_0^\eta (\eta - s)^{\gamma-1} f(s) ds. \qquad (2)$$

Definition 2. *The fractional-order derivative Caputo's operator of $h(\eta)$ is defined as [25,26]*

$$D_\eta^\gamma f(\eta) = I^{m-\gamma} f^m, \; m - 1 < \gamma < m, \; m \in \mathbb{N}$$
$$\frac{d^m}{d\eta_m} f(\eta), \; \gamma = m, \; m \in \mathbb{N}. \qquad (3)$$

Definition 3. *Shehu transform is modern and similar to other integral transform described for exponential order functions. In set A, we take a function is represented by [23,24,27]*

$$A = \{ f(\eta) : \exists, \rho_1, \rho_2 > 0, |f(\eta)| < Me^{\frac{|\eta|}{\rho_i}}, \; if \; \eta \in [0, \infty). \qquad (4)$$

The Shehu transform which is given by $S(.)$ for a function $f(\eta)$ is defined as

$$S\{f(\eta)\} = F(s, u) = \int_0^\infty f(\eta) e^{\frac{-s\eta}{u}} f(\eta) d\eta, \; \eta > 0, \; s > 0. \qquad (5)$$

The Shehu transform of a function $f(\eta)$ is $V(s, u)$: then $f(\eta)$ is called the inverse of $V(s, u)$ which is given as

$$S^{-1}\{F(s, u)\} = f(\eta), \; for \; \eta \geq 0, \; S^{-1} \; is \; inverse \; Shehu \; transformation. \qquad (6)$$

Definition 4. *Consider $f^{(m)}(\eta)$ be the m-th order classical derivative of the function $f(\eta) \in A$, then its Shehu integral transform is given by the following formula [23,24,27]:*

$$S\{f^{(m)}(\eta)\} = \left(\frac{s}{u}\right)^m F(s, u) - \sum_{k=0}^{m-1} \left(\frac{s}{u}\right)^{m-k-1} f^{(k)}(0), \; m \in \mathbb{N}. \qquad (7)$$

Definition 5. *The fractional order derivatives of Shehu transformation for [23,24,27]*

$$S\{f^{(\gamma)}(\eta)\} = \left(\frac{s}{u}\right)^\gamma F(s, u) - \sum_{k=0}^{m-1} \left(\frac{s}{u}\right)^{\gamma-k-1} f^{(k)}(0), \; m - 1 < \gamma \leq m. \qquad (8)$$

3. The Conceptualization of VITM

In this section discuses the VITM solution for FPDEs.

$$D_\eta^\gamma v(\xi,\zeta,\eta) + \tilde{\mathcal{G}}(\xi,\zeta,\eta) + \mathcal{N}(\xi,\zeta,\eta) - \mathcal{P}(\xi,\zeta,\eta) = 0, \quad m-1 < \gamma \leq m, \tag{9}$$

with the initial condition

$$v(\xi,\zeta,0) = g(\xi,\zeta), \tag{10}$$

where is $D_\eta^\gamma = \frac{\partial^\gamma}{\partial \eta^\gamma}$ the Caputo fractional derivative of order γ, $\tilde{\mathcal{G}}$, and $\mathcal{N}$, are linear and non-linear functions, respectively, and $\mathcal{P}$ are source operators.

The Shehu transform is implemented to Equation (9),

$$S[D_\eta^\gamma v(\xi,\zeta,\eta)] + S[\tilde{\mathcal{G}}(\xi,\zeta,\eta) + \mathcal{N}(\xi,\zeta,\eta) - \mathcal{P}(\xi,\zeta,\eta)] = 0. \tag{11}$$

Shehu transform the differentiation property is applying, we get

$$\frac{s^\gamma}{u^\gamma} S[v(\xi,\zeta,\eta)] - \frac{s^{\gamma-1}}{u^\gamma} v(\xi,\zeta,0) = -S[\tilde{\mathcal{G}}(\xi,\zeta,\eta) + \mathcal{N}(\xi,\zeta,\eta) - \mathcal{P}(\xi,\zeta,\eta)]. \tag{12}$$

The iterative scheme required the Lagrange multiplier as

$$\begin{aligned}S[v_{j+1}(\xi,\zeta,\eta)] = &S[v_j(\xi,\zeta,\eta)] + \lambda(s)\left[\frac{s^\gamma}{u^\gamma} S[v_j(\xi,\zeta,\eta)] - \frac{s^{\gamma-1}}{u^\gamma} v_j(\xi,\zeta,0)\right.\\ &\left. - S\{\tilde{\mathcal{G}}(\xi,\zeta,\eta) + \mathcal{N}(\xi,\zeta,\eta)\} - S[\mathcal{P}(\xi,\zeta,\eta)]\right].\end{aligned} \tag{13}$$

A Lagrange multiplier as

$$\lambda(s) = -\frac{u^\gamma}{s^\gamma}, \tag{14}$$

using inverse Shehu transformation S^{-1}, Equation (13) can be written as

$$v_{j+1}(\xi,\zeta,\eta) = v_j(\xi,\zeta,\eta) - S^{-1}\left[\frac{u^\gamma}{s^\gamma}\left[-S\{\tilde{\mathcal{G}}(\xi,\zeta,\eta) + \mathcal{N}(\xi,\zeta,\eta)\}\right] - S[\mathcal{P}(\xi,\zeta,\eta)]\right], \tag{15}$$

the initial value can be find as

$$v_0(\xi,\zeta,\eta) = S^{-1}\left[\frac{u^\gamma}{s^\gamma}\left\{\frac{s^{\gamma-1}}{u^\gamma} v(\xi,\zeta,0)\right\}\right]. \tag{16}$$

4. The Conceptualization of SDM

In this section, we discus the SDM solution of FPDEs.

$$D_\eta^\gamma v(\xi,\zeta,\eta) + \tilde{\mathcal{G}}(\xi,\zeta,\eta) + \mathcal{N}(\xi,\zeta,\eta) - \mathcal{P}(\xi,\zeta,\eta) = 0, \quad m-1 < \gamma \leq m, \tag{17}$$

with the initial condition

$$v(\xi,\zeta,0) = g(\xi,\zeta), \tag{18}$$

where is $D_\eta^\gamma = \frac{\partial^\gamma}{\partial \eta^\gamma}$ the Caputo fractional derivative of order γ, $\tilde{\mathcal{G}}$ and $\mathcal{N}$ are linear and non-linear functions, respectively, and $\mathcal{P}$ is source functions.

Apply Shehu transform to Equation (17),

$$S[D_\eta^\gamma v(\xi,\zeta,\eta)] + S[\tilde{\mathcal{G}}(\xi,\zeta,\eta) + \mathcal{N}(\xi,\zeta,\eta) - \mathcal{P}(\xi,\zeta,\eta)] = 0. \tag{19}$$

Applying the differentiation property of Shehu transform, we have

$$S[v(\xi,\zeta,\eta)] = \frac{1}{s}v(\xi,\zeta,0) + \frac{u^\gamma}{s^\gamma}S[\mathcal{P}(\xi,\zeta,\eta)] - \frac{u^\gamma}{s^\gamma}S\{\mathcal{G}(\xi,\zeta,\eta) + \mathcal{N}(\xi,\zeta,\eta)\}]. \quad (20)$$

SDM solution of infinite series $v(\xi,\zeta,\eta)$,

$$v(\xi,\zeta,\eta) = \sum_{j=0}^{\infty} v_m(\xi,\zeta,\eta). \quad (21)$$

The non-linear terms $\mathcal{N}$ is given as

$$\mathcal{N}(\xi,\zeta,\eta) = \sum_{j=0}^{\infty} \mathcal{A}_m. \quad (22)$$

The non-linear term can be find with the help of Adomian polynomials. So the Adomian polynomial formula is define as

$$\mathcal{A}_m = \frac{1}{j!}\left[\frac{\partial^m}{\partial \lambda^m}\left\{\mathcal{N}\left(\sum_{k=0}^{\infty}\lambda^k v_k\right)\right\}\right]_{\lambda=0}. \quad (23)$$

Putting Equations (21) and (22) into (20), gives

$$S\left[\sum_{j=0}^{\infty} v_m(\xi,\zeta,\eta)\right] = \frac{1}{s}v(\xi,\zeta,0) + \frac{u^\gamma}{s^\gamma}S\{\mathcal{P}(\xi,\zeta,\eta)\} - \frac{u^\gamma}{s^\gamma}S\left\{\mathcal{G}(\sum_{j=0}^{\infty}v_m) + \sum_{j=0}^{\infty}\mathcal{A}_m\right\}. \quad (24)$$

Using the inverse Shehu transform to Equation (24),

$$\sum_{j=0}^{\infty}v_m(\xi,\zeta,\eta) = S^{-1}\left[\frac{1}{s}v(\xi,\zeta,0) + \frac{u^\gamma}{s^\gamma}S\{\mathcal{P}(\xi,\zeta,\eta)\} - \frac{u^\gamma}{s^\gamma}S\left\{\mathcal{G}\left(\sum_{j=0}^{\infty}v_m\right) + \sum_{j=0}^{\infty}\mathcal{A}_m\right\}\right]. \quad (25)$$

Identify the following terms,

$$v_0(\xi,\zeta,\eta) = S^{-1}\left[\frac{1}{s}v(\xi,\zeta,0) + \frac{u^\gamma}{s^\gamma}S\{\mathcal{P}(\xi,\zeta,\eta)\}\right], \quad (26)$$

$$v_1(\xi,\zeta,\eta) = -S^{-1}\left[\frac{u^\gamma}{s^\gamma}S\{\mathcal{G}_1(v_0) + \mathcal{A}_0\}\right].$$

In general for $m \geq 1$, is define as

$$v_{j+1}(\xi,\zeta,\eta) = -S^{-1}\left[\frac{u^\gamma}{s^\gamma}S\{\mathcal{G}(v_m) + \mathcal{A}_m\}\right].$$

5. Implementation of Techniques

Example 1. *Consider the following fractional-order nonlinear Fornberg–Whitham:*

$$D_\eta^\gamma v - D_{\xi\xi\eta}v + D_\xi v = vD_{\xi\xi\xi}v - vD_\xi v + 3D_\xi v D_{\xi\xi}v, \quad 0 < \gamma \leq 1, \quad (27)$$

with the initial condition

$$v(\xi,0) = e^{\left(\frac{\xi}{2}\right)}. \quad (28)$$

Taking Shehu transform of (27),

$$\frac{s^\gamma}{u^\gamma}S[v(\xi,\eta)] - \frac{s^{\gamma-1}}{u^\gamma}v(\xi,0) = S\left[D_{\xi\xi\eta}v - D_\xi v + vD_{\xi\xi\xi}v - vD_\xi v + 3D_\xi v D_{\xi\xi}v\right].$$

Applying inverse Shehu transform

$$v(\xi,\eta) = S^{-1}\left[\frac{v(\xi,0)}{s} - \frac{u^\gamma}{s^\gamma}S\left[D_{\xi\xi\eta}v - D_\xi v + vD_{\xi\xi\xi}v - vD_\xi v + 3D_\xi v D_{\xi\xi}v\right]\right].$$

Using ADM procedure, we get

$$v_0(\xi,\eta) = S^{-1}\left[\frac{v(\xi,0)}{s}\right] = S^{-1}\left[\frac{e^{\left(\frac{\xi}{2}\right)}}{s}\right],$$

$$v_0(\xi,t) = e^{\left(\frac{\xi}{2}\right)}, \tag{29}$$

$$\sum_{j=0}^{\infty} v_{j+1}(\xi,\eta) = S^{-1}\left[\frac{u^\gamma}{s^\gamma}S\left[\sum_{j=0}^{\infty}(D_{\xi\xi\eta}v)_j - \sum_{j=0}^{\infty}(D_\xi v)_j + \sum_{j=0}^{\infty}A_j - \sum_{j=0}^{\infty}B_j + 3\sum_{j=0}^{\infty}C_j\right]\right], \quad j=0,1,2,\cdots$$

$$A_0(vD_{\xi\xi\xi}v) = v_0 D_{\xi\xi\xi} v_0,$$
$$A_1(vD_{\xi\xi\xi}v) = v_0 D_{\xi\xi\xi} v_1 + v_1 D_{\xi\xi\xi} v_0,$$
$$A_2(vD_{\xi\xi\xi}v) = v_1 D_{\xi\xi\xi} v_2 + v_1 D_{\xi\xi\xi} v_1 + v_2 D_{\xi\xi\xi} v_0,$$

$$B_0(vD_\xi v) = v_0 D_\xi v_0,$$
$$B_1(vD_\xi v) = v_0 D_\xi v_1 + v_1 D_\xi v_0,$$
$$B_2(vD_\xi v) = v_1 D_\xi v_2 + v_1 D_\xi v_1 + v_2 D_\xi v_0,$$

$$C_0(D_\xi v D_{\xi\xi} v) = D_\xi v_0 D_{\xi\xi} v_0,$$
$$C_1(D_\xi v D_{\xi\xi} v) = D_\xi v_0 D_{\xi\xi} v_1 + D_\xi v_1 D_{\xi\xi} v_0,$$
$$C_2(D_\xi v D_{\xi\xi} v) = D_\xi v_1 D_{\xi\xi} v_2 + D_\xi v_1 D_{\xi\xi} v_1 + D_\xi v_2 D_{\xi\xi} v_0,$$

for $j=1$

$$v_1(\xi,\eta) = S^{-1}\left[\frac{u^\gamma}{s^\gamma}S\left[D_{\xi\xi\eta}v_0 - D_\xi v_0 + A_0 - B_0 + 3C_0\right]\right],$$

$$v_1(\xi,t) = -\frac{1}{2}S^{-1}\left[\frac{u^\gamma e^{\left(\frac{\xi}{2}\right)}}{s^{\gamma+1}}\right] = -\frac{1}{2}e^{\left(\frac{\xi}{2}\right)}\frac{\eta^\gamma}{\Gamma(\gamma+1)}. \tag{30}$$

for $j=2$

$$v_2(\xi,\eta) = S^{-1}\left[\frac{u^\gamma}{s^\gamma}S\left[D_{\xi\xi\eta}v_1 - D_\xi v_1 + A_1 - B_1 + 3C_1\right]\right],$$

$$v_2(\xi,\eta) = -\frac{1}{8}e^{\left(\frac{\xi}{2}\right)}\frac{\eta^{2\gamma-1}}{\Gamma(2\gamma)} + \frac{1}{4}e^{\left(\frac{\xi}{2}\right)}\frac{\eta^{2\gamma}}{\Gamma(2\gamma+1)}, \tag{31}$$

for $j=3$

$$v_3(\xi,\eta) = S^{-1}\left[\frac{u^\gamma}{s^\gamma}S\left[D_{\xi\xi\eta}v_2 - D_\xi v_2 + A_2 - B_2 + 3C_2\right]\right],$$

$$v_3(\xi,\eta) = -\frac{1}{32}e^{\left(\frac{\xi}{2}\right)}\frac{\eta^{3\gamma-2}}{\Gamma(3\gamma-1)} + \frac{1}{8}e^{\left(\frac{\xi}{2}\right)}\frac{\eta^{3\gamma-1}}{\Gamma(3\gamma)} - \frac{1}{8}e^{\left(\frac{\xi}{2}\right)}\frac{\eta^{3\gamma}}{\Gamma(3\gamma+1)}, \tag{32}$$

The SDM solution for example (1) is

$$v(\xi,\eta) = v_0(\xi,\eta) + v_1(\xi,\eta) + v_2(\xi,\eta) + v_3(\xi,\eta) + v_4(\xi,\eta) + \cdots,$$

$$v(\xi,\eta) = e^{\left(\frac{\xi}{2}\right)} - \frac{1}{2}e^{\left(\frac{\xi}{2}\right)}\frac{\eta^\gamma}{\Gamma(\gamma+1)} - \frac{1}{8}e^{\left(\frac{\xi}{2}\right)}\frac{\eta^{2\gamma-1}}{\Gamma(2\gamma)} + \frac{1}{4}e^{\left(\frac{\xi}{2}\right)}\frac{\eta^{2\gamma}}{\Gamma(2\gamma+1)} - \frac{1}{32}e^{\left(\frac{\xi}{2}\right)}\frac{\eta^{3\gamma-2}}{\Gamma(3\gamma-1)}$$
$$+ \frac{1}{8}e^{\left(\frac{\xi}{2}\right)}\frac{\gamma^{3\gamma-1}}{\Gamma(3\gamma)} - \frac{1}{8}e^{\left(\frac{\xi}{2}\right)}\frac{\eta^{3\gamma}}{\Gamma(3\gamma+1)} - \cdots.$$
(33)

The simplification of Equation (33)

$$v(\xi,\eta) = e^{\left(\frac{\xi}{2}\right)}\left[1 - \frac{\eta^\gamma}{2\Gamma(\gamma+1)} - \frac{1}{8}\frac{\eta^{2\gamma-1}}{\Gamma(2\gamma)} + \frac{1}{4}\frac{\eta^{2\gamma}}{\Gamma(2\gamma+1)} - \frac{1}{32}\frac{\eta^{3\gamma-2}}{\Gamma(3\gamma-1)} + \frac{1}{8}\frac{\eta^{3\gamma-1}}{\Gamma(3\gamma)} - \frac{1}{8}\frac{\eta^{3\gamma}}{\Gamma(3\gamma+1)} + \cdots\right]. \quad (34)$$

The approximate solution by VITM.
The iteration formulas for Equation (27), we have

$$v_{j+1}(\xi,\eta) = v_j(\xi,\eta) - S^{-1}\left[\frac{u^\gamma}{s^\gamma}S\left\{\frac{s^\gamma}{u^\gamma}D_\eta v_j - D_{\xi\xi\eta}v_j + D_\xi v_j - v_j D_{\xi\xi\xi}v_j + v_j D_\xi v_j\right.\right.$$
$$\left.\left. - 3D_\xi v_j D_{\xi\xi}v_j\right\}\right], \quad (35)$$

where

$$v_0(\xi,t) = e^{\left(\frac{\xi}{2}\right)}. \quad (36)$$

For $j = 0, 1, 2, \cdots$

$$v_1(\xi,\eta) = v_0(\xi,\eta) - S^{-1}\left[\frac{u^\gamma}{s^\gamma}S\left\{\frac{s^\gamma}{u^\gamma}D_\eta v_0 - D_{\xi\xi\eta}v_0 + D_\xi v_0 - v_0 D_{\xi\xi\xi}v_0\right.\right.$$
$$\left.\left.+ v_0 D_\xi v_0 - 3D_\xi v_0 D_{\xi\xi}v_0\right\}\right],$$
$$v_1(\xi,\eta) = -\frac{1}{2}e^{\left(\frac{\xi}{2}\right)}\frac{\eta^\gamma}{\Gamma(\gamma+1)}, \quad (37)$$

$$v_2(\xi,\eta) = v_1(\xi,\eta) - S^{-1}\left[\frac{u^\gamma}{s^\gamma}S\left\{\frac{s^\gamma}{u^\gamma}D_\eta v_1 - D_{\xi\xi\eta}v_1 + D_\xi v_1 - v_1 D_{\xi\xi\xi}v_1\right.\right.$$
$$\left.\left.+ v_1 D_\xi v_1 - 3D_\xi v_1 D_{\xi\xi}v_1\right\}\right],$$
$$v_2(\xi,\eta) = -\frac{1}{8}e^{\left(\frac{\xi}{2}\right)}\frac{\eta^{2\gamma-1}}{\Gamma(2\gamma)} + \frac{1}{4}e^{\left(\frac{\xi}{2}\right)}\frac{\eta^{2\gamma}}{\Gamma(2\gamma+1)}, \quad (38)$$

$$v_3(\xi,\eta) = v_2(\xi,\eta) - S^{-1}\left[\frac{u^\gamma}{s^\gamma}S\left\{\frac{s^\gamma}{u^\gamma}D_\eta v_2 - D_{\xi\xi\eta}v_2 + D_\xi v_2 - v_2 D_{\xi\xi\xi}v_2\right.\right.$$
$$\left.\left.+ v_2 D_\xi v_2 - 3D_\xi v_2 D_{\xi\xi}v_2\right\}\right],$$
$$v_3(\xi,\eta) = -\frac{1}{32}e^{\left(\frac{\xi}{2}\right)}\frac{\eta^{3\gamma-2}}{\Gamma(3\gamma-1)} + \frac{1}{8}e^{\left(\frac{\xi}{2}\right)}\frac{\eta^{3\gamma-1}}{\Gamma(3\gamma)} - \frac{1}{8}e^{\left(\frac{\xi}{2}\right)}\frac{\eta^{3\gamma}}{\Gamma(3\gamma+1)}, \quad (39)$$

$$v(\xi,\eta) = \sum_{m=0}^\infty v_m(\xi,\zeta) = e^{\left(\frac{\xi}{2}\right)} - \frac{1}{2}e^{\left(\frac{\xi}{2}\right)}\frac{\eta^\gamma}{\Gamma(\gamma+1)} - \frac{1}{8}e^{\left(\frac{\xi}{2}\right)}\frac{\eta^{2\gamma-1}}{\Gamma(2\gamma)} + \frac{1}{4}e^{\left(\frac{\xi}{2}\right)}\frac{\eta^{2\gamma}}{\Gamma(2\gamma+1)}$$
$$- \frac{1}{32}e^{\left(\frac{\xi}{2}\right)}\frac{\eta^{3\gamma-2}}{\Gamma(3\gamma-1)} + \frac{1}{8}e^{\left(\frac{\xi}{2}\right)}\frac{\gamma^{3\gamma-1}}{\Gamma(3\gamma)} - \frac{1}{8}e^{\left(\frac{\xi}{2}\right)}\frac{\eta^{3\gamma}}{\Gamma(3\gamma+1)} - \cdots. \quad (40)$$

The exact solution of Equation (27) at $\gamma = 1$,

$$v(\xi,\eta) = e^{\left(\frac{\xi}{2} - \frac{2\eta}{3}\right)}. \quad (41)$$

Example 2. *Consider the following fractional-order nonlinear Fornberg–Whitham:*

$$D_\eta^\gamma v - D_{\xi\xi\eta} v + D_\xi v = v D_{\xi\xi\xi} v - v D_\xi v + 3 D_\xi v D_{\xi\xi} v, \quad \eta > 0, \quad 0 < \gamma \leq 1, \quad (42)$$

with the initial condition

$$v(\xi, 0) = \cosh^2\left(\frac{\xi}{4}\right). \quad (43)$$

Taking Shehu transform of (42),

$$\frac{s^\gamma}{u^\gamma} S[v(\xi,\eta)] - \frac{s^{\gamma-1}}{u^\gamma} v(\xi,0) = S\left[D_{\xi\xi\eta} v - D_\xi v + v D_{\xi\xi\xi} v - v D_\xi v + 3 D_\xi v D_{\xi\xi} v\right].$$

Applying inverse Shehu transform

$$v(\xi,\eta) = S^{-1}\left[\frac{v(\xi,0)}{s} - \frac{u^\gamma}{s^\gamma} S\{D_{\xi\xi\eta} v - D_\xi v + v D_{\xi\xi\xi} v - v D_\xi v + 3 D_\xi v D_{\xi\xi} v\}\right].$$

Using ADM procedure, we get

$$v_0(\xi,\eta) = S^{-1}\left[\frac{v(\xi,0)}{s}\right] = S^{-1}\left[\frac{\exp\left(\cosh^2\left(\frac{\xi}{4}\right)\right)}{s}\right],$$

$$v_0(\xi,t) = \cosh^2\left(\frac{\xi}{4}\right), \quad (44)$$

$$\sum_{j=0}^\infty v_{j+1}(\xi,\eta) = S^{-1}\left[\frac{u^\gamma}{s^\gamma} S\left[\sum_{j=0}^\infty (D_{\xi\xi\eta} v)_j - \sum_{j=0}^\infty (D_\xi v)_j + \sum_{j=0}^\infty A_j - \sum_{j=0}^\infty B_j + 3\sum_{j=0}^\infty C_j\right]\right], \quad j = 0,1,2,\cdots$$

for $j = 0$

$$v_1(\xi,\eta) = S^{-1}\left[\frac{u^\gamma}{s^\gamma} S[D_{\xi\xi\eta} v_0 - D_\xi v_0 + A_0 - B_0 + 3C_0]\right],$$

$$v_1(\xi,\eta) = -\frac{11}{32} S^{-1}\left[\frac{u^\gamma \sinh\left(\frac{x}{2}\right)}{s^{\gamma+1}}\right] = -\frac{11}{32} \sinh\left(\frac{\xi}{4}\right)\frac{\eta^\gamma}{\Gamma(\gamma+1)}. \quad (45)$$

for $j = 1$

$$v_2(\xi,\eta) = S^{-1}\left[\frac{u^\gamma}{s^\gamma} S[D_{\xi\xi\eta} v_1 - D_\xi v_1 + A_1 - B_1 + 3C_1]\right],$$

$$v_2(\xi,\eta) = -\frac{11}{28}\sinh\left(\frac{\xi}{4}\right)\frac{\eta^\gamma}{\Gamma(\gamma+1)} + \frac{121}{1024}\cosh\left(\frac{\xi}{4}\right)\frac{\eta^{2\gamma}}{\Gamma(2\gamma+1)}, \quad (46)$$

for $j = 2$

$$v_3(\xi,\eta) = S^{-1}\left[\frac{u^\gamma}{s^\gamma} S[D_{\xi\xi\eta} v_2 - D_\xi v_2 + A_2 - B_2 + 3C_2]\right],$$

$$v_3(\xi,\eta) = -\frac{11}{512}\sinh\left(\frac{\xi}{4}\right)\frac{\eta^\gamma}{\Gamma(\gamma+1)} + \frac{121}{2048}\cosh\left(\frac{\xi}{4}\right)\frac{\eta^{2\gamma}}{\Gamma(2\gamma+1)} - \frac{1331}{49152}\sinh\left(\frac{\xi}{4}\right)\frac{\eta^{3\gamma}}{\Gamma(3\gamma+1)}, \quad (47)$$

The SDM solution for example (2) is

$$v(\xi,\eta) = v_0(\xi,\eta) + v_1(\xi,\eta) + v_2(\xi,\eta) + v_3(\xi,\eta) + v_4(\xi,\eta) + \cdots,$$

$$v(\xi,\eta) = \cosh^2\left(\frac{\xi}{4}\right) - \frac{11}{32}\sinh\left(\frac{\xi}{4}\right)\frac{\eta^\gamma}{\Gamma(\gamma+1)} - \frac{11}{28}\sinh\left(\frac{\xi}{4}\right)\frac{\eta^\gamma}{\Gamma(\gamma+1)} + \frac{121}{1024}\cosh\left(\frac{\xi}{4}\right)\frac{\eta^{2\gamma}}{\Gamma(2\gamma+1)}$$
$$- \frac{11}{512}\sinh\left(\frac{\xi}{4}\right)\frac{\eta^\gamma}{\Gamma(\gamma+1)} + \frac{121}{2048}\cosh\left(\frac{\xi}{4}\right)\frac{\eta^{2\gamma}}{\Gamma(2\gamma+1)} - \frac{1331}{49152}\sinh\left(\frac{\xi}{4}\right)\frac{\eta^{3\gamma}}{\Gamma(3\gamma+1)} \cdots . \tag{48}$$

The approximate solution by VITM. The iteration formulas for Equation (42), we have

$$v_{j+1}(\xi,\eta) = v_j(\xi,\eta) - S^{-1}\left[\frac{u^\gamma}{s^\gamma}S\left\{\frac{s^\gamma}{u^\gamma}D_\eta v_j - D_{\xi\xi\eta}v_j + D_\xi v_j - v_j D_{\xi\xi\xi}v_j + v_j D_\xi v_j - 3D_\xi v_j D_{\xi\xi}v_j\right\}\right], \tag{49}$$

where

$$v_0(\xi,t) = \cosh^2\left(\frac{\xi}{4}\right). \tag{50}$$

For $j = 0, 1, 2, \cdots$

$$v_1(\xi,\eta) = v_0(\xi,\eta) - S^{-1}\left[\frac{u^\gamma}{s^\gamma}S\left\{\frac{s^\gamma}{u^\gamma}D_\eta v_0 - D_{\xi\xi\eta}v_0 + D_\xi v_0 - v_0 D_{\xi\xi\xi}v_0 + v_0 D_\xi v_0 - 3D_\xi v_0 D_{\xi\xi}v_0\right\}\right],$$
$$v_1(\xi,\eta) = \cosh^2\left(\frac{\xi}{4}\right) - \frac{11}{32}\sinh\left(\frac{\xi}{4}\right)\frac{\eta^\gamma}{\Gamma(\gamma+1)}, \tag{51}$$

$$v_2(\xi,\eta) = v_1(\xi,\eta) - S^{-1}\left[\frac{u^\gamma}{s^\gamma}S\left\{\frac{s^\gamma}{u^\gamma}D_\eta v_1 - D_{\xi\xi\eta}v_1 + D_\xi v_1 - v_1 D_{\xi\xi\xi}v_1 + v_1 D_\xi v_1 - 3D_\xi v_1 D_{\xi\xi}v_1\right\}\right],$$
$$v_2(\xi,\eta) = \cosh^2\left(\frac{\xi}{4}\right) - \frac{11}{32}\sinh\left(\frac{\xi}{4}\right)\frac{\eta^\gamma}{\Gamma(\gamma+1)} - \frac{11}{28}\sinh\left(\frac{\xi}{4}\right)\frac{\eta^\gamma}{\Gamma(\gamma+1)} + \frac{121}{1024}\cosh\left(\frac{\xi}{4}\right)\frac{\eta^{2\gamma}}{\Gamma(2\gamma+1)}, \tag{52}$$

$$v_3(\xi,\eta) = v_2(\xi,\eta) - S^{-1}\left[\frac{u^\gamma}{s^\gamma}S\left\{\frac{s^\gamma}{u^\gamma}D_\eta v_2 - D_{\xi\xi\eta}v_2 + D_\xi v_2 - v_2 D_{\xi\xi\xi}v_2 + v_2 D_\xi v_2 - 3D_\xi v_2 D_{\xi\xi}v_2\right\}\right],$$
$$v_3(\xi,\eta) = \cosh^2\left(\frac{\xi}{4}\right) - \frac{11}{32}\sinh\left(\frac{\xi}{4}\right)\frac{\eta^\gamma}{\Gamma(\gamma+1)} - \frac{11}{28}\sinh\left(\frac{\xi}{4}\right)\frac{\eta^\gamma}{\Gamma(\gamma+1)} + \frac{121}{1024}\cosh\left(\frac{\xi}{4}\right)\frac{\eta^{2\gamma}}{\Gamma(2\gamma+1)}, \tag{53}$$
$$- \frac{11}{512}\sinh\left(\frac{\xi}{4}\right)\frac{\eta^\gamma}{\Gamma(\gamma+1)} + \frac{121}{2048}\cosh\left(\frac{\xi}{4}\right)\frac{\eta^{2\gamma}}{\Gamma(2\gamma+1)} - \frac{1331}{49152}\sinh\left(\frac{\xi}{4}\right)\frac{\eta^{3\gamma}}{\Gamma(3\gamma+1)},$$

$$v(\xi,\eta) = \sum_{m=0}^\infty v_m(\xi,\zeta) = \cosh^2\left(\frac{\xi}{4}\right) - \frac{11}{32}\sinh\left(\frac{\xi}{4}\right)\frac{\eta^\gamma}{\Gamma(\gamma+1)} - \frac{11}{28}\sinh\left(\frac{\xi}{4}\right)\frac{\eta^\gamma}{\Gamma(\gamma+1)} + \frac{121}{1024}\cosh\left(\frac{\xi}{4}\right)\frac{\eta^{2\gamma}}{\Gamma(2\gamma+1)}, \tag{54}$$
$$- \frac{11}{512}\sinh\left(\frac{\xi}{4}\right)\frac{\eta^\gamma}{\Gamma(\gamma+1)} + \frac{121}{2048}\cosh\left(\frac{\xi}{4}\right)\frac{\eta^{2\gamma}}{\Gamma(2\gamma+1)} - \frac{1331}{49152}\sinh\left(\frac{\xi}{4}\right)\frac{\eta^{3\gamma}}{\Gamma(3\gamma+1)} - \cdots .$$

The exact solution of Equation (42) at $\gamma = 1$,

$$v(\xi,\eta) = \cosh^2\left(\frac{\xi}{4} - \frac{11\eta}{24}\right). \tag{55}$$

6. Results and Discussion

The present research work aims to find an analytical solution of time-fractional Fornberg–Whitham equations, implemented the efficient analytical methods. The variational iteration transform technique and Shehu decomposition technique are used to solve the targeted problems. To check the validity of the proposed methods, the solution of some illustrative problems are suggested. The solutions graphs are plotted for both fractional and integer-order problems. In Figure 1, (a) the exact and the approximate solution of example 1 at $\gamma = 1$ and (b) the analytical solution of different fractional-order of $\gamma = 1, 0.8, 0.6$ and 0.4. In Figure 2, (a) 3d graph of the exact and (b) the SDM and VITM solutions are plotted at $\gamma = 1$. It is observed that the exact, SDM and VITM solutions are in close contact with the exact result of the given problems. Also in Figure 3, (a) the exact and VITM and SDM solutions plot of example 1, (b) are calculated at different fractional-order $\gamma = 0.8, 0.6$ and Figure 4 show fractional-order $\gamma = 0.4$. It is confirmed that VITM and SDM results are in strong agreement with each other. The similar graphical analysis and discussion can be made for the solutions of example 2 in Figure 5, the 3d graph (a) the exact solution and (b) the SDM and VITM solution are discussed at $\gamma = 1$. Also in Figure 6, (a) the exact and VITM and SDM results plot of example 2 and (b) are calculated at different fractional-order $\gamma = 0.8, 0.6, 0.4$. In these graphs, it is investigated that both methods have a sufficient degree of accuracy. In Table 1 the SDM and VITM results are compared in terms of absolute errors for different fractional-order respectively. It has been shown that the proposed techniques have identical accuracy. It is investigated that results of fractional-order problems are convergent to an integer-order result as fractional-order analysis to integer-order. The same phenomenon of convergence of fractional-order solutions towards integral-order solutions is observed.

Table 1. The comparison between SDM and VITM for the approximate solution of example 1.

η	ζ	$\|Exact - SDM\|$	$\|Exact - SDM\|$	$\|Exact - VITM\|$	$\|Exact - VITM\|$
		$\gamma = 0.5$	$\gamma = 1$	$\gamma = 0.7$	$\gamma = 1$
0.1	0.5	$2.0515098570 \times 10^{-4}$	$4.0570000000 \times 10^{-8}$	$3.4157500000 \times 10^{-6}$	$4.0570000000 \times 10^{-8}$
	1	$8.4542014000 \times 10^{-4}$	$5.3500000000 \times 10^{-9}$	$1.4746800000 \times 10^{-7}$	$5.3500000000 \times 10^{-9}$
	1.5	$6.8110913000 \times 10^{-5}$	$7.5600000000 \times 10^{-10}$	$2.3936000000 \times 10^{-7}$	$7.5600000000 \times 10^{-10}$
	2	$7.4324428000 \times 10^{-4}$	$5.7400000000 \times 10^{-9}$	$1.3258200000 \times 10^{-6}$	$5.7400000000 \times 10^{-9}$
	2.5	$5.3344053000 \times 10^{-4}$	$8.5560000000 \times 10^{-9}$	$1.3236200000 \times 10^{-6}$	$8.5560000000 \times 10^{-9}$
	3	$7.4491757000 \times 10^{-3}$	$6.3450000000 \times 10^{-8}$	$3.6455200000 \times 10^{-6}$	$6.3450000000 \times 10^{-8}$
	3.5	$2.0565077000 \times 10^{-4}$	$6.4160000000 \times 10^{-8}$	$5.2393400000 \times 10^{-6}$	$6.4160000000 \times 10^{-8}$
	4	$4.4514678000 \times 10^{-4}$	$5.6400000000 \times 10^{-9}$	$4.5667200000 \times 10^{-6}$	$5.6400000000 \times 10^{-9}$
	4.5	$6.0056729000 \times 10^{-4}$	$4.4300000000 \times 10^{-9}$	$3.5344000000 \times 10^{-7}$	$4.4300000000 \times 10^{-9}$
	5	$7.4339041000 \times 10^{-4}$	$3.3700000000 \times 10^{-9}$	$2.3356500000 \times 10^{-7}$	$3.3700000000 \times 10^{-9}$

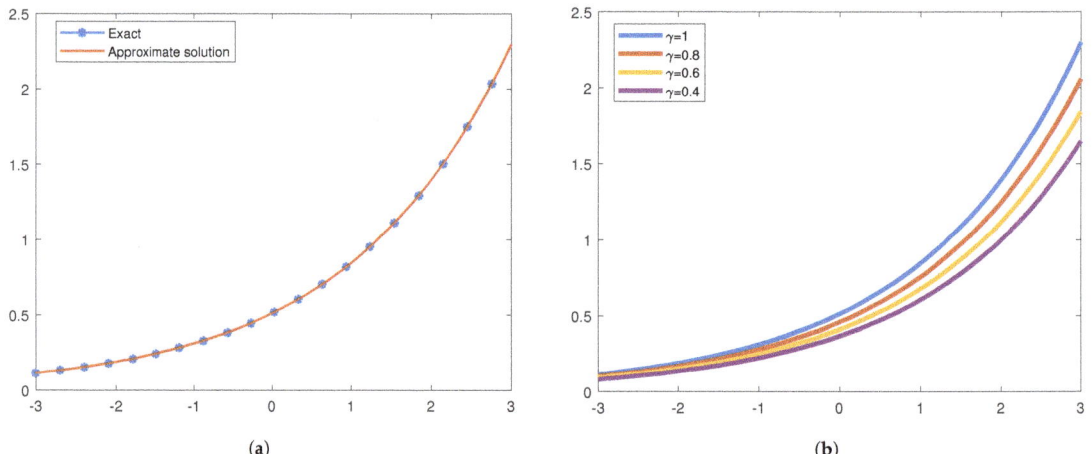

Figure 1. (a) Exact and approximate solution plot at $\gamma = 1$ of example 1. (b) Approximate solution plot of different fractional of example 1.

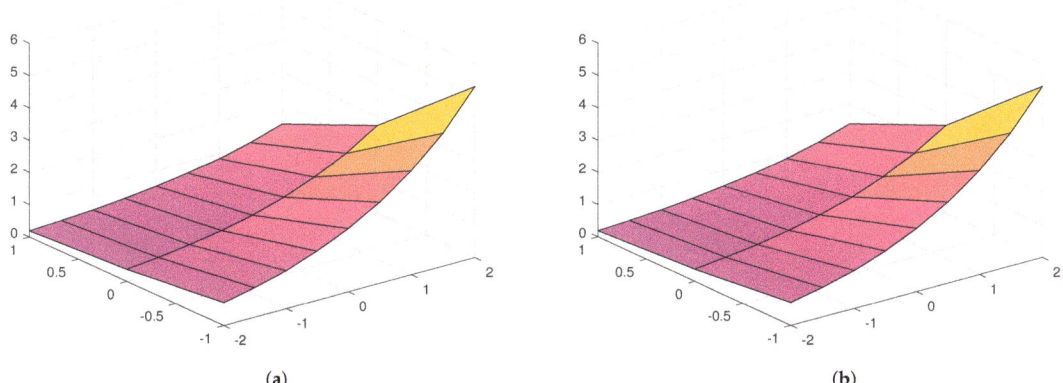

Figure 2. (**a**) Exact plot of example 1. (**b**) Comparison between approximate solution by SDM and VITM plot of example 1 at $\gamma = 1$.

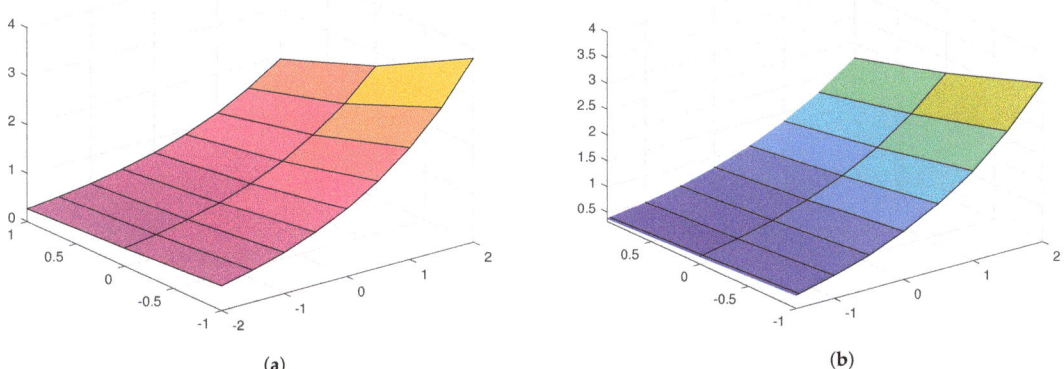

Figure 3. (**a**) Comparison between approximate solution by SDM and VITM plot of example 1 at $\gamma = 0.8$. (**b**) Comparison between approximate solution by SDM and VITM plot of example 1 at $\gamma = 0.6$.

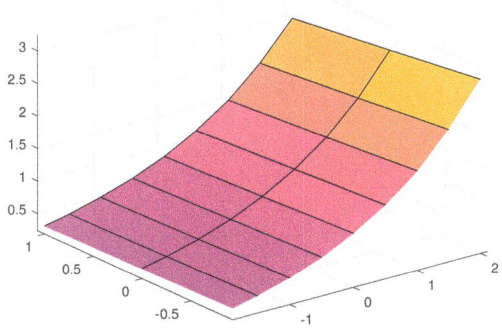

Figure 4. Comparison between approximate solution by SDM and VITM plot of example 1 at $\gamma = 0.4$.

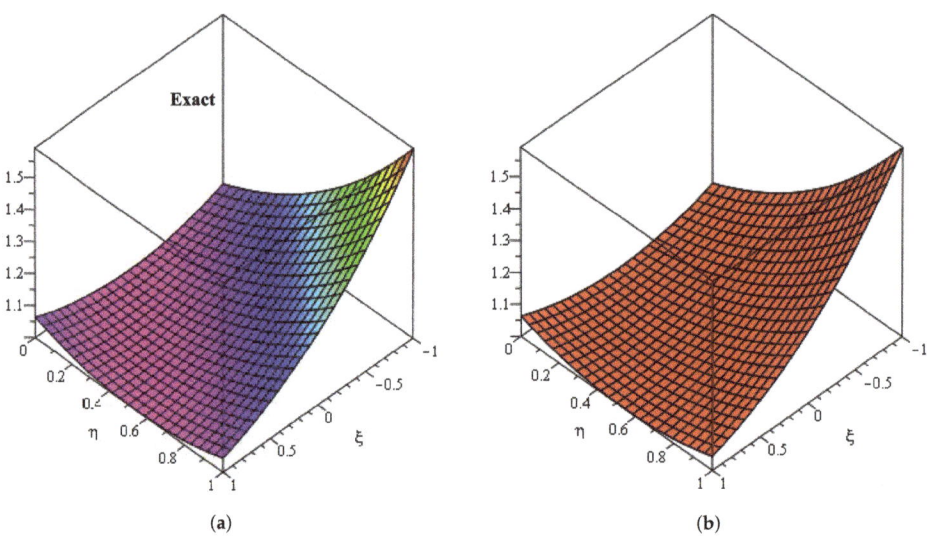

Figure 5. (**a**) Exact solution plot of example 2. (**b**) Comparison between approximate solution by SDM and VITM plot of Example 2 at $\gamma = 1$.

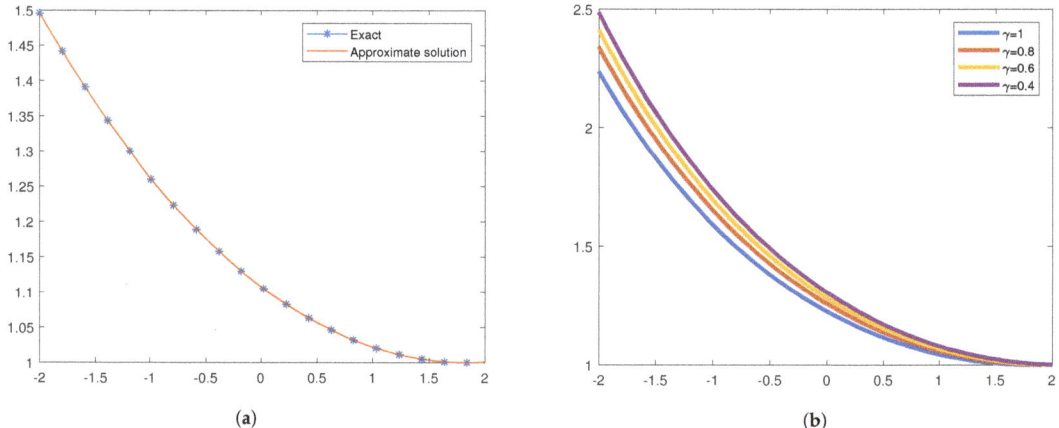

Figure 6. (**a**) Exact and approximate solution plot of example 2. (**b**) Approximate solution plot of different fractional of $\gamma = 1$ of example 2.

7. Conclusions

In this paper, we implemented Shehu decomposition method and variational iteration transform method for solving time-fractional Fornberg–Whitham equation. Some examples of the analytical solution are measured to confirm the accuracy and efficiency of the available method. Graphs and table of the solutions are plotted to show the closed contact between the obtained and exact solutions. The proposed techniques are easier and faster in their concepts and more effective in solving linear and non-linear fractional-order partial differential equation and useful technique for solving a broader class of non-linear fractional models in high precision applied mathematics.

Author Contributions: Conceptualization, N.A.S. and E.R.E.-Z.; methodology, N.A.S.; software, I.D. and E.R.E.-Z.; validation, S.T.; formal analysis, N.A.S. and I.D.; data curation, S.T.; writing–original draft preparation N.A.S.; writing–review and editing, I.D.; supervision, J.D.C.; project administration,

N.A.S.; funding acquisition, J.D.C. All authors have read and agreed to the published version of the manuscript.

Funding: This research received no external funding.

Acknowledgments: This work was supported by Korea Institute of Energy Technology Evaluation and Planning (KETEP) grant funded by the Korea government (MOTIE) (No. 20192010107020, Development of hybrid adsorption chiller using unutilized heat source of low temperature). S. Taherifar, would like to express her sincere gratitude to the Research Council of Shahid Chamran University of Ahvaz for its financial support (Grant No. SCU.MC99.29826).

Conflicts of Interest: The authors have no conflict of interest.

References

1. Hilfer, R. (Ed.) *Applications of Fractional Calculus in Physics*; World Scientific: Singapore, 2000; Volume 35, pp. 87–130.
2. Magin, R.L. *Fractional Calculus in Bioengineering*; Begell House: Redding, CA, USA, 2006; Volume 2.
3. Sabatier, J.A.T.M.J.; Agrawal, O.P.; Machado, J.T. *Advances in Fractional Calculus*; Springer: Dordrecht, The Netherlands, 2007; Volume 4.
4. Al-luhaibi, M.S. An analytical treatment to fractional Fornberg–Whitham equation. *Math. Sci.* **2017**, *11*, 1–6. [CrossRef]
5. Camacho, J.C.; Rosa, M.; Gandarias, M.L.; Bruzon, M.S. Classical symmetries, travelling wave solutions and conservation laws of a generalized Fornberg–Whitham equation. *J. Comput. Appl. Math.* **2017**, *318*, 149–155. [CrossRef]
6. Bruzon, M.S.; Marquez, A.P.; Garrido, T.M.; Recio, E.; de la Rosa, R. Conservation laws for a generalized seventh order KdV equation. *J. Comput. Appl. Math.* **2019**, *354*, 682–688. [CrossRef]
7. Whitham, G.B. Variational methods and applications to water waves. Proceedings of the Royal Society of London. Series A. *Math. Phys. Sci.* **1967**, *299*, 6–25.
8. Fornberg, B.; Whitham, G.B. A numerical and theoretical study of certain nonlinear wave phenomena. Philosophical Transactions of the Royal Society of London. *Ser. A Math. Phys. Sci.* **1978**, *289*, 373–404.
9. Kumar, D.; Singh, J.; Baleanu, D. A new analysis of the Fornberg–Whitham equation pertaining to a fractional derivative with Mittag-Leffler-type kernel. *Eur. Phys. J. Plus* **2018**, *133*, 1–10. [CrossRef]
10. Hashemi, M.S.; Haji-Badali, A.; Vafadar, P. Group invariant solutions and conservation laws of the Fornberg–Whitham equation. *Z. Naturforschung A* **2014**, *69*, 489–496. [CrossRef]
11. Lu, J. An analytical approach to the Fornberg–Whitham type equations by using the variational iteration method. *Comput. Math. Appl.* **2011**, *61*, 2010–2013. [CrossRef]
12. Merdan, M.; Gokdogan, A.; Yildirim, A.; Mohyud-Din, S.T. Numerical simulation of fractional Fornberg–Whitham equation by differential transformation method. *Abstr. Appl. Anal.* **2012**, *2012*, 965367. [CrossRef]
13. Ramadan, M. New Iterative Method for Solving the Fornberg-Whitham Equation and Comparison with Homotopy Perturbation Transform Method. *Br. J. Math. Comput. Sci.* **2014**, *4*, 1213–1227. [CrossRef]
14. Abidi, F.; Omrani, K. Numerical solutions for the nonlinear Fornberg–Whitham equation by He's methods. *Int. J. Mod. Phys. B* **2011**, *25*, 4721–4732. [CrossRef]
15. Wang, K.; Liu, S. Application of new iterative transform method and modified fractional homotopy analysis transform method for fractional Fornberg–Whitham equation. *J. Nonlinear Sci. Appl.* **2016**, *9*, 2419–2433. [CrossRef]
16. He, J.H. Approximate solution of nonlinear differential equations with convolution product nonlinearities. *Comput. Methods Appl. Mech. Eng.* **1998**, *167*, 69–73. [CrossRef]
17. He, J.H. Variational iteration method for autonomous ordinary differential systems. *Appl. Math. Comput.* **2000**, *114*, 115–123. [CrossRef]
18. Wu, G.C.; Baleanu, D. Variational iteration method for fractional calculus-a universal approach by Laplace transform. *Adv. Differ. Equ.* **2013**, *2013*, 1–9. [CrossRef]
19. Anjum, N.; He, J.H. Laplace transform: Making the variational iteration method easier. *Appl. Math. Lett.* **2019**, *92*, 134–138. [CrossRef]
20. Dehghan, M. Finite difference procedures for solving a problem arising in modeling and design of certain optoelectronic devices. *Math. Comput. Simul.* **2006**, *71*, 16–30. [CrossRef]
21. Adomian, G. *Solving Frontier Problems of Physics: The Decomposition Method*; Kluwer Academic Publishers: Boston, MA, USA, 1994.
22. Khalouta, A.; Kadem, A. A New Method to Solve Fractional Differential Equations: Inverse Fractional Shehu Transform Method. *Appl. Appl. Math.* **2019**, *14*, 926–941.
23. Bokhari, A.; Baleanu, D.; Belgacem, R. Application of Shehu transform to Atangana-Baleanu derivatives. *J. Math. Comput. Sci.* **2019**, *20*, 101–107. [CrossRef]
24. Belgacem, R.; Baleanu, D.; Bokhari, A. Shehu Transform and Applications to Caputo-Fractional Differential Equations. *Int. J. Anal. Appl.* **2019**, *17*, 917–927.
25. Machado, J.; Baleanu, D.; Chen, W.; Sabatier, J. New trends in fractional dynamics. *J. Vib. Control. SAGE Publ.* **2014**, *20*, 963. [CrossRef]

26. Baleanu, D.; Guvenc, Z.; Machado, J. *New Trends in Nanotechnology and Fractional Calculus Applications*; Springer: Dordrecht, The Netherlands, 2010.
27. Maitama, S.; Zhao, W. New integral transform: Shehu transform a generalization of Sumudu and Laplace transform for solving differential equations. *arXiv* **2019**, arXiv:1904.11370.

 *mathematics*

Article

On the Geometric Description of Nonlinear Elasticity via an Energy Approach Using Barycentric Coordinates

Odysseas Kosmas *, Pieter Boom and Andrey P. Jivkov

Department of MACE, University of Manchester, Oxford Road, Manchester M13 9PL, UK; pieter.boom@manchester.ac.uk (P.B.); andrey.jivkov@manchester.ac.uk (A.P.J.)
* Correspondence: odysseas.kosmas@manchester.ac.uk; Tel.: +44-(0)161-306-3727

Abstract: The deformation of a solid due to changing boundary conditions is described by a deformation gradient in Euclidean space. If the deformation process is reversible (conservative), the work done by the changing boundary conditions is stored as potential (elastic) energy, a function of the deformation gradient invariants. Based on this, in the present work we built a "discrete energy model" that uses maps between nodal positions of a discrete mesh linked with the invariants of the deformation gradient via standard barycentric coordinates. A special derivation is provided for domains tessellated by tetrahedrons, where the energy functionals are constrained by prescribed boundary conditions via Lagrange multipliers. The analysis of these domains is performed via energy minimisation, where the constraints are eliminated via pre-multiplication of the discrete equations by a discrete null-space matrix of the constraint gradients. Numerical examples are provided to verify the accuracy of the proposed technique. The standard barycentric coordinate system in this work is restricted to three-dimensional (3-D) convex polytopes. We show that for an explicit energy expression, applicable also to non-convex polytopes, the general barycentric coordinates constitute fundamental tools. We define, in addition, the discrete energy via a gradient for general polytopes, which is a natural extension of the definition for discrete domains tessellated by tetrahedra. We, finally, prove that the resulting expressions can consistently describe the deformation of solids.

Keywords: nonlinear elasticity; general barycentric coordinates; energy minimisation; Lagrange multipliers; null-space method

1. Introduction and Motivation

Computational solid mechanics provides approximate solutions for the deformation of continuous domains subjected to changes in boundary conditions [1–6]. The deformation process itself is described by using "intensive quantities"—stresses and strains—and a constitutive relation between them. These quantities have a geometric nature and form continuous tensor fields. The constitutive relation between stresses and strains may vary in the degree of complexity, depending on how the intensive quantities are related to the "extensive quantities"—forces and displacements. For example, the strains can be defined as linearised or nonlinear functions of the displacement gradient, but in all cases they must be symmetric tensors in order to fulfil physical objectivity. On the other hand, stresses can be defined as distributed forces with respect to a specific domain configuration, where the known true or Cauchy stresses are defined with respect to the current/deformed configuration. Furthermore, the simultaneous fulfilment of the balance of linear and angular momenta generates the symmetry of the stress tensor. As a consequence, the differential relations representing the strains as functions of displacements and equilibrium of stresses, together with the constitutive law, form a system of equations, the approximate solution of which is sought either by discretising the underlying solution space or by discretising the operators involved.

For the first approach (discretisation of the solution space), the most prominent example is the well-known finite element method. In this method, the standard finite

Citation: Kosmas, O.; Boom, P.; Jivkov, A.P. On the Geometric Description of Nonlinear Elasticity via an Energy Approach Using Barycentric Coordinates. *Mathematics* **2021**, *9*, 1689. https://doi.org/10.3390/math9141689

Academic Editor: Dumitru Baleanu

Received: 5 May 2021
Accepted: 7 July 2021
Published: 19 July 2021

Publisher's Note: MDPI stays neutral with regard to jurisdictional claims in published maps and institutional affiliations.

Copyright: © 2021 by the authors. Licensee MDPI, Basel, Switzerland. This article is an open access article distributed under the terms and conditions of the Creative Commons Attribution (CC BY) license (https://creativecommons.org/licenses/by/4.0/).

element formulations, which dominate commercial finite element analysis platforms, are based on a limited number of simple element geometries: triangles and quadrilaterals in 2D, and tetrahedra and hexahedra in 3D. While these are sufficient for most practical problems and make the implementation and the solution quite efficient, there are, however, situations where the use of general polyhedra as the indivisible units covering the domain can be really more advantageous. One obvious example of this kind is related to the representation of large polycrystalline microstructures or cellular assemblies, where the need to insert additional discretisation in the polyhedra may lead to computationally very expensive problems. This has led to developments of finite elements of the form of general polyhedra, including those using an arbitrary number of vertices and faces, those using generally non-convex polyhedra, and those using polyhedra with nonplanar faces [7–9]. In parallel, such general polyhedra proved to be the driving force for the recent development of the virtual element method [10,11]. However, to the best of our knowledge, methods that use general polyhedral meshing tools and then employ the subsequent solvers have not become fully established to date, and they remain in the academic domain.

The second approach (discretisation of the operators) is, to a large extent, based on the discrete differential geometry and was kept under development during the last 20 years. In this method, the discrete structure of the analysed solid at a given length-scale is considered as a starting point, i.e., the discretised computational domain is defined via the finite discrete nature of the solid constitution, and can be seen as an assembly of cells of arbitrary sizes and shapes. Concrete examples of this approach put further effort in order to preserve key properties of the system in terms of important invariants, such as energy, by proper discretisation of the operators. Even though these schemes have been well figured out/formulated and tested for a wide range of physical problems involving scalar fields, only a few of them have been proven to be stable when solving solid mechanics problems involving vector fields [12–14]. A notable approximation within this approach is the representation of the discrete system with a graph (contour) that allows rather simple formulations for the elasticity [15], the elasto-plasticity [16] and the elasto-plasticity involving damage [17].

For both of the aforementioned approaches in computational solid mechanics, the mesh quality plays crucial role in numerical simulations. For example, in several methods that rely on Voronoi meshes there may appear spurious solutions, mainly due to different scales of edges and faces (presence of small edges and/or faces), see, e.g., in [18] and references therein. Similar problems arising from mesh quality are present in several other methods, see, for example, in [13]. A common approach utilised to overcome such difficulties is the application of re-meshing: an initial tetrahedral mesh of any quality is used to create a new one with improved quality by appropriate merging of neighbouring tetrahedra. Examples of this technique can be found, e.g., in [19], using mesh-free methods, and in [20] using discontinuous Galerkin methods. Such a treatment, however, is not applicable in situations where a mesh representing some physically-based structure is required, e.g., an assembly of polytopes, and possible large differences in scales need to be handled. The effect of scale differences is quite strong due to the representation of differential operators in either approach, and could be overcome by an energy-based formulation.

The main aim of this work, is the consideration of the above open questions, focusing on the derivation of an appropriate energy-based model within the field of computational solid mechanics. This model would combine a continuum geometric description for the stresses and strains in the context of nonlinear elasticity, and a discrete energy formulation for tetrahedra as well as arbitrary convex polyhedra. The paper is structured as follows. We first recall the geometric description of deformation and the continuous definition of elastic (stored, conservative) energy in Section 2. This is subsequently used to derive a discrete energy representation in tetrahedral elements through the use of standard barycentric coordinates, Section 3. The problem of elastic deformation is formulated as an "energy minimisation problem", where the boundary conditions are imposed via Lagrange multipliers. The null-space method is then employed to eliminate the Lagrange multipliers, Section 4. The formulation of ... and the solution procedure are validated in Section 5 by comparison with analytical solutions for two examples: a cantilever beam subjected to uniformly distributed load, in Section 5.1, and a domain with a spherical hole subjected to remote tension, in Section 5.2. Finally, an energy model for general polytopes is proposed in Section 6. This is achieved by extending the definition of the standard barycentric coordinates to such polytopes, deriving weighted ones, and proving that these can define an energy functional that fully describes the physical system.

2. Deformation and Energy of Conservative Solids

We will first review some of the basic definitions of nonlinear elasticity from a geometric perspective. We start by identifying a material body with a (smooth) Riemannian manifold B and consider a time-dependent deformation of this body to the ambient space Riemannian manifold S described by [1]

$$\varphi_t : B \to \varphi_t(B), \qquad (1)$$

or, for simplicity,

$$\varphi : B \to S, \qquad (2)$$

see Figure 1. The points within the body are given with their coordinates with respect to a global coordinate system: $\mathbb{X} = [X_1 \ X_2 \ X_3]^T$—in the initial (reference) configuration, and $\mathbb{x} = [x_1 \ x_2 \ x_3]^T$—in the current (deformed) configuration. For these we can rewrite the deformation map (2) as

$$\mathbb{x} = \varphi(\mathbb{X}) \equiv \mathbb{x}(\mathbb{X}). \qquad (3)$$

The map φ is considered to be a diffeomorphism, i.e., an invertible differentiable map with differentiable inverse. Manifolds B and S are considered to be equipped with a metric tensor field G. This positive definite second-order tensor field is expressed by symmetric tensors in the tangent space at points of the manifold, denoted by $T_{\mathbb{X}}B$ on B and $T_{\mathbb{x}}S$ on S.

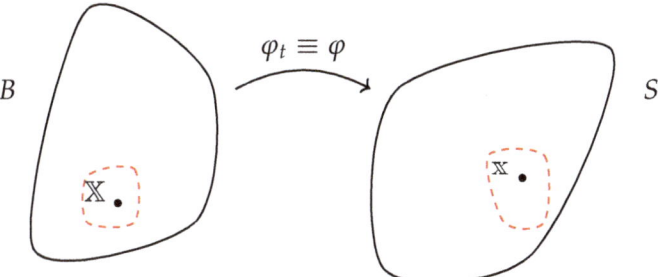

Figure 1. Initial B and current S configurations of a domain related by map $\varphi_t \equiv \varphi$.

A deformation (3) can also be represented by the deformation gradient $\mathcal{F}$, which is the tangent map of φ, i.e., the map between the tangent space on B and the tangent space on S [1,2]:

$$\mathcal{F}(\mathbb{X}) : T_{\mathbb{X}}B \to T_{\mathbb{x}}S. \qquad (4)$$

In the local coordinate charts for $\mathbb{X}$ and $\mathbb{x}$, the components $\mathcal{F}_{ij}$ of $\mathcal{F}$ are given by

$$\mathcal{F}_{ij} = \frac{\partial x_i}{\partial X_j} = x_{i,j} \quad \text{for} \quad i,j = 1,2,3. \qquad (5)$$

The deformation gradient is a non-singular two-point tensor, i.e., maps the tangent spaces of the two configurations, with a positive determinant, denoted by $\mathbb{J}$. The determinant measures the ratio between the current and initial infinitesimal volume at a given material point, and we note that the condition $\mathbb{J} = 1$ represents a volume preserving deformation. $\mathcal{F}$ can be multiplicatively decomposed in two possible ways:

$$\mathcal{F} = \mathcal{V}\mathcal{R} = \mathcal{R}\mathcal{U}, \tag{6}$$

where $\mathcal{R}$ is a proper orthogonal rotation tensor (considering that body and space are of the same Riemannian manifold), and $\mathcal{V}$ and $\mathcal{U}$ are the so-called left (spatial, current) and right (material, reference) stretch tensors, respectively, which are symmetric positive-definite as $\mathbb{J} > 0$. This reflects the two possible representations of the motion: (1) first rotation of a reference unit triad to a current unit triad, followed by its stretching in the current configuration, and (2) stretching of a reference unit triad, followed by rotation to a current triad. The two stretch tensors have identical three positive eigenvalues—λ_1, λ_2, and λ_3—representing the principal stretches of the deformation.

In this work, we will consider solids undergoing conservative deformation, i.e., where the solid stores no energy on a complete reversal of the deformation [5]. This behaviour covers the cases of linear and nonlinear elasticity, where all work done on the system by changing boundary conditions from one (initial) to another (current) configuration is stored as an elastic energy, which is exactly equal to the energy required to restore the initial configuration by reversed change of boundary conditions.

An elastic energy formulation in terms of deformation must be invariant with respect to rigid body rotations [1,2,4], thus existing formulations are based on the stretch tensors or some functions of their invariants. We will use one such formulation, which is based on invariants of the so-called left Cauchy–Green strain tensor $\mathcal{B}$, given by the map $\mathcal{B}(\mathbf{x}) : T_\mathbf{x} S \to T_\mathbf{x} S$ or by

$$\mathcal{B} = \mathcal{V}^2 \equiv \mathcal{F}\mathcal{F}^T, \tag{7}$$

where $\mathcal{F}^T$ maps covectors in the cotangent bundle of S (or T^*S) to covectors in the cotangent bundle of B (or T^*B), see also in [21–25]. It can be easily shown that $\mathcal{B}$ is objective, i.e., frame-independent, tensor.

One set of invariants of $\mathcal{B}$ is given by [1,2,4]

$$\mathbb{I}_1 = tr\left(\mathcal{F}\mathcal{F}^T\right), \quad \mathbb{I}_2 = \frac{1}{2}\left[\left(tr\left(\mathcal{F}\mathcal{F}^T\right)\right)^2 - \left(tr\left(\mathcal{F}\mathcal{F}^T\right)^2\right)\right], \quad \mathbb{I}_3 = det(\mathcal{F}\mathcal{F}^T) = \mathbb{J}^2 \tag{8}$$

which can be written in terms of the three principal stretches as

$$\mathbb{I}_1 = \lambda_1^2 + \lambda_2^2 + \lambda_3^2, \quad \mathbb{I}_2 = (\lambda_1\lambda_2)^2 + (\lambda_1\lambda_3)^2 + (\lambda_2\lambda_3)^2, \quad \mathbb{I}_3 = \lambda_1\lambda_2\lambda_3, \tag{9}$$

Another set of invariants, used to define a large class of non-linear elastic behaviours, is derived from (9) as

$$\bar{\mathbb{I}}_1 = \frac{\mathbb{I}_1}{\mathbb{J}^{2/3}}, \quad \bar{\mathbb{I}}_2 = \frac{\mathbb{I}_2}{\mathbb{J}^{4/3}}, \quad \bar{\mathbb{I}}_3 = \sqrt{det(\mathcal{F}\mathcal{F}^T)} = \mathbb{J}. \tag{10}$$

The elastic energy density of a simple generalised Neo-Hookean material is defined in terms of the second set by [2,4]

$$\mathcal{H} = \frac{\mu}{2}(\bar{\mathbb{I}}_1 - 3) + \frac{\kappa}{2}(\mathbb{J} - 1)^2, \tag{11}$$

where μ and κ are material-dependent parameters, which in the small strain approximation are known as shear and bulk moduli, respectively.

The integral of the energy density over the solid domain gives the total elastic (stored, potential) energy, which by the principle of stationary action must be minimum for the true deformation; derivation is shown in Appendix A. This can be understood as the system storing the minimal amount of energy for the change of boundary conditions between the initial and the current configuration, or as the change of boundary conditions doing the minimal amount of work (which is equal to the stored energy) to deform the solid from the initial to the current configuration.

While the solid deformation will be formulated as an elastic energy minimisation problem in this work, using the energy density expression (11), the stress tensor will be required for comparisons with known solutions of test problems. The (true) Cauchy stress tensor, σ, is the derivative of the elastic energy density function with respect to $\mathcal{B}$, which for the case of Neo–Hookean materials can be found as

$$\sigma_{ij} = \frac{\mu}{\mathbb{J}^{5/3}}\left(\mathcal{B}_{ij} - \frac{1}{3}\mathcal{B}_{kk}\delta_{ij}\right) + \kappa(\mathbb{J}-1)\delta_{ij}, \tag{12}$$

where δ_{ij} is the Kroneckers delta.

Interesting relations between the material parameters and energy can be established via the derivatives of the energy function with respect to the invariants of $\mathcal{F}$; these are shown in the Appendix C where the formulation is specialised to linear elasticity, i.e., infinitesimal deformation approximation.

3. Discrete Energy of Tetrahedral Cells

First, we consider a subdivision of the material manifold B into tetrahedra. For a given tetrahedron in $\mathbb{R}^3$ with vertices $\mathbb{X}^a, \mathbb{X}^b, \mathbb{X}^c$ and $\mathbb{X}^d$, any point $\mathbb{X}$ induces a partition described via

$$\mathbb{X} = \gamma^a \mathbb{X}^a + \gamma^b \mathbb{X}^b + \gamma^c \mathbb{X}^c + \gamma^d \mathbb{X}^d, \tag{13}$$

where $\gamma^a, \gamma^b, \gamma^c, \gamma^d \in \mathbb{R}$ are generalised barycentric coordinates. These are the ratios of the partitioned signed volumes V_i and the tetrahedral volume (V^t), see Figure 2. We introduce the vector of barycentric coordinates as

$$\Gamma = \begin{bmatrix} \gamma^a & \gamma^b & \gamma^c & \gamma^d \end{bmatrix}^T. \tag{14}$$

Further, we define a 4×4 matrix $\mathcal{S}^r$ describing the tetrahedron shape in the reference configuration by

$$\mathcal{S}^r = \begin{bmatrix} \tilde{\mathbb{X}}^a & \tilde{\mathbb{X}}^b & \tilde{\mathbb{X}}^c & \tilde{\mathbb{X}}^d \end{bmatrix}, \tag{15}$$

where each column contains corresponding nodal coordinates in the reference system with an additional element "1", e.g., for the first node we have

$$\tilde{\mathbb{X}}^a = \begin{bmatrix} X_1^a & X_2^a & X_3^a & 1 \end{bmatrix}^T, \tag{16}$$

and similarly for the remaining three nodes (upper indexes here indicate vertices, see Figure 3, and lower the i-th component of it, $i = 1, 2, 3$). Using this, any point $\mathbb{X}$ in the reference configuration can be expressed by

$$\tilde{\mathbb{X}} = \mathcal{S}^r \Gamma. \tag{17}$$

Similarly we define a 4×4 matrix $\mathcal{S}^d$ describing the tetrahedron shape in the deformed configuration by

$$\mathcal{S}^d = \begin{bmatrix} \tilde{\mathbb{x}}^a & \tilde{\mathbb{x}}^b & \tilde{\mathbb{x}}^c & \tilde{\mathbb{x}}^d \end{bmatrix}. \tag{18}$$

Using this, any point $\mathbb{x}$ in the deformed configuration can be expressed by

$$\tilde{\mathbb{x}} = \mathcal{S}^d \Gamma. \tag{19}$$

These expressions enable us to define the map between the reference and current configuration for any tetrahedral cell (see Figure 3) by

$$\tilde{\mathbb{x}} = \mathcal{S}^d (\mathcal{S}^r)^{-1} \tilde{\mathbb{X}}. \tag{20}$$

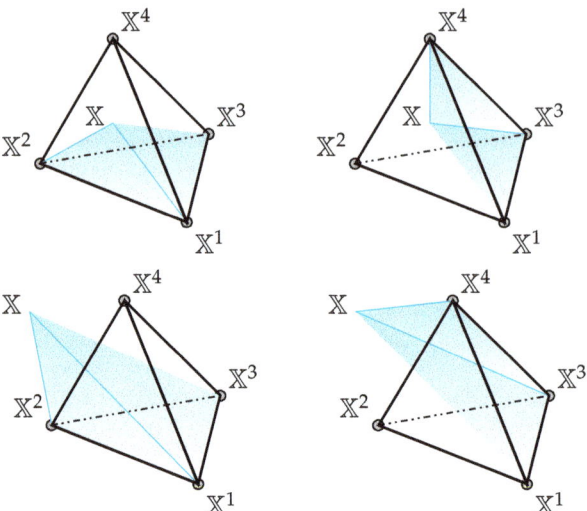

Figure 2. Examples of partitioned volumes V_I associated with point $\mathbb{X}$: (**top**) two figures illustrate two volumes for point inside the tetrahedron; (**bottom**) two figures illustrate two volumes for a point outside the tetrahedron.

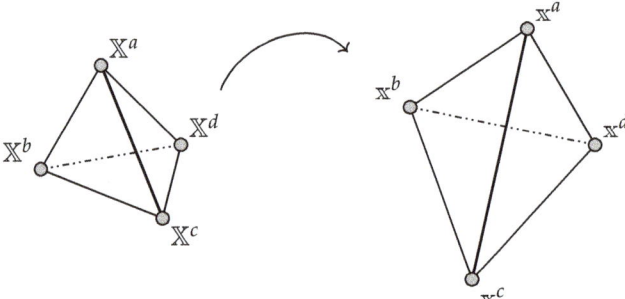

Figure 3. The deformation of a 3D tetrahedral element.

From another side, the physical map between the reference and the current configuration of a tetrahedron can be given by

$$\mathbb{x} = \mathcal{F}\mathbb{X} + \mathfrak{t}, \tag{21}$$

where $\mathfrak{t} = [t_i]$, $i = 1, 2, 3$ are the components of a translation vector, and $\mathcal{F}$ is the deformation gradient which is assumed to have positive determinant.

After some algebra, it can be shown that $S^d(S^r)^{-1}$ is the following a 4×4 block matrix:

$$S^d(S^r)^{-1} = \left[\begin{array}{c|c} \mathcal{F} & \mathfrak{t} \\ \hline \mathbb{O}^T & 1 \end{array}\right], \tag{22}$$

where $\mathbb{O}$ is a zero vector of size three.

With the knowledge of $\mathcal{F}$, the discrete energy of a tetrahedron is calculated by Equation (11), using the invariants given in Equation (10). The sum of energies of all tetrahedrons defines the discrete energy functional of the system.

4. Lagrange Multipliers Using Null-Space Method

When using the discrete energy functional proposed in Section 3 the Euler–Lagrange Equation (A4) are incomplete, and need to be complemented by prescribing Dirichlet (essential) and Neumann (natural) boundary conditions, see Appendix B. For the proposed formulation via energy minimisation, direct application of the boundary conditions is challenging and in such cases Lagrange multipliers have been extensively used [26]. This has been motivated by the fact that both essential and natural boundary conditions can be expressed as constraints and thus enforced by Lagrange multipliers, resulting in the following constrained Euler–Lagrange equations:

$$\frac{d}{dX_j} \frac{\partial \mathcal{H}}{\partial (\partial x_i / \partial X_j)} - \frac{\partial \mathcal{H}}{\partial x_i} - [C(X_j)]^T \lambda^j = 0, \quad (23)$$

for $i, j = 1, 2, 3$, where $C(X_j)$ are the constraints and λ^j are the Lagrange multipliers.

The introduction of Lagrange multipliers increases the number of unknowns, and in order to reduce them to the number of unknown displacements in the system we use the discrete null-space method of [26], which eliminates all Lagrange multipliers. For this, we define a null-space matrix $N(X_j)$, which satisfies

$$C(X_j) N(X_j) = 0. \quad (24)$$

Multiplying from the left with its transpose, Equation (23) becomes

$$[N(X_j)]^T \left(\frac{d}{dX_j} \frac{\partial \mathcal{H}}{\partial (\partial x_i / \partial X_j)} - \frac{\partial \mathcal{H}}{\partial x_i} \right) = 0. \quad (25)$$

This leads to a number of equations equal to the number of unknown degrees of freedom. Importantly, this technique has been proven to be energy consistent, meaning that energy is neither dissipated nor gained artificially during the numerical process [26–31].

5. Numerical Examples

A canonical way to test a proposal for numerical solution of boundary value problems in elasticity is to examine the solution behaviour for several simple deformation modes: volumetric expansion, pure shear, and possibly unconstrained uniaxial extension/compression. While we have tested these modes successfully, the inclusion of the results would not be of significant value to this work. Instead, we provide results for two known elasticity problems, where the combined effect of the different deformation modes is tested: a cantilever beam subjected to a uniformly distributed load and a cube with a spherical hole subjected to tension. We will present and compare results for displacements in the cantilever case, and for stresses in the cube case.

5.1. Cantilever Beam Subjected to a Regular Distributed Load

First, we consider the deformation of a three-dimensional cantilever beam subjected to a uniformly distributed load [4]. The beam has dimensions $10 \times 2 \times 2$ and is discretised into 5802 tetrahedral elements using 1322 nodes, see Figure 4. The material of the beam has properties $E = 3 \times 10^7$ kPa and $\nu = 0.3$.

The uniformly distributed load is applied in ten increments with step $f_i = 4$ kN/cm^2, and the solution is compared with linear and geometrically nonlinear finite elements analyses performed with identical tetrahedral elements. The comparison shown in Figure 5 illustrates that the calculated deflection is in excellent agreement with the geometrically nonlinear finite element solution. This is the first demonstration that the proposed method based on the minimisation of energy obtained by the barycentric map.

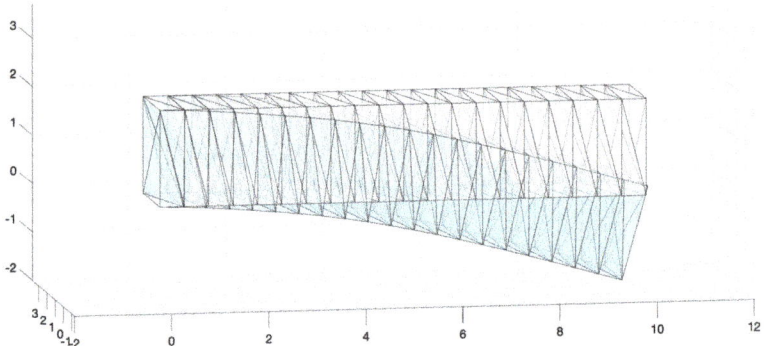

Figure 4. 3d cantilever beam.

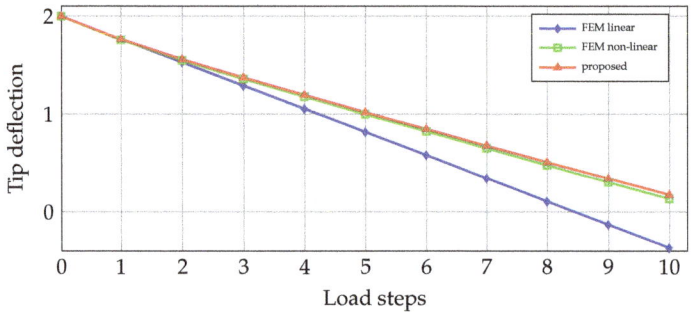

Figure 5. The deflection of the geometrically nonlinear case of a cantilever beam subjected to a regular distributed load calculated using finite element method with tetrahedral elements (FEM-tet) and the proposed scheme.

5.2. Cube with a Spherical Hole

Second, we consider the deformation of a cube with a spherical hole subjected to tensile load (Figure 6). The cube dimensions are $20 \times 20 \times 20$, and the spherical cavity has a radius $r = 1$ and centre at the cube centre. Due to symmetries, only one-eight of the cube is considered and tessellated with approximately 100 tetraherdrons. The material properties are the same as in the cantilever example. Uniform tensile load parallel to the x axis is applied.

The problem of a continuum domain with a spherical hole subjected to remote stress has an analytical solution [32]. Specifically the normal stress to the x, y plane ($z = 0$) is

$$\sigma_{33} = \frac{4-5\nu}{2(7-5\nu)}\left(\frac{r}{x}\right)^3 + \frac{9}{2(7-5\nu)}\left(\frac{r}{x}\right)^5 + 1. \tag{26}$$

This analytical solution is compared with the results obtained with the proposed method in Figure 7: analytical solution is plotted with blue line, calculated stresses are plotted with red line. The demonstrated good agreement between the two lends further support to the proposed approach.

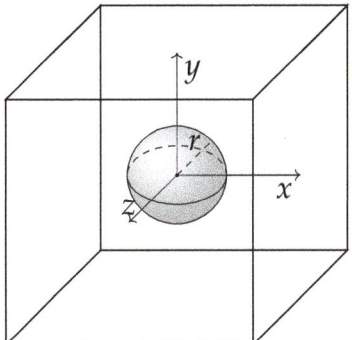

Figure 6. Cube with a spherical hole.

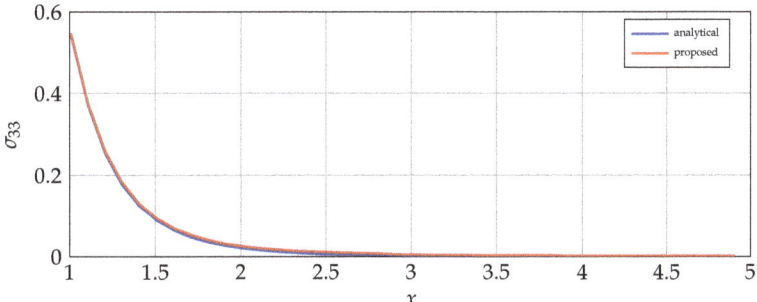

Figure 7. Stress distribution around the hole for distance $x > 1$ from the centre of the hole (size does not corresponds to example).

The approach can be tested further against various analytical solutions, but the implementation requires additional work to reduce the computational cost. Additionally, more work must be done on the mesh quality, in order to demonstrate how the number, size and shape of the tetrahedra matter in the calculations. One part of an ongoing work is an implementation of a parallel solver that will massively reduce that time.

6. Discrete Energy on General Polytopes Using Weighted Barycentric Coordinates

In order to define a discrete energy for general three-dimensional elements, we will follow an approach similar to the one described in Section 3. The extension requires first to define general/weighted barycentric coordinates on general polytopes and then to use them to express points of the material domain with respect to the tessellation nodes.

6.1. Standard Barycentric Coordinates Revisited

We start with rewriting the standard barycentric coordinates in a form suitable for generalisation. With respect to a convex polytope with vertices $\mathbb{X}_I$ for $I = 1, \ldots, n$ (where $n \geq 4$), any point $\mathbb{X} \in \mathbb{R}^3$ can written as [33]

$$\mathbb{X} = \sum_{I=1}^{n} \gamma_I \mathbb{X}_I, \qquad \sum_{I=1}^{n} \gamma_I = 1, \tag{27}$$

where γ_I are the generalised barycentric coordinates of $\mathbb{X}$. This can be also written in the form

$$\sum_{I=1}^{n} w_I(\mathbb{X}_I - \mathbb{X}) = 0, \qquad \sum_{I=1}^{n} w_I \neq 0, \quad \text{with} \quad \gamma_I = \frac{w_I}{\sum_{I=1}^{n} w_I}, \tag{28}$$

where the weight functions w_I can be appropriately defined. In [33] for example, the authors define the weight functions via the partition volumes

$$V_I = \{\mathbb{X}_1, \mathbb{X}_2, \ldots, \mathbb{X}_{I-1}, \mathbb{X}, \mathbb{X}_{I+1}, \ldots, \mathbb{X}_n\}_{\text{volume}} \tag{29}$$

and the positive functions $c_I > 0$, so that

$$w_I = \frac{c_{I+1} V_{I+1} + c_I V_I + c_{I-1} V_{I-1}}{V_{I+1} V_{I-1}}. \tag{30}$$

The sum of the weight functions becomes

$$W = \sum_{I=1}^{n} w_I = \sum_{I=1}^{n} \frac{c_I V}{V_{I+1} V_{I-1}}, \tag{31}$$

where V is the volume of the polytope.

The requirement for c_I is that these are arbitrary positive functions. A rather general definition has been proposed in [33]:

$$c_I = |\mathbb{X}_I - \mathbb{X}|^\alpha. \tag{32}$$

Notably, the selection $\alpha = 0$ results in the known Wachspress coordinates, while the selection $\alpha = 1$ provides the mean value coordinates.

6.2. Weighted Barycentric Coordinates on General Polytopes

We will now propose an extended version of barycentric coordinates on general polytopes that will be used to formulate an expression of the internal energy. To do so, we use the signed partitioned volumes given by Equation (29) and extend the definition of weight functions given by Equation (31).

Extending the barycentric coordinate expressions to general polytopes is challenging, because one needs to address issues arising from the definition of the weight functions in Equation (31). The problems stem mainly from the denominator, the product of the volumes V_{I-1} and V_{I+1} (or areas in two dimensions). For non-convex polytopes, this product might become negative. In the following, we restrict ourselves to arbitrary (non-platonic) tetrahedral elements, but the generalisation to any general polytope follows clearly. To bypass the possibility of negative denominator, we define the volume using cross-products in the following way:

$$V = \frac{1}{6} |(\mathbb{X}_1 - \mathbb{X}_2) \times (\mathbb{X}_1 - \mathbb{X}_3)| \left| \mathbb{h}_{\mathbb{X}_4, (\mathbb{X}_1, \mathbb{X}_2, \mathbb{X}_3)} \right|, \tag{33}$$

where $\mathbb{h}_{\mathbb{X}_I, (\mathbb{X}_1, \mathbb{X}_2, \mathbb{X}_3)}$ is the vector normal to the triangle face forming from points $(\mathbb{X}_1, \mathbb{X}_2, \mathbb{X}_3)$ to the point $\mathbb{X}_I$.

We can now rewrite the weights of (31) using the proposed volume definition to obtain

$$\begin{aligned} W &= \sum_{I=1}^{n} \frac{6^2 c_I V}{|(\mathbb{X}_1 - \mathbb{X}_2) \times (\mathbb{X}_1 - \mathbb{X}_3)| \left| \mathbb{h}_{\mathbb{X}, (\mathbb{X}_1, \mathbb{X}_2, \mathbb{X}_3)} \right| |(\mathbb{X}_1 - \mathbb{X}_3) \times (\mathbb{X}_1 - \mathbb{X}_4)| \left| \mathbb{h}_{\mathbb{X}, (\mathbb{X}_1, \mathbb{X}_3, \mathbb{X}_4)} \right|} \\ &= \sum_{I=1}^{n} \frac{6 c_I \left| \mathbb{h}_{\mathbb{X}_4, (\mathbb{X}_1, \mathbb{X}_2, \mathbb{X}_3)} \right|}{|(\mathbb{X}_1 - \mathbb{X}_3) \times (\mathbb{X}_1 - \mathbb{X}_4)| \left| \mathbb{h}_{\mathbb{X}, (\mathbb{X}_1, \mathbb{X}_2, \mathbb{X}_3)} \right| \left| \mathbb{h}_{\mathbb{X}, (\mathbb{X}_1, \mathbb{X}_3, \mathbb{X}_4)} \right|} \\ &= \sum_{I=1}^{n} \frac{6 c_I \left| \mathbb{h}_{\mathbb{X}_4, (\mathbb{X}_1, \mathbb{X}_2, \mathbb{X}_3)} \right|}{|\mathbb{X}_1 - \mathbb{X}_3||\mathbb{X}_1 - \mathbb{X}_4| \left| \mathbb{h}_{\mathbb{X}, (\mathbb{X}_1, \mathbb{X}_2, \mathbb{X}_3)} \right| \left| \mathbb{h}_{\mathbb{X}, (\mathbb{X}_1, \mathbb{X}_3, \mathbb{X}_4)} \right| \sin\left((\mathbb{X}_1 - \mathbb{X}_3), (\mathbb{X}_1 - \mathbb{X}_4)\right)}, \end{aligned} \tag{34}$$

With some functions $d_I > 0$ this can be written as

$$W = \sum_{I=1}^{n} \frac{d_I}{|\mathbb{X}_1 - \mathbb{X}_3||\mathbb{X}_1 - \mathbb{X}_4| \sin((\mathbb{X}_1 - \mathbb{X}_3), (\mathbb{X}_1 - \mathbb{X}_4))}$$
$$= \sum_{I=1}^{n} d_I \frac{\cot((\mathbb{X}_1 - \mathbb{X}_3), (\mathbb{X}_1 - \mathbb{X}_4))}{(\mathbb{X}_1 - \mathbb{X}_3) \cdot (\mathbb{X}_1 - \mathbb{X}_4)}. \tag{35}$$

As long as the dot product in the denominator is not zero, the barycentric coordinates that use the proposed weight functions are well defined for both convex and non-convex polytopes. Furthermore, the standard barycentric coordinates can be recovered from this definition.

6.3. Energy from Angles and Lengths

In order to understand more the angles introduced in (35), we will relate them to appropriate lengths of edges. For illustration, we will restrict ourselves to two dimensions, although the extension to three dimensions follows a similar path. We consider the triangle formed by points with coordinates $\mathbb{X}_a$, $\mathbb{X}_b$ and $\mathbb{X}_c$ (Figure 8). The three angles θ_a, θ_b and θ_c are opposite to the edges of lengths $|\mathbb{h}_{\mathbb{X}_b,\mathbb{X}_c}|$, $|\mathbb{h}_{\mathbb{X}_a,\mathbb{X}_c}|$ and $|\mathbb{h}_{\mathbb{X}_a,\mathbb{X}_b}|$, respectively.

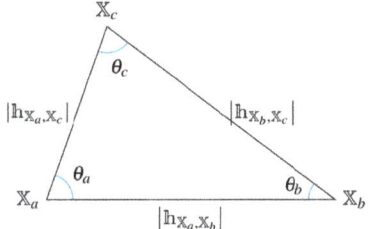

Figure 8. Two-dimensional triangle formed from points with nodal positions $\mathbb{X}_a$, $\mathbb{X}_b$ and $\mathbb{X}_c$.

Considering each angle to be a function of edge lengths, we can write the following expressions:

$$\cos(\theta_a) = \frac{|\mathbb{h}_{\mathbb{X}_a,\mathbb{X}_c}|^2 + |\mathbb{h}_{\mathbb{X}_a,\mathbb{X}_b}|^2 - |\mathbb{h}_{\mathbb{X}_b,\mathbb{X}_c}|^2}{2|\mathbb{h}_{\mathbb{X}_a,\mathbb{X}_c}||\mathbb{h}_{\mathbb{X}_a,\mathbb{X}_b}|}. \tag{36}$$

By taking the derivative with respect to $|\mathbb{h}_{\mathbb{X}_b,\mathbb{X}_c}|$, we have

$$\frac{\partial \theta_a}{\partial |\mathbb{h}_{\mathbb{X}_b,\mathbb{X}_c}|} = \frac{|\mathbb{h}_{\mathbb{X}_b,\mathbb{X}_c}|}{|\mathbb{h}_{\mathbb{X}_a,\mathbb{X}_c}||\mathbb{h}_{\mathbb{X}_a,\mathbb{X}_b}| \sin(\theta_a)}, \tag{37}$$

which, writing the area of the triangle as

$$A = \frac{1}{2} |\mathbb{h}_{\mathbb{X}_a,\mathbb{X}_c}||\mathbb{h}_{\mathbb{X}_a,\mathbb{X}_b}| \sin(\theta_a) \tag{38}$$

results in

$$\frac{\partial \theta_a}{\partial |\mathbb{h}_{\mathbb{X}_b,\mathbb{X}_c}|} = \frac{|\mathbb{h}_{\mathbb{X}_b,\mathbb{X}_c}|}{2A}. \tag{39}$$

Similarly, we can calculate the derivative of (36) with respect to $|\mathbb{h}_{\mathbb{X}_a,\mathbb{X}_c}|$ as

$$\frac{\partial \theta_a}{\partial |\mathbb{h}_{\mathbb{X}_a,\mathbb{X}_c}|} = -\frac{|\mathbb{h}_{\mathbb{X}_b,\mathbb{X}_c}| \cos(\theta_c)}{2A}. \tag{40}$$

Finally, to connect the cotangent of an angle, required in (35), we define

$$\zeta_a = \frac{1}{2}|\mathbbm{h}_{\mathbb{X}_b,\mathbb{X}_c}|^2, \qquad \zeta_b = \frac{1}{2}|\mathbbm{h}_{\mathbb{X}_a,\mathbb{X}_c}|^2, \qquad \zeta_c = \frac{1}{2}|\mathbbm{h}_{\mathbb{X}_a,\mathbb{X}_b}|^2 \qquad (41)$$

and observe that

$$\frac{\partial \cot(\theta_a)}{\partial \zeta_b} = \frac{1}{|\mathbbm{h}_{\mathbb{X}_a,\mathbb{X}_c}|} \frac{\partial \cot(\theta_a)}{\partial |\mathbbm{h}_{\mathbb{X}_a,\mathbb{X}_c}|}. \qquad (42)$$

The last expression, combined with (40), provides

$$\frac{\partial \cot(\theta_a)}{\partial \zeta_b} = \frac{|\mathbbm{h}_{\mathbb{X}_b,\mathbb{X}_c}|\cos(\theta_c)}{2\sin^2(\theta_a)|\mathbbm{h}_{\mathbb{X}_a,\mathbb{X}_c}|}. \qquad (43)$$

This result gives us a perspective to understand the weights defined by (35) via the derivatives with respect to edge lengths. In addition, due to symmetries we can obtain

$$\frac{\partial \cot(\theta_b)}{\partial \zeta_a} = \frac{|\mathbbm{h}_{\mathbb{X}_b,\mathbb{X}_c}|\cos(\theta_c)}{2\sin^2(\theta_a)|\mathbbm{h}_{\mathbb{X}_a,\mathbb{X}_c}|} \qquad (44)$$

and thus

$$\frac{\partial \cot(\theta_a)}{\partial \zeta_b} = \frac{\partial \cot(\theta_b)}{\partial \zeta_a}. \qquad (45)$$

The expressions relating cotangent of angles with lengths can be used to formulate an energy expression.

Total energy given by (A2) can be calculated using the energy of any triangle element, i.e., (A1) as

$$h_i \simeq \int_{\zeta_a,\zeta_b,\zeta_c} \sum_{I=1}^{n} w_I d\zeta_i \simeq \int_{\zeta_a,\zeta_b,\zeta_c} \sum_{a,b,c} \cot(\theta_i) d\zeta_i. \qquad (46)$$

6.4. Discrete Energy via Weighted Barycentric Coordinates

We will now prove that the energy expression of (46) can be used to determine the energy at each element. To that end, we here restrict to two-dimensional case, and thus we first prove that the integrant of (46), which can be identified as the differential form

$$\omega = \sum_{a,b,c} \cot(\theta_i) d\zeta_i = \cot(\theta_a) d\zeta_a + \cot(\theta_b) d\zeta_b + \cot(\theta_c) d\zeta_c \qquad (47)$$

is a closed 1-form, see in [12–14]. The proof can be based on observing that $d\omega$ can be written as

$$\begin{aligned} d\omega &= \left[\frac{\partial \cot(\theta_b)}{\partial \zeta_a} - \frac{\partial \cot(\theta_a)}{\partial \zeta_b}\right] d\zeta_a \wedge d\zeta_b \\ &+ \left[\frac{\partial \cot(\theta_c)}{\partial \zeta_b} - \frac{\partial \cot(\theta_b)}{\partial \zeta_c}\right] d\zeta_b \wedge d\zeta_c \\ &+ \left[\frac{\partial \cot(\theta_a)}{\partial \zeta_c} - \frac{\partial \cot(\theta_c)}{\partial \zeta_a}\right] d\zeta_c \wedge d\zeta_a. \end{aligned} \qquad (48)$$

To show that $d\omega = 0$ is then straightforward using (45).

Finally, the differential form defined in (46) is exact and thus the integration is strictly path-dependent, and thus completely defines an energy functional for the system.

7. Summary and Conclusions

In this work, a geometric formulation of nonlinear elasticity, based on discrete energy functional, is presented. In the first step, discrete energy of tetrahedral elements has been formulated through a map between initial and current positions of their vertices and the use of standard barycentric coordinates. The energy functional of the resulted boundary value problem has been minimised using energy consistent technique for constrained systems, where the constraints are enforced by Lagrange multipliers and are eliminated via pre-multiplication of the discrete equations of motion by a discrete null-space matrix of the constraint gradient. Although not tested specifically here, the convergence of the proposed scheme should inherit the convergence of the well-known methods for solving constrained systems by utilising the discrete null-space method. The numerical examples presented—cantilever beam and cube with a spherical hole—demonstrate the capabilities of the approach.

Because the use of standard barycentric coordinates is restricted to three-dimensional convex polytopes, a natural extension of the existing definitions to discrete domains consisting of arbitrary polytopes has been proposed. This opens the possibility to analyse domains with arbitrary cell shapes, including non-convex cells that posses specific microstructural features. The proposed technique is presently suited to conservative problems, i.e., linear and nonlinear elasticity, but it can be extended to dissipative systems, provided that the dissipation mechanism is given in terms of the deformations and stresses calculated in this work. Such extensions are the subject of future work.

Author Contributions: Conceptualization, O.K.; methodology, O.K. and A.P.J.; investigation, O.K., P.B. and A.P.J.; writing—original draft preparation, O.K. and A.P.J.; writing—review & editing, O.K., P.B and A.P.J.; visualization, O.K. and P.B. All authors have read and agreed to the published version of the manuscript.

Funding: This research was funded by Engineering and Physical Sciences Research Council (EPSRC) UK grant number EP/N026136/1.

Acknowledgments: Authors wish to acknowledge the support of Engineering and Physical Sciences Research Council (EPSRC) UK via grand EP/N026136/1 "Geometric Mechanics of Solids".

Conflicts of Interest: The authors declare no conflict of interest.

Appendix A. Principle of Stationary Action in Elasticity

In order to derive the equations that describe the deformation of the material we consider its energy per unit volume h_i as a function of the points on the deformed configuration x_i and the relative displacements of neighbouring points $\frac{\partial x_i}{\partial X_j}$, i.e.,

$$h_i \equiv h_i\left(x_i, \frac{\partial x_i}{\partial X_j}\right), \tag{A1}$$

for more details see [3]. The total energy of the body can be then calculated as the volume integral

$$\mathcal{H} = \int h_i dV \tag{A2}$$

or

$$\mathcal{H} = \iiint h_i\left(x_i, \frac{\partial x_i}{\partial X_j}\right) dX_1 dX_2 dX_3, \qquad i,j = 1,2,3. \tag{A3}$$

The principle of stationary action states that this functional must be stationary for the true deformation of the body, i.e., $\delta\mathcal{H} = 0$, which can be interpreted as body points under deformation move so as to minimise this energy. Calculating the variation of the energy functional leads to the Euler–Lagrange equations [1]

$$\frac{d}{dX_j}\frac{\partial \mathcal{H}}{\partial(\partial x_i/\partial X_j)} - \frac{\partial \mathcal{H}}{\partial x_i} = 0, \qquad i,j = 1,2,3. \tag{A4}$$

The later three equations are the differential equations of elasticity, applicable to both infinitesimal and finite deformations.

The total energy (A3) can be represented as a sum of an energy associated with deformation $\mathcal{H}^D$ and an energy associated with body forces $\mathcal{H}^F$, where the former is a function of relative positions only

$$\mathcal{H}^D \equiv \mathcal{H}^D\left(\frac{\partial x_i}{\partial X_j}\right), \tag{A5}$$

and the latter is a function of absolute positions only [1,4]

$$\mathcal{H}^F \equiv \mathcal{H}^F(x_i). \tag{A6}$$

Importantly, $\mathcal{H}^D$ must be invariant of coordinate translations and rotations, leading to a requirement for the deformation energy to be a function of some combination of the principal invariants of the gradient of φ defined by (3), see also [1–4].

Appendix B. Boundary Conditions

The boundary conditions for Equation (A4) are Dirichlet for prescribed (known) displacements and Neumann for prescribed (known) forces/ tractions. The application of the Dirichlet boundary conditions is straightforward in our formulation as the primal unknowns are the nodal displacements. For the Neumann boundary conditions we derive the following.

The equilibrium of the entire domain is expressed by [1–3,6]

$$\mathbb{F} = \int_\Omega f dV = -\int_{\partial\Omega} t dS = \mathbb{T} \tag{A7}$$

which shows that that the resultant body force $\mathbb{F}$ must be equal and opposite to the resultant of the applied forces on the boundary.

With the energy definition of Section 2 for a deformation of a body, the internal forces can be defined as the negative gradient of the energy, i.e.,

$$\mathbb{F} = -\nabla_\mathbf{x} \mathcal{H} \tag{A8}$$

or

$$F_i = -\iiint \frac{\partial \mathcal{H}}{\partial x_i} dX_1 dX_2 dX_3 \tag{A9}$$

which, when using (A4) becomes

$$F_i = -\iiint \frac{d}{dX_j} \frac{\partial \mathcal{H}}{\partial(\partial x_i/\partial X_j)} dX_1 dX_2 dX_3. \tag{A10}$$

If we further apply the divergence theorem we have and expression of the i-th component of the force

$$F_i = -\int \frac{\partial \mathcal{H}}{\partial(\partial x_i/\partial X_j)} dA_j \tag{A11}$$

at a surface defined its area vector dA_j. The balance of these forces with the surface forces as in (A7) leads to an expression for the the surface forces that uses the definition of the energy per unit volume, i.e.,

$$dT_i = \frac{\partial \mathcal{H}}{\partial(\partial x_i/\partial X_j)} dA_j. \tag{A12}$$

This expression for the Neumann boundary conditions is used in the current work (see also [6]).

Appendix C. Navier–Cauchy Equations of Linear Elasticity

Following the work in [6], we consider the displacement field $\mathbf{u} = \mathbf{x} - \mathbb{X}$ and define the symmetric part of its gradient by

$$u_{ik} = \frac{1}{2}\left(\frac{\partial u_i}{\partial X_k} + \frac{\partial u_k}{\partial X_i}\right). \tag{A13}$$

The energy of (A3) can be considered as

$$\mathcal{H} = \mathcal{H}^d = \mathcal{H}^d\Big|_0 + \frac{\lambda}{2}u_{ii}^2 + \mu u_{ik}^2 \tag{A14}$$

where $\mathcal{H}^d|_0$ corresponds to no change of energy state, thus no deformation. The parameters λ and μ are the Lamé parameters that can be calculated as [6]:

$$\begin{aligned}\lambda =\ & 4\left(\frac{\partial^2 \mathcal{H}^d}{\partial \mathbb{I}_1 \partial \mathbb{I}_1}\Big|_0\right) + 16\left(\frac{\partial^2 \mathcal{H}^d}{\partial \mathbb{I}_2 \partial \mathbb{I}_1}\Big|_0\right) + 4\left(\frac{\partial^2 \mathcal{H}^d}{\partial \mathbb{I}_3 \partial \mathbb{I}_1}\Big|_0\right) + 16\left(\frac{\partial^2 \mathcal{H}^d}{\partial \mathbb{I}_2 \partial \mathbb{I}_2}\Big|_0\right) \\ & + 8\left(\frac{\partial^2 \mathcal{H}^d}{\partial \mathbb{I}_3 \partial \mathbb{I}_2}\Big|_0\right) + \left(\frac{\partial^2 \mathcal{H}^d}{\partial \mathbb{I}_3 \partial \mathbb{I}_3}\Big|_0\right) - 2\frac{\partial \mathcal{H}^d}{\partial \mathbb{I}_1}\end{aligned} \tag{A15}$$

and

$$\mu = 2\left(\frac{\partial \mathcal{H}^d}{\partial \mathbb{I}_1} + \frac{\partial \mathcal{H}^d}{\partial \mathbb{I}_2}\right)\Big|_0. \tag{A16}$$

Using the energy of (A14) in the Euler-Lagrange Equation (A4), together with the definitions of the Lamé constants (A15) and (A16) we get the equilibrium equations for linear isotropic elastic materials (with no gravitational body force)

$$\mu \frac{\partial^2 u_i}{\partial (X_k)^2} + (\lambda + \mu)\frac{\partial^2 u_l}{\partial X_i \partial X_l} = 0, \tag{A17}$$

which can be written in terms of Youngs modulus

$$E = \frac{\mu(3\lambda + 2\mu)}{\lambda + \mu} \tag{A18}$$

and Poisson's ratio

$$\nu = \frac{\lambda}{2(\lambda + \mu)} \tag{A19}$$

as

$$\frac{E}{2(1+\nu)}\frac{\partial^2 u_i}{\partial (X_k)^2} + \frac{E}{2(1+\nu)(1-2\nu)}\frac{\partial^2 u_l}{\partial X_i \partial X_l} = 0. \tag{A20}$$

Equations (A17) and (A20) are the Navier-Cauchy equilibrium equations for linear elasticity.

References

1. Marsden, J.; Hughes, T. *Mathematical Foundations of Elasticity*; Dover Civil and Mechanical Engineering Series; Courier Corporation: Dover, UK, 1994.
2. Gurtin, M.E. The Linear Theory of Elasticity. In *Linear Theories of Elasticity and Thermoelasticity: Linear and Nonlinear Theories of Rods, Plates, and Shells*; Truesdell, C., Ed.; Springer: Berlin/Heidelberg, Germany, 1973; pp. 1–295.
3. Spencer, A. *Continuum Mechanics*; Dover Books on Physics; Dover Publications: Dover, UK, 2012.
4. Steinmann, P. *Geometrical Foundations of Continuum Mechanics: An Application to First- and Second-Order Elasticity and Elasto-Plasticity*; Lecture Notes in Applied Mathematics and Mechanics; Springer: Berlin/Heidelberg, Germany, 2015.
5. Shabana, A.A. *Computational Continuum Mechanics*; Cambridge University Press: Cambridge, UK, 2008.

6. Landau, L.; Pitaevskii, L.; Kosevich, A.; Lifshitz, E. *Theory of Elasticity: Volume 7*; Number τ. 7; Elsevier Science: Amsterdam, The Netherlands, 2012.
7. Rashid, M.M.; Selimotic, M. A three-dimensional finite element method with arbitrary polyhedral elements. *Int. J. Numer. Methods Eng.* **2006**, *67*, 226–252. [CrossRef]
8. Sohn, D.; Cho, Y.S.; Im, S. A novel scheme to generate meshes with hexahedral elements and poly-pyramid elements: The carving technique. *Comput. Methods Appl. Mech. Eng.* **2012**, *201–204*, 208–227. [CrossRef]
9. Sohn, D.; Han, J.; Cho, Y.S.; Im, S. A finite element scheme with the aid of a new carving technique combined with smoothed integration. *Comput. Methods Appl. Mech. Eng.* **2013**, *254*, 42–60. [CrossRef]
10. Beirão Da Veiga, L.; Brezzi, F.; Cangiani, A.; Manzini, G.; Marini, L.D.; Russo, A. Basic principles of Virtual Element Methods. *Math. Model. Methods Appl. Sci.* **2013**, *23*, 199–214. [CrossRef]
11. Gain, A.L.; Talischi, C.; Paulino, G.H. On the Virtual Element Method for three-dimensional linear elasticity problems on arbitrary polyhedral meshes. *Comput. Methods Appl. Mech. Eng.* **2014**, *282*, 132–160. [CrossRef]
12. Desbrun, M.; Hirani, A.N.; Leok, M.; Marsden, J.E. Discrete Exterior Calculus. *arXiv* **2005**, arXiv:math/0508341.
13. Gillette, A.; Bajaj, C. Dual formulations of mixed finite element methods with applications. *CAD Comput. Aided Des.* **2011**, *43*, 1213–1221. [CrossRef] [PubMed]
14. Kosmas, O.; Jivkov, A. Development of geometric formulation of elasticity. In Proceedings of the 1st International Conference on Theoretical, Applied, Experimental Mechanics, Cyprus, Greece, 17–20 June 2018; pp. 262–267.
15. Dassios, I.; Jivkov, A.; O'Ceeffe, G. A mathematical model for elasticity using calculus on discrete manifolds. *Math. Methods Appl. Sci.* **2018**, *41*, 9057–9070. [CrossRef]
16. Seruga, D.; Kosmas, O.; Jivkov, A. Geometric modelling of elastic and elastoplastic solids with separation of volumetric and distortional energies and Prandtl operators. *Int. J. Solids Struct.* **2020**, *198*, 136–148. [CrossRef]
17. Dassios, I.; Jivkov, A.; Abu-Muharib, A.; James, P. A mathematical model for plasticity and damage: A discrete calculus formulation. *J. Comput. Appl. Math.* **2017**, *312*, 27–38. [CrossRef]
18. Tsukerman, I. Spurious numerical solutions in electromagnetic resonance problems. *IEEE Trans. Magn.* **2003**, *39*, 1405–1408. [CrossRef]
19. Millán, D.; Sukumar, N.; Arroyo, M. Cell-based maximum-entropy approximants. *Comput. Methods Appl. Mech. Eng.* **2015**, *284*, 712–731. [CrossRef]
20. Bassi, F.; Botti, L.; Colombo, A.; Pietro, D.D.; Tesini, P. On the flexibility of agglomeration based physical space discontinuous Galerkin discretizations. *J. Comput. Phys.* **2012**, *231*, 45–65. [CrossRef]
21. Sansour, C. On the geometric structure of the stress and strain tensors, dual variables and objective rates in continuum mechanics. *Arch. Mech.* **1992**, *44*, 527–556.
22. Svendsen, B. A local frame formulation of dual-strain pairs and time derivatives. *Arch. Mech.* **1995**, *111*, 13–40. [CrossRef]
23. van der Giessen, E.; Kollmann, F.G. On Mathematical Aspects of Dual Variables in Continuum Mechanics. Part 1: Mathematical Principles. *ZAMM J. Appl. Math. Mech. Z. Angew. Math. Mech.* **1996**, *76*, 447–462. [CrossRef]
24. Stumpf, H.; Hoppe, U. The Application of Tensor Algebra on Manifolds to Nonlinear Continuum Mechanics: Invited Survey Article. *ZAMM J. Appl. Math. Mech. Z. Angew. Math. Mech.* **1997**, *77*, 327–339. [CrossRef]
25. Kadianakis, N. On the Geometry of Lagrangian and Eulerian Descriptions in Continuum Mechanics. *ZAMM J. Appl. Math. Mech. Z. Angew. Math. Mech.* **1999**, *79*, 131–138. [CrossRef]
26. Betsch, P.; Leyendecker, S. The discrete null space method for the energy consistent integration of constrained mechanical systems. Part II: multibody dynamics. *Int. J. Numer. Methods Eng.* **2006**, *67*, 499–552. [CrossRef]
27. Betsch, P. The discrete null space method for the energy consistent integration of constrained mechanical systems: Part I: Holonomic constraints. *Comput. Methods Appl. Mech. Eng.* **2005**, *194*, 5159–5190. [CrossRef]
28. Kosmas, O.; Papadopoulos, D.; Vlachos, D. Geometric Derivation and Analysis of Multi-Symplectic Numerical Schemes for Differential Equations. *Comput. Math. Var. Anal.* **2020**, *159*, 207–226.
29. Kosmas, O.; Leyendecker, S. Family of higher order exponential variational integrators for split potential systems. *J. Phys. Conf. Ser.* **2015**, *574*, 012002. [CrossRef]
30. Kosmas, O.; Vlachos, D. A space-time geodesic approach for phase fitted variational integrators. *J. Phys. Conf. Ser.* **2016**, *738*, 012133. [CrossRef]
31. Leitz, T.; Leyendecker, S. Galerkin Lie-group variational integrators based on unit quaternion interpolation. *Comput. Methods Appl. Mech. Eng.* **2018**, *338*, 333–361. [CrossRef]
32. Chati, M.K.; Mukherjee, S.; Paulino, G.H. The meshless hypersingular boundary node method for three-dimensional potential theory and linear elasticity problems. *Eng. Anal. Bound. Elem.* **2001**, *25*, 639–653. [CrossRef]
33. Floater, M.S.; Hormann, K.; Kós, G. A general construction of barycentric coordinates over convex polygons. *Adv. Comput. Math.* **2006**, *24*, 311–331. [CrossRef]

Variational Problems with Time Delay and Higher-Order Distributed-Order Fractional Derivatives with Arbitrary Kernels

Fátima Cruz †, Ricardo Almeida *,† and Natália Martins †

Center for Research and Development in Mathematics and Applications, Department of Mathematics, University of Aveiro, 3810-193 Aveiro, Portugal; fatima.cruz@live.ua.pt (F.C.); natalia@ua.pt (N.M.)
* Correspondence: ricardo.almeida@ua.pt
† These authors contributed equally to this work.

Abstract: In this work, we study variational problems with time delay and higher-order distributed-order fractional derivatives dealing with a new fractional operator. This fractional derivative combines two known operators: distributed-order derivatives and derivatives with respect to another function. The main results of this paper are necessary and sufficient optimality conditions for different types of variational problems. Since we are dealing with generalized fractional derivatives, from this work, some well-known results can be obtained as particular cases.

Keywords: fractional calculus; calculus of variations; Euler–Lagrange equations; isoperimetric problems; holonomic problems; higher-order derivatives

1. Introduction

Fractional calculus is a mathematical area that deals with the generalization of the classical notions of derivative and integral to a noninteger order. This fascinating theory has attracted the interest of the scientific community over the last few decades due to the fact that it is a powerful tool to deal with the dynamics of complex systems. Its importance is notable not only in Mathematics but also in Physics [1], Chemistry [2], Biology [3], Epidemiology [4], Control Theory [5], etc. (for completeness, we also point out that partial differential equations from classical calculus properly fit in the modeling of real problems; see, for instance, Refs. [6–8] for models from mathematical biology).

Since the beginning of the fractional calculus in 1695, numerous definitions of fractional integrals and derivatives were introduced by important mathematicians such as Leibniz, Euler, Fourier, Liouville, Riemann, Letnikov, etc. Many of these fractional derivatives can be related between them by an explicit formula [9,10]. Later on, in 1969, Caputo introduced the distributed-order fractional integrals and derivatives [11,12]. These operators can be seen as a new kind of generalization of the classical fractional operators, since these operators involve a weighted integral of different orders of differentiation. Another way that allows a generalization of the classical fractional operators is considering the notions of fractional integrals and derivatives with respect to another function [9,13,14].

The specificity of fractional calculus that can be considered the cause of its success in applications to real world problems is that the large number of fractional operators allows researchers to choose the most suitable one to model the problem under investigation.

In the recent paper [15], the authors introduced new notions of fractional derivatives combining the distributed-order derivatives and fractional derivatives with respect to an arbitrary smooth function, creating a new type of derivatives: distributed-order fractional derivatives with arbitrary kernels. In this paper, we are going to deal with these kinds of generalized fractional derivatives in order to study different types of problems of the calculus of variations.

The fractional calculus of variations was initiated by Riewe in 1996 [16,17] with the deduction of the Euler–Lagrange equation for problems where the Lagrangian depends on Riemann–Liouville fractional derivatives in order to deal with linear non-conservative forces. Since then, several authors have developed the fractional calculus of variations considering different types of fractional derivatives and different types of variational problems (see, e.g., [18–23] and references therein). For more details on fractional calculus of variations, we refer to the books [24–26].

It is well known that, in real world problems, delays are important to model certain processes and dynamical systems [22,27,28]. However, there are still few works in the literature dedicated to the fractional calculus of variations with time delay. To fill this gap, we will study in this paper time-delayed variational problems involving distributed-order fractional derivatives with arbitrary smooth kernels. We will also study variational problems involving higher-order distributed-order fractional derivatives with arbitrary smooth kernels.

The paper is organized as follows: in Section 2, we recall the new concepts of distributed-order fractional derivatives with respect to another function recently introduced in [15] and then we proceed with the extension to the higher-order case. We finalize Section 2 with the proof of the integration by parts formulae involving the higher-order distributed-order fractional derivatives with arbitrary smooth kernels. Section 3 is devoted to the main results of this paper: necessary and sufficient optimality conditions for variational problems with time delay and higher-order distributed-order fractional derivatives with arbitrary smooth kernels. In Section 4, we present three examples that illustrate the applicability of some of our main results. We finalize the paper with concluding remarks and also mentioning some possibilities for future research.

2. Preliminaries and Notations

We assume that the reader is familiar with the definitions and properties of the Riemann–Liouville and Caputo fractional operators with respect to another function (cf. [9,13], resp.).

In this paper, we consider variational problems involving the new concepts of distributed-order fractional derivatives with respect to an arbitrary smooth kernel recently introduced in [15]. For the reader's convenience, we recall here the definitions introduced in [15].

Let $\phi : [0,1] \to [0,1]$ be a continuous function such that

$$\int_0^1 \phi(\alpha) d\alpha > 0.$$

Definition 1 ([15]). *Let $x : [a,b] \to \mathbb{R}$ be an integrable function and $\psi \in C^1([a,b], \mathbb{R})$ be an increasing function such that $\psi'(t) \neq 0$, for all $t \in [a,b]$. The left and right Riemann–Liouville distributed-order fractional derivatives of a function x with respect to ψ are defined by:*

$$D_{a+}^{\phi(\alpha),\psi} x(t) := \int_0^1 \phi(\alpha) D_{a+}^{\alpha,\psi} x(t) d\alpha \quad \text{and} \quad D_{b-}^{\phi(\alpha),\psi} x(t) := \int_0^1 \phi(\alpha) D_{b-}^{\alpha,\psi} x(t) d\alpha,$$

where $D_{a+}^{\alpha,\psi}$ and $D_{b-}^{\alpha,\psi}$ are the left and right ψ-Riemann–Liouville fractional derivatives of order α, respectively.

Definition 2 ([15]). *Let $x, \psi \in C^1([a,b], \mathbb{R})$ be two functions such that ψ is increasing and $\psi'(t) \neq 0$, for all $t \in [a,b]$. The left and right Caputo distributed-order fractional derivatives of x with respect to ψ are defined by*

$$^C D_{a+}^{\phi(\alpha),\psi} x(t) := \int_0^1 \phi(\alpha) {^C D_{a+}^{\alpha,\psi}} x(t) d\alpha \quad \text{and} \quad ^C D_{b-}^{\phi(\alpha),\psi} x(t) := \int_0^1 \phi(\alpha) {^C D_{b-}^{\alpha,\psi}} x(t) d\alpha,$$

where $^C D_{a+}^{\alpha,\psi}$ and $^C D_{b-}^{\alpha,\psi}$ are the left and right ψ-Caputo fractional derivatives of order α, respectively.

Now, we will extend the definitions introduced in [15] to the higher-order case.

In the following, we assume that $n \in \mathbb{N}$ and $\phi : [n-1, n] \to [0,1]$ is a continuous function such that
$$\int_{n-1}^{n} \phi(\alpha) d\alpha > 0.$$

To the best of our knowledge, this is the first work that deals with higher-order distributed-order fractional derivatives.

Definition 3. *Let $x : [a, b] \to \mathbb{R}$ be an integrable function and $\psi \in C^n([a,b], \mathbb{R})$ be an increasing function such that $\psi'(t) \neq 0$, for all $t \in [a,b]$. The left and right Riemann–Liouville distributed-order fractional derivatives of a function x with respect to the kernel ψ are defined by:*

$$D_{a+}^{\phi(\alpha),\psi} x(t) := \int_{n-1}^{n} \phi(\alpha) D_{a+}^{\alpha,\psi} x(t) d\alpha \quad \text{and} \quad D_{b-}^{\phi(\alpha),\psi} x(t) := \int_{n-1}^{n} \phi(\alpha) D_{b-}^{\alpha,\psi} x(t) d\alpha,$$

where $D_{a+}^{\alpha,\psi}$ and $D_{b-}^{\alpha,\psi}$ are the left and right ψ-Riemann–Liouville fractional derivatives of order $\alpha \in [n-1, n]$, respectively.

Definition 4. *Let $x, \psi \in C^n([a,b], \mathbb{R})$ be two functions such that ψ is increasing and $\psi'(t) \neq 0$, for all $t \in [a, b]$. The left and right Caputo distributed-order fractional derivatives of x with respect to ψ are defined by*

$$^C D_{a+}^{\phi(\alpha),\psi} x(t) := \int_{n-1}^{n} \phi(\alpha) {}^C D_{a+}^{\alpha,\psi} x(t) d\alpha \quad \text{and} \quad {}^C D_{b-}^{\phi(\alpha),\psi} x(t) := \int_{n-1}^{n} \phi(\alpha) {}^C D_{b-}^{\alpha,\psi} x(t) d\alpha,$$

where ${}^C D_{a+}^{\alpha,\psi}$ and ${}^C D_{b-}^{\alpha,\psi}$ are the left and right ψ-Caputo fractional derivatives of order $\alpha \in [n-1, n]$, respectively.

In the following, we use the notations

$$I_{a+}^{n-\phi(\alpha),\psi} x(t) := \int_{n-1}^{n} \phi(\alpha) I_{a+}^{n-\alpha,\psi} x(t) d\alpha \quad \text{and} \quad I_{b-}^{n-\phi(\alpha),\psi} x(t) := \int_{n-1}^{n} \phi(\alpha) I_{b-}^{n-\alpha,\psi} x(t) d\alpha,$$

where $I_{a+}^{n-\alpha,\psi}$ and $I_{b-}^{n-\alpha,\psi}$ are, respectively, the left and right Riemann–Liouville fractional integrals of order $n - \alpha$ with respect to the kernel ψ. In addition, we fix two functions ϕ and ψ satisfying the assumptions above. In order to simplify notation, we will use the abbreviated symbol

$$x_\psi^{[m]}(t) := \left(\frac{1}{\psi'(t)} \frac{d}{dt}\right)^m x(t).$$

Next, we prove the integration by parts formulae, which are fundamental tools for the proofs of our main results. In our previous work, we proved a similar result when the fractional order is between 0 and 1 [15] [Theorem 3.1]. In this paper, we present a generalization of such result for the case when function ϕ is defined on the interval $[n-1, n]$.

Theorem 1 (Integration by parts formulae). *Let $x : [a, b] \to \mathbb{R}$ be a continuous function and $y \in C^n([a,b], \mathbb{R})$. Then,*

$$\int_a^b x(t) {}^C D_{a+}^{\phi(\alpha),\psi} y(t) dt = \int_a^b \left(D_{b-}^{\phi(\alpha),\psi} \frac{x(t)}{\psi'(t)} \right) \psi'(t) y(t) dt$$
$$+ \left[\sum_{k=0}^{n-1} \left(\frac{-1}{\psi'(t)} \frac{d}{dt} \right)^k \left(I_{b-}^{n-\phi(\alpha),\psi} \frac{x(t)}{\psi'(t)} \right) y_\psi^{[n-k-1]}(t) \right]_{t=a}^{t=b}$$

and

$$\int_a^b x(t)\,^C D_{b-}^{\phi(\alpha),\psi} y(t)dt = \int_a^b \left(D_{a+}^{\phi(\alpha),\psi} \frac{x(t)}{\psi'(t)} \right) \psi'(t) y(t) dt$$
$$+ \left[\sum_{k=0}^{n-1} (-1)^{n-k} \left(\frac{1}{\psi'(t)} \frac{d}{dt} \right)^k \left(I_{a+}^{n-\phi(\alpha),\psi} \frac{x(t)}{\psi'(t)} \right) y_\psi^{[n-k-1]}(t) \right]_{t=a}^{t=b}.$$

Proof. Using the definition of the left ψ-Caputo distributed-order fractional derivative, we have

$$\int_a^b x(t)\,^C D_{a+}^{\phi(\alpha),\psi} y(t) dt = \int_a^b x(t) \int_{n-1}^n \phi(\alpha)\,^C D_{a+}^{\alpha,\psi} y(t) d\alpha\, dt$$
$$= \int_a^b x(t) \int_{n-1}^n \frac{\phi(\alpha)}{\Gamma(n-\alpha)} \int_a^t \left(\frac{1}{\psi'(s)} \frac{d}{ds} \right)^n y(s) \cdot (\psi(t)-\psi(s))^{n-\alpha-1} \psi'(s) ds d\alpha\, dt$$
$$= \int_a^b x(t) \int_{n-1}^n \frac{\phi(\alpha)}{\Gamma(n-\alpha)} \int_a^t \left(\frac{1}{\psi'(s)} \frac{d}{ds} \right) y_\psi^{[n-1]}(s) \cdot (\psi(t)-\psi(s))^{n-\alpha-1} \psi'(s) ds d\alpha\, dt$$
$$= \int_{n-1}^n \frac{\phi(\alpha)}{\Gamma(n-\alpha)} \int_a^b x(t) \int_a^t \frac{d}{ds} y_\psi^{[n-1]}(s) \cdot (\psi(t)-\psi(s))^{n-\alpha-1} ds dt\, d\alpha.$$

Applying Dirichlet's formula, we get

$$\int_{n-1}^n \frac{\phi(\alpha)}{\Gamma(n-\alpha)} \int_a^b x(t) \int_a^t \frac{d}{ds} y_\psi^{[n-1]}(s) \cdot (\psi(t)-\psi(s))^{n-\alpha-1} ds dt\, d\alpha$$
$$= \int_{n-1}^n \frac{\phi(\alpha)}{\Gamma(n-\alpha)} \int_a^b \frac{d}{ds} y_\psi^{[n-1]}(s) \int_s^b x(t)(\psi(t)-\psi(s))^{n-\alpha-1} dt ds\, d\alpha.$$

Integrating by parts, we have

$$\int_a^b \frac{d}{ds} y_\psi^{[n-1]}(s) \int_s^b x(t)(\psi(t)-\psi(s))^{n-\alpha-1} dt\, ds$$
$$= \left[\int_s^b x(t)(\psi(t)-\psi(s))^{n-\alpha-1} dt \cdot y_\psi^{[n-1]}(s) \right]_{s=a}^{s=b}$$
$$- \int_a^b y_\psi^{[n-1]}(s) \frac{d}{ds} \left(\int_s^b x(t)(\psi(t)-\psi(s))^{n-\alpha-1} dt \right) ds$$
$$= \left[\int_s^b x(t)(\psi(t)-\psi(s))^{n-\alpha-1} dt \cdot y_\psi^{[n-1]}(s) \right]_{s=a}^{s=b}$$
$$+ \int_a^b \left(\frac{-1}{\psi'(s)} \frac{d}{ds} \right) \left(\int_s^b x(t)(\psi(t)-\psi(s))^{n-\alpha-1} dt \right) \cdot \frac{d}{ds} y_\psi^{[n-2]}(s) ds.$$

Using integration by parts in the last integral, we obtain

$$\int_a^b \left(\frac{-1}{\psi'(s)} \frac{d}{ds} \right) \left(\int_s^b x(t)(\psi(t)-\psi(s))^{n-\alpha-1} dt \right) \cdot \frac{d}{ds} y_\psi^{[n-2]}(s) ds$$
$$= \left[\left(\frac{-1}{\psi'(s)} \frac{d}{ds} \right) \left(\int_s^b x(t)(\psi(t)-\psi(s))^{n-\alpha-1} dt \right) \cdot y_\psi^{[n-2]}(s) \right]_{s=a}^{s=b}$$
$$- \int_a^b y_\psi^{[n-2]}(s) \frac{d}{ds} \left(\frac{-1}{\psi'(s)} \frac{d}{ds} \right) \left(\int_s^b x(t)(\psi(t)-\psi(s))^{n-\alpha-1} dt \right) ds$$
$$= \left[\left(\frac{-1}{\psi'(s)} \frac{d}{ds} \right) \left(\int_s^b x(t)(\psi(t)-\psi(s))^{n-\alpha-1} dt \right) \cdot y_\psi^{[n-2]}(s) \right]_{s=a}^{s=b}$$
$$+ \int_a^b \left(\frac{1}{\psi'(s)} \frac{d}{ds} \right)^2 \left(\int_s^b x(t)(\psi(t)-\psi(s))^{n-\alpha-1} dt \right) \cdot \frac{d}{ds} y_\psi^{[n-3]}(s) ds.$$

Since

$$\int_a^b \left(\frac{1}{\psi'(s)}\frac{d}{ds}\right)^2 \left(\int_s^b x(t)(\psi(t)-\psi(s))^{n-\alpha-1}dt\right) \cdot \frac{d}{ds}y_\psi^{[n-3]}(s)ds$$

$$= \left[\left(\frac{1}{\psi'(s)}\frac{d}{ds}\right)^2 \left(\int_s^b x(t)(\psi(t)-\psi(s))^{n-\alpha-1}dt\right) \cdot y_\psi^{[n-3]}(s)\right]_{s=a}^{s=b}$$

$$- \int_a^b y_\psi^{[n-3]}(s)\frac{d}{ds}\left[\left(\frac{1}{\psi'(s)}\frac{d}{ds}\right)^2 \left(\int_s^b x(t)(\psi(t)-\psi(s))^{n-\alpha-1}dt\right)\right]ds$$

$$= \left[\left(\frac{1}{\psi'(s)}\frac{d}{ds}\right)^2 \left(\int_s^b x(t)(\psi(t)-\psi(s))^{n-\alpha-1}dt\right) \cdot y_\psi^{[n-3]}(s)\right]_{s=a}^{s=b}$$

$$+ \int_a^b \left(\frac{-1}{\psi'(s)}\frac{d}{ds}\right)^3 \left(\int_s^b x(t)(\psi(t)-\psi(s))^{n-\alpha-1}dt\right) \cdot \frac{d}{ds}y_\psi^{[n-4]}(s)ds,$$

then we get

$$\int_a^b \frac{d}{ds}y_\psi^{[n-1]}(s) \int_s^b x(t)(\psi(t)-\psi(s))^{n-\alpha-1}dt\, ds$$

$$= \left[\sum_{k=0}^{2}\left(\frac{-1}{\psi'(s)}\frac{d}{ds}\right)^k \left(\int_s^b x(t)(\psi(t)-\psi(s))^{n-\alpha-1}dt\right) \cdot y_\psi^{[n-k-1]}(s)\right]_{s=a}^{s=b}$$

$$+ \int_a^b \left(\frac{-1}{\psi'(s)}\frac{d}{ds}\right)^3 \left(\int_s^b x(t)(\psi(t)-\psi(s))^{n-\alpha-1}dt\right) \cdot \frac{d}{ds}y_\psi^{[n-4]}(s)ds.$$

Repeating the process of integration by parts $n-3$ more times, we prove the formula. Using similar techniques, we deduce the integration by parts formula involving the operator $^C D_{b^-}^{\phi(\alpha),\psi}$. □

3. Main Results

3.1. Variational Problems with Time Delay

We begin this section by studying variational problems involving distributed-order fractional derivatives with time delay. For clarity of presentation, we restrict ourselves to the case where $\alpha \in [0,1]$, that is, considering the definitions introduced in [15].

Consider two continuous functions $\phi, \varphi : [0,1] \to [0,1]$ satisfying the following conditions

$$\int_0^1 \phi(\alpha)d\alpha > 0 \quad \text{and} \quad \int_0^1 \varphi(\alpha)d\alpha > 0.$$

In what follows, $a, b \in \mathbb{R}$ are such that $a < b$ and τ is a fixed real number satisfying the condition $0 \leq \tau < b-a$.

We are now in position to present the first problem under study.

Problem 1 ((P_τ)). *Determine a curve $x \in C^1([a-\tau,b],\mathbb{R})$, subject to $x(t) = \mu(t)$ for all $t \in [a-\tau,a]$, where $\mu \in C^1([a-\tau,a],\mathbb{R})$ is a given initial function, that minimizes or maximizes the following functional:*

$$\mathcal{J}(x) := \int_a^b L\left(t, x(t), x(t-\tau), {}^C D_{a^+}^{\phi(\alpha),\psi}x(t), {}^C D_{b^-}^{\varphi(\alpha),\psi}x(t)\right)dt, \tag{1}$$

where $L : [a,b] \times \mathbb{R}^4 \to \mathbb{R}$ is assumed to be continuously differentiable with respect to the second, third, fourth, and fifth variables. We will consider the variational problem (P_τ) with and without fixed terminal boundary condition, and also with isoperimetric or holonomic constraints.

Let us fix the following notations: by $\partial_i L$, we denote the partial derivative of L with respect to its ith-coordinate and

$$[x]_\tau(t) := \left(t, x(t), x(t-\tau), {}^C D_{a+}^{\phi(\alpha),\psi} x(t), {}^C D_{b-}^{\varphi(\alpha),\psi} x(t)\right).$$

To simplify the presentation of our results, we consider the following conditions:

$$C_\phi^-[H, i, b-\tau]: \quad t \to \left(D_{(b-\tau)-}^{\phi(\alpha),\psi} \frac{\partial_i H[x]_\tau}{\psi'}\right)(t) \text{ is continuous for all } t \in [a, b-\tau]$$

$$C_\phi^-[H, i, b]: \quad t \to \left(D_{b-}^{\phi(\alpha),\psi} \frac{\partial_i H[x]_\tau}{\psi'}\right)(t) \text{ is continuous for all } t \in [b-\tau, b]$$

$$C_\phi^+[H, i, a]: \quad t \to \left(D_{a+}^{\varphi(\alpha),\psi} \frac{\partial_i H[x]_\tau}{\psi'}\right)(t) \text{ is continuous for all } t \in [a, b-\tau]$$

$$C_\phi^+[H, i, b-\tau]: \quad t \to \left(D_{(b-\tau)+}^{\varphi(\alpha),\psi} \frac{\partial_i H[x]_\tau}{\psi'}\right)(t) \text{ is continuous for all } t \in [b-\tau, b]$$

where H is a function and $i \in \mathbb{N}$.

Theorem 2 (Fractional Euler–Lagrange equations and natural boundary condition for problem (P_τ)). *Suppose that L satisfies the conditions $C_\phi^-[L, 4, b-\tau]$, $C_\phi^+[L, 5, a]$, $C_\phi^-[L, 4, b]$ and $C_\phi^+[L, 5, b-\tau]$. If $x \in C^1([a-\tau, b], \mathbb{R})$ is an extremizer of functional $\mathcal{J}$, then x satisfies the following Euler–Lagrange equations*

$$\partial_2 L[x]_\tau(t) + \partial_3 L[x]_\tau(t+\tau) + \left(D_{(b-\tau)-}^{\phi(\alpha),\psi} \frac{\partial_4 L[x]_\tau(t)}{\psi'(t)}\right)\psi'(t) + \left(D_{a+}^{\varphi(\alpha),\psi} \frac{\partial_5 L[x]_\tau(t)}{\psi'(t)}\right)\psi'(t) \\ - \int_0^1 \frac{\phi(\alpha)}{\Gamma(1-\alpha)} \frac{d}{dt} \int_{b-\tau}^b (\psi(s)-\psi(t))^{-\alpha} \partial_4 L[x]_\tau(s) ds d\alpha = 0, \forall t \in [a, b-\tau] \quad (2)$$

and

$$\partial_2 L[x]_\tau(t) + \left(D_{b-}^{\phi(\alpha),\psi} \frac{\partial_4 L[x]_\tau(t)}{\psi'(t)}\right)\psi'(t) + \left(D_{(b-\tau)+}^{\varphi(\alpha),\psi} \frac{\partial_5 L[x]_\tau(t)}{\psi'(t)}\right)\psi'(t) \\ + \int_0^1 \frac{\varphi(\alpha)}{\Gamma(1-\alpha)} \frac{d}{dt} \int_a^{b-\tau} (\psi(t)-\psi(s))^{-\alpha} \partial_5 L[x]_\tau(s) ds d\alpha = 0, \forall t \in [b-\tau, b]. \quad (3)$$

If $x(b)$ is free, then the following natural boundary condition holds:

$$I_{b-}^{1-\phi(\alpha),\psi} \frac{\partial_4 L[x]_\tau(b)}{\psi'(b)} = I_{a+}^{1-\varphi(\alpha),\psi} \frac{\partial_5 L[x]_\tau(b)}{\psi'(b)}. \quad (4)$$

Proof. Consider that $h \in C^1([a-\tau, b], \mathbb{R})$ is an arbitrary function such that $h(t) = 0$, $a - \tau \leq t \leq a$. Define the function j by $j(\epsilon) := \mathcal{J}(x + \epsilon h)$, $\epsilon \in \mathbb{R}$. Since x is an extremizer of $\mathcal{J}$, $j'(0) = 0$, and we have that

$$\int_a^b \left(\partial_2 L[x]_\tau(t) \cdot h(t) + \partial_3 L[x]_\tau(t) \cdot h(t-\tau) + \partial_4 L[x]_\tau(t) \cdot {}^C D_{a+}^{\phi(\alpha),\psi} h(t) \right. \\ \left. + \partial_5 L[x]_\tau(t) \cdot {}^C D_{b-}^{\varphi(\alpha),\psi} h(t)\right) dt = 0. \quad (5)$$

Since

$$\int_a^b \partial_3 L[x]_\tau(t) \cdot h(t-\tau) dt = \int_{a-\tau}^a \partial_3 L[x]_\tau(t+\tau) \cdot h(t) dt + \int_a^{b-\tau} \partial_3 L[x]_\tau(t+\tau) \cdot h(t) dt,$$

and $h(t) = 0$ for $t \in [a-\tau, a]$, then we get

$$\int_a^b \partial_3 L[x]_\tau(t) \cdot h(t-\tau) dt = \int_a^{b-\tau} \partial_3 L[x]_\tau(t+\tau) \cdot h(t) dt. \tag{6}$$

Replacing (6) into (5), we get

$$\int_a^{b-\tau} \left(\partial_2 L[x]_\tau(t) + \partial_3 L[x]_\tau(t+\tau) \right) \cdot h(t) dt + \int_{b-\tau}^b \partial_2 L[x]_\tau(t) \cdot h(t) dt$$
$$+ \int_a^b \left(\partial_4 L[x]_\tau(t) \cdot {}^C D_{a+}^{\phi(\alpha),\psi} h(t) + \partial_5 L[x]_\tau(t) \cdot {}^C D_{b-}^{\phi(\alpha),\psi} h(t) \right) dt = 0. \tag{7}$$

Note that, for all $t \in [a, b-\tau]$, we have

$$D_{b-}^{\phi(\alpha),\psi} \frac{\partial_4 L[x]_\tau(t)}{\psi'(t)} = D_{(b-\tau)-}^{\phi(\alpha),\psi} \frac{\partial_4 L[x]_\tau(t)}{\psi'(t)}$$
$$- \int_0^1 \frac{\phi(\alpha)}{\Gamma(1-\alpha)} \left(\frac{1}{\psi'(t)} \frac{d}{dt} \right) \int_{b-\tau}^b (\psi(s) - \psi(t))^{-\alpha} \partial_4 L[x]_\tau(s) ds d\alpha \tag{8}$$

and, for all $t \in [b-\tau, b]$, we have

$$D_{a+}^{\varphi(\alpha),\psi} \frac{\partial_5 L[x]_\tau(t)}{\psi'(t)} = D_{(b-\tau)+}^{\varphi(\alpha),\psi} \frac{\partial_5 L[x]_\tau(t)}{\psi'(t)}$$
$$+ \int_0^1 \frac{\varphi(\alpha)}{\Gamma(1-\alpha)} \left(\frac{1}{\psi'(t)} \frac{d}{dt} \right) \int_a^{b-\tau} (\psi(t) - \psi(s))^{-\alpha} \partial_5 L[x]_\tau(s) ds d\alpha = 0. \tag{9}$$

Using Theorem 1 and (8), we obtain

$$\int_a^b \partial_4 L[x]_\tau(t) \cdot {}^C D_{a+}^{\phi(\alpha),\psi} h(t) dt = \int_a^{b-\tau} \left(\left(D_{(b-\tau)-}^{\phi(\alpha),\psi} \frac{\partial_4 L[x]_\tau(t)}{\psi'(t)} \right) \psi'(t) \right.$$
$$\left. - \int_0^1 \frac{\phi(\alpha)}{\Gamma(1-\alpha)} \frac{d}{dt} \int_{b-\tau}^b (\psi(s) - \psi(t))^{-\alpha} \partial_4 L[x]_\tau(s) ds d\alpha \right) h(t) dt \tag{10}$$
$$+ \int_{b-\tau}^b \left(D_{b-}^{\phi(\alpha),\psi} \frac{\partial_4 L[x]_\tau(t)}{\psi'(t)} \right) \psi'(t) h(t) dt + \left[\left(I_{b-}^{1-\phi(\alpha),\psi} \frac{\partial_4 L[x]_\tau(t)}{\psi'(t)} \right) h(t) \right]_{t=a}^{t=b}.$$

Once again, by Theorem 1 and (9), we obtain

$$\int_a^b \partial_5 L[x]_\tau(t) \cdot {}^C D_{b-}^{\varphi(\alpha),\psi} h(t) dt = \int_{b-\tau}^b \left(\left(D_{(b-\tau)+}^{\varphi(\alpha),\psi} \frac{\partial_5 L[x]_\tau(t)}{\psi'(t)} \right) \psi'(t) \right.$$
$$\left. + \int_0^1 \frac{\varphi(\alpha)}{\Gamma(1-\alpha)} \frac{d}{dt} \int_a^{b-\tau} (\psi(t) - \psi(s))^{-\alpha} \partial_5 L[x]_\tau(s) ds d\alpha \right) h(t) dt \tag{11}$$
$$+ \int_a^{b-\tau} \left(D_{a+}^{\varphi(\alpha),\psi} \frac{\partial_5 L[x]_\tau(t)}{\psi'(t)} \right) \psi'(t) h(t) dt - \left[\left(I_{a+}^{1-\varphi(\alpha),\psi} \frac{\partial_5 L[x]_\tau(t)}{\psi'(t)} \right) h(t) \right]_{t=a}^{t=b}.$$

Replacing (10) and (11) into (7), we get that

$$\int_a^{b-\tau} \left(\partial_2 L[x]_\tau(t) + \partial_3 L[x]_\tau(t+\tau) + \left(D_{(b-\tau)^-}^{\phi(\alpha),\psi} \frac{\partial_4 L[x]_\tau(t)}{\psi'(t)} \right) \psi'(t) \right.$$
$$\left. - \int_0^1 \frac{\phi(\alpha)}{\Gamma(1-\alpha)} \frac{d}{dt} \int_{b-\tau}^b (\psi(s)-\psi(t))^{-\alpha} \partial_4 L[x]_\tau(s) ds\, d\alpha + \left(D_{a^+}^{\varphi(\alpha),\psi} \frac{\partial_5 L[x]_\tau(t)}{\psi'(t)} \right) \psi'(t) \right) h(t) dt$$
$$+ \int_{b-\tau}^b \left(\partial_2 L[x]_\tau(t) + \left(D_{b^-}^{\phi(\alpha),\psi} \frac{\partial_4 L[x]_\tau(t)}{\psi'(t)} \right) \psi'(t) + \left(D_{(b-\tau)^+}^{\varphi(\alpha),\psi} \frac{\partial_5 L[x]_\tau(t)}{\psi'(t)} \right) \psi'(t) \right.$$
$$\left. + \int_0^1 \frac{\varphi(\alpha)}{\Gamma(1-\alpha)} \frac{d}{dt} \int_a^{b-\tau} (\psi(t)-\psi(s))^{-\alpha} \partial_5 L[x]_\tau(s) ds\, d\alpha \right) h(t) dt \qquad (12)$$
$$+ \left[\left(I_{b^-}^{1-\phi(\alpha),\psi} \frac{\partial_4 L[x]_\tau(t)}{\psi'(t)} \right) h(t) \right]_{t=a}^{t=b} - \left[\left(I_{a^+}^{1-\varphi(\alpha),\psi} \frac{\partial_5 L[x]_\tau(t)}{\psi'(t)} \right) h(t) \right]_{t=a}^{t=b} = 0.$$

From the arbitrariness of h, we get the desired Equations (2)–(4). □

Next, we consider the case where we add to problem (P_τ) an isoperimetric restriction.

Problem 2 $((P_{I_\tau}))$. *The isoperimetric problem with a time delay τ can be formulated in the following way: minimize or maximize the functional $\mathcal{J}$ in* (1) *subject to an integral constraint of type*

$$\mathcal{I}(x) := \int_a^b G[x]_\tau(t) dt = k, \qquad (13)$$

where $k \in \mathbb{R}$ is fixed and $G : [a,b] \times \mathbb{R}^4 \to \mathbb{R}$ is a continuously differentiable function with respect to the second, third, fourth, and fifth variables.

The following theorem presents necessary conditions for x to be a solution of the fractional isoperimetric problem (P_{I_τ}) under the assumption that x is not an extremal for G.

Theorem 3 (Necessary optimality conditions for problem (P_{I_τ})—Case I). *Let $x \in C^1([a-\tau, b], \mathbb{R})$ be a curve such that $\mathcal{J}$ attains an extremum at x, when subject to the integral constraint* (13). *Assume that x does not satisfy the Euler–Lagrange Equation* (2) *or* (3) *with respect to G. Moreover, suppose that L satisfies the conditions $C_\phi^-[L, 4, b-\tau]$, $C_\varphi^+[L, 5, a]$, $C_\phi^-[L, 4, b]$ and $C_\varphi^+[L, 5, b-\tau]$, and G satisfies the conditions $C_\phi^-[G, 4, b-\tau]$, $C_\varphi^+[G, 5, a]$, $C_\phi^-[G, 4, b]$ and $C_\varphi^+[G, 5, b-\tau]$. Then, there exists $\lambda \in \mathbb{R}$ such that x is a solution of the equations*

$$\partial_2 H[x]_\tau(t) + \partial_3 H[x]_\tau(t+\tau) + \left(D_{(b-\tau)^-}^{\phi(\alpha),\psi} \frac{\partial_4 H[x]_\tau(t)}{\psi'(t)} \right) \psi'(t) + \left(D_{a^+}^{\varphi(\alpha),\psi} \frac{\partial_5 H[x]_\tau(t)}{\psi'(t)} \right) \psi'(t)$$
$$- \int_0^1 \frac{\phi(\alpha)}{\Gamma(1-\alpha)} \frac{d}{dt} \int_{b-\tau}^b (\psi(s)-\psi(t))^{-\alpha} \partial_4 H[x]_\tau(s) ds\, d\alpha = 0, \forall t \in [a, b-\tau] \qquad (14)$$

and

$$\partial_2 H[x]_\tau(t) + \left(D_{b^-}^{\phi(\alpha),\psi} \frac{\partial_4 H[x]_\tau(t)}{\psi'(t)} \right) \psi'(t) + \left(D_{(b-\tau)^+}^{\varphi(\alpha),\psi} \frac{\partial_5 H[x]_\tau(t)}{\psi'(t)} \right) \psi'(t)$$
$$+ \int_0^1 \frac{\varphi(\alpha)}{\Gamma(1-\alpha)} \frac{d}{dt} \int_a^{b-\tau} (\psi(t)-\psi(s))^{-\alpha} \partial_5 H[x]_\tau(s) ds\, d\alpha = 0, \forall t \in [b-\tau, b], \qquad (15)$$

where $H := L + \lambda G$.
If $x(b)$ is free, then

$$I_{b^-}^{1-\phi(\alpha),\psi} \frac{\partial_4 H[x]_\tau(b)}{\psi'(b)} = I_{a^+}^{1-\varphi(\alpha),\psi} \frac{\partial_5 H[x]_\tau(b)}{\psi'(b)}. \qquad (16)$$

Proof. The proof follows from the ideas presented in Theorem 2 and Theorem 3.3 of [15]. □

Now, we present necessary optimality conditions for the case when the solution of the isoperimetric problem is an extremal for the fractional isoperimetric functional (13).

Theorem 4 (Necessary optimality conditions for fractional problem (P_{I_τ})—Case II). *Let x be a curve such that $\mathcal{J}$ attains an extremum at x, when subject to the integral constraint (13). Moreover, suppose that L satisfies the conditions $C_\phi^-[L, 4, b-\tau]$, $C_\phi^+[L, 5, a]$, $C_\phi^-[L, 4, b]$ and $C_\phi^+[L, 5, b-\tau]$, and G satisfies the conditions $C_\phi^-[G, 4, b-\tau]$, $C_\phi^+[G, 5, a]$, $C_\phi^-[G, 4, b]$ and $C_\phi^+[G, 5, b-\tau]$. Then, there exists a vector $(\lambda_0, \lambda) \in \mathbb{R}^2 \setminus \{(0,0)\}$ such that x is a solution of Equations (14) and (15), with the Hamiltonian H defined as $H := \lambda_0 L + \lambda G$. If $x(b)$ is free, then x must satisfy Equation (16).*

Proof. The result is an immediate consequence of Theorem 3. □

In the following, we study variational problems with a holonomic constraint. For this purpose, we now assume that x is a two-dimensional vector function and $L : [a, b] \times \mathbb{R}^8 \to \mathbb{R}$ is assumed to be continuously differentiable with respect to the ith variable, with $i = 2, \ldots, 9$.

Problem 3 ((P_{C_τ})). *Consider the variational problem (P_τ) but in the presence of a holonomic constraint:*

$$g(t, x(t)) = 0, \quad t \in [a, b], \quad (17)$$

where $g : [a, b] \times \mathbb{R}^2 \to \mathbb{R}$ is a C^1 function. The state variable x is a two-dimensional vector function $x = (x_1, x_2)$, where $x_1, x_2 \in C^1([a-\tau, b], \mathbb{R})$. Moreover, the boundary condition

$$x(t) = \mu(t), \, t \in [a-\tau, a], \quad (18)$$

where $\mu \in C^1([a-\tau, a], \mathbb{R}) \times C^1([a-\tau, a], \mathbb{R})$ is a given function, is imposed.

Theorem 5 (Necessary optimality conditions for problem (P_{C_τ})). *Consider the functional*

$$\mathcal{J}(x) = \int_a^b L[x]_\tau(t) dt, \quad (19)$$

defined on $C^1([a-\tau, b], \mathbb{R}) \times C^1([a-\tau, b], \mathbb{R})$ and subject to the constraints (17) and (18). Suppose that L satisfies the conditions $C_\phi^-[L, i+5, b-\tau]$, $C_\phi^+[L, i+7, a]$, $C_\phi^-[L, i+5, b]$ and $C_\phi^+[L, i+7, b-\tau]$, with $i = 1, 2$.

If x is an extremizer of functional $\mathcal{J}$ and if

$$\partial_3 g(t, x(t)) \neq 0, \quad \forall t \in [a, b],$$

then there exists a continuous function $\lambda : [a, b] \to \mathbb{R}$ such that x is a solution of

$$\partial_{i+1} L[x]_\tau(t) + \partial_{i+3} L[x]_\tau(t+\tau) + \left(D_{(b-\tau)^-}^{\phi(\alpha), \psi} \frac{\partial_{i+5} L[x]_\tau(t)}{\psi'(t)}\right) \psi'(t)$$
$$+ \left(D_{a^+}^{\phi(\alpha), \psi} \frac{\partial_{i+7} L[x]_\tau(t)}{\psi'(t)}\right) \psi'(t) - \int_0^1 \frac{\phi(\alpha)}{\Gamma(1-\alpha)} \frac{d}{dt} \int_{b-\tau}^b (\psi(s) - \psi(t))^{-\alpha} \partial_{i+5} L[x]_\tau(s) ds d\alpha \quad (20)$$
$$+ \lambda(t) \cdot \partial_{i+1} g(t, x(t)) = 0, \quad \forall t \in [a, b-\tau], \, i = 1, 2$$

and

$$\partial_{i+1} L[x]_\tau(t) + \left(D_{b^-}^{\phi(\alpha), \psi} \frac{\partial_{i+5} L[x]_\tau(t)}{\psi'(t)}\right) \psi'(t) + \left(D_{(b-\tau)^+}^{\phi(\alpha), \psi} \frac{\partial_{i+7} L[x]_\tau(t)}{\psi'(t)}\right) \psi'(t)$$
$$+ \int_0^1 \frac{\phi(\alpha)}{\Gamma(1-\alpha)} \frac{d}{dt} \int_a^{b-\tau} (\psi(t) - \psi(s))^{-\alpha} \partial_{i+7} L[x]_\tau(s) ds d\alpha + \lambda(t) \cdot \partial_{i+1} g(t, x(t)) = 0, \quad (21)$$
$$\forall t \in [b-\tau, b], \, i = 1, 2.$$

If $x(b)$ is free, then, for $i = 1, 2$,

$$I_{b^-}^{1-\phi(\alpha),\psi} \frac{\partial_{i+5} L[x]_\tau(b)}{\psi'(b)} = I_{a^+}^{1-\phi(\alpha),\psi} \frac{\partial_{i+7} L[x]_\tau(b)}{\psi'(b)}. \tag{22}$$

Proof. The proof follows combining the ideas from Theorem 2 above with Theorem 3.5 from [15]. □

Now, we focus our attention on sufficient optimality conditions for all the variational problems studied previously.

Definition 5. *Function $f(t, x_2, x_3, ..., x_n)$ defined on $U \subseteq \mathbb{R}^n$ is called convex (resp. concave) if $\partial_i f(t, x_2, x_3, ..., x_n)$, $i = 2, ..., n$, exist and are continuous, and if*

$$f(t, x_2 + h_2, x_3 + h_3, ..., x_n + h_n) - f(t, x_2, x_3, ..., x_n) \geq (\text{resp. } \leq) \sum_{i=2}^{n} \partial_i f(t, x_2, x_3, ..., x_n) h_i$$

for all $(t, x_2, x_3, ..., x_n), (t, x_2 + h_2, x_3 + h_3, ..., x_n + h_n) \in U$.

Theorem 6 (Sufficient optimality conditions for problem (P_τ)). *Let L be convex (resp. concave) in $[a, b] \times \mathbb{R}^4$. Then, each solution $\bar{x}$ of the fractional Euler–Lagrange Equations (2) and (3) minimizes (resp. maximizes) the functional $\mathcal{J}$ given in (1), subject to the boundary conditions $x(t) = \mu(t)$, $t \in [a - \tau, a]$ and $x(b) = \bar{x}(b)$. If $x(b)$ is free, then each solution $\bar{x}$ of the Equations (2)–(4) minimizes (resp. maximizes) $\mathcal{J}$.*

Proof. We prove the case when L is convex. The other case is similar. Consider $h \in C^1([a - \tau, b], \mathbb{R})$ an arbitrary function. Since L is convex, we can conclude that

$$\mathcal{J}(\bar{x} + h) - \mathcal{J}(\bar{x}) \geq \int_a^b \Big(\partial_2 L[\bar{x}]_\tau(t) \cdot h(t) + \partial_3 L[\bar{x}]_\tau(t) \cdot h(t - \tau) + \partial_4 L[\bar{x}]_\tau(t) \cdot {}^C D_{a^+}^{\phi(\alpha),\psi} h(t) + \partial_5 L[\bar{x}]_\tau(t) \cdot {}^C D_{b^-}^{\phi(\alpha),\psi} h(t) \Big) dt.$$

Using the same techniques used in the proof of Theorem 2, we get

$$\mathcal{J}(\bar{x} + h) - \mathcal{J}(\bar{x}) \geq \int_a^{b-\tau} \Bigg(\partial_2 L[\bar{x}]_\tau(t) + \partial_3 L[\bar{x}]_\tau(t + \tau) + \Big(D_{(b-\tau)^-}^{\phi(\alpha),\psi} \frac{\partial_4 L[\bar{x}]_\tau(t)}{\psi'(t)} \Big) \psi'(t)$$
$$- \int_0^1 \frac{\phi(\alpha)}{\Gamma(1-\alpha)} \frac{d}{dt} \int_{b-\tau}^b (\psi(s) - \psi(t))^{-\alpha} \partial_4 L[\bar{x}]_\tau(s) ds d\alpha + \Big(D_{a^+}^{\phi(\alpha),\psi} \frac{\partial_5 L[\bar{x}]_\tau(t)}{\psi'(t)} \Big) \psi'(t) \Bigg) h(t) dt$$
$$+ \int_{b-\tau}^b \Bigg(\partial_2 L[\bar{x}]_\tau(t) + \Big(D_{b^-}^{\phi(\alpha),\psi} \frac{\partial_4 L[\bar{x}]_\tau(t)}{\psi'(t)} \Big) \psi'(t) + \Big(D_{(b-\tau)^+}^{\phi(\alpha),\psi} \frac{\partial_5 L[\bar{x}]_\tau(t)}{\psi'(t)} \Big) \psi'(t) \tag{23}$$
$$+ \int_0^1 \frac{\phi(\alpha)}{\Gamma(1-\alpha)} \frac{d}{dt} \int_a^{b-\tau} (\psi(t) - \psi(s))^{-\alpha} \partial_5 L[\bar{x}]_\tau(s) ds d\alpha \Bigg) h(t) dt$$
$$+ \Bigg[\Big(I_{b^-}^{1-\phi(\alpha),\psi} \frac{\partial_4 L[\bar{x}]_\tau(t)}{\psi'(t)} \Big) h(t) \Bigg]_{t=a}^{t=b} - \Bigg[\Big(I_{a^+}^{1-\phi(\alpha),\psi} \frac{\partial_5 L[\bar{x}]_\tau(t)}{\psi'(t)} \Big) h(t) \Bigg]_{t=a}^{t=b}.$$

If $x(b)$ is fixed then $h(a) = h(b) = 0$, and so from (23) we obtain

$$\mathcal{J}(\bar{x}+h) - \mathcal{J}(\bar{x}) \geq \int_a^{b-\tau} \left(\partial_2 L[\bar{x}]_\tau(t) + \partial_3 L[\bar{x}]_\tau(t+\tau) + \left(D_{(b-\tau)^-}^{\phi(\alpha),\psi} \frac{\partial_4 L[\bar{x}]_\tau(t)}{\psi'(t)} \right) \psi'(t) \right.$$
$$\left. - \int_0^1 \frac{\phi(\alpha)}{\Gamma(1-\alpha)} \frac{d}{dt} \int_{b-\tau}^b (\psi(s)-\psi(t))^{-\alpha} \partial_4 L[\bar{x}]_\tau(s) ds d\alpha + \left(D_{a^+}^{\phi(\alpha),\psi} \frac{\partial_5 L[\bar{x}]_\tau(t)}{\psi'(t)} \right) \psi'(t) \right) h(t) dt$$
$$+ \int_{b-\tau}^b \left(\partial_2 L[\bar{x}]_\tau(t) + \left(D_{b^-}^{\phi(\alpha),\psi} \frac{\partial_4 L[\bar{x}]_\tau(t)}{\psi'(t)} \right) \psi'(t) + \left(D_{(b-\tau)^+}^{\phi(\alpha),\psi} \frac{\partial_5 L[\bar{x}]_\tau(t)}{\psi'(t)} \right) \psi'(t) \right.$$
$$\left. + \int_0^1 \frac{\phi(\alpha)}{\Gamma(1-\alpha)} \frac{d}{dt} \int_a^{b-\tau} (\psi(t)-\psi(s))^{-\alpha} \partial_5 L[\bar{x}]_\tau(s) ds d\alpha \right) h(t) dt.$$

Since $\bar{x}$ is a solution of the fractional Euler–Lagrange Equations (2) and (3), then we conclude that $\mathcal{J}(\bar{x}+h) - \mathcal{J}(\bar{x}) \geq 0$. The case when $x(b)$ is free follows by considering $h(t) = 0$, $t \in [a-\tau, a]$ and $h(b)$ non-zero in (23). □

Using similar techniques as the ones used in the proof of the last theorem, we can prove the following two results.

Theorem 7 (Sufficient optimality conditions for problem (P_{I_τ})). *Let us assume that, for some constant λ, the functions L and λG are convex (resp. concave) in $[a,b] \times \mathbb{R}^4$ and define the function H as $H = L + \lambda G$. Then, each solution $\bar{x}$ of the fractional Equations (14) and (15) minimizes (resp. maximizes) the functional $\mathcal{J}$ given in (1), subject to the restrictions $x(t) = \mu(t)$, $t \in [a-\tau, a]$ and $x(b) = \bar{x}(b)$, and the integral constraint (13). If $x(b)$ is free, then each solution $\bar{x}$ of the fractional Equations (14)–(16) minimizes (resp. maximizes) $\mathcal{J}$ subject to (13).*

Theorem 8 (Sufficient optimality conditions for problem (P_{C_τ})). *Consider the functional $\mathcal{J}$ defined in (19), where the Lagrangian function L is convex (resp. concave) in $[a,b] \times \mathbb{R}^7$. Define function $\lambda : [a,b] \to \mathbb{R}$ by*

$$\lambda(t) := -\frac{1}{\partial_3 g(t, x(t))} \left(\partial_3 L[x]_\tau(t) + \partial_5 L[x]_\tau(t+\tau) + \left(D_{(b-\tau)^-}^{\phi(\alpha),\psi} \frac{\partial_7 L[x]_\tau(t)}{\psi'(t)} \right) \psi'(t) \right.$$
$$\left. + \left(D_{a^+}^{\phi(\alpha),\psi} \frac{\partial_9 L[x]_\tau(t)}{\psi'(t)} \right) \psi'(t) - \int_0^1 \frac{\phi(\alpha)}{\Gamma(1-\alpha)} \frac{d}{dt} \int_{b-\tau}^b (\psi(s)-\psi(t))^{-\alpha} \partial_7 L[x]_\tau(s) ds d\alpha \right),$$

for $t \in [a, b-\tau]$, and

$$\lambda(t) := -\frac{1}{\partial_3 g(t, x(t))} \left(\partial_3 L[x]_\tau(t) + \left(D_{b^-}^{\phi(\alpha),\psi} \frac{\partial_7 L[x]_\tau(t)}{\psi'(t)} \right) \psi'(t) \right.$$
$$\left. + \left(D_{(b-\tau)^+}^{\phi(\alpha),\psi} \frac{\partial_9 L[x]_\tau(t)}{\psi'(t)} \right) \psi'(t) + \int_0^1 \frac{\phi(\alpha)}{\Gamma(1-\alpha)} \frac{d}{dt} \int_a^{b-\tau} (\psi(t)-\psi(s))^{-\alpha} \partial_9 L[x]_\tau(s) ds d\alpha \right),$$

for $t \in [b-\tau, b]$, where g is a C^1 function, such that $\partial_3 g(t, x(t)) \neq 0$ for all $t \in [a,b]$. Then, each solution $\bar{x} = (\bar{x}_1, \bar{x}_2)$ of the Equations (20) and (21) minimizes (resp. maximizes) the functional $\mathcal{J}$, subject to the restrictions $x(t) = \mu(t)$, $t \in [a-\tau, a]$ and $x(b) = \bar{x}(b)$, and the holonomic constraint (17). In addition, if $x(b)$ is free, then each solution $\bar{x}$ of the fractional Equations (20)–(22) minimizes (resp. maximizes) $\mathcal{J}$ subject to (17).

3.2. Higher-Order Variational Problems

In this section, we consider the general case with respect to fractional orders. Thus, the distributions ϕ_i, φ_i have domain $[i-1, i], i = 1, \ldots, n$, where $n \in \mathbb{N}$ is fixed, with

$$\int_{i-1}^{i} \phi_i(\alpha) d\alpha > 0 \quad \text{and} \quad \int_{i-1}^{i} \varphi_i(\alpha) d\alpha > 0.$$

The problem is formulated as follows:

Problem 4 ((P_n)). *Find a curve $x \in C^n([a,b], \mathbb{R})$ for which the functional*

$$\mathcal{J}(x) := \int_a^b L\left(t, x(t), {}^C D_{a+}^{\phi_1(\alpha), \psi} x(t), {}^C D_{b-}^{\varphi_1(\alpha), \psi} x(t), \ldots, {}^C D_{a+}^{\phi_n(\alpha), \psi} x(t), {}^C D_{b-}^{\varphi_n(\alpha), \psi} x(t)\right) dt, \quad (24)$$

attains a minimum or a maximum value, where $L : [a,b] \times \mathbb{R}^{2n+1} \to \mathbb{R}$ is a continuously differentiable function. In addition, the following boundary conditions

$$x^{(i)}(a) = x_a^i \quad \text{and} \quad x^{(i)}(b) = x_b^i, \text{ with } x_a^i, x_b^i \in \mathbb{R}, \ i = 0, \ldots, n-1 \quad (25)$$

may be assumed.

We will consider the variational problem (P_n) with and without fixed boundary conditions (25), and also with isoperimetric or holonomic constraints.

As done previously, we use the abbreviations

$$[x]_n(t) := \left(t, x(t), {}^C D_{a+}^{\phi_1(\alpha), \psi} x(t), {}^C D_{b-}^{\varphi_1(\alpha), \psi} x(t), \ldots, {}^C D_{a+}^{\phi_n(\alpha), \psi} x(t), {}^C D_{b-}^{\varphi_n(\alpha), \psi} x(t)\right)$$

and

$$C_{\phi_i}^-[H, j] : \quad t \to \left(D_{b-}^{\phi_i(\alpha), \psi} \frac{\partial_j H[x]_n}{\psi'}\right)(t) \text{ is continuous for all } t \in [a,b]$$

$$C_{\varphi_i}^+[H, j] : \quad t \to \left(D_{a+}^{\varphi_i(\alpha), \psi} \frac{\partial_j H[x]_n}{\psi'}\right)(t) \text{ is continuous for all } t \in [a,b]$$

where H is a function and $i, j \in \mathbb{N}$.

Theorem 9 (Fractional Euler–Lagrange equation and natural boundary conditions for problem (P_n)). *Let $x \in C^n([a,b], \mathbb{R})$ be an extremizer of functional $\mathcal{J}$ defined by (24). If conditions $C_{\phi_i}^-[L, 2i+1]$ and $C_{\varphi_i}^+[L, 2i+2]$ hold, for all $i \in \{1, \ldots, n\}$, then x satisfies the following Euler–Lagrange equation:*

$$\partial_2 L[x]_n(t) + \sum_{i=1}^n \left[\left(D_{b-}^{\phi_i(\alpha), \psi} \frac{\partial_{2i+1} L[x]_n(t)}{\psi'(t)}\right) \psi'(t) + \left(D_{a+}^{\varphi_i(\alpha), \psi} \frac{\partial_{2i+2} L[x]_n(t)}{\psi'(t)}\right) \psi'(t)\right] = 0, \quad (26)$$

for all $t \in [a,b]$. In addition, if $x^{(i)}(a)$ are free, for $i = 0, \ldots, n-1$, then

$$\sum_{k=i+1}^n \left[\left(\left(-\frac{1}{\psi'(t)} \frac{1}{dt}\right)^{k-i-1} \left(I_{b-}^{k-\phi_k(\alpha), \psi} \frac{\partial_{2k+1} L[x]_n(t)}{\psi'(t)}\right)\right)\right.$$

$$\left. + (-1)^{i+1} \left(\frac{1}{\psi'(t)} \frac{1}{dt}\right)^{k-i-1} \left(I_{a+}^{k-\varphi_k(\alpha), \psi} \frac{\partial_{2k+2} L[x]_n(t)}{\psi'(t)}\right)\right] = 0, \quad \text{at } t = a, \quad (27)$$

and if $x^{(i)}(b)$ are free, for $i = 0, \ldots, n-1$, then

$$\sum_{k=i+1}^{n} \left[\left(\left(-\frac{1}{\psi'(t)} \frac{d}{dt} \right)^{k-i-1} \left(I_{b-}^{k-\phi_k(\alpha),\psi} \frac{\partial_{2k+1} L[x]_n(t)}{\psi'(t)} \right) \right. \right.$$
$$\left. \left. + (-1)^{i+1} \left(\frac{1}{\psi'(t)} \frac{d}{dt} \right)^{k-i-1} \left(I_{a+}^{k-\varphi_k(\alpha),\psi} \frac{\partial_{2k+2} L[x]_n(t)}{\psi'(t)} \right) \right) \right] = 0, \quad \text{at } t = b. \quad (28)$$

Proof. Let $h \in C^n([a,b], \mathbb{R})$ be a function. Observe that, given $i \in \{0, \ldots, n-1\}$, if $x^{(i)}(a)$ or $x^{(i)}(b)$ are fixed, then we need to assume that $h^{(i)}(a) = 0$ or $h^{(i)}(b) = 0$, respectively, and so

$$\left(\frac{1}{\psi'(t)} \frac{d}{dt} \right)^i h(t) = 0, \quad \text{at } t = a \text{ or } t = b,$$

respectively. Defining j as $j(\epsilon) := \mathcal{J}(x + \epsilon h)$, $\epsilon \in \mathbb{R}$, then $j'(0) = 0$, and so

$$\int_a^b \left(\partial_2 L[x]_n(t) \cdot h(t) + \sum_{i=1}^n \left(\partial_{2i+1} L[x]_n(t) \cdot {}^C D_{a+}^{\phi_i(\alpha),\psi} h(t) \right. \right.$$
$$\left. \left. + \partial_{2i+2} L[x]_n(t) \cdot {}^C D_{b-}^{\varphi_i(\alpha),\psi} h(t) \right) \right) dt = 0.$$

Using Theorem 1, we obtain, for each $i \in \{1, \ldots, n\}$,

$$\int_a^b \partial_{2i+1} L[x]_n(t) \cdot {}^C D_{a+}^{\phi_i(\alpha),\psi} h(t) dt = \int_a^b \left(D_{b-}^{\phi_i(\alpha),\psi} \frac{\partial_{2i+1} L[x]_n(t)}{\psi'(t)} \right) \psi'(t) h(t) dt$$
$$+ \sum_{k=0}^{i-1} \left[\left(-\frac{1}{\psi'(t)} \frac{d}{dt} \right)^k \left(I_{b-}^{i-\phi_i(\alpha),\psi} \frac{\partial_{2i+1} L[x]_n(t)}{\psi'(t)} \right) \cdot h_\psi^{[i-k-1]}(t) \right]_{t=a}^{t=b}$$

and

$$\int_a^b \partial_{2i+2} L[x]_n(t) \cdot {}^C D_{b-}^{\varphi_i(\alpha),\psi} h(t) dt = \int_a^b \left(D_{a+}^{\varphi_i(\alpha),\psi} \frac{\partial_{2i+2} L[x]_n(t)}{\psi'(t)} \right) \psi'(t) h(t) dt$$
$$+ \sum_{k=0}^{i-1} \left[(-1)^{i-k} \left(\frac{1}{\psi'(t)} \frac{d}{dt} \right)^k \left(I_{a+}^{i-\varphi_i(\alpha),\psi} \frac{\partial_{2i+2} L[x]_n(t)}{\psi'(t)} \right) \cdot h_\psi^{[i-k-1]}(t) \right]_{t=a}^{t=b}.$$

Therefore,

$$\int_a^b \left(\partial_2 L[x]_n(t) + \sum_{i=1}^n \left[\left(D_{b-}^{\phi_i(\alpha),\psi} \frac{\partial_{2i+1} L[x]_n(t)}{\psi'(t)} \right) \psi'(t) \right. \right.$$
$$\left. \left. + \left(D_{a+}^{\varphi_i(\alpha),\psi} \frac{\partial_{2i+2} L[x]_n(t)}{\psi'(t)} \right) \psi'(t) \right] \right) h(t) dt$$
$$+ \sum_{i=1}^n \sum_{k=0}^{i-1} \left[\left(\left(-\frac{1}{\psi'(t)} \frac{d}{dt} \right)^k \left(I_{b-}^{i-\phi_i(\alpha),\psi} \frac{\partial_{2i+1} L[x]_n(t)}{\psi'(t)} \right) \right. \right.$$
$$\left. \left. + (-1)^{i-k} \left(\frac{1}{\psi'(t)} \frac{d}{dt} \right)^k \left(I_{a+}^{i-\varphi_i(\alpha),\psi} \frac{\partial_{2i+2} L[x]_n(t)}{\psi'(t)} \right) \right) h_\psi^{[i-k-1]}(t) \right]_{t=a}^{t=b} = 0.$$

Since

$$\sum_{i=1}^{n}\sum_{k=0}^{i-1}\left[\left(\left(-\frac{1}{\psi'(t)}\frac{1}{dt}\right)^k\left(\mathrm{I}_{b^-}^{i-\phi_i(\alpha),\psi}\frac{\partial_{2i+1}L[x]_n(t)}{\psi'(t)}\right)\right.\right.$$
$$\left.\left.+(-1)^{i-k}\left(\frac{1}{\psi'(t)}\frac{1}{dt}\right)^k\left(\mathrm{I}_{a^+}^{i-\varphi_i(\alpha),\psi}\frac{\partial_{2i+2}L[x]_n(t)}{\psi'(t)}\right)\right)h_\psi^{[i-k-1]}(t)\right]_{t=a}^{t=b}$$
$$=\sum_{i=0}^{n-1}h_\psi^{[i]}(t)\sum_{k=i+1}^{n}\left[\left(\left(-\frac{1}{\psi'(t)}\frac{1}{dt}\right)^{k-i-1}\left(\mathrm{I}_{b^-}^{k-\phi_k(\alpha),\psi}\frac{\partial_{2k+1}L[x]_n(t)}{\psi'(t)}\right)\right.\right.$$
$$\left.\left.+(-1)^{i+1}\left(\frac{1}{\psi'(t)}\frac{1}{dt}\right)^{k-i-1}\left(\mathrm{I}_{a^+}^{k-\varphi_k(\alpha),\psi}\frac{\partial_{2k+2}L[x]_n(t)}{\psi'(t)}\right)\right)\right]_{t=a}^{t=b},$$

from the arbitrariness of h, we prove (26), (27), and (28). □

When in the presence of an isoperimetric or holonomic contraint, similar results are proven for this new variational problem. To simplify, we will assume that the boundary conditions (25) hold. In addition, the proofs will be omitted since they follow the same pattern as the ones presented before.

Problem 5 ((P_{In})). *The isoperimetric problem can be formulated as follows: minimize or maximize the functional $\mathcal{J}$ in (24) assuming the boundary conditions (25) and also an integral restriction*

$$\mathcal{I}(x) = \int_a^b G[x]_n(t)dt = k, \quad k \in \mathbb{R}, \tag{29}$$

where $G : [a,b] \times \mathbb{R}^{2n+1} \to \mathbb{R}$ is a C^1 function.

Theorem 10 (Necessary optimality conditions for problem (P_{In})—Case I). *Let $x \in C^n([a,b], \mathbb{R})$ be a solution of problem (P_{In}). Suppose that there exists some $t \in [a,b]$ such that*

$$\partial_2 G[x]_n(t) + \sum_{i=1}^{n}\left[\left(\mathrm{D}_{b^-}^{\phi_i(\alpha),\psi}\frac{\partial_{2i+1}G[x]_n(t)}{\psi'(t)}\right)\psi'(t) + \left(\mathrm{D}_{a^+}^{\varphi_i(\alpha),\psi}\frac{\partial_{2i+2}G[x]_n(t)}{\psi'(t)}\right)\psi'(t)\right] \neq 0. \tag{30}$$

If conditions $C_{\phi_i}^-[L, 2i+1]$, $C_{\varphi_i}^+[L, 2i+2]$, $C_{\phi_i}^-[G, 2i+1]$, and $C_{\varphi_i}^+[G, 2i+2]$ hold, for all $i \in \{1, ..., n\}$, then there exists a real number λ such that x is a solution of the equation

$$\partial_2 H[x]_n(t) + \sum_{i=1}^{n}\left[\left(\mathrm{D}_{b^-}^{\phi_i(\alpha),\psi}\frac{\partial_{2i+1}H[x]_n(t)}{\psi'(t)}\right)\psi'(t) + \left(\mathrm{D}_{a^+}^{\varphi_i(\alpha),\psi}\frac{\partial_{2i+2}H[x]_n(t)}{\psi'(t)}\right)\psi'(t)\right] = 0, \tag{31}$$

for all $t \in [a,b]$, where $H := L + \lambda G$.

Theorem 11 (Necessary optimality conditions for problem (P_{In})—Case II). *Let $x \in C^n([a,b], \mathbb{R})$ be a solution of problem (P_{In}). If conditions $C_{\phi_i}^-[L, 2i+1]$, $C_{\varphi_i}^+[L, 2i+2]$, $C_{\phi_i}^-[G, 2i+1]$, and $C_{\varphi_i}^+[G, 2i+2]$ hold, for all $i \in \{1, ..., n\}$, then there exists a vector $(\lambda_0, \lambda) \in \mathbb{R}^2 \setminus \{(0,0)\}$ such that x is a solution of Equation (31) for all $t \in [a,b]$, with the Hamiltonian H defined as $H := \lambda_0 L + \lambda G$.*

To finish this section, we will study problem (P_n) with a holonomic constraint.

Problem 6 ((P_{Cn})). *The objective is to find $x \in C^n([a,b], \mathbb{R}) \times C^n([a,b], \mathbb{R})$ that minimizes or maximizes the functional*

$$\mathcal{J}(x) = \int_a^b L[x]_n(t)dt, \tag{32}$$

defined on $C^n([a,b], \mathbb{R}) \times C^n([a,b], \mathbb{R})$ and subject a constraint

$$g(t, x(t)) = 0, \quad t \in [a,b], \tag{33}$$

where $g : [a,b] \times \mathbb{R}^2 \to \mathbb{R}$ is a C^n function. In addition, boundary conditions

$$x^{(i)}(a) = x_a^{(i)} \text{ and } x^{(i)}(b) = x_b^{(i)}, \quad x_a^i, x_b^i \in \mathbb{R}^2 \text{ for } i = 0, ..., n-1 \tag{34}$$

are imposed on the variational problem.

Theorem 12 (Necessary optimality conditions for problem (P_{C_n})). *Let x be an extremizer of functional $\mathcal{J}$ defined by (32) and subject to the constraints (33)–(34). If conditions $C_{\phi_i}^-[L, 4i+j-1]$ and $C_{\phi_i}^+[L, 4i+j+1]$ hold for all $i \in \{1, ..., n\}$ and $j = 1, 2$, and if*

$$\partial_3 g(t, x(t)) \neq 0, \ \forall \, t \in [a,b],$$

then there exists a continuous function $\lambda : [a,b] \to \mathbb{R}$ such that x is a solution of

$$\partial_{j+1} L[x]_n(t) + \sum_{i=1}^n \left[\left(D_{b-}^{\phi_i(\alpha), \psi} \frac{\partial_{4i+j-1} L[x]_n(t)}{\psi'(t)} \right) \psi'(t) + \left(D_{a+}^{\phi_i(\alpha), \psi} \frac{\partial_{4i+j+1} L[x]_n(t)}{\psi'(t)} \right) \psi'(t) \right] \\ + \lambda(t) \partial_{j+1} g(t, x(t)) = 0, \tag{35}$$

for all $t \in [a,b]$ and $j = 1, 2$.

Remark 1. *In a similar way, we can prove that, in case function L is convex (resp. concave), then the conditions given in Theorems 9–12 are also sufficient conditions to ensure that the candidates of extremizers are indeed minimizers (resp. maximizers) of the functional.*

4. Illustrative Examples

Some illustrative examples are provided to demonstrate the applicability of our results.

Example 1. *Suppose we intend to find a function $\bar{x} \in C^3([0,1], \mathbb{R})$, subject to the initial conditions $x(0) = (\psi(1) - \psi(0))^5$, $x'(0) = -5\psi'(0)(\psi(1) - \psi(0))^4$, $x''(0) = -5\psi''(0)(\psi(1) - \psi(0))^4 + 20(\psi'(0))^2(\psi(1) - \psi(0))^3$, and terminal conditions $x(1) = x'(1) = x''(1) = 0$, that extremizes the functional*

$$\mathcal{J}(x) = \int_0^1 \left({}^C D_{0+}^{\phi_3(\alpha), \psi} x(t) \cdot (\psi(1) - \psi(t))^5 \psi'(t) \right. \\ \left. - x(t) \cdot \frac{(\psi(1) - \psi(t))^3 - (\psi(1) - \psi(t))^2}{\ln(\psi(1) - \psi(t))} \psi'(t) \right) dt,$$

where $\phi_3 : [2, 3] \to [0, 1]$ is defined by

$$\phi_3(\alpha) = \frac{\Gamma(6-\alpha)}{5!}.$$

The Euler–Lagrange equation associated is the following (cf. Theorem 9):

$$-\frac{(\psi(1) - \psi(t))^3 - (\psi(1) - \psi(t))^2}{\ln(\psi(1) - \psi(t))} + D_{1-}^{\phi_3(\alpha), \psi} \left((\psi(1) - \psi(t))^5 \right) = 0.$$

By ([14] Lemma 14),

$$D_{1-}^{\alpha, \psi} \left((\psi(1) - \psi(t))^5 \right) = \frac{5!}{\Gamma(6-\alpha)} (\psi(1) - \psi(t))^{5-\alpha},$$

and so
$$D_{1-}^{\phi_3(\alpha),\psi}((\psi(1)-\psi(t))^5) = \frac{(\psi(1)-\psi(t))^3 - (\psi(1)-\psi(t))^2}{\ln(\psi(1)-\psi(t))},$$
proving that the function $\overline{x}(t) = (\psi(1)-\psi(t))^5$, $t \in [0,1]$, is a candidate to be an extremizer of the proposed problem.

Example 2. We want to find a curve $\overline{x} \in C^1([-1,2],\mathbb{R})$, subject to the condition $x(t) = \mu(t)$, $t \in [-1,0]$, where $\mu \in C^1([-1,0],\mathbb{R})$ is a fixed initial function with $\mu(0) = (\psi(2)-\psi(0))^2$, that minimizes the following functional:

$$\begin{aligned}\mathcal{J}(x) &= \int_0^2 \Bigg(\left(x(t-1)-(\psi(2)-\psi(t-1))^2\right)^2 \\ &\quad + \left({}^C D_{2-}^{\varphi(\alpha),\psi} x(t) - \frac{\psi(t)-\psi(2)+(\psi(2)-\psi(t))^2}{\ln(\psi(2)-\psi(t))}\right)^2\Bigg) dt,\end{aligned}$$

where $\varphi:[0,1] \to [0,1]$ is defined by

$$\varphi(\alpha) = \frac{\Gamma(3-\alpha)}{2}.$$

By Lemma 1 in [13], if $\overline{x}:[-1,2]\to\mathbb{R}$ is defined by $\overline{x}(t) = (\psi(2)-\psi(t))^2$ if $t \in [0,2]$, and $\overline{x}(t) = \mu(t)$, if $t \in [-1,0]$, then

$$^C D_{2-}^{\alpha,\psi}\overline{x}(t) = \frac{2}{\Gamma(3-\alpha)}(\psi(2)-\psi(t))^{2-\alpha}, \quad t \in [0,2],$$

and so the distributed-order derivative with respect to ψ is given by

$$^C D_{2-}^{\varphi(\alpha),\psi}\overline{x}(t) = \int_0^1 \varphi(\alpha)\,{}^C D_{2-}^{\alpha,\psi}\overline{x}(t)\,d\alpha = \frac{\psi(t)-\psi(2)+(\psi(2)-\psi(t))^2}{\ln(\psi(2)-\psi(t))}.$$

Note that $\overline{x}$ satisfies the assumptions of Theorem 2 and also the Euler–Lagrange Equations (2) and (3), as well as the transversality condition (4), proving that $\overline{x}$ is a candidate to be a local minimizer of $\mathcal{J}$. Since the Lagrangian function is convex, we conclude by Theorem 6 that $\overline{x}$ is a minimizer of $\mathcal{J}$.

Example 3. Determine $\overline{x}$ that minimizes the functional

$$\begin{aligned}\mathcal{J}(x) &= \int_0^1 \Bigg(\left({}^C D_{0+}^{\phi_2(\alpha),\psi} x(t) - \frac{\psi(t)-\psi(0)-1}{\ln(\psi(t)-\psi(0))}\right)^2 \\ &\quad + \left({}^C D_{1-}^{\varphi_2(\alpha),\psi} x(t) - \frac{\psi(1)-\psi(t)-1}{\ln(\psi(1)-\psi(t))}\right)^2\Bigg) dt,\end{aligned}$$

in the class of functions $C^2([0,1],\mathbb{R})$ subject to the boundary conditions $x(0) = x'(0) = 0$, where $\phi_2, \varphi_2:[1,2]\to[0,1]$ are defined by

$$\phi_2(\alpha) = \frac{\Gamma(3-\alpha)}{2} = \varphi_2(\alpha).$$

Again, by [13, Lemma 1], if $\overline{x}(t) = (\psi(t)-\psi(0))^2$, $t \in [0,1]$, then

$$^C D_{0+}^{\alpha,\psi}\overline{x}(t) = \frac{2}{\Gamma(3-\alpha)}(\psi(t)-\psi(0))^{2-\alpha},$$

and so
$$^C\mathrm{D}_{0+}^{\phi_2(\alpha),\psi}\overline{x}(t) = \int_1^2 \phi_2(\alpha) {}^C\mathrm{D}_{0+}^{\alpha,\psi}\overline{x}(t)d\alpha = \frac{\psi(t)-\psi(0)-1}{\ln(\psi(t)-\psi(0))}.$$

In addition, observe that
$$\begin{aligned} {}^C\mathrm{D}_{1-}^{\alpha,\psi}\overline{x}(t) &= {}^C\mathrm{D}_{1-}^{\alpha,\psi}((\psi(1)-\psi(t))+(\psi(0)-\psi(1)))^2 \\ &= {}^C\mathrm{D}_{1-}^{\alpha,\psi}(\psi(1)-\psi(t))^2 = \frac{2}{\Gamma(3-\alpha)}(\psi(1)-\psi(t))^{2-\alpha}, \end{aligned}$$

and therefore
$$^C\mathrm{D}_{1-}^{\varphi_2(\alpha),\psi}\overline{x}(t) = \int_1^2 \varphi_2(\alpha) {}^C\mathrm{D}_{1-}^{\alpha,\psi}\overline{x}(t)d\alpha = \frac{\psi(1)-\psi(t)-1}{\ln(\psi(1)-\psi(t))}.$$

We can easily verify that $\overline{x}$ satisfies assumptions of Theorem 9, the Euler–Lagrange Equation (26), and the natural boundary condition (28), proving that $\overline{x}$ is a candidate to be a local minimizer of $\mathcal{J}$. Since the Lagrangian function is convex, we conclude that $\overline{x}$ is a minimizer of $\mathcal{J}$.

5. Conclusions and Future Work

In this article, we continue the study started in [15], considering now new problems in the calculus of variations. Namely, two distinct types are considered: when the Lagrangian function involves a time delay and derivatives of order greater than 1. Necessary and sufficient optimization conditions are proved, for the basic problem and when in the presence of additional constraints to the problem. The study is formulated in the context of fractional calculus, where the derivative of the state curve is of the fractional type involving distributed-orders and the kernel involves an arbitrary smooth function.

In the future, we intend to study variational problems of Herglotz type and some generalizations involving distributed-order fractional derivatives with arbitrary smooth kernels.

Author Contributions: Conceptualization, formal analysis, investigation, writing—review and editing: F.C., R.A. and N.M. All authors have read and agreed to the published version of the manuscript.

Funding: This research was supported by Portuguese funds through the CIDMA—Center for Research and Development in Mathematics and Applications, and the Portuguese Foundation for Science and Technology (FCT-Fundação para a Ciência e a Tecnologia), reference UIDB/04106/2020.

Institutional Review Board Statement: Not applicable.

Informed Consent Statement: Not applicable.

Data Availability Statement: Not applicable.

Conflicts of Interest: The authors declare no conflict of interest.

References

1. Hilfer, R. *Applications of Fractional Calculus in Physics*; World Scientific: Singapore, 2000.
2. Oldham, K.B. Fractional differential equations in electrochemistry. *Adv. Eng. Softw.* **2010**, *41*, 9–12. [CrossRef]
3. Magin, R.L. Fractional calculus models of complex dynamics in biological tissues. *Comput. Math. Appl.* **2010**, *59*, 1586–1593. [CrossRef]
4. Almeida, R.; Brito da Cruz, A.M.C.; Martins, N.; Monteiro, T. An epidemiological MSEIR model described by the Caputo fractional derivative. *Int. J. Dynam. Control* **2019**, *7*, 776–784. [CrossRef]
5. Bergounioux, M.; Bourdin, L. Pontryagin maximum principle for general Caputo fractional optimal control problems with Bolza cost and terminal constraints. *ESAIM Control Optim. Calc. Var.* **2020**, *26*, 35. [CrossRef]
6. Li, T.; Pintus, N.; Viglialoro, G. Properties of solutions to porous medium problems with different sources and boundary conditions. *Z. Angew. Math. Phys.* **2019**, *70*, 18. [CrossRef]
7. Li, T.; Viglialoro, G. Boundedness for a nonlocal reaction chemotaxis model even in the attraction-dominated regime. *Differ. Integral Equ.* **2021**, *34*, 315–336.
8. Viglialoro, G.; Woolley, T.E. Solvability of a Keller–Segel system with signal-dependent sensitivity and essentially sublinear production. *Appl. Anal.* **2020**, *99*, 2507–2525. [CrossRef]

9. Kilbas, A.A.; Srivastava, H.M.; Trujillo, J.J. *Theory and Applications of Fractional Differential Equations*; North-Holland Mathematics Studies, 204; Elsevier Science B.V.: Amsterdam, The Netherlands, 2006.
10. Samko, S.G.; Kilbas, A.A.; Marichev, O.I. *Fractional Integrals and Derivatives, Translated from the 1987 Russian Original*; Gordon and Breach: Yverdon, Switzerland, 1993.
11. Caputo, M. *Elasticità e Dissipazione*; Zanichelli: Bologna, Italy, 1969.
12. Caputo, M. Mean fractional-order-derivatives differential equations and filters. *Ann. Univ. Ferrara* **1995**, *41*, 73–84.
13. Almeida, R. A Caputo fractional derivative of a function with respect to another function. *Commun. Nonlinear Sci. Numer. Simul.* **2017**, *44*, 460–481. [CrossRef]
14. Almeida, R. Further properties of Osler's generalized fractional integrals and derivatives with respect to another function. *Rocky Mt. J. Math.* **2019**, *49*, 2459–2493. [CrossRef]
15. Cruz, F.; Almeida, R.; Martins, N. Optimality conditions for variational problems involving distributed-order fractional derivatives with arbitrary kernels. *AIMS Math.* **2021**, *6*, 5351-5369. [CrossRef]
16. Riewe, F. Nonconservative Lagrangian and Hamiltonian mechanics. *Phys. Rev. E* **1996**, *53*, 1890–1899. [CrossRef]
17. Riewe, F. Mechanics with fractional derivatives. *Phys. Rev. E* **1997**, *55*, 3581–3592. [CrossRef]
18. Agrawal, O.P. Formulation of Euler–Lagrange equations for fractional variational problems. *J. Math. Anal. Appl.* **2002**, *272*, 368–379. [CrossRef]
19. Agrawal, O.P. Fractional variational calculus and the transversality conditions. *J. Phys. A Math. Gen.* **2006**, *39*, 10375–10384. [CrossRef]
20. Almeida, R. Optimality conditions for fractional variational problems with free terminal time. *arXiv* **2017**, arXiv:1702.00976.
21. Baleanu, D.; Muslih, S.I.; Rabei, E.M. On fractional Euler–Lagrange and Hamilton equations and the fractional generalization of total time derivative. *Nonlinear Dyn.* **2008**, *53*, 67–74. [CrossRef]
22. Jarad, F.; Abdeljawad, T.; Baleanu, D. Fractional variational principles with delay within Caputo derivatives. *Rep. Math. Phys.* **2010**, *65*, 17–28. [CrossRef]
23. Malinowska, A.B.; Torres, D.F.M. Generalized natural boundary conditions for fractional variational problems in terms of the Caputo derivative. *Comput. Math. Appl.* **2010**, *59*, 3110–3116. [CrossRef]
24. Almeida, R.; Pooseh, S.; Torres, D.F.M. *Computational Methods in the Fractional Calculus of Variations*; Imperial College Press: London, UK, 2015.
25. Malinowska, A.B.; Torres, D.F.M. *Introduction to the Fractional Calculus of Variations*; Imperial College Press: London, UK, 2012.
26. Malinowska, A.B.; Odzijewicz, T.; Torres, D.F.M. *Advanced Methods in the Fractional Calculus of Variations*; SpringerBriefs in Applied Sciences and Technology; Springer: Cham, Switzerland, 2015.
27. Džurina, J.; Grace, S.R.; Jadlovská, I.; Li, T. Oscillation criteria for second-order Emden–Fowler delay differential equations with a sublinear neutral term. *Math. Nachrichten* **2020**, *293*, 910–922. [CrossRef]
28. Jhinga, A.; Daftardar-Gejji, V. A new numerical method for solving fractional delay differential equations. *Comput. Appl. Math.* **2019**, *38*, 166. [CrossRef]

Article

Quadratic First Integrals of Time-Dependent Dynamical Systems of the Form $\ddot{q}^a = -\Gamma^a_{bc}\dot{q}^b\dot{q}^c - \omega(t)Q^a(q)$

Antonios Mitsopoulos * and Michael Tsamparlis

Faculty of Physics, Department of Astronomy-Astrophysics-Mechanics, University of Athens, Panepistemiopolis, 15783 Athens, Greece; mtsampa@phys.uoa.gr
* Correspondence: antmits@phys.uoa.gr

Citation: Mitsopoulos, A.; Tsamparlis, M. Quadratic First Integrals of Time-Dependent Dynamical Systems of the Form $\ddot{q}^a = -\Gamma^a_{bc}\dot{q}^b\dot{q}^c - \omega(t)Q^a(q)$. *Mathematics* **2021**, *9*, 1503. https://doi.org/10.3390/math9131503

Academic Editor: José Velhinho

Received: 23 April 2021
Accepted: 24 June 2021
Published: 27 June 2021

Publisher's Note: MDPI stays neutral with regard to jurisdictional claims in published maps and institutional affiliations.

Copyright: © 2021 by the authors. Licensee MDPI, Basel, Switzerland. This article is an open access article distributed under the terms and conditions of the Creative Commons Attribution (CC BY) license (https://creativecommons.org/licenses/by/4.0/).

Abstract: We consider the time-dependent dynamical system $\ddot{q}^a = -\Gamma^a_{bc}\dot{q}^b\dot{q}^c - \omega(t)Q^a(q)$ where $\omega(t)$ is a non-zero arbitrary function and the connection coefficients Γ^a_{bc} are computed from the kinetic metric (kinetic energy) of the system. In order to determine the quadratic first integrals (QFIs) I we assume that $I = K_{ab}\dot{q}^a\dot{q}^b + K_a\dot{q}^a + K$ where the unknown coefficients K_{ab}, K_a, K are tensors depending on t, q^a and impose the condition $\frac{dI}{dt} = 0$. This condition leads to a system of partial differential equations (PDEs) involving the quantities $K_{ab}, K_a, K, \omega(t)$ and $Q^a(q)$. From these PDEs, it follows that K_{ab} is a Killing tensor (KT) of the kinetic metric. We use the KT K_{ab} in two ways: a. We assume a general polynomial form in t both for K_{ab} and K_a; b. We express K_{ab} in a basis of the KTs of order 2 of the kinetic metric assuming the coefficients to be functions of t. In both cases, this leads to a new system of PDEs whose solution requires that we specify either $\omega(t)$ or $Q^a(q)$. We consider first that $\omega(t)$ is a general polynomial in t and find that in this case the dynamical system admits two independent QFIs which we collect in a Theorem. Next, we specify the quantities $Q^a(q)$ to be the generalized time-dependent Kepler potential $V = -\frac{\omega(t)}{r^\nu}$ and determine the functions $\omega(t)$ for which QFIs are admitted. We extend the discussion to the non-linear differential equation $\ddot{x} = -\omega(t)x^\mu + \phi(t)\dot{x}$ ($\mu \neq -1$) and compute the relation between the coefficients $\omega(t), \phi(t)$ so that QFIs are admitted. We apply the results to determine the QFIs of the generalized Lane–Emden equation.

Keywords: time-dependent dynamical systems; quadratic first integrals; Killing tensors; kinetic metric; Kepler potential; oscillator; Lane-Emden equation

1. Introduction

The equations of motion of a dynamical system define in the configuration space a Riemannian structure with the metric of the kinetic energy (kinetic metric). This metric is inherent in the structure of the dynamical system; therefore, we expect that it will determine the first integrals (FIs) of the system which are important in its evolution. On the other hand a metric is fixed by its symmetries, that is, the linear collineations: Killing vectors (KVs), homothetic vectors (HVs), conformal Killing vectors (CKVs), affine collineations (ACs), projective collineations (PCs); the quadratic collineations: second order Killing tensors (KTs). The question then is how the FIs of the dynamical system and the geometric symmetries of the kinetic metric are related.

The standard way to determine the FIs of a differential equation is the use of Lie/Noether symmetries which applies to the point as well as the generalized Lie/Noether symmetries. The relation of the Lie/Noether symmetries with the symmetries of the kinetic metric has been considered mostly in the case of point symmetries for autonomous conservative dynamical systems moving in a Riemannian space. In particular, it has been shown (see, e.g., [1–4]) that the Lie point symmetries are generated by the special projective algebra of the kinetic metric whereas the Noether point symmetries are generated by the homothetic algebra of the kinetic metric, the latter being a subalgebra of the projective algebra. A recent clear statement of these results is discussed in [5].

In addition to the autonomous conservative systems this method has been applied to the time-dependent potentials $W(t,q) = \omega(t)V(q)$, that is, for equations of the form $\ddot{q}^a = -\Gamma^a_{bc}\dot{q}^b\dot{q}^c - \omega(t)V^{,a}(q)$ (see, e.g., [6–12]). In this case it has been shown that the Lie point symmetries, the Noether point symmetries and the associated FIs are computed in terms of the collineations of the kinetic metric plus a set of constraint conditions involving the time-dependent potential and the collineation vectors. These time-dependent potentials are important because (among others) they contain the time-dependent oscillator (see, e.g., [8,10,13–15]) and the time-dependent Kepler potential (see, e.g., [12,16–18]). A further development in the same line is the extension of this method to time-dependent potentials $W(t,q)$ with linear damping terms [12]. It has been shown that under a suitable time transformation the damping term can be removed and the problem reduces to a time-dependent potential of the form $W(t,q) = \bar{\omega}(t)V(q)$ but with different $\bar{\omega}(t)$. Finally the Lie/Noether method has been applied to the study of partial differential equations (PDEs) [4,19–21].

Besides the aforementioned Lie/Noether method there is a different method which computes the FIs in terms of the collineations of the kinetic metric without using Lie symmetries. This method we shall apply in this paper. It has as follows.

One assumes the generic quadratic first integral (QFI) to be of the form (the linear FIs (LFIs) are also included for $K_{ab} = 0$)

$$I = K_{ab}\dot{q}^a\dot{q}^b + K_a\dot{q}^a + K \tag{1}$$

where the coefficients K_{ab}, K_a, K are tensors depending on the coordinates t, q^a and imposes the condition $\frac{dI}{dt} = 0$. Using again the equations of motion to replace the quantities $\ddot{q}^a$ whenever they appear, this condition leads to a system of PDEs involving the unknown quantities K_{ab}, K_a, K and the dynamical elements, i.e., the potential and the generalized forces of the system. The solution of this system of PDEs provides the QFIs (1). For future reference we shall call this method the *direct method*.

The system of PDEs consists of two parts: a. The geometric part which is independent of the dynamical quantities; b. the dynamical part which contains the scalar K and the dynamical quantities. The main conclusion of the geometric part is that the tensor K_{ab} is a KT of the kinetic metric whereas the vector K_a is related to the linear collineations of that metric. The dynamical part involves the scalar K which is determined by a set of constraint conditions which involve K_{ab}, K_a, K, the potential and the generalized forces. Once K is computed one gets the corresponding QFI I.

The direct method can always be related to the Noether symmetries. Indeed assuming that the system has a regular Lagrangian (which is always the case since we assume that there exists the kinetic energy) it can be shown by using the inverse Noether theorem (see [22] and section II in [23]) that to each QFI I one determines an associated gauged generalized Noether symmetry with generator $\eta_a = -2K_{ab}\dot{q}^b - K_a$ and Noether function $f = -K_{ab}\dot{q}^a\dot{q}^b + K$ whose Noether integral is the considered QFI. Therefore, we conclude that all QFIs of the form (1) are Noetherian, provided the Lagrangian is regular, that is, the dynamical equations can be solved in terms of $\ddot{q}^a$.

Moreover, the direct method has been employed in the literature (see [17,24–26]) both for autonomous and time-dependent dynamical systems. A recent account of this method in the case of autonomous conservative systems together with relevant references can be found in [27]. This approach being geometric is powerful and convenient because with minimal calculations it allows the computation of the FIs by using known results from differential geometry.

The purpose of the present work is to apply the direct method to compute the QFIs of time-dependent equations of the form $\ddot{q}^a = -\Gamma^a_{bc}\dot{q}^b\dot{q}^c - \omega(t)Q^a(q)$. Because many well-known dynamical systems fall in this category we intend to recover in a direct single approach all the known results derived from the Lie/Noether symmetry method, which are scattered in a large number of papers.

As explained above, the solution of the system requires that the tensor K_{ab} is a KT of the kinetic metric. In general, the computation of the KTs of a metric is a major task. However, for spaces of constant curvature, this problem has been solved (see [28–30]). Therefore, in this paper, we restrict our discussion to Euclidean spaces only. Since the KT K_{ab} is a function of t, q^a we suggest two procedures of work: (a). The polynomial method; (b). the basis method.

In the polynomial method, one assumes a general polynomial form in the variable t both for the KT K_{ab} and the vector K_a and replaces in the equations of the relevant system. In the basis method, one first computes a basis of the KTs of order 2 of the kinetic metric and then expresses in this basis the KT K_{ab} with the coefficients to be functions of t. The vector K_a and the FIs follow from the solution of the system of PDEs. Both methods are suitable for autonomous dynamical systems but for time-dependent systems it appears that the basis method is preferable.

Concerning the quantities $\omega(t)$ and $Q^a(q)$, again, there are two ways to proceed.

(a) Consider a general form for the function $\omega(t)$ and let the quantities Q^a unspecified. In this case, the quantities Q^a act as constraints;
(b) Specify the quantities Q^a and determine for which functions $\omega(t)$ the resulting dynamical system admits QFIs.

In the following, we shall consider both the polynomial method and the basis method, starting from the former. As a first application, we assume the KT $K_{ab} = N(t)\gamma_{ab}$ where $N(t)$ is an arbitrary function and show that we recover all the point Noether integrals found in [12]. As a second application, we assume that $\omega(t) = b_0 + b_1 t + ... + b_\ell t^\ell$ with $b_\ell \neq 0$ and $\ell \geq 1$ whereas the quantities Q^a are unspecified. We find that in this case, the system admits two families of independent QFIs as stated in Theorem 1.

Subsequently, we consider the basis method. This is carried out in two steps. In the first step, we assume that we know a basis $\{C_{(N)ab}(q)\}$ of the space of KTs of the kinetic metric and require that K_{ab} has the form $K_{ab}(t,q) = \sum_{N=1}^{m} \alpha_N(t) C_{(N)ab}(q)$. In the second step, we specify the generalized forces to be conservative with the time-dependent Newtonian generalized Kepler potential $V = -\frac{\omega(t)}{r^\nu}$ where ν is a non-zero real constant and $r = \sqrt{x^2 + y^2 + z^2}$. This potential for $\nu = -2, 1$ includes, respectively, the three-dimensional (3d) time-dependent oscillator and the time-dependent Kepler potential. For other values of ν it reduces to other important dynamical systems, for example, for $\nu = 2$ one obtains the Newton–Cotes potential (see, e.g., [31]). We determine the QFIs of the time-dependent generalized Kepler potential and recover in a systematic way the known results concerning the QFIs of the 3d time-dependent oscillator, the time-dependent Kepler potential and the Newton–Cotes potential. For easier reference, we collect the results in Table 2 of Section 14.

Using the well-known result that by a reparameterization the linear damping term $\phi(t)\dot{q}^a$ of a dynamical equation is absorbed to a time-dependent force of the form $\omega(t)Q^a(q)$, we also study the non-linear differential equation $\ddot{x} = -\omega(t)x^\mu + \phi(t)\dot{x}$ ($\mu \neq -1$) and compute the relation between the coefficients $\omega(t), \phi(t)$ for which QFIs are admitted. It is found that a family of 'frequencies' $\tilde{\omega}(s)$ is admitted which for $\mu = 0, 1, 2$ is parameterized with functions whereas for $\mu \neq -1, 0, 1, 2$ is parameterized with constants. As a further application, we study the integrability of the well-known generalized Lane–Emden equation.

The structure of the paper is as follows. In Section 2, we determine the system of PDEs resulting form the condition $dI/dt = 0$. In Section 3, we assume that the KT is proportional to the kinetic metric and derive the point Noether FIs of the time-dependent dynamical system (2). In Section 4, we consider the polynomial method and define the general forms of the KT K_{ab} and the vector K_a which lead to a new form of the system of PDEs. In Section 5, we assume that $\omega(t)$ is a general polynomial of t and we find that the resulting time-dependent system admits two independent QFIs as stated in Theorem 1. In Section 6, we discuss some special cases of the QFI I_n of Theorem 1. In Section 7, we consider the basis method. In Section 8, we find a basis for the KTs in E^3 in order to apply the basis method to 3d Newtonian systems. In Sections 9–13, we study the time-dependent generalized Kepler potential and find for which functions $\omega(t)$ admits QFIs. Particularly, in Section 13, we study a special class of time-dependent oscillators with frequency $\omega_{3O}(t)$ as given in Equation (123). We collect our results for the several values of ν in Table 2 of Section 14. In Section 15, we use the independent LFIs I_{41i}, I_{42i} given in Equations (125) and (126) to integrate the equations of the time-dependent oscillators defined in Section 13; the FIs L_i, E_2, A_i determined in Section 11.1 to integrate the time-dependent Kepler potential with $\omega(t) = \frac{k}{b_0 + b_1 t}$ where $kb_1 \neq 0$. In Section 16, we consider the second order non-linear time-dependent differential Equation (154) and show that it is integrable with an associated QFI given in Equation (175) iff the functions $\omega(t), \phi(t)$ are related as shown in Equation (174). For the special values $\mu = 0, 1, 2$ we find also that there exist additional relations between $\omega(t), \phi(t)$ for which the resulting differential equation admits a QFI. For $\mu = 1$ Equation (154) admits the general solution (166) provided that condition (165) is satisfied. We apply these results in Section 16.1 and we study the properties of the well-known generalized Lane–Emden equation. Finally, in Section 17, we draw our conclusions and, in the Appendix A, we give the proof of Theorem 1.

2. The System of Equations

We consider the dynamical system

$$\ddot{q}^a = -\Gamma^a_{bc} \dot{q}^b \dot{q}^c - \omega(t) Q^a(q) \tag{2}$$

where Γ^a_{bc} are the Riemannian connection coefficients determined by the kinetic metric γ_{ab} (kinetic energy) of the system and $-\omega(t)Q^a(q)$ are the time-dependent generalized forces. Einstein summation convention is assumed and the metric γ_{ab} is used for lowering and raising the indices.

We next consider a function $I(t, q^a, \dot{q}^a)$ of the form

$$I = K_{ab}(t,q)\dot{q}^a\dot{q}^b + K_a(t,q)\dot{q}^a + K(t,q) \tag{3}$$

where K_{ab} is a symmetric tensor, K_a is a vector and K is an invariant.

We demand I be a FI of (2) by imposing the condition

$$\frac{dI}{dt} = 0. \tag{4}$$

Using the dynamical Equations (2) to replace $\ddot{q}^a$ whenever it appears, we find the system of equations

$$K_{(ab;c)} = 0 \tag{5}$$

$$K_{ab,t} + K_{(a;b)} = 0 \tag{6}$$

$$-2\omega K_{ab} Q^b + K_{a,t} + K_{,a} = 0 \tag{7}$$

$$K_{,t} - \omega K_a Q^a = 0 \tag{8}$$

$$K_{a,tt} + \omega \left(K_b Q^b\right)_{,a} - 2\omega_{,t} K_{ab} Q^b - 2\omega K_{ab,t} Q^b = 0 \tag{9}$$

$$K_{[a;b],t} - 2\omega \left(K_{[a|c|} Q^c\right)_{;b]} = 0 \tag{10}$$

where the last two Equations (9) and (10) express the integrability conditions $K_{,[at]} = 0$ and $K_{,[ab]} = 0$, respectively, for the scalar K. We also note that round and square brackets indicate symmetrization and antisymmetrization, respectively, of the enclosed indices; indices enclosed between vertical lines are overlooked by symmetrization or antisymmetrization symbols; a comma indicates partial derivative and a semicolon Riemannian covariant derivative.

Equation (5) implies that K_{ab} is a KT of order 2 (possibly zero) of the kinetic metric γ_{ab}.

The solution of the system requires the function $w(t)$ and the quantities $Q^a(q)$ both being quantities which are characteristic of the given dynamical system. There are two ways to proceed.

(a) Consider a general form for the function $w(t)$ and let the quantities $Q^a(q)$ unspecified. In this case the quantities $Q^a(q)$ act as constraints.
(b) Specify the quantities $Q^a(q)$ and determine for which functions $w(t)$ the resulting dynamical system admits FIs.

However, before continuing with this kind of considerations, we first proceed with the simple geometric choice $K_{ab} = N(t)\gamma_{ab}$ where $N(t)$ is an arbitrary smooth function. By specifying the KT K_{ab} as above both the function $w(t)$ and the quantities $Q^a(q)$ stay unspecified and act as constraints.

3. The Point Noether FIs of the Time-Dependent Dynamical System (2)

We consider the simplest choice

$$K_{ab} = N(t)\gamma_{ab} \tag{11}$$

where $N(t)$ is an arbitrary smooth function. This choice is purely geometric; therefore, the function $w(t)$ and the quantities $Q^a(q)$ are unspecified and act as constraints, whereas the vector K_a is identified with a collineation of the kinetic metric. With this K_{ab}, the system of Equations (5)–(10) become (Equation (5) vanishes trivially)

$$N_{,t}\gamma_{ab} + K_{(a;b)} = 0 \tag{12}$$
$$-2wNQ_a + K_{a,t} + K_{,a} = 0 \tag{13}$$
$$K_{,t} - wK_aQ^a = 0 \tag{14}$$
$$K_{a,tt} + w\left(K_bQ^b\right)_{,a} - 2w_{,t}NQ_a - 2wN_{,t}Q_a = 0 \tag{15}$$
$$K_{[a;b],t} - 2wNQ_{[a;b]} = 0. \tag{16}$$

We consider the following cases.

3.1. Case $K_a = K_a(q)$ is the HV of γ_{ab} with Homothety Factor ψ

In this case, $K_{a,t} = 0$ and $K_{(a;b)} = \psi\gamma_{ab}$ where ψ is an arbitrary constant. Equation (12) gives

$$N_{,t} = -\psi \implies N = -\psi t + c$$

where c is an arbitrary constant.
Equation (16) implies that (take $w \neq 0$)

$$Q_{[a;b]} = 0 \implies Q_a = V_{,a}$$

where $V = V(q)$ is an arbitrary potential.
Replacing in (13) we find that

$$K_{,a} = 2w(-\psi t + c)V_{,a} \implies K = 2w(-\psi t + c)V + M(t)$$

where $M(t)$ is an arbitrary function.
Substituting the function $K(t,q)$ in (14) we get

$$wK_aV^{,a} - 2w_{,t}(-\psi t + c)V + 2w\psi V - M_{,t} = 0. \tag{17}$$

The remaining condition (15) is just the partial derivative of (17), and hence is satisfied trivially.

Moreover, since $\omega \neq 0$, Equation (17) can be written in the form

$$K_a V^{,a} - 2(\ln \omega)_{,t}(-\psi t + c)V + 2\psi V - \frac{M_{,t}}{\omega} = 0 \tag{18}$$

which implies that

$$2(\ln \omega)_{,t}(-\psi t + c) = c_1 \tag{19}$$
$$M_{,t} = c_2 \omega \tag{20}$$

where c_1, c_2 are arbitrary constants.

Therefore, Equation (18) becomes

$$K_a V^{,a} + (2\psi - c_1)V - c_2 = 0. \tag{21}$$

The QFI is

$$I_1 = (-\psi t + c)\gamma_{ab}\dot{q}^a \dot{q}^b + K_a(q)\dot{q}^a + 2\omega(-\psi t + c)V + M(t) \tag{22}$$

where $Q_a = V_{,a}$ and the quantities $\omega(t), M(t), V(q), K_a(q)$ satisfy the conditions (19)–(21).

3.2. Case $K_a = -M(t)S_{,a}(q)$ Where $S_{,a}$ Is the Gradient HV of γ_{ab}

In this case $S_{;ab} = \psi \gamma_{ab}$ and $M(t) \neq 0$ is an arbitrary function.

Equation (12) implies $N_{,t} = \psi M$.

From Equation (16) we find that there exists a potential function $V(q)$ such that $Q_a = V_{,a}$.

Replacing the above results in (13) we obtain

$$K_{,a} = 2\omega N V_{,a} + M_{,t} S_{,a} \implies K = 2\omega N V + M_{,t} S + C(t)$$

where $C(t)$ is an arbitrary function.

Substituting in (14) we get (take $\omega M \neq 0$)

$$\omega M S_{,a} V^{,a} + 2\omega_{,t} N V + 2\omega \psi M V + M_{,tt} S + C_{,t} = 0 \implies$$

$$S_{,a} V^{,a} + 2\psi V + \frac{2(\ln \omega)_{,t} N}{M} V + \frac{M_{,tt}}{\omega M} S + \frac{C_{,t}}{\omega M} = 0$$

which implies that

$$\frac{2(\ln \omega)_{,t} N}{M} = d_1 \tag{23}$$

$$\frac{M_{,tt}}{\omega M} = m \tag{24}$$

$$\frac{C_{,t}}{\omega M} = k \tag{25}$$

$$S_{,a} V^{,a} + (2\psi + d_1)V + mS + k = 0 \tag{26}$$

where d_1, m, k are arbitrary constants. The remaining condition (15) is satisfied identically.

The QFI is

$$I_2 = N\gamma_{ab}\dot{q}^a \dot{q}^b - MS_{,a}\dot{q}^a + 2\omega NV + M_{,t}S + C(t) \tag{27}$$

where $Q_a = V_{,a}, N_{,t} = \psi M$ and the conditions (23)–(26) must be satisfied.

3.3. Case $Q_a = V_{,a}$ and $K_a = -M(t)V_{,a}(q)$ Where $V_{,a}$ Is the Gradient HV of γ_{ab}

Equation (12) implies $N_{,t} = \psi M$ where ψ is the homothety factor of $V_{,a}$.

From Equation (13), we obtain
$$K_{,a} = 2\omega N V_{,a} + M_{,t} V_{,a} \implies K = 2\omega N V + M_{,t} V + C(t)$$

where $C(t)$ is an arbitrary function.

Substituting in (14) we get (take $\omega M \neq 0$)
$$\omega M V_{,a} V^{,a} + 2\omega_{,t} N V + 2\omega \psi M V + M_{,tt} V + C_{,t} = 0 \implies$$
$$V_{,a} V^{,a} + 2\psi V + \frac{2(\ln \omega)_{,t} N}{M} V + \frac{M_{,tt}}{\omega M} V + \frac{C_{,t}}{\omega M} = 0$$

which implies that
$$\frac{M_{,tt}}{\omega M} + \frac{2(\ln \omega)_{,t} N}{M} = d_2 \tag{28}$$
$$\frac{C_{,t}}{\omega M} = k \tag{29}$$
$$V_{,a} V^{,a} + (2\psi + d_2) V + k = 0 \tag{30}$$

where d_2, k are arbitrary constants. The remaining conditions are satisfied identically.

The QFI is
$$I_3 = N \gamma_{ab} \dot{q}^a \dot{q}^b - M V_{,a} \dot{q}^a + (2\omega N + M_{,t}) V + C \tag{31}$$

where $Q_a = V_{,a}$, $N_{,t} = \psi M$ and the conditions (28)–(30) must be satisfied.

The above results reproduce Theorem 2 of [12] which states that the point Noether symmetries of the time-dependent potentials of the form $\omega(t)V(q)$ are generated by the homothetic algebra of the kinetic metric (provided the Lagrangian is regular).

It is interesting to observe that the QFIs (22), (27) and (31) produced by point Noether symmetries can be also produced by generalized (gauged) Noether symmetries using the inverse Noether theorem. This proves that a Noether FI may not associated with a unique Noether symmetry.

4. The Polynomial Method for Computing the QFIs

In the polynomial approach, one assumes a polynomial form in t of the KT $K_{ab}(t,q)$ and the vector $K_a(t,q)$ and solves the resulting system for given $\omega(t), Q^a(q)$. One application of this method can be found in [27] where a general theorem is given which allows the finding of the QFIs of an autonomous conservative dynamical system. In the present work, we generalize the considerations made in [27] and assume that the quantity $K_{ab}(t,q)$ has the form
$$K_{ab}(t,q) = C_{(0)ab}(q) + \sum_{N=1}^{n} C_{(N)ab}(q) \frac{t^N}{N} \tag{32}$$

where $C_{(N)ab}$, $N = 0, 1, ..., n$, is a sequence of arbitrary KTs of order 2 of the kinetic metric γ_{ab}.

This choice of K_{ab} and Equation (6) indicate that we set
$$K_a(t,q) = \sum_{M=0}^{m} L_{(M)a}(q) t^M \tag{33}$$

where $L_{(M)a}(q)$, $M = 0, 1, ..., m$, are arbitrary vectors.

We note that both powers n, m in the above polynomial expressions may be infinite.

Substituting (32) and (33) in the system of Equations (5)–(10) (Equation (5) is identically zero since $C_{(N)ab}$ are KTs) we obtain the system of equations

$$0 = C_{(1)ab} + C_{(2)ab}t + ... + C_{(n)ab}t^{n-1} + L_{(0)(a;b)} + L_{(1)(a;b)}t + ... + L_{(m)(a;b)}t^m \tag{34}$$

$$0 = -2\omega C_{(0)ab}Q^b - 2\omega C_{(1)ab}Q^b t - ... - 2\omega C_{(n)ab}Q^b \frac{t^n}{n} + L_{(1)a} + 2L_{(2)a}t + ... + mL_{(m)a}t^{m-1} + K_{,a} \tag{35}$$

$$0 = K_{,t} - \omega L_{(0)a}Q^a - \omega L_{(1)a}Q^a t - ... - \omega L_{(m)a}Q^a t^m \tag{36}$$

$$0 = \left(-2C_{(0)ab}Q^b - 2C_{(1)ab}Q^b t - ... - 2C_{(n)ab}Q^b \frac{t^n}{n}\right)\omega_{,t} - 2\omega C_{(1)ab}Q^b - 2\omega C_{(2)ab}Q^b t - ... - 2\omega C_{(n)ab}Q^b t^{n-1} +$$
$$+ 2L_{(2)a} + 6L_{(3)a}t + ... + m(m-1)L_{(m)a}t^{m-2} + \omega\left(L_{(0)b}Q^b\right)_{,a} + \omega\left(L_{(1)b}Q^b\right)_{,a}t + ... + \omega\left(L_{(m)b}Q^b\right)_{,a}t^m \tag{37}$$

$$0 = 2\omega\left(C_{(0)[a|c|}Q^c\right)_{;b]} + 2\omega\left(C_{(1)[a|c|}Q^c\right)_{;b]}t + ... + 2\omega\left(C_{(n)[a|c|}Q^c\right)_{;b]}\frac{t^n}{n} - L_{(1)[a;b]} -$$
$$- 2L_{(2)[a;b]}t - ... - mL_{(m)[a;b]}t^{m-1}. \tag{38}$$

In this system of PDEs the pairs $\omega(t), Q^a(q)$ are not specified. As we explained in the introduction, we shall fix a general form of ω and find the admitted QFIs in terms of the (unspecified) Q^a. In the following section, we choose $\omega(t)$ to be a general polynomial in t; however, any other choice is possible.

5. The Case $\omega(t) = b_0 + b_1 t + \cdots + b_\ell t^\ell$ with $b_\ell \neq 0, \ell \geq 1$

We assume that

$$\omega(t) = b_0 + b_1 t + ... + b_\ell t^\ell, \quad b_\ell \neq 0, \quad \ell \geq 1 \tag{39}$$

where ℓ is the degree of the polynomial. Substituting the function (39) in the system of Equations (34)–(38) we find that there are two independent QFIs as given in Theorem 1 (the proof of Theorem 1 is in the Appendix A).

Theorem 1. *The independent QFIs of the time-dependent dynamical system (2) where $\omega(t) = b_0 + b_1 t + ... + b_\ell t^\ell$ with $b_\ell \neq 0$ and $\ell \geq 1$ are the following:*

Integral 1.

$$I_n = \left(C_{(0)ab} + \sum_{k=1}^{n}\frac{t^k}{k}C_{(k)ab}\right)\dot{q}^a\dot{q}^b + \sum_{k=0}^{n}t^k L_{(k)a}\dot{q}^a + \sum_{k=0}^{n}\sum_{r=0}^{\ell}\left(L_{(k)a}Q^a b_r \frac{t^{k+r+1}}{k+r+1}\right) + G(q)$$

where $n = 0, 1, 2, ..., C_{(0)ab}$ is a KT, the KTs $C_{(N)ab} = -L_{(N-1)(a;b)}$ for $N = 1, ..., n$, $L_{(n)a}$ is a KV, $G(q)$ is an arbitrary function defined by the condition

$$G_{,a} = 2b_0 C_{(0)ab}Q^b - L_{(1)a} \tag{40}$$

s is an arbitrary constant defined by the condition

$$L_{(n)a}Q^a = s \tag{41}$$

and the following conditions are satisfied

$$\sum_{s=0}^{\ell-1}\left[-\frac{2(r+s)b_{(r+s\leq\ell)}}{n-s}C_{(n-s\geq0)ab}Q^b - 2b_{(r+s\leq\ell)}C_{(n-s>0)ab}Q^b + b_{(r+s\leq\ell)}\left(L_{(n-s-1\geq0)b}Q^b\right)_{,a}\right] = 0, \quad r = 1, 2, ..., \ell \tag{42}$$

$$-\sum_{s=1}^{\ell}\left[\frac{2sb_s}{n-s}C_{(n-s\geq0)ab}Q^b\right] + \sum_{s=0}^{\ell}\left[-2b_s C_{(n-s>0)ab}Q^b + b_s\left(L_{(n-s-1\geq0)b}Q^b\right)_{,a}\right] = 0 \tag{43}$$

$$k(k-1)L_{(k)a} - \sum_{s=1}^{\ell}\left[\frac{2sb_s}{k-s-1}C_{(k-s-1\geq 0)ab}Q^b\right] + \sum_{s=0}^{\ell}\left[-2b_sC_{(k-s-1\geq 0)ab}Q^b + b_s\left(L_{(k-s-2\geq 0)b}Q^b\right)_{,a}\right] = 0 \quad (44)$$

with $k = 2, 3, ... n$.

Integral 2.

$$I_e = I_e(\ell = 1) = -e^{\lambda t}L_{(a;b)}\dot{q}^a\dot{q}^b + \lambda e^{\lambda t}L_a\dot{q}^a + \left(b_0 - \frac{b_1}{\lambda}\right)e^{\lambda t}L_aQ^a + b_1 t e^{\lambda t}L_aQ^a$$

where $L_{(a;b)}$ is a KT, $\left(L_bQ^b\right)_{,a} = \frac{\lambda^3}{b_1}L_a$ and $\lambda^3 L_a = -2b_1L_{(a;b)}Q^b$.

We note that the FI I_e exists only when $\omega(t) = b_0 + b_1 t$, that is, for $\ell = 1$.

6. Special Cases of the QFI I_n

The parameter n in the case Integral 1 of Theorem 1 runs over all positive integers, i.e., $n = 0, 1, 2, ...$. This results in a sequence of QFIs $I_0, I_1, I_2, ...$, one QFI I_n for each value n. A significant characteristic of this sequence is that $I_k < I_{k+1}$, that is, each QFI I_k where $k = 0, 1, 2, ...$ can be derived from the next QFI I_{k+1} as a subcase.

In the following, we consider some special cases of the QFI I_n for small values of n.

6.1. The QFI I_0

For $n = 0$ we have

$$I_0 = C_{(0)ab}\dot{q}^a\dot{q}^b + L_{(0)a}\dot{q}^a + b_\ell s\frac{t^{\ell+1}}{\ell+1} + ... + b_1 s\frac{t^2}{2} + b_0 st$$

where $C_{(0)ab}$ is a KT, $L_{(0)a}$ is a KV, $L_{(0)a}Q^a = s$ and $C_{(0)ab}Q^b = 0$.

This QFI consists of the independent FIs

$$I_{0a} = C_{(0)ab}\dot{q}^a\dot{q}^b, \quad I_{0b} = L_{(0)a}\dot{q}^a + b_\ell s\frac{t^{\ell+1}}{\ell+1} + ... + b_1 s\frac{t^2}{2} + b_0 st.$$

6.2. The QFI I_1

For $n = 1$ the conditions (41)–(44) become

$$L_{(1)a}Q^a = s \quad (45)$$

$$\left(L_{(0)b}Q^b\right)_{,a} = -2(\ell+1)L_{(0)(a;b)}Q^b \quad (46)$$

$$kb_k C_{(0)ab}Q^b = -(\ell-k+1)b_{k-1}L_{(0)(a;b)}Q^b, \quad k = 1, ..., \ell. \quad (47)$$

Since $b_\ell \neq 0$ the last condition for $k = \ell$ gives

$$C_{(0)ab}Q^b = -\frac{b_{\ell-1}}{\ell b_\ell}L_{(0)(a;b)}Q^b$$

and the remaining equations become

$$\left[(\ell-k+1)b_{k-1} - \frac{kb_k b_{\ell-1}}{\ell b_\ell}\right]L_{(0)(a;b)}Q^b = 0, \quad k = 1, ..., \ell-1.$$

The last set of equations exists only for $\ell \geq 2$. From these equations, using mathematical induction, we prove after successive substitutions that

$$\left(b_0 - \frac{b_{\ell-1}^\ell}{\ell^\ell b_\ell^{\ell-1}}\right)L_{(0)(a;b)}Q^b = 0.$$

The QFI is (I_0 is a subcase of I_1)

$$I_1 = \left(-tL_{(0)(a;b)} + C_{(0)ab}\right)\dot{q}^a\dot{q}^b + tL_{(1)a}\dot{q}^a + L_{(0)a}\dot{q}^a + sb_\ell\frac{t^{\ell+2}}{\ell+2} + \left(sb_{\ell-1} + b_\ell L_{(0)a}Q^a\right)\frac{t^{\ell+1}}{\ell+1} + \ldots +$$
$$+ \left(sb_0 + b_1 L_{(0)a}Q^a\right)\frac{t^2}{2} + b_0 L_{(0)a}Q^a t + G(q)$$

where $C_{(0)ab}$, $L_{(0)(a;b)}$ are KTs, $L_{(1)a}$ is a KV, $L_{(1)a}Q^a = s$, $\left(L_{(0)b}Q^b\right)_{,a} = -2(\ell+1)L_{(0)(a;b)}Q^b$, $C_{(0)ab}Q^b = -\frac{b_{\ell-1}}{\ell b_\ell}L_{(0)(a;b)}Q^b$, $\left[(\ell-k+1)b_{k-1} - \frac{kb_k b_{\ell-1}}{\ell b_\ell}\right]L_{(0)(a;b)}Q^b = 0$ where $k = 1, \ldots, \ell-1$ and $G_{,a} = 2b_0 C_{(0)ab}Q^b - L_{(1)a}$.

For some values of the degree ℓ of the polynomial $\omega(t)$ we have:

(1) For $\ell = 1$.

We have $\omega = b_0 + b_1 t$ and the QFI is

$$I_1 = \left(-tL_{(0)(a;b)} + C_{(0)ab}\right)\dot{q}^a\dot{q}^b + tL_{(1)a}\dot{q}^a + L_{(0)a}\dot{q}^a + sb_1\frac{t^3}{3} + \left(sb_0 + b_1 L_{(0)a}Q^a\right)\frac{t^2}{2} + b_0 L_{(0)a}Q^a t + G(q)$$

where $C_{(0)ab}$, $L_{(0)(a;b)}$ are KTs, $L_{(1)a}$ is a KV, $L_{(1)a}Q^a = s$, $\left(L_{(0)b}Q^b\right)_{,a} = -4L_{(0)(a;b)}Q^b$, $C_{(0)ab}Q^b = -\frac{b_0}{b_1}L_{(0)(a;b)}Q^b$ and $G_{,a} = 2b_0 C_{(0)ab}Q^b - L_{(1)a}$.

(2) For $\ell = 2$.

We have $\omega = b_0 + b_1 t + b_2 t^2$ and the QFI is

$$I_1 = \left(-tL_{(0)(a;b)} + C_{(0)ab}\right)\dot{q}^a\dot{q}^b + tL_{(1)a}\dot{q}^a + L_{(0)a}\dot{q}^a + sb_2\frac{t^4}{4} + \left(sb_1 + b_2 L_{(0)a}Q^a\right)\frac{t^3}{3}$$
$$+ \left(sb_0 + b_1 L_{(0)a}Q^a\right)\frac{t^2}{2} + b_0 L_{(0)a}Q^a t + G(q)$$

where $C_{(0)ab}$, $L_{(0)(a;b)}$ are KTs, $L_{(1)a}$ is a KV, $L_{(1)a}Q^a = s$, $\left(L_{(0)b}Q^b\right)_{,a} = -6L_{(0)(a;b)}Q^b$, $C_{(0)ab}Q^b = -\frac{b_1}{2b_2}L_{(0)(a;b)}Q^b$, $\left(b_0 - \frac{b_1^2}{4b_2}\right)L_{(0)(a;b)}Q^b = 0$ and $G_{,a} = 2b_0 C_{(0)ab}Q^b - L_{(1)a}$.

(3) For $\ell = 3$.

We have $\omega = b_0 + b_1 t + b_2 t^2 + b_3 t^3$ and the QFI is

$$I_1 = \left(-tL_{(0)(a;b)} + C_{(0)ab}\right)\dot{q}^a\dot{q}^b + tL_{(1)a}\dot{q}^a + L_{(0)a}\dot{q}^a + sb_3\frac{t^5}{5} + \left(sb_2 + b_3 L_{(0)a}Q^a\right)\frac{t^4}{4} + \left(sb_1 + b_2 L_{(0)a}Q^a\right)\frac{t^3}{3} +$$
$$+ \left(sb_0 + b_1 L_{(0)a}Q^a\right)\frac{t^2}{2} + b_0 L_{(0)a}Q^a t + G(q)$$

where $C_{(0)ab}$, $L_{(0)(a;b)}$ are KTs, $L_{(1)a}$ is a KV, $L_{(1)a}Q^a = s$, $\left(L_{(0)b}Q^b\right)_{,a} = -8L_{(0)(a;b)}Q^b$, $C_{(0)ab}Q^b = -\frac{b_2}{3b_3}L_{(0)(a;b)}Q^b$, $\left(b_0 - \frac{b_1 b_2}{9b_3}\right)L_{(0)(a;b)}Q^b = 0$, $\left(b_1 - \frac{b_2^2}{3b_3}\right)L_{(0)(a;b)}Q^b = 0$ and $G_{,a} = 2b_0 C_{(0)ab}Q^b - L_{(1)a}$.

7. The Basis Method for Computing QFIs

As it has been explained in the introduction, in the basis method instead of considering the KT K_{ab} to be given as a polynomial in t with coefficients arbitrary KTs (see Equation (32)) one defines the KT $K_{ab}(t,q)$ by the requirement

$$K_{ab}(t,q) = \sum_{N=1}^{m} \alpha_N(t) C_{(N)ab}(q) \tag{48}$$

where $\alpha_N(t)$ are arbitrary smooth functions and the m linearly independent KTs $C_{(N)ab}(q)$ constitute a basis of the space of KTs of the kinetic metric $\gamma_{ab}(q)$. In this case, one does not assume a form for the vector $K_a(t,q)$ which is determined from the resulting system of Equations (5)–(10).

The basis method has been used previously by Katzin and Levine in [17] in order to determine the QFIs for the time-dependent Kepler potential. As we shall apply the basis method to 3d Newtonian systems, we need a basis of KTs (and other collineations) of the Euclidean space E^3.

8. The Geometric Quantities of E^3

In E^3 the general KT of order 2 has independent components

$$\begin{aligned}
C_{11} &= \frac{a_6}{2}y^2 + \frac{a_1}{2}z^2 + a_4 yz + a_5 y + a_2 z + a_3 \\
C_{12} &= \frac{a_{10}}{2}z^2 - \frac{a_6}{2}xy - \frac{a_4}{2}xz - \frac{a_{14}}{2}yz - \frac{a_5}{2}x - \frac{a_{15}}{2}y + a_{16}z + a_{17} \\
C_{13} &= \frac{a_{14}}{2}y^2 - \frac{a_4}{2}xy - \frac{a_1}{2}xz - \frac{a_{10}}{2}yz - \frac{a_2}{2}x + a_{18}y - \frac{a_{11}}{2}z + a_{19} \\
C_{22} &= \frac{a_6}{2}x^2 + \frac{a_7}{2}z^2 + a_{14}xz + a_{15}x + a_{12}z + a_{13} \\
C_{23} &= \frac{a_4}{2}x^2 - \frac{a_{14}}{2}xy - \frac{a_{10}}{2}xz - \frac{a_7}{2}yz - (a_{16}+a_{18})x - \frac{a_{12}}{2}y - \frac{a_8}{2}z + a_{20} \\
C_{33} &= \frac{a_1}{2}x^2 + \frac{a_7}{2}y^2 + a_{10}xy + a_{11}x + a_8 y + a_9
\end{aligned} \tag{49}$$

where a_I with $I=1,2,\ldots,20$ are arbitrary real constants.

The vector L^a generating the KT $C_{ab} = L_{(a;b)}$ is

$$L_a = \begin{pmatrix} -a_{15}y^2 - a_{11}z^2 + a_5 xy + a_2 xz + 2(a_{16}+a_{18})yz + a_3 x + 2a_4 y + 2a_1 z + a_6 \\ -a_5 x^2 - a_8 z^2 + a_{15}xy - 2a_{18}xz + a_{12}yz + 2(a_{17}-a_4)x + a_{13}y + 2a_7 z + a_{14} \\ -a_2 x^2 - a_{12}y^2 - 2a_{16}xy + a_{11}xz + a_8 yz + 2(a_{19}-a_1)x + 2(a_{20}-a_7)y + a_9 z + a_{10} \end{pmatrix} \tag{50}$$

and the generated KT is

$$C_{ab} = \begin{pmatrix} a_5 y + a_2 z + a_3 & -\frac{a_5}{2}x - \frac{a_{15}}{2}y + a_{16}z + a_{17} & -\frac{a_2}{2}x + a_{18}y - \frac{a_{11}}{2}z + a_{19} \\ -\frac{a_5}{2}x - \frac{a_{15}}{2}y + a_{16}z + a_{17} & a_{15}x + a_{12}z + a_{13} & -(a_{16}+a_{18})x - \frac{a_{12}}{2}y - \frac{a_8}{2}z + a_{20} \\ -\frac{a_2}{2}x + a_{18}y - \frac{a_{11}}{2}z + a_{19} & -(a_{16}+a_{18})x - \frac{a_{12}}{2}y - \frac{a_8}{2}z + a_{20} & a_{11}x + a_8 y + a_9 \end{pmatrix} \tag{51}$$

which is a subcase of the general KT (49) for $a_1 = a_4 = a_6 = a_7 = a_{10} = a_{14} = 0$.

We note that the covariant expression of the most general KT M_{ij} of order 2 of E^3 is (see [32,33])

$$M_{ij} = (\varepsilon_{ikm}\varepsilon_{jln} + \varepsilon_{jkm}\varepsilon_{iln}) A^{mn} q^k q^l + (B^l_{(i}\varepsilon_{j)kl} + \lambda_{(i}\delta_{j)k} - \delta_{ij}\lambda_k) q^k + D_{ij} \tag{52}$$

where A^{mn}, B^l_i, D_{ij} are constant tensors all being symmetric and B^l_i also being traceless; λ^k is a constant vector; ε_{ijk} is the 3d Levi-Civita symbol. This result is obtained from the solution of the Killing tensor equation in the Euclidean space.

Observe that A^{mn}, D_{ij} have each six independent components; B^l_i has five independent components; λ^k has three independent components. Therefore, M_{ij} depends on $6+6+5+$

3 = 20 arbitrary real constants, a result which is in accordance with the one given above in Equation (49).

9. The Time-Dependent Newtonian Generalized Kepler Potential

The time-dependent Newtonian generalized Kepler potential is $V = -\frac{\omega(t)}{r^\nu}$ where ν is a non-zero real constant and $r = (x^2 + y^2 + z^2)^{\frac{1}{2}}$. This potential contains (among others) the 3d time-dependent oscillator [8,10,13–15] for $\nu = -2$, the time-dependent Kepler potential [12,16–18] for $\nu = 1$ and the Newton–Cotes potential for $\nu = 2$ [31]. The integrability of these systems has been studied in numerous works over the years using various methods, mainly the Noether symmetries. Our purpose is to recover the results of these works—and also new ones—using the basis method.

The Lagrangian of the system is

$$L = \frac{1}{2}(\dot{x}^2 + \dot{y}^2 + \dot{z}^2) + \frac{\omega(t)}{r^\nu} \tag{53}$$

and the corresponding Euler–Lagrange equations are

$$\ddot{x} = -\frac{\nu\omega(t)}{r^{\nu+2}}x, \quad \ddot{y} = -\frac{\nu\omega(t)}{r^{\nu+2}}y, \quad \ddot{z} = -\frac{\nu\omega(t)}{r^{\nu+2}}z. \tag{54}$$

For this system the $Q^a = \frac{\nu q^a}{r^{\nu+2}}$ where $q^a = (x, y, z)$ whereas the $\omega(t)$ is unspecified. We shall determine those $\omega(t)$ for which the resulting FIs are not combinations of the angular momentum.

The LFIs and the QFIs of the autonomous generalized Kepler potential, that is, $\omega(t) = k = const$, have been determined in [27] using the direct method and are listed in Table 1.

Table 1. The LFIs/QFIs of the autonomous generalized Kepler potential for $\omega(t) = k = const$.

$V = -\frac{k}{r^\nu}$	LFIs and QFIs
$\forall \nu$	$L_1 = y\dot{z} - z\dot{y}$, $L_2 = z\dot{x} - x\dot{z}$, $L_3 = x\dot{y} - y\dot{x}$, $H_\nu = \frac{1}{2}(\dot{x}^2 + \dot{y}^2 + \dot{z}^2) - \frac{k}{r^\nu}$
$\nu = -2$	$B_{ij} = \dot{q}_i\dot{q}_j - 2kq_iq_j$
$\nu = -2, k > 0$	$I_{3a\pm} = e^{\pm\sqrt{2k}t}(\dot{q}_a \mp \sqrt{2k}q_a)$
$\nu = -2, k < 0$	$I_{3a\pm} = e^{\pm i\sqrt{-2k}t}(\dot{q}_a \mp i\sqrt{-2k}q_a)$
$\nu = 1$	$R_i = (\dot{q}^j\dot{q}_j)q_i - (\dot{q}^jq_j)\dot{q}_i - \frac{k}{r}q_i$
$\nu = 2$	$I_1 = -H_2t^2 + t(\dot{q}^iq_i) - \frac{r^2}{2}$, $I_2 = -H_2t + \frac{1}{2}(\dot{q}^iq_i)$

In Table 1, H_ν is the Hamiltonian of the system, L_i are the components of the angular momentum, R_i are the components of the Runge–Lenz vector and B_{ij} are the components of the Jauch–Hill–Fradkin tensor.

Using $Q^a = \frac{vq^a}{r^{v+2}}$, conditions (5)–(10) become (see [17])

$$K_{(ab;c)} = 0 \tag{55}$$

$$K_{(a;b)} + K_{ab,t} = 0 \tag{56}$$

$$K_{,a} - \frac{2v\omega}{r^{v+2}} K_{ab} q^b + K_{a,t} = 0 \tag{57}$$

$$K_{,t} - \frac{v\omega}{r^{v+2}} K_a q^a = 0 \tag{58}$$

$$K_{a,tt} + v\omega \left(\frac{K_b q^b}{r^{v+2}}\right)_{,a} - \frac{2v\omega_{,t}}{r^{v+2}} K_{ab} q^b - \frac{2v\omega}{r^{v+2}} K_{ab,t} q^b = 0 \tag{59}$$

$$K_{[a;b],t} - 2v\omega \left(\frac{K_{[a|c|} q^c}{r^{v+2}}\right)_{;b]} = 0. \tag{60}$$

From the Lagrangian (53), we infer that the kinetic metric is $\delta_{ij} = diag(1,1,1)$.
According to the basis approach, the KT $K_{ab}(t, q)$ of (55) is the KT given by (49) but the 20 arbitrary constants a_I are assumed to be time-dependent functions $a_I(t)$.
Condition (56) gives

$$K_{a,b} + K_{b,a} = -2K_{ab,t} \implies$$

$$K_{1,1} = -K_{11,t} \tag{61}$$
$$K_{2,2} = -K_{22,t} \tag{62}$$
$$K_{3,3} = -K_{33,t} \tag{63}$$
$$K_{1,2} + K_{2,1} = -2K_{12,t} \tag{64}$$
$$K_{1,3} + K_{3,1} = -2K_{13,t} \tag{65}$$
$$K_{2,3} + K_{3,2} = -2K_{23,t}. \tag{66}$$

From the first three conditions (61)–(63) we find

$$K_1 = -\frac{\dot{a}_6}{2} xy^2 - \frac{\dot{a}_1}{2} xz^2 - \dot{a}_4 xyz - \dot{a}_5 xy - \dot{a}_2 xz - \dot{a}_3 x + A(y, z, t)$$

$$K_2 = -\frac{\dot{a}_6}{2} yx^2 - \frac{\dot{a}_7}{2} yz^2 - \dot{a}_{14} xyz - \dot{a}_{15} xy - \dot{a}_{12} yz - \dot{a}_{13} y + B(x, z, t)$$

$$K_3 = -\frac{\dot{a}_1}{2} zx^2 - \frac{\dot{a}_7}{2} zy^2 - \dot{a}_{10} xyz - \dot{a}_{11} xz - \dot{a}_8 yz - \dot{a}_9 z + C(x, y, t)$$

where A, B, C are arbitrary functions.
Substituting these results in (64)–(66) we obtain

$$0 = \dot{a}_{10} z^2 - 3\dot{a}_6 xy - 2\dot{a}_4 xz - 2\dot{a}_{14} yz - 2\dot{a}_5 x - 2\dot{a}_{15} y + 2\dot{a}_{16} z + 2\dot{a}_{17} + A_{,2} + B_{,1} \tag{67}$$

$$0 = \dot{a}_{14} y^2 - 2\dot{a}_4 xy - 3\dot{a}_1 xz - 2\dot{a}_{10} yz - 2\dot{a}_2 x + 2\dot{a}_{18} y - 2\dot{a}_{11} z + 2\dot{a}_{19} + A_{,3} + C_{,1} \tag{68}$$

$$0 = \dot{a}_4 x^2 - 2\dot{a}_{14} xy - 2\dot{a}_{10} xz - 3\dot{a}_7 yz - 2(\dot{a}_{16} + \dot{a}_{18})x - 2\dot{a}_{12} y - 2\dot{a}_8 z + 2\dot{a}_{20} + B_{,3} + C_{,2}. \tag{69}$$

By taking the second partial derivatives of (67) with respect to (wrt) x, y, of (68) wrt x, z and of (69) wrt y, z we find that

$$a_1 = c_1, \quad a_6 = c_2, \quad a_7 = c_3$$

are arbitrary constants.
Then, Equations (67)–(69) become

$$0 = \dot{a}_{10} z^2 - 2\dot{a}_4 xz - 2\dot{a}_{14} yz - 2\dot{a}_5 x - 2\dot{a}_{15} y + 2\dot{a}_{16} z + 2\dot{a}_{17} + A_{,2} + B_{,1} \tag{70}$$

$$0 = \dot{a}_{14} y^2 - 2\dot{a}_4 xy - 2\dot{a}_{10} yz - 2\dot{a}_2 x + 2\dot{a}_{18} y - 2\dot{a}_{11} z + 2\dot{a}_{19} + A_{,3} + C_{,1} \tag{71}$$

$$0 = \dot{a}_4 x^2 - 2\dot{a}_{14} xy - 2\dot{a}_{10} xz - 2(\dot{a}_{16} + \dot{a}_{18})x - 2\dot{a}_{12} y - 2\dot{a}_8 z + 2\dot{a}_{20} + B_{,3} + C_{,2}. \tag{72}$$

By suitable differentiations of the above equations, we obtain

$$
\begin{aligned}
A_{,22} &= 2\dot{a}_{14}z + 2\dot{a}_{15} \\
A_{,33} &= 2\dot{a}_{10}y + 2\dot{a}_{11} \\
B_{,11} &= 2\dot{a}_{4}z + 2\dot{a}_{5} \\
B_{,33} &= 2\dot{a}_{10}x + 2\dot{a}_{8} \\
C_{,11} &= 2\dot{a}_{4}y + 2\dot{a}_{2} \\
C_{,22} &= 2\dot{a}_{14}x + 2\dot{a}_{12}.
\end{aligned}
$$

Then,

$$
\begin{aligned}
A &= \dot{a}_{14}zy + \dot{a}_{10}yz^2 + \dot{a}_{15}y^2 + \dot{a}_{11}z^2 + \sigma_1(t)yz + \sigma_2(t)y + \sigma_3(t)z + \sigma_4(t) \\
B &= \dot{a}_{4}zx^2 + \dot{a}_{10}xz^2 + \dot{a}_{5}x^2 + \dot{a}_{8}z^2 + \tau_1(t)xz + \tau_2(t)x + \tau_3(t)z + \tau_4(t) \\
C &= \dot{a}_{4}yx^2 + \dot{a}_{14}xy^2 + \dot{a}_{2}x^2 + \dot{a}_{12}y^2 + \eta_1(t)xy + \eta_2(t)x + \eta_3(t)y + \eta_4(t)
\end{aligned}
$$

where $\sigma_k(t), \tau_k(t), \eta_k(t)$ for $k=1,2,3,4$ are arbitrary functions.

Substituting in (70)–(72) we find

$$
\begin{aligned}
(70) &\implies a_{10} = c_4,\ \sigma_1 = -\tau_1 - 2\dot{a}_{16},\ \sigma_2 = -\tau_2 - 2\dot{a}_{17} \\
(71) &\implies a_{14} = c_5,\ \eta_1 = -\sigma_1 - 2\dot{a}_{18},\ \eta_2 = -\sigma_3 - 2\dot{a}_{19} \\
(72) &\implies a_4 = c_6,\ \tau_1 = -\eta_1 + 2(\dot{a}_{16} + \dot{a}_{18}),\ \tau_3 = -\eta_3 - 2\dot{a}_{20}
\end{aligned}
$$

from which we finally have

$$
a_{10} = c_4,\ a_{14} = c_5,\ a_4 = c_6,\ \tau_1 = 2\dot{a}_{18},\ \eta_1 = 2\dot{a}_{16},\ \sigma_1 = -2(\dot{a}_{16} + \dot{a}_{18}),
$$

$$
\tau_2 = -\sigma_2 - 2\dot{a}_{17},\ \eta_2 = -\sigma_3 - 2\dot{a}_{19},\ \eta_3 = -\tau_3 - 2\dot{a}_{20}
$$

where c_4, c_5, c_6 are arbitrary constants.

Therefore, the KT K_{ab} is

$$
\begin{aligned}
K_{11} &= \frac{c_2}{2}y^2 + \frac{c_1}{2}z^2 + c_6 yz + a_5 y + a_2 z + a_3 \\
K_{12} &= \frac{c_4}{2}z^2 - \frac{c_2}{2}xy - \frac{c_6}{2}xz - \frac{c_5}{2}yz - \frac{a_5}{2}x - \frac{a_{15}}{2}y + a_{16}z + a_{17} \\
K_{13} &= \frac{c_5}{2}y^2 - \frac{c_6}{2}xy - \frac{c_1}{2}xz - \frac{c_4}{2}yz - \frac{a_2}{2}x + a_{18}y - \frac{a_{11}}{2}z + a_{19} \\
K_{22} &= \frac{c_2}{2}x^2 + \frac{c_3}{2}z^2 + c_5 xz + a_{15}x + a_{12}z + a_{13} \\
K_{23} &= \frac{c_6}{2}x^2 - \frac{c_5}{2}xy - \frac{c_4}{2}xz - \frac{c_3}{2}yz - (a_{16}+a_{18})x - \frac{a_{12}}{2}y - \frac{a_8}{2}z + a_{20} \\
K_{33} &= \frac{c_1}{2}x^2 + \frac{c_3}{2}y^2 + c_4 xy + a_{11}x + a_8 y + a_9
\end{aligned} \quad (73)
$$

and the vector K_a is

$$
\begin{aligned}
K_1 &= \dot{a}_{15}y^2 + \dot{a}_{11}z^2 - \dot{a}_5 xy - \dot{a}_2 xz - 2(\dot{a}_{16}+\dot{a}_{18})yz - \dot{a}_3 x + \sigma_2 y + \sigma_3 z + \sigma_4 \\
K_2 &= \dot{a}_5 x^2 + \dot{a}_8 z^2 - \dot{a}_{15}xy + 2\dot{a}_{18}xz - \dot{a}_{12}yz - (\sigma_2 + 2\dot{a}_{17})x - \dot{a}_{13}y + \tau_3 z + \tau_4 \\
K_3 &= \dot{a}_2 x^2 + \dot{a}_{12}y^2 + 2\dot{a}_{16}xy - \dot{a}_{11}xz - \dot{a}_8 yz - (\sigma_3 + 2\dot{a}_{19})x - (\tau_3 + 2\dot{a}_{20})y - \dot{a}_9 z + \eta_4.
\end{aligned} \quad (74)
$$

Replacing the above results in the constraint (60) we find the following set of equations:

$$
a_2 = a_{12},\ a_5 = a_8,\ a_{11} = a_{15},\ a_{16} = a_{18} = 0 \quad (75)
$$

$$
(\nu-1)a_2 = 0,\ (\nu-1)a_5 = 0,\ (\nu-1)a_{11} = 0 \quad (76)
$$

$$
(\nu+2)a_{17} = 0,\ (\nu+2)a_{19} = 0,\ (\nu+2)a_{20} = 0,\ (\nu+2)(a_3 - a_9) = 0,\ (\nu+2)(a_3 - a_{13}) = 0 \quad (77)
$$

$$\ddot{a}_2 = \ddot{a}_5 = \ddot{a}_{11} = 0, \ \dot{\sigma}_2 = -\ddot{a}_{17}, \ \dot{\sigma}_3 = -\ddot{a}_{19}, \ \dot{\tau}_3 = -\ddot{a}_{20}. \tag{78}$$

We consider three cases depending on the value of ν:

- $\forall \nu$. The general case.
- $\nu = 1$. Time-dependent Kepler potential.
- $\nu = -2$. Time-dependent 3d oscillator.

The Newton–Cotes potential ($\nu = 2$) is contained as a subcase of the general case.

10. The General Case

This case holds for any value of ν and conditions (75)–(78) give

$$a_2 = a_5 = a_8 = a_{11} = a_{12} = a_{15} = a_{16} = a_{17} = a_{18} = a_{19} = a_{20} = 0,$$

$$a_3 = a_9 = a_{13}, \ \sigma_2 = c_7, \ \sigma_3 = c_8, \ \tau_3 = c_9$$

where c_7, c_8, c_9 are arbitrary constants.

Substituting in the constraint (59), we find that

$$\ddot{a}_3 = 0, \ (\nu - 2)\omega \dot{a}_3 - 2\dot{\omega} a_3 = 0 \tag{79}$$

$$\dot{\sigma}_4 = \dot{\tau}_4 = \dot{\eta}_4 = 0, \ \omega \sigma_4 = \omega \tau_4 = \omega \eta_4 = 0 \implies \sigma_4 = \tau_4 = \eta_4 = 0.$$

Therefore, the KT K_{ab} becomes

$$K_{ab} = \begin{pmatrix} \frac{c_2}{2}y^2 + \frac{c_1}{2}z^2 + c_6 yz + a_3 & \frac{c_4}{2}z^2 - \frac{c_2}{2}xy - \frac{c_6}{2}xz - \frac{c_5}{2}yz & \frac{c_5}{2}y^2 - \frac{c_6}{2}xy - \frac{c_1}{2}xz - \frac{c_4}{2}yz \\ \frac{c_4}{2}z^2 - \frac{c_2}{2}xy - \frac{c_6}{2}xz - \frac{c_5}{2}yz & \frac{c_2}{2}x^2 + \frac{c_3}{2}z^2 + c_5 xz + a_3 & \frac{c_6}{2}x^2 - \frac{c_5}{2}xy - \frac{c_4}{2}xz - \frac{c_3}{2}yz \\ \frac{c_5}{2}y^2 - \frac{c_6}{2}xy - \frac{c_1}{2}xz - \frac{c_4}{2}yz & \frac{c_6}{2}x^2 - \frac{c_5}{2}xy - \frac{c_4}{2}xz - \frac{c_3}{2}yz & \frac{c_1}{2}x^2 + \frac{c_3}{2}y^2 + c_4 xy + a_3 \end{pmatrix} \tag{80}$$

and the vector

$$K_a = \begin{pmatrix} -\dot{a}_3 x + c_7 y + c_8 z \\ -c_7 x - \dot{a}_3 y + c_9 z \\ -c_8 x - c_9 y - \dot{a}_3 z \end{pmatrix}. \tag{81}$$

Since the ten parameters $a_3(t)$ and c_A where $A = 1, 2, \ldots, 9$ are independent (i.e., they generate different FIs) we consider the following two cases.

10.1. $a_3(t) = 0$

In this case, the conditions (79) are satisfied identically leaving the function $\omega(t)$ free. Therefore, the KT (80) becomes

$$K_{ab} = \begin{pmatrix} \frac{c_2}{2}y^2 + \frac{c_1}{2}z^2 + c_6 yz & \frac{c_4}{2}z^2 - \frac{c_2}{2}xy - \frac{c_6}{2}xz - \frac{c_5}{2}yz & \frac{c_5}{2}y^2 - \frac{c_6}{2}xy - \frac{c_1}{2}xz - \frac{c_4}{2}yz \\ \frac{c_4}{2}z^2 - \frac{c_2}{2}xy - \frac{c_6}{2}xz - \frac{c_5}{2}yz & \frac{c_2}{2}x^2 + \frac{c_3}{2}z^2 + c_5 xz & \frac{c_6}{2}x^2 - \frac{c_5}{2}xy - \frac{c_4}{2}xz - \frac{c_3}{2}yz \\ \frac{c_5}{2}y^2 - \frac{c_6}{2}xy - \frac{c_1}{2}xz - \frac{c_4}{2}yz & \frac{c_6}{2}x^2 - \frac{c_5}{2}xy - \frac{c_4}{2}xz - \frac{c_3}{2}yz & \frac{c_1}{2}x^2 + \frac{c_3}{2}y^2 + c_4 xy \end{pmatrix}$$

and the vector (81) becomes the general non-gradient KV

$$K_a = \begin{pmatrix} c_7 y + c_8 z \\ -c_7 x + c_9 z \\ -c_8 x - c_9 y \end{pmatrix}.$$

Then, the constraint (58) implies that (since $K_a q^a = 0$) $K = G(x, y, z)$ which when replaced in (57) gives (since $K_{ab} q^b = 0$) $G_{,a} = 0$. Hence $K = const \equiv 0$.

The QFI $I = K_{ab}\dot{q}^a \dot{q}^b + K_a \dot{q}^a$ leads only to the three components L_i of the angular momentum. We note that I contains nine independent parameters, each of them defining an FI: (a) c_7, c_8, c_9 lead to the components $L_1 = y\dot{z} - z\dot{y}$, $L_2 = z\dot{x} - x\dot{z}$, $L_3 = x\dot{y} - y\dot{x}$ of the angular momentum (LFIs); (b) $c_1, c_2, c_3, c_4, c_5, c_6$ lead to the products (QFIs depending on L_i) $L_1^2, L_2^2, L_3^2, L_1 L_2, L_1 L_3$ and $L_2 L_3$.

We have the following result.

Proposition 1. *The time-dependent generalized Kepler potential $V(t,q) = -\frac{\omega(t)}{r^\nu}$ for a general smooth function $\omega(t)$ admits only the LFIs of the angular momentum L_i. Independent QFIs in general do not exist, they are all quadratic combinations of L_i.*

10.2. $c_A = 0$ where $A = 1, 2, \ldots, 9$

In this case, the conditions (79) imply that $a_3(t) = b_0 + b_1 t + b_2 t^2$ and

$$\omega_{(\nu)}(t) = k\left(b_0 + b_1 t + b_2 t^2\right)^{\frac{\nu-2}{2}} \tag{82}$$

where k, b_0, b_1, b_2 are arbitrary constants and the index (ν) denotes the dependence of $\omega(t)$ on the value of ν.

Since $c_A = 0$ the quantities (80) and (81) become

$$K_{ab} = a_3 \delta_{ab}, \quad K_a = -\dot{a}_3 q_a.$$

Substituting in the remaining constraints (57) and (58), we find

$$K = b_2 r^2 - \frac{2k(b_0 + b_1 t + b_2 t^2)^{\nu/2}}{r^\nu}.$$

The QFI is

$$J_\nu = (b_0 + b_1 t + b_2 t^2)\left[\frac{\dot{q}^i \dot{q}_i}{2} - \frac{k(b_0 + b_1 t + b_2 t^2)^{\frac{\nu-2}{2}}}{r^\nu}\right] - \frac{b_1 + 2b_2 t}{2} q^i \dot{q}_i + \frac{b_2 r^2}{2}. \tag{83}$$

We note that the resulting time-dependent generalized Kepler potential

$$V = -\frac{\omega_\nu(t)}{r^\nu}, \quad \omega_\nu = k\left(b_0 + b_1 t + b_2 t^2\right)^{\frac{\nu-2}{2}} \tag{84}$$

is a subcase of the Case III potential of [18] if we set the function

$$U\left(\frac{r}{\phi}\right) = k_1 \frac{r^2}{\phi^2} - \frac{k\phi^\nu}{r^\nu}$$

with

$$\phi = \sqrt{b_0 + b_1 t + b_2 t^2}, \quad k_1 = \frac{b_0 b_2}{2} - \frac{b_1^2}{8}.$$

Then, the associated QFI (3.13) of [18] (for $K_1 = K_2 = 0$) reduces to the QFI J_ν.

For some values of ν, we have the following results:

- $\nu = 1$ (time-dependent Kepler potential).

  The $\omega_{(1)}(t) = k(b_0 + b_1 t + b_2 t^2)^{-1/2}$ and the QFI $J_1 = E_3$ (see Section 11.2 below).

- $\nu = 2$ (Newton–Cotes potential [31]).

  The $\omega_{(2)} = k = const$ and the QFI is

$$\begin{aligned} J_2 &= (b_0 + b_1 t + b_2 t^2)\left(\frac{\dot{q}^i \dot{q}_i}{2} - \frac{k}{r^2}\right) - \frac{b_1 + 2b_2 t}{2} q^i \dot{q}_i + \frac{b_2}{2} r^2 \\ &= b_0 H_2 - b_1 I_2 - b_2 I_1. \end{aligned}$$

This expression contains the independent QFIs

$$H_2 = \frac{\dot{q}^i \dot{q}_i}{2} - \frac{k}{r^2}, \quad I_1 = -t^2 H_2 + t q^i \dot{q}_i - \frac{r^2}{2}, \quad I_2 = -t H_2 + \frac{\dot{q}^i \dot{q}_i}{2}$$

where H_2 is the Hamiltonian of the system. These are the FIs found in [27] (see also Table 1) in the case of the autonomous generalized Kepler potential for $\nu = 2$.

- $\nu = -2$ (time-dependent oscillator).

The $\omega_{(-2)} = k(b_0 + b_1 t + b_2 t^2)^{-2}$ and the QFI is

$$J_{-2} = (b_0 + b_1 t + b_2 t^2)\left[\frac{\dot{q}^i \dot{q}_i}{2} - \frac{k}{(b_0 + b_1 t + b_2 t^2)^2} r^2\right] - \frac{b_1 + 2b_2 t}{2}q^i \dot{q}_i + \frac{b_2 r^2}{2}.$$

This is the trace of the QFIs (111) found below for $a_3(t) = b_0 + b_1 t + b_2 t^2$. Substituting this $a_3(t)$ in (110) and (111) we find, respectively, that the $\omega = \omega_{(-2)}$ with constant $k = -\frac{1}{8}(b_1^2 - 4b_2 b_0 + 2c_0)$ and the QFIs are

$$I_{ij} = \Lambda_{ij}(a_3 = b_0 + b_1 t + b_2 t^2) = (b_0 + b_1 t + b_2 t^2)(\dot{q}_i \dot{q}_j - 2\omega q_i q_j) - (b_1 + 2b_2 t)q_{(i}\dot{q}_{j)} + b_2 q_i q_j. \tag{85}$$

Therefore, the trace $Tr[I_{ij}] = I_{11} + I_{22} + I_{33} = 2J_{-2}$. Note that $r^2 = q^i q_i$.

We infer the following new general result which includes the time-dependent Kepler potential and the time-dependent oscillator as subcases.

Proposition 2 (3d time-dependent generalized Kepler potentials which admit FIs). *For all functions $\omega(t)$ the time-dependent generalized Kepler potential $V(t, q) = -\frac{\omega(t)}{r^\nu}$ admits the LFIs of the angular momentum and QFIs which are products of the components of the angular momentum. However for the function $\omega(t) = \omega_{(\nu)}(t) = k(b_0 + b_1 t + b_2 t^2)^{\frac{\nu-2}{2}}$ the resulting time-dependent generalized Kepler potential admits the additional QFI J_ν given by (83).*

11. The Time-Dependent Kepler Potential

In this case, $\nu = 1$ and conditions (75)–(78) give

$$a_{16} = a_{17} = a_{18} = a_{19} = a_{20} = 0, \quad a_5 = a_8, \quad a_2 = a_{12}, \quad a_3 = a_9 = a_{13}, \quad a_{11} = a_{15}$$

$$\ddot{a}_2 = \ddot{a}_5 = \ddot{a}_{11} = 0$$

$$\sigma_2 = c_7, \quad \sigma_3 = c_8, \quad \tau_3 = c_9.$$

Then, constraint (59) gives

$$\dddot{a}_3 = 0, \quad \sigma_4 = \tau_4 = \eta_4 = 0$$

and

$$a_3 \omega^2 = c_{10}, \quad a_2 \omega = c_{11}, \quad a_5 \omega = c_{12}, \quad a_{11}\omega = c_{13}$$

where $c_{10}, c_{11}, c_{12}, c_{13}$ are arbitrary constants.

Finally, we have

$$\begin{aligned}
K_{11} &= \frac{c_2}{2}y^2 + \frac{c_1}{2}z^2 + c_6 yz + a_5 y + a_2 z + a_3 \\
K_{12} &= \frac{c_4}{2}z^2 - \frac{c_2}{2}xy - \frac{c_6}{2}xz - \frac{c_5}{2}yz - \frac{a_5}{2}x - \frac{a_{11}}{2}y \\
K_{13} &= \frac{c_5}{2}y^2 - \frac{c_6}{2}xy - \frac{c_1}{2}xz - \frac{c_4}{2}yz - \frac{a_2}{2}x - \frac{a_{11}}{2}z \\
K_{22} &= \frac{c_2}{2}x^2 + \frac{c_3}{2}z^2 + c_5 xz + a_{11}x + a_2 z + a_3 \\
K_{23} &= \frac{c_6}{2}x^2 - \frac{c_5}{2}xy - \frac{c_4}{2}xz - \frac{c_3}{2}yz - \frac{a_2}{2}y - \frac{a_5}{2}z \\
K_{33} &= \frac{c_1}{2}x^2 + \frac{c_3}{2}y^2 + c_4 xy + a_{11}x + a_5 y + a_3
\end{aligned}$$

and
$$K_1 = \dot{a}_{11}y^2 + \dot{a}_{11}z^2 - \dot{a}_5 xy - \dot{a}_2 xz - \dot{a}_3 x + c_7 y + c_8 z$$
$$K_2 = \dot{a}_5 x^2 + \dot{a}_5 z^2 - \dot{a}_{11} xy - \dot{a}_2 yz - c_7 x - \dot{a}_3 y + c_9 z$$
$$K_3 = \dot{a}_2 x^2 + \dot{a}_2 y^2 - \dot{a}_{11} xz - \dot{a}_5 yz - c_8 x - c_9 y - \dot{a}_3 z$$

where

$$\ddot{a}_2 = \ddot{a}_5 = \ddot{a}_{11} = 0, \ \dddot{a}_3 = 0, \ a_3 \omega^2 = c_{10}, \ a_2 \omega = c_{11}, \ a_5 \omega = c_{12}, \ a_{11} \omega = c_{13}. \tag{86}$$

From the last conditions follow that in order QFIs to be admitted the function $\omega(t)$ can have only three possible forms:

- $\omega(t)$ a general function;
- $\omega(t) = \omega_{2K}(t) = \frac{c_{11}}{b_0 + b_1 t}$ where $c_{11} b_1 \neq 0$;
- $\omega(t) = \omega_{3K}(t) = \frac{k}{(b_0 + b_1 t + b_2 t^2)^{1/2}}$ where $k \neq 0$ and $b_1^2 - 4 b_2 b_0 \neq 0$.

This result confirms the results found previously in [12,17,18]. We note that the time-dependent Kepler potential $V = -\frac{\omega_{2K}(t)}{r}$ is a subcase of the Case II potential of [18] for $\mu_0 = c_{11}$ and $\phi = b_0 + b_1 t$, whereas the potential $V = -\frac{\omega_{3K}(t)}{r}$ is a subcase of the Case III potential of [18] (see Section 10.2).

In the following, we discuss the cases for the special functions $\omega_{2K}(t)$ and $\omega_{3K}(t)$ because the case for a general function $\omega(t)$ reproduces the results of Section 10.1.

11.1. $\omega(t) = \omega_{2K}(t) = \frac{c_{11}}{b_0 + b_1 t}, \ c_{11} b_1 \neq 0$

In that case, conditions (86) give

$$a_2 = b_0 + b_1 t, \ a_3 = \frac{c_{10}}{c_{11}^2}(b_0 + b_1 t)^2, \ a_5 = \frac{c_{12}}{c_{11}}(b_0 + b_1 t), \ a_{11} = \frac{c_{13}}{c_{11}}(b_0 + b_1 t).$$

Substituting the resulting vector K_a and the KT K_{ab} in (58) we find the solution

$$K(q,t) = -\frac{2 c_{10} b_1 t}{c_{11} r} + G(q).$$

Replacing this solution in the remaining constraint (57) we find

$$G(x,y,z) = -\frac{2 c_{10} b_0}{c_{11} r} - \frac{c_{13} x + c_{12} y + c_{11} z}{r} + \frac{c_{10} b_1^2}{c_{11}^2} r^2.$$

Therefore,

$$K(x,y,z,t) = \frac{c_{10} b_1^2 r^2}{c_{11}^2} - \frac{2 c_{10}(b_0 + b_1 t)}{c_{11} r} - \frac{c_{13} x + c_{12} y + c_{11} z}{r}.$$

The QFI is

$$I = \frac{c_3}{2} L_1^2 + \frac{c_1}{2} L_2^2 + \frac{c_2}{2} L_3^2 - c_4 L_1 L_2 - c_5 L_1 L_3 - c_6 L_2 L_3 - c_9 L_1 + c_8 L_2 - c_7 L_3 + \frac{2 c_{10}}{c_{11}^2} E_2 +$$
$$+ \frac{c_{13}}{c_{11}} A_1 + \frac{c_{12}}{c_{11}} A_2 + A_3$$

where $\omega_{2K}(t) = \frac{c_{11}}{b_0+b_1 t}$ and

$$L_i \equiv \dot{q}_{i+1}\dot{q}_{i+2} - q_{i+2}\dot{q}_{i+1} \tag{87}$$

$$E_2 \equiv (b_0+b_1 t)^2 \left[\frac{\dot{q}^i\dot{q}_i}{2} - \frac{c_{11}}{r(b_0+b_1 t)}\right] - b_1(b_0+b_1 t)q^i\dot{q}_i + \frac{b_1^2 r^2}{2} \tag{88}$$

$$\tilde{R}_i \equiv (\dot{q}^j\dot{q}_j)q_i - (\dot{q}^j q_j)\dot{q}_i - \frac{c_{11}}{r(b_0+b_1 t)}q_i \tag{89}$$

$$A_i \equiv (b_0+b_1 t)\tilde{R}_i + b_1(q_{i+2}L_{i+1} - q_{i+1}L_{i+2}). \tag{90}$$

We note that $i = 1, 2, 3$, $q_i = (x, y, z)$ and $q_i \equiv q_{i+3k}$ for all $k \in \mathbb{N}$, that is

$$x = q_1 = q_4 = q_7 = ..., \quad y = q_2 = q_5 = q_8 = ..., \quad z = q_3 = q_6 = q_9.$$

The QFI I contains the already found LFIs L_i of the angular momentum; the QFI E_2 which for $b_1 = 0$ reduces to the Hamiltonian of the Kepler potential $V = -\frac{c_{11}}{b_0 r}$; the QFIs A_i which may be considered as a generalization of the Runge–Lenz vector $R_i\left(k = \frac{c_{11}}{b_0}\right)$ for time-dependence $\omega_{2K}(t) = \frac{c_{11}}{b_0+b_1 t}$. Indeed we have $A_i(b_1 = 0) = b_0 R_i\left(k = \frac{c_{11}}{b_0}\right)$.

The expressions (88)–(90) are written compactly as follows

$$E_2 \equiv c_{11}^2 \left[\frac{1}{\omega_{2K}^2}\left(\frac{\dot{q}^i\dot{q}_i}{2} - \frac{\omega_{2K}}{r}\right) - \frac{1}{2}\frac{d}{dt}\left(\frac{1}{\omega_{2K}}\right)^2 q^i\dot{q}_i + \frac{d^2}{dt^2}\left(\frac{1}{\omega_{2K}}\right)^2 \frac{r^2}{4}\right] \tag{91}$$

$$\tilde{R}_i \equiv (\dot{q}^j\dot{q}_j)q_i - (\dot{q}^j q_j)\dot{q}_i - \frac{\omega_{2K}}{r}q_i \tag{92}$$

$$A_i \equiv c_{11}\left[\frac{1}{\omega_{2K}}\tilde{R}_i - \frac{(\ln\omega_{2K})^\cdot}{\omega_{2K}}(q_{i+2}L_{i+1} - q_{i+1}L_{i+2})\right] \tag{93}$$

where $\omega_{2K}(t) = \frac{c_{11}}{b_0+b_1 t}$.

We remark that only five of the seven FIs E_2, L_i, A_i are functionally independent because they are related as follows

$$\mathbf{A} \cdot \mathbf{L} = 0, \quad 2E_2 \mathbf{L}^2 + c_{11}^2 = \mathbf{A}^2. \tag{94}$$

For $b_1 = 0$, $b_0 \neq 0$ we have $\omega_{2K} = \frac{c_{11}}{b_0} \equiv k = const$, $E_2 = b_0^2 H$, $\tilde{R}_i = R_i$ and $A_i = b_0 R_i$ where H is the Hamiltonian and R_i the Runge–Lenz vector for the Kepler potential $V = -\frac{k}{r}$. Then, as expected, Equation (94) reduces to the well-known relation

$$2H\mathbf{L}^2 + k^2 = \mathbf{R}^2.$$

11.2. $\omega(t) = \omega_{3K}(t) = \frac{k}{(b_0+b_1 t+b_2 t^2)^{1/2}}$, $k \neq 0$, $b_1^2 - 4b_2 b_0 \neq 0$

In that case (observe that if $b_1^2 - 4b_2 b_0 = 0$, this case reduces to the case of the Section 11.1 because equation $b_0 + b_1 t + b_2 t^2 = 0$ has a double root t_0 and can be factored in the form $b_2(t - t_0)^2$), conditions (86) give

$$a_2 = a_5 = a_{11} = 0, \quad c_{11} = c_{12} = c_{13} = 0, \quad a_3 = \frac{c_{10}}{k^2}(b_0 + b_1 t + b_2 t^2).$$

Substituting the K_a and K_{ab} of that case in (58) we find the solution

$$K(q,t) = -\frac{2c_{10}}{r\omega_{3K}} + G(q).$$

When this solution is introduced in the remaining constraint (57) gives $G(x, y, z) = \frac{b_2 c_{10}}{k^2} r^2$. Therefore,

$$K(x, y, z, t) = \frac{b_2 c_{10}}{k^2} r^2 - \frac{2c_{10}}{r\omega_{3K}}.$$

The QFI is

$$I = \frac{c_3}{2}L_1^2 + \frac{c_1}{2}L_2^2 + \frac{c_2}{2}L_3^2 - c_4 L_1 L_2 - c_5 L_1 L_3 - c_6 L_2 L_3 - c_9 L_1 + c_8 L_2 - c_7 L_3 + \frac{2c_{10}}{k^2} E_3$$

where

$$E_3 \equiv (b_0 + b_1 t + b_2 t^2)\left[\frac{\dot{q}^i \dot{q}_i}{2} - \frac{k}{r(b_0 + b_1 t + b_2 t^2)^{1/2}}\right] - \frac{b_1 + 2b_2 t}{2} q^i \dot{q}_i + \frac{b_2 r^2}{2} \quad (95)$$

is the only new independent QFI. This QFI is written equivalently

$$E_3 = k^2 \left[\frac{1}{\omega_{3K}^2}\left(\frac{\dot{q}^i \dot{q}_i}{2} - \frac{\omega_{3K}}{r}\right) - \frac{1}{2}\frac{d}{dt}\left(\frac{1}{\omega_{3K}}\right)^2 q^i \dot{q}_i + \frac{d^2}{dt^2}\left(\frac{1}{\omega_{3K}}\right)^2 \frac{r^2}{4}\right]. \quad (96)$$

For $b_1 = b_2 = 0$, E_2 reduces to the well-known Hamiltonian of the time-independent Kepler potential.

We note also that the QFIs (88) and (95) can be written compactly as (see Equation (2.86) in [17])

$$E_\mu = k^2 \left[\frac{1}{\omega_{\mu K}^2}\left(\frac{\dot{q}^i \dot{q}_i}{2} - \frac{\omega_{\mu K}}{r}\right) - \frac{1}{2}\frac{d}{dt}\left(\frac{1}{\omega_{\mu K}}\right)^2 q^i \dot{q}_i + \frac{d^2}{dt^2}\left(\frac{1}{\omega_{\mu K}}\right)^2 \frac{r^2}{4}\right] \quad (97)$$

where $\mu = 2, 3$, $\omega_{2K}(t) = \frac{k}{b_0 + b_1 t}$ and $\omega_{3K}(t) = \frac{k}{(b_0 + b_1 t + b_2 t^2)^{1/2}}$.

Proposition 3 (Time-dependent Kepler potentials which admit additional FIs [17]). *The time-dependent Kepler potential $V(t, q) = -\frac{\omega(t)}{r}$ for the function $\omega_{2K}(t) = \frac{c_{11}}{b_0 + b_1 t}$, $c_{11} b_1 \neq 0$ and the function $\omega_{3K}(t) = \frac{k}{(b_0 + b_1 t + b_2 t^2)^{1/2}}$ where $k \neq 0$ and $b_1^2 - 4b_2 b_0 \neq 0$ admits additional QFIs given by (88), (90) and (95), respectively.*

12. The 3d Time-Dependent Oscillator

In this case, $\nu = -2$ and conditions (75)–(78) give

$$a_2 = a_5 = a_8 = a_{11} = a_{12} = a_{15} = a_{16} = a_{18} = 0$$

and

$$\dot{\sigma}_2 = -\ddot{a}_{17}, \quad \dot{\sigma}_3 = -\ddot{a}_{19}, \quad \dot{\tau}_3 = -\ddot{a}_{20}. \quad (98)$$

Then, the constraint (59) implies that

$$\ddot{\sigma}_4 - 2\omega \sigma_4 = 0, \quad \ddot{\tau}_4 - 2\omega \tau_4 = 0, \quad \ddot{\eta}_4 - 2\omega \eta_4 = 0, \quad (99)$$

$$\dddot{a}_3 - 8\omega \dot{a}_3 - 4\dot{\omega} a_3 = 0, \quad \dddot{a}_9 - 8\omega \dot{a}_9 - 4\dot{\omega} a_9 = 0, \quad \dddot{a}_{13} - 8\omega \dot{a}_{13} - 4\dot{\omega} a_{13} = 0, \quad (100)$$

$$\dddot{a}_{17} - 8\omega \dot{a}_{17} - 4\dot{\omega} a_{17} = 0, \quad \dddot{a}_{19} - 8\omega \dot{a}_{19} - 4\dot{\omega} a_{19} = 0, \quad \dddot{a}_{20} - 8\omega \dot{a}_{20} - 4\dot{\omega} a_{20} = 0. \quad (101)$$

Therefore,
$$\begin{aligned}
K_{11} &= \frac{c_2}{2}y^2 + \frac{c_1}{2}z^2 + c_6 yz + a_3 \\
K_{12} &= \frac{c_4}{2}z^2 - \frac{c_2}{2}xy - \frac{c_6}{2}xz - \frac{c_5}{2}yz + a_{17} \\
K_{13} &= \frac{c_5}{2}y^2 - \frac{c_6}{2}xy - \frac{c_1}{2}xz - \frac{c_4}{2}yz + a_{19} \\
K_{22} &= \frac{c_2}{2}x^2 + \frac{c_3}{2}z^2 + c_5 xz + a_{13} \\
K_{23} &= \frac{c_6}{2}x^2 - \frac{c_5}{2}xy - \frac{c_4}{2}xz - \frac{c_3}{2}yz + a_{20} \\
K_{33} &= \frac{c_1}{2}x^2 + \frac{c_3}{2}y^2 + c_4 xy + a_9
\end{aligned} \qquad (102)$$

and
$$\begin{aligned}
K_1 &= -\dot{a}_3 x + \sigma_2 y + \sigma_3 z + \sigma_4 \\
K_2 &= -(\sigma_2 + 2\dot{a}_{17})x - \dot{a}_{13} y + \tau_3 z + \tau_4 \\
K_3 &= -(\sigma_3 + 2\dot{a}_{19})x - (\tau_3 + 2\dot{a}_{20})y - \dot{a}_9 z + \eta_4.
\end{aligned} \qquad (103)$$

Before we proceed with considering various subcases it is important that we discuss the ordinary differential equations (ODEs) (100) and (101).

12.1. The Lewis Invariant

Equations of the form
$$\dddot{a} - 8\omega \dot{a} - 4\dot{\omega} a = 0 \qquad (104)$$
where $a = a(t)$ can be written as follows
$$a\ddot{a} - \frac{1}{2}\dot{a}^2 - 4\omega a^2 = c_0 = \text{const}. \qquad (105)$$

By putting $a = -\rho^2$ where $\rho = \rho(t)$, Equation (105) becomes
$$\ddot{\rho} - 2\omega \rho - \frac{c_0}{2\rho^3} = 0. \qquad (106)$$

For $2\omega(t) = -\psi^2(t)$, Equation (106) is written
$$\ddot{\rho} + \psi^2 \rho - \frac{c_0}{2\rho^3} = 0. \qquad (107)$$

Equation (107) is the auxiliary Equation (see [8,34,35]) that should be introduced in order to derive the Lewis invariant for the one-dimensional (1d) time-dependent oscillator
$$\ddot{x} + \psi^2 x = 0. \qquad (108)$$

By eliminating the ψ^2 using (108) and multiplying with the factor $x\dot{\rho} - \rho\dot{x}$ Equation (107) gives
$$\ddot{\rho} - \frac{\rho}{x}\ddot{x} - \frac{c_0}{2\rho^3} = 0 \implies \left[\frac{1}{2}(x\dot{\rho} - \rho\dot{x})^2 + \frac{c_0}{4}\left(\frac{x}{\rho}\right)^2 \right]^{\cdot} = 0 \implies$$
$$I \equiv \frac{1}{2}(x\dot{\rho} - \rho\dot{x})^2 + \frac{c_0}{4}\left(\frac{x}{\rho}\right)^2 = \text{const} \qquad (109)$$

which is the well-known Lewis invariant for the 1d time-dependent harmonic oscillator or, equivalently, a FI for the two-dimensional (2d) time-dependent system with equations of motion (107) and (108).

12.2. The System of Equations (98)–(101)

The conditions (99) are not involved into the conditions (98), (100) and (101). This means that the parameters σ_4, τ_4, η_4 give different independent FIs from the remaining parameters $a_3, a_9, a_{13}, a_{17}, a_{19}, a_{20}$. Therefore, without loss of generality they can be treated separately. This leads to the following two cases.

12.2.1. $a_3 \neq 0$, $\sigma_4 = \tau_4 = \eta_4 = 0$

Because the ODEs (100) and (101) are independent (i.e., each one leads to a different FI) and are of the same form without loss of generality we assume

$$a_9 = k_1 a_3, \quad a_{13} = k_2 a_3, \quad a_{17} = k_3 a_3, \quad a_{19} = k_4 a_3, \quad a_{20} = k_5 a_3$$

where k_1, k_2, k_3, k_4, k_5 are arbitrary constants.

From the discussion of Section 12.1 and the assumption $a_3 \neq 0$ condition (100) concerning $a_3(t)$ becomes (see Equation (9.2) in [8])

$$\dddot{a}_3 - 8\omega \dot{a}_3 - 4\dot{\omega} a_3 = 0 \implies a_3 \ddot{a}_3 - \frac{1}{2}\dot{a}_3^2 - 4\omega a_3^2 = c_0 \implies \omega(t) = \frac{\ddot{a}_3}{4a_3} - \frac{1}{8}\left(\frac{\dot{a}_3}{a_3}\right)^2 - \frac{c_0}{4a_3^2} \quad (110)$$

where c_0 is an arbitrary constant and $a_3(t)$ is an arbitrary non-zero function.

Moreover, conditions (98) become

$$\sigma_2 = -\dot{a}_{17}, \quad \sigma_3 = -\dot{a}_{19}, \quad \tau_3 = -\dot{a}_{20}$$

because any additional constant (in general $\sigma_2 = -\dot{a}_{17} + m_1$ where m_1 is a constant) leads to the usual LFIs of the angular momentum.

Then the KT (102) and the vector (103) become (we set $c_1 = \ldots = c_6 = 0$ because they generate the already-found FIs of the angular momentum)

$$K_{ab} = a_3 \begin{pmatrix} 1 & k_3 & k_4 \\ k_3 & k_2 & k_5 \\ k_4 & k_5 & k_1 \end{pmatrix}, \quad K_a = -\dot{a}_3 \begin{pmatrix} x + k_3 y + k_4 z \\ k_3 x + k_2 y + k_5 z \\ k_4 x + k_5 y + k_1 z \end{pmatrix}.$$

Substituting in the constraints (57) and (58) we find

$$K = \frac{\dot{a}_3^2 + 2c_0}{4a_3}\left(x^2 + k_2 y^2 + k_1 z^2 + 2k_3 xy + 2k_4 xz + 2k_5 yz\right).$$

Using Equation (110) we can write $\frac{\dot{a}_3^2 + 2c_0}{4a_3} = \frac{\ddot{a}_3}{2} - 2\omega a_3$.

The QFI is

$$\begin{aligned} I &= a_3\left(\dot{x}^2 + k_2 \dot{y}^2 + k_1 \dot{z}^2 + 2k_3 \dot{x}\dot{y} + 2k_4 \dot{x}\dot{z} + 2k_5 \dot{y}\dot{z}\right) - \dot{a}_3(x + k_3 y + k_4 z)\dot{x} - \\ &\quad - \dot{a}_3(k_3 x + k_2 y + k_5 z)\dot{y} - \dot{a}_3(k_4 x + k_5 y + k_1 z)\dot{z} + \\ &\quad + \left(\frac{\ddot{a}_3}{2} - 2\omega a_3\right)\left(x^2 + k_2 y^2 + k_1 z^2 + 2k_3 xy + 2k_4 xz + 2k_5 yz\right). \end{aligned}$$

This expression contains six QFIs which are the components of the symmetric tensor (see Equations (1.4) and (6.24) in [8])

$$\Lambda_{ij} = a_3\left(\dot{q}_i \dot{q}_j - 2\omega q_i q_j\right) - \dot{a}_3 q_{(i} \dot{q}_{j)} + \frac{\ddot{a}_3}{2} q_i q_j. \quad (111)$$

This tensor for $a_3 = const \neq 0$ reduces to the Jauch–Hill–Fradkin tensor B_{ij} for $\omega = -\frac{c_0}{4a_3^2} = const$.

If we make the transformation (see Section 12.1) $a_3(t) = -\rho^2(t)$ and $2\omega(t) = -\psi^2(t)$, Equation (54) becomes

$$\ddot{q}^a - 2\omega q^a = 0 \implies \ddot{q}^a + \psi^2 q^a = 0 \quad (112)$$

and the QFIs (111) give

$$\Lambda_{ij} = -(\rho\dot{q}_i - \dot{\rho}q_i)(\rho\dot{q}_j - \dot{\rho}q_j) - \frac{c_0}{2}\rho^{-2}q_iq_j \tag{113}$$

where the condition (110) takes the form (107).

The symmetric tensor (113) may be thought of as a 3d generalization of the 1d Lewis invariant (109). Moreover, Equation (113) coincides with Equation (8) in [14] and Equation (1.4) in [8] when $c_0 = 2$.

12.2.2. $a_3 = a_9 = a_{13} = a_{17} = a_{19} = a_{20} = 0, \sigma_4 \neq 0$

In this case, the conditions (100) and (101) vanish identically; the conditions (98) imply that $\sigma_2 = c_7, \sigma_3 = c_8$ and $\tau_3 = c_9$.

Since the remaining ODEs (99) are all independent (i.e., each one generates an independent FI) and of the same form without loss of generality we assume

$$\tau_4 = k_1\sigma_4, \quad \eta_4 = k_2\sigma_4$$

where k_1, k_2 are arbitrary constants.

From (99) for $\sigma_4 \neq 0$ we get

$$\omega(t) = \frac{\ddot{\sigma}_4}{2\sigma_4}. \tag{114}$$

The parameters c_A where $A = 1, 2, ..., 9$ produce the FIs of the angular momentum and we fix them to zero. Therefore

$$K_{ab} = 0, \quad K_a = \sigma_4(1, k_1, k_2).$$

Substituting in the remaining constraints (57) and (58) we find

$$K = -\dot{\sigma}_4(x + k_1 y + k_2 z).$$

The QFI is

$$I = \sigma_4\dot{x} - \dot{\sigma}_4 x + k_1(\sigma_4\dot{y} - \dot{\sigma}_4 y) + k_2(\sigma_4\dot{z} - \dot{\sigma}_4 z)$$

which contains the irreducible LFIs (see Equation (6.25) in [8])

$$I_{4i} = f\dot{q}_i - \dot{f}q_i \tag{115}$$

where $f(t)$ is an arbitrary non-zero function satisfying (114). We note that the LFIs (115) can be derived directly from the equations of motion for $\omega(t) = \frac{\ddot{f}}{2f}$.

From the above two cases, we arrive at the following conclusion.

Proposition 4 (3d time-dependent oscillators which admit additional FIs). *For the function $\omega(t) = \frac{\ddot{a}_3}{4a_3} - \frac{1}{8}\left(\frac{\dot{a}_3}{a_3}\right)^2 - \frac{c_0}{4a_3^2}$ where $a_3(t) \neq 0$, c_0 is an arbitrary constant and the function $\omega(t) = \frac{\ddot{f}}{2f}$ where $f(t) \neq 0$ the resulting 3d time-dependent oscillator $V(t, q) = -\omega(t)r^2$ admits the QFIs (111) and the LFIs (115), respectively.*

13. A Special Class of Time-Dependent Oscillators

In Proposition 4, it has been shown that the time-dependent oscillator ($\nu = -2$) for the frequency

$$\omega_{10}(t) = \frac{\ddot{f}}{4f(t)} - \frac{1}{8}\left(\frac{\dot{f}}{f}\right)^2 - \frac{c_0}{4f^2} \tag{116}$$

where $f(t)$ is an arbitrary non-zero function admits the six QFIs

$$\Lambda_{ij} = f(t)\left(\dot{q}_i \dot{q}_j - 2\omega q_i q_j\right) - \dot{f} q_{(i} \dot{q}_{j)} + \frac{\ddot{f}}{2} q_i q_j \tag{117}$$

and for the frequency

$$\omega_{2O}(t) = \frac{\ddot{g}}{2g(t)} \tag{118}$$

where $g(t)$ is an arbitrary non-zero function admits the three LFIs

$$I_{4i} = g(t)\dot{q}_i - \dot{g}q_i. \tag{119}$$

We consider the class of the 3d time-dependent oscillators for which $\omega_{1O}(t) = \omega_{2O}(t)$. These oscillators admit both the six QFIs Λ_{ij} and the three LFIs I_{4i}.

The condition $\omega_{1O}(t) = \omega_{2O}(t)$ relates the functions $f(t), g(t)$ as follows

$$\omega_{3O}(t) = \frac{\ddot{f}}{4f(t)} - \frac{1}{8}\left(\frac{\dot{f}}{f}\right)^2 - \frac{c_0}{4f^2} = \frac{\ddot{g}}{2g(t)}. \tag{120}$$

It can be easily proved that

$$g = f^{1/2}\cos\theta, \quad \dot{\theta} = \left(\frac{c_0}{2}\right)^{1/2} f^{-1} \implies \theta(t) = \left(\frac{c_0}{2}\right)^{1/2} \int \frac{dt}{f(t)} \tag{121}$$

and

$$g = f^{1/2}\sin\theta, \quad \dot{\theta} = \left(\frac{c_0}{2}\right)^{1/2} f^{-1} \implies \theta(t) = \left(\frac{c_0}{2}\right)^{1/2} \int \frac{dt}{f(t)} \tag{122}$$

satisfy the requirement (120) for any non-zero function $f(t)$. In other words, all the time-dependent oscillators with frequency

$$\omega_{3O}(t) = \frac{\ddot{f}}{4f(t)} - \frac{1}{8}\left(\frac{\dot{f}}{f}\right)^2 - \frac{c_0}{4f^2} \tag{123}$$

admit the six QFIs

$$\Lambda_{ij} = f(t)\left(\dot{q}_i \dot{q}_j - 2\omega q_i q_j\right) - \dot{f} q_{(i} \dot{q}_{j)} + \frac{\ddot{f}}{2} q_i q_j \tag{124}$$

and the six LFIs

$$I_{41i} = \left(\frac{c_0}{2}\right)^{1/2} f^{-1/2} q_i \sin\theta + \left(f^{1/2}\dot{q}_i - \frac{\dot{f}}{2}f^{-1/2}q_i\right)\cos\theta \tag{125}$$

$$I_{42i} = -\left(\frac{c_0}{2}\right)^{1/2} f^{-1/2} q_i \cos\theta + \left(f^{1/2}\dot{q}_i - \frac{\dot{f}}{2}f^{-1/2}q_i\right)\sin\theta. \tag{126}$$

These are the LFIs J_3^k, J_4^k derived in Equations (44) and (45) in [10] using Noether point symmetries and Noether's theorem.

We note that

$$\frac{dI_{42i}}{d\theta} = I_{41i} \tag{127}$$

and

$$\Lambda_{ij} = I_{41i}I_{41j} + I_{42i}I_{42j}. \tag{128}$$

Next, we consider the LFIs of the angular momentum $L_i = q_{i+1}\dot{q}_{i+2} - q_{i+2}\dot{q}_{i+1}$ which can be expressed equivalently as components of the totally antisymmetric tensor

$$L_{ij} = q_i \dot{q}_j - q_j \dot{q}_i = \varepsilon_{ijk} L^k \tag{129}$$

where ε_{ijk} is the 3d Levi-Civita symbol and $L^i = L_i$ since the kinetic metric $\gamma_{ij} = \delta_{ij}$. Then (see Equation (51) in [10])

$$L_{ij} = \left(\frac{2}{c_0}\right)^{1/2} (I_{41i}I_{42j} - I_{41j}I_{42i}). \tag{130}$$

Proposition 5. *For the class of 3d time-dependent oscillators with potential $V(t,q) = -\omega(t)r^2$ where $\omega(t)$ is defined in terms of an arbitrary non-zero (smooth) function $f(t)$ as in (123), the only independent FIs are the LFIs I_{41i}, I_{42i}.*

In order to recover the results of [10], we assume a time-dependent oscillator with $\omega_{3O}(t)$ given by (123) and we write the non-zero function $f(t)$ in the form $f(t) = \rho^2(t)$. Then Equation (123) becomes

$$\omega_{3O}(t) = \frac{\ddot{\rho}}{2\rho} - \frac{c_0}{4\rho^4}. \tag{131}$$

The relations (121) and (122) become

$$g = \rho\cos\theta, \quad \dot{\theta} = \left(\frac{c_0}{2}\right)^{1/2}\rho^{-2} \implies \theta(t) = \left(\frac{c_0}{2}\right)^{1/2}\int\frac{dt}{\rho^2} \tag{132}$$

$$g = \rho\sin\theta, \quad \dot{\theta} = \left(\frac{c_0}{2}\right)^{1/2}\rho^{-2} \implies \theta(t) = \left(\frac{c_0}{2}\right)^{1/2}\int\frac{dt}{\rho^2} \tag{133}$$

and the LFIs (125) and (126) take the form

$$I_{41i} = \left(\frac{c_0}{2}\right)^{1/2}\rho^{-1}q_i\sin\theta + (\rho\dot{q}_i - \dot{\rho}q_i)\cos\theta \tag{134}$$

$$I_{42i} = -\left(\frac{c_0}{2}\right)^{1/2}\rho^{-1}q_i\cos\theta + (\rho\dot{q}_i - \dot{\rho}q_i)\sin\theta. \tag{135}$$

These latter expressions for $c_0 = 2$ coincide with the independent LFIs (44) and (45) found in [10].

Finally, we note that if we consider in this special class of oscillators the simple case $f = 1$, we find $\omega_{3O}(t) = const = -\frac{c_0}{4} \equiv k$ which is the 3d autonomous oscillator (for $k < 0$). Then it can be shown that the exponential LFIs $I_{3i\pm}$ (see Table 1) found in [27] can be written in terms of I_{41i}, I_{42j}. Indeed we have $I_{3i\pm}(k>0) = I_{41i} \mp iI_{42i}$ and $I_{3i\pm}(k<0) = I_{41i} \pm iI_{42i}$.

14. Collection of Results

We collect the results concerning the time-dependent generalized Kepler potential for all values of ν in Table 2. We note that for $\nu = -2, 1, 2$ the dynamical system is the time-dependent 3d oscillator, the time-dependent Kepler potential and the Newton–Cotes potential, respectively. Concerning notation, we have $q^i = (x,y,z)$, $q_i \equiv q_{i+3k}$ for all $k \in \mathbb{N}$ and $\tilde{R}_i = (\dot{q}^j\dot{q}_j)q_i - (\dot{q}^jq_j)\dot{q}_i - \frac{k}{r(b_0+b_1t)}q_i$.

Table 2. The LFIs/QFIs of the time-dependent generalized Kepler potential $V = -\frac{\omega(t)}{r^\nu}$.

ν	$\omega(t)$	LFIs and QFIs
$\forall \nu$	$\forall \omega$ k $\omega_\nu = k(b_0 + b_1 t + b_2 t^2)^{\frac{\nu-2}{2}}$	$L_i = q_{i+1}\dot{q}_{i+2} - q_{i+2}\dot{q}_{i+1}, \; L_{ij} = q_i\dot{q}_j - q_j\dot{q}_i = \varepsilon_{ijk}L^k$ $H_\nu = \frac{1}{2}\dot{q}^i\dot{q}_i - \frac{k}{r^\nu}$ $J_\nu = (b_0 + b_1 t + b_2 t^2)\left(\frac{\dot{q}^i\dot{q}_i}{2} - \frac{\omega_\nu}{r^\nu}\right) - \frac{b_1+2b_2 t}{2}q^i\dot{q}_i + \frac{b_2 r^2}{2}$
-2	k $k > 0$ $k < 0$ $\frac{k}{(b_0+b_1 t+b_2 t^2)^2}$	$B_{ij} = \dot{q}_i\dot{q}_j - 2kq_i q_j$ $I_{3a\pm} = e^{\pm\sqrt{2k}t}(\dot{q}_a \mp \sqrt{2k}q_a)$ $I_{3a\pm} = e^{\pm i\sqrt{-2k}t}(\dot{q}_a \mp i\sqrt{-2k}q_a)$ $I_{ij} = (b_0 + b_1 t + b_2 t^2)(\dot{q}_i\dot{q}_j - 2\omega q_i q_j) - (b_1 + 2b_2 t)q_{(i}\dot{q}_{j)} + b_2 q_i q_j$
	$\frac{\ddot{f}}{4f(t)} - \frac{1}{8}\left(\frac{\dot{f}}{f}\right)^2 - \frac{c_0}{4f^2}$	$L_{ij} = \left(\frac{2}{c_0}\right)^{1/2}(I_{41i}I_{42j} - I_{41j}I_{42i}),$ $\Lambda_{ij} = f(t)(\dot{q}_i\dot{q}_j - 2\omega q_i q_j) - \dot{f}q_{(i}\dot{q}_{j)} + \frac{\ddot{f}}{2}q_i q_j = I_{41i}I_{41j} + I_{42i}I_{42j},$ $I_{41i} = \left(\frac{c_0}{2}\right)^{1/2} f^{-1/2} q_i \sin\theta + \left(f^{1/2}\dot{q}_i - \frac{\dot{f}}{2}f^{-1/2}q_i\right)\cos\theta,$ $I_{42i} = -\left(\frac{c_0}{2}\right)^{1/2} f^{-1/2} q_i \cos\theta + \left(f^{1/2}\dot{q}_i - \frac{\dot{f}}{2}f^{-1/2}q_i\right)\sin\theta$ where $\theta = \left(\frac{c_0}{2}\right)^{1/2}\int f^{-1}dt$
	$\frac{\ddot{g}}{2g(t)}$	$I_{4i} = g(t)\dot{q}_i - \dot{g}q_i$
1	k $\frac{k}{b_0+b_1 t}$ $\frac{k}{(b_0+b_1 t+b_2 t^2)^{1/2}}$	$R_i = (\dot{q}^j\dot{q}_j)q_i - (\dot{q}^j q_j)\dot{q}_i - \frac{k}{r}q_i$ $E_2 = (b_0 + b_1 t)^2\left[\frac{\dot{q}^i\dot{q}_i}{2} - \frac{k}{r(b_0+b_1 t)}\right] - b_1(b_0 + b_1 t)q^i\dot{q}_i + \frac{b_1^2 r^2}{2},$ $A_i = (b_0 + b_1 t)\bar{R}_i + b_1(q_{i+2}L_{i+1} - q_{i+1}L_{i+2})$ where $\bar{R}_i = (\dot{q}^j\dot{q}_j)q_i - (\dot{q}^j q_j)\dot{q}_i - \frac{k}{r(b_0+b_1 t)}q_i$ $E_3 = (b_0 + b_1 t + b_2 t^2)\left[\frac{\dot{q}^i\dot{q}_i}{2} - \frac{k}{r(b_0+b_1 t+b_2 t^2)^{1/2}}\right] - \frac{b_1+2b_2 t}{2}q^i\dot{q}_i + \frac{b_2 r^2}{2}$
2	k	$I_1 = -H_2 t^2 + t(\dot{q}^i q_i) - \frac{r^2}{2}, \; I_2 = -H_2 t + \frac{1}{2}(\dot{q}^i q_i)$

15. Integrating the Equations

In this section, we use the independent LFIs I_{41i}, I_{42i} to integrate the equations of the special class of 3d time-dependent oscillators ($\nu = -2$) defined in Section 13 with $\omega(t)$ given by (123). We also use the FIs L_i, E_2, A_i to integrate the time-dependent Kepler potential ($\nu = 1$) with $\omega(t) = \frac{k}{b_0+b_1 t}$ where $kb_1 \neq 0$ (see Section 11.1).

15.1. The 3d Time-Dependent Oscillator with $\omega(t)$ Given by (123)

Using the LFIs (125) and (126) we find

$$q_i(t) = \left(\frac{2}{c_0}\right)^{1/2} f^{1/2}\left(I_{41i}\sin\theta - I_{42i}\cos\theta\right) \tag{136}$$

where $I_{41i}, I_{42i}, i = 1, 2, 3$, are arbitrary constants (real or imaginary) and $\theta(t) = \left(\frac{c_0}{2}\right)^{1/2}\int f^{-1}dt$.

The solution (136) coincides with the solution (52) in [10].

In the case of the 1d time-dependent oscillator, if we set $2\omega(t) = -\psi^2(t)$, $c_0 = 2$ and $f(t) = \rho^2(t)$, Equation (54) and the defining relation (123) for $\omega(t)$ become

$$\ddot{x} = -\psi^2 x \tag{137}$$
$$\ddot{\rho} = -\psi^2 \rho + \rho^{-3}. \tag{138}$$

The LFIs (134) and (135) become

$$I_{41} = \rho^{-1}x\sin\theta + (\rho\dot{x} - x\dot{\rho})\cos\theta \tag{139}$$
$$I_{42} = -\rho^{-1}x\cos\theta + (\rho\dot{x} - x\dot{\rho})\sin\theta. \tag{140}$$

The general solution (136) is

$$x(t) = \rho(t)\left(I_{41}\sin\theta - I_{42}\cos\theta\right) \tag{141}$$

where $\dot{\theta} = \rho^{-2}$ and $\rho(t)$ is a given non-zero function which defines $\psi(t)$ through (138). This is the 1d solution (9) in [10].

15.2. The Solution of the Time-Dependent Kepler Potential with $\omega_{2K}(t) = \frac{k}{b_0+b_1 t}$ Where $kb_1 \neq 0$

In Section 11.1, it is shown that this system admits the following FIs:

$$L_1 = y\dot{z} - z\dot{y}, \quad L_2 = z\dot{x} - x\dot{z}, \quad L_3 = x\dot{y} - y\dot{x}$$

$$E_2 = (b_0 + b_1 t)^2\left[\frac{\dot{q}^i\dot{q}_i}{2} - \frac{k}{r(b_0+b_1 t)}\right] - b_1(b_0+b_1 t)q^i\dot{q}_i + \frac{b_1^2 r^2}{2}$$

$$A_i = (b_0+b_1 t)\tilde{R}_i + b_1(q_{i+2}L_{i+1} - q_{i+1}L_{i+2})$$

where $\tilde{R}_i = (\dot{q}^j\dot{q}_j)q_i - (\dot{q}^j q_j)\dot{q}_i - \frac{k}{r(b_0+b_1 t)}q_i$. The components of the generalized Runge–Lenz vector are written

$$A_1 = (b_0+b_1 t)(\dot{y}L_3 - \dot{z}L_2) + b_1(zL_2 - yL_3) - \frac{k}{r}x$$

$$A_2 = (b_0+b_1 t)(\dot{z}L_1 - \dot{x}L_3) + b_1(xL_3 - zL_1) - \frac{k}{r}y$$

$$A_3 = (b_0+b_1 t)(\dot{x}L_2 - \dot{y}L_1) + b_1(yL_1 - xL_2) - \frac{k}{r}z.$$

Since the angular momentum is an FI, the motion is on a plane. We choose, without loss of generality, the plane $z=0$ and on that the polar coordinates $x = r\cos\theta$, $y = r\sin\theta$. Then,

$$L_1 = L_2 = 0, \quad L_3 = r^2\dot{\theta}, \quad E_2 = (b_0+b_1 t)^2\left[\frac{\dot{r}^2 + r^2\dot{\theta}^2}{2} - \frac{k}{r(b_0+b_1 t)}\right] - b_1(b_0+b_1 t)r\dot{r} + \frac{b_1^2 r^2}{2}$$

$$A_1 = L_3\left[(b_0+b_1 t)\dot{r} - b_1 r\right]\sin\theta + \left[(b_0+b_1 t)L_3 r\dot{\theta} - k\right]\cos\theta$$

$$A_2 = -L_3\left[(b_0+b_1 t)\dot{r} - b_1 r\right]\cos\theta + \left[(b_0+b_1 t)L_3 r\dot{\theta} - k\right]\sin\theta, \quad A_3 = 0.$$

Using the relation $\dot{\theta} = \frac{L_3}{r^2}$ to replace $\dot{\theta}$, the above relations are written

$$E_2 = (b_0+b_1 t)^2\left[\frac{\dot{r}^2}{2} + \frac{L_3^2}{2r^2} - \frac{k}{r(b_0+b_1 t)}\right] - b_1(b_0+b_1 t)r\dot{r} + \frac{b_1^2 r^2}{2} \tag{142}$$

$$A_1 = L_3\left[(b_0+b_1 t)\dot{r} - b_1 r\right]\sin\theta + \left[(b_0+b_1 t)\frac{L_3^2}{r} - k\right]\cos\theta \tag{143}$$

$$A_2 = -L_3\left[(b_0+b_1 t)\dot{r} - b_1 r\right]\cos\theta + \left[(b_0+b_1 t)\frac{L_3^2}{r} - k\right]\sin\theta. \tag{144}$$

By multiplying Equation (143) with $\cos\theta$ and (144) with $\sin\theta$ we find that

$$\frac{1}{r} = \frac{k}{L_3^2(b_0+b_1 t)}(1 + k_1\cos\theta + k_2\sin\theta) \implies r = \frac{L_3^2(b_0+b_1 t)}{k(1+k_1\cos\theta + k_2\sin\theta)} \tag{145}$$

where $k_1 \equiv \frac{A_1}{k}$ and $k_2 \equiv \frac{A_2}{k}$.

Applying the transformation $k_1 = \alpha \cos\beta$ and $k_2 = \alpha \sin\beta$, Equation (145) is written (see also Section 5 in [17])

$$\frac{1}{r} = \frac{\omega_{2K}}{L_3^2}\left[1 + \alpha\cos(\theta - \beta)\right] \implies r = \frac{L_3^2 \omega_{2K}^{-1}}{1 + \alpha\cos(\theta - \beta)} \quad (146)$$

which for $\omega_{2K}(t) = const$ (standard Kepler problem) reduces to the analytical equation of a conic section in polar coordinates. In that case α is the eccentricity.

It is also worthwhile mentioning that the relation (94) becomes

$$2E_2 L_3^2 + k^2 = \alpha^2 k^2 \implies 2E_2 L_3^2 = k^2(\alpha^2 - 1).$$

Moreover, Equation (142) gives

$$\left[\frac{d}{dt}\left(\frac{r}{b_0 + b_1 t}\right)\right]^2 = -2(b_0 + b_1 t)^{-2}\left[\frac{L_3^2}{2r^2} - \frac{k}{r(b_0 + b_1 t)} - \frac{E_2}{(b_0 + b_1 t)^2}\right].$$

Finally, in the polar plane the equations of motion (54) for $\nu = 1$ become

$$\ddot{r} - r\dot{\theta}^2 + \frac{\omega_{2K}}{r^2} = 0 \quad (147)$$

$$r\ddot{\theta} + 2\dot{r}\dot{\theta} = 0. \quad (148)$$

Equation (148) implies the FI of the angular momentum $L_3 = r^2\dot{\theta}$. It can be easily checked that the solution (145) satisfies Equation (147) by replacing $\ddot{\theta}$ from (148) and $\dot{\theta}$ with $\frac{L_3}{r^2}$. The solution (145) into the FI L_3 gives

$$\int \frac{k^2 dt}{L_3^3(b_0 + b_1 t)^2} = \int \frac{d\theta}{(1 + k_1 \cos\theta + k_2 \sin\theta)^2} \implies \frac{k}{L_3^2(b_0 + b_1 t)} = -\frac{b_1 L_3}{k}\int \frac{d\theta}{(1 + k_1\cos\theta + k_2\sin\theta)^2}. \quad (149)$$

Substituting (149) in (145) we obtain

$$\frac{1}{r} = -\frac{b_1 L_3}{k}(1 + k_1\cos\theta + k_2\sin\theta)\int \frac{d\theta}{(1 + k_1\cos\theta + k_2\sin\theta)^2} \quad (150)$$

which coincides with Equation (5.17) in [17].

16. A Class of 1d Non-Linear Time-Dependent Equations

In this section, we use the well-known result [12] that the non-linear dynamical system

$$\ddot{q}^a = -\Gamma^a_{bc}\dot{q}^b\dot{q}^c - \omega(t)Q^a(q) + \phi(t)\dot{q}^a \quad (151)$$

is equivalent to the linear dynamical system (without damping term)

$$\frac{d^2 q^a}{ds^2} = -\Gamma^a_{bc}\frac{dq^b}{ds}\frac{dq^c}{ds} - \bar{\omega}(s)Q^a(q) \quad (152)$$

where $\phi(t)$ is an arbitrary function such that

$$s(t) = \int e^{\int \phi(t)dt} dt, \quad \bar{\omega}(s) = \omega(t(s))\left(\frac{dt}{ds}\right)^2 \iff \omega(t) = \bar{\omega}(s(t))e^{2\int \phi(t)dt}. \quad (153)$$

We apply this result to the following problem:
Consider the second order differential equation

$$\ddot{x} = -\omega(t)x^\mu + \phi(t)\dot{x} \quad (154)$$

where the constant $\mu \neq -1$ and determine the relation between the functions $\omega(t), \phi(t)$ for which the equation admits a QFI; therefore, it is integrable.

This problem has been considered previously in [36,37] (see Equation (28a) in [36] and Equation (17) in [37]) and has been answered partially using different methods. In [36], the author used the Hamiltonian formalism where one looks for a canonical transformation to bring the Hamiltonian in a time-separable form. In [37], the author used a direct method for constructing FIs by multiplying the equation with an integrating factor. In [37], it is shown that both methods are equivalent and that the results of [37] generalize those of [36]. In the following, we shall generalize the results of [37]; in addition, we discuss a number of applications.

Equation (154) is equivalent to the equation

$$\frac{d^2 x}{ds^2} = -\bar{\omega}(s) x^\mu, \quad \mu \neq -1 \tag{155}$$

where the function $\bar{\omega}(s)$ is given by (153).

Replacing $Q^1 = x^\mu$ in the system of Equations (5)–(10) (in 1d Euclidean space, the KT condition (5) $K_{(ab;c)} = 0$ becomes $K_{11,1} = 0 \implies K_{11} = K_{11}(s)$, that is, it is an arbitrary function of s), we find that $K_{11} = K_{11}(s)$ and the following conditions

$$K_1(s, x) = -\frac{dK_{11}}{ds} x + b_1(s) \tag{156}$$

$$K(s, x) = 2\bar{\omega} K_{11} \frac{x^{\mu+1}}{\mu+1} + \frac{d^2 K_{11}}{ds^2} \frac{x^2}{2} - \frac{db_1}{ds} x + b_2(s) \tag{157}$$

$$0 = \left(\frac{2 \frac{d\bar{\omega}}{ds} K_{11}}{\mu+1} + \frac{2\bar{\omega} \frac{dK_{11}}{ds}}{\mu+1} + \bar{\omega} \frac{dK_{11}}{ds} \right) x^{\mu+1} - \bar{\omega} b_1 x^\mu + \\ + \frac{d^3 K_{11}}{ds^3} \frac{x^2}{2} - \frac{d^2 b_1}{ds^2} x + \frac{db_2}{ds} \tag{158}$$

where $b_1(s), b_2(s)$ are arbitrary functions. Then, the general QFI (3) becomes

$$I = K_{11}(s) \left(\frac{dx}{ds} \right)^2 + K_1(s,x) \frac{dx}{ds} + K(s,x). \tag{159}$$

We consider the solution of the system (156)–(158) for various values of μ.

As will be shown for $\mu \neq -1$ results a family of 'frequencies' $\bar{\omega}(s)$ parameterized with constants. However, for the specific values $\mu = 0, 1, 2$ there results a family of 'frequencies' $\bar{\omega}(s)$ parameterized with functions.

(1) Case $\mu = 0$.

We find the QFI

$$I = K_{11} \left(\frac{dx}{ds} \right)^2 - \frac{dK_{11}}{ds} x \frac{dx}{ds} + b_1(s) \frac{dx}{ds} + c_3 x^2 + 2\bar{\omega}(s) K_{11} x - \frac{db_1}{ds} x + \int b_1(s) \bar{\omega}(s) ds \tag{160}$$

where $K_{11} = c_1 + c_2 s + c_3 s^2$, c_1, c_2, c_3 are arbitrary constants and the functions $b_1(s), \bar{\omega}(s)$ satisfy the condition

$$\frac{d^2 b_1}{ds^2} = 2 \frac{d\bar{\omega}}{ds} K_{11} + 3\bar{\omega} \frac{dK_{11}}{ds}. \tag{161}$$

Using the transformation (153), Equations (160) and (161) become

$$I = \left[c_1 + c_2 \int e^{\int \phi(t)dt} dt + c_3 \left(\int e^{\int \phi(t)dt} dt\right)^2\right] e^{-2\int \phi(t)dt} \dot{x}^2 - \left[c_2 + 2c_3 \int e^{\int \phi(t)dt} dt\right] e^{-\int \phi(t)dt} x\dot{x} +$$
$$+ b_1(s(t))e^{-\int \phi(t)dt} \dot{x} + c_3 x^2 + 2\omega(t)\left[c_1 + c_2 \int e^{\int \phi(t)dt} dt + c_3 \left(\int e^{\int \phi(t)dt} dt\right)^2\right] e^{-2\int \phi(t)dt} x -$$
$$- \dot{b}_1 e^{-\int \phi(t)dt} x + \int b_1(s(t))\omega(t) e^{-\int \phi(t)dt} dt \tag{162}$$

and

$$\ddot{b}_1 - \phi \dot{b}_1 = 2 e^{-\int \phi(t)dt}(\dot{\omega} - 2\phi\omega)\left[c_1 + c_2 \int e^{\int \phi(t)dt} dt + c_3 \left(\int e^{\int \phi(t)dt} dt\right)^2\right] +$$
$$+ 3\omega\left[c_2 + 2c_3 \int e^{\int \phi(t)dt} dt\right]. \tag{163}$$

(2) Case $\mu = 1$.

We again derive the results of the time-dependent oscillator (see Table 2 for $\nu = -2$) in one dimension. Using the transformation (153), we deduce that the original equation

$$\ddot{x} = -\omega(t)x + \phi(t)\dot{x} \tag{164}$$

for the frequency

$$\omega(t) = -\rho^{-1}\ddot{\rho} + \phi(\ln \rho)^{\cdot} + \rho^{-4} e^{2\int \phi(t)dt} \tag{165}$$

admits the general solution

$$x(t) = \rho(t)(A \sin \theta + B \cos \theta) \tag{166}$$

where $\rho(t) \equiv \rho(s(t))$ and $\theta(s(t)) = \int \rho^{-2}(t) e^{\int \phi(t)dt} dt$.

(3) Case $\mu = 2$.

We find the function $\tilde{\omega} = K_{11}^{-5/2}$ and the QFI

$$I = K_{11}(s)\left(\frac{dx}{ds}\right)^2 - \frac{dK_{11}}{ds} x \frac{dx}{ds} + (c_4 + c_5 s)\frac{dx}{ds} + \frac{2}{3} K_{11}^{-3/2} x^3 + \frac{d^2 K_{11}}{ds^2} \frac{x^2}{2} - c_5 x \tag{167}$$

where c_4, c_5 are arbitrary constants and the function $K_{11}(s)$ is given by

$$\frac{d^3 K_{11}}{ds^3} = 2(c_4 + c_5 s) K_{11}^{-5/2}. \tag{168}$$

Using the transformation (153), the above results become

$$\omega(t) = K_{11}^{-5/2} e^{2\int \phi(t)dt} \tag{169}$$

$$I = K_{11} e^{-2\int \phi(t)dt} \dot{x}^2 - \dot{K}_{11} e^{-2\int \phi(t)dt} x\dot{x} + \left[c_4 + c_5 \int e^{\int \phi(t)dt} dt\right] e^{-\int \phi(t)dt} \dot{x} + \frac{2}{3} K_{11}^{-3/2} x^3 +$$
$$+ (\ddot{K}_{11} - \phi \dot{K}_{11}) e^{-2\int \phi(t)dt} \frac{x^2}{2} - c_5 x \tag{170}$$

and

$$\dddot{K}_{11} - 3\phi \ddot{K}_{11} - \dot{\phi} \dot{K}_{11} + 2\phi^2 \dot{K}_{11} = 2\left[c_4 + c_5 \int e^{\int \phi(t)dt} dt\right] e^{3\int \phi(t)dt} K_{11}^{-5/2} \tag{171}$$

where the function $K_{11} = K_{11}(s(t))$.

We note that for $\mu = 2$ Equation (154), or to be more specific its equivalent (155), arises in the solution of Einstein field equations when the gravitational field is spherically symmetric and the matter source is a shear-free perfect fluid (see, e.g., [38–43]).

(4) Case $\mu \neq -1$.

In this case, $b_1 = b_2 = 0$, $K_{11} = c_1 + c_2 s + c_3 s^2$ and $\bar{\omega}(s) = (c_1 + c_2 s + c_3 s^2)^{-\frac{\mu+3}{2}}$ where c_1, c_2, c_3 are arbitrary constants.

The QFI (159) becomes
$$I = (c_1 + c_2 s + c_3 s^2)\left(\frac{dx}{ds}\right)^2 - (c_2 + 2c_3 s)x\frac{dx}{ds} + \frac{2}{\mu+1}(c_1 + c_2 s + c_3 s^2)^{-\frac{\mu+1}{2}} x^{\mu+1} + c_3 x^2 \tag{172}$$

and the function
$$\bar{\omega}(s) = (c_1 + c_2 s + c_3 s^2)^{-\frac{\mu+3}{2}}. \tag{173}$$

It can be checked that (172) and (173) for $\mu = 0, 1, 2$ give results compatible with the ones we found for these values of μ.

Using the transformation (153), we deduce that the original system (154) is integrable iff the functions $\omega(t), \phi(t)$ are related as follows
$$\omega(t) = \left[c_1 + c_2 \int e^{\int \phi(t)dt} dt + c_3 \left(\int e^{\int \phi(t)dt} dt\right)^2\right]^{-\frac{\mu+3}{2}} e^{2\int \phi(t)dt}. \tag{174}$$

In this case, the associated QFI (172) is
$$I = \left[c_1 + c_2 \int e^{\int \phi(t)dt} dt + c_3 \left(\int e^{\int \phi(t)dt} dt\right)^2\right] e^{-2\int \phi(t)dt} \dot{x}^2 - \left[c_2 + 2c_3 \int e^{\int \phi(t)dt} dt\right] e^{-\int \phi(t)dt} x\dot{x} +$$
$$+ \frac{2}{\mu+1}\left[c_1 + c_2 \int e^{\int \phi(t)dt} dt + c_3 \left(\int e^{\int \phi(t)dt} dt\right)^2\right]^{-\frac{\mu+1}{2}} x^{\mu+1} + c_3 x^2. \tag{175}$$

These expressions generalize the expressions given in [37]. Indeed, if we introduce the notation $\omega(t) \equiv \alpha(t)$, $\phi(t) \equiv -\beta(t)$, then Equations (174) and (175) for $c_3 = 0$ become Equarions (25) and (26) of [37].

16.1. The Generalized Lane–Emden Equation

Consider the 1d generalized Lane–Emden Equation (see Equation (6) in [44])
$$\ddot{x} = -\omega(t)x^\mu - \frac{k}{t}\dot{x} \tag{176}$$

where k is an arbitrary constant. This equation is well-known in the literature because of its many applications in astrophysical problems (see Refs. in [44]). In general, to find explicit analytic solutions of Equation (176) it is a major task. For example, such solutions have only been found for the special values $\mu = 0, 1, 5$, in the case that the function $\omega(t) = 1$ and the constant $k = 2$. New, exact solutions, or at least the Liouville integrability, of Equation (176) are guaranteed, if we find a way to determine its FIs. We see that Equation (176) is a subcase of the original Equation (154) for $\phi(t) = -\frac{k}{t}$; therefore, we can apply the results found earlier in Section 16.

In what follows, we only discuss the fourth case where $\mu \neq -1$ in order to compare our results with those found in Table 1 of [44]. In particular, for $\phi(t) = -\frac{k}{t}$ the function (174) and the associated QFI (175) become
$$\omega(t) = t^{-2k}\left(c_1 + c_2 M + c_3 M^2\right)^{-\frac{\mu+3}{2}} \tag{177}$$

and
$$I = t^{2k}\left(c_1 + c_2 M + c_3 M^2\right)\dot{x}^2 - t^k(c_2 + 2c_3 M)x\dot{x} + \frac{2}{\mu+1}\left(c_1 + c_2 M + c_3 M^2\right)^{-\frac{\mu+1}{2}} x^{\mu+1} + c_3 x^2 \tag{178}$$

where the function $M(t) = \int t^{-k} dt$.

Concerning the form of the function $M(t)$ there are two cases to consider: (a) $k = 1$; (b) $k \neq 1$.

(a) Case $k = 1$.

We have $M = \ln t$ and Equations (177) and (178) give

$$\omega(t) = t^{-2}\left[c_1 + c_2 \ln t + c_3 (\ln t)^2\right]^{-\frac{\mu+3}{2}} \tag{179}$$

and

$$I = t^2\left[c_1 + c_2 \ln t + c_3 (\ln t)^2\right]\dot{x}^2 - t(c_2 + 2c_3 \ln t)x\dot{x} +$$
$$+ \frac{2}{\mu+1}\left[c_1 + c_2 \ln t + c_3 (\ln t)^2\right]^{-\frac{\mu+1}{2}} x^{\mu+1} + c_3 x^2. \tag{180}$$

We consider the following subcases:

- $c_2 = c_3 = 0, c_1 \neq 0$.

Equations (179) and (180) give the function $\omega(t) = At^{-2}$ and the QFI (divide I with $2c_1$)

$$I = \frac{t^2}{2}\dot{x}^2 + \frac{A}{\mu+1}x^{\mu+1}$$

where the constant $A = c_1^{-\frac{\mu+3}{2}}$. This is the Case 5 in Table 1 of [44].

- $c_1 = c_3 = 0, c_2 \neq 0$.

Equations (179) and (180) give the function $\omega(t) = At^{-2}(\ln t)^{-\frac{\mu+3}{2}}$ and the QFI (divide I with $2c_2$)

$$I = \frac{1}{2}t^2(\ln t)\dot{x}^2 - \frac{t}{2}x\dot{x} + \frac{A}{\mu+1}(\ln t)^{-\frac{\mu+1}{2}} x^{\mu+1}$$

where the constant $A = c_2^{-\frac{\mu+3}{2}}$. This is the Case 6 in Table 1 of [44].

- $c_1 = c_2 = 0, c_3 \neq 0$.

Equations (181) and (182) give the function $\omega(t) = At^{-2}(\ln t)^{-\mu-3}$ and the QFI (divide I with $2c_3$)

$$I = \frac{1}{2}(t \ln t)^2 \dot{x}^2 - t(\ln t)x\dot{x} + \frac{A}{\mu+1}(\ln t)^{-\mu-1} x^{\mu+1} + \frac{x^2}{2}$$

where the constant $A = c_3^{-\frac{\mu+3}{2}}$. This is the Case 7 in Table 1 of [44].

(b) Case $k \neq 1$.

We have $M = \frac{t^{1-k}}{1-k}$ and Equations (177) and (178) give

$$\omega(t) = t^{-2k}\left[c_1 + \frac{c_2}{1-k}t^{1-k} + \frac{c_3}{(1-k)^2}t^{2(1-k)}\right]^{-\frac{\mu+3}{2}} \tag{181}$$

and

$$I = t^{2k}\left[c_1 + \frac{c_2}{1-k}t^{1-k} + \frac{c_3}{(1-k)^2}t^{2(1-k)}\right]\dot{x}^2 - t^k\left(c_2 + \frac{2c_3}{1-k}t^{1-k}\right)x\dot{x} +$$
$$+ \frac{2}{\mu+1}\left[c_1 + \frac{c_2}{1-k}t^{1-k} + \frac{c_3}{(1-k)^2}t^{2(1-k)}\right]^{-\frac{\mu+1}{2}} x^{\mu+1} + c_3 x^2. \tag{182}$$

We consider the following subcases:

- $c_2 = c_3 = 0$, $c_1 \neq 0$.

Equations (181) and (182) give the function $w(t) = At^{-2k}$ and the QFI (divide I with $2c_1$)

$$I = \frac{t^{2k}}{2}\dot{x}^2 + \frac{A}{\mu+1}x^{\mu+1}$$

where the constant $A = c_1^{-\frac{\mu+3}{2}}$. This is the Case 2 in Table 1 of [44].

- $c_1 = c_3 = 0$, $c_2 \neq 0$.

Equations (181) and (182) give the function $w(t) = At^{\frac{1}{2}(k\mu-k-\mu-3)}$ and the QFI (multiply I with $\frac{1-k}{c_2}$)

$$I = t^{k+1}\dot{x}^2 + (k-1)t^k x\dot{x} + \frac{2A}{\mu+1}t^{\frac{1}{2}(\mu+1)(k-1)}x^{\mu+1}$$

where the constant $A = \left(\frac{c_2}{1-k}\right)^{-\frac{\mu+3}{2}}$. This is the Case 3 in Table 1 of [44].

We note also that for $k = \frac{\mu+3}{\mu-1}$ where $\mu \neq 1$ the function $w(t) = A = const$. This reproduces the first subcase of Case 1 in Table 1 of [44] which is the Case 5.1 of [45].

- $c_1 = c_2 = 0$, $c_3 \neq 0$.

Equations (181) and (182) give the function $w(t) = At^{k\mu+k-\mu-3}$ and the QFI (multiply I with $\frac{(1-k)^2}{2c_3}$)

$$I = \frac{t^2}{2}\dot{x}^2 + (k-1)tx\dot{x} + \frac{A}{\mu+1}t^{(\mu+1)(k-1)}x^{\mu+1} + \frac{1}{2}(k-1)^2x^2$$

where the constant $A = \left(\frac{1-k}{\sqrt{c_3}}\right)^{\mu+3}$. This is the Case 4 in Table 1 of [44].

We note also that for $k = \frac{\mu+3}{\mu+1}$ the function $w(t) = A = const$. This recovers the second subcase of Case 1 in Table 1 of [44] which is the Case 5.2 of [45].

We conclude that the seven cases 1–7 found in Table 1 of [44] are just subcases of the above two general cases a) and b). To compare with these results one must adopt the notation $w = f$, $k = n$ and $\mu = p$.

17. Conclusions

The purpose of the present work was to compute the QFIs of time-dependent dynamical systems of the form $\ddot{q}^a = -\Gamma^a_{bc}\dot{q}^b\dot{q}^c - w(t)Q^a(q)$, where the connection coefficients are computed from the kinetic metric, using the direct method instead of the Noether symmetries as it is usually done. In the direct method, one assumes that the QFI is of the form $I = K_{ab}\dot{q}^a\dot{q}^b + K_a\dot{q}^a + K$ and demands that $dI/dt = 0$. This leads to a system of PDEs whose solution provides the QFIs. One key result is that the tensor K_{ab} is a KT of the kinetic metric.

We have discussed the solution of the system of equations at two levels. The first level is purely geometric and concerns the KT K_{ab}; the second level is the physical, which concerns the quantities $w(t), Q^a(q)$ defining the dynamical system.

Concerning the first level we have applied two different methods:

a. The polynomial method in which one assumes a general polynomial form in the variable t both for the KT K_{ab} and for the vector K_a.
b. The basis method where one computes first a basis of the KTs of order 2 of the kinetic metric and then expresses K_{ab} in this basis assuming that the 'components' are functions of t.

In both methods, the key point is to compute the scalar K.

Concerning the dynamical quantities $w(t), Q^a(q)$ we have chosen to work in two ways:

a. First, we considered the polynomial method and assumed the function $\omega(t)$ to be a polynomial leaving the quantities Q^a unspecified. It is found that in this case, the resulting dynamical system admits two independent QFIs whose explicit expression together with conditions involving the quantities Q^a and the collineations of the kinetic metric are given in Theorem 1.
b. In the basis method we worked the other way. That is, we assumed the quantities $Q^a(q)$ to be given by the time-dependent generalized Kepler potential $V = -\frac{\omega(t)}{r^\nu}$ and determined the functions $\omega(t)$ for which QFIs exist. The results of this detailed study are displayed in Table 2 for all values of ν. For the values $\nu = -2, 1, 2$ we recovered the known results concerning the time-dependent 3d oscillator, the time-dependent Kepler potential and the Newton–Cotes potential, respectively. We note that these latter results have appeared over the years in many works whereas in the present discussion occur as particular cases of a single geometric approach.

The last part of our considerations concerns the well-known proposition that under a reparameterization the linear damping $\phi(t)\dot{q}^a$ can be absorbed to a time-dependent generalized force. We used this proposition in the case of a 1d non-linear second order time-dependent differential equation, we determined the condition that the time-dependent coefficients of the equation must satisfy in order a QFI to exist and we computed this QFI. As an application, we studied the properties of the well-known generalized Lane–Emden equation.

We note that one is possible to consider other dynamical quantities and/or kinetic metric and compute the QFIs. What is the same in all cases is the method of work which we hope we have presented adequately in the present paper.

Author Contributions: Methodology, M.T.; formal analysis, A.M.; investigation, A.M. and M.T.; writing—original draft preparation, A.M.; writing—review and editing, A.M. and M.T.; supervision, M.T. All authors have read and agreed to the published version of the manuscript.

Funding: This research received no external funding.

Conflicts of Interest: The authors declare no conflict of interest.

Appendix A

Substituting the polynomial function $\omega(t)$ given by (39) in the system of Equations (34)–(38) we have the following cases.

I. Case n = m (both n, m finite)

From Equation (34) we obtain

$$C_{(k)ab} = -L_{(k-1)(a;b)}, \quad k = 1, ..., n, \quad L_{(n)(a;b)} = 0. \tag{A1}$$

Therefore, $L_{(n)a}$ is a KV of γ_{ab}.

Condition (37) gives

$$0 = -2\left(b_1 + 2b_2 t + ... + \ell b_\ell t^{\ell-1}\right)\left(C_{(0)ab}Q^b + C_{(1)ab}Q^b t + ... + C_{(n)ab}Q^b \frac{t^n}{n}\right) + 2L_{(2)a} + 6L_{(3)a}t + ... +$$
$$+ n(n-1)L_{(n)a}t^{n-2} - 2\left(b_0 + b_1 t + ... + b_\ell t^\ell\right)\left(C_{(1)ab}Q^b + C_{(2)ab}Q^b t + ... + C_{(n)ab}Q^b t^{n-1}\right) +$$
$$+ \left(b_0 + b_1 t + ... + b_\ell t^\ell\right)\left[\left(L_{(0)b}Q^b\right)_{,a} + \left(L_{(1)b}Q^b\right)_{,a} t + ... + \left(L_{(n-1)b}Q^b\right)_{,a} t^{n-1} + \left(L_{(n)b}Q^b\right)_{,a} t^n\right].$$

This is a polynomial of the general form $P_{(0)a}(q) + P_{(1)a}(q)t + ... + P_{(n+\ell)a}(q)t^{n+\ell} = 0$. The vanishing of the coefficients $P_{(k)a}(q)$ in the last polynomial implies that

$$L_{(n)a}Q^a = s = const \tag{A2}$$

$$\sum_{s=0}^{\ell-1}\left[-\frac{2(k+s)b_{(k+s\leq\ell)}}{n-s}C_{(n-s\geq 0)ab}Q^b - 2b_{(k+s\leq\ell)}C_{(n-s>0)ab}Q^b + b_{(k+s\leq\ell)}\left(L_{(n-s-1\geq 0)b}Q^b\right)_{,a}\right] = 0 \tag{A3}$$

where $k = 1, 2, ..., \ell$,

$$-\sum_{s=1}^{\ell}\left[\frac{2sb_s}{n-s}C_{(n-s\geq 0)ab}Q^b\right] + \sum_{s=0}^{\ell}\left[-2b_s C_{(n-s>0)ab}Q^b + b_s\left(L_{(n-s-1\geq 0)b}Q^b\right)_{,a}\right] = 0 \tag{A4}$$

and

$$k(k-1)L_{(k)a} - \sum_{s=1}^{\ell}\left[\frac{2sb_s}{k-s-1}C_{(k-s-1\geq 0)ab}Q^b\right] + \sum_{s=0}^{\ell}\left[-2b_s C_{(k-s-1>0)ab}Q^b + b_s\left(L_{(k-s-2\geq 0)b}Q^b\right)_{,a}\right] = 0 \tag{A5}$$

where $k = 2, 3, ...n$.

We note that in the $n + \ell + 1$ formulae (A3)–(A5), when the undefined quantity $\frac{C_{(0)ab}}{0}$ appears in the calculations, it must be replaced by $C_{(0)ab}$ in order to have a consistent result.

We continue with the remaining constraints (35) and (36) in order to determine the scalar coefficient $K(t, q)$.

The solution of (36) is

$$K_{,t} = L_{(0)a}Q^a\left(b_0 + b_1 t + ... + b_\ell t^\ell\right) + L_{(1)a}Q^a\left(b_0 t + b_1 t^2 + ... + b_\ell t^{\ell+1}\right) + ... +$$
$$+ L_{(n-1)a}Q^a\left(b_0 t^{n-1} + b_1 t^n + ... + b_\ell t^{n+\ell-1}\right) + s\left(b_0 t^n + b_1 t^{n+1} + ... + b_\ell t^{n+\ell}\right) \implies$$

$$K = L_{(0)a}Q^a\left(b_0 t + b_1 \frac{t^2}{2} + ... + b_\ell \frac{t^{\ell+1}}{\ell+1}\right) + L_{(1)a}Q^a\left(b_0 \frac{t^2}{2} + b_1 \frac{t^3}{3} + ... + b_\ell \frac{t^{\ell+2}}{\ell+2}\right) + ... +$$
$$+ L_{(n-1)a}Q^a\left(b_0 \frac{t^n}{n} + b_1 \frac{t^{n+1}}{n+1} + ... + b_\ell \frac{t^{n+\ell}}{n+\ell}\right) + s\left(b_0 \frac{t^{n+1}}{n+1} + b_1 \frac{t^{n+2}}{n+2} + ... + b_\ell \frac{t^{n+\ell+1}}{n+\ell+1}\right) + G(q).$$

Replacing K in (35) and using the conditions (A2)–(A5) we find that

$$G_{,a} = 2b_0 C_{(0)ab}Q^b - L_{(1)a}.$$

Condition (38) is satisfied trivially from the above solutions.

The QFI is

$$I = \left(\frac{t^n}{n}C_{(n)ab} + ... + tC_{(1)ab} + C_{(0)ab}\right)\dot{q}^a\dot{q}^b + t^n L_{(n)a}\dot{q}^a + ... + tL_{(1)a}\dot{q}^a + L_{(0)a}\dot{q}^a +$$
$$+ L_{(0)a}Q^a\left(b_0 t + b_1 \frac{t^2}{2} + ... + b_\ell \frac{t^{\ell+1}}{\ell+1}\right) + L_{(1)a}Q^a\left(b_0 \frac{t^2}{2} + b_1 \frac{t^3}{3} + ... + b_\ell \frac{t^{\ell+2}}{\ell+2}\right) + ... +$$
$$+ L_{(n-1)a}Q^a\left(b_0 \frac{t^n}{n} + b_1 \frac{t^{n+1}}{n+1} + ... + b_\ell \frac{t^{n+\ell}}{n+\ell}\right) + s\left(b_0 \frac{t^{n+1}}{n+1} + b_1 \frac{t^{n+2}}{n+2} + ... + b_\ell \frac{t^{n+\ell+1}}{n+\ell+1}\right) + G(q)$$

where $C_{(0)ab}$ is a KT, the KTs $C_{(k)ab} = -L_{(k-1)(a;b)}$ for $k = 1, ..., n$, $L_{(n)a}$ is a KV such that $L_{(n)a}Q^a = s$, $G_{,a} = 2b_0 C_{(0)ab}Q^b - L_{(1)a}$ and the conditions (A3)–(A5) are satisfied.

II. Case n $\neq$ m. (one of n or m may be infinite)

We find QFIs that are subcases of those found in **Case I** and **Case III** which follows.

III. Both n, m are infinite.

In this case, we consider the solution to have the form

$$K_{ab}(t,q) = g(t)C_{ab}(q), \quad K_a(t,q) = f(t)L_a(q)$$

where the functions $g(t), f(t)$ are analytic so that they may be represented by polynomial functions as follows

$$g(t) = \sum_{k=0}^{n} c_k t^k = c_0 + c_1 t + ... + c_n t^n$$

$$f(t) = \sum_{k=0}^{m} d_k t^k = d_0 + d_1 t + ... + d_m t^m.$$

In the above expressions, the coefficients $c_0, c_1, ..., c_n$ and $d_0, d_1, ..., d_m$ are arbitrary constants. We find that only the following subcase gives a new independent FI. All other subcases give results already found.

Subcase ($g = e^{\lambda t}, f = e^{\mu t}$), $\lambda\mu \neq 0$.
In this case, the system of Equations (34)–(37) (Equation (38) is satisfied trivially from the solutions found below) becomes:

$$\lambda e^{\lambda t} C_{ab} + e^{\mu t} L_{(a;b)} = 0 \tag{A6}$$

$$-2\left(b_0 + b_1 t + ... + b_\ell t^\ell\right) e^{\lambda t} C_{ab} Q^b + \mu e^{\mu t} L_a + K_{,a} = 0 \tag{A7}$$

$$K_{,t} - (b_0 + b_1 t + ... + b_\ell t^\ell) e^{\mu t} L_a Q^a = 0 \tag{A8}$$

$$-2\left(b_1 + 2b_2 t + ... + \ell b_\ell t^{\ell-1}\right) e^{\lambda t} C_{ab} Q^b - 2\lambda(b_0 + b_1 t + ... + b_\ell t^\ell) e^{\lambda t} C_{ab} Q^b +$$
$$+\mu^2 e^{\mu t} L_a + (b_0 + b_1 t + ... + b_\ell t^\ell) e^{\mu t} \left(L_b Q^b\right)_{,a} = 0. \tag{A9}$$

We consider the following subcases.

a. For $\lambda \neq \mu$:

From (A6) we have that $C_{ab} = 0$ and L_a is a KV.
From (A9) we find that $L_a = 0$.
Therefore, the QFI $I_e(\lambda \neq \mu) = const$ which is trivial.

b. For $\lambda = \mu$:

From (A6) we have that $C_{ab} = -\frac{1}{\lambda} L_{(a;b)}$. Therefore, $L_{(a;b)}$ is a KT.
We consider two cases according to the degree ℓ of the polynomial $\omega(t)$.

- Case $\ell = 1$.

From (A9) we find that

$$\left(L_b Q^b\right)_{,a} = 2\lambda C_{ab} Q^b \tag{A10}$$

$$\lambda^2 L_a + b_0 \left(L_b Q^b\right)_{,a} - 2(b_1 + \lambda b_0) C_{ab} Q^b = 0. \tag{A11}$$

Replacing with $C_{ab} = -\frac{1}{\lambda}L_{(a;b)}$ and by substituting (A10) in (A11) we obtain

$$\left(L_b Q^b\right)_{,a} = -2L_{(a;b)} Q^b \tag{A12}$$

$$\lambda^3 L_a + 2b_1 L_{(a;b)} Q^b = 0. \tag{A13}$$

The solution of (A8) is

$$K = \left(\frac{b_0}{\lambda} - \frac{b_1}{\lambda^2}\right) e^{\lambda t} L_a Q^a + \frac{b_1}{\lambda} t e^{\lambda t} L_a Q^a + G(q)$$

which when replaced in (A7) gives $G_{,a} = 0$, that is $G = const \equiv 0$.

The QFI is

$$I_e(\ell = 1) = -e^{\lambda t} L_{(a;b)} \dot{q}^a \dot{q}^b + \lambda e^{\lambda t} L_a \dot{q}^a + \left(b_0 - \frac{b_1}{\lambda}\right) e^{\lambda t} L_a Q^a + b_1 t e^{\lambda t} L_a Q^a \tag{A14}$$

where $L_{(a;b)}$ is a KT, $\left(L_b Q^b\right)_{,a} = \frac{\lambda^3}{b_1} L_a$ and $\lambda^3 L_a = -2b_1 L_{(a;b)} Q^b$.

- Case $\ell > 1$.

From (A9) we find that $\left(L_b Q^b\right)_{,a} = 2\lambda C_{ab} Q^b$, $C_{ab} Q^b = 0$ and $\lambda^2 L_a = 2b_1 C_{ab} Q^b$.

Therefore, $L_a = 0$ and hence $C_{ab} = -\frac{1}{\lambda} L_{(a;b)} = 0$. We end up with a trivial FI $I_e = const$.

References

1. Katzin, G.H.; Levine, J. Dynamical symmetries and constants of the motion for classical particle systems. *J. Math. Phys.* **1974**, *15*, 1460. [CrossRef]
2. Tsamparlis, M.; Paliathanasis, A. Two-dimensional dynamical systems which admit Lie and Noether symmetries. *J. Phys. A Math. Theor.* **2011**, *44*, 175202. [CrossRef]
3. Tsamparlis, M.; Paliathanasis, A.; Karpathopoulos, L. Autonomous three-dimensional Newtonian systems which admit Lie and Noether point symmetries. *J. Phys. A Math. Theor.* **2012**, *45*, 275201. [CrossRef]
4. Paliathanasis, A.; Tsamparlis, M. Lie point symmetries of a general class of PDEs: The heat equation. *J. Geom. Phys.* **2012**, *62*, 2443. [CrossRef]
5. Tsamparlis, M. Geometrization of Lie and Noether symmetries and applications. *Int. J. Mod. Phys. Conf. Ser.* **2015**, *38*, 1560078. [CrossRef]
6. Katzin, G.H.; Levine, J. A gauge invariant formulation of time-dependent dynamical symmetry mappings and associated constants of motion for Lagrangian particle mechanics. I. *J. Math. Phys.* **1976**, *17*, 1345. [CrossRef]
7. Katzin, G.H.; Levine, J.; Sane, R.N. Time-dependent dynamical symmetry mappings and associated constants of motion for classical particles. II. *J. Math. Phys.* **1977**, *18*, 424. [CrossRef]
8. Katzin, G.H.; Levine, J. Time-dependent dynamical symmetries and constants of motion. III. Time-dependent harmonic oscillator. *J. Math. Phys.* **1977**, *18*, 1267. [CrossRef]
9. Ray, J.R.; Reid, J.L. Noether's theorem, time-dependent invariants and nonlinear equations of motion. *J. Math. Phys.* **1979**, *20*, 2054. [CrossRef]
10. Prince, G.E.; Eliezer, C.J. Symmetries of the time-dependent N-dimensional oscillator. *J. Phys. A Math. Gen.* **1980**, *13*, 815. [CrossRef]
11. Ray, J.R. Noether's theorem and exact invariants for time-dependent systems. *J. Phys. A Math. Gen.* **1980**, *13*, 1969. [CrossRef]
12. Karpathopoulos, L.; Paliathanasis, A.; Tsamparlis, M. Lie and Noether point symmetries for a class of nonautonomous dynamical systems. *J. Math. Phys.* **2017**, *58*, 082901. [CrossRef]
13. Lewis, H.R. Class of Exact Invariants for Classical and Quantum Time-dependent Harmonic Oscillators. *J. Math. Phys.* **1968**, *9*, 1976. [CrossRef]
14. Günther, N.J.; Leach, P.G.L. Generalized invariants for the time-dependent harmonic oscillator. *J. Math. Phys.* **1977**, *18*, 572. [CrossRef]
15. Ray, J.R.; Reid, J.L. More exact invariants for the time-dependent harmonic oscillator. *Phys. Lett. A* **1979**, *71*, 317. [CrossRef]
16. Prince, G.E.; Eliezer, C.J. On the Lie symmetries of the classical Kepler problem. *J. Phys. A Math. Gen.* **1981**, *14*, 587. [CrossRef]
17. Katzin, G.H.; Levine, J. Time-dependent quadratic constants of motion, symmetries, and orbit equations for classical particle dynamical systems with time-dependent Kepler potentials. *J. Math. Phys.* **1982**, *23*, 552. [CrossRef]

18. Leach, P.G.L. Classes of potentials of time-dependent central force fields which possess first integral quadratic in the momenta. *J. Math. Phys.* **1985**, *26*, 1613. [CrossRef]
19. Rosenhaus, V.; Katzin, G.H. On symmetries, conservation laws, and variational problems for partial differential equations. *J. Math. Phys.* **1994**, *35*, 1998. [CrossRef]
20. Bozhkov, Y.; Freire, I.L. Special conformal groups of a Riemannian manifold and Lie point symmetries of the nonlinear Poisson equation. *J. Differ. Equat.* **2010**, *249*, 872. [CrossRef]
21. Tsamparlis, M.; Paliathanasis, A. Symmetries of second-order PDEs and conformal Killing vectors. *J. Phys. Conf. Ser.* **2015**, *621*, 012014. [CrossRef]
22. Djukic, D.S.; Vujanovic, B.D. Noether's Theory in Classical Nonconservative Mechanics. *Acta Mechanica* **1975**, *23*, 17. [CrossRef]
23. Tsamparlis, M.; Mitsopoulos, A. First integrals of holonomic systems without Noether symmetries. *J. Math. Phys.* **2020**, *61*, 122701. [CrossRef]
24. Katzin, G.H. Related integral theorem. II. A method for obtaining quadratic constants of the motion for conservative dynamical systems admitting symmetries. *J. Math. Phys.* **1973**, *14*, 1213. [CrossRef]
25. Katzin, G.H.; Levine, J. Geodesic first integrals with explicit path-parameter dependence in Riemannian space-times. *J. Math. Phys.* **1981**, *22*, 1878. [CrossRef]
26. Katzin, G.H.; Levine, J. Time-dependent vector constants of motion, symmetries, and orbit equations for the dynamical system $\ddot{\mathbf{r}} = \hat{\imath}_r \{[\dot{U}(t)/U(t)]r - [\mu_0/U(t)]r^{-2}\}$. *J. Math. Phys.* **1983**, *24*, 1761. [CrossRef]
27. Tsamparlis, M.; Mitsopoulos, A. Quadratic first integrals of autonomous conservative dynamical systems. *J. Math. Phys.* **2020**, *61*, 072703. [CrossRef]
28. Thompson, G. Polynomial constants of motion in flat space. *J. Math. Phys.* **1984**, *25*, 3474. [CrossRef]
29. Thompson, G. Killing tensors in spaces of constant curvature. *J. Math. Phys.* **1986**, *27*, 2693. [CrossRef]
30. Horwood, J.T. On the theory of algebraic invariants of vector spaces of Killing tensors. *J. Geom. Phys.* **2008**, *58*, 487. [CrossRef]
31. Ibragimov, N.H.; Kara, A.H.; Mahomed, F.H. Lie-Bäcklund and Noether Symmetries with Applications. *Nonlinear Dyn.* **1998**, *15*, 115. [CrossRef]
32. Crampin, M. Hidden Symmetries and Killing Tensors. *Rep. Math. Phys.* **1984**, *20*, 31. [CrossRef]
33. Chanu, C.; Degiovanni, L.; McLenaghan, R.G. Geometrical classification of Killing tensors on bidimensional flat manifolds. *J. Math. Phys.* **2006**, *47*, 073506. [CrossRef]
34. Leach, P.G.L. Generalized Ermakov systems. *Phys. Lett. A* **1991**, *158*, 102–106. [CrossRef]
35. Tsamparlis, M.; Paliathanasis, A. Generalizing the autonomous Kepler-Ermakov system in a Riemannian space. *J. Phys. A Math. Theor.* **2012**, *45*, 275202. [CrossRef]
36. Da Silva, M.R.M.C. A transformation approach for finding first integrals of motion of dynamical systems. *Int. J. Non-Linear Mech.* **1974**, *9*, 241. [CrossRef]
37. Sarlet, W.; Bahar, L.Y. A direct construction of first integrals for certain non-linear dynamical systems. *Int. J. Non-Linear Mech.* **1980**, *15*, 133. [CrossRef]
38. Stephani, H.; Kramer, D.; Maccallum, M.; Hoenselaers, C.; Herlt, E. *Exact Solutions to Einstein's Field Equations*, 2nd ed.; Cambridge U.P.: Cambridge, UK, 2003.
39. Stephani, H. A new interior solution of Einstein's field equations for a spherically symmetric perfect fluid in shear-free motion. *J. Phys. A Math. Gen.* **1983**, *16*, 3529. [CrossRef]
40. Srivastana, D.C. Exact solutions for shear-free motion of spherically symmetric perfect fluid distributions in general relativity. *Class. Quant. Grav.* **1987**, *4*, 1093. [CrossRef]
41. Leach, P.G.L. A first integral for a class of time-dependent anharmonic oscillators with multiple anharmonicities. *J. Math. Phys.* **1992**, *33*, 2023. [CrossRef]
42. Leach, P.G.L.; Maartens, R.; Maharaj, S.D. Self-similar solutions of the generalized Emden–Fowler equation. *Int. J. Non-Linear Mech.* **1992**, *27*, 575. [CrossRef]
43. Maharaj, S.D.; Leach, P.G.L.; Maartens, R. Expanding Spherically Symmetric Models without Shear. *Gen. Rel. Grav.* **1996**, *28*, 35. [CrossRef]
44. Muatjetjeja, B.; Khalique, C.M. Exact solutions of the generalized Lane–Emden equations of the first and second kind. *Pramana J. Phys.* **2011**, *77*, 545. [CrossRef]
45. Khalique, C.M.; Mahomed, F.M.; Muatjetjeja, B. Lagrangian formulation of a generalized Lane–Emden equation and double reduction. *J. Nonlin. Math. Phys.* **2008**, *15*, 152. [CrossRef]

Article

Closed-Loop Nash Equilibrium in the Class of Piecewise Constant Strategies in a Linear State Feedback Form for Stochastic LQ Games

Vasile Drăgan [1,2,†], Ivan Ganchev Ivanov [3,†], Ioan-Lucian Popa [4,*,†] and Ovidiu Bagdasar [5,†]

[1] "Simion Stoilow" Institute of Mathematics, Romanian Academy, P.O. Box 1-764, 014700 Bucharest, Romania; Vasile.Dragan@imar.ro
[2] The Academy of the Romanian Scientists, Str. Ilfov, 3, 050044 Bucharest, Romania
[3] Faculty of Economics and Business Administration, Sofia University St. Kliment Ohridski, 1113 Sofia, Bulgaria; i_ivanov@feb.uni-sofia.bg
[4] Department of Computing, Mathematics and Electronics, "1 Decembrie 1918" University of Alba Iulia, 510009 Alba Iulia, Romania
[5] School of Computing and Engineering, University of Derby, Derby DE22 1GB, UK; O.Bagdasar@derby.ac.uk
* Correspondence: lucian.popa@uab.ro
† These authors contributed equally to this work.

Abstract: In this paper, we examine a sampled-data Nash equilibrium strategy for a stochastic linear quadratic (LQ) differential game, in which admissible strategies are assumed to be constant on the interval between consecutive measurements. Our solution first involves transforming the problem into a linear stochastic system with finite jumps. This allows us to obtain necessary and sufficient conditions assuring the existence of a sampled-data Nash equilibrium strategy, extending earlier results to a general context with more than two players. Furthermore, we provide a numerical algorithm for calculating the feedback matrices of the Nash equilibrium strategies. Finally, we illustrate the effectiveness of the proposed algorithm by two numerical examples. As both situations highlight a stabilization effect, this confirms the efficiency of our approach.

Keywords: nash equilibria; stochastic LQ differential games; sampled-data controls; equilibrium strategies; optimal trajectories

MSC: 91A23; 93E20; 49N10; 49N70

1. Introduction

Stochastic control problems governed by Itô's differential equations have been the subject of intensive research over the last decades. This generated a rich literature and fundamental results such as the H_2 and LQ robust sampled-data control problems under a unified framework studied in [1,2], classes of uncertain sampled-data systems with random jumping parameters characterized by finite state semi-Markov process analysed in [3], or stochastic differential games investigated in [4–7].

Dynamical games have been used to solve many real life problems (see e.g., [8]). For example, the concept of Nash equilibrium is very important for dynamical games, where for controlled systems the closed-loop and open-loop equilibria strategies present special interest. Various aspects of open-loop Nash equilibria are studied for a LQ differential game in [9], other results being reported in [10–12]. In addiytion, in [13] applications to gas network optimisation are studied via open-loop sampled-data Nash equilibrium strategy. The framework in which state vector measurements for a class of differential games are available only at discrete times was first studied in [14]. There, a two-player differential game was considered, and necessary conditions for the sample data controls were obtained using a backward translation method starting at the last time interval, and following the previous state measurements. This case has been extended to a stochastic framework in [15], where the players have access to sample-data state information with sampling interval. For other results dealing with closed-loop systems (see, e.g., [16]). Stochastic dynamical games are an important, but more challenging framework. First introduced in [17], stochastic LQ problems have been studied extensively (see, [18,19]).

In the present paper, we consider stochastic differential games governed by Itô's differential equation, with state multiplicative and control multiplicative white noise perturbations. The original contributions of this work are the following. First, we analyze the design of a Nash equilibrium strategy in a state feedback form in the class of piecewise constant admissible strategies. It is assumed that the state measurements are available only at some discrete times. The original problem is transformed into an equivalent one which asks to find some existence conditions for a Nash equilibrium strategy in a state feedback form for a LQ stochastic differential game described by a system of Itô differential equations controlled by impulses. Necessary and sufficient conditions for the existence of a Nash equilibrium strategy for the new LQ differential game are obtained based on methods from [20,21]. The feedback matrices of the equilibrium strategies for the original dynamical game are obtained from the general result using the structure of the matrix coefficients of the system controlled by impulses. Another major contribution of this paper consists of the numerical methods for computing the feedback matrices of the Nash equilibrium strategy.

To our knowledge, in the stochastic framework, there are few papers dealing with the problem of sampled-data Nash equilibrium strategy in both open-loop and closed-loop forms ([22,23]), the papers [13,14] mentioned before only considering the deterministic framework. In that case, the problem of sampled-data Nash equilibrium strategy can be transformed in a natural way into a problem stated in discrete-time framework. Such a transformation is not possible when the dynamical system contains state multiplicative and control multiplicative white noise perturbations. In [15], the stochastic character is due only to the presence of the additive white noise perturbations. In that case, the approach is not essentially different from the one used in the deterministic case.

The paper is organized as follows. In Section 2, we formulate the problem, introducing the L-players Nash equilibria concept. In Section 2.2, we state an equivalent form of the original problem and we introduce a system of matrix linear differential equations with jumps and algebraic constraints which is involved in the derivation of the feedback matrices of the equilibrium strategies. Then, in Section 2.3, we provide some necessary and sufficient conditions which guarantee the existence of a piecewise constant Nash equilibrium strategy. An algorithm implementing these developments is given in Section 3. The efficiency of the proposed algorithm is demonstrated by two numerical examples illustrating the behavior of the optimal trajectories generated by the equilibrium strategy. Section 4 is dedicated to conclusions.

2. Problem Formulation

2.1. Model Description and Problem Setting

Consider the controlled system having the state space representation described by

$$dx(t) = [Ax(t) + \sum_{k=1}^{L} B_k u_k(t)]dt + [Cx(t) + \sum_{k=1}^{L} D_k u_k(t)]dw(t),$$
$$x(t_0) = x_0, \quad t \in [t_0, t_f], \tag{1}$$

where $x(t) \in \mathbb{R}^n$ is the state vector, L is a positive integer, $u_k(t) \in \mathbb{R}^{m_k}$, $k = 1, \ldots, L$ are control parameters, and $\{w(t)\}_{t \geq 0}$ is a 1-dimensional standard Wiener process defined on a probability space $(\Omega, \mathcal{F}, \mathcal{P})$.

In the controlled system there are L players ($k = 1, 2, \ldots, L$) who change their behavior through their control function $u_k(\cdot)$, $k = 1, \ldots, L$. The matrices of the system $A, C \in \mathbb{R}^{n \times n}$ and matrices of the players $B_k, D_k \in \mathbb{R}^{n \times m_k}$, $k = 1, \ldots, L$, are known. In the field of the game theory, the controls $u_k(\cdot)$ are called admissible strategies (or policies) for the players.

The different classes of admissible strategies can be defined in various ways, depending on the available information.

Each player aims to minimize its own cost function (performance criterion), and for $k = 1, \ldots, L$ we have

$$J_k(t_0, x_0; u_1, \ldots, u_L) = \mathbb{E}\left[x_u^T(t_f) G_k x_u(t_f) + \int_{t_0}^{t_f} (x_u^T(t) M_k x_u(t) + \sum_{j=1}^{L} u_j^T(t) R_{kj} u_j(t)) dt\right]. \quad (2)$$

We make the following assumption regarding the weights matrices in (2):
H. $G_k \geq 0$, $M_k \geq 0$, $R_{kk} > 0$, and $R_{kl} \geq 0$, with $k, l = 1, \ldots, L$, and $l \neq k$.
Here we generalize Definition 2.1 given in [23].

Definition 1. *The L-tuple of admissible strategies $(\tilde{u}_1(\cdot), \tilde{u}_2(\cdot), \ldots, \tilde{u}_L(\cdot))$ is said to achieve a Nash equilibrium for the differential game described by the controlled system (1), the cost function (2), and the class of the admissible strategies $\mathcal{U} = \mathcal{U}_1 \times \mathcal{U}_2 \times \cdots \times \mathcal{U}_L$, if for all $u_k(\cdot) \in \mathcal{U}_k, k = 1, \ldots, L$ we have*

$$J_k(t_0, x_0; \tilde{u}_1, \tilde{u}_2, \ldots, \tilde{u}_L) \leq J_k(t_0, x_0; \tilde{u}_1, \tilde{u}_2, \ldots, \tilde{u}_{k-1}, u_k, \tilde{u}_{k+1}, \ldots, \tilde{u}_L). \quad (3)$$

In this paper we consider a special class of closed-loop admissible strategies in which the states $x(t)$ of the dynamical system are available for measurement at the discrete-times $0 \leq t_0 < t_1 < \ldots < t_{N-1} < t_N = t_f$, and the set of admissible strategies consists of piecewise constant stochastic processes of the form

$$u_k(t) = F_k(j) x(t_j), \quad t_j \leq t < t_{j+1}, \quad j = 0, 1, \ldots, N-1, \quad (4)$$

with $F_k(j) \in \mathbb{R}^{m_k \times n}$ are arbitrary matrices.

Our aim is to investigate the problem of designing a Nash equilibrium strategy in the class of piecewise constant admissible strategies of type (4) (the closed-loop admissible strategies), for a LQ differential game described by a dynamical system of type (1), under the performance criteria (2). Moreover, we also present a method for the numerical computation of the feedback gains of the equilibrium strategy.

We denote $\tilde{\mathcal{U}}^{pc} = \tilde{\mathcal{U}}_1^{pc} \times \tilde{\mathcal{U}}_2^{pc} \times \ldots \times \tilde{\mathcal{U}}_L^{pc}$ the set of the piecewise constant admissible strategies of type (4).

2.2. *The Equivalent Problem*

Define $v_k : [t_0, t_f] \to \mathbb{R}^{m_k}$ by $v_k(t) = u_k(j)$, $t_j \leq t < t_{j+1}, j = 0, 1, \ldots, N-1$, where $u_k(j)$ are arbitrary m_k-dimensional random vectors with finite second moments. If $x(t)$ is the solution of system (1) determined by the piecewise constant inputs $v_k(\cdot)$, we set $\xi(t) = (x^T(t) \ v_1^T(t) \ \ldots \ v_L^T(t))^T \in \mathbb{R}^{n+m}, m = \sum_{k=1}^{L} m_k$.

Direct calculations show that $\xi(t)$ is the solution of the initial value problem (IVP) associated to a linear stochastic system with finite jumps often called system controlled by impulses:

$$d\xi(t) = \mathbf{A}\xi(t)dt + \mathbf{C}\xi(t)dw(t), \quad t_j \leq t < t_{j+1} \quad (5a)$$

$$\xi(t_j^+) = \mathbf{A}_d \xi(t_j) + \sum_{k=1}^{L} \mathbf{B}_{dk} u_k(j), \quad j = 0, 1, \ldots, N-1, \quad (5b)$$

$$\xi(t_0) = (x_0^T \ 0^T \ldots 0^T)^T, \quad (5c)$$

under the notations:

$$\mathbf{A} = \begin{pmatrix} A & B_1 & B_2 & \cdots & B_L \\ 0_{mn} & 0_{mm_1} & 0_{mm_2} & \cdots & 0_{mm_L} \end{pmatrix},$$

$$\mathbf{C} = \begin{pmatrix} C & D_1 & D_2 & \cdots & D_L \\ 0_{mn} & 0_{mm_1} & 0_{mm_2} & \cdots & 0_{mm_L} \end{pmatrix}, \quad (6)$$

$$\mathbf{A}_d = \begin{pmatrix} I_n & 0_{nm_1} & 0_{nm_2} & \cdots & 0_{nm_l} \\ 0_{mn} & 0_{mm_1} & 0_{mm_2} & \cdots & 0_{mm_L} \end{pmatrix},$$

$$\mathbf{B}_{dk} = \begin{pmatrix} 0^T_{nm_k} & 0^T_{m_1 m_k} & \cdots & 0^T_{m_{k-1} m_k} & I_{m_k} & 0^T_{m_{k+1} m_k} & \cdots & 0^T_{m_L m_k} \end{pmatrix}^T,$$

where 0_{pq} denotes the zero matrix of size $p \times q$.

The performance criteria (2) becomes

$$J_k(t_0, \zeta_0; \mathbf{u}_1, \mathbf{u}_2, \ldots, \mathbf{u}_L) = \mathbb{E}[\xi^T(t_f) \mathbf{G}_k \xi(t_f) + \int_{t_0}^{t_f} \xi^T(t) \mathbf{M}_k \xi(t) dt]$$
$$+ \sum_{j=0}^{N-1} \mathbb{E}[\sum_{i=1}^{L} u_i^T(j) \mathbf{R}_{ki}(j) u_i(j)], \quad (7)$$

for all $\mathbf{u}_k = (u_k(0), \ldots, u_k(N-1))$, $u_k(j)$ are m_k-dimensional random vectors $\mathcal{F}_{t_j}$-measurable such that

$$\mathbb{E}[|u_k(j)|^2] < \infty.$$

Throughout the paper $\mathcal{F}_t$ denotes the σ-algebra generated by the random variables $w(s), 0 \leq s \leq t$. The matrices in (7) can be written as

$$\mathbf{G}_k = \text{diag}(G_k \ 0) \in \mathbb{R}^{(n+m) \times (n+m)}$$

$$\mathbf{M}_k = \text{diag}(M_k \ 0) \in \mathbb{R}^{(n+m) \times (n+m)} \quad (8)$$

$$\mathbf{R}_{ki}(j) = (t_{j+1} - t_j) R_{ki}.$$

Let $\mathcal{U}^{sd} = \mathcal{U}_1^{sd} \times \mathcal{U}_2^{sd} \times \cdots \times \mathcal{U}_L^{sd}$ be the set of the inputs of the form of sampled data linear state feedback, i.e., $\mathbf{u} = (\mathbf{u}_1, \mathbf{u}_2, \ldots, \mathbf{u}_L) \in \mathcal{U}^{sd}$ if and only if $\mathbf{u}_k = (u_k(0), \ldots, u_k(N-1))$ with

$$u_k(j) = \mathbf{F}_k(j) \xi(t_j), \quad 0 \leq j \leq N-1, \quad (9)$$

where $\mathbf{F}_k(j) \in \mathbb{R}^{m_k \times (n+m)}$ are arbitrary matrices and $\xi(t_j)$ are the values at the time instants t_j of the solution of the following IVP:

$$d\xi(t) = \mathbf{A}\xi(t) dt + \mathbf{C}\xi(t) dw(t), \quad t_j < t \leq t_{j+1} \quad (10a)$$

$$\xi(t_j^+) = (\mathbf{A}_d + \sum_{k=1}^{L} \mathbf{B}_{dk} \mathbf{F}_k(j)) \xi(t_j), \quad j = 0, 1, \ldots, N-1, \quad (10b)$$

$$\xi(t_0) = \zeta_0 \in \mathbb{R}^{n+m}. \quad (10c)$$

Let Φ_k be a matrix valued sequence of the form

$$\Phi_k = (\mathbf{F}_k(0), \mathbf{F}_k(1), \ldots, \mathbf{F}_k(N-1)), \quad (11)$$

where $\mathbf{F}_k(i) \in \mathbb{R}^{m_k \times (n+m)}$ are arbitrary matrices. We consider the set

$$\mathcal{U}_\Phi^{sd} = \{(\Phi_1, \Phi_2, \ldots, \Phi_L) : \Phi_k \text{ are arbitrary sequences defined as in (11)}\}. \quad (12)$$

Remark 1. *By (9) and (10), there is a one to one correspondence between the sets $\mathcal{U}^{sd}$ and $\mathcal{U}^{sd}_\Phi$. Each $\mathbf{u}_k$ from $\mathcal{U}^{sd}_k$ can be identified with the sequence $\Phi_k = (\Phi_k(0), \Phi_k(1), \ldots, \Phi_k(N-1))$ of its feedback matrices.*

Based on this remark we can rewrite the performance criterion (7) as:

$$\mathcal{J}_k(t_0, \xi_0; \Phi_1, \Phi_2, \ldots, \Phi_L) = \mathbb{E}[\xi^T(t_f)\mathbf{G}_k\xi(t_f) + \int_{t_0}^{t_f} \xi^T(t)\mathbf{M}_k\xi(t)dt]$$
$$+ \sum_{j=0}^{N-1} \mathbb{E}[\sum_{i=1}^{L} \xi^T(t_j)\mathbf{F}_i^T(j)\mathbf{R}_{ki}(j)\mathbf{F}_i(j)\xi(t_j)], \tag{13}$$

for all $(\Phi_1, \Phi_2, \ldots, \Phi_L) \in \mathcal{U}^{sd}_\Phi$.

Similarly to Definition 1, one can define a Nash equilibrium strategy for the LQ differential game described by the controlled system (5), the performance criteria (13) and the class of admissible strategies $\mathcal{U}^{sd}_\Phi$ described by (12).

Definition 2. *The L-tuple of admissible strategies $(\tilde{\Phi}_1, \tilde{\Phi}_2, \ldots, \tilde{\Phi}_L)$ is said to achieve a Nash equilibrium for the differential game described by the controlled system (5), the cost function (13), and the class of the admissible strategies $\mathcal{U}^{sd}_\Phi$, if for all $(\Phi_1, \Phi_2, \ldots, \Phi_L) \in \mathcal{U}^{sd}_\Phi$, we have*

$$\mathcal{J}_k(t_0, \xi_0; \tilde{\Phi}_1, \tilde{\Phi}_2, \ldots, \tilde{\Phi}_L) \leq \mathcal{J}_k(t_0, \xi_0; \tilde{\Phi}_1, \tilde{\Phi}_2, \ldots, \tilde{\Phi}_{k-1}, \Phi_k, \tilde{\Phi}_{k+1}, \ldots, \tilde{\Phi}_L). \tag{14}$$

Remark 2.

(a) Based on the Remark 1 we may infer that if $(\tilde{\Phi}_1, \tilde{\Phi}_2, \ldots, \tilde{\Phi}_L)$ is an equilibrium strategy in the sense of the Definition 2, then $(\tilde{\mathbf{u}}_1, \tilde{\mathbf{u}}_2, \ldots, \tilde{\mathbf{u}}_L)$ given by (9) using the matrix components of $\tilde{\Phi}_k$, provides an equilibrium strategy for the LQ differential game described by (5), (7) and the family of admissible strategies $\mathcal{U}^{sd}$.

(b) Among the feedback matrices from (9) some have the form:

$$\mathbf{F}_k(j) = (F_k(j) \quad 0_{m_k m}), \tag{15}$$

where $F_k(j) \in \mathbb{R}^{m_k \times n}$. Hence, some admissible strategies (9) are of type (4). Hence, if the feedback matrices of the Nash equilibrium strategy $(\tilde{\Phi}_1, \tilde{\Phi}_2, \ldots, \tilde{\Phi}_L)$ have the structure given in (15), then the strategy of type (9) with these feedback matrices provide the Nash equilibrium strategy for the LQ differential game described by (1), (2) and (4).

To obtain explicit formulae for the feedback matrices of a Nash equilibrium strategy of type (9) (or, equivalently (11), (12)), we use the following system of matrix linear differential equations (MLDEs) with jumps and algebraic constraints:

$$-\dot{P}_k(t) = \mathbf{A}^T P_k(t) + P_k(t)\mathbf{A} + \mathbf{C}^T P_k(t)\mathbf{C} + \mathbf{M}_k, \quad t_j \leq t < t_{j+1} \tag{16a}$$

$$P_k(t_j^-) = \mathbf{A}_{[-k]}^T(j) P_k(t_j) \mathbf{A}_{[-k]}(j) - \mathbf{A}_{[-k]}^T(j) P_k(t_j) \mathbf{B}_{dk} \times$$

$$\times (\mathbf{R}_{kk}(j) + \mathbf{B}_{dk}^T P_k(t_j) \mathbf{B}_{dk})^\dagger \mathbf{B}_{dk}^T P_k(t_j) \mathbf{A}_{[-k]}(j) + \mathbf{M}_{[-k]}(j) \tag{16b}$$

$$\sum_{i=1}^{k-1} \mathbf{B}_{dk}^T P_k(t_j) \mathbf{B}_{di} \mathbf{F}_i(j) + (\mathbf{R}_{kk}(j) + \mathbf{B}_{dk}^T P_k(t_j) \mathbf{B}_{dk}) \mathbf{F}_k(j)$$

$$+ \sum_{i=k+1}^{L} \mathbf{B}_{dk}^T P_k(t_j) \mathbf{B}_{di} \mathbf{F}_i(j) = -\mathbf{B}_{dk}^T P_k(t_j) \mathbf{A}_d \tag{16c}$$

$$P_k(t_N^-) = \mathbf{G_k}, \quad \mathbf{k} = 1,\ldots, \mathbf{L}, \tag{16d}$$

where we have denoted

$$\mathbf{A}_{[-k]}(j) = \mathbf{A}_d + \sum_{i=1, i\neq k}^{L} \mathbf{B}_{di} \mathbf{F}_i(j) \tag{17}$$

and

$$\mathbf{M}_{[-k]}(j) = \sum_{i=1, i\neq k}^{L} \mathbf{F}_i^T(j) \mathbf{R}_{ki}(j) \mathbf{F}_i(j), \tag{18}$$

while the superscript † denotes the generalized inverse of a matrix.

Remark 3. *A solution of the terminal value problem (TVP) with algebraic constraints (16) is a 2L-uple of the form $(P_1(\cdot), P_2(\cdot), \ldots, P_L(\cdot); \mathbf{F}_1(\cdot), \mathbf{F}_2(\cdot), \ldots, \mathbf{F}_L(\cdot))$ where, for each $1 \leq k \leq L$, $P_k(\cdot)$ is a solution of the TVP (16a), (16b), (16d) and $\mathbf{F}_k(j) \in \mathbb{R}^{m_k \times (n+m)}, 0 \leq j \leq N-1$. On the interval $[t_{N-1}, t_N]$, $P_k(\cdot)$ is the solution of the TVP described by the perturbed Lyapunov-type equation from (16a) and the terminal value given in (16d). On each interval $[t_{j-1}, t_j)$, $j \leq N-1$, the terminal value $P_k(t_j^-)$ of $P_k(\cdot)$ is computed via (16b) together with (17) and (18) provided that $(\mathbf{F}_1(j), \mathbf{F}_2(j), \ldots, \mathbf{F}_L(j))$ to be obtained as solution of (16c). So, the TVPs solved by $P_k(\cdot), 1 \leq k \leq L$ are interconnected via (16c).*

To facilitate the statement of the main result of this section, we rewrite (16c) in a compact form as:

$$\Pi_d(P_1(t_j), \ldots, P_L(t_j), j) \mathbb{F}(j) = -\Gamma_d(P_1(t_j), \ldots, P_L(t_j)), \tag{19}$$

where $\mathbb{F}(j) = (\mathbf{F}_1^T(j) \ \mathbf{F}_2^T(j) \ \ldots \ \mathbf{F}_L^T(j))^T$ and the matrices $\Pi_d(P_1(t_j), \ldots, P_L(t_j), j)$ and $\Gamma_d(P_1(t_j), \ldots, P_L(t_j))$ are obtained using the block components of (16c).

2.3. Sampled Data Nash Equilibrium Strategy

First we derive a necessary and sufficient condition for the existence of an equilibrium strategy of type (9) for the LQ differential game given by the controlled system (5), the performance criteria (7) and the set of the admissible strategies $\mathcal{U}^{sd}$. To this end we adapt the argument used in the proof of ([22], Theorem 4).

We prove:

Theorem 1. *Under the assumption H. the following are equivalent:*

(i) *the LQ differential game defined by the dynamical system controlled by impulses (5), the performance criteria (7) and the class of the admissible strategies of type (9) has a Nash equilibrium strategy*

$$\tilde{u}_k(j) = \tilde{\mathbf{F}}_k(j) \xi(t_j), \ 0 \leq j \leq N-1, 1 \leq k \leq L. \tag{20}$$

(ii) *the TVP with constraints (16) has a solution* $(\tilde{P}_1(\cdot), \tilde{P}_2(\cdot), \ldots, \tilde{P}_L(\cdot); \tilde{F}_1(\cdot), \tilde{F}_2(\cdot), \ldots, \tilde{F}_L(\cdot))$ *defined on the whole interval* $[t_0, t_f]$ *and satisfying the conditions below for* $0 \leq j \leq N-1$:

$$\Pi_d(\tilde{P}_1(t_j), \ldots, \tilde{P}_L(t_j), j)\Pi_d(\tilde{P}_1(t_j), \ldots, \tilde{P}_L(t_j), j)^{\dagger}\Gamma_d(\tilde{P}_1(t_j), \ldots, \tilde{P}_L(t_j)) = \\ = \Gamma_d(\tilde{P}_1(t_j), \ldots, \tilde{P}_L(t_j)). \quad (21)$$

If condition (21) holds, then the feedback matrices of a Nash equilibrium strategy of type (9) are the matrix components of the solution of the TVP (16) and are given by

$$(\tilde{F}_1^T(j) \ \tilde{F}_2^T(j) \ \ldots \ \tilde{F}_L^T(j))^T = -\Pi_d(\tilde{P}_1(t_j), \ldots, \tilde{P}_L(t_j), j)^{\dagger}\Gamma_d(\tilde{P}_1(t_j), \ldots, \tilde{P}_L(t_j)), \\ 0 \leq j \leq N-1. \quad (22)$$

The minimal value of the cost of the k-th player is $\xi_0^T \tilde{P}_k(t_0^-)\xi_0$.

Proof. From (14) and Remarks 1 and 2(a), one can see that a strategy of type (9) defines a Nash equilibrium strategy for the linear differential game described by the controlled system (5), the performance criteria (7) (or equivalently (13)) if and only if for each $1 \leq k \leq L$ the optimal control problem described by the controlled system

$$d\xi(t) = \mathbf{A}\xi(t)dt + \mathbf{C}\xi(t)dw(t), \ t_j < t \leq t_{j+1} \quad (23a)$$

$$\xi(t_j^+) = \tilde{\mathbf{A}}_{[-k]}(j)\xi(t_j) + \mathbf{B}_{dk}u_k(j), \ j = 0, 1, \ldots, N-1, \quad (23b)$$

$$\xi(t_0) = \xi_0 \in \mathbb{R}^{n+m}, \quad (23c)$$

and the quadratic functional

$$\mathcal{J}_{[-k]}(t_0, \xi_0; \mathbf{u}_k) = \mathbb{E}[\xi^T(t_f)\mathbf{G}_k\xi(t_f) + \int_{t_0}^{t_f} \xi^T(t)\mathbf{M}_k\xi(t)dt] \\ + \sum_{j=0}^{N-1} \mathbb{E}[\xi^T(t_j)\tilde{\mathbf{M}}_{[-k]}(j)\xi(t_j) + u_k^T(j)\mathbf{R}_{kk}(j)u_k(j)], \quad (24)$$

has an optimal control in a state feedback form. The controlled system (23) and the performance criterion (24) are obtained substituting $\tilde{u}_\ell(j) = \tilde{F}_\ell(j)\xi(t_j), 1 \leq k, \ell \leq L, \ell \neq k$ in (5) and (7), respectively. $\tilde{A}_{[-k]}$ and $\tilde{M}_{[-k]}$ are computed as in (17) and (18), respectively, but with $F_i(j)$ replaced by $\tilde{F}_i(j)$.

To obtain necessary and sufficient conditions for the existence of the optimal control in a linear state feedback form we employ the results proved in [20]. First, notice that in the case of the optimal control problem (23)–(24), the TVP (16a), (16b), (16d) plays the role of the TVP (19)–(23) from [20].

Using Theorem 3 in [20] in the case of the optimal control problem described by (23) and (24) we deduce that the existence of the Nash equilibrium strategy of the form (9) for the differential game described by the controlled system (5), the performance criteria (7) (or its equivalent form (13)), is equivalent to the solvability of the TVP described by (16). The feedback matrix $\tilde{F}_k(j)$ of the optimal control solves the equation:

$$(\mathbf{R}_{kk}(j) + \mathbf{B}_{dk}^T\tilde{P}_k(t_j)\mathbf{B}_{dk})\tilde{F}_k(j) = -\mathbf{B}_{dk}^T\tilde{P}_k(t_j)\tilde{\mathbf{A}}_{[-k]}(j). \quad (25)$$

Substituting the formulae of $\tilde{A}_{[-k]}$ in (25) we deduce that the feedback matrices of the Nash equilibrium strategy solve an equation of the form (16c) written for $\tilde{F}_k(j)$ instead of $F_k(j)$. This equation may be written in the compact form:

$$\Pi_d(\tilde{P}_1(t_j), \ldots, \tilde{P}_L(t_j), j)\tilde{\mathbb{F}}(j) = -\Gamma_d(\tilde{P}_1(t_j), \ldots, \tilde{P}_L(t_j)), \quad (26)$$

where $\tilde{\mathbb{F}}(j) = (\tilde{F}_1^T(j) \ \tilde{F}_2^T(j) \ \ldots \ \tilde{F}_L^T(j))^T$.

By Lemma 2.7 in [21] we deduce that the Equation (26) has a solution if and only if the condition (21) holds. A solution of the Equation (26) is given by (22). The minimal value of the cost for the k-th player is obtained from Theorem 1 in [20] applied in the case of the optimal control problem described by (23), (24). Thus the proof is complete. □

Remark 4. *When the matrices* $\Pi_d(\tilde{P}_1(t_j),\ldots,\tilde{P}_L(t_j),j)$ *are invertible, the conditions (21) are satisfied automatically. In this case, the feedback matrices* $\tilde{\mathbf{F}}_k(j)$ *of a Nash equilibrium strategy of type (20) are obtained as the unique solution of the Equation (22), because in this case, the generalized inverse of each matrix* $\Pi_d(\tilde{P}_1(t_j),\ldots,\tilde{P}_L(t_j),j), 0 \leq j \leq N-1$ *is the usual inverse.*

Combining (6) and (16c), we deduce that the matrices $\tilde{\mathbf{F}}_k(j)$ provided by (22) have the structure $\tilde{\mathbf{F}}_k(j) = (\tilde{F}_k(j) \ 0_{m_k m})$. Hence, the Nash equilibrium strategy of the differential game described by the dynamical system (5), the performance criteria (7) and the admissible strategies of type (9) have the form

$$\tilde{u}_k(j) = (\tilde{F}_k(j) \ 0_{m_k m})\xi(t_j) = \tilde{F}_k(j)x(t_j), \ 0 \leq j \leq N-1.$$

Now we obtain the following Nash equilibrium strategy of the differential game.

Theorem 2. *Assume that the conditions* **H.** *and (ii) in Theorem 1 are satisfied. Then, a Nash equilibrium strategy in a state feedback form with sampled measurements of type (4) of the differential game described by the dynamical system (1) and the performance criteria (2) are given by:*

$$\tilde{u}_k(t) = \tilde{F}_k(j)x(t_j), \ t_j \leq t \leq t_{j+1}, \ 0 \leq j \leq N-1, \ 1 \leq k \leq L. \tag{27}$$

The feedback matrices $\tilde{F}_k(j)$ *from (27) are given by the first n columns of the matrices* $\tilde{\mathbf{F}}_k(j)$*, which are obtained as solutions of Equation (26). In (27),* $x(t_j)$ *are the values measured at the times* $t_j, 0 \leq j \leq N-1$*, of the solution of the closed-loop system obtained when (27) is plugged into (1). The minimal value of the cost (2) associated to the k-th player is given by*

$$(x_0^T \ \ 0_{nm})\tilde{P}_k(t_0^-)(x_0^T \ \ 0_{nm})^T.$$

In the next section, we present an algorithm which allows the numerical computation of the matrices $\tilde{F}_k(j)$ arising in (27) for an LQ differential game with two players.

3. Numerical Computations and the Algorithm

In what follows we assume that $L = 2$ and $t_{j+1} - t_j = h > 0.0 \leq j \leq N-1$.
We propose a numerical approach to compute the optimal strategies

$$\tilde{u}_k(j) = \tilde{F}_k(j)\tilde{x}(t_j), \ j = 0, 1, \ldots, N-1. \tag{28}$$

The algorithm consists of two steps:
- We first compute the feedback matrices $\tilde{F}_k(j), j = 0, 1, \ldots, N-1, k = 1, 2$ of the Nash equilibrium strategy, based on the solution $\tilde{P}_1(\cdot), \tilde{P}_2(\cdot)$:

$$-\dot{P}_k(t) = \mathbf{A}^T P_k(t) + P_k(t)\mathbf{A} + \mathbf{C}^T P_k(t)\mathbf{C} + \mathbf{M}_k, \ t_j \leq t < t_{j+1}. \tag{29}$$

STEP 1.A. We take $P_k(t_N^-) = \mathbf{G}_k, \ k = 1, 2$, and compute

$$\tilde{P}_k(t_{N-1}) = e^{\mathcal{L}^* h}[\mathbf{G}_k] + \mathbb{M}_k, \ k = 1, 2, \ \text{where} \tag{30}$$

$$\mathbb{M}_k = h\mathbf{M}_k + \frac{h^2}{2}\mathcal{L}^*[\mathbf{M}_k] + \frac{h^3}{6}(\mathcal{L}^*)^2[\mathbf{M}_k] + \cdots + \frac{h^p}{p!}(\mathcal{L}^*)^{p-1}[\mathbf{M}_k] \tag{31}$$

$$e^{\mathcal{L}^* h}[\mathbf{X}] \simeq \sum_{\ell=0}^{q} \frac{h^\ell}{\ell!} \mathcal{L}^{*\ell}[\mathbf{X}] = \mathbf{X} + h\mathcal{L}^*[\mathbf{X}] + \frac{h^2}{2}(\mathcal{L}^*)[\mathcal{L}^*[\mathbf{X}]] + \ldots + \frac{h^q}{q!}(\mathcal{L}^*)^q[\mathbf{X}],$$

with $p \geq 1$ and $q \geq 1$ sufficiently large.
For the operator $\mathcal{L}^*[X]$ we have

$$\mathcal{L}^*[X] = \mathbf{A}^T X + X\mathbf{A} + \mathbf{C}^T X \mathbf{C} \tag{32}$$

for all $X = X^T \in \mathbb{R}^{(n+m_1+m_2)\times(n+m_1+m_2)}$.
The iterations $\mathcal{L}^\ell[\mathbf{X}]$ are computed from:

$$\mathcal{L}^{*\ell}[\mathbf{X}] = \mathbf{A}^T \mathcal{L}^{*(\ell-1)}[\mathbf{X}] + \mathcal{L}^{*(\ell-1)}[\mathbf{X}]\mathbf{A} + \mathbf{C}^T \mathcal{L}^{*(\ell-1)}[\mathbf{X}]\mathbf{C} \tag{33}$$

for $\ell \geq 1$ with $\mathcal{L}^0[\mathbf{X}] = \mathbf{X}$ where $\mathbf{X} = P_k(t_{j+1}^-)$ or $\mathbf{X} = \mathbf{M}_k$, respectively.
We compute the feedback matrices $\tilde{F}_k(N-1) \in \mathbb{R}^{m_k \times n}$ as solutions of the linear equation

$$\begin{pmatrix} R_{11} + h^{-1}\tilde{P}_{1,11}(t_{N-1}) & h^{-1}\tilde{P}_{1,12}(t_{N-1}) \\ h^{-1}\tilde{P}_{2,12}^T(t_{N-1}) & R_{22} + h^{-1}\tilde{P}_{2,22}(t_{N-1}) \end{pmatrix} \begin{pmatrix} \tilde{F}_1(N-1) \\ \tilde{F}_2(N-1) \end{pmatrix} =$$
$$- \begin{pmatrix} h^{-1}\tilde{P}_{1,01}^T(t_{N-1}) \\ h^{-1}\tilde{P}_{2,02}^T(t_{N-1}) \end{pmatrix} \tag{34}$$

STEP 1.B. We set

$$\tilde{\mathbf{F}}_k(N-1) = (\tilde{F}_k(N-1) \quad 0 \quad 0) \in \mathbb{R}^{m_k \times (n+m_1+m_2)}, k = 1,2.$$

Next, we compute $\tilde{P}_k(t_{N-1}^-), k = 1,2,$:

$$\tilde{P}_1(t_{N-1}^-) = (\mathbf{A}_d + \mathbf{B}_{d2}\tilde{\mathbf{F}}_2(N-1))^T \tilde{P}_1(t_{N-1})(\mathbf{A}_d + \mathbf{B}_{d2}\tilde{\mathbf{F}}_2(N-1))$$
$$- (\mathbf{A}_d + \mathbf{B}_{d2}\tilde{\mathbf{F}}_2(N-1))^T \tilde{P}_1(t_{N-1})\mathbf{B}_{d1}(hR_{11} + \mathbf{B}_{d1}^T \tilde{P}_1(t_{N-1})\mathbf{B}_{d1})^{-1}$$
$$\cdot \mathbf{B}_{d1}^T \tilde{P}_1(t_{N-1})(\mathbf{A}_d + \mathbf{B}_{d2}\tilde{\mathbf{F}}_2(N-1)) + h\tilde{\mathbf{F}}_2^T(N-1)R_{12}\tilde{\mathbf{F}}_2(N-1) \tag{35}$$

and

$$\tilde{P}_2(t_{N-1}^-) = (\mathbf{A}_d + \mathbf{B}_{d1}\tilde{\mathbf{F}}_1(N-1))^T \tilde{P}_2(t_{N-1})(\mathbf{A}_d + \mathbf{B}_{d1}\tilde{\mathbf{F}}_1(N-1))$$
$$- (\mathbf{A}_d + \mathbf{B}_{d1}\tilde{\mathbf{F}}_1(N-1))^T \tilde{P}_2(t_{N-1})\mathbf{B}_{d2}(hR_{22} + \mathbf{B}_{d2}^T \tilde{P}_2(t_{N-1})\mathbf{B}_{d2})^{-1}$$
$$\cdot \mathbf{B}_{d2}^T \tilde{P}_2(t_{N-1})(\mathbf{A}_d + \mathbf{B}_{d1}\tilde{\mathbf{F}}_1(N-1)) + h\tilde{\mathbf{F}}_1^T(N-1)R_{21}\tilde{\mathbf{F}}_1(N-1). \tag{36}$$

STEP 2.A. Fix j such that $j \leq N-2$. Assuming that $\tilde{P}_k(t_{j+1}^-)$ have already been computed for a $j \leq N-2$, $k = 1,2$, we compute

$$\tilde{P}_k(t_j) = e^{\mathcal{L}^* h}[\tilde{P}_k(t_{j+1}^-)] + \mathbb{M}_k, k = 1,2, \tag{37}$$

where $\mathbb{M}_k$ is computed as in (31).
We compute the feedback gains $\tilde{F}_k(j) \in \mathbb{R}^{m_k \times n}$ as solution of the linear equation

$$\begin{pmatrix} R_{11} + h^{-1}\tilde{P}_{1,11}(t_j) & h^{-1}\tilde{P}_{1,12}(t_j) \\ h^{-1}\tilde{P}_{2,12}^T(t_j) & R_{22} + h^{-1}\tilde{P}_{2,22}(t_j) \end{pmatrix} \begin{pmatrix} \tilde{F}_1(j) \\ \tilde{F}_2(j) \end{pmatrix} = - \begin{pmatrix} h^{-1}\tilde{P}_{1,01}^T(t_j) \\ h^{-1}\tilde{P}_{2,02}^T(t_j) \end{pmatrix} \tag{38}$$

STEP 2.B. Setting $\tilde{\mathbf{F}}_k(j) = \begin{pmatrix} \tilde{F}_k(j) & 0 & 0 \end{pmatrix} \in \mathbb{R}^{m_k \times (n+m_1+m_2)}$, $k = 1, 2$ we compute $\tilde{P}_k(t_j^-)$ as in the formulae below

$$\tilde{P}_1(t_j^-) = (\mathbf{A}_d + \mathbf{B}_{d2}\tilde{\mathbf{F}}_2(j))^T \tilde{P}_1(t_j)(\mathbf{A}_d + \mathbf{B}_{d2}\tilde{\mathbf{F}}_2(j))$$
$$- (\mathbf{A}_d + \mathbf{B}_{d2}\tilde{\mathbf{F}}_2(j))^T \tilde{P}_1(t_j) \mathbf{B}_{d1}(hR_{11} + \mathbf{B}_{d1}^T \tilde{P}_1(t_j) \mathbf{B}_{d1})^{-1}$$
$$\cdot \mathbf{B}_{d1}^T \tilde{P}_1(t_j)(\mathbf{A}_d + \mathbf{B}_{d2}\tilde{\mathbf{F}}_2(j)) + h\tilde{\mathbf{F}}_2^T(j) R_{12} \tilde{\mathbf{F}}_2(j) \quad (39)$$

and

$$\tilde{P}_2(t_j^-) = (\mathbf{A}_d + \mathbf{B}_{d1}\tilde{\mathbf{F}}_1(j))^T \tilde{P}_2(t_j)(\mathbf{A}_d + \mathbf{B}_{d1}\tilde{\mathbf{F}}_1(j))$$
$$- (\mathbf{A}_d + \mathbf{B}_{d1}\tilde{\mathbf{F}}_1(j))^T \tilde{P}_2(t_j) \mathbf{B}_{d2}(hR_{22} + \mathbf{B}_{d2}^T \tilde{P}_2(t_j) \mathbf{B}_{d2})^{-1}$$
$$\mathbf{B}_{d2}^T \tilde{P}_2(t_j)(\mathbf{A}_d + \mathbf{B}_{d1}\tilde{\mathbf{F}}_1(j)) + h\tilde{\mathbf{F}}_1^T(j) R_{21} \tilde{\mathbf{F}}_1(j). \quad (40)$$

- In the second step, the computation of the optimal trajectory $\tilde{x}(t)$ involves the initial vector x_0 and the equilibrium strategy values $u_k(j)$, $k = 1, 2$.
  Then, we illustrate the mean squares of the optimal trajectory $\mathbb{E}[|\tilde{x}(t)|^2]$ and of the equilibrium strategy $\mathbb{E}[|\tilde{u}_k(t)|^2]$, $k = 1, 2$. We set $\tilde{\xi}(t) = (\tilde{x}^T(t) \; \tilde{u}_1^T(t) \; \tilde{u}_2^T(t))^T$ and define $X(t) = \mathbb{E}[\tilde{\xi}(t)\tilde{\xi}^T(t)]$.
  We have $t \to X(t)$ solves the forward linear differential equation with finite jumps:

$$\dot{X}(t) = LX(t), \quad t_j \leq t < t_{j+1}. \quad (41)$$

For $t_j = jh$ we write:

$$X(t_j^+) = (\mathbf{A}_d + \mathbf{B}_{d1}\tilde{\mathbf{F}}_1(j) + \mathbf{B}_{d2}\tilde{\mathbf{F}}_2(j)) X(t_j) \cdot (\mathbf{A}_d + \mathbf{B}_{d1}\tilde{\mathbf{F}}_1(j) + \mathbf{B}_{d2}\tilde{\mathbf{F}}_2(j))^T \quad (42)$$

$0 \leq j \leq N - 1$, $t_j = jh$, where

$$LX = \mathbf{A}X + X\mathbf{A}^T + \mathbf{C}X\mathbf{C}^T. \quad (43)$$

Then, we have used the values to make plots

$$\mathbb{E}[|\tilde{x}(i\delta + jh)|^2] = Tr[X_{11}(i\delta + jh)]$$
$$\mathbb{E}[|\tilde{u}_1(i\delta + jh)|^2] = Tr[X_{22}(i\delta + jh)]$$
$$\mathbb{E}[|\tilde{u}_2(i\delta + jh)|^2] = Tr[X_{33}(i\delta + jh)],$$

where

$$X(i\delta + jh) = \begin{pmatrix} X_{11}(i\delta + jh) & X_{12}(i\delta + jh) & X_{13}(i\delta + jh) \\ X_{12}^T(i\delta + jh) & X_{22}(i\delta + jh) & X_{23}(i\delta + jh) \\ X_{13}^T(i\delta + jh) & X_{23}^T(i\delta + jh) & X_{33}(i\delta + jh) \end{pmatrix}$$

such that $X_{11}(i\delta + jh) \in \mathbb{R}^{n \times n}$, $X_{22}(i\delta + jh) \in \mathbb{R}^{m_1 \times m_1}$ and $X_{33}(i\delta + jh) \in \mathbb{R}^{m_2 \times m_2}$.

This algorithm enables us to compute the equilibrium strategies values $u_k(j)$ of the players. The experiments illustrate that the optimal strategies are piecewise constant, which seems to indicate that we have a stabilization effect.

Further, we consider two examples for the LQ differential game described by the dynamical system (1), the performance criteria (2) and the class of piecewise constant admissible strategies of type (28).

Example 1. *We consider the controlled system (1) in the special form $n = m_1 = m_2 = 2$. The coefficient matrices A, B_k, C, D_k, M_k, G_k, R_{kk}, $R_{k\ell}$, $k, \ell = 1, 2$, $k \neq \ell$ are defined as*

$$A = \begin{pmatrix} 1.5 & 0.17 \\ 0.07 & -1.4 \end{pmatrix} \quad B_1 = \begin{pmatrix} 1.5 & 0.7 \\ 0.3 & 0.4 \end{pmatrix} \quad B_2 = \begin{pmatrix} 1.2 & 0.95 \\ 0.8 & 0.7 \end{pmatrix}$$

$$C = \begin{pmatrix} 0.7 & 0.19 \\ 0.24 & 0.9 \end{pmatrix} \quad D_1 = \begin{pmatrix} 0.2 & 0.04 \\ 0.4 & 0.5 \end{pmatrix} \quad D_2 = \begin{pmatrix} 0.1 & 0.06 \\ 0.2 & 0.3 \end{pmatrix}$$

$$M_1 = \begin{pmatrix} 0.8 & 0.7 \\ 0.7 & 0.95 \end{pmatrix} \quad M_2 = \begin{pmatrix} 0.09 & 0.04 \\ 0.04 & 0.08 \end{pmatrix}$$

$$G_1 = \begin{pmatrix} 1.2 & 0.45 \\ 0.45 & 1.5 \end{pmatrix} \quad G_2 = \begin{pmatrix} 0.95 & 0.8 \\ 0.8 & 1.15 \end{pmatrix}$$

$$R_{11} = \begin{pmatrix} 0.6 & 0.25 \\ 0.25 & 0.8 \end{pmatrix} \quad R_{22} = \begin{pmatrix} 0.3 & 0.15 \\ 0.15 & 0.4 \end{pmatrix}$$

$$R_{12} = \begin{pmatrix} 0.05 & 0.04 \\ 0.04 & 0.08 \end{pmatrix} \quad R_{21} = \begin{pmatrix} 0.06 & 0.07 \\ 0.07 & 0.09 \end{pmatrix}.$$

The evolution of the mean square values $\mathbb{E}[|\tilde{x}(t)|]^2$ and $\mathbb{E}[|u_{opt}(t)|]^2$ of the optimal trajectory $\tilde{x}(t)$ (with the initial point $x_0^T = (0.03 \; 0.01)$) and the equilibrium strategies $u_{1,opt}(t)$ and $u_{2,opt}(t)$ is depicted in Figure 1 on the intervals $[0, 1]$, and in Figure 2 for $[0, 2]$, respectively. The values of the optimal trajectory $\tilde{x}(t)$ equilibrium strategies of both players are very close to zero in both the short-term and long-term periods.

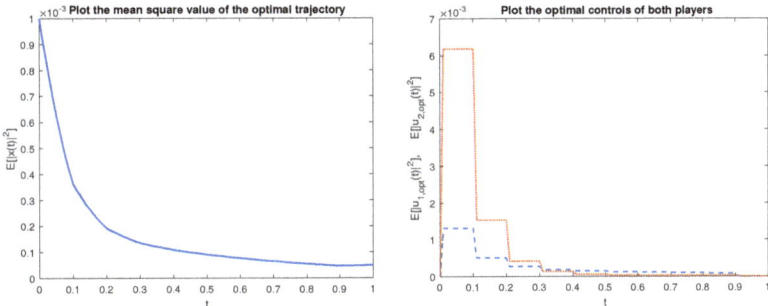

Figure 1. (**left**) $\mathbb{E}[|\tilde{x}(t)|^2]$; Interval $[t_0, \tau] = [0, 1]$; (**right**) $\mathbb{E}[|u_{1,opt}(t)|^2]$ and $\mathbb{E}[|u_{2,opt}(t)|^2]$; Interval $[t_0, \tau] = [0, 1]$.

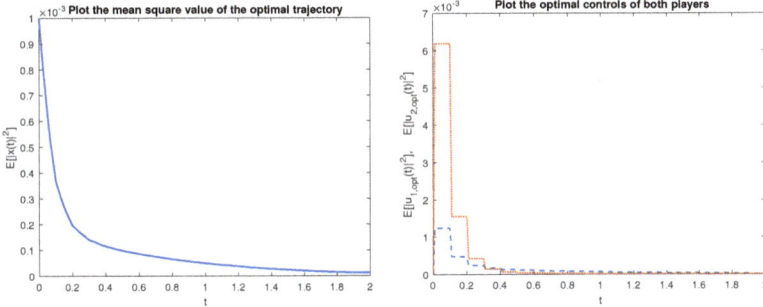

Figure 2. (**left**) $\mathbb{E}[|\tilde{x}(t)|^2]$; Interval $[t_0, \tau] = [0, 2]$; (**right**) $\mathbb{E}[|u_{1,opt}(t)|^2]$ and $\mathbb{E}[|u_{2,opt}(t)|^2]$; Interval $[t_0, \tau] = [0, 2]$.

Example 2. *We consider the controlled system (1) in the special form $n = 4$ and $m_1 = m_2 = 2$. We define the matrix coefficients A, B_k, C, D_k, M_k, G_k, R_{kk}, $R_{k\ell}$, $k, \ell = 1, 2, k \neq \ell$ as follows:*

$$A = \begin{pmatrix} 0.5 & 0.17 & 0.07 & 0.9 \\ 0.07 & 0.54 & 0.2 & 0.25 \\ 0.6 & 0.8 & 0.92 & 0.06 \\ 0.35 & 0.45 & 0.04 & -0.99 \end{pmatrix} \quad B_1 = \begin{pmatrix} 4.05 & -0.4 \\ 0.4 & -0.8 \\ 1 & 0.9 \\ 0 & -0.8 \end{pmatrix}$$

$$C = \begin{pmatrix} 0.07 & 0.19 & 0.8 & 0 \\ 0.4 & 0.18 & 0.24 & 0.7 \\ 0.06 & 0.3 & 0.15 & 0.4 \\ 0.45 & 0.37 & 0.09 & 0.08 \end{pmatrix} \quad D_1 = \begin{pmatrix} 0.15 & 0 \\ -0.2 & 0.25 \\ 0 & 0.035 \\ 0.04 & -0.2 \end{pmatrix}$$

$$B_2 = \begin{pmatrix} 0.4 & 0.05 \\ 0.05 & -0.07 \\ 0 & 0.07 \\ 0.3 & -0.05 \end{pmatrix} \quad D_2 = \begin{pmatrix} 0.25 & 0.525 \\ 1.25 & -0.025 \\ 0.35 & -0.75 \\ 0.25 & -0.9 \end{pmatrix}$$

$$M_1 = \begin{pmatrix} 0.78 & 0 & 0 & 0 \\ 0 & 0.82 & 0 & 0 \\ 0 & 0 & 0.6 & 0 \\ 0 & 0 & 0 & 0.5 \end{pmatrix} \quad M_2 = \begin{pmatrix} 0.6 & 0 & 0 & 0 \\ 0 & 0.8 & 0 & 0 \\ 0 & 0 & 0.48 & 0 \\ 0 & 0 & 0 & 1.05 \end{pmatrix}$$

$$G_1 = \begin{pmatrix} 0.9 & 0.05 & 0.25 & 0.35 \\ 0.05 & 1 & 0.2 & 0.07 \\ 0.25 & 0.2 & 1.05 & 0.3 \\ 0.35 & 0.07 & 0.3 & 0.9 \end{pmatrix} \quad G_2 = \begin{pmatrix} 1.25 & 0.75 & 0.21 & 0.65 \\ 0.75 & 0.88 & 0.45 & 0.76 \\ 0.21 & 0.45 & 1 & 0.87 \\ 0.65 & 0.76 & 0.87 & 0.99 \end{pmatrix}$$

$$R_{11} = \begin{pmatrix} 1.26 & 0.25 & 0.25 & 0.8 \\ 0.25 & 0.95 & 0.15 & 0.4 \\ 0.25 & 0.15 & 0.96 & 0.3 \\ 0.8 & 0.4 & 0.3 & 0.88 \end{pmatrix} \quad R_{22} = \begin{pmatrix} 0.6 & 0.15 & 0.15 & 0.4 \\ 0.15 & 0.85 & 0.36 & 0.4 \\ 0.15 & 0.36 & 0.4 & 0.25 \\ 0.4 & 0.4 & 0.25 & 0.87 \end{pmatrix}$$

$$R_{12} = \begin{pmatrix} 0.98 & 0.04 & 0.36 & 0.4 \\ 0.04 & 0.8 & 0.36 & 0.45 \\ 0.36 & 0.36 & 0.64 & 0.1 \\ 0.4 & 0.45 & 0.1 & 0.89 \end{pmatrix} \quad R_{21} = \begin{pmatrix} 0.6 & 0.07 & 0.35 & 0.28 \\ 0.07 & 0.8 & 0.39 & 0.25 \\ 0.35 & 0.39 & 1.2 & 0.48 \\ 0.28 & 0.25 & 0.48 & 1.01 \end{pmatrix}.$$

The evolution of the mean square values $\mathbb{E}[||\tilde{x}(t)||]^2$ and $\mathbb{E}[||u_{opt}(t)||]^2$ of the optimal trajectory $\tilde{x}(t)$ (with the initial point $x_0^T = (0.15 \ 0.01 \ 0.02 \ 0.03 \ )$) and the equilibrium strategies $u_{1,opt}(t)$ and $u_{2,opt}(t)$ on the intervals $[0, 1]$ (Figure 3) and $[0, 5]$ (Figure 4), respectively. The values of the optimal trajectory $\tilde{x}(t)$ equilibrium strategies of both players are very close to zero in short-term and long-term period.

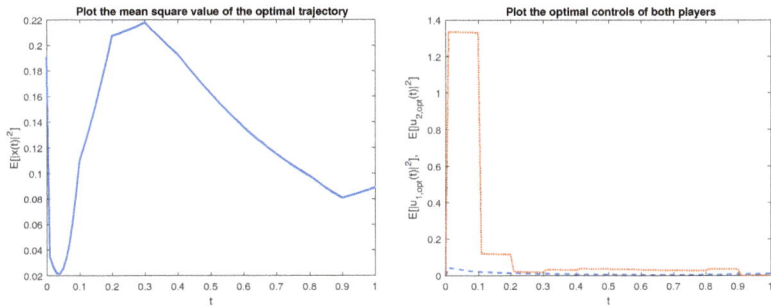

Figure 3. (**left**) $\mathbb{E}[|\tilde{x}(t)|^2]$; Interval $[t_0, \tau] = [0,1]$; (**right**) $\mathbb{E}[|u_{1,opt}(t)|^2]$ and $\mathbb{E}[|u_{2,opt}(t)|^2]$; Interval $[t_0, \tau] = [0,1]$.

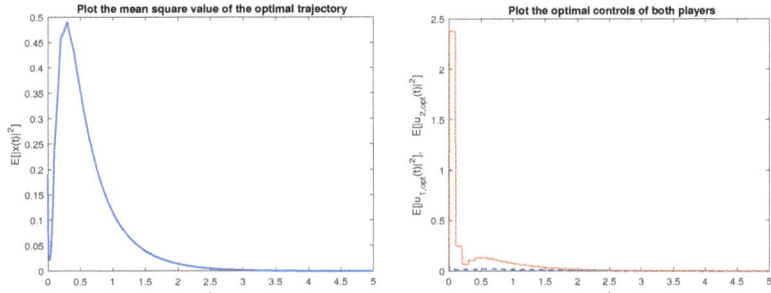

Figure 4. (**left**) $\mathbb{E}[|\tilde{x}(t)|^2]$; Interval $[t_0, \tau] = [0,5]$; (**right**) $\mathbb{E}[|u_{1,opt}(t)|^2]$ and $\mathbb{E}[|u_{2,opt}(t)|^2]$; Interval $[t_0, \tau] = [0,5]$.

4. Concluding Remarks

In this paper, we have investigated the formulation of existence conditions for the Nash equilibria strategy in a state feedback form, in the piecewise constant admissible strategies case. These conditions are expressed through the solvability of the algebraic Equation (26). The solutions of these equations provide the feedback matrices of the desired Nash equilibrium strategy. To obtain such conditions for the existence of a sampled-data Nash equilibrium strategy, we have transformed the original problem into an equivalent one which requires to find a Nash equilibrium strategy in a state feedback form for a stochastic differential game, in which the dynamic is described by Itô type differential equations controlled by impulses. Unlike for the deterministic case, when the problem of finding of a sampled-data Nash equilibrium strategy can be transformed into an equivalent problem in discrete-time, in the stochastic framework when the controlled system is described by Itô type differential equations, such a transformation to the discrete-time case is not possible. The developments from the present work clarify and extend the results from Section 5 of [23], where only the particular case $L = 2$ was considered. The key method used for obtaining the feedback matrices of the Nash equilibrium strategy via the Equation (26) is the solution $\tilde{P}_k(\cdot), 1 \leq k \leq L$ of the TVP (16). On each interval $(t_{j-1}, t_j), 1 \leq j \leq N$, (16a) consists of L uncoupled backward linear differential equation. The boundary values $\tilde{P}_k(t_j^-)$ are computed via (16d) for $j = N$ and via (16b) for $j \leq N - 1$. Finally, we gave an algorithm for calculating the equilibrium strategies of the players, and the numerical experiments suggest a stabilization effect.

Author Contributions: Conceptualization, V.D., I.G.I., I.-L.P. and O.B.; methodology, V.D., I.G.I., I.-L.P. and O.B.; software, V.D., I.G.I., I.-L.P. and O.B.; validation, V.D., I.G.I., I.-L.P. and O.B.; investigation, V.D., I.G.I., I.-L.P. and O.B.; resources, V.D., I.G.I., I.-L.P. and O.B.; writing—original draft preparation, V.D., I.G.I., I.-L.P. and O.B.; writing—review and editing, V.D., I.G.I., I.-L.P. and O.B. All authors have read and agreed to the published version of the manuscript.

Funding: This research was funded by "1 Decembrie 1918" University of Alba Iulia through scientific research funds.

Institutional Review Board Statement: Not applicable.

Informed Consent Statement: Not applicable.

Data Availability Statement: Not applicable.

Conflicts of Interest: The authors declare no conflict of interest.

References

1. Hu, L.S.; Cao, Y.Y.; Shao, H.H. Constrained robust sampled-data control for nonlinear uncertain systems. *Int. J. Robust Nonlinear Control* **2002**, *12*, 447–464. [CrossRef]
2. Hu, L.-S.; Lam, J.; Cao, Y.-Y.; Shao, H.-H. A linear matrix inequality (LMI) approach to robust H/sub 2/sampled-data control for linear uncertain systems. *IEEE Trans. Syst. Man Cybern. Part B Cybern.* **2003**, *33*, 149–155. [CrossRef]
3. Hu, L.; Shi, P.; Huang, B. Stochastic stability and robust control for sampled-data systems with Markovian jump parameters. *J. Math. Anal. Appl.* **2006**, 504–517. [CrossRef]
4. Ramachandran, K.; Tsokos, C. *Stochastic Differential Games Theory and Applications*; Atlantis Studies in Probability and Statistics; Atlantis Press: Dordrecht, The Netherlands, 2012.
5. Yeung, D.K.; Petrosyan, L.A. *Cooperative Stochastic Differential Games*; Springer Series in Operations Research and Financial Engineering; Springer: New York, NY, USA, 2006.
6. Zhang, J. *Backward Stochastic Differential Equations: From Linear to Fully Nonlinear Theory*; Probability Theory and Stochastic Modelling; Springer: New York, NY, USA, 2017; Volume 86.
7. Dockner, E.; Jorgensen, S.; Long, N.; Sorger, G. *Differential Games in Economics and Management Science*; Cambridge University Press: Cambridge, UK, 2000. [CrossRef]
8. Başar, T.; Olsder, G.J. *Dynamic Noncooperative Game Theory*; Classics in Applied Mathematics; Society for Industrial and Applied Mathematics: Philadelphia, PA, USA, 1999; Volume 23.
9. Engwerda, J. On the open-loop Nash equilibrium in LQ-games. *J. Econ. Dyn. Control* **1998**, *22*, 729–762. [CrossRef]
10. Engwerda, J. Computational aspects of the open-loop Nash equilibrium in linear quadratic games. *J. Econ. Dyn. Control* **1998**, *22*, 1487–1506. [CrossRef]
11. Engwerda, J. Open-loop Nash equilibria in the non-cooperative infinite-planning horizon LQ game. *J. Frankl. Inst.* **2014**, *351*, 2657–2674. [CrossRef]
12. Nian, X.; Duan, Z.; Tang, W. Analytical solution for a class of linear quadratic open-loop Nash game with multiple players. *J. Control Theory Appl.* **2006**, *4*, 239–244. [CrossRef]
13. Azevedo-Perdicoúlis, T.P.; Jank, G. Disturbance Attenuation of Linear Quadratic OL-Nash Games on Repetitive Processes with Smoothing on the Gas Dynamics. *Multidimens. Syst. Signal Process.* **2012**, *23*, 131–153. [CrossRef]
14. Imaan, M.; Cruz, J. Sampled-data Nash controls in non-zero-sum differential games. *Int. J. Control* **1973**, *17*, 1201–1209. [CrossRef]
15. Başar, T. On the existence and uniqueness of closed-loop sampled-data nash controls in linear-quadratic stochastic differential games. In *Optimization Techniques*; Iracki, K., Malanowski, K., Walukiewicz, S., Eds.; Lecture Notes in Control and Information Sciences; Springer: Berlin/Heidelberg, Germany, 1980; Volume 22, pp. 193–203.
16. Engwerda, J. A numerical algorithm to find soft-constrained Nash equilibria in scalar LQ-games. *Int. J. Control* **2006**, *79*, 592–603. [CrossRef]
17. Wonham, W.M. On a Matrix Riccati Equation of Stochastic Control. *SIAM J. Control* **1968**, *6*, 681–697. [CrossRef]
18. Yong, J.S.J. Linear–quadratic stochastic two-person nonzero-sum differential games: Open-loop and closed-loop Nash equilibria. *Stoch. Process. Appl.* **2019**, 381–418. [CrossRef]
19. Sun, J.; Li, X.; Yong, J. Open-Loop and Closed-Loop Solvabilities for Stochastic Linear Quadratic Optimal Control Problems. *SIAM J. Control Optim.* **2016**, *54*, 2274–2308. [CrossRef]
20. Drăgan, V.; Ivanov, I.G. On the stochastic linear quadratic control problem with piecewise constant admissible controls. *J. Frankl. Inst.* **2020**, *357*, 1532–1559. [CrossRef]
21. Rami, M.; Moore, J.; Zhou, X. Indefinite stochastic linear quadratic control and generalized differential Riccati equation. *Siam J. Control Optim.* **2001**, *40*, 1296–1311. [CrossRef]

22. Drăgan, V.; Ivanov, I.G.; Popa, I.L. Stochastic linear quadratic differential games in a state feedback setting with sampled measurements. *Syst. Control Lett.* **2019**, 104563. [CrossRef]
23. Drăgan, V.; Ivanov, I.G.; Popa, I.L. On the closed loop Nash equilibrium strategy for a class of sampled data stochastic linear quadratic differential games. *Chaos Solitons Fractals* **2020**, 109877. [CrossRef]

Article

High-Order Filtered PID Controller Tuning Based on Magnitude Optimum

Damir Vrančić [1],* and Mikuláš Huba [2]

1. Jožef Stefan Institute, SI-1000 Ljubljana, Slovenia
2. Faculty of Electrical Engineering and Information Technology, Slovak University of Technology in Bratislava, Ilovičova 3, 81219 Bratislava, Slovakia; mikulas.huba@stuba.sk
* Correspondence: damir.vrancic@ijs.si

Abstract: The paper presents a tuning method for PID controllers with higher-order derivatives and higher-order controller filters (HO-PID), where the controller and filter orders can be arbitrarily chosen by the user. The controller and filter parameters are tuned according to the magnitude optimum criteria and the specified noise gain of the controller. The advantages of the proposed approach are twofold. First, all parameters can be obtained from the process transfer function or from the measured input and output time responses of the process as the steady-state changes. Second, the a priori defined controller noise gain limits the amount of HO-PID output noise. Therefore, the method can be successfully applied in practice. The work shows that the HO-PID controllers can significantly improve the control performance of various process models compared to the standard PID controllers. Of course, the increased efficiency is limited by the selected noise gain. The proposed tuning method is illustrated on several process models and compared with two other tuning methods for higher-order controllers.

Keywords: higher-order controllers; PID controller; magnitude optimum; controller tuning; noise attenuation

1. Introduction

The PID controllers are widespread in many industries and are frequently included in embedded solutions [1–4]. This is not surprising, since the basic PID control algorithm is very simple and the control performance, when the controller is tuned appropriately, is usually very good. However, the control performance can be improved by increasing the controller order. The improvement depends on the process order. While the first-order process can be efficiently controlled by the PI controller and the second-order process by the PID controller, the control efficiency for higher-order processes can be improved by increasing the controller order beyond the PID control.

In practice the PI controllers are used more often than the PID controllers, since the latter significantly increase the controller output noise. Naturally, with higher degrees of controllers, the problem becomes aggravated. Therefore, the appropriate higher-order controller filter is inevitable in practical applications.

For easier classification of the HO-PID controllers according to the controller (m) and filter (n) order, let us denote them as PID_n^m. A general PID_n^m controller transfer function $G_{CF}(s)$ can be defined as follows:

$$G_{CF}(s) = G_C(s) G_F(s), \text{ where}$$
$$G_C(s) = \left(K_{-1}s^{-1} + K_0 + K_1 s + \cdots + K_m s^m\right) \quad (1)$$
$$G_F(s) = \frac{1}{(1+T_F s)^n}$$

where $K_{-1}, K_0, K_1, \ldots K_m$ are controller gains, and $G_F(s)$ is the binomial filter with filter time constant T_F. In practical applications, in order to limit the higher-frequency controller output noise, $n \geq m$. Note that PID_0^0 denotes the PI controller ($K_I = K_{-1}$, $K_P = K_0$) and PID_1^1 denotes the PID controller ($K_I = K_{-1}$, $K_P = K_0$, $K_D = K_1$) with the first-order filter ($n = 1$).

Several tuning methods for HO-PID controllers have been proposed so far. The majority of them are made for proportional-integrative-derivative-accelerative (PIDA) controllers (PID_n^2). The controller structure is either 1 degree of freedom (1-DOF) [5–20] or 2 degrees of freedom (2-DOF) [21–23] which can optimise the tracking and control performance.

The tuning methods for the mentioned PIDA controllers are derived either for the first-order process with delay [20,22,23], third order process [5,11,13,14,21], first-order double integrating process [5,11,16], second-order integrating process [8,9,11,16], double integrating process with time delay [10], fourth-order system [18], for different types of process models [6,17,18] or for the automatic voltage regulator (AVR) in the generator excitation system [7,15,19]. Unfortunately, only a few of the mentioned PIDA controller tuning methods take into account the controller filter in the controller design stage [5–7,10,15,23]. Therefore, the practical implementation of other PIDA tuning methods remains questionable.

Besides PIDA controllers, some higher-order controller tuning methods also exist [24–27]. The tuning method for the PID_0^3 controller (the controller filter is not considered), where the controlled process is a model of the ship power plant, including the heat exchanger, is given in [24]. The method optimises the IAE for disturbance rejection while limiting the peak of the closed-loop amplitude frequency response.

Tuning methods for even higher-order controllers ($m > 3$) were developed for the integrating process model with a time delay (IPTD) [25–27]. Although the type of the process model seems to be limited, we have to mention that many stable process models can be modelled as IPTD processes [1]. For HO-PID control of stable time-delayed processes, a new method was also proposed by generalizing Skogestad's method SIMC [28]. The basic version is based on the approximation of processes by transfer functions with multiple time constants (obtained, for example, by an appropriate identification method); however, a suitable model can also be obtained from a more general description of the process reduced by the modified "half-rule" method [29]. Although not specifically designed for HO-PID controllers, we should also mention that the tuning approach is based on the design of multiple dominant closed-loop poles for delayed processes, applied to the PI and PID controllers [30], which can be easily extended to HO-PID controllers.

The developed tuning methods for the PID_n^m controllers reveal that the HO-PID controllers can be much more efficient than the ordinary PID controllers without significant increase of the controller output noise.

This paper presents the PID_n^m controller and filter tuning method, which is based on the parametric or the non-parametric process description. It means that the process can be given by the general transfer function (of the arbitrary order and time delay) or by the process input and output time-responses during the steady-state change of the process. The only user-defined parameters will be the controller (m) and the filter (n) order and the desired high-frequency gain of the controller. As will be shown later, the controller parameters will be calculated analytically.

Therefore, the main advantages of the proposed method are the flexibility of the process description (the process model is not required), simple specifications by the user and simple calculation of the controller and filter parameters.

The content of the paper is as follows. The tuning method for the PID_n^m controllers is covered in Section 2. The calculation of the controller and controller filter time constant, according to the desired closed-loop high-frequency gain, is derived in Section 3. The comparison with some other tuning methods is carried out in Section 4. The paper concludes with Section 5.

2. HO-PID Controller Tuning

The HO-PID controller parameters will be derived according to the magnitude optimum multiple integration (MOMI) tuning method, which is based on the magnitude optimum (MO) criteria [31–37]. The main advantages of the MOMI method are that it combines frequency-domain MO tuning criterion (providing a fast and non-oscillatory closed-loop process output response) with the time-domain method of moments (the calculation of the process characteristic areas directly from the process time responses).

The process

The general order process transfer function with time delay is defined by the following expression:

$$G_P(s) = \frac{K_{PR}(1 + b_1 s + b_2 s^2 + \cdots + b_r s^r)}{1 + a_1 s + a_2 s^2 + \cdots + a_p s^p} e^{-s T_{del}} \quad (2)$$

where K_{PR} is the process gain, T_{del} is the process time delay and a_1 to a_p and b_1 to b_r are the process dynamic parameters. To simplify the derivation, let us assume that the process transfer function is developed into an infinite Taylor series around $s = 0$:

$$G_P(s) = G_{P0} + G_{P1} s + \frac{G_{P2}}{2!} s^2 + \frac{G_{P3}}{3!} s^3 + \cdots, \quad (3)$$

where G_{Pk} are the k-th derivatives of the $G_P(s)$ over s around $s = 0$. The moments can be calculated from the process impulse response $h(t)$ in the following way [1,38]:

$$G_P^{(k)}(0) = G_{Pk} = (-1)^k \int_0^\infty t^k h(t) dt \quad (4)$$

Besides measuring the process impulse response, the moments can also be calculated from the process steady-state change by measuring the process input and output time responses [32,34]. By integrating the process input and output time responses, the so-called characteristic areas A_k are obtained, which are related to the process moments as follows:

$$A_k = \frac{(-1)^k}{k!} G_{Pk} \quad (5)$$

The process transfer function, based on the characteristic areas, can be derived from (3) and (5) as follows:

$$G_P(s) = A_0 - A_1 s + A_2 s^2 - A_3 s^3 + \cdots. \quad (6)$$

Since the calculation of the mentioned areas from the process input and output time responses, during arbitrary steady-state change, are already covered in detail in [36], it will not be repeated herein.

The process moments (4) and, therefore, the characteristic areas A_k (5), can also be calculated from the process transfer function (2) by calculating the derivatives of $G_P(s)$ over s around $s = 0$. The result is the following [32,34]:

$$\begin{aligned} A_0 &= K_{PR} \\ A_1 &= K_{PR}(a_1 - b_1 + T_{del}) \\ A_2 &= A_1 a_1 + K_{PR}\left(b_2 - a_2 - T_{del} b_1 + \frac{T_{del}^2}{2!}\right) \\ &\vdots \\ A_k &= \sum_{i=1}^{k-1}(-1)^{k+i-1} A_1 a_{k-i} + (-1)^{k+1} K_{PR}(a_k - b_k) + K_{PR} \sum_{i=1}^{k} \frac{(-1)^{k+i}}{i!} T_{del}^i b_{k-i} \end{aligned} \quad (7)$$

Therefore, the characteristic areas in expression (6) can be calculated either from the process time response or from the process transfer function. This is a very important advantage, since the actual process model can be used, but is not required.

In order to simplify the derivation of the controller parameters, the controller binomial filter $G_F(s)$ (1) will be considered as a part of the process. Since the above areas are calculated for the process without the filter, the areas A_i should be modified, accordingly. If the filter

$G_F(s)$ (1) is added to the process (2) and developed into a Taylor series, it can be derived that the new areas, denoted by A_{iF}, can be simply calculated as:

$$A_{VF} = M_F^n A_V, \text{ where}$$

$$M_F = \begin{bmatrix} 1 & 0 & 0 & 0 & 0 & 0 \\ T_F & 1 & 0 & 0 & 0 & 0 \\ T_F^2 & T_F & 1 & 0 & 0 & 0 \\ T_F^3 & T_F^2 & T_F & 1 & 0 & 0 \\ T_F^4 & T_F^3 & T_F^2 & T_F & 1 & 0 \\ \vdots & \vdots & \vdots & \vdots & T_F & \ddots \end{bmatrix}, A_V = \begin{bmatrix} A_0 \\ A_1 \\ A_2 \\ A_3 \\ A_4 \\ \vdots \end{bmatrix}, A_{VF} = \begin{bmatrix} A_{0F} \\ A_{1F} \\ A_{2F} \\ A_{3F} \\ A_{4F} \\ \vdots \end{bmatrix} \quad (8)$$

Note that n is the binomial filter order (1). Naturally, the chosen size of the matrix and the vectors depends on the number of the required areas.

Note that the characteristic areas with the included controller filter can be obtained a-posteriori, when the process areas A_i are already measured either from the process time response (5) or calculated from the process transfer function (7).

For further reference, please note that the process areas with the included controller binomial filter are denoted with index F (A_{iF}) and the process areas without the controller filter are denoted without index F (A_i).

The closed-loop transfer function

In the paper, the process and the HO-PID controller (1) will be considered, as shown in Figure 1. Signals r, r_f, e, u, d, n and y stand for the reference, filtered reference, control error, controller output, process input disturbance, process output noise and the process output, respectively. Block G_{FR} represents the second order filter for the reference signal in order to reduce excessive controller output change on reference changes:

$$G_{FR}(s) = \frac{1}{(1 + T_{FR}s)^2}, \quad (9)$$

where T_{FR} denotes the reference filter time constant. Due to simplicity, the filter order in (9) is fixed. However, note that the filter order may be increased by increasing the controller order so as to additionally attenuate the swings of the signal u for step-like changes of the reference signal r.

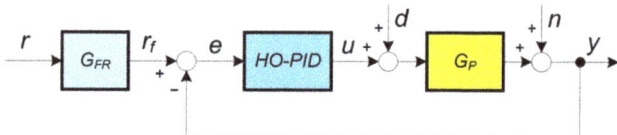

Figure 1. The control loop with HO-PID controller and the process.

Let us now calculate the process closed-loop transfer function $G_{CL}(s)$ from the filtered reference (r_f) to the process output (y). The closed-loop transfer function is then defined as:

$$G_{CL}(s) = \frac{Y(s)}{R_F(s)} = \frac{G_C G_P}{1 + G_C G_P}, \quad (10)$$

where $Y(s)$ and $R(s)$ are the Laplace transforms of the process output and the reference signals, respectively.

When applying the process (6) and the controller (1) transfer functions to (10), and considering that the controller binomial filter is a part of the process (in the process transfer function (6) the areas A_i are replaced by A_{iF}), the closed-loop transfer function becomes:

$$G_{CL}(s) = \frac{G_{OL}(s)}{1+G_{OL}(s)},$$
$$G_{OL}(s) = A_{0F}K_{-1}s^{-1} + (A_{0F}K_0 - A_{1F}K_{-1}) + s(A_{0F}K_1 - A_{1F}K_0 + A_{2F}K_{-1})$$
$$+ s^2(A_{0F}K_2 - A_{1F}K_1 + A_{2F}K_0 - A_{3F}K_{-1}) + \cdots \quad (11)$$
$$+ s^k \sum_{i=0}^{k+1} (-1)^i A_{iF}K_{k-i} + \cdots$$

where $G_{OL}(s)$ denotes the open-loop transfer function $G_{OL}(s) = G_C(s)G_P(s)$.

The MO criteria

According to [35], the MO tuning criterion states that the closed-loop amplitude (magnitude) should be 1 in as wide a frequency bandwidth as possible (starting from frequency $\omega = 0$). This can be achieved if the open-loop transfer function $G_{OL}(j\omega)$, in the Nyquist diagram, follows the vertical line with the real value -0.5 (according to M and N circles in control theory).

Replacing s with complex frequency $j\omega$ in $G_{OL}(s)$ (11) yields:

$$G_{OL}(s) = -jA_{0F}K_{-1}\omega^{-1} + (A_{0F}K_0 - A_{1F}K_{-1}) + j\omega(A_{0F}K_1 - A_{1F}K_0 + A_{2F}K_{-1})$$
$$- \omega^2(A_{0F}K_2 - A_{1F}K_1 + A_{2F}K_0 - A_{3F}K_{-1}) + \cdots \quad (12)$$
$$+ (j\omega)^k \sum_{i=0}^{k+1} (-1)^i A_{iF}K_{k-i} + \cdots$$

where j denotes the imaginary component $j = \sqrt{-1}$.

Since merely the real part of the open-loop transfer function is required, only the even powers over frequency in (12) are needed. Therefore:

$$Re\{G_{OL}(s)\} = (A_{0F}K_0 - A_{1F}K_{-1}) - \omega^2(A_{0F}K_2 - A_{1F}K_1 + A_{2F}K_0 - A_{3F}K_{-1}) + \cdots$$
$$+ (-1)^q \omega^{2q} \sum_{i=0}^{2q+1} (-1)^i A_{iF}K_{2q-i} + \cdots \quad (13)$$

In order to achieve that the $Re\{G_{OL}(s)\} = -0.5$ for as high frequencies as possible, the following conditions should be fulfilled:

$$-A_{1F}K_{-1} + A_{0F}K_0 = -0.5$$
$$-A_{3F}K_{-1} + A_{2F}K_0 - A_{1F}K_1 + A_{0F}K_2 = 0$$
$$-A_{5F}K_{-1} + A_{4F}K_0 - A_{3F}K_1 + A_{2F}K_2 - A_{1F}K_3 + A_{0F}K_4 = 0 \quad (14)$$
$$\vdots$$

or in matrix form:

$$MK_V = C, \text{ where}$$

$$M_F = \begin{bmatrix} -A_{1F} & A_{0F} & 0 & 0 & 0 & \cdots \\ -A_{3F} & A_{2F} & -A_{1F} & A_{0F} & 0 & \cdots \\ -A_{5F} & A_{4F} & -A_{3F} & A_{2F} & -A_{1F} & \cdots \\ -A_{7F} & A_{6F} & -A_{5F} & A_{4F} & -A_{3F} & \cdots \\ -A_{9F} & A_{8F} & -A_{7F} & A_{6F} & -A_{5F} & \cdots \\ \vdots & \vdots & \vdots & \vdots & \vdots & \end{bmatrix}, K_V = \begin{bmatrix} A_{-1} \\ K_0 \\ K_1 \\ K_2 \\ K_3 \\ \vdots \end{bmatrix}, C = \begin{bmatrix} -0.5 \\ 0 \\ 0 \\ 0 \\ 0 \\ \vdots \end{bmatrix} \quad (15)$$

Note that the matrix and vector dimensions depend on the number of controller parameters $(m + 2)$:

$$M_{(m+2)\times(m+2)}, K_{V_{(m+2)\times 1}}, C_{(m+2)\times 1} \quad (16)$$

The controller parameters (gains) can then be simply calculated from (15):

$$K_V = M^{-1}C \qquad (17)$$

The calculation of the controller and filter parameters is straightforward. However, to make it even simpler, we have provided online MATLAB/Octave scripts via the OctaveOnline Bucket website [39]. The provided scripts calculate all the controller parameters for the given process transfer function and the filter time constant. The website layout is shown in Figure 2. The calculation procedure proceeds as follows:

1. Select the appropriate Octave (MATLAB) script (test_HO_TF.m).
2. Provide the process parameters, the filter time constant, the controller order and filter order,
3. press the "Save" button, and
4. press the "Run" button.

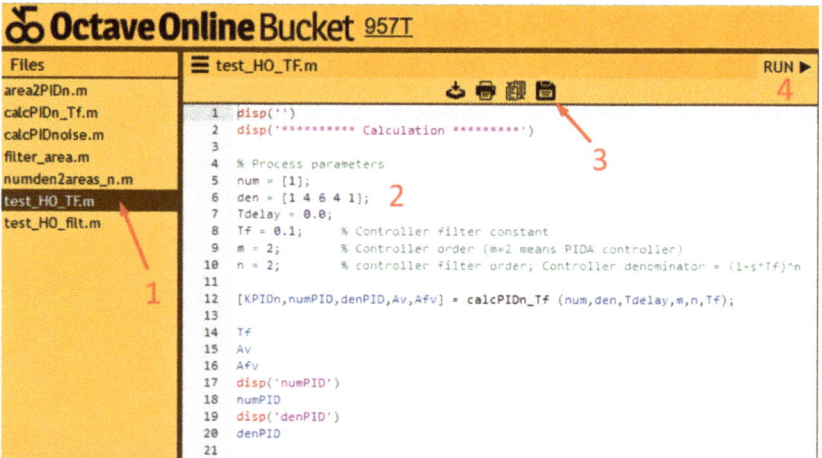

Figure 2. The layout of the OctaveOnline Bucket website (function test_HO_TF.m).

The script then calculates the characteristic areas, the controller and the filter parameters. The results are then shown on the right panel of the website.

Illustrative example 1

The D_1^1, PID_2^2 and PID_3^3 controller parameters will be calculated for the following processes:

$$\begin{aligned} G_{P1}(s) &= \frac{1}{(1+s)^4} \\ G_{P2}(s) &= \frac{e^{-0.5s}}{(1+s)^2} \end{aligned} \qquad (18)$$

The chosen controller filter time constants is $T_F = 0.1$. The characteristic areas, without (7), and with controller filter (8) are given in Table 1.

Table 1. The calculated areas for the processes (18) without and with the controller filter.

	A_0	A_1	A_2	A_3	A_4	A_5	A_6	A_7	A_8	A_9
Areas G_{P1}	1	4	10	20	35	56	84	120	165	220
Areas G_{P1} with controller PID_1^1 filter	1	4.1	10.41	21.041	37.104	59.71				
Areas G_{P1} with controller PID_2^2 filter	1	4.2	10.83	22.124	39.317	63.64	96.34	138.63		
Areas G_{P1} with controller PID_3^3 filter	1	4.3	11.26	23.25	41.642	67.81	103.12	148.94	206.66	277.63
Areas G_{P2}	1	2.5	4.125	5.771	7.419	9.068	10.717	12.365	14.014	15.663
Areas G_{P2} with controller PID_1^1 filter	1	2.6	4.385	6.209	8.040	9.872				
Areas G_{P2} with controlle PID_2^2 filter	1	2.7	4.655	6.675	8.708	10.743	12.778	14.814		
Areas G_{P2} with controller PID_3^3 filter	1	2.8	4.935	7.168	9.425	11.685	13.947	16.208	18.470	20.732

The calculated controller parameters (17) are given in Table 2.

Table 2. The calculated controller parameters.

	K_{-1}	K_0	K_1	K_2	K_3
G_{P1}—controller PID_1^1	0.438	1.295	1.041	-	-
G_{P1}—controller PID_2^2	0.812	2.911	3.599	1.556	-
G_{P1}—controller PID_3^3	1.810	7.282	11.008	7.417	1.883
G_{P2}—controller PID_1^1	0.890	1.814	0.934	-	-
G_{P2}—controller PID_2^2	1.140	2.578	1.738	0.300	-
G_{P2}—controller PID_3^3	1.304	3.152	2.459	0.678	0.0674

In order to reduce the excessive swing of the controller output when changing the reference, the following reference filter time constant (9) is used for both processes:

$$T_{FR} = 0.5 \tag{19}$$

Note that the second order reference filter is used (9).

The closed-loop responses for the processes $G_{P1}(s)$ and $G_{P2}(s)$, for all three types of controllers, are shown in Figures 3 and 4. It is clear that tracking and control performance increase by the controller order. Note that the controller output response of PID_3^3 controller is not shown entirely in order to see the responses of PID_1^1 and PID_2^2 controllers more clearly.

When comparing process output responses when using controllers PID_1^1 and PID_3^3 in Figures 3 and 4, it can be seen that the relative difference in performance is larger on higher-order process $G_{P1}(s)$. This is expected, since lower-order processes can already be optimally controlled by lower-order controllers (e.g., the first-order process with PID_0^0 and the second-order process with the PID_1^1 controller). Since the second-order process $G_{P2}(s)$ has an additional delay, the closed-loop performance can still be slightly increased with the PID_3^3 controller.

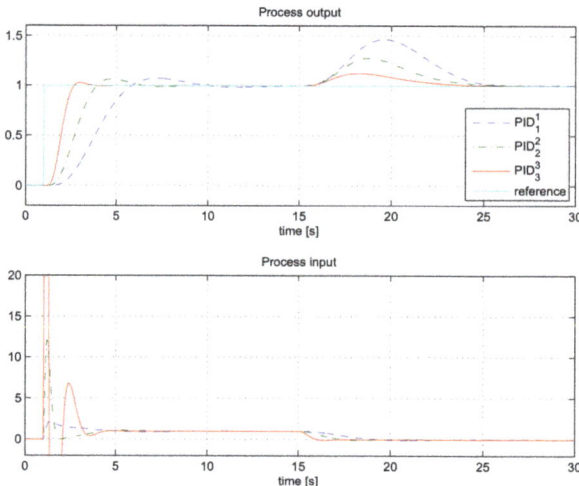

Figure 3. The closed-loop responses for the process $G_{P1}(s)$ when using controllers PID_1^1, PID_2^2 and PID_3^3.

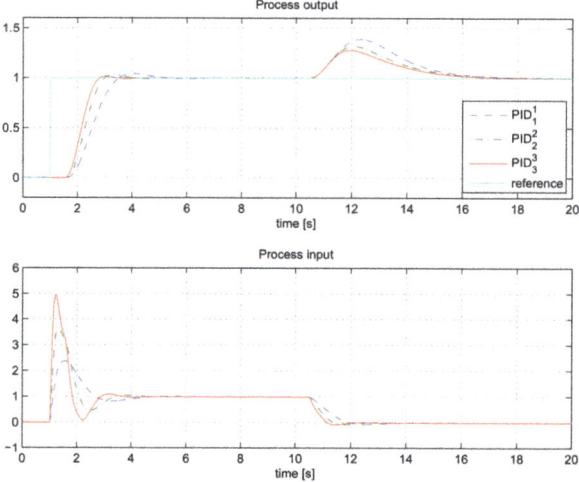

Figure 4. The closed-loop responses for the process $G_{P2}(s)$ when using controllers PID_1^1, PID_2^2 and PID_3^3.

According to the closed-loop responses, it can be concluded that HO-PID controllers can significantly improve the closed-loop performance, especially for higher-order processes. The only required parameter from the user is the controller filter time constant T_F. Namely, the amplification of the process output measurement noise depends on the chosen T_F. However, the relation between T_F and the actual amplification of the high-frequency (HF) noise depends on several other controller parameters and is a rather complex function. Therefore, in practice, it would be more appropriate to define the desired HF noise amplification than the controller filter time constant.

3. HO-PID Controller with Specified HF Noise Amplification

As mentioned in the previous section, the n-th order controller filter $G_F(s)$ (1) is primarily used to decrease the controller output noise due to the measurement noise (in addition to making the entire controller transfer function proper or strictly proper and, therefore, realisable in practice). High controller amplification of the measurement noise is never desired, since it may also cause large swings of the control output signals and thus may decrease the actuator's life span. In order to limit the amplification of the process measurement noise, the user can try different values of T_F until the desired amplification (attenuation) of the noise is achieved. In practice, this may take too long, since the function between T_F and the noise amplification is complex and non-linear. Therefore, from the user's perspective, it is easier to define the desired noise amplification of the controller than select filter time constant T_F.

The process output noise (n_y) is amplified by the controller (1) in the closed-loop configuration as follows:

$$U_N = G_{CN}(s)N_y = \frac{G_{CF}(s)}{1 + G_{CF}(s)G_P(s)} N_y = \left(G_P(s) + \frac{1}{G_{CF}(s)}\right)^{-1} N_y, \quad (20)$$

where N_y and U_N are Laplace transforms of the measurement noise and the controller output noise, respectively. The negative sign is omitted to simplify the derivation. From (20) it can be seen that at lower frequencies, the transfer function $G_{CN}(s)$ is mostly dominated by the process transfer function $G_P(s)$, while at higher frequencies, it is mostly dominated by the controller transfer function $G_{CF}(s)$. At lower frequencies, the process can be approximated by its gain K_{PR}, while at higher frequencies the controller gains K_{-1} and K_0 can be neglected. Therefore, $G_{CN}(s)$ can be approximated by the following transfer function:

$$G_{CN}(s) \approx \frac{K_{PR}^{-1} + K_1 s + K_2 s^2 + \cdots + K_m s^m}{(1 + T_F s)^n}. \quad (21)$$

On the other hand, the desired controller output noise (U_{ND}) should be similar to:

$$U_{ND} = K_{HF} N_y, \quad (22)$$

where K_{HF} is a chosen noise amplification factor. Since amplitudes U_N and U_{ND} cannot be compared directly due to different frequency characteristics, it is easier to compare noise powers of both signals in some chosen frequency bandwidth (from ω_1 to ω_2). Namely, due to Parseval theorem, the power of the controller output signal (P_{UN}) is proportional to:

$$P_{UN} \propto \int_{\omega_1}^{\omega_2} |G_{CN}(\omega) N_y(\omega)|^2 d\omega. \quad (23)$$

The desired noise power is, according to (22), proportional to:

$$P_{UND} \propto \int_{\omega_1}^{\omega_2} |K_{HF} N_y(\omega)|^2 d\omega. \quad (24)$$

When considering the N_y as a white noise with amplitude over frequency as $N_y(\omega) = 1$, the powers P_{UN} and P_{UND} would become the same when:

$$\begin{aligned}
\int_{\omega_1}^{\omega_2} \frac{F_0 + F_1 \omega^2 + F_2 \omega^4 + \cdots + F_m \omega^{2m}}{(1 + T_F^2 \omega^2)^n} d\omega &= K_{HF}^2 (\omega_2 - \omega_1), \text{ where } K_0 = K_{PR}^{-1} \text{ and} \\
F_0 &= K_0^2 \\
F_1 &= K_1^2 - 2K_0 K_2 \\
&\vdots \\
F_k &= K_k^2 + 2\sum_{i=0}^{k-1} (-1)^{k+i} K_i K_{2k-i} \\
&\vdots \\
F_m &= K_m^2
\end{aligned} \quad (25)$$

However, the solution of the integral in (25), due to the denominator (controller filter), becomes very complex and highly non-linear in respect to T_F. Therefore, some search algorithm (optimization) must be applied for each calculation of the T_F.

This would seriously impact the simplicity of the proposed method. Therefore, it is decided to simplify the function inside the above integral. Since at higher frequencies, the most dominant controller term becomes the one with the highest derivative (K_m), the function can be simplified as follows:

$$\frac{F_0 + F_1\omega^2 + F_2\omega^4 + \cdots + F_m\omega^{2m}}{(1+T_F^2\omega^2)^n} \approx \begin{cases} F_m\omega^{2m} & ;\omega \leq \frac{1}{T_F} \\ \frac{F_m\omega^{2(m-n)}}{T_F^{2n}} & ;\omega > \frac{1}{T_F} \end{cases}. \qquad (26)$$

According to (26), the expression (25) simplifies into:

$$\int_{\omega_1}^{\omega_F} F_m\omega^{2m}d\omega + \int_{\omega_F}^{\omega_2} F_m\omega^{2(m-n)}\omega_F^{2n}d\omega \approx K_{HF}^2(\omega_2 - \omega_1)$$
$$\int_{\omega_1}^{\omega_F} F_m\omega^{2m}d\omega = \frac{F_m\left(\omega_F^{2m+1}-\omega_1^{2m+1}\right)}{(2m+1)}$$
$$\int_{\omega_F}^{\omega_2} F_m\omega^{2(m-n)}\omega_F^{2n}d\omega = \begin{cases} \frac{F_m\omega_F^{2n}\left(\omega_2^{2(m-n)+1}-\omega_F^{2(m-n)+1}\right)}{(2m-2n+1)} & n > m \\ F_m\omega_F^{2n}(\omega_2-\omega_F) & n=m \end{cases} \qquad (27)$$
$$\omega_F = \frac{1}{T_F}$$

The contribution of noise power in the frequency region below ω_F is usually much smaller than at higher frequencies. Therefore, in order to even further simplify the derivation, we can choose $\omega_1 = 0$ without making any significant error in the calculation. Selection of the upper frequency (ω_2) in the integral, due to the Shannon theorem, depends on the controller sampling frequency. Without loss of generality, the upper frequency can be selected as:

$$\omega_2 = \omega_S = \frac{2\pi}{T_S}, \qquad (28)$$

where ω_S is controller sampling frequency (in rad/s) and T_S is controller sampling time. By taking into account that:

$$\omega_S \gg \omega_F, \qquad (29)$$

and $\omega_1 = 0$, the expression (27) simplifies even further:

$$\int_0^{\omega_F} F_m\omega^{2m}d\omega = \frac{F_m\omega_F^{2m+1}}{2m+1}$$
$$\int_{\omega_F}^{\omega_S} \frac{F_m\omega^{2(m-n)}}{T_F^{2n}}d\omega \approx \begin{cases} \frac{F_m\omega_F^{2m+1}}{2(n-m)-1} & n > m \\ F_m\omega_F^{2n}\omega_S & n=m \end{cases} \qquad (30)$$

Therefore, the final expression, when taking into account that $F_m = K_m^2$, reads as:

$$\begin{matrix} K_m^2\omega_F^{2m+1}\left(\frac{1}{2m+1}+\frac{1}{2(n-m)-1}\right) \approx K_{HF}^2\omega_S & n>m \\ K_m^2\omega_F^{2m} \approx K_{HF}^2 & n=m \end{matrix}, \qquad (31)$$

Therefore, the filter time constant ($T_F = 1/\omega_F$) can be estimated as follows:

$$T_F \approx \sqrt[2m+1]{\frac{K_m^2\left(\frac{1}{2m+1}+\frac{1}{2(n-m)-1}\right)}{K_{HF}^2\omega_S}} \quad ; n>m$$
$$T_F \approx \sqrt[m]{\frac{|K_m|}{K_{HF}}} \quad ; n=m \qquad (32)$$

Note that the above derivation of the filter time constant takes into account approximations (26) and (29). This means that the final output noise power of the controller may differ from that defined by the selected high frequency gain K_{HF}. However, if the above approximations are not taken into account, then the final expressions for the calculation of ω_F in (31) would become those of the higher order without analytic solution for T_F. This would significantly complicate the filter calculation.

The entire procedure for the calculation of the controller parameters for a given process is given in Figure 5.

1. Calculate the moments from the given $G_P(s)$ (7) or from the process response in time domain (Vrančić et al., 2001; Vrančić, 2011).
2. Choose some initial filter time constant T_F.
3. For a given filter order (n), calculate modified areas according to the chosen T_F from (8).
4. For a given model order (m) calculate the controller parameters from (17).
5. Calculate constant T_F from (32).
6. Repeat steps 3–5 a few times (3 times is usually enough) until value T_F settles.

Figure 5. Calculation of the filter and controller parameters.

As shown in Figure 5, the calculation of the controller and filter parameters is straightforward. However, to make it even simpler, as mentioned before, we have provided online MATLAB/Octave scripts via OctaveOnline Bucket website [39]. The website layout is shown in Figure 6. The calculation procedure proceeds as follows:

1. Select the appropriate Octave (MATLAB) script (test_HO_filt.m).
2. Provide the process parameters, the desired noise gain, the controller sampling time, the controller order and filter order,
3. press the "Save" button, and
4. press the "Run" button.

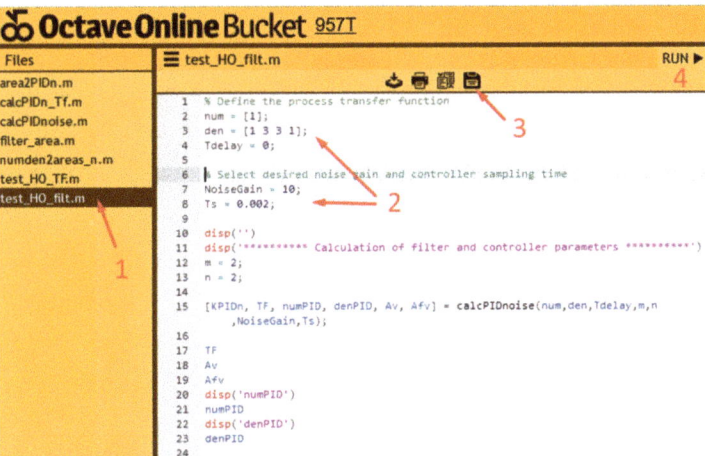

Figure 6. The layout of the OctaveOnline Bucket website (function test_HO_filt.m).

The script then calculates the filter time constant, the characteristic areas and the controller parameters. The results are shown on the right panel of the website.

Illustrative example 2

Consider the following fourth-order process transfer function $G_{P3}(s)$ (18):

$$G_{P3}(s) = \frac{e^{-0.2s}}{(1+s)^4} \qquad (33)$$

The initially chosen controller filter time constants is $T_F = 0.1$. For all the experiments in this section, the chosen sampling time is $T_S = 0.002$ s. In order to retain clarity of the derivations, the characteristic areas of the process are not mentioned herein; however, they can be calculated (besides all the controller and the filter parameters) on the aforementioned website [39].

a. Changing the parameter K_{HF}

According to the procedure given in Figure 5, when choosing parameter K_{HF}, controller PID_4^3 and repeating steps 3–5 a few times (in our case, 3 times), the calculated filter time constants, and the calculated controller parameters (17) are given in Table 3.

Table 3. The calculated filter time constants T_F and controller parameters at different noise gains K_{HF}.

	T_F	K_{-1}	K_0	K_1	K_2	K_3	σ_{rel}
$K_{HF} = 2$	0.209	0.679	2.445	3.282	1.954	0.440	1.85
$K_{HF} = 5$	0.155	0.773	2.684	3.426	1.896	0.382	4.60
$K_{HF} = 10$	0.124	0.844	2.873	3.562	1.885	0.352	9.2
$K_{HF} = 20$	0.100	0.914	3.062	3.710	1.890	0.329	18.3

Again, in order to reduce the excessive swing of the controller output when changing the reference, the following second-order reference filter time constant (9) is used:

$$T_{FR} = 0.2 \qquad (34)$$

The closed-loop responses for different values of K_{HF} are given in Figure 7.

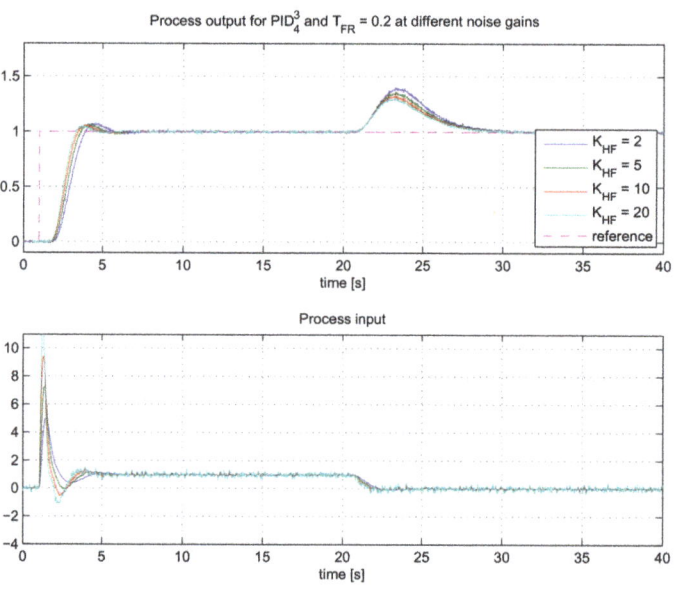

Figure 7. The closed-loop responses for the process $G_{P3}(s)$ when using controllers PID_4^3, at different K_{HF}.

As expected, the speed of the closed-loop response and the controller output signal noise increases by increasing the noise gain factor K_{HF}. However, the improvement of the closed-loop speed is not so significant at the highest factors K_{HF}. On the other hand, the controller output noise increases at higher factors K_{HF}. As expected, there is a trade-off between the closed-loop speed and the amount of the controller output noise. Therefore, in practice, the allowed noise gain should be chosen wisely according to the amount of noise present in the system.

The actual "amplification" of the measurement noise (the actually achieved noise gain K_{HF}) is measured by dividing standard deviations of the controller output signal (u) and the process output (n) when the process is in the steady-state:

$$\sigma_{rel} = \frac{\sigma_u}{\sigma_y}. \tag{35}$$

The actual amplifications of the measurement noise signals are given in Table 3. It is obvious that the actual gains of the noise (σ_{rel}) are very similar to the desired ones (K_{HF}).

b. Changing the filter order (n)

On the other hand, the speed of the closed-loop response, for the same K_{HF} and the controller order (m), can also be altered by changing the filter order. In this regard, we tested the performance of the controllers PID_n^3, where n varies from 3 to 6.

According to the procedure given in Figure 5, when choosing $K_{HF} = 10$ and repeating steps 3–5 3 times, the calculated filter time constants and the controller parameters (17) are given in Table 4.

Table 4. The calculated filter time constants T_F and controller parameters at different n.

Controller Structure	T_F	K_{-1}	K_0	K_1	K_2	K_3	σ_{rel}
PID_3^3	0.396	0.619	2.402	3.547	2.388	0.629	10.1
PID_4^3	0.124	0.844	2.873	3.562	1.885	0.352	9.17
PID_5^3	0.109	0.799	2.731	3.410	1.824	0.348	5.05
PID_6^3	0.104	0.742	2.564	3.247	1.777	0.352	3.33

The closed-loop responses for different controller filter orders ($n = 3$ to 6) are given in Figure 8.

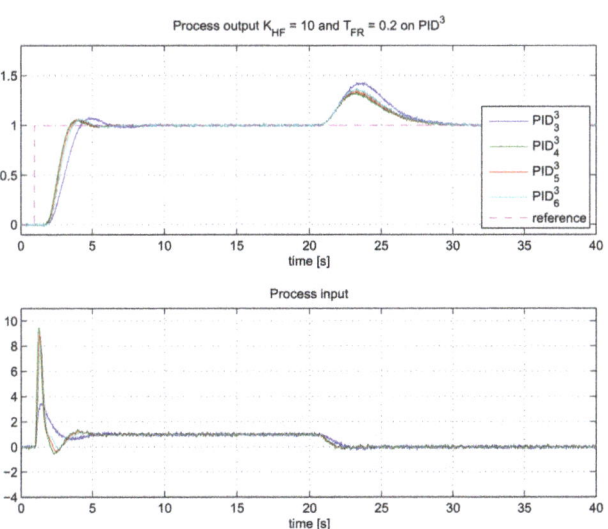

Figure 8. The closed-loop responses for the process $G_{P3}(s)$ when using controllers with different filter orders PID_n^3, at $K_{HF} = 10$.

As can be seen, the speed of the closed-loop response is the highest for controller PID_4^3. The speed of controllers with higher-order filters ($n > 4$) are slightly slower. The speed of response for $n > 4$ is not improving since a higher-order filter also adds some complexity to the closed-loop transfer function. This, in return, may result in lower closed-loop speeds.

The practical question is how to find the most optimal controller filter order in advance, before making the closed-loop experiment on the process. This can be answered by calculating the integral of control error (IE), which can be considered as a measure of the closed-loop speed:

$$IE = \int_{t=0}^{\infty} (r - y) dt \quad (36)$$

If the closed-loop responses have small overshoots, the higher values of IE indicate slower closed-loop responses. For such responses, the IE can be a useful tool to measure the closed-loop speed. The IE value can be relatively easily calculated by transforming the Equation (36) into Laplace domain. It can be shown that:

$$IE = \frac{1}{K_{PR} K_{-1}}. \quad (37)$$

Therefore, for the process with the same steady-state gain K_{PR} (2), the closed-loop speed is inversely proportional to the integrating gain (K_{-1}) of the controller. Therefore, the controller with the highest gain K_{-1} will produce the fastest closed-loop response (providing that the closed-loop responses have small or negligible overshoots). Indeed, from Table 4 it is evident that the highest gain K_{-1} is calculated for controller PID_4^3. This corresponds to our previous observations.

The actual amplifications of the measurement noise signals, according to (35), are given in Table 4. The actual noise gains (σ_{rel}) are very similar to the desired ones (K_{HF}) for filter orders 3 and 4, while for higher-order filters the actual noise gain is lower. This is due to various assumptions (simplifications) made when deriving the filter time constant (32).

c. Changing the controller order (m)

As is already known, the speed of the closed-loop response can also be altered by changing the controller order. In this regard, we tested the performance of the controllers PID_n^m, where m varies from 1 to 4. In all cases the controller filter is chosen to be 1 order higher than the controller order ($n = m + 1$). The desired noise gain remains the same as in the previous experiment ($K_{HF} = 10$).

The calculated filter time constants and the controller parameters (17) are given in Table 5.

Table 5. The calculated filter time constants T_F and controller parameters at different controller order m ($n = m + 1$).

Controller Structure	T_F	K_{-1}	K_0	K_1	K_2	K_3	K_3	σ_{rel}
PID_2^1	0.015	0.517	1.323	0.904	-	-	-	10.9
PID_3^2	0.078	0.766	2.36	2.45	0.863	-	-	9.7
PID_4^3	0.124	0.844	2.873	3.562	1.885	0.352	-	9.2
PID_5^4	0.161	0.876	3.270	4.694	3.225	1.068	0.143	8.9

The closed-loop responses for different controller orders ($m = 1$ to 4) are given in Figure 9.

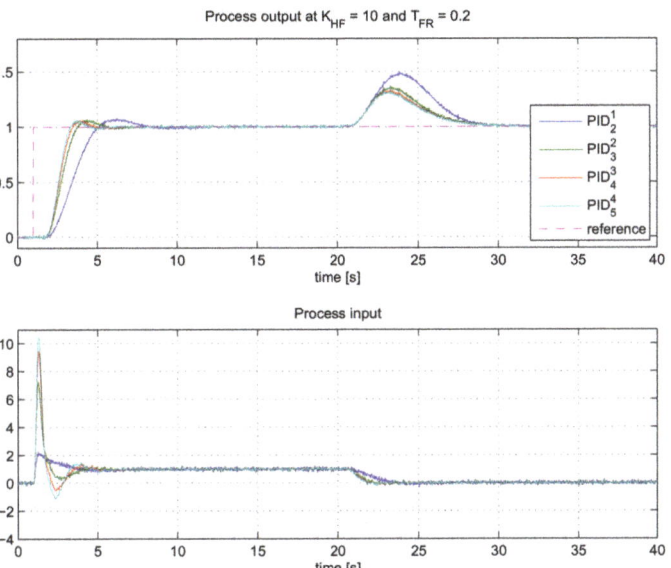

Figure 9. The closed-loop responses for the process $G_{P3}(s)$ when using controllers with different controller orders PID_n^m, at $K_{HF} = 10$ and $n = m + 1$.

As can be seen, the closed-loop speed increases by increased controller order, similar to the results in Figures 3 and 4. The difference is that now the controller output noise is under control ($K_{HF} = 10$), so the level of control noise is similar for all of the controllers. The fastest responses are obtained with PID_5^4. In a similar manner as in the previous case, the speed of responses can be estimated by comparing the values of the calculated integrating gains (K_{-1}) in Table 5. Indeed, K_{-1} is the highest for PID_5^4.

The actual amplifications of the measurement noise signals, according to (35), are given in Table 5. The actual gains of the noise (σ_{rel}) are very similar to the desired ones (K_{HF}) for all controller orders.

4. Robustness

The proposed design of HO-PID controllers results in a relatively fast and non-oscillatory response. In addition, the controller noise is under control by choosing parameter K_{HF}. However, the designed closed-loop system can still be not robust enough to process variations. Namely, due to nonlinearity or time-variations of the process, its characteristics (gain, delay, time constants, etc.) can vary by working point or by time.

The robustness of a stable closed-loop system is usually measured by maximum sensitivity (M_S) [1,38]. Maximum sensitivity is related to the distance of the open-loop transfer function $G_C(j\omega)G_P(j\omega)$ from the critical point ($-1+j0$). Namely, M_S is the inverse of the minimum distance between the open-loop transfer function and the critical point. Generally, a smaller value of M_S denotes a more robust closed-loop system to process variations. Usual values of M_S for stable processes are between 1.4 and 2.0 [1,38].

The robustness of the closed-loop system for the proposed HO-PID controllers has been tested on the following third-order process with delay:

$$G_{P4}(s) = \frac{K_{PR}e^{-T_{del}s}}{(1+sT)^3}, \tag{38}$$

where the nominal values are $K_{PR} = 1$, $T_{del} = 1$ and $T = 1$. Three different HO-PID controllers are selected: PID_3^2, PID_4^3, and PID_5^4. The calculated controller parameters, when choosing

$K_{HF} = 10$, $T_S = 0.002$ s and according to the proposed tuning method, are shown in Table 6. The calculated values of the maximum sensitivity M_S, for all three controllers, are shown in the same table. It can be seen that the M_S values slightly increase with the increased controller order. However, the differences are not large and all the values are below 2.0.

Table 6. The calculated filter time constants T_F and controller parameters at different controller orders m ($n = m + 1$) for $G_{P4}(s)$.

Controller Structure	T_F	K_{-1}	K_0	K_1	K_2	K_3	K_3	M_S
PID_3^2	0.0702	0.498	1.597	1.752	0.668	-	-	1.78
PID_4^3	0.125	0.554	1.992	2.674	1.596	0.362	-	1.86
PID_5^4	0.170	0.579	2.308	3.629	2.832	1.117	0.185	1.91

Besides calculating the M_S values, we were also simulating the closed-loop responses using all three controllers on the nominal process, and on the changed process ($\pm 10\%$ change of process gain K_{PR}, time-delay T_{del} and time constant T). The closed-loop responses are shown in Figures 10–12. It is evident that the closed-loop responses under perturbed parameters are still stable without significant oscillations. When comparing Figures 10 and 12 it can be noticed that the perturbed parameters with controller PID_5^4 result in slightly more deviation from the nominal response than with controller PID_3^2. This is all in accordance with the calculated values of M_S in Table 6.

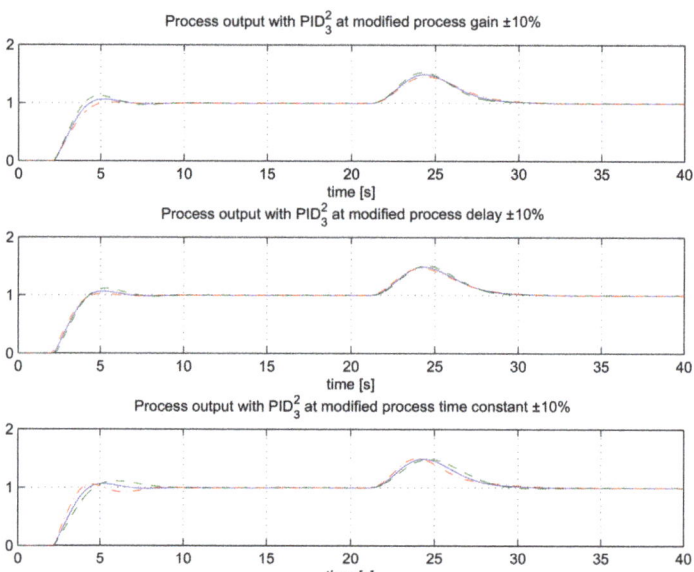

Figure 10. The closed-loop responses for the process $G_{P4}(s)$, using controller PID_3^2 at $K_{HF} = 10$ for nominal (solid line), 10% increased (dashed line) and 10% decreased (dash-dotted line) process parameters.

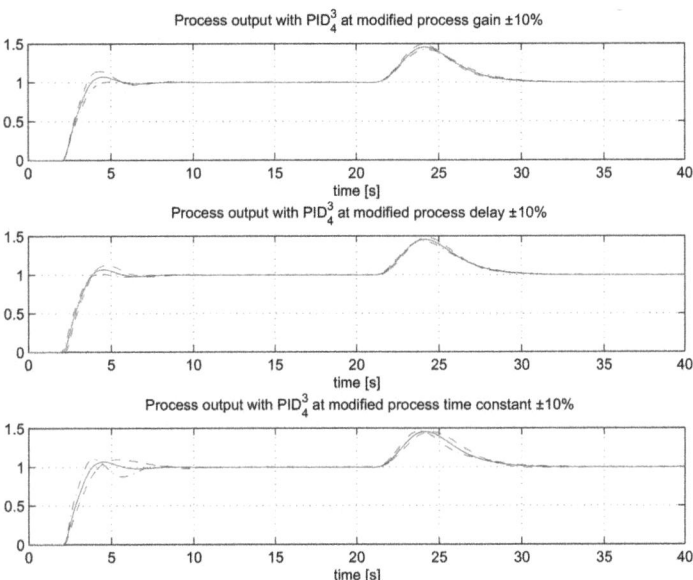

Figure 11. The closed-loop responses for the process $G_{P4}(s)$, using controller PID_4^3 at $K_{HF} = 10$ for nominal (solid line), 10% increased (dashed line) and 10% decreased (dash-dotted line) process parameters.

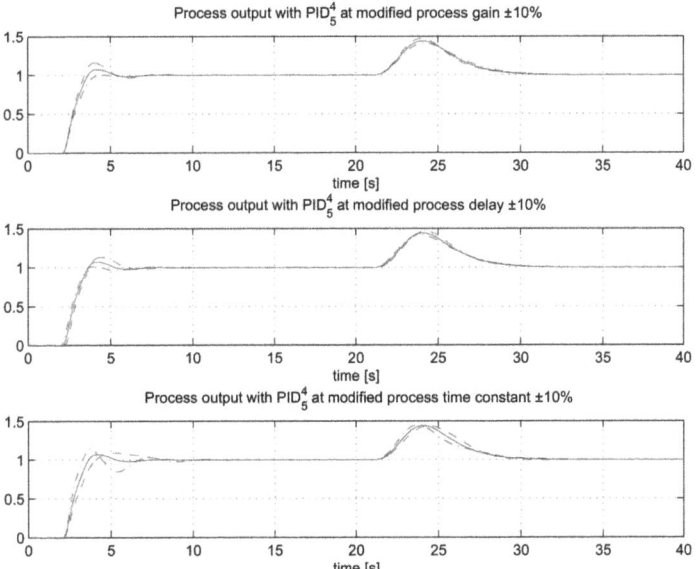

Figure 12. The closed-loop responses for the process $G_{P4}(s)$, using controller PID_5^4 at $K_{HF} = 10$ for nominal (solid line), 10% increased (dashed line) and 10% decreased (dash-dotted line) process parameters.

5. Comparison with Other Tuning Methods

The proposed tuning method was compared with some other methods for PIDA controllers. The chosen methods, which were tested on a particular process model, are from

Lurang and Puangdownreong [21] (denoted as the Lurang method from here on) and Jung and Dorf [11] (denoted as the Jung method from here on). The Lurang method involves calculating the PIDA controller parameters by optimizing the tracking and disturbance rejection response under several limitations given on rise time, overshoot, settling time, steady-state error and similar. The optimization is carried out with a modified bat algorithm proposed by the authors. The Jung method analytically calculates the PIDA controller parameters for the third-order process according to provided desired overshoot and settling time. Both methods do not take into account the controller's filter. Therefore, the actual implementation in practice could be questionable if the filter dynamics become slower.

Case 1

The following process model has been selected, according to [21]:

$$G_{P5}(s) = \frac{1}{(1+s)(1+0.5s)\left(1+\frac{s}{3}\right)} \tag{39}$$

The Lurang method suggests the following PIDA controller parameters:

$$K_{-1} = 2.20,\ K_0 = 3.60,\ K_1 = 1.60,\ K_2 = 0.06 \tag{40}$$

The chosen controller filter time constant was very low ($T_F = 0.01$), since we did not want to spoil the closed-loop response of the Lurang method. Namely, as already mentioned, the Lurang method does not take into account the controller filter in the design phase.

For comparison, we chose the controller structures with the lowest possible controller filter order n: PID_2^2. For illustrative purposes, the one-order higher controller structure (PID_3^3) was also tested. Note that the closed-loop results of our proposed method, for the same level of controller noise, can be improved by using $n > m$.

The calculated controller parameters, for the given process and controller filter were the following:

$$\begin{aligned}PID_2^2 &: K_{-1} = 25.06,\ K_0 = 45.95,\ K_1 = 25.07,\ K_2 = 4.18 \\ PID_3^3 &: K_{-1} = 37.53,\ K_0 = 69.42,\ K_1 = 38.88,\ K_2 = 6.88,\ K_3 = 0.104\end{aligned} \tag{41}$$

We tested, separately, the tracking response and the disturbance rejection when using all three controllers. For tracking response, the reference (r) changed from 0 to 1 at $t = 1$ s and for disturbance response the process input disturbance (d) changed from 0 to 1 at $t = 1$ s.

The closed-loop responses are shown in Figure 13.

As can be seen, the responses of the proposed method with PID_2^2 controller are superior to the Lurang method. Certainly, the one-order higher controller (PID_3^3) has a better result.

For a more objective comparison, the integral of squared error (ISE) signal has been calculated for all three controllers. The results are shown in Table 7. It is obvious that the ISE values for the PID_2^2 controller are much lower than the ones for the Lurang controller.

Table 7. The ISE values for all three controllers in tracking and disturbance rejection.

ISE	PID_2^2	PID_3^3	Lurang
Tracking	0.0228	0.0131	0.322
disturbance rejection	4.38×10^{-7}	1.95×10^{-7}	0.061

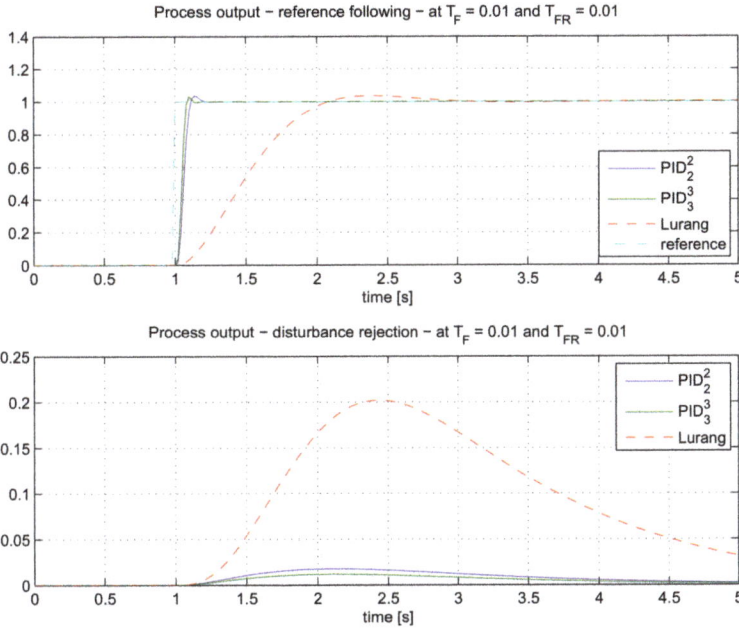

Figure 13. The comparison of the closed-loop responses for the process $G_{P5}(s)$ when using PID_2^2, PID_3^3 and the Lurang controller.

Case 2

The second process model has been selected according to [11]:

$$G_{P6}(s) = \frac{0.0556}{(1+s)\left(1+\frac{s}{3}\right)\left(1+\frac{s}{6}\right)} \quad (42)$$

The Jung method suggests the following PIDA controller parameters:

$$K_{-1} = 529.8, \; K_0 = 516.5, \; K_1 = 179.2, \; K_2 = 26.3 \quad (43)$$

As before, the controller filter time constant was chosen very low ($T_F = 0.005$), since we wanted to preserve the closed-loop response of the Jung method, which was obtained without the controller filter.

The calculated PID_2^2 and PID_3^3 controller parameters, for the given process and controller filter were the following:

$$\begin{aligned} PID_2^2 &: K_{-1} = 902, \; K_0 = 1353, \; K_1 = 501, \; K_2 = 50.1 \\ PID_3^3 &: K_{-1} = 1351, \; K_0 = 2037, \; K_1 = 767, \; K_2 = 81.3, \; K_3 = 0.6 \end{aligned} \quad (44)$$

As in the previous case, the closed-loop responses were tested on the tracking response and the disturbance rejection. The closed-loop responses are shown in Figure 14.

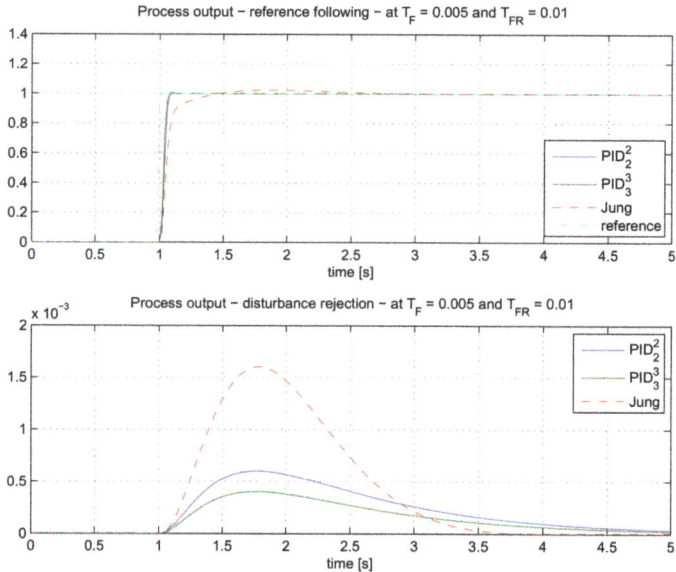

Figure 14. The comparison of the closed-loop responses for the process $G_{P6}(s)$ when using PID_2^2, PID_3^3 and the Jung controller.

Again, the responses of the proposed method with PID_2^2 and PID_3^3 controllers are superior to the Jung method. The comparison of ISE values in Table 8 shows PID_2^2 controller has lower values than the Jung controller. However, note that the disturbance rejection settling time is the best with the Jung method.

Table 8. The ISE values for all three controllers in tracking and disturbance rejection.

ISE	PID_2^2	PID_3^3	Jung
Tracking	8.12×10^{-3}	4.11×10^{-3}	1.97×10^{-2}
disturbance rejection	4.38×10^{-7}	1.95×10^{-7}	2.18×10^{-6}

Case 3

The fourth-order process model has been selected according to [6]:

$$G_{P7}(s) = \frac{1}{(1+s)\left(1+\frac{s}{2}\right)\left(1+\frac{s}{4}\right)\left(1+\frac{s}{8}\right)} \quad (45)$$

The Puangdownreong method suggests the following PIDA controller parameters:

$$K_{-1} = 1.647, \ K_0 = 2.684, \ K_1 = 1.105, \ K_2 = -2.65 \cdot 10^{-3} \quad (46)$$

The method calculated the following controller filter:

$$G_F(s) = \frac{1}{1 + 0.0132s + 5.26 \cdot 10^{-5} s^2} \quad (47)$$

which was also used in design of the proposed PID_2^2 controller parameters. For the given process and controller filter transfer function, the following controller parameters were calculated:

$$PID_2^2: \ K_{-1} = 4.36, \ K_0 = 7.735, \ K_1 = 3.97, \ K_2 = 0.60 \quad (48)$$

As in the previous case, the closed-loop responses were tested on the tracking response and the disturbance rejection. The closed-loop responses are shown in Figure 15.

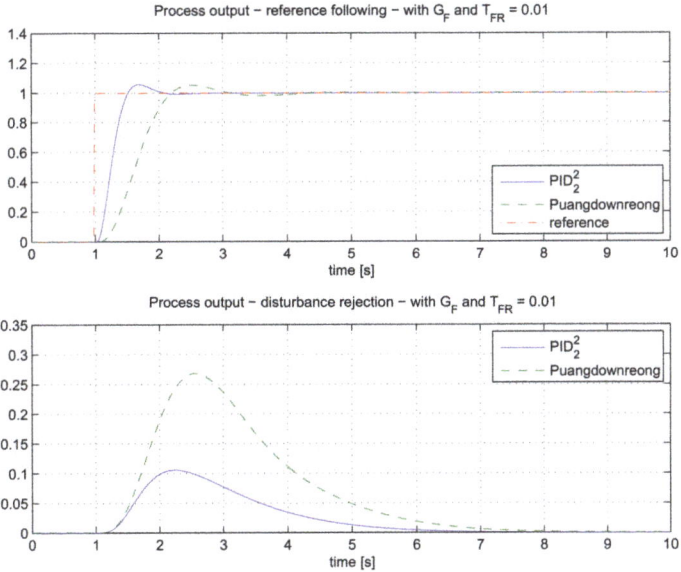

Figure 15. The comparison of the closed-loop responses for the process $G_{P6}(s)$ when using PID_2^2 and the Puangdownreong controller.

Again, the responses of the proposed method with the PID_2^2 controller are superior to the Puangdownreong method. The comparison of ISE values in Table 9 shows the PID_2^2 controller has lower values than the Puangdownreong controller.

Table 9. The ISE values for both controllers in tracking and disturbance rejection.

ISE	PID_2^2	Puangdownreong
Tracking	0.172	0.466
disturbance rejection	0.0162	0.107

6. Conclusions

In the paper, the method for tuning the parameters of the m-th order controller with the n-th order binomial filter has been presented. The proposed tuning method is based on the MO criteria which aims to produce non-oscillatory and fast closed-loop reference step responses. The calculation of the controller parameters is analytical and does not require any kind of optimization. An additional advantage of the proposed method is that the process can be described either by the process model or by the process time responses during the steady-state change.

To keep the noise gain of the controller under control, the filter time constant of the controller can also be calculated according to the specified noise gain. The calculation procedure is still analytical, and the results confirm that the level of controller noise is consistent with the given noise gain. The only exception is the use of larger relative degrees between the controller and the filter order, which is the consequence of some simplifications in the calculation of the filter time constant.

The proposed method was tested on six different process models (from second to fourth-order process models with or without time delay). The results confirmed that the control performance can be improved by increasing the controller order or by selecting the filter order appropriately without increasing the controller output noise. The study shows that increasing the filter order improves the performance only up to a certain level, after which the performance starts to decrease. The optimum degree of controller and filter order can be easily determined by the value of integral gain of the controller.

The tuning method was compared with three other tuning methods for PIDA controllers (Lurang [21], Jung [11] and Puangdownreong [6] methods). Although the selected process models were the same as in the aforementioned methods, the proposed method resulted in a better control performance.

Therefore, the proposed higher-order controller design is efficient, and the controller output noise gain is under control. However, it does not mean that the proposed method cannot be improved. Indeed, the proposed method is based on optimizing the reference tracking performance. In our further research, we plan to improve the disturbance rejection performance as well. Namely, the article shows that the MO controller design leads to a strong asymmetry in the dynamics of tracking and disturbance rejection behaviour. While the HO-PID controller design leads to an increase in the number of pulses of the control signal after reference step changes, the responses of the control signal after the change of disturbance remain monotonic. This motivates us to deal with the modification of the MO controller design with regard to a faster response to disturbances.

Moreover, we also plan to design a method that will find the most optimal controller and filter order for the given process and noise amplification considering the complexity of the controller and filter order. We plan to calculate the optimal parameters of the reference filter to control the change of the controller output signal when the reference signal is changed.

Another planned modification is adding a user-defined parameter for changing the speed of the closed-loop control. Slowing down the control speed would further increase the robustness of the system.

Author Contributions: Writing-original draft preparation, D.V. and M.H. Simulations, D.V. and M.H. Editing, D.V. and M.H. Project administration, D.V. All authors have read and agreed to the published version of the manuscript.

Funding: This research was funded by the grants P2-0001 financed by the Slovenian Research Agency, APVV SK-IL-RD-18-0008 platoon modelling and control for mixed autonomous and conventional vehicles: a laboratory experimental analysis, and VEGA 1/0745/19 control and modelling of mechatronic systems in e-mobility.

Acknowledgments: Supported by Slovenská e-akadémia, n. o.

Conflicts of Interest: The authors declare no conflict of interest.

References

1. Åström, K.J.; Hägglund, T. *PID Controllers: Theory, Design, and Tuning*, 2nd ed.; Instrument Society of America: Pittsburgh, PA, USA, 1995.
2. Vilanova, R.; Visioli, A. *PID Control in the Third Millennium*, 1st ed.; Vilanova, R., Visioli, A., Eds.; Advances in Industrial Control; Springer: London, UK, 2012; ISBN 978-1-4471-2424-5.
3. Alfaro, V.M.; Vilanova, R. *Model-Reference Robust Tuning of PID Controllers*; Springer International Publishing: Cham, Switzerland, 2016. [CrossRef]
4. Visioli, A. *Practical PID Control*; Springer: London, UK, 2016. [CrossRef]
5. Jung, S.; Dorf, R.C. Analytic PIDA controller design technique for a third order system. In Proceedings of the 35th IEEE on Decision and Control, Kobe, Japan, 13 December 1996; Volume 3. [CrossRef]
6. Puangdownreong, D. Application of Current Search to Optimum PIDA Controller Design. *Intell. Control Autom.* **2012**, *3*, 303–312. [CrossRef]
7. Sambariya, D.K.; Paliwal, D. Design of PIDA Controller Using Bat Algorithm for AVR Power System. *Adv. Energy Power* **2016**, *4*, 1–6. [CrossRef]
8. Ukakimaparn, P.; Pannil, P.; Boonchuay, P.; Trisuwannawat, T. PIDA Controller Designed by Kitti's Method. In Proceedings of the ICCAS-SICE, Fukuoka, Japan, 18–21 August 2009; pp. 1547–1550.

9. Smerpitak, K.; Ukakimaparn, P.; Trisuwannawat, T.; La-orsri, P. Discrete-time PIDA Controller designed by Kitti's method with Bilinear transform. In Proceedings of the 12th International Conference on Control, Automation and Systems, JeJu Island, Korea, 17–21 October 2012; pp. 1585–1590.
10. Huba, M. Filtered PIDA Controller for the Double Integrator Plus Dead Time. *IFAC PapersOnLine* **2019**, *52*, 106–113. [CrossRef]
11. Jung, A.; Dorf, R.C. Novel Analytic Technique for PID and PIDA Controller Design. *IFAC Proc. Vol.* **1996**, *29*, 1146–1151. [CrossRef]
12. Sharma, A.; Sharma, H.; Bhargava, A.; Sharma, N. Optimal design of PIDA controller for induction motor using Spider Monkey Optimization algorithm. *Int. J. Metaheuristics* **2016**, *5*, 278–290. [CrossRef]
13. Jitwang, T.; Nawikavatan, A.; Puangdownreong, D. Optimal PIDA Controller Design for Three-Tank Liquid-Level Control System with Model Uncertainty by Cuckoo Search. *Int. J. Circuits Syst. Signal Process.* **2019**, *13*, 60–65, ISSN 1998-4464.
14. Kumar, M.; Hote, Y.V. Robust CDA-PIDA Control Scheme for Load Frequency Control of Interconnected Power Systems. *IFAC PapersOnLine* **2018**, *51*, 616–621. [CrossRef]
15. Mosaad, A.M.; Attia, M.A.; Abdelaziz, A.Y. Whale optimization algorithm to tune PID and PIDA controllers on AVR system. *Ain Shams Eng. J.* **2019**, *10*, 755–767. [CrossRef]
16. Dal-Young, H.; Ihn-Yong, L.; Young-Seung, C.; Young-Do, L.; BooKwi, C. The design of PIDA controller with pre-compensator [for induction motors]. In Proceedings of the 2001 IEEE International Symposium on Industrial Electronics Proceedings (Cat. No.01TH8570), Pusan, Korea, 12–16 June 2001; Volume 2, pp. 798–804. [CrossRef]
17. Raju, M.; Saikia, L.C.; Sinha, N. Automatic generation control of a multi-area system using ant lion optimizer algorithm based PID plus second order derivative controller. *Int. J. Electr. Power Energy Syst.* **2016**, *80*, 52–63. [CrossRef]
18. Guha, D.; Roy, P.K.; Banerjee, S. Multi-verse optimisation: A novel method for solution of load frequency control problem in power system. *IET Gener. Transm. Distrib.* **2017**, *11*, 3601–3611. [CrossRef]
19. Sahib, M.A. A novel optimal PID plus second order derivative controller for AVR system. *Eng. Sci. Technol. Int. J.* **2015**, *18*, 194–206. [CrossRef]
20. Bisták, P.; Huba, M. Analysis of Higher Derivative Degree PID Controllers via Virtual Laboratory. In Proceedings of the 27th Mediterranean Conference on Control and Automation (MED), Akko, Israel, 1–4 July 2019; pp. 256–261. [CrossRef]
21. Lurang, K.; Puangdownreong, D. Two-degree-of-freedom PIDA controllers design optimization for liquid-level system by using modified mat algorithm. *Int. J. Innov. Comput. Inf. Control* **2020**, *16*, 715–732. [CrossRef]
22. Ozbey, N.; Yeroglu, C.; Baykant Alagoz, B.; Herencsar, N.; Kartci, A.; Sotner, R. 2DOF multi-objective optimal tuning of disturbance reject fractional order PIDA controllers according to improved consensus oriented random search method. *Int. J. Innov. Comput. J. Adv. Res.* **2020**, *25*, 159–170. [CrossRef]
23. Huba, M.; Vrančić, D. Comparing filtered PI, PID and PIDD control for the FOTD plants. *IFAC PapersOnLine* **2018**, *51*, 954–959. [CrossRef]
24. Simanenkov, A.L.; Rozhkov, S.A.; Borisova, V.A. An algorithm of optimal settings for PIDD2D3-controllers in ship power plant. In Proceedings of the 2017 IEEE 37th International Conference on Electronics and Nanotechnology (ELNANO), Kiev, Ukraine, 18–20 April 2017; pp. 152–155. [CrossRef]
25. Huba, M.; Vrančić, D. Introduction to the Discrete Time PIDmn Control for the PDT Plant. In Proceedings of the 15th IFAC International Conference on Programmable Devices and Embedded Systems, Ostrava, Czech Republic, 23–25 May 2018.
26. Bistak, P. Disturbance Analysis Virtual Laboratory for PID Controllers with Higher Derivative Degrees. In Proceedings of the 2018 16th International Conference on Emerging eLearning Technologies and Applications (ICETA), Stary Smokovec, Slovakia, 15–16 November 2018; pp. 69–74. [CrossRef]
27. Huba, M.; Vrančić, D.; Bisták, P. PIDmn Control for IPDT Plants. Part 1: Disturbance Response. In Proceedings of the 26th Mediterranean Conference on Control and Automation (MED), Zadar, Croatia, 19–22 June 2018; pp. 1–6. [CrossRef]
28. Skogestad, S. Simple analytic rules for model reduction and PID controller tuning. *J. Process Control* **2003**, *13*, 291–309. [CrossRef]
29. Huba, M.; Vrancic, D. Extending the Model-Based Controller Design to Higher-Order Plant Models and Measurement Noise. *Symmetry* **2021**, *13*, 798. [CrossRef]
30. Vítečkova, M.; Vítečěk, A. 2DOF PI and PID controllers tuning. In Proceedings of the 9th IFAC Workshop on Time Delay Systems, Prague, Czech Republic, 7–9 June 2010; Volume 9, pp. 343–348.
31. Vrančić, D.; Strmčnik, S.; Hanus, R. Magnitude optimum tuning using non-parametric data in the frequency domain. In Proceedings of the PID'00: Preprints: IFAC Workshop on Digital Control: Past, Present and Future of PID Control, Terrassa, Spain, 5–7 April 2000; pp. 438–443.
32. Vrančić, D.; Strmčnik, S.; Juričić, Ð. A magnitude optimum multiple integration method for filtered PID controller. *Automatica* **2001**, *37*, 1473–1479. [CrossRef]
33. Vrančić, D.; Strmčnik, S.; Kocijan, J.; de Moura Oliveira, P.B. Improving disturbance rejection of PID controllers by means of the magnitude optimum method. *ISA Trans.* **2010**, *49*, 47–56, ISSN 0019-0578. [CrossRef]
34. Vrančić, D. Magnitude optimum techniques for PID controllers. In *Introduction to PID Controllers: Theory, Tuning and Application to Frontiers Areas*; Panda, R.C., Ed.: InTech Cop.: Rijeka, Croatia, 2011; pp. 75–102.
35. Whiteley, A.L. Theory of servo systems, with particular reference to stabilization. *J. IEE Part II* **1946**, *93*, 353–372.
36. Preuss, H.P. Model-free PID-controller design by means of the method of gain optimum. *Automatisierungstechnik* **1991**, *39*, 15–22. (In German) [CrossRef]

37. Kessler, C. Über die Vorausberechnung optimal abgestimmter Regelkreise Teil III. Die optimale Einstellung des Reglers nach dem Betragsoptimum. *Regelungstechnik* **1955**, *3*, 40–49.
38. Åström, K.J.; Panagopoulos, H.; Hägglund, T. Design of PI Controllers based on Non-Convex Optimization. *Automatica* **1998**, *34*, 585–601. [CrossRef]
39. Octave Online Bucket Website. Available online: https://octave-online.net/bucket~{}957TukXTyYuXNMsxeL75FP (accessed on 8 April 2021).

Article

Feedforward of Measurable Disturbances to Improve Multi-Input Feedback Control

Javier Rico-Azagra *,† and Montserrat Gil-Martínez †

Control Engineering Research Group, Electrical Engineering Department, University of La Rioja, 26004 Logroño, Spain; montse.gil@unirioja.es
* Correspondence: javier.rico@unirioja.es; Tel.: +34-941-299-479
† These authors contributed equally to this work.

Abstract: The availability of multiple inputs (plants) can improve output performance by conveniently allocating the control bandwidth among them. Beyond that, the intervention of only the useful plants at each frequency implies the minimum control action at each input. Secondly, in single input control, the addition of feedforward loops from measurable external inputs has been demonstrated to reduce the amount of feedback and, subsequently, palliate its sideband effects of noise amplification. Thus, one part of the action calculated by feedback is now provided by feedforward. This paper takes advantage of both facts for the problem of robust rejection of measurable disturbances by employing a set of control inputs; a previous work did the same for the case of robust reference tracking. Then, a control architecture is provided that includes feedforward elements from the measurable disturbance to each control input and feedback control elements that link the output error to each control input. A methodology is developed for the robust design of the named control elements that distribute the control bandwidth among the cheapest inputs and simultaneously assures the prescribed output performance to correct the disturbed output for a set of possible plant cases (model uncertainty). The minimum necessary feedback gains are used to fight plant uncertainties at the control bandwidth, while feedforward gains achieve the nominal output response. Quantitative feedback theory (QFT) principles are employed. An example illustrates the method and its benefits versus a control architecture with only feedback control elements, which have much more gain beyond the control bandwidth than when feedforward is employed.

Keywords: mid-ranging; valve position control; input resetting control; parallel control; MISO; robust control; QFT; frequency domain; feedforward

Citation: Rico-Azagra, J; Gil-Martínez, M. Feedforward of Measurable Disturbances to Improve Multi-Input Feedback Control. *Mathematics* **2021**, *9*, 2114. https://doi.org/10.3390/math9172114

Academic Editor: Dimplekumar N. Chalishajar

Received: 30 June 2021
Accepted: 27 August 2021
Published: 1 September 2021

Publisher's Note: MDPI stays neutral with regard to jurisdictional claims in published maps and institutional affiliations.

Copyright: © 2021 by the authors. Licensee MDPI, Basel, Switzerland. This article is an open access article distributed under the terms and conditions of the Creative Commons Attribution (CC BY) license (https://creativecommons.org/licenses/by/4.0/).

1. Introduction

Uncertainties such as nonmeasurable disturbances or unavoidable simplifications in plant modelling justify feedback control loops, which, by permanently supervising the output, can correct its deviation from the reference or track reference changes. Better performances of the output response are linked to larger control bandwidths, which are provided by larger gains of feedback controllers (magnitude frequency response). Limited actuator ranges usually constrain the bandwidth and performance. Even for unlimited linear ranges or very powerful actuators, sensor noise amplifications at the control inputs impose an important constraint to the bandwidth to avoid fatigue or even saturation of actuators (Horowitz [1] labelled this fact as 'the cost of feedback'). With this in mind, Quantitative Feedback Theory (QFT) [1–3] proposes incorporating feedforward controllers when external inputs are available (reference or measurable disturbance inputs [4]), reducing feedback gain to only that strictly necessary to compensate for the uncertainties. However, reduction of the feedback gain increases the feedforward gain to maintain a specific performance that is linked with the chosen closed-loop bandwidth. Then, the control action is univocally conditioned by the plant frequency response and the desired performance, but its convenient allocation between feedback and feedforward control actions can prevent excessive sensor noise amplification linked with feedback gain. These facts, which are common knowledge in single-input control, have not yet been fully exploited in multi-input control.

The use of multiple control inputs can undoubtedly improve closed-loop performance. A great variety of control structures and design methods are available in the scientific literature. Some works focused on widening the range of operating points for the output [5,6]. Other works focused on improving the output dynamic performance and simultaneously searched for a profitable combination of control inputs, branding them as input (valve) position control, mid-ranging control [7], or input resetting control [8]—their foundation [9] has inspired a set of works in the robust framework of QFT with the named missions of feedback and feedforward [10–13]. Thus, the robustly designed control elements determine the intervention or inhibition of plants (one for each input) along the frequency band. Let us consider the following facts: (i) some plants could provide the performance using less control action than others, p.e., those plants of larger magnitude, considering that magnitude dominance can change over the frequency band; (ii) plants that do not significantly contribute to the performance at certain frequencies are advised to be inhibited; (iii) the collaboration of productive plants can reduce the control action that is needed at their inputs—the virtual total control effort is divided among them. The frequency inhibition of unproductive plants is relevant for several reasons. It prevents high-frequency signals from exciting the actuators of plants that are useless at high frequencies [10]. Similarly, it also avoids inconvenient steady-state displacements of the operating point of plants that are useless at low frequencies [11]; applied works such as [14,15] highlight the relevance of resetting the steady-state points of high-frequency intervention plants. Finally, stability issues become critical when plants are out of phase, despite the fact that their magnitude contribution may be large and nearly the same [16,17]; Reference [12] presented an appropriate intervention of the magnitude frequency response of plants that were not minimum phase.

Structures with exclusive feedback controllers to the control inputs are the only possibility for rejection at the output of nonmeasurable disturbances. In [10,11], robust design methods of the feedback controllers distributed the frequency band among the most favourable plants to minimise the control action at each input (any number of inputs were possible) while achieving the desired performance of the output response. The control architecture of [10] allowed the collaboration of plants over the same frequency band while the architecture of [11] required separated work-bands in favour of an easier design method; unstable, nonminimum phase, or delayed plants were investigated in [12].

The reference tracking problem admits feedforward elements that can reduce the gain of feedback controllers to palliate noise amplification at control inputs [13]. Beyond that, the priority of the method in [13] was achieving correct distribution of the bandwidth among the inputs (plants) to obtain the performance using the minimum possible control action at each input.

The fact that disturbances are sometimes measurable variables opens the possibility of connecting feedforward paths to the control inputs, which can be exploited by this work. A control architecture with feedback and feedforward elements will be presented for robust disturbance rejection. The method will distribute the frequency band among the most favourable inputs (those that demand less control action). Finally, a robust design of the control elements will guarantee the prescribed performance and stability for a set of possible plant models. Feedforward will reduce feedback, reporting important benefits with regard to excessive sensor noise amplification at the control inputs that could saturate actuators and spoil the expected performance in feedback-only control structures. Whenever external disturbances are measurable, the contribution of this work can be of importance in a great variety of fields where multi-input control has been successfully applied. Remarkable application fields include bioprocesses [14,15], thermal systems [18], medical systems [19,20], scanner imaging [21,22], massive data storage devices [23,24], fuel engines [25] and electrical vehicles [26], robotics [27–29], and unmanned aerial vehicles [30].

2. Control Architecture and Robust Design Method

Figure 1 depicts the multiple-input single-output (MISO) system and the proposed control architecture. The y output deviation is modelled by the influence of $u_{i=1,...n}$ control inputs and a d disturbance input, achieving a vector of $(n+1)$ transfer functions (plants) $P(s) = [p_{i=1,...n}(s), p_d(s)]$. Let us consider a total number z of uncertain parameters in these dynamical models. By defining q_l as a vector of those uncertain parameters in a set of all possible values of $\mathcal{Q}$ in $\mathbb{R}^z$, the MISO uncertain system can be formally defined as

$$\mathcal{P} = \{P(s; q_l) : q_l \in \mathcal{Q}\}. \tag{1}$$

Henceforth, labels p_i or p_d denote plant models of delimited uncertainty.

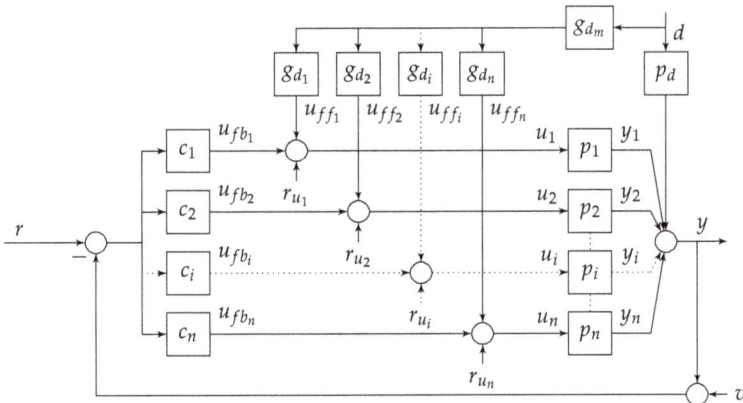

Figure 1. Feedback–feedforward control structure for robust rejection of measurable disturbances in multi-input systems.

An appropriate control must compensate for the output deviation from the constant reference, $e = r - y$, when a d disturbance occurs; reference tracking problems were discussed in [13]. Measurable disturbances are considered in the new design method. In such a case, the robust control specification is posed in the frequency domain as

$$\left|\frac{e}{d}\right| = \left|\frac{p_d + (\sum_{i=1}^{n} p_i g_{d_i}) g_{d_m}}{1 + \sum_{i=1}^{n} p_i c_i}\right| \leq W_d; \quad \forall P \in \mathcal{P}, \forall \omega, \tag{2}$$

where W_d is an upper tolerance on the set of $|e/d|$ frequency responses.

As demonstrated in [10], when d is nonmeasurable (i.e., $g_{d_i} = g_{d_m} = 0$), the parallel structure of feedback controllers $c_{i=1,...,n}$ allows any distribution of frequencies for $u_{i=1,...n}$ participation to fulfil $|e/d| \leq W_d$. Several p_i plants could even collaborate over the same frequencies to reduce each u_i. On the other hand, a series structure of feedback controllers [11] obliges to a predefined location of plants inside the structure and requires separated frequency work-bands for the u_i inputs. In spite of this, a method was provided to sort the plants and assign a convenient frequency band to each input to use the least u_i possible.

Beyond those solutions, feedforward loops from the external input d to the control inputs u_i are now being added. Individual elements g_{d_i} allow the frequency band distribution for u_i inputs with regard to feedforward tasks, while the feedforward master g_{d_m} locates the responses e, taking advantage of the measurable information d; as long as there is a set of possible plants (1), there is a bunch of responses. The dispersion of frequency responses is constrained by feedback, which can be freely distributed among u_i by controllers c_i. In summary, a total feedforward

$$l_{g_d} = \sum_{i=1}^{n} l_{g_{d_i}} = \left(\sum_{i=1}^{n} p_i g_{d_i} \right) g_{d_m} = p_{d_m} g_{d_m} \qquad (3)$$

is contributed by individual feedforward channels $l_{g_{d_i}}$, which supply u_{ff_i}, and a total feedback

$$l_t = \sum_{i=1}^{n} l_i = \sum_{i=1}^{n} p_i c_i \qquad (4)$$

is contributed by individual feedback loops l_i, which supply u_{fb_i}. Both components u_{ff_i} and u_{fb_i} build the control action u_i, which, for d handling, can be written and overbounded as

$$\left| \frac{u_i}{d} \right| = \left| \frac{u_{fb_i}}{d} + \frac{u_{ff_i}}{d} \right| = \left| -\frac{p_d + l_{g_d}}{1 + l_t} c_i + g_{d_i} g_{d_m} \right| \leq W_d |c_i| + |g_{d_i} g_{d_m}|; \quad \forall P \in \mathcal{P}, \forall \omega. \qquad (5)$$

In SISO control ($i = n = 1$), the desired performance for e/d univocally fixes the only control action u_1/d, which can be distributed as desired between feedback and feedforward components. QFT prioritises feedforward to reduce as much feedback as possible and its said drawbacks; [4] provided a design solution inside a tracking error structure such as ours, which pursues the smallest $p_1 c_1$ gain that guarantees the existence of $p_1 g_d$ to meet (2); in this way, the amplification of sensor noise v at the control input u_1 that depends on c_1 gain is also reduced as much as possible. However, evaluating (5), a reduction of u_{fb_1}/d occurs at the expense of an increase in u_{ff_1}/d, since u_1 is unique to provide the performance, i.e., the gain of $g_d = g_{d_1} g_{d_m}$ increases.

On the other hand, a multi-input availability offers many more possibilities. Let us note that despite the distribution between l_t and l_{g_d} that was selected to achieve the performance (2), infinite combinations of l_i (4) and $l_{g_{d_i}}$ (3) could build them. The goal is to find the solution that uses the set of smaller control inputs u_i/d. The authors of [13] provided a method for the problem of robust reference tracking ($r \neq$ constant). The key point was the more the gain of a plant, the less the need of control action to contribute to the performance, which foresaw the use of inputs towards plants with higher gains at each frequency.

In the current case, let us suppose a single input u_i (plant p_i) participates in the disturbance rejection. If plant models are perfectly known, the control action $u_i = -p_d/p_i$ would cancel the d disturbance influence on the y output. Here, the whole set of plant uncertainties is being considered in the robust design. Then, the frequency response

$$k_i = \frac{p_{d,\max}}{p_{i,\min}}, \quad \forall P \in \mathcal{P}, \forall \omega \qquad (6)$$

is a rough approximation of the less favourable u_i if only p_i participates in the d disturbance rejection; $p_{i,\min}$ is the plant p_i of least magnitude at a particular ω inside the uncertain set $|p_i(j\omega)|$; and $p_{d,\max}$ is the plant p_d of largest magnitude at ω inside $|p_d(j\omega)|$.

Next, the k_i frequency responses of all inputs $i = 1, \ldots, n$ are compared at each frequency to decide which inputs are of sufficient interest for participation; those that yield the smallest k_i magnitude are considered. At any frequency, the contribution of as many inputs as possible is desired, if it yields a total plant

$$p_{d_m} = \sum_{i=1}^{n} p_i g_{d_i}, \qquad (7)$$

with *significantly* greater magnitude than the individuals p_i (let us advance that g_{d_i} will be designed as filters with unitary gain at the pass band). Thus, the potential collaboration of plants would reduce individual feedforward actuations $|u_{ff_i}/d|$ because the virtual need of total feedforward $|\sum u_{ff_i}/d| \approx |p_d/p_{d_m}|$ would be significantly reduced. A two-in-two comparison of k_i is advised. As a rule of thumb, a difference in $k_i(j\omega)$ magnitude greater than $20\log 2 = 6$ dB makes the plant associated with larger $k_i(j\omega)$ magnitude useless. When a plant cannot report benefits at a certain frequency, its disconnection is recommended to avoid useless signals reaching the actuators. A second relevant point is to check that the $k_i(j\omega)$ phase-shift of those plants that are likely to collaborate is less than $90°$, since the vector sum of plants in the counter-phase would reduce the total magnitude of p_{d_m} (7). The disconnection of useless plans in the counter-phase is a priority for stability issues [12].

The k_i comparisons decide the smallest u_i input at each frequency, i.e., the desired frequency band allocation among inputs. Then, the design of g_{d_i} and c_i must attain the planned distribution and, simultaneously, g_{d_i}, c_i, and g_{d_m} must achieve the specification (2). The design method is described as follows: First, g_{d_i} are designed as filters with unitary gain over the pass-band. This yields a convenient plant p_{d_m} (7) that selects the most powerful p_i plants at each frequency for feedforward tasks. Subsequently, feedback l_t must reduce the influence of p_{d_m} uncertainty in $|e/d|$ deviations around zero only to the extent that a master feedforward g_{d_m} can further position the magnitude frequency responses inside tolerance $\pm W_d$. The required amount of feedback l_t could be provided with several combinations of c_i, but the one according to the planned distribution will save the control action by using the most powerful plants at each frequency for feedback tasks too. The set of controllers c_i are designed via loop-shaping of $l_i(j\omega)$ to satisfy the bounds $\beta_{l_i}(\omega)$ at a discrete set of frequencies $\Omega = \{\omega\}$. The QFT bounds β_{l_i} translate the closed loop specification into terms of restrictions for $l_i = c_i p_i$ nominal at specific frequencies ω that are conveniently selected according to the plant and specifications; the bounds are depicted on a mod-arg plot [2,3]. During $l_i(j\omega)$ shaping, when it lies exactly on the bounds, it guarantees the minimum gain of the c_i controller to achieve the specification by the whole set of plant cases. A sequential process between the $i = 1, ..., n$ loops is arbitrated. Thus, if at some point the controller c_i is to be adjusted and the other controllers $c_{k \neq i}$ take known values in the sequence, the robust disturbance rejection specification (2) can be rewritten as

$$\left|\frac{e}{d}\right| = \left|\frac{p_d + g_{d_m} p_{d_m}}{1 + \sum_{k \neq i} p_k c_k + p_i c_i}\right| \leq W_d; \quad \forall P \in \mathcal{P}, \forall \omega, \tag{8}$$

and their representative β_{l_i} bounds can be computed by choosing $A = p_{d_m}$, $B = p_d$, $C = 1 + \sum_{k \neq i} p_k c_k$, $D = p_i$, $G = c_i$, $G_f = g_{d_m}$, and $W = W_d$ in the solution given to

$$\left|\frac{AG_f + B}{C + DG}\right| \leq W \tag{9}$$

in [13]; this work provided the formulation to make the design of c_i and g_{d_m} independent. After the bound computation, the essence of loop-shaping is that c_i reaches the necessary gain at the frequencies where the p_i plant must work and filters (gain below 0 dB) those frequencies where p_i must not work. Special attention must be paid to the frequencies where several inputs must collaborate. A detailed explanation of the global procedure is given in [10].

The full achievement of (2) ends with the design of the master feedforward g_{d_m}. The specification format can now be adapted to $|(A + BG)/(C + DG)| \leq W$ of function gndbnds in the QFT toolbox [31]. By choosing $A = p_d$, $B = p_{d_m}$, $C = 1 + l_t$, $D = 0$, $G = g_{d_m}$, and $W = W_d$, the regions that are permitted for g_{d_m} on a mod-arg plot are determined; the loop-shaping of $g_{d_m}(j\omega)$ is conducted on these bounds.

Considering the whole set of external inputs, the output error responds to

$$e = -\frac{p_d + l_{g_d}}{1 + l_t} d + \frac{1}{1 + l_t}(r - v) - \sum_{i=1}^{n} \frac{p_i}{1 + l_t} r_{u_i}, \tag{10}$$

and the control inputs are

$$u_i = \left[-\frac{p_d + l_{g_d}}{1 + l_t} c_i + g_{d_i} g_{d_m}\right] d + \frac{c_i}{1 + l_t}(r - v) + \frac{(1 + l_{-i})}{1 + l_t} r_{u_i} - \sum_{k \neq i} \frac{c_i p_k}{1 + l_t} r_{u_k}, \quad (11)$$

where $l_{-i} = l_t - l_i$. Two benefits are mentioned. The availability of multiple inputs made it possible to select the intervention of the more favourable plants p_i at each frequency to achieve $|e/d| < W_d$ using the minimum $|u_i/d|$. Individual feedforward g_{d_i} and individual feedback c_i either disconnected or not the commanded inputs at each frequency; integrators or derivators are recommended to connect or disconnect plants at low frequency to fully eliminate steady-state errors [13]. Further, c_i and g_{d_m} were in charge of providing $|e/d| < W_d$; let us recall that g_{d_i} were filters of unitary gain at the pass-band. The use of feedforward g_{d_m} allows reducing the amount of feedback $|c_i|$; in fact, the formal QFT method pursues the minimum set of $|c_i|$ for the existence of g_{d_m}. As $|c_i|$ reduces, $|u_i/v|$ (11) also reduces in comparison with $g_{d_m} = 0$ solutions (feedback-only control structures are the only option when disturbances are nonmeasurable, as in [10,12]).

An additional flexibility of multi-input systems is the possibility of moving the system operating point $u_i(t = \infty)$ by changing the input resetting point $r_{u_i}(t)$ of the plants that do not work at low frequencies [9,12,32].

The output reference $r(t)$ is considered constant in the present work. For tracking control problems, feedforwarding $r(t)$ can achieve important benefits; a control architecture and design method were provided in [13].

3. Example

The following theoretical example illustrates the new method of designing feedback and feedforward elements. In addition to analysing how the specification of robust disturbance rejection is achieved with the minimum set of control actions, a comparison with a control structure with only feedback elements is conducted, proving the superiority of the feedback–feedforward structure. References [10,12] collected other examples with only feedback elements.

A system with two control inputs obeys the following models y/u_i, $i = 1, 2$, with parametric uncertainty:

$$p_1(s) = \frac{a_1}{\left(\frac{a_2}{a_1} s + 1\right)^2}, \quad a_1 \in [1.60, 2.40], \quad a_2 \in [0.17, 18.00];$$
$$p_2(s) = \frac{b_1}{b_2 s + 1}, \quad b_1 \in [0.98, 1.02], \quad b_2 \in [0.33, 1.00]. \quad (12)$$

The d disturbance input influence follows the uncertain parametric model y/d:

$$p_d(s) = \frac{c_1}{s + c_2}, \quad c_1 \in [2.00, 3.00], \quad c_2 \in [1.00, 2.00]. \quad (13)$$

Robust stability specifications

$$|T_i(j\omega)| = \left|\frac{l_i(j\omega)}{1 + l_t(j\omega)}\right| \leq W_{s_i}, i = 1, 2; \quad \forall P \in \mathcal{P}, \forall \omega, \quad (14)$$

seek minimum phase margins of $40°$ for both feedback loops $i = 1, 2$ by taking

$$W_{s_i} = \left|\frac{0.5}{\cos(\pi(180 - PM)/360)}\right|, \quad PM = 40°. \quad (15)$$

Their representative bounds will delimit forbidden regions around the critical point that cannot be violated by $l_i = c_i p_i / (1 + \sum_{j \neq i} l_j)$ at any ω-frequency during loop-shaping [11,12,32]. These bounds can be computed with traditional CAD tools in the QFT toolbox [31].

The specification for the robust rejection of measurable d-disturbances (2) adopts the tolerance

$$W_d(\omega) = \left| \frac{0.2s}{(0.5s+1)^2} \right|_{s=j\omega}, \tag{16}$$

whose magnitude frequency response is plotted together with the magnitude frequency responses of plants in Figure 2a. The error tolerance $W_d(\omega)$ will allow reducing the feedback to zero as soon as possible over $\omega > 4$. However, as $W_d(\omega) < |p_d(j\omega)|$, a small feedforward action will be needed at those frequencies. The problem arises when only feedback action is used, since feedback can never be neglected at high frequencies. Thus, a new specification

$$W_{dfb}(\omega) = \left| \frac{0.2s(0.1s+1)}{(0.5s+1)^2} \right|_{s=j\omega} \tag{17}$$

is defined for the comparison of the new control architecture with the feedback-only architecture. Let us remark that time-domain performance will not be appreciatively altered between the use of (16) or (17) since their differences occur after the control bandwidth (see Figure 2a).

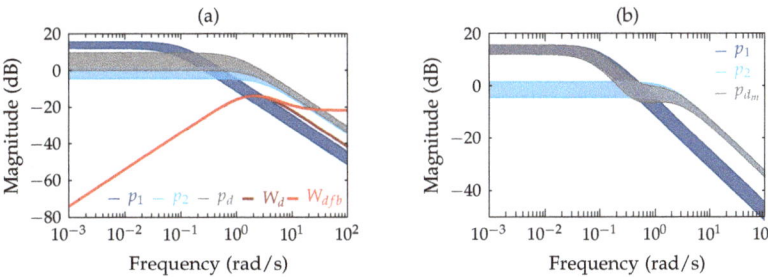

Figure 2. Magnitude frequency responses of plants: (**a**) performance specifications; (**b**) outcome plant after individual feedforward prefiltering.

The set of discrete frequencies

$$\Omega = \{0.01,\ 0.1,\ 0.2,\ 0.4,\ 0.8,\ 1,\ 4,\ 8,\ 10,\ 20\}\,[\text{rad/s}] \tag{18}$$

will be used for the assignment of working frequencies to inputs (plants) for bound calculations and to guide loop-shaping in the QFT framework. These have been selected considering the frequency response of plants and of the open-loop and closed-loop transfer functions.

3.1. Design Methodology

The frequency band allocation that minimises u_i is founded on the k_i frequency responses (6), which are depicted in Figure 3. The criteria argued in Section 2 advise that p_1 works over $\omega < 0.2$ and p_2 works over $\omega > 1.0$ since their respective k_i magnitudes are the lesser over those frequencies. Additionally, the collaboration of both plants over $0.2 \leq \omega \leq 1.0$ is advised since the difference between k_i-magnitudes is less than 6 dB, and the difference between k_i-phases is less than $90°$. Table 1 summarises all these conclusions.

Table 1. Frequency-band allocation that minimises u_i.

ω	0.01	0.1	0.2	0.4	0.8	1	4	8	10	20
p_1	×	×	×	×	×	×				
p_2			×	×	×	×	×	×	×	×

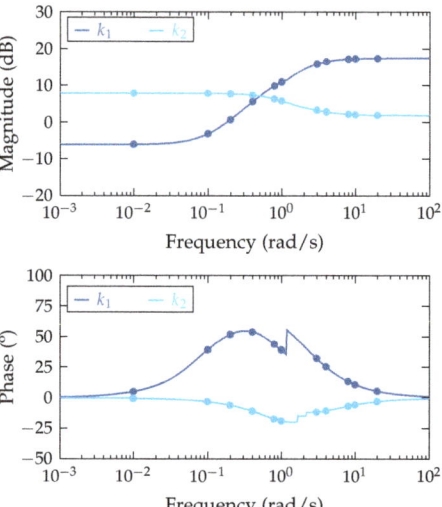

Figure 3. Frequency responses of $k_{1,2}$ (6).

According to the desired frequency band allocation (Table 1), the design of the individual feedforward elements yields

$$g_{d_1}(s) = \frac{1}{s+1}, \quad g_{d_2}(s) = \frac{s}{s+0.2}. \qquad (19)$$

The low-pass filter g_{d_1} attains a cut-off frequency of $\omega_c = 1$, and the high-pass filter g_{d_2} attains a cut-off frequency of $\omega_c = 0.2$. The use of individual filters $g_{d_{i=1,2}}$ modifies the outcome plant p_{d_m} (7) to be handled by feedback $c_{i=1,2}$ and the remaining feedforward g_{d_m}. Figure 2b proves how p_{d_m} selects the more powerful part of plants $p_{i=1,2}$, which will minimise u_{ff_i} to satisfy the performance specification (2) and (16).

For the design of feedback controllers c_i, the bounds β_{l_i} that represent performance (2) and (16) and stability (14) and (15) specifications are computed. Then, each l_i nominal, $l_{i_o} = p_{i_o} c_i$, is shaped to meet the bounds considering the frequency band allocation that minimises u_{fb_i} (see Table 1). Figure 4 depicts the bounds and loop-shapings; nominal plants p_{i_o} correspond to parameters $a = 0.16, b = 1.36, c = 0.98, d = 1.00$ in (12). The resulting controllers are

$$c_1(s) = \frac{1.575(s+0.08)}{s(s+0.12)(s+1.5)}, \quad c_2(s) = \frac{1.5(s+0.6)}{(s+0.3)^2}. \qquad (20)$$

Finally, the bounds on the feedforward master are computed, and the loop-shaping (see Figure 4) yields

$$g_{d_m}(s) = \frac{-1.1849(s+0.1)(s+0.175)(s+2)}{(s+0.052)(s^2+0.8563s+0.2072)}. \qquad (21)$$

If no feedforward loops are employed ($g_{d_1} = g_{d_2} = g_{d_m} = 0$), feedback controllers $c_{i=1,2}$ should complete the whole job. In such a case, after computing the bounds that represent the specifications of robust disturbance rejection (2) and (17) and robust stability (14) and (15), the shaping of l_{i_o}, $i = 1, 2$, yields

$$c_1 = \frac{108(s+0.1)}{s(s+10)(s+0.4)}, \quad c_2 = \frac{964.49(s+2.5)^2(s+0.2)}{(s+74)(s+7.8)(s^2+0.45s+0.0625)}. \qquad (22)$$

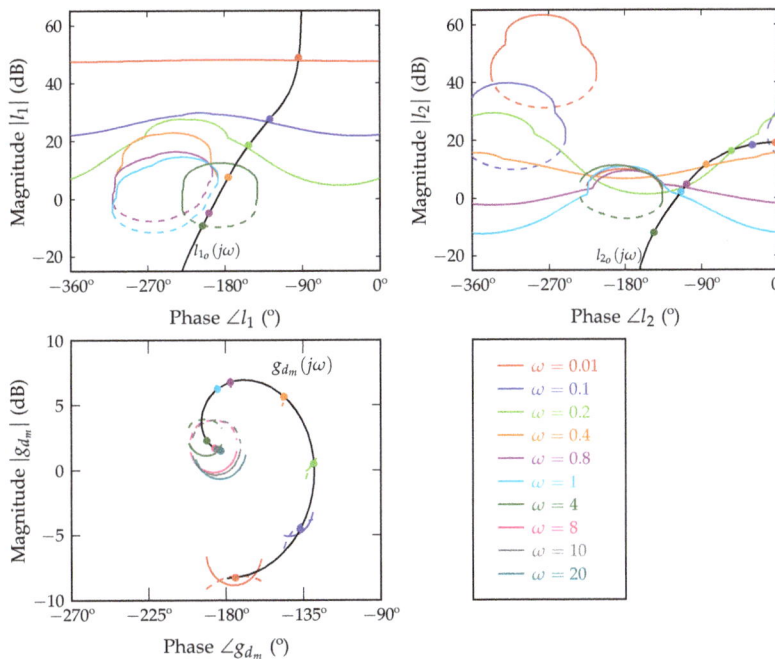

Figure 4. Bounds and loop-shaping for (north west) c_1, (north east) c_2, and (south west) g_{d_m}.

3.2. Analysis and Comparatives

Figure 5 shows several magnitude frequency responses of interest; the feedback-feedforward solution is depicted in blue and the feedback-only solution is in red; where applicable, several plant cases (12) are depicted.

In particular, closed-loop frequency responses of subplots (a) and (b) in Figure 5 prove the fulfilment of robust specifications on disturbance rejection and stability, respectively. A tight achievement of performance tolerance in the control bandwidth ($\omega \leq 4$) can be noticed because some plant cases are close to or on the tolerance $W_d(\omega)$; to achieve it, observe how l_{1_o} is onto β_{l_1} at $\omega = \{0.01, 0.1, 0.2\}$ and l_{2_o} onto β_{l_2} at $\omega = \{0.2, 0.4, 0.8, 1\}$ in Figure 4, which requires a relatively high order of the controllers (20) and (22). In addition, Table 1 planning has been executed successfully: l_1-l_{g_1} of the feedback–feedforward solution and l_1 of the feedback-only solution work alongside the low-frequency band, and l_2-l_{g_2} of feedback–feedforward and l_2 of feedback-only work alongside the high-frequency band (see subplots (e) and (f) in Figure 5).

The expected benefits of the above are using the minimum $|u_i/d|$ over $\omega \leq 4$ (see subplot (g) in Figure 5). Regarding the frequency band distribution among plants, let us note, p.e., that if p_2 were forced to work at low frequency instead of p_1, $|u_2/d(j0)|$ would be $|p_1/p_2(j0)|$ larger than the current $|u_1/d(j0)|$. Regarding the tight achievement of bounds for each input design, it seeks the strictly necessary $|u_i/d|$ to achieve the specification; observe how $|u_1/d|$ along $\omega \leq 1$ and $|u_2/d|$ along $0.2 \leq \omega \leq 4$ are very similar for both solutions. The minimum effort in the control bandwidth pursues that $|u_i/v|$ can be reduced as soon as possible at high frequencies (see subplot (h) in Figure 5). However, the collaboration of feedback l_i and feedforward l_{g_i} to build u_i/d yields smaller magnitudes $|l_i|$ than when only feedback intervenes (see subplot (e) in Figure 5). Then, feedback gains $|c_i|$ are smaller not only in the control bandwidth but also beyond the work-band of each input (see subplot (c) in Figure 5). The end effect $|u_1/v|$ over $\omega > 1$ is smaller for the feedback–feedforward solution than for the feedback-only solution, and the same occurs for $|u_2/v|$ over $\omega > 4$ (see subplot (h) in Figure 5). In fact, a huge noise amplification is expected at the second control input in the feedback-only solution.

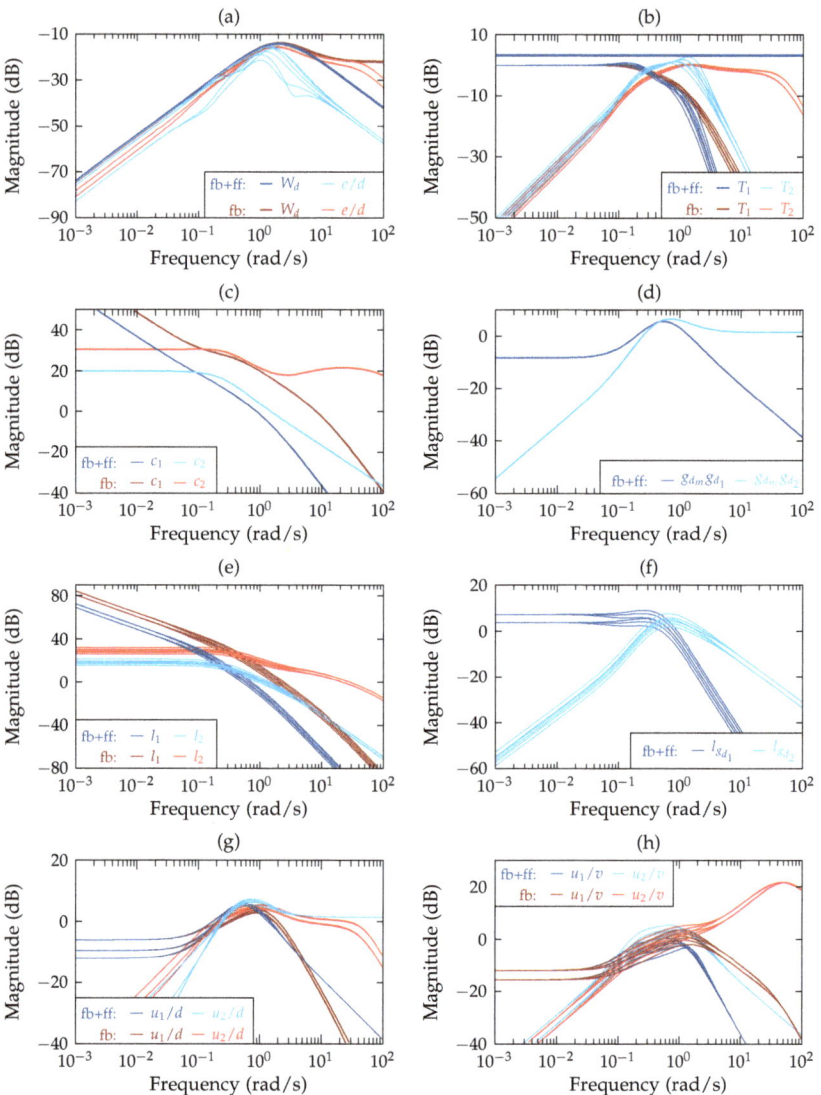

Figure 5. Magnitude frequency responses: (**a**) Output error, (**b**) stability, (**c**) feedback controllers, (**d**) feedforward elements, (**e**) feedback open-loops, (**f**) feedforward open-loops, (**g**) control inputs for disturbance rejection, (**h**) sensor noise at the control inputs.

Figure 6 shows the time-domain behaviour. External inputs are a unit step change of disturbance $d(t)$ at $t = 1$ s and a sensor noise $v(t)$ that is built with a band-limited, white-noise source of Simulink® (power of 0.00005 and sample time of 0.01 s); the reference input $r(t)$ is constant and equal to zero. Blue and red colours distinguish the responses of feedback–feedforward and feedback-only solutions, respectively. Several plant cases are represented.

As expected, the output response $y(t)$ is built by the faster response $y_2(t)$ of the plant p_2, which works at high frequencies, and by the slower response $y_1(t)$ of the plant p_1, which progressively takes control of the steady-state. Ignoring the noise, the control actions $u_1(t)$ and $u_2(t)$, which command the plants p_1 and p_2, corroborate the same. Let us also remark how the input u_2, which does not work at steady-state, recovers the initial operating point $r_{u_2} = 0$. Further, observe that $y(t)$ finally recovers the initial steady-state of zero. Both steady-state conditions $y = r$ and $u_2 = r_{u_2}$ require an integrator in c_1 (20) and (22) and a differentiator in g_{d_2} (19). Regarding the control actions, $u_i(t)$ is built with $u_{ff_i}(t)$ and $u_{fb_i}(t)$ in the feedback–feedforward solution, while $u_i(t) = u_{fb_i}(t)$ is built in the feedback-only solution. The main difference between both solutions is the $v(t)$ noise amplification at the output and, mainly, at the control inputs. The huge noise amplification at $u_2(t)$ of the feedback-only solution would cause fatigue of the actuator or might saturate it and spoil the theoretical performance. In such a case, a more conservative specification for disturbance rejection e/d would be indicated in true-life control (higher tolerance W_d in the control bandwidth). All these corroborate the superiority of feedback–feedforward schemes.

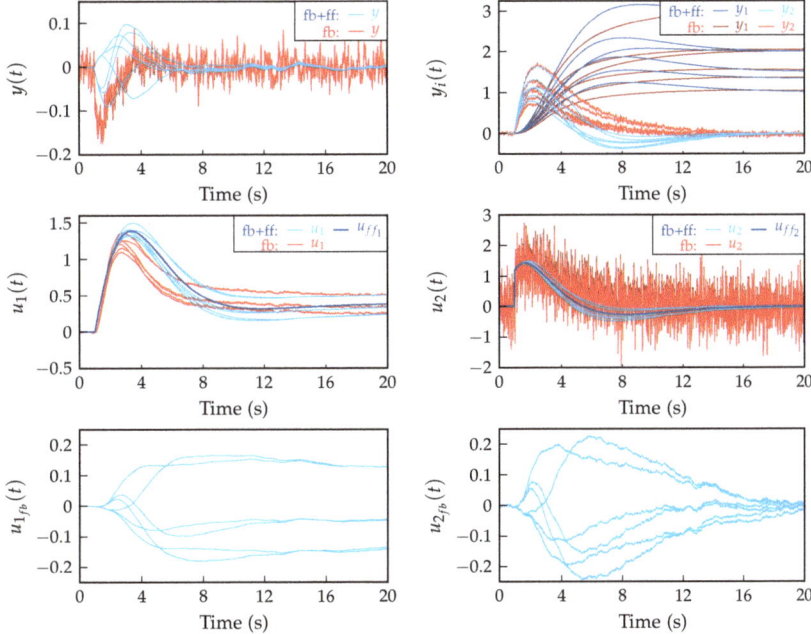

Figure 6. Time-domain responses.

4. Conclusions

A new control architecture and design methodology has been proposed for the robust rejection of measurable disturbances when multiple control inputs are available to correct the output deviation. The multi-input character allowed selecting the most favourable plants (inputs) at each frequency to provide the performance. Thus, individual feedback and feedforward controllers to each input allowed distributing the control bandwidth as desired among the inputs; the allocation criterion was minimising the control action to provide the performance. Beyond that, the main benefit of the new structure is the presence of feedforward loops. This allowed reducing the amount of feedback and, consequently, the sensor noise amplification at the output and, mainly, at the control inputs. The advantages would be notorious in real-life systems, since excessive noise at actuators could sacrifice the achievement of the aggressive performance of the output. Finally, it is important to recall the robust character of the control system, which guaranteed the expected performance for a set of possible plant models.

Author Contributions: Conceptualization, J.R.-A. and M.G.-M.; software, J.R.-A.; data curation, J.R.-A.; writing—original draft preparation, M.G.-M.; writing—review and editing, J.R.-A. and M.G.-M.; funding acquisition, M.G.-M. All authors have read and agreed to the published version of the manuscript.

Funding: This research was funded by the University of La Rioja under grant REGI 2020/23.

Data Availability Statement: The data used to support the findings of this study are available from the corresponding author upon request.

Conflicts of Interest: The authors declare no conflict of interest.

Abbreviations

The following abbreviations are used in this manuscript:

QFT	quantitative feedback theory
MISO	multiple-input single-output
SISO	single-input single-output
CAD	computer-aided design

References

1. Horowitz, I. Survey of quantitative feedback theory (QFT). *Int. J. Robust Nonlinear Control.* **2001**, *11*, 887–921. [CrossRef]
2. Houpis, C.; Rasmussen, S.; Garcia-Sanz, M. *Quantitative Feedback Theory. Fundamentals and Applications*; CRC Press Book: Boca Raton, FL, USA, 2006.
3. García-Sanz, M. *Robust Control Engineering: Practical QFT Solutions*; CRC Press: Boca Raton, FL, USA, 2017; pp. 1–556. [CrossRef]
4. Elso, J.; Gil-Martínez, M.; García-Sanz, M. Quantitative feedback-feedforward control for model matching and disturbance rejection. *IET Control. Theory Appl.* **2013**, *7*, 894–900. [CrossRef]
5. Reyes-Lúa, A.; Skogestad, S. Multiple-input single-output control for extending the steady-state operating range-use of controllers with different setpoints. *Processes* **2019**, *7*, 941. [CrossRef]
6. Reyes-Lúa, A.; Skogestad, S. Multi-input single-output control for extending the operating range: Generalized split range control using the baton strategy. *J. Process. Control* **2020**, *91*, 1–11. [CrossRef]
7. Hägglund, T. A feedforward approach to mid-ranging control. *Control. Eng. Pract.* **2021**, *108*, 104713. [CrossRef]
8. Sun, B.; Skogestad, S.; Lu, J.; Zhang, W. Dual SIMC-PI Controller Design for Cascade Implement of Input Resetting Control with Application. *Ind. Eng. Chem. Res.* **2018**, *57*, 6947–6955. [CrossRef]
9. Allison, B.J.; Ogawa, S. Design and tuning of valve position controllers with industrial applications. *Trans. Inst. Meas. Control.* **2003**, *25*, 3–16. [CrossRef]
10. Rico-Azagra, J.; Gil-Martínez, M.; Elso, J. Quantitative feedback control of multiple input single output systems. *Math. Probl. Eng.* **2014**, *2014*, 1–17. [CrossRef]
11. Gil-Martínez, M.; Rico-Azagra, J.; Elso, J. Frequency domain design of a series structure of robust controllers for multi-input single-output systems. *Math. Probl. Eng.* **2018**, *2018*. [CrossRef]
12. Gil-Martínez, M.; Rico-Azagra, J. Robust Feedback Control for Nonminimum Phase, Delayed, or Unstable Systems with Multiple Inputs. *Math. Probl. Eng.* **2020**, *2020*. [CrossRef]
13. Rico-Azagra, J.; Gil-Martínez, M. Feedforward for robust reference tracking in multi-input feedback control. *IEEE Access* **2021**, *9*, 92553–92567. [CrossRef]
14. Johnsson, O.; Sahlin, D.; Linde, J.; Lidén, G.; Hägglund, T. A mid-ranging control strategy for non-stationary processes and its application to dissolved oxygen control in a bioprocess. *Control. Eng. Pract.* **2015**, *42*, 89–94. [CrossRef]
15. Nájera, S.; Gil-Martínez, M.; Rico-Azagra, J. Dual-control of autothermal thermophilic aerobic digestion using aeration and solid retention time. *Water* **2017**, *9*, 426. [CrossRef]
16. Schroeck, S.J.; Messner, W.C.; McNab, R.J. On compensator design for linear time-invariant dual-input single-output systems. *IEEE/ASME Trans. Mechatron.* **2001**, *6*, 50–57. [CrossRef]
17. Alvarez-Ramirez, J.; Velasco, A.; Fernandez-Anaya, G. A note on the stability of habituating process control. *J. Process. Control.* **2004**, *14*, 939–945. [CrossRef]
18. Zotică, C.; Pérez-Piñeiro, D.; Skogestad, S. Supervisory control design for balancing supply and demand in a district heating system with thermal energy storage. *Comput. Chem. Eng.* **2021**, *149*, 107306. [CrossRef]
19. Van Heusden, K.; Ansermino, J.M.; Dumont, G.A. Robust MISO control of propofol-remifentanil anesthesia guided by the neurosense Monitor. *IEEE Trans. Control. Syst. Technol.* **2018**, *26*, 1758–1770. [CrossRef]

20. Eskandari, N.; van Heusden, K.; Dumont, G.A. Extended habituating model predictive control of propofol and remifentanil anesthesia. *Biomed. Signal Process. Control* **2020**, *55*, 101656. [CrossRef]
21. Soltani Bozchalooi, I.; Youcef-Toumi, K. Multi-actuation and PI control: A simple recipe for high-speed and large-range atomic force microscopy. *Ultramicroscopy* **2014**, *146*, 117–124. [CrossRef]
22. Soltani Bozchalooi, I.; Careaga Houck, A.; AlGhamdi, J.; Youcef-Toumi, K. Design and control of multi-actuated atomic force microscope for large-range and high-speed imaging. *Ultramicroscopy* **2016**, *160*, 213–224. [CrossRef]
23. Li, H.; Du, C.; Wang, Y. Optimal reset control for a dual-stage actuator system in HDDs. *IEEE/ASME Trans. Mechatron.* **2011**, *16*, 480–488. [CrossRef]
24. Zheng, J.; Fu, M. A unified dual-stage actuator control scheme for track seeking and following in hard disk drives. *IET Control Theory Appl.* **2012**, *6*, 1468–1477. [CrossRef]
25. Jade, S.; Larimore, J.; Hellstrom, E.; Jiang, L.; Stefanopoulou, A.G. Enabling large load transitions on multicylinder recompression HCCI engines using fuel governors. In Proceedings of the American Control Conference, Washington, DC, USA, 17–19 June 2013; pp. 4423–4428. [CrossRef]
26. Wu, J.; Liang, J.; Ruan, J.; Zhang, N.; Walker, P. A robust energy management strategy for EVs with dual input power-split transmission. *Mech. Syst. Signal Process.* **2018**, *111*, 442–455. [CrossRef]
27. Ma, Z.; Poo, A.N.; Ang, M.H., Jr.; Hong, G.S.; See, H.H. Design and control of an end-effector for industrial finishing applications. *Robot. Comput.-Integr. Manuf.* **2018**, *53*, 240–253. [CrossRef]
28. Nainer, C.; Furci, M.; Seuret, A.; Zaccarian, L.; Franchi, A. Hierarchical Control of the Over-Actuated ROSPO Platform via Static Input Allocation. *IFAC-PapersOnLine* **2017**, *50*, 12698–12703. [CrossRef]
29. Schneider, U.; Olofsson, B.; Sörnmo, O.; Drust, M.; Robertsson, A.; Hägele, M.; Johansson, R. Integrated approach to robotic machining with macro/micro-actuation. *Robot. Comput.-Integr. Manuf.* **2014**, *30*, 636–647. [CrossRef]
30. Haus, T.; Ivanovic, A.; Car, M.; Orsag, M.; Bogdan, S. Mid-Ranging Control Concept for a Multirotor UAV with Moving Masses. In Proceedings of the MED 2018-26th Mediterranean Conference on Control and Automation, Zadar, Croatia, 19–22 June 2018; pp. 339–344. [CrossRef]
31. Borghesani, C.; Chait, Y.; Yaniv, O. *Quantitative Feedback Theory Toolbox. For Use with Matlab*, 2nd ed.; Terasoft: San Diego, CA, USA, 2002.
32. Rico-Azagra, J.; Gil-Martínez, M.; Rico, R.; Maisterra, P. QFT bounds for robust stability specifications defined on the open-loop function. *Int. J. Robust Nonlinear Control* **2018**, *28*, 1116–1125. [CrossRef]

Article

Leveraging Elasticity to Uncover the Role of Rabinowitsch Suspension through a Wavelike Conduit: Consolidated Blood Suspension Application

Sara I. Abdelsalam [1,2,*] and Abdullah Z. Zaher [3]

1. Basic Science, Faculty of Engineering, The British University in Egypt, Al-Shorouk City, Cairo 11837, Egypt
2. Instituto de Matemáticas—Juriquilla, Universidad Nacional Autónoma de México, Blvd. Juriquilla 3001, Querétaro 76230, Mexico
3. Engineering Mathematics and Physics Department, Faculty of Engineering, Shubra-Benha University, Cairo 11629, Egypt; abdullah.zaher@feng.bu.edu.eg
* Correspondence: sara.abdelsalam@bue.edu.eg or siabdelsalam@im.unam.mx

Citation: Abdelsalam, S.I.; Zaher, A.Z. Leveraging Elasticity to Uncover the Role of Rabinowitsch Suspension through a Wavelike Conduit: Consolidated Blood Suspension Application. *Mathematics* **2021**, *9*, 2008. https://doi.org/10.3390/math9162008

Academic Editor: Efstratios Tzirtzilakis

Received: 28 June 2021
Accepted: 18 August 2021
Published: 22 August 2021

Publisher's Note: MDPI stays neutral with regard to jurisdictional claims in published maps and institutional affiliations.

Copyright: © 2021 by the authors. Licensee MDPI, Basel, Switzerland. This article is an open access article distributed under the terms and conditions of the Creative Commons Attribution (CC BY) license (https://creativecommons.org/licenses/by/4.0/).

Abstract: The present work presents a mathematical investigation of a Rabinowitsch suspension fluid through elastic walls with heat transfer under the effect of electroosmotic forces (EOFs). The governing equations contain empirical stress-strain equations of the Rabinowitsch fluid model and equations of fluid motion along with heat transfer. It is of interest in this work to study the effects of EOFs, which are rigid spherical particles that are suspended in the Rabinowitsch fluid, the Grashof parameter, heat source, and elasticity on the shear stress of the Rabinowitsch fluid model and flow quantities. The solutions are achieved by taking long wavelength approximation with the creeping flow system. A comparison is set between the effect of pseudoplasticity and dilatation on the behaviour of shear stress, axial velocity, and pressure rise. Physical behaviours have been graphically discussed. It was found that the Rabinowitsch and electroosmotic parameters enhance the shear stress while they reduce the pressure gradient. A biomedical application to the problem is presented. The present analysis is particularly important in biomedicine and physiology.

Keywords: elasticity; electroosmotic forces; heat transfer; Rabinowitsch fluid; suspension

1. Introduction

The movement of blood liquids is an important study for the mathematical simulation of medical applications. Rabinowitsch fluid is one of the fluids that simulate blood movement because the Rabinowitsch model effectively relies on studying the result of lubricant additives, for a wide range of shear rates, and studying their experimental data. Over the past decades, scientists have made active efforts to increase the ability of solidifying the features of non-Newtonian lubricants using long-chain quantities by adding a very small addition of the polymer solution. A very important result from this is that this result reduces the lubricant sensitivity. Additionally, a non-linear relationship appears between the shear stress rate and shear pressure. Through those recent actions based on the Rabinowitsch model, Akbar and Butt [1] studied the flow of the Rabinowitsch model due to the cilia located on the wall. Moreover, Singh et al. [2] studied the movement of Rabinowitsch fluid through peristaltic flow. In addition, Vaidya [3] investigated the movement of Rabinowitsch fluid through the oblique wall of a channel, while Sadaf and Nadeem [4] studied the Rabinowitsch model through a non-uniform conduit with peristalsis. Choudhari et al. [5] also studied the effect of slipping on the oscillating transmission of a Rabinowitsch model in a non-uniform channel.

In recent years, microfluidic systems have been developed through the use of Electric-Double-Layer (EDL). This increased interest is reflected in references [6–8]. Electrical osmosis is defined as the movement of a liquid in relation to a fixed surface due to the presence of an externally applied electric field. One of the first studies that have studied the application of these external forces is by Ross [9]. The idea is that electrical ripening comes into contact with the aqueous electrolytic solution with the solids and then generates a relatively electrical charge. In addition, the opposite ion charge is attracted to that charge on the surface and the opposite process from the ions on the surface and shows the double layer, and thus, the surface becomes electrically charged. As a result of this phenomenon, a process of acceleration of the liquid by migrating ions occurs, and the resulting flow is called electromagnetic flow.

The study of the movement of suspended particles inside the fluid is considered the most important medical application. The movement of the fluid that contains particles is similar to the movement of the blood plasma since the blood consists of solid materials, that is, it is a liquid in which those substances swim. In that sense, there are a lot of species studied such as sickle cell (Hb SS), plasma cell dyscrasias, normal blood, controlled hypertension, uncontrolled hypertension, and polycythaemia. Each of these types is known by a specific haematocrit, i.e., C = 0.248, C = 0.28, C = 0.426, C = 0.4325, C = 0.4331, and C = 0.632 [10]. In addition, the study of the movement of suspended particles inside fluids is very interesting because they resemble white blood cells, red blood cells, and/or platelets that move inside the blood. Many experimental and analytical studies have focused on studying suspended particles because of their great importance in improving and understanding the blood flow and the distribution of proteins within it [11–13].

The geometrical shape of fluid flow has an important role in understanding various properties of different fluid flows such as blood flow and other important applications. Most studies that have discussed fluid movement have relied on solid ducts and tubes [14–24]. Because biological flows depend on their flexible flow fields, and this appears through their flexible nature, the flow and the movement of Newtonian and non-Newtonian fluids through walls of a flexible nature carry many important medical applications such as blood flow through the arteries, small blood vessels, heart systems, and others, which, according to some studies, revealed that the velocity of the blood is greatly affected by the elastic placement of the walls. Some of the work that has been interested in discussing the flow rate through elastic nature can be found in the refs. [25–31].

Accordingly, this work attempts to fill the void of the movement of the particulate suspension under the effects of electroosmotic forces using Rabinowitsch fluid. Analytical solution is used to obtain the physical parameters of the problem subjected to appropriate boundary conditions. The impact of relevant parameters is discussed graphically.

2. The Mathematical Model and the Rabinowitsch Fluid Equation

Consider a particulate suspension swimming in a Rabinowitsch fluid through elastic peristaltic walls of a channel with amplitude a and half width b. In addition, consider that the deformation on the wall is α as shown in Figure 1. Furthermore, the inlet pressure is defined as p_i and the outlet pressure is defined as p_o, as shown in Figure 1. The effect of the electroosmotic forces on the Rabinowitsch fluid through the elastic peristaltic walls is taken into account. The velocity of the particulate suspension and Rabinowitsch fluid are denoted by $\vec{V}(\overline{U}_p, \overline{V}_p)$, $\vec{V}(\overline{U}_f, \overline{V}_f)$. The mathematical geometry of the channel wall is given by

$$H(\overline{X}, t) = \pm \left(d + a \sin \frac{2\pi}{\lambda} (\overline{X} - c\, t) \right), \qquad (1)$$

Here, d is the radius of the artery channel, a is the amplitude of the wall, λ is the amplitude of the peristaltic wave, and c is the blood velocity.

The isotropic rheological equation of a Rabinowitsch fluid takes the following form:

$$\overline{\tau}_{\overline{XY}} + \mu_o \overline{\tau}_{\overline{XY}}^3 = \mu_S(C) \frac{\partial \overline{U}}{\partial \overline{Y}}, \qquad (2)$$

where the coefficient μ_o represents pseudo-plasticity of the fluid, which takes a fundamental role in determining the nature of fluids; $\mu_S(C)$ is the viscosity of suspension; $\overline{\tau}_{XY}$ is the stress tensor; $\overline{U}$ is the velocity component; and C is the volume fraction. The model represents a pseudoplastic state for $\mu_o > 0$, a Newtonian state for $\mu_o = 0$, and an expanded fluid model for $\mu_S < 1$.

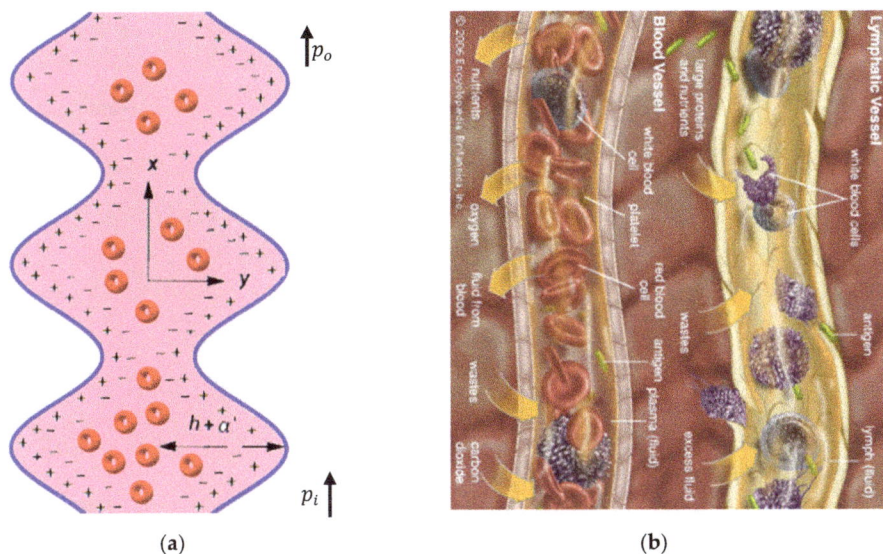

Figure 1. (a) Physical modelling of the problem. (b) Example for extracellular fluid that contains plasma.

The momentum and continuity equations for the problem of both particle and fluid phases are given in the following form [32].

Model of Fluid Phase

$$\frac{\partial \overline{U}_f}{\partial \overline{X}} + \frac{\partial \overline{V}_f}{\partial \overline{Y}} = 0, \qquad (3)$$

$$\rho_f\, C_{PH} \left(\frac{\partial \overline{U}_f}{\partial t} + \overline{U}_f \frac{\partial \overline{U}_f}{\partial \overline{X}} + \overline{V}_f \frac{\partial \overline{U}_f}{\partial \overline{Y}} \right)$$
$$= -C_{PH}\frac{\partial \overline{P}}{\partial \overline{X}} + C_{PH}\left[\frac{\partial \tau_{\overline{XX}}}{\partial \overline{X}} + \frac{\partial \tau_{\overline{XY}}}{\partial \overline{Y}}\right] + \rho_e E_x + \rho_f \gamma g\,(T - T_0) - C\,S\left(\overline{U}_f - \overline{U}_P\right), \qquad (4)$$

$$\rho_f\, C_{PH}\left(\frac{\partial \overline{V}_f}{\partial t} + \overline{U}_f \frac{\partial \overline{V}_f}{\partial \overline{X}} + \overline{V}_f \frac{\partial \overline{V}_f}{\partial \overline{Y}}\right)$$
$$= -C_{PH}\frac{\partial \overline{P}}{\partial \overline{Y}} + C_{PH}\left[\frac{\partial \tau_{\overline{XX}}}{\partial \overline{X}} + \frac{\partial \tau_{\overline{XY}}}{\partial \overline{Y}}\right] - C\,S\left(\overline{V}_f - \overline{V}_P\right), \qquad (5)$$

$$(\rho C)_f \left(\frac{\partial T_f}{\partial t} + \overline{U}_f \frac{\partial T_f}{\partial \overline{X}} + \overline{V}_f \frac{\partial T_f}{\partial \overline{Y}} \right) = k\left(\frac{\partial^2 T}{\partial \overline{X}^2} + \frac{\partial^2 T}{\partial \overline{Y}^2}\right) + H_S, \qquad (6)$$

Model of Particle Phase

$$\frac{\partial \overline{U}_P}{\partial \overline{X}} + \frac{\partial \overline{V}_P}{\partial \overline{Y}} = 0, \qquad (7)$$

$$\rho_P\, C_{PH}\left(\frac{\partial \overline{U}_P}{\partial t} + \overline{U}_P \frac{\partial \overline{U}_P}{\partial \overline{X}} + \overline{V}_P \frac{\partial \overline{U}_P}{\partial \overline{Y}}\right) = -C_{PH}\frac{\partial \overline{P}}{\partial \overline{X}} + C\,S\left(\overline{U}_f - \overline{U}_P\right), \qquad (8)$$

$$\rho_f\, C_{PH}\left(\frac{\partial \overline{V}_P}{\partial t} + \overline{U}_P \frac{\partial \overline{V}_P}{\partial \overline{X}} + \overline{V}_P \frac{\partial \overline{V}_P}{\partial \overline{Y}}\right) = -C_{PH}\frac{\partial \overline{P}}{\partial \overline{Y}} + C\,S\left(\overline{V}_f - \overline{V}_P\right), \qquad (9)$$

where $C_{PH} = 1 - C$, S is the drag coefficient and $\mu_S(C)$ is the viscosity of suspension, $\rho_{f,p}$ is the fluid and particle density, ρ_e is the electrical charge density, E_x is the axial electric field, γ is the thermal expansion coefficient, g is the gravitational acceleration, k is the thermal conductivity, and H_S is the constant heat absorption or heat generation. The empirical relation for S and $\mu_S(C)$ can be described as

$$\mu_S = 1/(1 - m\,C), \quad m = 0.07 * Exp\left[2.49 * C - \tfrac{1107}{273} * Exp[-1.69 * C]\right],$$
$$S = \tfrac{9\mu_0}{2\in^2}\gamma(C), \quad \gamma(C) = \tfrac{4+3\sqrt{8C-3C^2}+3C}{(2-3C)^2}. \tag{10}$$

Here, μ_0 is the viscosity of fluid for suspending medium, and $\in$ is the radius of a particle.

Now, we use the convenient transformation to convert from fixed frame to wave frame as follows:

$$\bar{x} = \overline{X} - ct, \quad \bar{y} = \overline{Y}, \quad \bar{u} = \overline{U} - c, \quad p = P. \tag{11}$$

Then, the mathematical formulation and Rabinowitsch fluid Equations (1)–(9) take the following form:

Rabinowitsch fluid equation

$$\overline{\tau_{xy}} + \mu_0 \overline{\tau_{xy}}^3 = \mu_s(C)\frac{\partial \bar{u}_f}{\partial \bar{y}}, \tag{12}$$

Model of fluid phase

$$\rho_f\,C_{PH}\left(\bar{u}_f\frac{\partial \bar{u}_f}{\partial \bar{x}} + \bar{v}_f\frac{\partial \bar{u}_f}{\partial \bar{y}}\right) \tag{13}$$

$$\rho_f\,C_{PH}\left(\bar{u}_f\frac{\partial \overline{V}_f}{\partial \bar{x}} + \bar{v}_f\frac{\partial \bar{v}_f}{\partial \bar{y}}\right) = -C_{PH}\frac{\partial \bar{p}}{\partial \bar{y}} + C_{PH}\left[\frac{\partial \tau_{yx}}{\partial \bar{x}^2} + \frac{\partial \tau_{yy}}{\partial \bar{y}^2}\right] - C\,S\left(\bar{v}_f - \bar{v}_P\right), \tag{14}$$

$$(\rho C)_f\left(\frac{\partial T_f}{\partial t} + \bar{u}_f\frac{\partial T_f}{\partial \bar{x}} + \bar{v}_f\frac{\partial T_f}{\partial \bar{y}}\right) = k\left(\frac{\partial^2 T}{\partial \bar{x}^2} + \frac{\partial^2 T}{\partial \bar{y}^2}\right) + H_S, \tag{15}$$

Model of particle phase

$$\rho_P\,C_{PH}\left(\bar{u}_P\frac{\partial \bar{u}_P}{\partial \bar{x}} + \bar{v}_P\frac{\partial \bar{u}_P}{\partial \bar{y}}\right) = -C_{PH}\frac{\partial \bar{p}}{\partial \bar{x}} + C\,S\left(\bar{u}_f - \bar{u}_P\right), \tag{16}$$

$$\rho_f\,C_{PH}\left(\bar{u}_P\frac{\partial \bar{v}_P}{\partial \bar{x}} + \bar{v}_P\frac{\partial \bar{v}_P}{\partial \bar{y}}\right) = -C_{PH}\frac{\partial \bar{p}}{\partial \bar{y}} + C\,S\left(\bar{v}_f - \bar{v}_P\right), \tag{17}$$

3. Electroosmotic Flow

The Poisson–Boltzmann equation:

$$\nabla^2 \bar{\varphi} = \frac{\rho_e}{\epsilon}, \tag{18}$$

where ρ_e is a charge density, ϵ is the electric permittivity, and $\bar{\varphi}$ is the electroosmotic potential function.

The charge density ρ_e of the fluid in a unit volume is given by:

$$\rho_e = \varepsilon\,e\,(n^+ - n^-) = -2\varepsilon\,e\,n_0\,\sinh\left\{\frac{\varepsilon\,e\,\bar{\varphi}}{k_B\,T_{av}}\right\}, \tag{19}$$

$$n^- = n_0\,e^{\frac{\varepsilon\,e\,\bar{\varphi}}{k_B T_{av}}}, \quad n^+ = n_0\,e^{\frac{-\varepsilon\,e\,\bar{\varphi}}{k_B T_{av}}}, \tag{20}$$

where ε, n^+, n^-, e, k_B, and T_{av} are the valence of ions, the number densities of positive and negative ions, electric charge, Boltzmann's constant, local absolute temperature of the electrolytic solution, and bulk volume concentration of positive or negative ions, respectively. In addition, using the Debye–Huckel linearisation principle, $\left\{\frac{\varepsilon e \varphi'}{k_B T_{av}} \ll 1\right\}$. Equation (19) reduces to

$$\rho_e = \frac{-\epsilon}{\Gamma^2}\overline{\varphi}, \qquad (21)$$

where $\Gamma = (\varepsilon\,e)^{-1}\sqrt{\frac{\epsilon\,k_B T_{av}}{2\,n_0}}$ is the Debye–Huckel parameter, which describes the properties of the EDL thickness. The solution for the distribution of the electroosmotic potential can easily be achieved using the Poisson–Boltzmann equation:

$$\frac{\partial^2 \overline{\varphi}}{\partial \overline{x}^2} + \frac{\partial^2 \overline{\varphi}}{\partial \overline{y}^2} = \frac{1}{\Gamma^2}\overline{\varphi}, \qquad (22)$$

4. Non-Dimensional Physical Parameters

The non dimensionless quantities are introduced in the following expression

$$\begin{array}{c} u_{P,f} = \frac{\overline{u}_{P,f}}{c}, y = \frac{\overline{y}}{a}, v_{P,f} = \frac{\overline{v}_{P,f}}{\delta c}, p = \frac{a^2}{\lambda\,c\,\mu_0}\overline{p}, \delta = \frac{a}{\lambda}, \vartheta = \frac{\overline{\varphi}}{\zeta}, Re = \frac{\rho_f\,c\,a}{\mu_0}, \\ Gr = \frac{\rho_f\gamma g\,a^2\,T_0}{\mu_0\,c}, \theta = \frac{T-T_0}{T_0}, \overline{\mu} = \frac{\mu_s(C)}{\mu_0}, \tau = \frac{a}{c\mu_0}\overline{\tau}, U_{HS} = -\frac{E_x\,\epsilon\,\zeta}{\mu_0\,c}, \\ K = \frac{\mu_s(C)c^2\mu_0^2}{a^2}, m = \frac{a}{k^2}, M = \frac{Sa^2}{\mu_s(C)(1-C)}, Q = \frac{H_s a^2}{\mu_0\,T_0}, p_r = \frac{\mu_0 C_f}{k}, \\ h = \frac{H}{d}, \phi = \frac{a}{d} \end{array} \qquad (23)$$

where K, m, Q, p_r, U_{HS}, Gr, and Re are, respectively, the Rabinowitsch fluid parameter, electroosmotic parameter, heat source, Prandtl number, electroosmotic velocity, Grashof number, and Reynolds number. The non-dimensional formulation of the mathematical geometry for the channel wall is given by

$$h(x) = \pm(1 + \phi \sin 2\pi\,x),$$

where ϕ is the amplitude ratio.

After using the non-dimensional physical parameters given by Equation (23) in the governing Equations (12)–(17) and in Equation (22), we find:

Non-dimensional Rabinowitsch fluid equations

$$\tau_{xy} + K\,\tau_{xy}^3 = \overline{\mu}\frac{\partial u_f}{\partial y}, \qquad (24)$$

Non-dimensional model of fluid phase

$$Re\,\delta\,C_{PH}\left(u_f\frac{\partial u_f}{\partial x} + v_f\frac{\partial u_f}{\partial y}\right) = -C_{PH}\frac{\partial p}{\partial x} + C_{PH}\left[\delta\frac{\partial \tau_{xx}}{\partial x} + \frac{\partial \tau_{xy}}{\partial y}\right] + m^2 U_{HS}\cosh my + G_r\,(T-T_0) - C\,C_{PH}\,\overline{\mu}\,M\left(u_f - u_P\right), \qquad (25)$$

$$Re\,\delta\,C_{PH}\left(u_f\frac{\partial v_f}{\partial x} + v_f\frac{\partial v_f}{\partial y}\right) = -C_{PH}\frac{\partial p}{\partial y} + C_{PH}\left[\frac{\partial \tau_{yx}}{\partial x} + \frac{\partial \tau_{yy}}{\partial y}\right] - C\,C_{PH}\,\overline{\mu}\,M\left(v_f - v_P\right), \qquad (26)$$

$$Re\,p_r\delta\left(u_f\frac{\partial \theta}{\partial x} + v_f\frac{\partial \theta}{\partial y}\right) = \left(\frac{\partial^2 \theta}{\partial x^2} + \frac{\partial^2 \theta}{\partial y^2}\right) + Q, \qquad (27)$$

Non-dimensional model of particle phase

$$\frac{\rho_P}{\rho_f}CR_e\delta\left(u_P\frac{\partial u_P}{\partial \overline{x}} + v_P\frac{\partial u_P}{\partial \overline{y}}\right) = -C\frac{\partial p}{\partial x} + C\,C_{PH}\,\overline{\mu}\,M\left(u_f - u_P\right), \qquad (28)$$

$$\frac{\rho_P}{\rho_f}CR_e\delta\left(u_P\frac{\partial v_P}{\partial x} + v_P\frac{\partial v_P}{\partial y}\right) = -C\frac{\partial p}{\partial y} + C\,C_{PH}\,\overline{\mu}\,M\,\delta\left(v_f - v_P\right), \qquad (29)$$

with dimensionless boundary conditions

$$u = -1, \quad \theta = 0, \quad \vartheta = 1 \quad \text{at} \quad y = h(x),$$
$$u = -1, \quad \theta = 0, \quad \vartheta = 1 \quad \text{at} \quad y = -h(x) \tag{30}$$
$$\tau_{xy} = 0 \text{ at } y = 0.$$

5. Methodology

Taking a long wavelength approximation and a creeping flow system, i.e., $\delta \ll 1$, the solution of Equations (24)–(29) takes the following form

$$\theta(y) = \frac{1}{2}Q(h-y)(h+y), \tag{31}$$

$$\tau_{xy} = \frac{6\,P\,y + G_r\,Q\,y(-3h^2 + y^2) - 6\,m\,U_{HS}\,\frac{\sinh\,(my)}{\cosh\,(mh)}}{6\,C_{PH}}, \tag{32}$$

$$\begin{aligned}u(y) = c_0 \{ & c_1 + c_2\,y^{10} + c_3\,y^2 + c_4\,y^8 + c_5\,y^6 + c_6\,\text{Cosh}(3my) + c_7\,y\,\text{Sinh}(2my) + c_8\,P_1(y) \\ & + \text{Cosh}(2my)(c_9 + c_{10}\,P_2(y)) + y\,\text{Sinh}(my)(c_{16} + c_{12}\,P_1(y)P_2(y)) + c_{13}\,P_3(y)) + c_{17} \\ & + \text{Cosh}(my)(c_{18} + c_{19}\,P_4(y)) + c_{20}\,y^4 + c_{21}\,y^2 + (c_{23} - c_{14}\,y^2(P_1(y))^2)) \}.\end{aligned} \tag{33}$$

where P, P_j ($j = 1 \to 4$) and the constants c_i ($i = 1 \to 23$) are given in the Appendix A.

6. Theoretical Determination of Pressure Gradient and Pressure Rise Application in Blood Flows

In this section, the deformation in the walls that is defined by elasticity in the channel walls is taken into account, which appears from the pressure shown in Figure 1. According to Rubinow and Keller [28], the flow rate and pressure gradient are related by the following expression:

$$Q = -\sigma(p_i - p_o)\frac{\partial p}{\partial x}, \tag{34}$$

The flow rate is defined as

$$Q = \int_0^h u(y)dy, \tag{35}$$

Following the hypothesis of elastic walls, according to Rubinow and Keller [28], and using Equations (33)–(35), it is found that the flow rate takes the following form as follows

$$Q = \sigma_1(p_i - p_o)\left(-\frac{\partial p}{\partial x}\right)^3 + \sigma_2(p_i - p_o)\left(-\frac{\partial p}{\partial x}\right)^2 + \sigma_3(p_i - p_o)\left(-\frac{\partial p}{\partial x}\right) + c_{24} \tag{36}$$

such that c_{24} is given in the Appendix A.
Where

$$\sigma_1(p_i - p_o) = \frac{\alpha(x)^5 k}{5A\,M^3}, \tag{37}$$

$$\begin{aligned}\sigma_2(p_i - p_o) = & \tfrac{1}{8640\bar{\mu}\,m^6M^3}\left(\tfrac{13824}{7}G_r\,\alpha(x)^7\,K\,m^6Q + 103680\,\alpha(x)K\,m^4\,U_{HS}\right. \\ & + 25920\,\alpha(x)K\,m^4(2 + \alpha(x)^2m^2)\,U_{hs} - 155520\,K\,m^3\,U_{HS}\,\tanh\,(\alpha(x)m) \\ & \left. - 77760\,\alpha\,(x)^2\,K\,m^5\,U_{HS}\,\tanh(\alpha(x)m)\right),\end{aligned} \tag{38}$$

$$\begin{aligned}
\sigma_3(p_i - p_o) = {} & \tfrac{1}{8640\bar{\mu}\, m^6 M^3}\Big(-2880\ \alpha(x)^3 m^6 M^2 - \tfrac{5312}{7} G_r^2\ \alpha(x)^9 K m^6 Q^2 \\
& +4320\ \alpha(x)^3 K m^8 U_{HS}{}^2 \operatorname{sech}^2(\alpha(x)m)) + 414720\ G_r\ \alpha(x)\ K\ Q\ U_{HS} \\
& -17280\ G_r\ \alpha(x)^3 K\ m^4 Q\ U_{HS} + 17280\ G_r\ \alpha(x)\ K\ m^2\ (24 - \alpha(x)^2 m^2)\ Q\ U_{HS} \\
& -17280\ G_r\ \alpha(x)\ K m^2(-12 - 3\,\alpha(x)^2 m^2 + \alpha(x)^4 m^4)\ Q\ U_{HS} \\
& +6480\ \ \alpha(x)\ K\ m^6\ U_{HS}{}^2 \operatorname{sech}(\alpha(x)m)\sinh(\alpha(x)m) - 622080\ G_r\ K\ m\ Q\ U_{HS}\tanh(\alpha(x)m) \\
& -103680\ G_r\ \alpha(x)^2 K\ m^3\ Q\ U_{HS}\tanh(\alpha(x)m) + 17280\ G_r\ \alpha(x)^4\ K\ m^5\ Q\ U_{HS}\tanh(\alpha(x)m) \\
& +17280\ G_r\ \alpha(x)^2 K\ m^3\ (-12 + \alpha(x)^2 m^2)\ Q\ U_{HS}\tanh(\alpha(x)m) \\
& -51840\ G_r\ K\ m\ (8 + \alpha(x)^2 m^2)\ Q\ U_{HS}\tanh(\alpha(x)m) \\
& -3240\ K\ m^5\ U_{HS}{}^2\ \operatorname{sech}(\alpha(x)m)\sinh(\alpha(x)m) \\
& -6480\ \alpha(x)^2\ K\ m^7 U_{HS}\ \operatorname{sech}(\alpha(x)m)\sinh(\alpha(x)m)\Big),
\end{aligned} \qquad (39)$$

Here, $\alpha(x) = h(x) + \alpha'$, where $h(x)$ and α' are the radii of the channel for peristalsis and elasticity, respectively. Additionally, the pressure rise is defined as

$$\Delta p = \int_0^1 \left(\frac{dp}{dx}\right) dx. \qquad (40)$$

7. Graphical Results and Discussion

The goal of this section is to study the effect of the pertinent parameters on the resulted physical expression. In doing so, the Mathematica program is used in order to investigate the impact of Rabinowitsch parameter K, Prandlt number Pr, heat source Q, electroosmotic parameter m, volume fraction C, Grashof number Gr, maximum electroosmotic velocity U_{HS}, and radius of the channel for elasticity α' on the shear stress τ_{xy}, axial velocity $U(y)$, pressure gradient $\frac{dp}{dx}$, and pressure rise Δp. A graphical comparison is also set to compare between pseudoplastic and dilatant fluids.

Figures 2–9 are plotted to investigate the impact of U_{HS}, C, Gr, m, K, and α' on τ_{xy} for sundry values of the parameters of interest. It is observed from Figures 2–7 that the Rabinowitsch shear stress improves prominently with increasing all the parameters, even with increasing the curviness of the conduit in both the lower and upper halves of the channel. Figures 8 and 9 demonstrate a comparison between the impact of pseudoplasticity and dilatation on the shear stress profile through x and y axes, respectively. It is notable from the latter figures that for pseudoplastic fluid, τ_{xy} is enhanced along the conduit through the x-axis, whereas for the case of dilatant fluids, a reverse effect is observed. It is also seen that τ_{xy} behaves differently along the y-axis where it is seen that, for the pseudoplastic fluids, τ_{xy} decays near the lower wall of the channel and improves with an increase in the curviness of the channel. An exact opposite behaviour is seen for dilatant fluids, as seen in Figure 9.

Figures 10–16 illustrate the impact of K, U_{HS}, Gr, C, m, and α' on $U(y)$ for various values of the pertinent parameters. It is noticed that K, U_{HS}, and α' play a distinguished role in lessening the fluid velocity, as seen in Figures 10, 11 and 15. It is also depicted that Gr, C, and m disturb the velocity profile significantly, as observed in Figures 12–14. It is noticed that the latter parameters barely have an effect on $U(y)$ near the walls of the channel, whereas they enhance the flow in the centre part of the channel. It is generally noticed that $U(y)$ has a parabolic shape along the conduit for all the parameters under consideration. Figure 16 is plotted to spot the difference in the behaviour of $U(y)$ for pseudoplastic and dilated fluids. It is demonstrated that for pseudoplastic fluids, $U(y)$ is not disturbed at all near the walls of the conduit, whereas it is noticed that for dilated fluids, the flow is decelerated at the centre of the channel.

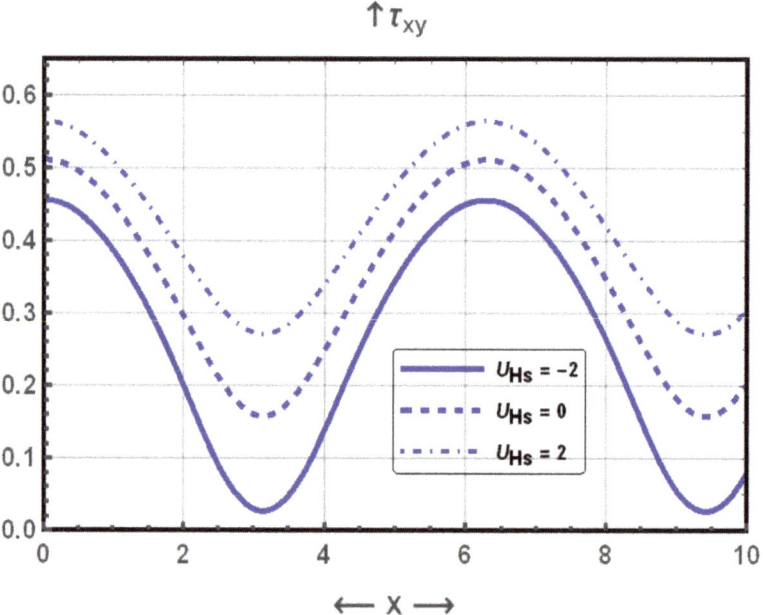

Figure 2. Display of shear stress profile for different values of U_{HS}.

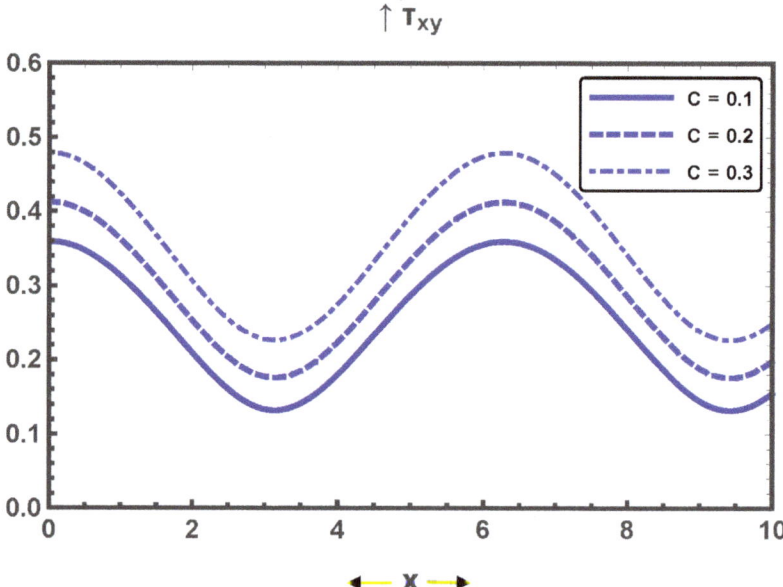

Figure 3. Display of shear stress profile for different values of C.

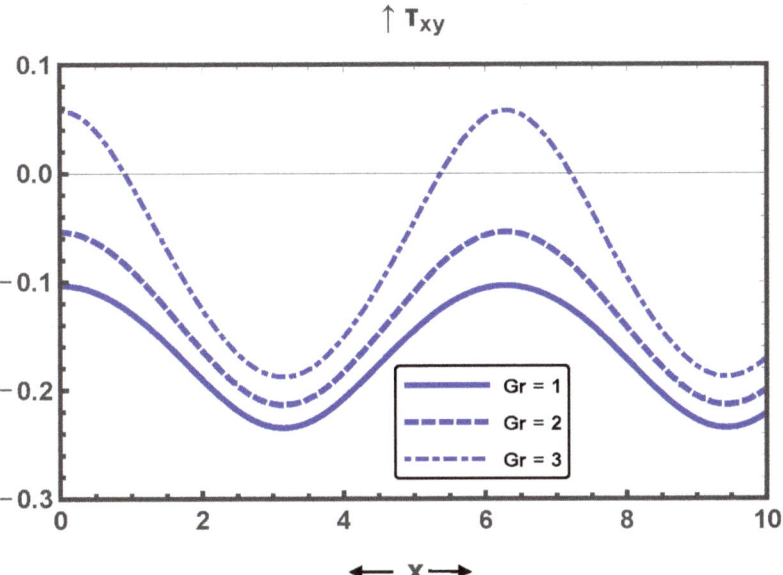

Figure 4. Display of shear stress profile for different values of Gr.

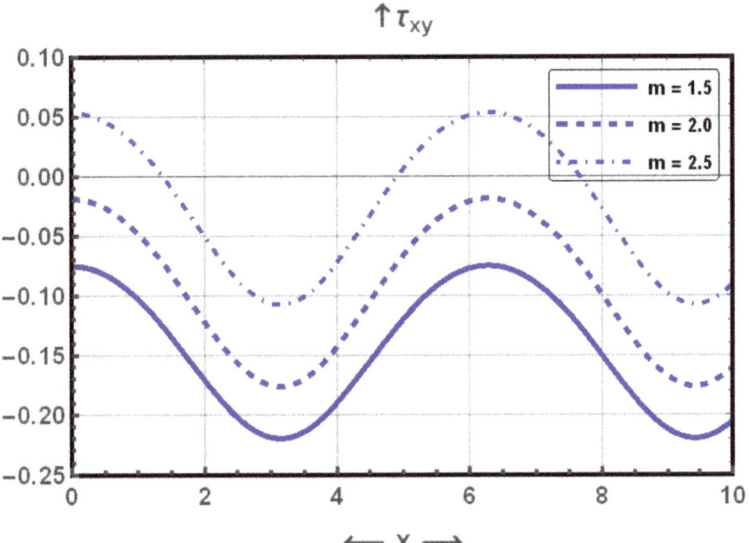

Figure 5. Display of shear stress profile for different values of m.

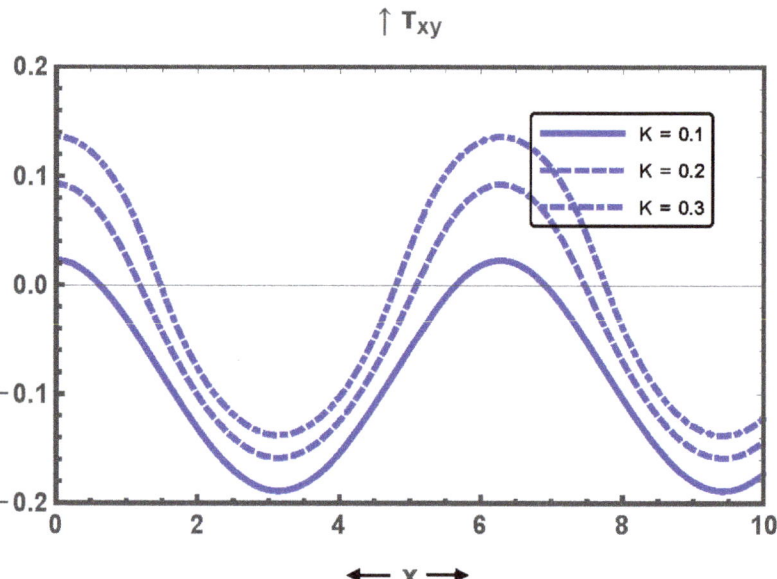

Figure 6. Display of shear stress profile for different values of K.

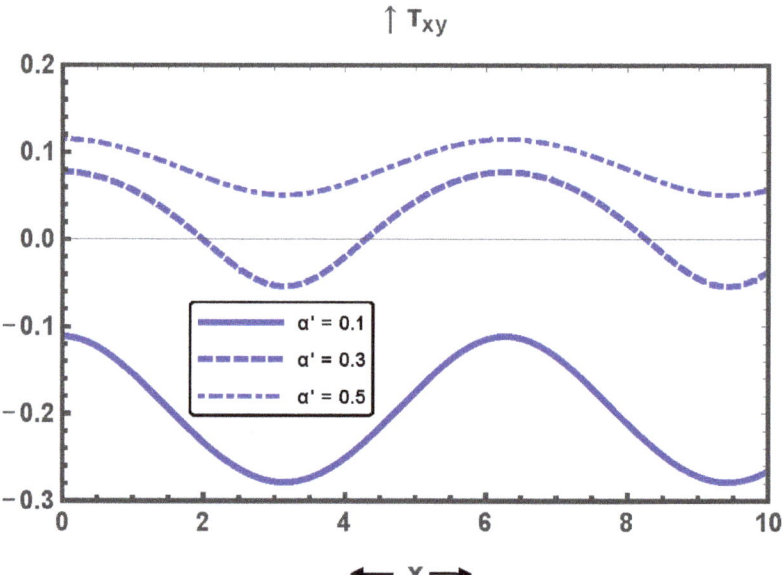

Figure 7. Display of shear stress profile for different values of α'.

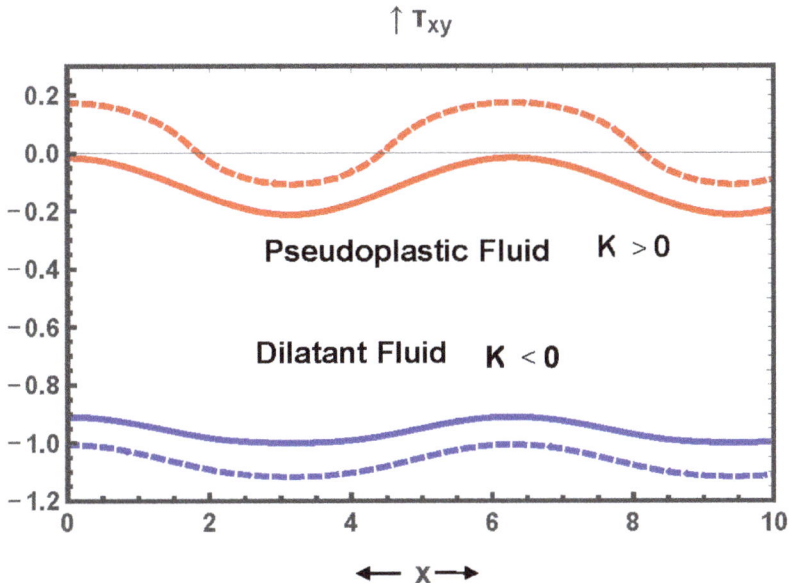

Figure 8. Display of shear stress profile via x for pseudoplastic and dilatant fluids.

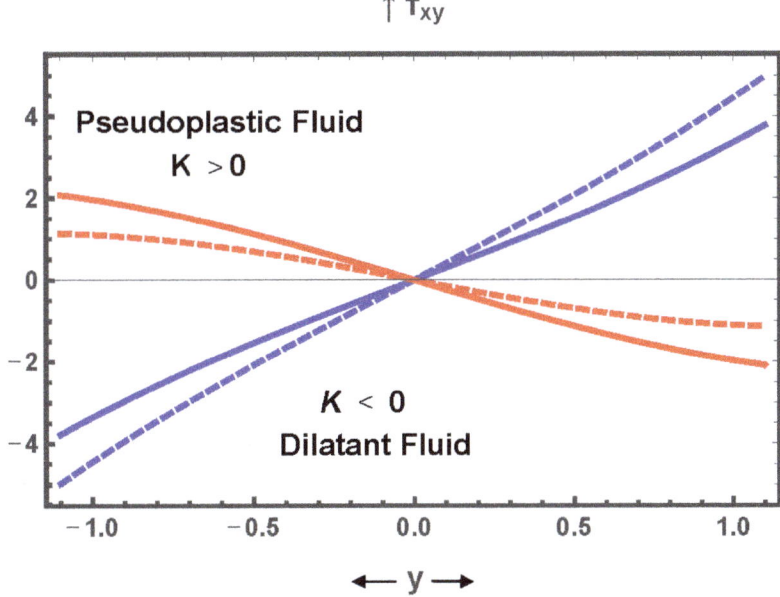

Figure 9. Display of shear stress profile via y for pseudoplastic and dilatant fluids.

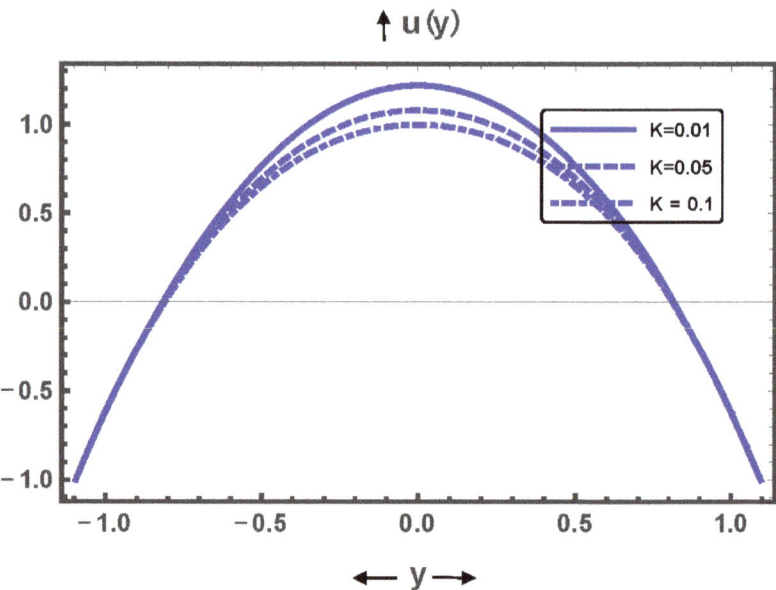

Figure 10. Display of axial velocity for different values of K.

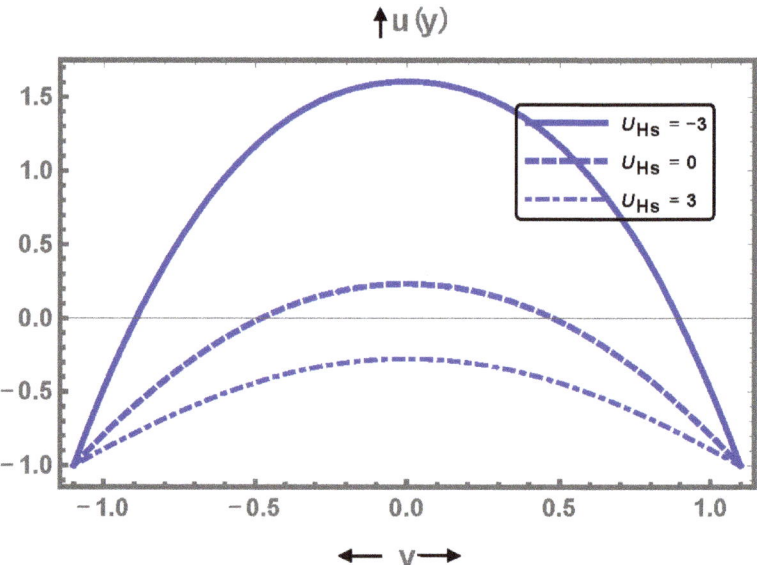

Figure 11. Display of axial velocity for different values of U_{HS}.

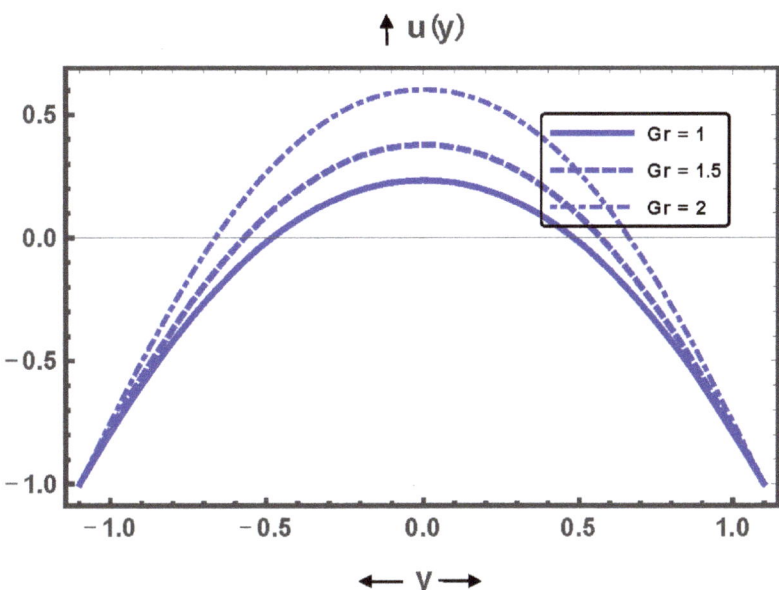

Figure 12. Display of axial velocity for different values of *Gr*.

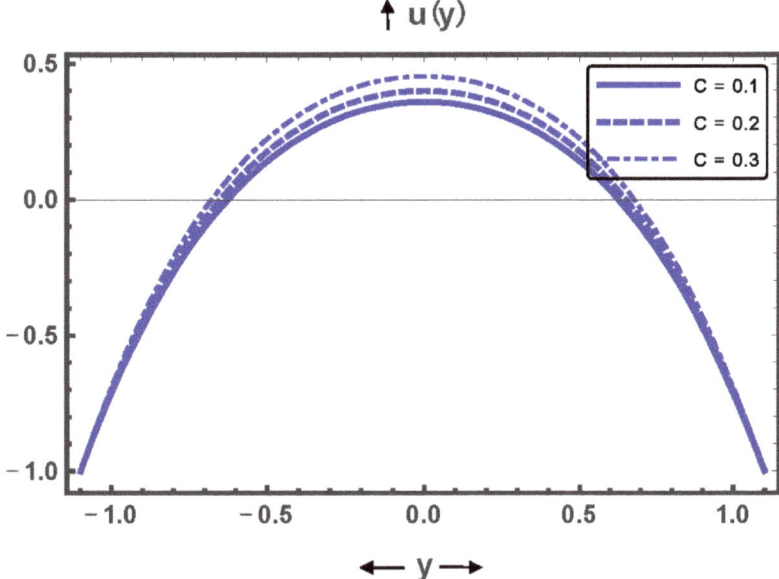

Figure 13. Display of axial velocity for different values of *C*.

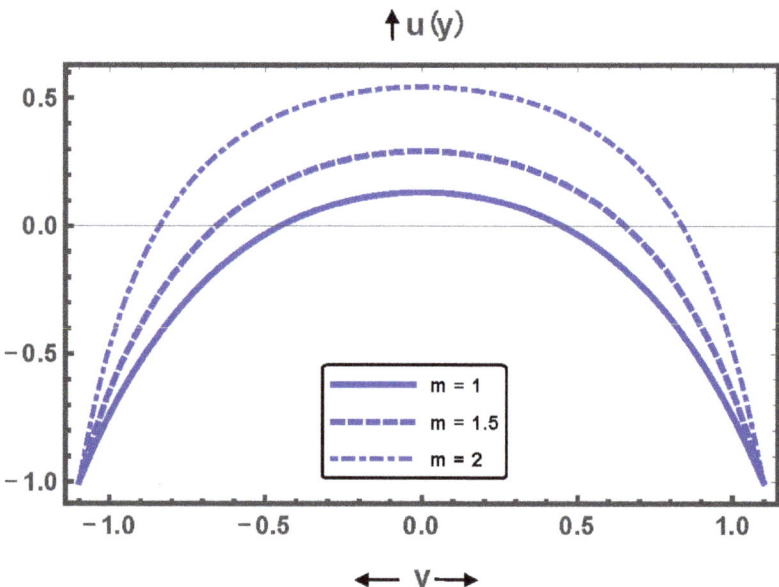

Figure 14. Display of axial velocity for different values of m.

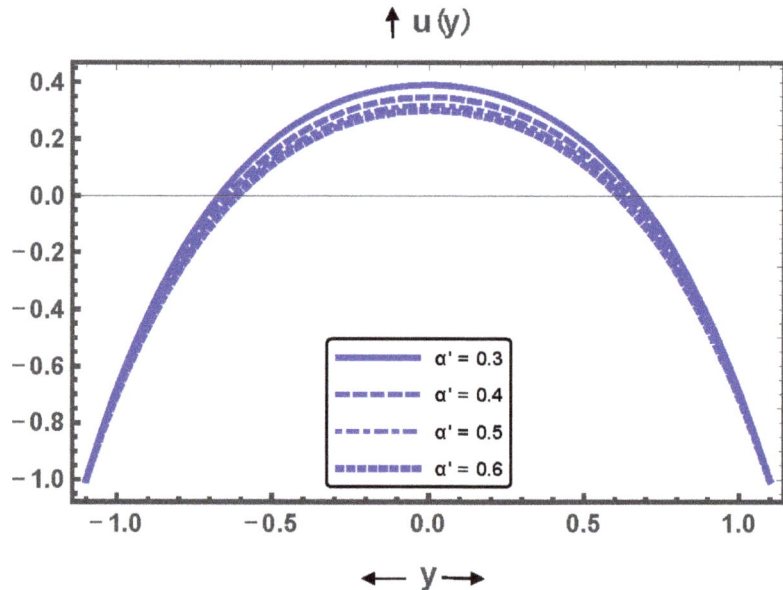

Figure 15. Display of axial velocity for different values of α'.

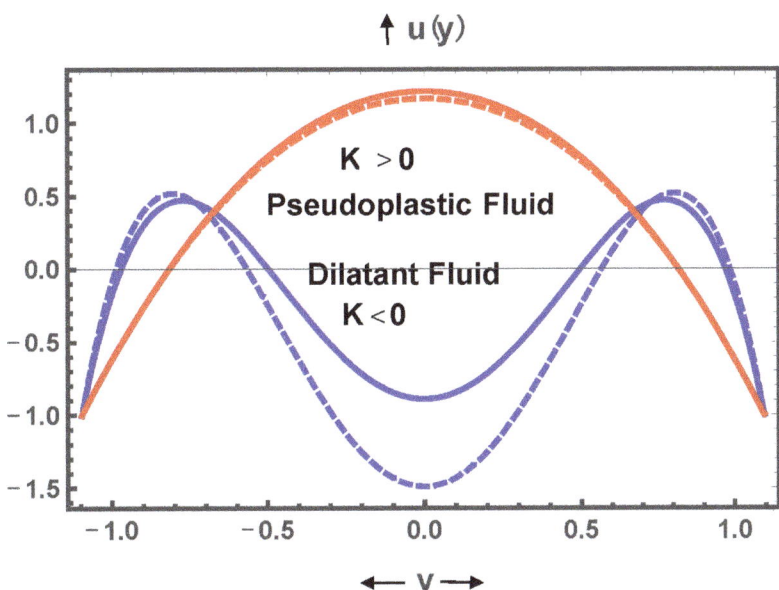

Figure 16. Display of axial velocity for pseudoplastic and dilatant fluids.

Figures 17–22 are prepared in order to see the behaviour of $\frac{dp}{dx}$ along the axis of the conduit under the effect of K, C, U_{HS}, Gr, m, and α'. It is seen that K, C, m, and α' serve to reduce $\frac{dp}{dx}$ for all values of the pertinent parameters, as noticed in Figures 17, 18, 21 and 22. It is also noticed from Figures 19 and 20 that $\frac{dp}{dx}$ grows for greater values of U_{HS} and Gr. It is also observed that for $x \in [0, 2]$ and $[3.9, 6]$, the pressure gradient is small and that the large pressure gradient occurs for $x \in [2.1, 4]$.

Figures 23–28 are prepared in order to spot the variation of Δp that is portrayed against the dimensionless time-averaged flux across one wavelength, Q, for several values of the parameters under consideration. The contributions of K, Gr, and m for Δp are displayed in Figures 23, 25 and 26, where it is noticed that Δp decays near the lower wall of the channel and grows afterwards with an increase in the channel curviness. It is also shown from Figures 24 and 27 that Δp attains smaller values as the channel curviness increases away from the wall of the conduit. Finally, Figure 28 displays the behaviour of Δp in case of dilatation and pseudoplasticity of fluids. It is seen that Δp is generally higher for dilated fluids than that of pseudoplastic ones. It is also observed that Δp decreases for dilated fluids all the way along, whereas it decreases for pseudoplastic fluids only until a specific value ($Q = 1$) away from the wall from which the behaviour is reversed.

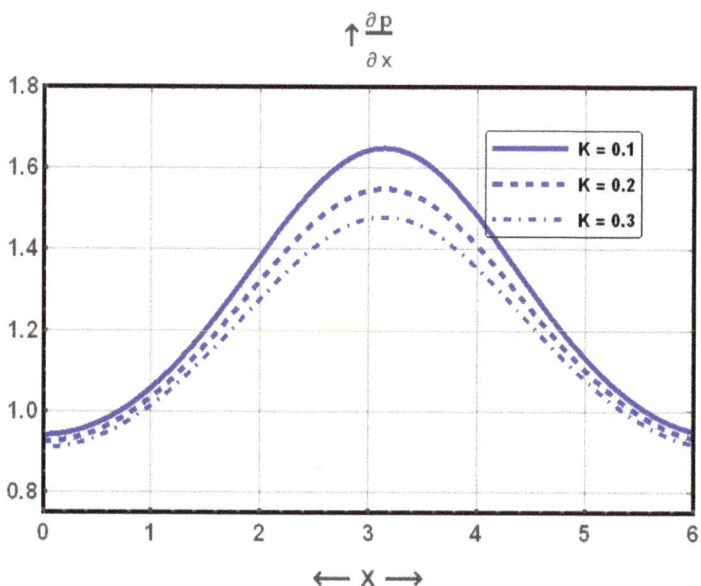

Figure 17. Display of pressure gradient for different values of K.

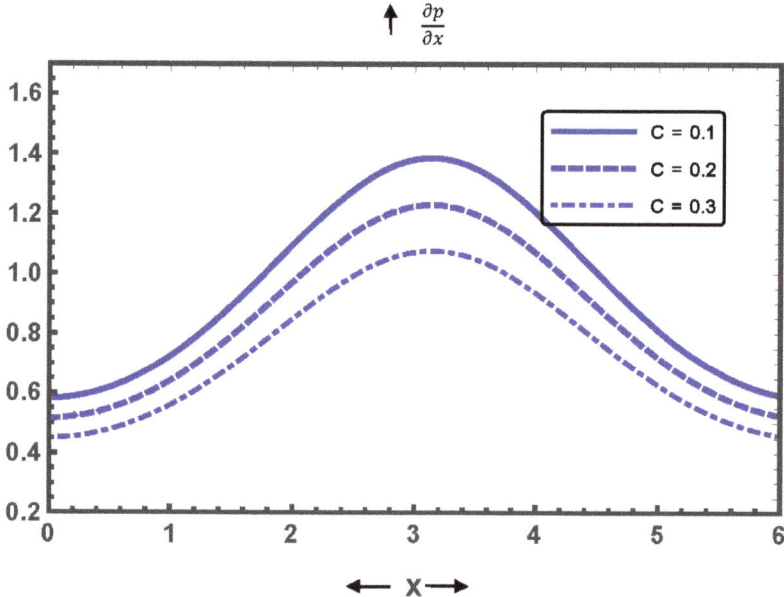

Figure 18. Display of pressure gradient for different values of C.

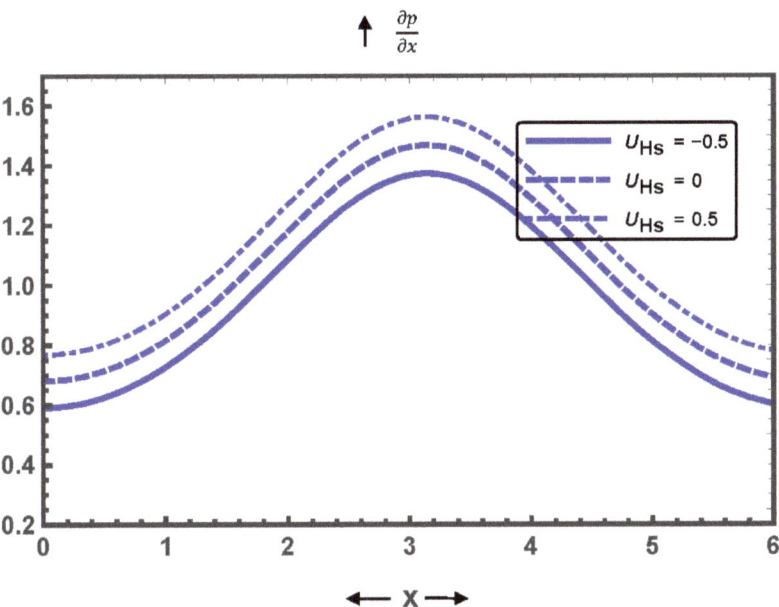

Figure 19. Display of pressure gradient for different values of U_{HS}.

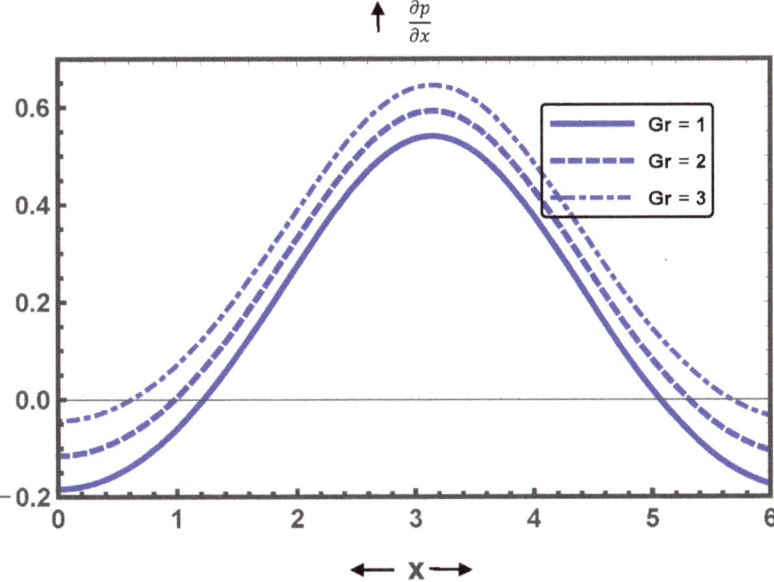

Figure 20. Display of pressure gradient for different values of Gr.

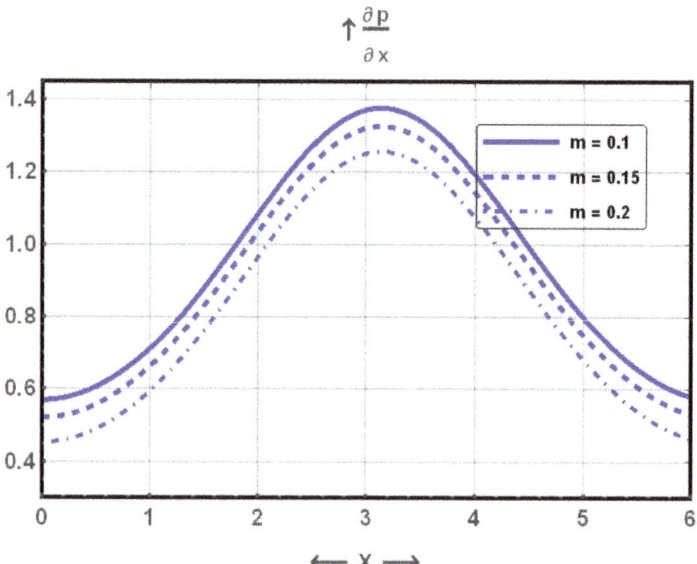

Figure 21. Display of pressure gradient for different values of m.

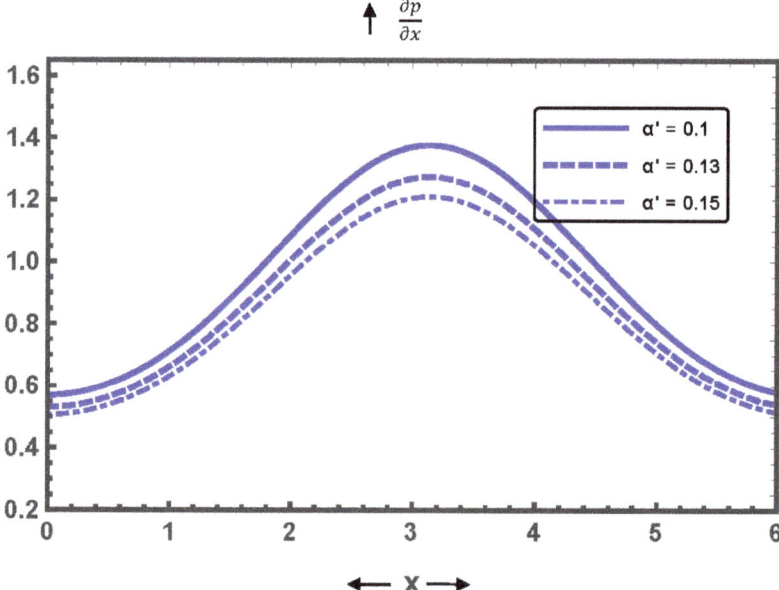

Figure 22. Display of pressure gradient for different values of α'.

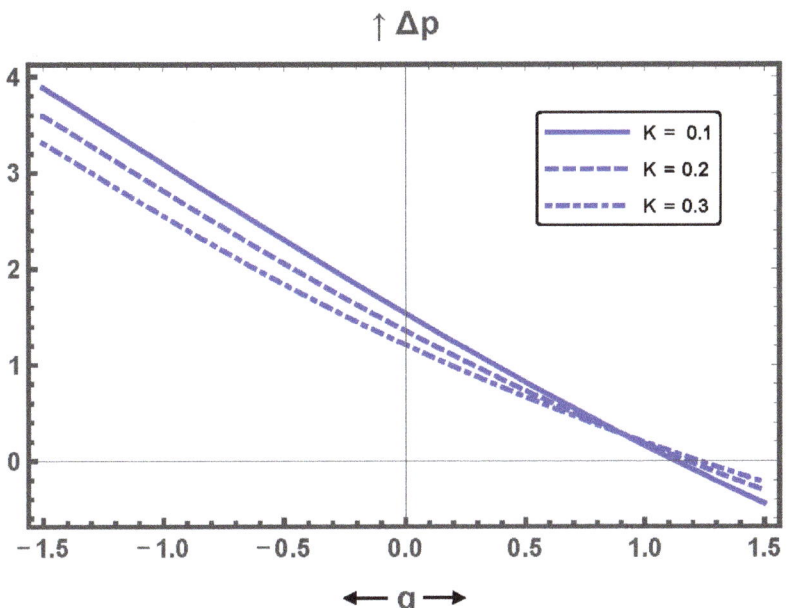

Figure 23. Display of pressure rise vs. volume flow rate for different values of K.

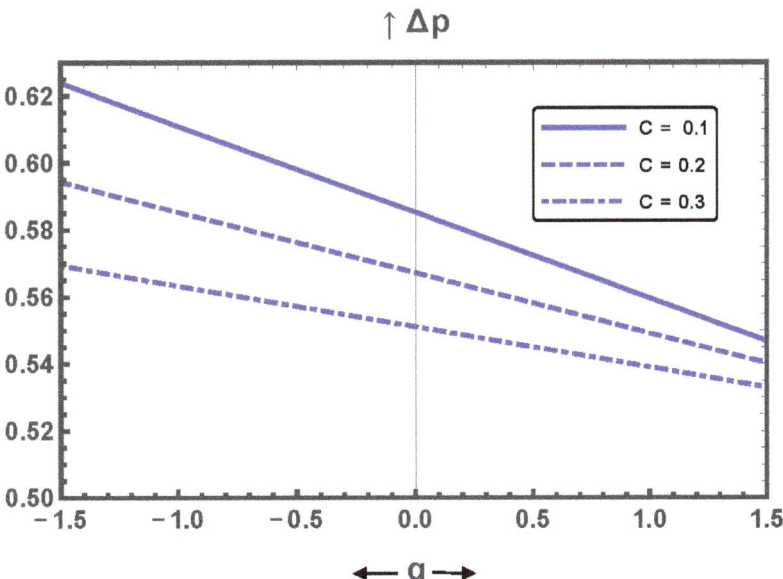

Figure 24. Display of pressure rise vs. volume flow rate for different values of C.

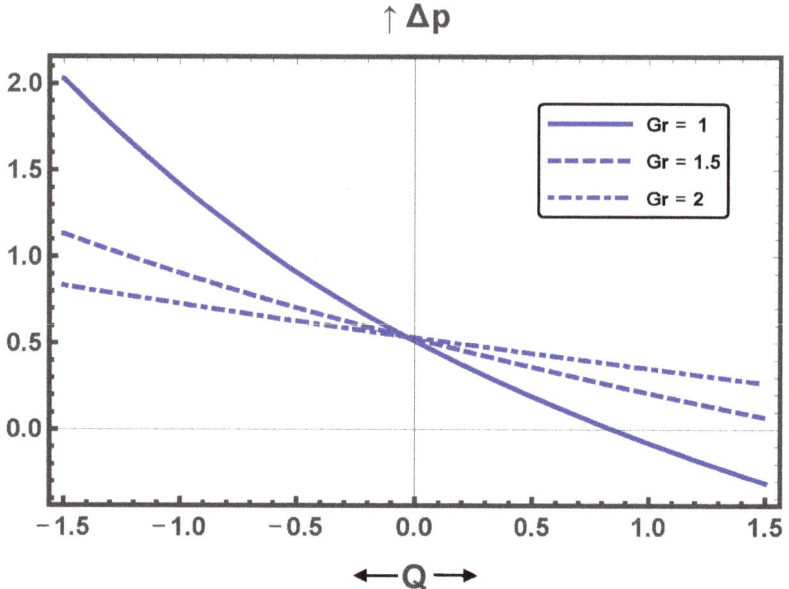

Figure 25. Display of pressure rise vs. volume flow rate for different values of *Gr*.

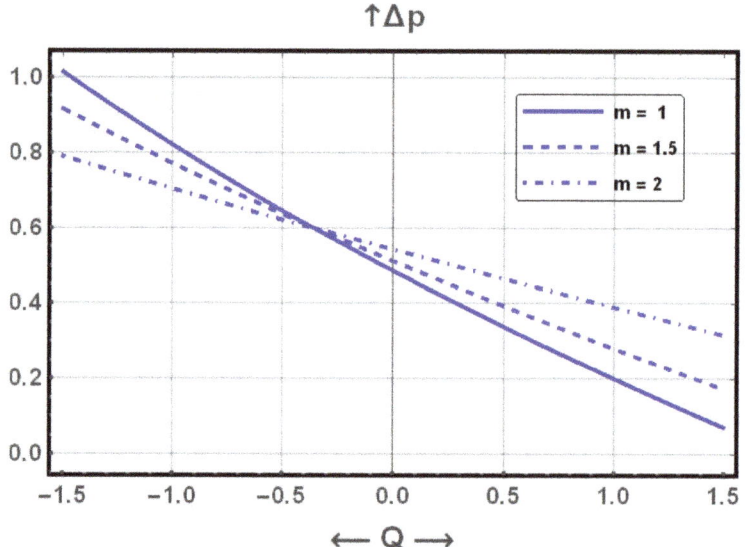

Figure 26. Display of pressure rise vs. volume flow rate for different values of *m*.

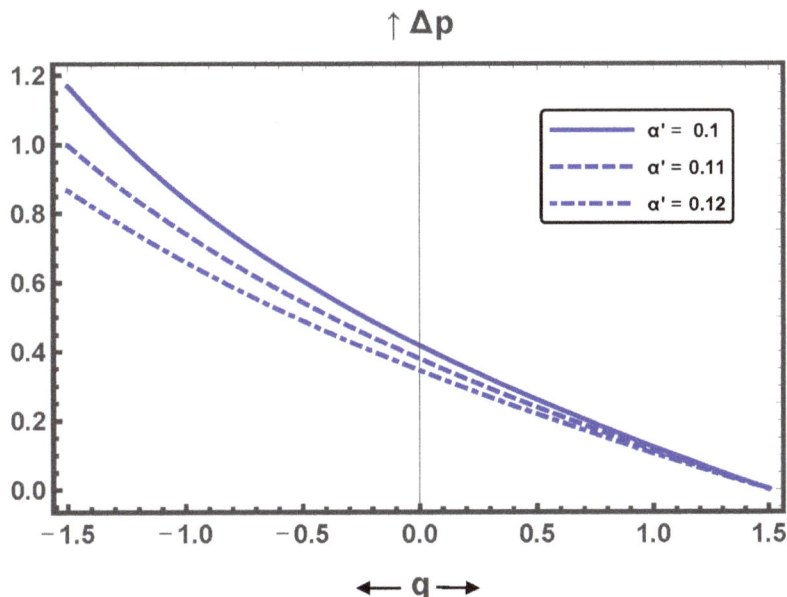

Figure 27. Display of pressure rise vs. volume flow rate for different values of α'.

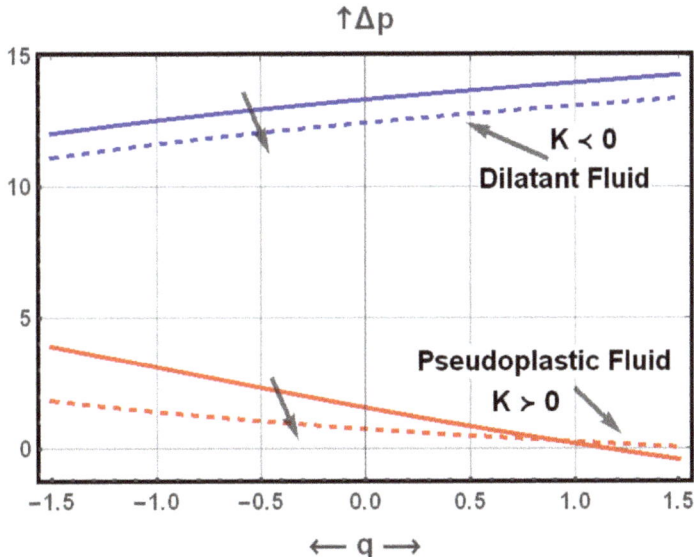

Figure 28. Display of pressure rise vs. volume flow rate for pseudoplastic and dilatant fluids.

8. Biomedical Application of the Problem

Shear stress of fluid circulation is an important diagnostic aspect for evaluating the properties of blood supply through the arteries. The evolution of shear stress in the consolidated system, combined with the dynamic rheology of the blood, describes the reduction of the circular region of the system over time. Wall shear stress plays a significant part in reshaping the arterial wall, which can contribute to arterial thickening. Table 1 illustrates the non-dimensional shear stresses of Rabinowitsch fluid, τ, through an artery for various values of the haematocrit, C, for diseased blood. It is noticed that as the C increases, τ increases.

Table 1. Rabinowitsch shear stress through an artery for various values C.

x	Shear Stress of Rabinowitsch Fluid τ					
	C = 0.248	C = 0.28	C = 0.426	C = 0.4325	C = 0.4331	C = 0.632
	Hb SS (Sickle Cell)	Plasma Cell Dyscrasias	Normal Blood	Hypertension (Controlled)	Hypertension (Uncontrolled)	Polycythemia
0.	0.508917	0.538364	0.707973	0.717319	0.718192	1.15146
0.2	0.505563	0.534945	0.704064	0.713379	0.714249	1.14586
0.4	0.495578	0.524771	0.69247	0.701695	0.702557	1.12931
0.6	0.479179	0.508091	0.673581	0.682663	0.683511	1.10248
0.8	0.456697	0.485281	0.64801	0.656909	0.657739	1.0665
1.	0.428523	0.456801	0.616547	0.625236	0.626047	1.02282
1.2	0.395056	0.423142	0.580099	0.588575	0.589366	0.973144
1.4	0.35665	0.384766	0.539639	0.54792	0.548692	0.919356
1.6	0.313594	0.34209	0.496165	0.504294	0.505052	0.86342
1.8	0.266209	0.295542	0.450704	0.458753	0.459502	0.807327
2.	0.215192	0.245805	0.404386	0.41245	0.4132	0.753059
2.2	0.162415	0.194396	0.358613	0.3668	0.367561	0.702604
2.4	0.111854	0.144497	0.315318	0.323729	0.324509	0.657972
2.6	0.0690173	0.101038	0.277209	0.285898	0.286704	0.621209
2.8	0.038254	0.0688821	0.24769	0.256637	0.257466	0.594302
3.	0.0213037	0.0508044	0.23019	0.2393	0.240144	0.578956
3.2	0.0183903	0.0476728	0.227071	0.236211	0.237058	0.576266
3.4	0.029497	0.0595737	0.238779	0.247809	0.248646	0.586434
3.6	0.0546015	0.0860756	0.26368	0.272484	0.2733	0.608713
3.8	0.0927918	0.125329	0.298654	0.307178	0.307969	0.641609
4.	0.140811	0.173205	0.340168	0.348438	0.349206	0.683216
4.2	0.19328	0.22449	0.385186	0.393288	0.394041	0.731496
4.4	0.245362	0.275183	0.431472	0.439514	0.440263	0.78442
4.6	0.294386	0.323171	0.477437	0.485523	0.486276	0.839995
4.8	0.339291	0.367516	0.521865	0.530076	0.530841	0.896238
5.	0.379664	0.407729	0.563701	0.572092	0.572875	0.95116

9. Deductions

In this article, the impact of Rabinowitsch suspension fluid through elastic walls with heat transfer under the effect of the electroosmotic forces is investigated. The solutions of the fluid model are achieved by taking a long wavelength approximation. A comparison is set between the effect of pseudoplasticity and dilatation on the behaviour of shear stress, axial velocity, and pressure rise. The impact of all the pertinent parameters are discussed graphically. The main observations are as follows:

i. Unlike the effect of the radius of the channel for elasticity on the shear stress, it tends to reduce the axial velocity, pressure gradient, and pressure rise.
ii. The volume fraction boosts the shear stress and the axial velocity, whereas the effect is totally reversed with the pressure gradient and pressure rise.

iii. The Grashof number accelerates the flow and increases shear stresses along with the pressure gradient.
iv. The maximum axial velocity takes place at the centre of the conduit.
v. The maximum electroosmotic velocity boosts the shear stress and pressure gradient but reduces the axial velocity.
vi. The influence of the Rabinowitsch and electroosmotic parameters is to enhance the shear stress, whereas their effect is totally reversed for the pressure gradient.
vii. The current model reduces to the case of dilatant fluid for $K < 0$, pseudoplastic fluid for $K > 0$.

Author Contributions: Conceptualization, S.I.A.; methodology, A.Z.Z.; software, A.Z.Z.; validation, S.I.A.; formal analysis, A.Z.Z.; investigation, S.I.A.; resources, A.Z.Z.; data curation, S.I.A. and A.Z.Z.; writing—original draft preparation, S.I.A. and A.Z.Z.; writing—review and editing, S.I.A.; visualization, A.Z.Z.; supervision, S.I.A.; project administration, S.I.A. All authors have read and agreed to the published version of the manuscript.

Funding: Not applicable.

Institutional Review Board Statement: Not applicable.

Informed Consent Statement: Not applicable.

Data Availability Statement: Not applicable.

Acknowledgments: Figure 1b is used by courtesy of Encyclopedia Britannica.

Conflicts of Interest: Authors declare no conflict of interest.

Appendix A

The constants given in Equations (32), (33) and (36) are defined as:

$P = \frac{dp}{dx}$.
$P_1(y) = 6P + QG_r(-3h^2 + y^2)$.
$P_2(y) = 2P + QG_r(-h^2 + y^2)$.
$P_3(y) = 12P + QG_r(-6h^2 + 5y^2)$.
$P_4(y) = -4P + QG_r(2h^2 - 5y^2)$.
$c_0 = \frac{1}{8640\,\overline{\mu}\,m^6 C_{PH}^3}$.
$c_1 = m^6(-8640\,\overline{\mu}\,C_{PH}^3$
$+h^2(540Km^2 U_{Hs}^2 Sech^2(hm)(12P - 5h^2 QG_r)$
$+360C_{PH}^2(-12P + 5h^2 QG_r)$
$+h^2 K(-2160(P)^3 + 2520h^2 QG_r(P)^2$
$-990h^4 Q^2 G_r^2 P + 131h^6 Q^3 G_r^3))$
$+90y^4(4QC_{PH}^2 G_r$
$+3K(-2m^2 QU hs^2 Sech^2(hm)G_r$
$+(2P - h^2 QG_r)^3)))$.
$c_2 = 4\,Km^6\,Q^3\,G_r^3$.
$c_3 = 1080\,m^6\,(-3Km^2 U_{Hs}^2 Sech^2(h(x)m) + 2C_{PH}^2)(2P - h^2 QG_r)$.
$c_4 = -45\,Km^6\,Q^2 G_r^2(-2P + h^2 QG_r)$.
$c_5 = 180\,K\,m^6\,Q\,G_r(-2P + h^2 QG_r)^2$.
$c_6 = -720\,K\,m^8\,U_{HS}^3\,Sech^3(hm)$.
$c_7 = 1620\,K\,m^5\,U_{HS}^2\,Q\,G_r\,Sech^2(hm)$.
$c_8 = 180\,m^2\,U_{HS}\,Sech(hm)$.
$c_9 = c_{11} Q\,G_r$
$c_{10} = 2m^2 c_{11}$.
$c_{11} = -810\,K\,m^4\,U_{HS}^2\,Sech^2(hm)$.

$$c_{12} = c_{15}\, m^4.$$
$$c_{13} = 4m^2 Q\, G_r\, c_{15}.$$
$$c_{14} = 90\, U_{HS}\, m^6 K\, Sech(hm).$$
$$c_{15} = 4320\, K\, m\, U_{HS}\, Sech(hm).$$
$$c_{16} = 120\, Q^2\, G_r^2.$$
$$\begin{aligned}c_{17} =\ & -720\, U_{HS}\, (9Km^8 U_{HS}^{\ 2} Sech^2(hm) + \\ & 4(-9Km^4(2+h^2m^2)(P)^2 - 3m^6 C_{PH}^2 + \\ & 6Km^2(-12-3h^2m^2+h^4m^4)QG_rP - K(180+ \\ & 54h^2m^2 - 6h^4m^4 + h^6m^6)Q^2 G_r^2)) \\ & Km(8m^7 U_{HS}^{\ 2} Cosh(3hm)Sech^2(hm) +) \\ & 9m^3 U_{HS}\, Cosh(2hm)Sech(hm)(4m^2 P + QG_r) + \\ & 6h(m^4 U_{HS}\, Sech(hm)\, Sinh(2hm)(-12\, m^2 P + \\ & (-3+4h^2m^2)QG_r) + 32\sinh(hm)(-3m^4 P^2 + \\ & m^2(-12+h^2m^2)QG_rP + (-30+h^2m^2)Q^2 G_r^2))).\end{aligned}$$
$$c_{18} = 90\, U_{HS}\, Sech(hm)(9Km^8 U_{HS}^{\ 2} Sech^2(hm) - 720 KQ^2 G_r^2) + c22.$$
$$c_{19} = 6480\, Km^2 QG_r\, U_{HS}\, Sech(hm).$$
$$c_{20} = -2700\, Q^2\, G_r^2\, m^4\, K\, U_{HS}\, Sech(hm).$$
$$c_{21} = 1080\, Q\, G_r(-2P+h^2 QG_r)\, U_{HS}\, Sech(hm) 6Km^4.$$
$$c_{22} = 1620\, K\, m^4\, U_{HS}\, (-2P+h^2 QG_r)^2\, Sech(hm).$$
$$c_{23} = -1080\, C_{PH}^2\, m^6\, U_{HS}\, Sech(hm).$$
$$\begin{aligned}c_{24} =\ & \tfrac{1}{8640\overline{\mu}m^6 M^3}\Big\{ -8640\, \overline{\mu}\, h(x) m^6 M^3 + 1152\, G_r\, h(x)^5 m^6 M^2 Q \\ & + \tfrac{7552}{77} G_r^{\ 3} h(x)^{11} K\, m^6\, Q^3 - 1728 c1^2 G_r\, h(x)^5 K\, m^8\, Q\, U_{HS}^{\ 2} + \\ & 8640\, h(x)\, m^6 M^2 U_{HS} + 1555200\, G_r^{\ 2} h(x)\, K\, Q^2 U_{HS} - \\ & 34560 G_r^{\ 2} h(x)^3 K m^2 Q^2 U_{HS} - 34560 G_r^{\ 2} h(x)\, K(-45+h^2m^2)\, Q^2 U_{HS} + \\ & 2880\, G_r^{\ 2} h(x)\, K(180+54h(x)^2 m^2 - 6h(x)^4 m^4 + h(x)^6 m^6)\, Q^2 U_{HS} - \\ & 6480 h(x)\, K\, m^8 U_{HS}^{\ 3}\, sech^2(h(x)\, m) + \\ & 3240 G_r h(x) K m^4 Q U_{HS}^{\ 2} \cosh(2h(x)m) sech^2(h(x)m) - \\ & 1080 G_r h(x)^3 K m^6 Q U_{HS}^{\ 2} \cosh(2h(x)m) sech^2(hm) + \\ & 720\, h(x) K m^8 U_{HS}^{\ 3} \cosh(3h(x)m) sech^3(h(x)m) - \\ & 8640\, m^5 M^2 U_{HS} \tanh(h(x)m) - \tfrac{2073600\, G_r^{\ 2} K Q^2 U_{HS} \tanh(h(x)m)}{m} - \\ & 466560\, G_r^{\ 2} h(x)^2 K m Q^2 U_{HS} \tanh(h(x)m) + \\ & G_r^{\ 2} h(x)^4 K m^3 Q^2 U_{HS} \tanh(h(x)m)(34560 - 2880 G_r^{\ 2} h(x)^2 m^2) + \\ & 17280\, G_r^{\ 2} h(x)^2 K m(-30+h(x)^2 m^2)\, Q^2 U_{HS} \tanh(h(x)m) - \\ & \tfrac{17280\, G_r^{\ 2} K(90+18 h(x)^2 m^2 - h(x)^4 m^4) Q^2 U_{HS} \tanh(h(x)m)}{m} + \\ & 6480\, Km^7 U_{HS}^{\ 3} \tanh(h(x)m)\, sech^2(h(x)m) - \\ & 1620\, G_r Km^3 Q U_{HS}^{\ 2} \tanh(h(x)m) - 1620\, G_r h(x)^2\, Km^5 Q U_{HS}^{\ 2} \tanh(h(x)m) + \\ & 2160\, G_r h(x)^4 Km^7 Q U_{HS}^{\ 2} \tanh(h(x)m) - \\ & 240\, Km^7 U_{HS}^{\ 3} \sinh(3h(x)m) sech^3(h(x)m) \Big\}.\end{aligned}$$

References

1. SherAkbar, N.; WahidButt, A. Heat transfer analysis of Rabinowitsch fluid flow due to metachronal wave of cilia. *Results Phys.* **2015**, *5*, 92–98.
2. Singh, B.K.; Singh, U.P. Analysis of peristaltic flow in a tube: Rabinowitsch fluid model. *Int. J. Fluids Eng.* **2014**, *6*, 1–8.
3. Vaidya, H.; Rajashekhar, C.; Manjunatha, G.; Prasad, K.V. Peristaltic mechanism of a Rabinowitsch fluid in an inclined channel with complaint wall; variable liquid properties. *J. Braz. Soc. Mech. Sci. Eng.* **2019**, *41*, 52. [CrossRef]
4. Sadaf, H.; Nadeem, S. Analysis of combined convective and viscous dissipation effects for peristaltic flow of Rabinowitsch fluid model. *J. Bionic Eng.* **2017**, *14*, 182–190. [CrossRef]
5. Choudhari, R. Analysis of peristaltic flow of Rabinowitsch fluid in a non-uniform channel: Analytical approach. *Lat. Am. Appl. Res.* **2020**, *50*, 151–158.
6. Mekheimer, K.; Zaher, A.; Hasona, W. Entropy of AC electro-kinetics for blood mediated gold or copper nanoparticles as a drug agent for thermotherapy of oncology. *Chin. J. Phys.* **2020**, *65*, 123–138. [CrossRef]
7. Mekheimer, K.S.; Zaher, A.Z.; Abo-Elkhair, R.E. Electro-magnetohydrodynamic oscillatory flow of a dielectric fluid through a porous medium with heat transfer: Brinkman model. *Bionanoscience* **2018**, *8*, 596–608.

8. Zaher, A.; Ali, K.K.; Mekheimer, K.S. Electroosmosis forces EOF driven boundary layer flow for a non-newtonian fluid with planktonic microorganism: Darcy Forchheimer model. *Int. J. Numer. Methods Heat Fluid Flow* **2021**, *31*, 2534–2559. [CrossRef]
9. Reuss, F.F. *Mémoires de la Société Impériale des Naturalistes de Moscou*; Imperial Moscow University: Moscow, Russian, 1809; Volume 2, pp. 327–337.
10. Mekheimer, K.S.; Zaher, A.; Abdellateef, A.I. Entropy hemodynamics particle-fluid suspension model through eccentric catheterization for time-variant stenotic arterial wall: Catheter injection. *Int. J. Geom. Methods Mod. Phys.* **2019**, *16*, 164–496. [CrossRef]
11. Zeeshan, A.; Ijaz, N.; Bhatti, M.M. Flow analysis of particulate suspension on an asymmetric peristaltic motion in a curved configuration with heat and mass transfer. *Mech. Ind.* **2018**, *19*, 401. [CrossRef]
12. Abdelsalam, S.I.; Vafai, K. Particulate suspension effect on peristaltically induced unsteady pulsatile flow in a narrow artery: Blood flow model. *Math. Biosci.* **2017**, *283*, 91–105. [CrossRef]
13. Khan, A.A.; Tariq, H. Influence of wall properties on the peristaltic flow of a dusty Walter's B fluid. *J. Braz. Soc. Mech. Sci. Eng.* **2018**, *40*, 368. [CrossRef]
14. Choi, S.U.S.; Eastman, J.A. Enhancing thermal conductivity of fluids with nanoparticles. In *Developments and Applications of Non-Newtonian Flows*; Siginer, D.A., Wang, H.P., Eds.; ASME: New York, NY, USA, 1995; pp. 99–105.
15. Sadaf, H.; Abdelsalam, S.I. Adverse effects of hybrid nanofluid in a wavy nonuniform annulus with convective boundary conditions. *RSC Adv.* **2019**, *10*, 15035–15043. [CrossRef]
16. Bhatti, M.M.; Ellahi, R.; Zeeshan, A.; Marin, M.; Abdelsalam, S.I. Swimming of motile gyrotactic microorganisms and movement of nanoparticles in blood flow through anisotropically tapered arteries. *Front. Phys.* **2020**, *8*, 1–9. [CrossRef]
17. Abdelsalam, S.I.; Bhatti, M.M. Anomalous reactivity of thermo-bioconvective nanofluid towards oxytactic microorganisms. *Appl. Math. Mech.* **2020**, *41*, 1–14. [CrossRef]
18. Mekheimer, K.; Hasona, W.; Abo-Elkhair, R.; Zaher, A. Peristaltic blood flow with gold nanoparticles as a third grade nanofluid in catheter: Application of cancer therapy. *Phys. Lett. A* **2018**, *382*, 85–93. [CrossRef]
19. Sohail, M.; Naz, R.; Abdelsalam, S.I. On the onset of entropy generation for a nanofluid with thermal radiation and gyrotactic microorganisms through 3D flows. *Phys. Scr.* **2020**, *95*, 045206. [CrossRef]
20. Abdelsalam, S.I.; Bhatti, M.M. The study of non-newtonian nanofluid with hall and ion slip effects on peristaltically induced motion in a non-uniform channel. *RSC Adv.* **2018**, *8*, 7904–7915. [CrossRef]
21. Nguyen-Thoi, T.; Sheikholeslami, M.; Hamid, M.; Haq, R.-U.; Shafee, A. CVFEM modeling for nanofluid behavior involving non-equilibrium model and Lorentz effect in appearance of radiation. *Phys. A Stat. Mech. Appl.* **2019**, *534*. [CrossRef]
22. Khan, Z.H.; Usman, M.; Zubair, T.; Hamid, M.; Haq, R.U. Brownian motion and thermophoresis effects on unsteady stagnation point flow of eyring–powell nanofluid: A Galerkin approach. *Commun. Theor. Phys.* **2020**, *72*, 125005. [CrossRef]
23. Khan, Z.H.; Khan, W.A.; Haq, R.; Usman, M.; Hamid, M. Effects of volume fraction on water-based carbon nanotubes flow in a right-angle trapezoidal cavity: FEM based analysis. *Int. Commun. Heat Mass Transf.* **2020**, *116*, 104640. [CrossRef]
24. Khan, Z.H.; Khan, W.A.; Hamid, M.; Liu, H. Finite element analysis of hybrid nanofluid flow and heat transfer in a split lid driven square cavity with Y-shaped obstacle. *Phys. Fluids* **2020**, *32*, 093609. [CrossRef]
25. Sochi, T. The flow of Newtonian and power law fluids in elastic tubes. *Int. J. Non-Linear Mech.* **2014**, *67*, 245–250. [CrossRef]
26. Sarkar, A.; Jayaraman, G. Non-linear analysis of oscillatory flow in the annulus of an elastic tube: Application to catheterized artery. *Phys. Fluids* **2001**, *13*, 2901–2911. [CrossRef]
27. Pedrizzetti, G. Fluid flow in a tube with an elastic membrane insertion. *J. Fluid Mech.* **1998**, *375*, 39–64. [CrossRef]
28. Rubinow, S.I.; Keller, J.B. Flow of a viscous fluid through an elastic tube with applications to blood flow. *J. Theor. Biol.* **1972**, *35*, 299–313. [CrossRef]
29. Marin, M.; Ellahi, R.; Chirila, A. On solutions of Saint-Venant's problem for elastic dipolar bodies with voids. *Carpathian J. Math.* **2017**, *33*, 219–232. [CrossRef]
30. Marin, M.; Ellahi, R.; Vlase, S.; Bhatti, M.M. On the decay of exponential type for the solutions in a dipolar elastic body. *J. Taibah Univ. Sci.* **2020**, *14*, 534–540. [CrossRef]
31. Marin, M.; Öchsner, A.; Ellahi, R.; Bhatti, M.M. A semigroup of contractions in elasticity of porous bodies. *Contin. Mech. Thermodyn.* **2021**, *33*, 2027–2037. [CrossRef]
32. Ijaz, N.; Zeeshan, A.; Bhatti, M. Peristaltic propulsion of particulate non-newtonian Ree-eyring fluid in a duct through constant magnetic field. *Alex. Eng. J.* **2018**, *57*, 1055–1060. [CrossRef]

Article

A Comparative Study among New Hybrid Root Finding Algorithms and Traditional Methods

Elsayed Badr [1,2,*], Sultan Almotairi [3,*] and Abdallah El Ghamry [4]

1 Scientific Computing Department, Faculty of Computers & Artificial Intelligence, Benha University, Benha 13518, Egypt
2 Higher Technological Institute, 10th of Ramadan City, Embassies District, Nasr City, Cairo 11765, Egypt
3 Department of Natural and Applied Sciences, Community College Majmaah University, Al-Majmaah 11952, Saudi Arabia
4 Computer Science Department, Faculty of Computers & Artificial Intelligence, Benha University, Benha 13518, Egypt; abdallah17163@fci.bu.edu.eg
* Correspondence: badrgraph@gmail.com (E.B.); almotairi@mu.edu.sa (S.A.)

Abstract: In this paper, we propose a novel blended algorithm that has the advantages of the trisection method and the false position method. Numerical results indicate that the proposed algorithm outperforms the secant, the trisection, the Newton–Raphson, the bisection and the regula falsi methods, as well as the hybrid of the last two methods proposed by Sabharwal, with regard to the number of iterations and the average running time.

Keywords: hybrid method; trisection; bisection; false position; Newton–Raphson; secant; dynamical systems

1. Introduction

There are many sciences (mathematics, computer science, dynamical systems in engineering, agriculture, biomedical, etc.) that require finding the roots of non-linear equations. When there is not an analytic solution, we try to determine a numerical solution. There is not a specific algorithm for solving every non-linear equation efficiently.

There are several pure methods for solving such problems, including the pure, metaheuristic and blended methods. Pure methods include classical techniques such as the bisection method, the false position method, the secant method and the Newton–Raphson method, etc. Metaheuristic methods use metaheuristic algorithms such as particle swarm optimization, firefly, and ant colony for root finding, whereas blended methods are hybrid combinations of two classical methods.

There is not a specific method for solving every non-linear equation efficiently. In general, we can see more details about classical methods in [1–4] and especially for the bisection and Newton–Raphson methods in [5–8]. Other problems such as minimization, target shooting, etc. are discussed in [9–14].

Sabharwal [15] proposed a novel blended method that is a dynamic hybrid of the bisection and false position methods. He deduced that his algorithm outperformed pure methods (bisection and false position). On the other hand, he observed that his algorithm outperformed the secant method and the Newton–Raphson method according to the number of iterations. Sabharwal did not analyze his algorithm according to the running time, but he was satisfied with the iterations number only. Perhaps there is a method that has a small number of iterations, but the execution time is large and vice versa. For this reason, the iteration number and the running time are important metrics to evaluate the algorithms. Unfortunately, most researchers have not paid attention to the details of finding the running time. Furthermore, they did not discuss and did not answer the following question: why does the running time change from one run to another on the used software package?

Citation: Badr, E.; Almotairi, S.; Ghamry, A.E. A Comparative Study among New Hybrid Root Finding Algorithms and Traditional Methods. Mathematics 2021, 9, 1306. https://doi.org/10.3390/math9111306

Academic Editor: Ioannis Dassios

Received: 29 April 2021
Accepted: 3 June 2021
Published: 7 June 2021

Publisher's Note: MDPI stays neutral with regard to jurisdictional claims in published maps and institutional affiliations.

Copyright: © 2021 by the authors. Licensee MDPI, Basel, Switzerland. This article is an open access article distributed under the terms and conditions of the Creative Commons Attribution (CC BY) license (https://creativecommons.org/licenses/by/4.0/).

The genetic algorithm was used to compare among the classical methods [9–11] based on the fitness ratio of the equations. The authors deduced that the genetic algorithm is more efficient than the classical algorithms for solving the functions $x^2 - x - 2$ [12] and $x^2 + 2x - 7$ [11]. Mansouri et al. [12] presented a new iterative method to determine the fixed point of a nonlinear function. Therefore, they combined ideas proposed in the artificial bee colony algorithm [13] and the bisection method [14]. They illustrate this method with four benchmark functions and compare results with others methods, such as artificial bee colony (ABC), particle swarm optimization (PSO), genetic algorithm (GA) and firefly algorithms.

For more details about the classical methods, hybrid methods and the metaheuristic approaches, the reader can refer to [16,17].

In this work, we propose a novel blended algorithm that has the advantages of the trisection method and the false position algorithm. The computational results show that the proposed algorithm outperforms the trisection and regula falsi methods. On the other hand, the introduced algorithm outperforms the bisection, Newton–Raphson and secant methods according to the iteration number and the average of running time. Finally, the implementation results show the superiority of the proposed algorithm on the blended bisection and false position algorithm, which was proposed by Sabharwal [15]. The results presented in this paper open the way for presenting new methods that compete with traditional methods and may replace them in software packages.

The rest of this work is organized as follows: The pure methods for determining the roots of non-linear equations are introduced in Section 2. The blended algorithms for finding the roots of non-linear equations are presented in Section 3. In Section 4, the numerical results analysis and statistical test among the pure methods and the blended algorithms are provided. Finally, conclusions are drawn in Section 5.

2. Pure Methods

In this section, we introduce five pure methods for finding the roots of non-linear equations. These methods are the bisection method, the trisection method, the false position method, the secant method and the Newton–Raphson method. We contribute to implementing the trisection algorithm with equal subintervals that overcomes the bisection algorithm on fifteen benchmark equations as shown in Section 3. On the other hand, the trisection algorithm also outperforms the false position method, secant method and Newton–Raphson method partially, as shown in Section 3.

2.1. Bisection Method

We assume that the function $f(x)$ is defined and continuous on the closed interval $[a, b]$, where the signals of $f(x)$ at the ends (a and b) are different. We divide the interval $[a, b]$ into two halves, where $x = \frac{a+b}{2}$, if $f(x) = 0$; then, x becomes a solution for the equation $f(x) = 0$. Otherwise, $(f(x) \neq 0)$ and we can choose one subinterval $[a, x]$ or $[x, b]$ that has different signals of $f(x)$ at its ends. We repeat dividing the new subinterval into two halves until we reach the exact solution x where $f(x) = 0$ or the approximate solution $f(x) \approx 0$ with tolerance, eps. The value of eps closes to zero as shown in Algorithm 1 and other algorithms.

The size of the interval was reduced by half at each iteration. Therefore the value eps is determined from the following formula:

$$eps = \frac{b-a}{2^n} \qquad (1)$$

where n is the number of iterations. From (1), the number of iterations is found by

$$n = \left\lceil \log_2\left(\frac{b-a}{eps}\right) \right\rceil \qquad (2)$$

Algorithm 1. Bisection(*f, a, b, eps*).

Input: The function $f(x)$,
The interval $[a, b]$ where the root lies in,
The absolute error (*eps*).
Output: The root (x),
The value of $f(x)$
Numbers of iterations (n),
The interval $[a, b]$ where the root lies in
$n := 0$
while true **do**
    $n := n + 1$
    $x := (a + b)/2$
    if $|f(x)| <= eps.$
        return $x, f(x), n, a, b$
    else if $f(a) * f(x) < 0$
        $b := x$
    else
        $a := x$
end (while)

The bisection method is a bracketing method, so it brackets the root in the interval $[a, b]$, and at each iteration, the size of the interval $[a, b]$ is halved. Accordingly, it reduces the error between the approximation root and the exact root for any iteration. On the other hand, the bisection method works quickly if the approximate root is far from the endpoint of the interval; otherwise, it needs more iterations to reach the root [17].

Advantages and Disadvantages of the Bisection Method

The bisection method is simple to implement, and its convergence is guaranteed. On the other hand, it has a relatively slow convergence, it needs different signs for the function values of the endpoints, and the test for checking this affects the complexity in the number of operations.

2.2. Trisection Method

The trisection method is like the bisection method, except that it divides the interval $[a, b]$ into three subintervals, while the bisection method divides the interval $[a, b]$ into two partial periods. Algorithm 2 divides the interval $[a, b]$ into three equal subintervals and searches for the root in the subinterval that contains different signs of the function values at the endpoints of this subinterval.

If the condition of termination is true, then the iteration has finished its task; otherwise, the algorithm repeats the calculations.

In order to divide the interval $[a, b]$ into equal three parts by x_1 and x_2, we need to know the locations of x_1 and x_2 as the following:

As shown in Figure 1, since

$$x_1 - a = b - x_2 \tag{3}$$

$$x_2 - x_1 = x_1 - a \tag{4}$$

Figure 1. How to divide the interval $[a, b]$ into three subintervals.

By solving Equations (3) and (4),
We get

$$x_1 = \frac{2a + b}{3}$$

And
$$x_2 = \frac{2b + a}{3}$$

The size of the interval $[a, b]$ decreases to a third with each repetition. Therefore, the value *eps* is determined from the following formula:

$$eps = \frac{b - a}{3^n} \quad (5)$$

where n is the number of iterations. From (5) the number of iterations is found by

$$n = \left\lceil \log_3\left(\frac{b-a}{eps}\right) \right\rceil \quad (6)$$

When we compare Equations (2) and (6), we conclude that the iterations number of the trisection algorithm is less than the iterations number of the bisection algorithm. We might think that the trisection algorithm is better than the bisection algorithm since it requires a few iterations. However, it might be the case that one iteration of the trisection algorithm has an execution time greater than the execution time of one iteration of the bisection algorithm. Therefore, we will consider both execution time and the number of iterations to evaluate the different algorithms.

Algorithm 2. Trisection(f, a, b, eps).

Input: The function $f(x)$,
  The interval $[a, b]$ where the root lies in,
  The absolute error (eps).
Output: The root (x),
  The value of $f(x)$
  Numbers of iterations (n),
  The interval $[a, b]$ where the root lies in
$n := 0$
while true **do**
  $n := n + 1$
  $x1 := (b + 2*a)/3$
  $x2 := (2*b + a)/3$
  if $|f(x1)| < |f(x2)|$
    $x := x1$
  else
    $x := x2$
  if $|f(x)| <= eps$
    return $x, f(x), n, a, b$
  else if $f(a) * f(x1) < 0$
    $b := x1$
  else if $f(x1) * f(x2) < 0$
    $a := x1$
    $b := x2$
  else
    $a := x2$
end (while)

Advantages and Disadvantages of the Trisection Method

The trisection method has the same advantages and disadvantages of the bisection method, in addition to being faster than it, as shown in Tables 1–9.

2.3. False Position (Regula Falsi) Method

There is no unique method suitable for finding the roots of all nonlinear functions. Each method has advantages and disadvantages. Hence, the false position method is a dynamic and fast method when the nature of the function is linear. The function $f(x)$, whose roots are in the interval $[a, b]$ must be continuous, and the values of $f(x)$ at the endpoints of the interval $[a, b]$ have different signs. The false position method uses two endpoints of the interval $[a, b]$ with initial values ($r_0 = a$, $r_1 = b$). The connecting line between the two points ($r_0, f(r_0)$) and ($r_1, f(r_1)$) intersects the x-axis at the next estimate, r_2. Now, we can determine the successive estimates, r_n from the following relationship

$$r_n = r_{n-1} - \frac{f(r_{n-1})(r_{n-1} - r_{n-2})}{f(r_{n-1}) - f(r_{n-2})} \tag{7}$$

for $n \geq 2$.

Remark: The regula falsi method is very similar to the bisection method. However, the next iteration point is not the midpoint of the interval but the intersection of the x-axis with a secant through $(a, f(a))$ and $(b, f(b))$.

Algorithm 3 uses the relation (7) to get the successive approximations by the false position method.

Algorithm 3. False Position(f, a, b, eps).

Input: The function (f),
The interval $[a, b]$ where the root lies in,
The absolute error (eps).
Output: The root (x),
The value of $f(x)$
Numbers of iterations (n),
The interval $[a, b]$ where the root lies in
$n := 0$
while true **do**
    $n := n + 1$;
    $x = a - (f(a)*(b - a))/(f(b) - f(a))$
    if $|f(x)| <= eps$
        return $x, f(x), n, a, b$
    else if $f(a) * f(x) < 0$
        $b := x$
    else
        $a := x$
end (while)

Advantages and Disadvantages of the Regula Falsi Method

It is guaranteed to converge, and it is fast when the function is linear. On the other hand, we cannot determine the iterations number needed for convergence. It is very slow when the function is not linear.

2.4. Newton–Raphson Method

This method depends on a chosen initial point x_0. This point plays an important role for Newton–Raphson method. The success of the method depends mainly on the point x_0, and then the method may converge to its root or diverge based on the choice of the point x_0. Therefore, the first estimate can be determined from the following relation.

$$x_1 = x_0 - \frac{f(x_0)}{f'(x_0)} \tag{8}$$

The successive approximations for the Newton–Raphson method can be found from the following relation:

$$x_{i+1} = x_i - \frac{f(x_i)}{f'(x_i)} \tag{9}$$

such that the $f'(x_i)$ is the first derivative of the function $f(x)$ at the point x_i.

Algorithm 4 uses the relation (9) to get the successive approximations by the Newton–Raphson method.

Algorithm 4. Newton(f, xi, eps).

This function implements Newton's method.
Input: The function (f),
        An initial root xi,
        The absolute error (eps).
Output: The root (x),
        The value of $f(x)$
        Numbers of iterations (n),
$g(x) := f'(x)$
$n = 0$
while true do
    $n := n + 1$
    $xi = xi - f(xi)/g(xi)$
    if $|f(x)| <= eps$
        return $xi, f(xi), n$
end (while)

Advantages and Disadvantages of the Newton–Raphson Method

It is very fast compared to other methods, but it sometimes fails, meaning that there is no guarantee of its convergence.

2.5. Secant Method

Just as there is the possibility of the Newton method failing, there is also the possibility that the secant method will fail. The Newton method uses the relation (9) to find the successive approximations, but the secant method uses the following relation:

$$x_{i+1} = x_i - \frac{x_i - x_{i-1}}{f(x_i) - f(x_{i-1})} f(x_i) \quad (10)$$

Algorithm 5 uses the relation (10) to get the successive approximations by the secant method.

Algorithm 5. Secant(f, a, b, eps).

This function implements the Secant method.
Input: The function (f),
        Two initial roots: a and b,
        The absolute error (eps).
Output: The root (x),
        The value of $f(x)$
        Numbers of iterations (n),
$n := 0$
while true do
    $n := n + 1$
    $x := b - f(b)*(b - a)/(f(b) - f(a))$
    if $|f(x)| <= eps$
        return $x, f(x), n$
    $a := b$
    $b := x$
end (while)

Advantages and Disadvantages of the Secant Method

It is very fast compared to other methods, but it sometimes fails, meaning that there is no guarantee of its convergence.

3. Hybrid Algorithms

In this section, instead of pure methods such as the bisection method, the trisection method, the false position method, the secant method and the Newton–Raphson method, we propose a new hybrid root-finding algorithm (trisection–false position), which outperforms the algorithm (bisection-false position) that was proposed by Sabharwal [15].

3.1. Blended Bisection and False Position

Sabharwal [15] proposed a new algorithm that has the advantages of both the bisection and the false position methods. He built a novel hybrid method, Algorithm 6, which overcame the pure methods (bisection and false position).

Algorithm 6. blendBF(f, a, b, eps).

This function implements the blended method of bisection and false position methods.
    Input: The function (f),
            The interval [a, b] where the root lies in,
            The absolute error (eps).
    Output: The root (x), The value of $f(x)$; Numbers of iterations (n),
            The interval [a, b] where the root lies in
    $n := 0$
    $a1 := a$
    $a2 := a$
    $b1 := b$
    $b2 := b$
    while true **do**
      $n := n + 1$
      $xB := (a + b)/2$
      $xF := a - (f(a)*(b - a))/(f(b) - f(a))$
      if $|f(xB)| < |f(xF)|$
          $x := xB$
      else
          $x := xF$
      if $|(fx)| <= eps$
          return $x, f(x), n, a, b$
      if $f(a)*f(xB) < 0$
          $b1 := xB$
      else
          $a1 := xB$
      if $f(a) * f(xF) < 0$
          $b2 := xF$
      else
          $a2 := xF$
      $a := max(a1, a2);$
      $b := min(b1, b2)$
    end (while)

Advantages and Disadvantages of the Blended Algorithm

It is guaranteed to converge, and it is efficient more than the classical methods but it sometimes takes a long time to get root.

3.2. Blended Trisection and False Position

We exploit the superiority of the trisection over the bisection method (as shown in Section 4) in order to present a new hybrid method (Algorithm 7) that overcomes the hybrid method presented by Sabharwal [15]. The blended method (trisection–false position) is based on calculating the segment line point in the false position method and also calculating two points that divide the interval [a, b] in the trisection method and then choosing the best of them, which converges to the approximating root. The number of iterations $n(eps)$ of the proposed hybrid method is less than or equal to $min\{n_f(eps), n_t(eps)\}$, where $n_f(eps)$ and $n_t(eps)$ are the number of iterations of the false position method and the trisection method, respectively. Algorithm 7 outperforms all the classical methods (Tables 1–9).

Algorithm 7. blendTF(*f*, *a*, *b*, *eps*).

This function implements the blended method of trisection and false position methods.
    Input: The function (*f*); The interval [*a*, *b*] where the root lies in,
         The absolute error (*eps*).
    Output: The root (*x*), The value of *f*(*x*), Numbers of iterations (*n*),
         The interval [*a*, *b*] where the root lies in
    $n = 0$; $a1 := a$; $a2 := a$; $b1 := b$, $b2 := b$
    while true **do**
      $n := n + 1$
      $xT1 := (b + 2*a)/3$
      $xT2 := (2*b + a)/3$
      $xF := a - (f(a)*(b - a))/(f(b) - f(a))$
      $x := xT1$
      $fx := fxT1$
      if $|f(xT2)| < |f(x)|$
         $x := xT2$
      if $|f(xF)| < |f(x)|$
         $x := xF$
      if $|f(x)| <= eps$
         return $x, f(x), n, a, b$
      if $fa * f(xT1) < 0$
         $b1 := xT1$
      else if $f(xT1) * f(xT2) < 0$
         $a1 := xT1$
         $b1 := xT2$
      else
         $a1 := xT2$
      if $fa*f(xF) < 0$
         $b2 := xF$;
      else
      $a2 := xF$;
      $a := max(a1, a2)$; $b := min(b1, b2)$
    end (while)

Advantages and Disadvantages of the Blended Algorithm (The Proposed Algorithm)

It is guaranteed to converge, and it is more efficient than the classical methods and the blended algorithm that was proposed in [15], as shown in Tables 1–9.

4. Computational Study

The numerical results of the pure methods bisection method, trisection method, false position method, secant method and Newton–Raphson method are proposed. In addition to the computational results for the hybrid methods, the bisection–false position and trisection–false position are proposed. We compare the pure method and the hybrid method with the proposed hybrid method according to the number of iterations and CPU time. We used fifteen benchmark problems for this comparison, as shown in Table 1. We ran each problem ten times, and then we computed the average of CPU time and the number of iterations.

Table 1. Fifteen benchmark problems.

No.	Problem	Intervals	References
P1	$x^2 - 3$	[1, 2]	Harder [18]
P2	$x^2 - 5$	[2, 7]	Srivastava [9]
P3	$x^2 - 10$	[3, 4]	Harder [18]
P4	$x^2 - x - 2$	[1, 4]	Moazzam [10]
P5	$x^2 + 2x - 7$	[1, 3]	Nayak [11]
P6	$x^3 - 2$	[0, 2]	Harder [18]
P7	$xe^x - 7$	[0, 2]	Callhoun [19]
P8	$x - \cos(x)$	[0, 1]	Ehiwario [6]
P9	$x\sin(x) - 1$	[0, 2]	Mathews [20]
P10	$x\cos(x) + 1$	[−2, 4]	Esfandiari [21]
P11	$x^{10} - 1$	[0, 1.3]	Chapra [17]
P12	$x^2 + e^{x/2} - 5$	[1, 2]	Esfandiari [21]
P13	$\sin(x)\sinh(x) + 1$	[3, 4]	Esfandiari [21]
P14	$e^x - 3x - 2$	[2, 3]	Hoffman [22]
P15	$\sin(x) - x^2$	[0.5, 1]	Chapra [17]

Table 2. Comparison among pure methods and blended algorithms according to iterations, AppRoot, error and interval bounds.

Method	Iter.	AppRoot	Error	LowerB	UpperB
Bisection	19	2.0000019073486328	0.0000057220495364	1.9999961853027344	2.0000076293945313
Trisection	1	2.0000000000000000	0.0000000000000000	1.0000000000000000	4.0000000000000000
FalsePosition	15	1.9999983893881288	0.0000048318330195	1.9999959734735644	4.0000000000000000
Secant	6	2.0000000786432022	0.0000002359296127	na	na
NewtonRaphson	5	2.0000000006984919	0.0001373332926100	na	na
Hybrid [15]	2	2.0000000000000000	0.0000000000000000	1.5000000000000000	2.5000000000000000
OurHybrid	1	2.0000000000000000	0.0000000000000000	1.0000000000000000	4.0000000000000000

Table 3. Solutions of fifteen problems by the bisection method.

			Bisection Method			
Problem	Iter	Average CPU Time	Approximate Root	Function Value	Lower Bound	Upper Bound
P1	44	0.514839	1.7320508075688963	0.0000000000000000	1.7320508075688394	1.7320508075689531
P2	44	0.339006	2.2360679774997720	0.0000000000000000	2.2360679774994878	2.2360679775000563
P3	44	0.330300	3.1622776601683995	0.0000000000000000	3.1622776601683427	3.1622776601684564
P4	45	0.339274	2.0000000000000284	0.0000000000000000	1.9999999999999432	2.0000000000001137
P5	48	0.413062	1.8284271247461916	0.0000000000000086	1.8284271247461845	1.8284271247461987
P6	49	0.373710	1.2599210498948743	0.0000000000000054	1.2599210498948707	1.2599210498948779
P7	46	0.381111	1.5243452049841437	−0.0000000000000075	1.5243452049841153	1.5243452049841721
P8	44	0.345850	0.7390851332151556	−0.0000000000000085	0.7390851332150987	0.7390851332152124
P9	46	0.556300	1.1141571408719244	−0.0000000000000079	1.1141571408718960	1.1141571408719528
P10	45	0.454494	2.0739328090912181	−0.0000000000000074	2.0739328090910476	2.0739328090913887
P11	44	0.338134	1.0000000000000058	0.0000000000000000	0.9999999999999318	1.0000000000000795
P12	48	0.379392	1.6490132683031895	−0.0000000000000028	1.6490132683031860	1.6490132683031931
P13	48	0.390438	3.2215883990939425	−0.0000000000000056	3.2215883990939389	3.2215883990939460
P14	46	0.354950	2.1253911988111298	−0.0000000000000007	2.1253911988111156	2.1253911988111440
P15	45	0.359546	0.8767262153950668	−0.0000000000000048	0.8767262153950526	0.8767262153950810

Table 4. Solutions of fifteen problems by the trisection method.

Problem	Trisection Method				
	Iter	Average CPU Time	Approximate Root	Function Value	Lower Bound	Upper Bound
P1	26	0.292349	1.7320508075688856	0.0000000000000000	1.7320508075680989	1.7320508075692791
P2	28	0.311319	2.2360679774997863	0.0000000000000000	2.2360679774993493	2.2360679775000047
P3	28	0.312939	3.1622776601683911	0.0000000000000000	3.1622776601683040	3.1622776601684350
P4	1	0.011161	2.0000000000000000	0.0000000000000000	1.0000000000000000	4.0000000000000000
P5	29	0.330426	1.8284271247461907	0.0000000000000036	1.8284271247461616	1.8284271247462491
P6	30	0.341553	1.2599210498948719	−0.0000000000000062	1.2599210498948623	1.2599210498948914
P7	31	0.349806	1.5243452049841439	−0.0000000000000049	1.5243452049841375	1.5243452049841473
P8	29	0.326833	0.7390851332151560	−0.0000000000000078	0.7390851332151415	0.7390851332151852
P9	28	0.773690	1.1141571408719348	0.0000000000000066	1.1141571408717601	1.1141571408720223
P10	28	0.316154	2.0739328090912146	0.0000000000000007	2.0739328090906901	2.0739328090914770
P11	26	0.297432	1.0000000000000393	0.0000000000000000	0.9999999999995278	1.0000000000010620
P12	26	0.299995	1.6490132683031904	0.0000000000000012	1.6490132683024035	1.6490132683035839
P13	31	0.360716	3.2215883990939425	−0.0000000000000056	3.2215883990939407	3.2215883990939456
P14	28	0.323873	2.1253911988111311	0.0000000000000065	2.1253911988110437	2.1253911988111747
P15	29	0.334640	0.8767262153950647	−0.0000000000000025	0.8767262153950502	0.8767262153950720

Table 5. Solutions of fifteen problems by the false position method.

Problem	False Position Method				
	Iter	Average CPU Time	Approximate Root	Function Value	Lower Bound	Upper Bound
P1	12	0.134719	1.7320508075688599	0.0000000000000000	1.7320508075686347	2.0000000000000000
P2	46	0.510051	2.2360679774997747	0.0000000000000000	2.2360679774997609	7.0000000000000000
P3	14	0.155169	3.1622776601683644	0.0000000000000000	3.1622776601682516	4.0000000000000000
P4	34	0.382718	1.9999999999999558	0.0000000000000000	1.9999999999998894	4.0000000000000000
P5	20	0.556411	1.8284271247461896	−0.0000000000000027	1.8284271247461874	3.0000000000000000
P6	40	0.455044	1.2599210498948719	−0.0000000000000062	1.2599210498948701	2.0000000000000000
P7	29	0.330403	1.5243452049841437	−0.0000000000000075	1.5243452049841419	2.0000000000000000
P8	11	0.124456	0.7390851332151551	−0.0000000000000092	0.7390851332150500	1.0000000000000000
P9	6	0.078088	1.1141571408719306	0.0000000000000008	1.0997501702946164	1.1141571408730828
P10	12	0.138026	2.0739328090912146	0.0000000000000007	2.0739328090912039	2.5157197710146586
P11	127	1.447224	0.9999999999999812	0.0000000000000000	0.9999999999999755	1.3000000000000000
P12	15	0.176429	1.6490132683031899	−0.0000000000000008	1.6490132683031871	2.0000000000000000
P13	44	0.507856	3.2215883990939416	0.0000000000000063	3.2215883990939407	4.0000000000000000
P14	44	0.504918	2.1253911988111285	−0.0000000000000079	2.1253911988111267	3.0000000000000000
P15	16	0.185620	0.8767262153950552	0.0000000000000080	0.8767262153950091	1.0000000000000000

Table 6. Solutions of fifteen problems by Newton's method.

Problem	Newton's Method			
	Iter	Average CPU Time	Approximate Root	Function Value
P1	6	0.240500	1.7320508075688774	0.0000000000000000
P2	5	0.186819	2.2360679774997898	0.0000000000000000
P3	5	0.185136	3.1622776601683795	0.0000000000000000
P4	7	0.244393	2.0000000000000000	0.0000000000000000
P5	6	0.214349	1.8284271247461901	−0.0000000000000002
P6			Fail	
P7	14	0.436972	1.5243452049841444	0.0000000000000002
P8	6	0.214512	0.7390851332151607	0.0000000000000001
P9			Fail	
P10	14	0.439575	4.9171859252871322	0.0000000000000011
P11			Fail	
P12	6	0.221387	1.6490132683031902	0.0000000000000002
P13	6	0.221157	3.2215883990939420	0.0000000000000004
P14	5	0.191465	2.1253911988111298	0.0000000000000017
P15	9	0.306000	0.8767262153950625	0.0000000000000000

Table 7. Solutions of fifteen problems by the secant method.

Problem	Secant Method			
	Iter	Average CPU Time	Approximate Root	Function Value
P1	6	0.068071	1.7320508075688772	0.0000000000000000
P2	7	0.077763	2.2360679774997898	0.0000000000000000
P3	5	0.055822	3.1622776601683764	0.0000000000000000
P4	8	0.089142	2.0000000000000000	0.0000000000000000
P5	6	0.066767	1.8284271247461907	0.0000000000000036
P6	10	0.114367	1.2599210498948716	-0.0000000000000073
P7	9	0.101345	1.5243452049841444	0.0000000000000002
P8	6	0.067514	0.7390851332151607	0.0000000000000001
P9	5	0.073486	1.1141571408719304	0.0000000000000004
P10	8	0.091206	2.0739328090912150	-0.0000000000000003
P11		Fail		
P12	6	0.069605	1.6490132683031902	0.0000000000000002
P13	8	0.093442	3.2215883990939420	0.0000000000000004
P14	7	0.081160	2.1253911988111298	-0.0000000000000007
P15	7	0.080784	0.8767262153950625	-0.0000000000000000

Table 8. Solutions of fifteen problems by the hybrid method bisection-false position.

Problem	Bisection-False Position Method					
	Iter	Average CPU Time	Approximate Root	Function Value	Lower Bound	Upper Bound
P1	8	0.121232	1.7320508075688772	0.0000000000000000	1.7320508075688001	1.7350578402209837
P2	10	0.148720	2.2360679774997889	0.0000000000000000	2.2360679774993639	2.2439291539836148
P3	7	0.103442	3.1622776601683702	0.0000000000000000	3.1622776601625873	3.1721597778622157
P4	2	0.030053	2.0000000000000000	0.0000000000000000	1.5000000000000000	2.5000000000000000
P5	5	0.074941	1.8284271247461901	-0.0000000000000002	1.8284271247430004	1.8284271247493797
P6	9	0.137275	1.2599210498948723	-0.0000000000000041	1.2599210498939839	1.2611286403176987
P7	11	0.165907	1.5243452049841444	0.0000000000000002	1.5243452049841386	1.5260333371087631
P8	8	0.120322	0.7390851332151607	0.0000000000000001	0.7390851332151470	0.7422270732175922
P9	6	0.101488	1.1141571408719302	0.0000000000000001	1.1132427327642707	1.1141571408719768
P10	10	0.150611	2.0739328090912150	-0.0000000000000003	2.0739328090911866	2.0789350033373930
P11	12	0.184145	0.9999999999999999	0.0000000000000000	0.9999999999999305	1.0003433632829859
P12	8	0.123939	1.6490132683031895	-0.0000000000000028	1.6490132683026435	1.6531557562694839
P13	9	0.139654	3.2215883990939420	0.0000000000000004	3.2215883990939242	3.2224168881395068
P14	9	0.139775	2.1253911988111289	-0.0000000000000055	2.1253911988104042	2.1275191334463157
P15	7	0.107493	0.8767262153950581	0.0000000000000048	0.8767262153886712	0.8772684454348731

Table 9. Solutions of fifteen problems by the hybrid method trisection-false position.

Problem	Trisection-False Position Method					
	Iter	Average CPU Time	Approximate Root	Function Value	Lower Bound	Upper Bound
P1	7	0.131418	1.7320508075688772	0.0000000000000000	1.7320508075687824	1.7324926951584967
P2	8	0.149270	2.2360679774997894	0.0000000000000000	2.2360679774987138	2.2373661277171197
P3	6	0.111271	3.1622776601683777	0.0000000000000000	3.1622776601623102	3.1638711488008444
P4	1	0.018535	2.0000000000000000	0.0000000000000000	1.0000000000000000	4.0000000000000000
P5	7	0.131906	1.8284271247461901	-0.0000000000000002	1.8284271247461521	1.8288267084339278
P6	8	0.152130	1.2599210498948730	-0.0000000000000009	1.2599210498938187	1.2602675857311345
P7	7	0.131670	1.5243452049841444	0.0000000000000002	1.5243452049840662	1.5244112793655715
P8	7	0.131345	0.7390851332151607	0.0000000000000001	0.7390851332151193	0.7396432352779715
P9	5	0.213409	1.1141571408719326	0.0000000000000035	1.1126440519145675	1.1141571409109841
P10	8	0.150378	2.0739328090912150	-0.0000000000000003	2.0739328090912079	2.0745363211703700
P11	9	0.170638	1.0000000000000000	0.0000000000000000	0.9999999999999090	1.0000567349034972
P12	6	0.115872	1.6490132683031897	-0.0000000000000018	1.6490132683015255	1.6496393349802922
P13	7	0.135481	3.2215883990939420	0.0000000000000004	3.2215883990931498	3.2217303732361522
P14	7	0.134990	2.1253911988111298	-0.0000000000000007	2.1253911988110636	2.1254846670968397
P15	5	0.096275	0.8767262153950616	0.0000000000000010	0.8767262151142412	0.8767286917958327

We used MATLAB v7.01 Software Package to implement all the codes. All codes were run under 64-bit Window 8.1 Operating System with Core(TM)i5 CPU M 460 @2.53GHz, 4.00 GB of memory.

Dataset and Evaluation Metrics

There are different ways to terminate the numerical algorithms such as the absolute error (eps) and the number of iterations. In this paper, we used the absolute error ($eps = 10^{-14}$) to terminate all the algorithms. Perhaps there is a method that has a small number of iterations, but the execution time is large and vice versa. For this reason, the iteration number and the running time are important metrics to evaluate the algorithms. Unfortunately, most researchers did not pay attention to the details of finding the running time. Furthermore, they did not discuss and did not answer the following question: why does the running time change from one run to another with the used software package? Therefore, we ran every algorithm ten times and calculated the average of the running time to obtain an accurate running time and avoid the problems of the operating systems.

In Table 2, the abbreviations AppRoot, Error, LowerB and UpperB are used to denote the approximation root, the difference between two successive roots, lower bound and upper bound, respectively. Table 2 shows the performance of all classical methods and blended algorithms for solving the Problem 4. It is clear that both the trisection and the proposed blended algorithm (trisection-false position) outperformed the other algorithms. Because it is not accurate enough to make a conclusion from one function, we used fifteen benchmark functions (Table 1) to evaluate the proposed algorithm.

Ali Demir [23] proved that the trisection method with k-Lucas number works faster than the bisection method. From Tables 3 and 4 and Figure 2, it is clear that the trisection method is better than the bisection method with respect to the running time for all problems except for problem 9. On the other hand, the trisection method determined the exact root (2.0000000000000000) of problem 4 after one iteration, but the bisection method found the approximate root (2.0000000000000284) after 45 iterations. Figure 3 shows that the trisection method always has fewer iterations than the bisection method. We can determine the number of iterations for the trisection method by $n = \left\lceil \log_3 \left(\frac{b-a}{eps} \right) \right\rceil$ and the number of iterations for the bisection method by $n = \left\lceil \log_2 \left(\frac{b-a}{eps} \right) \right\rceil$. The authors [6,11] explained that the secant method is better than the bisection and Newton–Raphson methods for problem 8. It is not accurate to draw a conclusion from one function [15], so we experimented on fifteen benchmark functions. From Table 7, it is clear that the secant method failed to solve problem 11.

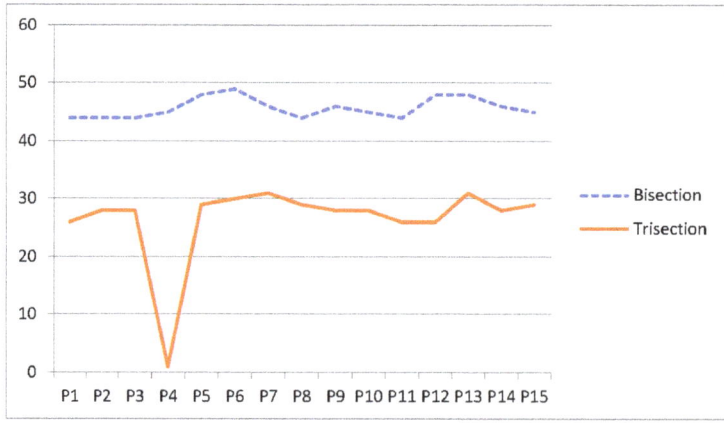

Figure 2. A comparison among 7 methods on 15 problems according to the number of iteration.

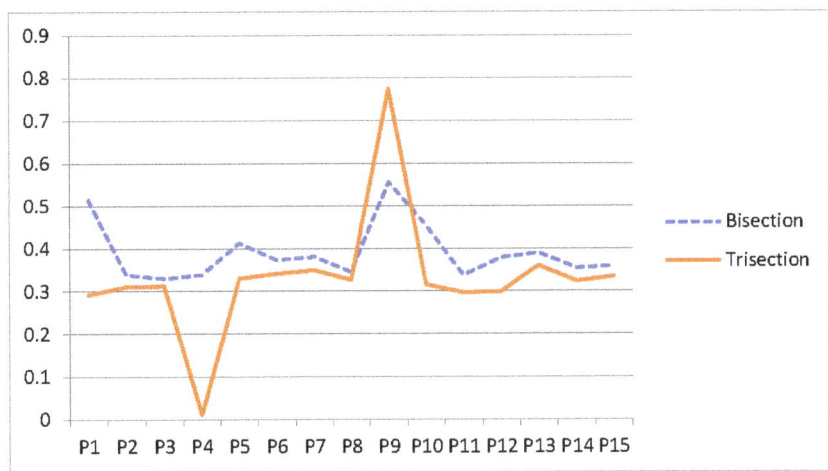

Figure 3. A comparison among 7 methods on 15 problems according to the CPU time.

From Tables 5–7, we deduce that the proposed hybrid algorithm (trisection-false position) is better than the Newton–Raphson, false-position and secant. The Newton–Raphson method failed to solve problems P6, P9 and P11, and the secant method failed to solve P11.

From Figure 4 and Tables 8 and 9, it is clear that the proposed blended algorithm (trisection–false position) has fewer iterations than the blended algorithm (bisection–false position) [15] on all the problems except problem 5 (i.e., according to the number of iterations, the proposed algorithm achieved 93.3% of fifteen problems but Sabharwal's algorithm achieved 6.6%).

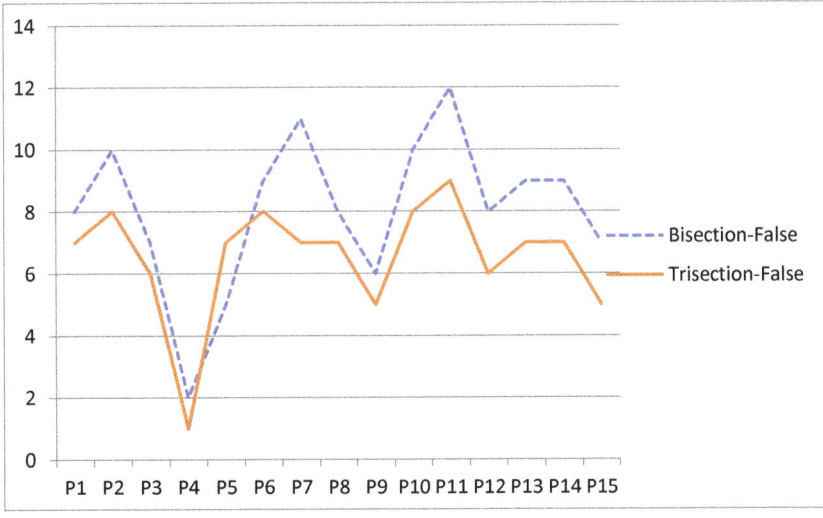

Figure 4. A comparison among 7 methods on 15 problems according to the number of iterations.

From Figure 5 and Tables 8 and 9, it is clear that the proposed blended algorithm (trisection–false position) outperforms the blended algorithm (bisection-false position) [15] for eight problems versus seven problems (i.e., the proposed algorithm achieved 53.3%

of fifteen problems but Sabharwal's algorithm achieved 46.6%). On the other hand, the trisection method determined the exact root (1.0000000000000000) of the problem 4 after nine iterations, but the bisection method found the approximate root (0.9999999999999999) after 12 iterations.

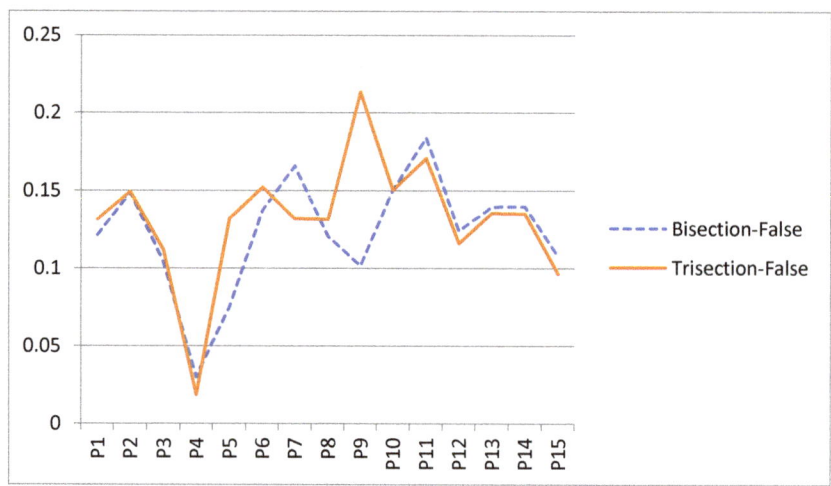

Figure 5. A comparison among 7 methods on 15 problems according to the CPU time.

5. Conclusions

In this work, we proposed a novel blended algorithm that has the advantages of the trisection method and the false position method. The computational results show that the proposed algorithm outperforms the trisection and regula falsi methods. On the other hand, the introduced algorithm outperforms the bisection, Newton–Raphson and secant methods according to the iteration number and the average running time. Finally, the implementation results show the superiority of the proposed algorithm on the blended bisection and false position algorithm, which was proposed by Sabharwal [15]. In future work, we will do more numerical studies using benchmark functions to evaluate the proposed algorithm and ensure that it competes with the traditional algorithms to replace it in software packages such as Matlab and Python. We will also propose some other hybrid algorithms that may be better than the proposed algorithm such as the bisection–Newton–Raphson method and trisection–Newton–Raphson.

Author Contributions: Conceptualization, E.B.; methodology, S.A.; software, A.E.G.; validation, E.B.; formal analysis, E.B.; investigation, S.A.; resources, A.E.G.; data curation, A.E.G.; writing—original draft preparation, E.B.; writing—review and editing, E.B.; visualization, E.B.; supervision, E.B.; project administration, E.B.; funding acquisition, S.A. All authors have read and agreed to the published version of the manuscript.

Funding: The authors extend their appreciation to the Deanship of Scientific Research at Majmaah University for funding this work under project number (R-2021-140).

Acknowledgments: The help from Higher Technological Institute, 10th of Ramadan City, Egypt for publishing is sincerely and greatly appreciated. We also thank the referees for suggestions to improve the presentation of this paper.

Conflicts of Interest: The authors declare no conflict of interest.

References

1. Hasan, A. Numerical Study of Some Iterative Methods for Solving Nonlinear Equations. *Int. J. Eng. Sci. Invent.* **2016**, *5*, 1–10.
2. Hasan, A.; Ahmad, N. Compartive study of a new iterative method with that Newtons Method for solving algebraic and transcesental equations. *Int. J. Comput. Math. Sci.* **2015**, *4*, 32–37.
3. Khirallah, M.Q.; Hafiz, M.A. Solving system of nonlinear equations using family of jarratt methods. *Int. J. Differ. Equ. Appl.* **2013**, *12*, 69–83. [CrossRef]
4. Remani, C. *Numerical Methods for Solving Systems of Nonlinear Equations*; Lakehead University: Thunder Bay, ON, Canada, 2012; p. 13.
5. Lally, C.H. A faster, high precision algorithm for calculating symmetric and asymmetric. *arXiv* **2015**, arXiv:1509.01831.
6. Ehiwario, J.C.; Aghamie, S.O. Comparative Study of Bisection, Newton-Raphson and Secant Methods of Root-Finding Problems. *IOSR J. Eng.* **2014**, *4*, 1–7.
7. Ait-Aoudia, S.; Mana, I. Numerical solving of geometric constraints by bisection: A distributed approach. *Int. J. Comput. Inf. Sci.* **2004**, *2*, 66.
8. Baskar, S.; Ganesh, S.S. *Introduction to Numerical Analysis*; Department of Mathematics, Indian Institute of Technology Bombay Powai: Mumbai, India, 2016.
9. Srivastava, R.B.; Srivastava, S. Comparison of numerical rate of convergence of bisection, Newton and secant methods. *J. Chem. Biol. Phys. Sci.* **2011**, *2*, 472–479.
10. Moazzam, G.; Chakraborty, A.; Bhuiyan, A. A robust method for solving transcendental equations. *Int. J. Comput. Sci. Issues* **2012**, *9*, 413–419.
11. Nayak, T.; Dash, T. Solution to quadratic equation using genetic algorithm. In Proceedings of the National Conference on AIRES-2012, Vishakhapatnam, India, 29–30 June 2012.
12. Mansouria, P.; Asadya, B.; Guptab, N. The Bisection–Artificial Bee Colony algorithm to solve fixed point problems. *Appl. Soft Comput.* **2015**, *26*, 143–148. [CrossRef]
13. Karaboga, D.; Basturk, B. A powerful and efficient algorithm for numerical func-tion optimization: Artificial Bee Colony (ABC) algorithm. *J. Glob. Optim.* **2007**, *39*, 459–471. [CrossRef]
14. Burden, L.R.; Douglas, F.J. *Numerical Analysis, Prindle, Weber & Schmidt*, 3rd ed.; Amazon: Seattle, WA, USA, 1 January 1985.
15. Sabharwal, C.L. Blended Root Finding Algorithm Outperforms Bisection and Regula Falsi Algorithms. *Mathematics* **2019**, *7*, 1118. [CrossRef]
16. Badr, E.M.; Elgendy, H. A hybrid water cycle-particle swarm optimization for solving the fuzzy underground water confined steady flow. *Indones. J. Electr. Eng. Comput. Sci.* **2020**, *19*, 492–504. [CrossRef]
17. Chapra, S.C.; Canale, R.P. *Numerical Methods for Engineers*, 7th ed.; McGraw-Hill: Boston, MA, USA, 2015.
18. Harder, D.W. Numerical Analysis for Engineering. Available online: https://ece.uwaterloo.ca/~{}\{\}dwharder/NumericalAnaly-sis/10RootFinding/falseposition/ (accessed on 11 June 2019).
19. Calhoun, D. Available online: https://math.boisestate.edu/~{}\{\}calhoun/teaching/matlab-tutorials/lab_16/html/lab_16.html (accessed on 13 June 2019).
20. Mathews, J.H.; Fink, K.D. *Numerical Methods Using Matlab*, 4th ed.; Prentice-Hall Inc.: Upper Saddle River, NJ, USA, 2004; ISBN 0-13-065248-2.
21. Esfandiari, R.S. *Numerical Methods for Engineers and Scientists Using MATLAB*; CRC Press: Boca Raton, FL, USA, 2013.
22. Joe, D.H. *Numerical Methods for Engineers and Scientists*, 2nd ed.; CRC Press: Boca Raton, FL, USA, 2001.
23. Demir, A. Trisection method by k-Lucas numbers. *Appl. Math. Comput.* **2008**, *198*, 339–345. [CrossRef]

Article

On a Riemann–Liouville Type Implicit Coupled System via Generalized Boundary Conditions †

Usman Riaz [1], Akbar Zada [1], Zeeshan Ali [2], Ioan-Lucian Popa [3,*], Shahram Rezapour [4,5,*] and Sina Etemad [4]

[1] Department of Mathematics, University of Peshawar, Peshawar, Khyber Pakhtunkhwa 25000, Pakistan; uriaz513@gmail.com (U.R.); zadababo@yahoo.com (A.Z.)
[2] School of Engineering, Monash University Malaysia, Selangor 47500, Malaysia; zeeshanmaths1@gmail.com or zeeshan.ali@monash.edu
[3] Department of Computing, Mathematics and Electronics, "1 Decembrie 1918" University of Alba Iulia, Alba Iulia 510009, Romania
[4] Department of Mathematics, Azarbaijan Shahid Madani University, Tabriz 51368, Iran; sina.etemad@azaruniv.ac.ir or sina.etemad@gmail.com
[5] Department of Medical Research, China Medical University Hospital, China Medical University, Taichung 404, Taiwan
* Correspondence: lucian.popa@uab.ro (I.-L.P.); rezapourshahram@yahoo.ca (S.R.)
† These authors contributed equally to this work.

Abstract: We study a coupled system of implicit differential equations with fractional-order differential boundary conditions and the Riemann–Liouville derivative. The existence, uniqueness, and at least one solution are established by applying the Banach contraction and Leray–Schauder fixed point theorem. Furthermore, Hyers–Ulam type stabilities are discussed. An example is presented to illustrate our main result. The suggested system is the generalization of fourth-order ordinary differential equations with anti-periodic, classical, and initial boundary conditions.

Keywords: Riemann–Liouville fractional derivative; coupled system; fractional order boundary conditions; green function; existence theory; Ulam stability

MSC: 26A33; 34B27; 45M10

1. Introduction

The generalization of ordinary derivatives leads us to the theory of fractional derivatives. The concept of fractional derivatives was established in 1695, after the well-known conversation of Leibniz and L'Hospital [1]. Mathematicians like Riemann, Liouville, Caputo, Hadamard, Fourier, and Laplace contributed a lot and made the area more interesting for researchers. A fractional-order derivative is a global operator, which may act as a tool to modify or modernize different physical phenomena like control theory [2], dynamical process [3], electro-chemistry [4], mathematical biology [5], image and signal processing [6], etc. For more applications of the fractional differential equations (FDEs), we refer the reader to the works in [7–11]. Furthermore, the theory of coupled systems of differential equations is referred to as an important theory in the applied sciences envisaging different areas of biochemistry, ecology, biology, and classical fields of physical sciences and engineering. For details see in [12–14].

The theory regarding the existence of solutions of FDEs, drew significant attention of the researchers working on different boundary conditions, e.g., classical, integral, multipoint, non-local, periodic, and anti-periodic [15–18]. Among the qualitative properties of FDEs, the stability property of the solution is the central one, particularly the Hyers–Ulam (HU) stability [19–26]. Stability theory in the sense of HU was first discussed by Ulam [27] in the form of a question in 1940 and the following year, Hyers [28] answered his question in the context of Banach spaces. Recently, generalized HU stability was discussed by

Alqifiary et al. [29] for linear differential equations. Razaei et al. [30] presented Laplace transform and HU stability of linear differential equations. Wang et al. [31] studied HU stability for two types of linear FDEs. Shen et al. [32] worked on the HU stability of linear FDEs with constant coefficients using Laplace transform method. Liu et al. [33] proved the HU stability of linear Caputo–Fabrizio FDEs. Liu et al. [34] studied the HU stability of linear Caputo–Fabrizio FDEs with the Mittag–Leffler kernel by Laplace transform method.

The above work motivate us to study the coupled implicit FDEs with fractional-order differential boundary conditions:

$$\begin{cases} \mathfrak{D}^\alpha v(t) - \chi_1(t, u(t), \mathfrak{D}^\alpha v(t)) = 0;\ t \in \mathfrak{J}, \\ \mathfrak{D}^\kappa u(t) - \chi_2(t, v(t), \mathfrak{D}^\kappa u(t)) = 0;\ t \in \mathfrak{J}, \\ \mathfrak{D}^{\alpha-4}v(0) = \eta_1 \mathfrak{D}^{\alpha-4}v(\sigma),\ \mathfrak{D}^{\alpha-3}v(0) = \eta_2 \mathfrak{D}^{\alpha-3}v(\sigma), \\ \mathfrak{D}^{\alpha-2}v(0) = \eta_3 \mathfrak{D}^{\alpha-2}v(\sigma),\ \mathfrak{D}^{\alpha-1}v(0) = \eta_4 \mathfrak{D}^{\alpha-1}v(\sigma), \\ \mathfrak{D}^{\kappa-4}u(0) = \eta_5 \mathfrak{D}^{\kappa-4}u(\sigma),\ \mathfrak{D}^{\kappa-3}u(0) = \eta_6 \mathfrak{D}^{\kappa-3}u(\sigma), \\ \mathfrak{D}^{\kappa-2}u(0) = \eta_7 \mathfrak{D}^{\kappa-2}u(\sigma),\ \mathfrak{D}^{\kappa-1}u(0) = \eta_8 \mathfrak{D}^{\kappa-1}u(\sigma), \end{cases} \quad (1)$$

where $3 < \alpha, \kappa \leq 4$, $\mathfrak{J} = [0, \sigma]$, $\sigma > 0$ and $\eta_i \neq 1$ for $i = 1, 2, \ldots, 8$. $\mathfrak{D}^\alpha, \mathfrak{D}^\kappa$ be the α, κ order denotes Riemann–Liouville fractional derivatives and $\chi_1, \chi_2 : \mathfrak{J} \times \mathcal{R} \times \mathcal{R} \to \mathcal{R}$ be continuous functions.

Higher-order ordinary differential equations (ODEs) can be used to model problems arising from the field of applied sciences and engineering [35,36]. The generalization of fourth-order ODEs are FDEs (1) if $\alpha = \kappa = 4$. Fourth-order differential equations have important applications in mechanics, thus have attracted considerable attention over the last three decades. The problem of static deflection of a uniform beam, which can be modeled as a fourth-order initial value problem is a good example of a real problem in engineering [37,38].

This problem has been extensively analyzed, some new techniques were developed and numerous general and impressive results regarding the existence of solutions were established in [39–42]. Sometimes, mathematical modeling of the various physical phenomena may arise as a coupled system of the forgoing ODEs. Furthermore, for $\eta_i = -1$ ($i = 1, 2, \ldots, 8$), we can obtain anti-periodic boundary conditions which are applicable in several mathematical models, some are given in [43,44].

The manuscript is categorized as follows. For our main results, we establish some basic notations, definitions, and lemma in Section 2. In Section 3, we present existence, uniqueness, and at least one solution of system (1) by applying the Banach contraction fixed point theorem and Leray–Schauder fixed point theorem. In Section 4, we discuss definitions of HU type stabilities, which help us to show that system (1) has HU type stabilities by two different approaches. In Section 5, by a particular example of the system (1), we show that our results are applicable.

2. Background Materials

In this fragment, we present basic notations with Banach spaces, definitions of the considered derivative and integral, and lemma, which will be utilized in the next sections.

Suppose $\mathbb{C}(\mathfrak{J})$ is a Banach space with a norm defined as $\|v\| = \sup_{t \in \mathfrak{J}} |v(t)|$. For $t \in \mathfrak{J}$, we define $v_r(t) = t^r v(t)$, $r \geq 0$. Suppose that $S_1 = \mathbb{C}_r(\mathfrak{J}) \subset \mathbb{C}(\mathfrak{J})$ be the space of all functions v such that $v_r \in S_1$ which yields to be a Banach space when endowed with the norm

$$\|v\|_{S_1} = \max\{\sup_{t \in \mathfrak{J}} t^r |v(t)|,\ \sup_{t \in \mathfrak{J}} t^r |\mathfrak{D}^\alpha v(t)|\}.$$

Similarly, $\|(v, u)\|_S = \|v\|_{S_1} + \|u\|_{S_2}$ is the norm defined on the product space, where $S = S_1 \times S_2$. Obviously $(S, \|(v, u)\|_S)$ is a Banach space.

Definition 1. [45] *For a continuous function* $v : \mathcal{R}^+ \to \mathcal{R}$, *the Riemann–Liouville integral of order* $\alpha > 0$ *is defined as*

$$\mathfrak{I}^\alpha v(t) = \frac{1}{\Gamma(\alpha)} \int_0^t \frac{v(\tau)}{(t-\tau)^{1-\alpha}} d\tau,$$

such that the integral is pointwise defined on $\mathcal{R}^+$.

Definition 2. [45] *For a continuous function* $v : \mathcal{R}^+ \to \mathcal{R}$, *the Riemann–Liouville derivative of order* $\alpha > 0$ *is defined as*

$$\mathfrak{D}^\alpha v(t) = \frac{1}{\Gamma(n-\alpha)} \left(\frac{d}{dt}\right)^n \int_0^t \frac{v(\tau)}{(t-\tau)^{\alpha-n+1}} d\tau,$$

where $[\alpha]$ *represents the integer part of* α *and* $n = [\alpha] + 1$. *We note that for* $\varrho > -1$, $\varrho \neq \alpha - 1, \alpha - 2, \ldots, \alpha - n$, *we have*

$$\mathfrak{D}^\alpha t^\varrho = \frac{\Gamma(\varrho+1)}{\Gamma(\varrho-\alpha+1)} t^{\varrho-\alpha}$$

and

$$\mathfrak{D}^\alpha t^{\alpha-i} = 0, \quad i = 1, 2, 3, \ldots, n.$$

Lemma 1. [45] *Solution of the following Riemann–Liouville FDE of order* $n - 1 < \alpha \leq n$

$$\mathfrak{D}^\alpha v(t) = \vartheta(t),$$

is

$$\mathfrak{I}^\alpha \mathfrak{D}^\alpha v(t) = \mathfrak{I}^\alpha \vartheta(t) + k_0 t^{\alpha-n} + k_1 t^{\alpha-n-1} + \cdots + k_{n-2} t^{\alpha-2} + k_{n-1} t^{\alpha-1},$$

where $k_i (i = 1, 2, 3, \ldots, n)$ *are unknowns.*

3. Existence Theory

This section is devoted to the equivalent integral form of the proposed problem.

Lemma 2. *Let* $\vartheta \in \mathbb{C}(\mathfrak{J})$, *the following* $\alpha \in (3, 4]$ *order FDE with boundary conditions*

$$\begin{cases} \mathfrak{D}^\alpha v(t) = \vartheta(t); \; t \in \mathfrak{J}, \\ \mathfrak{D}^{\alpha-4} v(0) = \eta_1 \mathfrak{D}^{\alpha-4} v(\sigma), \; \mathfrak{D}^{\alpha-3} v(0) = \eta_2 \mathfrak{D}^{\alpha-3} v(\sigma), \\ \mathfrak{D}^{\alpha-2} v(0) = \eta_3 \mathfrak{D}^{\alpha-2} v(\sigma), \; \mathfrak{D}^{\alpha-1} v(0) = \eta_4 \mathfrak{D}^{\alpha-1} v(\sigma), \end{cases} \quad (2)$$

have the solution

$$v(t) = \int_0^\sigma G_\alpha(t, \tau) \vartheta(\tau) d\tau,$$

where

$$G_\alpha(t,\tau) = \begin{cases} \dfrac{(t-\tau)^{\alpha-1}}{\Gamma(\alpha)} + \dfrac{\eta_1 t^{\alpha-4}(\sigma-\tau)^3}{6(1-\eta_1)\Gamma(\alpha-3)} + \dfrac{\left[(1-\eta_1)\eta_2 t^{\alpha-3}+\eta_1\eta_2\sigma t^{\alpha-4}(\alpha-3)\right](\sigma-\tau)^2}{2(1-\eta_1)(1-\eta_2)\Gamma(\alpha-2)} \\ + \dfrac{\eta_3 t^{\alpha-2}(\sigma-\tau)}{(1-\eta_3)\Gamma(\alpha-1)} + \dfrac{\eta_2\eta_3\sigma t^{\alpha-3}(\sigma-\tau)}{(1-\eta_2)(1-\eta_3)\Gamma(\alpha-2)} + \dfrac{\eta_1(1+\eta_2)\eta_3\sigma^2 t^{\alpha-4}(\sigma-\tau)}{2(1-\eta_1)(1-\eta_2)(1-\eta_3)\Gamma(\alpha-3)} \\ + \dfrac{\eta_4 t^{\alpha-1}}{(1-\eta_4)\Gamma(\alpha)} + \dfrac{\eta_3\eta_4\sigma t^{\alpha-2}}{(1-\eta_3)(1-\eta_4)\Gamma(\alpha-1)} + \dfrac{\eta_2(1+\eta_3)\eta_4\sigma^2 t^{\alpha-3}}{2(1-\eta_2)(1-\eta_3)(1-\eta_4)\Gamma(\alpha-2)} \\ + \dfrac{\eta_1\left((1+\eta_2)(1+\eta_3)+\eta_2+\eta_3\right)\eta_4\sigma^3 t^{\alpha-4}}{6(1-\eta_1)(1-\eta_2)(1-\eta_3)(1-\eta_4)\Gamma(\alpha-3)}, & 0 \leq \tau < t \leq \sigma, \\[1em] \dfrac{\eta_1 t^{\alpha-4}(\sigma-\tau)^3}{6(1-\eta_1)\Gamma(\alpha-3)} + \dfrac{\left[(1-\eta_1)\eta_2 t^{\alpha-3}+\eta_1\eta_2\sigma t^{\alpha-4}(\alpha-3)\right](\sigma-\tau)^2}{2(1-\eta_1)(1-\eta_2)\Gamma(\alpha-2)} \\ + \dfrac{\eta_3 t^{\alpha-2}(\sigma-\tau)}{(1-\eta_3)\Gamma(\alpha-1)} + \dfrac{\eta_2\eta_3\sigma t^{\alpha-3}(\sigma-\tau)}{(1-\eta_2)(1-\eta_3)\Gamma(\alpha-2)} + \dfrac{\eta_1(1+\eta_2)\eta_3\sigma^2 t^{\alpha-4}(\sigma-\tau)}{2(1-\eta_1)(1-\eta_2)(1-\eta_3)\Gamma(\alpha-3)} \\ + \dfrac{\eta_4 t^{\alpha-1}}{(1-\eta_4)\Gamma(\alpha)} + \dfrac{\eta_3\eta_4\sigma t^{\alpha-2}}{(1-\eta_3)(1-\eta_4)\Gamma(\alpha-1)} + \dfrac{\eta_2(1+\eta_3)\eta_4\sigma^2 t^{\alpha-3}}{2(1-\eta_2)(1-\eta_3)(1-\eta_4)\Gamma(\alpha-2)} \\ + \dfrac{\eta_1\left((1+\eta_2)(1+\eta_3)+\eta_2+\eta_3\right)\eta_4\sigma^3 t^{\alpha-4}}{6(1-\eta_1)(1-\eta_2)(1-\eta_3)(1-\eta_4)\Gamma(\alpha-3)}, & 0 \leq t < \tau \leq \sigma. \end{cases} \quad (3)$$

Proof. Using Lemma 1 on FDE (2), we have

$$v(t) = \frac{1}{\Gamma(\alpha)}\int_0^t (t-\tau)^{\alpha-1}\vartheta(\tau)d\tau + k_3 t^{\alpha-1} + k_2 t^{\alpha-2} + k_1 t^{\alpha-3} + k_0 t^{\alpha-4}. \quad (4)$$

Applying boundary conditions of (2) on (4), we get unknowns

$$k_0 = \frac{\eta_1}{(1-\eta_1)\Gamma(\alpha-3)}\Big[\frac{1}{6}\int_0^\sigma (\sigma-\tau)^3\vartheta(\tau)d\tau + \frac{\eta_2\sigma}{2(1-\eta_2)}\int_0^\sigma (\sigma-\tau)^2\vartheta(\tau)d\tau$$
$$+ \frac{(1+\eta_2)\eta_3\sigma^2}{2(1-\eta_2)(1-\eta_3)}\int_0^\sigma (\sigma-\tau)\vartheta(\tau)d\tau + \frac{((1+\eta_2)(1+\eta_3)+\eta_2+\eta_3)\eta_4\sigma^3}{6(1-\eta_2)(1-\eta_3)(1-\eta_4)}\int_0^\sigma \vartheta(\tau)d\tau\Big],$$
$$k_1 = \frac{\eta_2}{(1-\eta_2)\Gamma(\alpha-2)}\Big[\frac{1}{2}\int_0^\sigma (\sigma-\tau)^2\vartheta(\tau)d\tau + \frac{\eta_3\sigma}{(1-\eta_3)}\int_0^\sigma (\sigma-\tau)\vartheta(\tau)d\tau$$
$$+ \frac{(1+\eta_3)\eta_4\sigma^2}{2(1-\eta_3)(1-\eta_4)}\int_0^\sigma \vartheta(\tau)d\tau\Big],$$
$$k_2 = \frac{\eta_3}{(1-\eta_3)\Gamma(\alpha-1)}\Big[\int_0^\sigma (\sigma-\tau)\vartheta(\tau)d\tau + \frac{\eta_4\sigma}{(1-\eta_4)}\int_0^\sigma \vartheta(\tau)d\tau\Big],$$
$$k_3 = \frac{\eta_4}{(1-\eta_4)\Gamma(\alpha)}\int_0^\sigma \vartheta(\tau)d\tau.$$

Put the values of k_0, k_1, k_2 and k_3 in Equation (4), we obtain

$$v(t) = \frac{1}{\Gamma(\alpha)} \int_0^t (t-\tau)^{\alpha-1} \vartheta(\tau) d\tau + \frac{\eta_1 t^{\alpha-4}}{6(1-\eta_1)\Gamma(\alpha-3)} \int_0^\sigma (\sigma-\tau)^3 \vartheta(\tau) d\tau$$

$$+ \left[\frac{\eta_2 t^{\alpha-3}}{2(1-\eta_2)\Gamma(\alpha-2)} + \frac{\eta_1 \eta_2 \sigma t^{\alpha-4}}{2(1-\eta_1)(1-\eta_2)\Gamma(\alpha-3)}\right] \int_0^\sigma (\sigma-\tau)^2 \vartheta(\tau) d\tau$$

$$+ \left[\frac{\eta_3 t^{\alpha-2}}{(1-\eta_3)\Gamma(\alpha-1)} + \frac{\eta_2 \eta_3 \sigma t^{\alpha-3}}{(1-\eta_2)(1-\eta_3)\Gamma(\alpha-2)} + \frac{\eta_1(1+\eta_2)\eta_3 \sigma^2 t^{\alpha-4}}{2(1-\eta_1)(1-\eta_2)(1-\eta_3)\Gamma(\alpha-3)}\right]$$

$$\times \int_0^\sigma (\sigma-\tau)\vartheta(\tau) d\tau + \left[\frac{\eta_4 t^{\alpha-1}}{(1-\eta_4)\Gamma(\alpha)} + \frac{\eta_3 \eta_4 \sigma t^{\alpha-2}}{(1-\eta_3)(1-\eta_4)\Gamma(\alpha-1)}\right.$$

$$+ \frac{\eta_2(1+\eta_3)\eta_4 \sigma^2 t^{\alpha-3}}{2(1-\eta_2)(1-\eta_3)(1-\eta_4)\Gamma(\alpha-2)} +$$

$$+ \left.\frac{\eta_1((1+\eta_2)(1+\eta_3)+\eta_2+\eta_3)\eta_4 \sigma^3 t^{\alpha-4}}{6(1-\eta_1)(1-\eta_2)(1-\eta_3)(1-\eta_4)\Gamma(\alpha-3)}\right] \int_0^\sigma \vartheta(\tau) d\tau$$

$$= \int_0^\sigma \mathbf{G}_\alpha(t,\tau)\vartheta(\tau) d\tau, \tag{5}$$

where $\mathbf{G}_\alpha(t,\tau)$ is given by (3). □

Remark 1. *Let $\mu \in \mathbb{C}(\mathfrak{J})$, the following $\kappa \in (3,4]$ order FDE with boundary conditions*

$$\begin{cases} \mathfrak{D}^\kappa u(t) = \mu(t); \ t \in \mathfrak{J}, \\ \mathfrak{D}^{\kappa-4} u(0) = \eta_5 \mathfrak{D}^{\kappa-4} u(\sigma), \ \mathfrak{D}^{\kappa-3} u(0) = \eta_6 \mathfrak{D}^{\kappa-3} u(\sigma), \\ \mathfrak{D}^{\kappa-2} u(0) = \eta_7 \mathfrak{D}^{\kappa-2} u(\sigma), \ \mathfrak{D}^{\kappa-1} u(0) = \eta_8 \mathfrak{D}^{\kappa-1} u(\sigma) \end{cases}$$

has the solution

$$u(t) = \int_0^\sigma \mathbf{G}_\kappa(t,\tau)\mu(\tau) d\tau,$$

where $\mathbf{G}_\kappa(t,\tau)$ is given by

$$\mathbf{G}_\kappa(t,\tau) = \begin{cases} \frac{(t-\tau)^{\kappa-1}}{\Gamma(\kappa)} + \frac{\eta_5 t^{\kappa-4}(\sigma-\tau)^3}{6(1-\eta_5)\Gamma(\kappa-3)} + \frac{\left[(1-\eta_5)\eta_6 t^{\kappa-3}+\eta_5\eta_6\sigma t^{\kappa-4}(\kappa-3)\right](\sigma-\tau)^2}{2(1-\eta_5)(1-\eta_6)\Gamma(\kappa-2)} \\ + \frac{\eta_7 t^{\kappa-2}(\sigma-\tau)}{(1-\eta_7)\Gamma(\kappa-1)} + \frac{\eta_6\eta_7\sigma t^{\kappa-3}(\sigma-\tau)}{(1-\eta_6)(1-\eta_7)\Gamma(\kappa-2)} + \frac{\eta_5(1+\eta_6)\eta_7\sigma^2 t^{\kappa-4}(\sigma-\tau)}{2(1-\eta_5)(1-\eta_6)(1-\eta_7)\Gamma(\kappa-3)} \\ + \frac{\eta_8 t^{\kappa-1}}{(1-\eta_8)\Gamma(\kappa)} + \frac{\eta_7\eta_8\sigma t^{\kappa-2}}{(1-\eta_7)(1-\eta_8)\Gamma(\kappa-1)} + \frac{\eta_6(1+\eta_7)\eta_8\sigma^2 t^{\kappa-3}}{2(1-\eta_6)(1-\eta_7)(1-\eta_8)\Gamma(\kappa-2)} \\ + \frac{\eta_5\left((1+\eta_6)(1+\eta_7)+\eta_6+\eta_7\right)\eta_8\sigma^3 t^{\kappa-4}}{6(1-\eta_5)(1-\eta_6)(1-\eta_7)(1-\eta_8)\Gamma(\kappa-3)}, & 0 \leq \tau < t \leq \sigma, \\[6pt] \frac{\eta_5 t^{\kappa-4}(\sigma-\tau)^3}{6(1-\eta_5)\Gamma(\kappa-3)} + \frac{\left[(1-\eta_5)\eta_6 t^{\kappa-3}+\eta_5\eta_6\sigma t^{\kappa-4}(\kappa-3)\right](\sigma-\tau)^2}{2(1-\eta_5)(1-\eta_6)\Gamma(\kappa-2)} \\ + \frac{\eta_7 t^{\kappa-2}(\sigma-\tau)}{(1-\eta_7)\Gamma(\kappa-1)} + \frac{\eta_6\eta_7\sigma t^{\kappa-3}(\sigma-\tau)}{(1-\eta_6)(1-\eta_7)\Gamma(\kappa-2)} + \frac{\eta_5(1+\eta_6)\eta_7\sigma^2 t^{\kappa-4}(\sigma-\tau)}{2(1-\eta_5)(1-\eta_6)(1-\eta_7)\Gamma(\kappa-3)} \\ + \frac{\eta_8 t^{\kappa-1}}{(1-\eta_8)\Gamma(\kappa)} + \frac{\eta_7\eta_8\sigma t^{\kappa-2}}{(1-\eta_7)(1-\eta_8)\Gamma(\kappa-1)} + \frac{\eta_6(1+\eta_7)\eta_8\sigma^2 t^{\kappa-3}}{2(1-\eta_6)(1-\eta_7)(1-\eta_8)\Gamma(\kappa-2)} \\ + \frac{\eta_5\left((1+\eta_6)(1+\eta_7)+\eta_6+\eta_7\right)\eta_8\sigma^3 t^{\kappa-4}}{6(1-\eta_5)(1-\eta_6)(1-\eta_7)(1-\eta_8)\Gamma(\kappa-3)}, & 0 \leq t < \tau \leq \sigma. \end{cases}$$

Remark 2. *Putting $\alpha = 4$ and $\eta_1 = \eta_2 = \eta_3 = \eta_4 = -1$ in (3), gives Green's function $\mathbf{G}_\alpha(t,\tau)$ of fourth-order ODE with anti-periodic boundary conditions.*

Remark 3. *Putting $\alpha = 4$ and $\eta_1 = \eta_2 = \eta_3 = \eta_4 = 0$ in (5), gives the solution of fourth-order ODE having initial conditions.*

For the reason of advantage, we set the following notations:

$$\mathcal{Q}_\alpha = \max\left\{\frac{\sigma^4}{\Gamma(\alpha+1)} + \left|\frac{\eta_1\sigma^4}{24(1-\eta_1)\Gamma(\alpha-3)}\right| + \left|\frac{\eta_2(1-\eta_1)\sigma^4 + \eta_1\eta_2\sigma^4(\alpha-3)}{6(1-\eta_1)(1-\eta_2)\Gamma(\alpha-2)}\right|\right.$$
$$+ \left|\frac{\eta_3(1-\eta_2)\sigma^4 + \eta_2\eta_3\sigma^4(\alpha-2)}{2(1-\eta_2)(1-\eta_3)\Gamma(\alpha-1)}\right| + \left|\frac{\eta_1(1+\eta_2)\eta_3\sigma^4}{2(1-\eta_1)(1-\eta_2)(1-\eta_3)\Gamma(\alpha-3)}\right|$$
$$+ \left|\frac{(1-\eta_3)\eta_4\sigma^4 + \eta_3\eta_4\sigma^4(\alpha-1)}{(1-\eta_3)(1-\eta_4)\Gamma(\alpha)}\right| + \left|\frac{\eta_2(1+\eta_3)\eta_4\sigma^4}{2(1-\eta_2)(1-\eta_3)(1-\eta_4)\Gamma(\alpha-2)}\right|$$
$$\left. + \left|\frac{\eta_1((1+\eta_2)(1+\eta_3)+\eta_2+\eta_3)\eta_4\sigma^4}{6(1-\eta_1)(1-\eta_2)(1-\eta_3)(1-\eta_4)\Gamma(\alpha-3)}\right|\right\} \tag{6}$$

and

$$\mathcal{Q}_\kappa = \max\left\{\frac{\sigma^4}{\Gamma(\kappa+1)} + \left|\frac{\eta_5\sigma^4}{24(1-\eta_5)\Gamma(\kappa-3)}\right| + \left|\frac{\eta_6(1-\eta_5)\sigma^4 + \eta_5\eta_6\sigma^4(\kappa-3)}{6(1-\eta_5)(1-\eta_6)\Gamma(\kappa-2)}\right|\right.$$
$$+ \left|\frac{\eta_7(1-\eta_6)\sigma^4 + \eta_6\eta_7\sigma^4(\kappa-2)}{2(1-\eta_6)(1-\eta_7)\Gamma(\kappa-1)}\right| + \left|\frac{\eta_5(1+\eta_6)\eta_7\sigma^4}{2(1-\eta_5)(1-\eta_6)(1-\eta_7)\Gamma(\kappa-3)}\right|$$
$$+ \left|\frac{(1-\eta_7)\eta_8\sigma^4 + \eta_7\eta_8\sigma^4(\kappa-1)}{(1-\eta_7)(1-\eta_8)\Gamma(\kappa)}\right| + \left|\frac{\eta_6(1+\eta_7)\eta_8\sigma^4}{2(1-\eta_6)(1-\eta_7)(1-\eta_8)\Gamma(\kappa-2)}\right|$$
$$\left. + \left|\frac{\eta_5((1+\eta_6)(1+\eta_7)+\eta_6+\eta_7)\eta_8\sigma^4}{6(1-\eta_5)(1-\eta_6)(1-\eta_7)(1-\eta_8)\Gamma(\kappa-3)}\right|\right\} \tag{7}$$

If solution of system (1) is (v, u) and $t \in \mathfrak{J}$, then

$$v(t) = \frac{1}{\Gamma(\alpha)}\int_0^t (t-\tau)^{\alpha-1}\chi_1(\tau, u(\tau), \mathfrak{D}^\alpha v(\tau))d\tau$$
$$+ \frac{\eta_1 t^{\alpha-4}}{6(1-\eta_1)\Gamma(\alpha-3)}\int_0^\sigma (\sigma-\tau)^3 \chi_1(\tau, u(\tau), \mathfrak{D}^\alpha v(\tau))d\tau$$
$$+ \left[\frac{\eta_2 t^{\alpha-3}}{2(1-\eta_2)\Gamma(\alpha-2)} + \frac{\eta_1\eta_2\sigma t^{\alpha-4}}{2(1-\eta_1)(1-\eta_2)\Gamma(\alpha-3)}\right]\int_0^\sigma (\sigma-\tau)^2 \chi_1(\tau, u(\tau), \mathfrak{D}^\alpha v(\tau))d\tau$$
$$+ \left[\frac{\eta_3 t^{\alpha-2}}{(1-\eta_3)\Gamma(\alpha-1)} + \frac{\eta_2\eta_3\sigma t^{\alpha-3}}{(1-\eta_2)(1-\eta_3)\Gamma(\alpha-2)} + \frac{\eta_1(1+\eta_2)\eta_3\sigma^2 t^{\alpha-4}}{2(1-\eta_1)(1-\eta_2)(1-\eta_3)\Gamma(\alpha-3)}\right]$$
$$\times \int_0^\sigma (\sigma-\tau)\chi_1(\tau, u(\tau), \mathfrak{D}^\alpha v(\tau))d\tau + \left[\frac{\eta_4 t^{\alpha-1}}{(1-\eta_4)\Gamma(\alpha)} + \frac{\eta_3\eta_4\sigma t^{\alpha-2}}{(1-\eta_3)(1-\eta_4)\Gamma(\alpha-1)}\right.$$
$$\left. + \frac{\eta_2(1+\eta_3)\eta_4\sigma^2 t^{\alpha-3}}{2(1-\eta_2)(1-\eta_3)(1-\eta_4)\Gamma(\alpha-2)} + \frac{\eta_1((1+\eta_2)(1+\eta_3)+\eta_2+\eta_3)\eta_4\sigma^3 t^{\alpha-4}}{6(1-\eta_1)(1-\eta_2)(1-\eta_3)(1-\eta_4)\Gamma(\alpha-3)}\right]$$
$$\times \int_0^\sigma \chi_1(\tau, u(\tau), \mathfrak{D}^\alpha v(\tau))d\tau$$
$$= \int_0^\sigma G_\alpha(t, \tau)\chi_1(\tau, u(\tau), \mathfrak{D}^\alpha v(\tau))d\tau,$$

and

$$u(t) = \frac{1}{\Gamma(\kappa)} \int_0^t (t-\tau)^{\kappa-1} \chi_2(\tau, v(\tau), \mathfrak{D}^\kappa u(\tau)) d\tau$$

$$+ \frac{\eta_5 t^{\kappa-4}}{6(1-\eta_5)\Gamma(\kappa-3)} \int_0^\sigma (\sigma-\tau)^3 \chi_2(\tau, v(\tau), \mathfrak{D}^\kappa u(\tau)) d\tau$$

$$+ \left[\frac{\eta_6 t^{\kappa-3}}{2(1-\eta_6)\Gamma(\kappa-2)} + \frac{\eta_5 \eta_6 \sigma t^{\kappa-4}}{2(1-\eta_5)(1-\eta_6)\Gamma(\kappa-3)} \right] \int_0^\sigma (\sigma-\tau)^2 \chi_2(\tau, v(\tau), \mathfrak{D}^\kappa u(\tau)) d\tau$$

$$+ \left[\frac{\eta_7 t^{\kappa-2}}{(1-\eta_7)\Gamma(\kappa-1)} + \frac{\eta_6 \eta_7 \sigma t^{\kappa-3}}{(1-\eta_6)(1-\eta_7)\Gamma(\kappa-2)} + \frac{\eta_5(1+\eta_6)\eta_7 \sigma^2 t^{\kappa-4}}{2(1-\eta_5)(1-\eta_6)(1-\eta_7)\Gamma(\kappa-3)} \right]$$

$$\times \int_0^\sigma (\sigma-\tau) \chi_2(\tau, v(\tau), \mathfrak{D}^\kappa u(\tau)) d\tau + \left[\frac{\eta_8 t^{\kappa-1}}{(1-\eta_8)\Gamma(\kappa)} + \frac{\eta_7 \eta_8 \sigma t^{\kappa-2}}{(1-\eta_7)(1-\eta_8)\Gamma(\kappa-1)} \right.$$

$$+ \frac{\eta_6(1+\eta_7)\eta_8 \sigma^2 t^{\kappa-3}}{2(1-\eta_6)(1-\eta_7)(1-\eta_8)\Gamma(\kappa-2)} + \frac{\eta_5((1+\eta_6)(1+\eta_7)+\eta_6+\eta_7)\eta_8 \sigma^3 t^{\kappa-4}}{6(1-\eta_5)(1-\eta_6)(1-\eta_7)(1-\eta_8)\Gamma(\kappa-3)} \right]$$

$$\times \int_0^\sigma \chi_2(\tau, v(\tau), \mathfrak{D}^\kappa u(\tau)) d\tau$$

$$= \int_0^\sigma G_\kappa(t,\tau) \chi_2(\tau, v(\tau), \mathfrak{D}^\kappa u(\tau)) d\tau.$$

We use the following notations for convenience:

$$Y(t) = \chi_1(t, u(t), \mathfrak{D}^\alpha v(t)) = \chi_1(t, u(t), Y(t))$$
$$X(t) = \chi_2(t, v(t), \mathfrak{D}^\kappa u(t)) = \chi_2(t, v(t), X(t)).$$

Now, transform system (1) to the fixed point problem, let $F : S \to S$ is an operator defined by

$$F(v,u)(t) = \begin{pmatrix} \int_0^t G_\alpha(t,\tau) \chi_1(\tau, u(\tau), Y(\tau)) d\tau \\ \int_0^t G_\kappa(t,\tau) \chi_2(\tau, v(\tau), X(\tau)) d\tau \end{pmatrix} = \begin{pmatrix} F_\alpha(u,Y)(t) \\ F_\kappa(v,X)(t) \end{pmatrix} = \begin{pmatrix} F_\alpha(v)(t) \\ F_\kappa(u)(t) \end{pmatrix}. \quad (8)$$

Then, the fixed point of F and the solution of system (1) coincided, i.e.,

$$F_\alpha(v)(t) =$$
$$\frac{1}{\Gamma(\alpha)} \int_0^t (t-\tau)^{\alpha-1} Y(\tau) d\tau + \frac{\eta_1 t^{\alpha-4}}{6(1-\eta_1)\Gamma(\alpha-3)} \int_0^\sigma (\sigma-\tau)^3 Y(\tau) d\tau$$

$$+ \left[\frac{\eta_2 t^{\alpha-3}}{2(1-\eta_2)\Gamma(\alpha-2)} + \frac{\eta_1 \eta_2 \sigma t^{\alpha-4}}{2(1-\eta_1)(1-\eta_2)\Gamma(\alpha-3)} \right] \int_0^\sigma (\sigma-\tau)^2 Y(\tau) d\tau$$

$$+ \left[\frac{\eta_3 t^{\alpha-2}}{(1-\eta_3)\Gamma(\alpha-1)} + \frac{\eta_2 \eta_3 \sigma t^{\alpha-3}}{(1-\eta_2)(1-\eta_3)\Gamma(\alpha-2)} + \frac{\eta_1(1+\eta_2)\eta_3 \sigma^2 t^{\alpha-4}}{2(1-\eta_1)(1-\eta_2)(1-\eta_3)\Gamma(\alpha-3)} \right]$$

$$\times \int_0^\sigma (\sigma-\tau) Y(\tau) d\tau + \left[\frac{\eta_4 t^{\alpha-1}}{(1-\eta_4)\Gamma(\alpha)} + \frac{\eta_3 \eta_4 \sigma t^{\alpha-2}}{(1-\eta_3)(1-\eta_4)\Gamma(\alpha-1)} \right.$$

$$+ \frac{\eta_2(1+\eta_3)\eta_4 \sigma^2 t^{\alpha-3}}{2(1-\eta_2)(1-\eta_3)(1-\eta_4)\Gamma(\alpha-2)} + \frac{\eta_1((1+\eta_2)(1+\eta_3)+\eta_2+\eta_3)\eta_4 \sigma^3 t^{\alpha-4}}{6(1-\eta_1)(1-\eta_2)(1-\eta_3)(1-\eta_4)\Gamma(\alpha-3)} \right] \int_0^\sigma Y(\tau) d\tau$$

and

$$F_\kappa(u)(t) =$$

$$\frac{1}{\Gamma(\kappa)} \int_0^t (t-\tau)^{\kappa-1} \chi(\tau) d\tau + \frac{\eta_5 t^{\kappa-4}}{6(1-\eta_5)\Gamma(\kappa-3)} \int_0^\sigma (\sigma-\tau)^3 \chi(\tau) d\tau$$

$$+ \left[\frac{\eta_6 t^{\kappa-3}}{2(1-\eta_6)\Gamma(\kappa-2)} + \frac{\eta_5 \eta_6 \sigma t^{\kappa-4}}{2(1-\eta_5)(1-\eta_6)\Gamma(\kappa-3)} \right] \int_0^\sigma (\sigma-\tau)^2 \chi(\tau) d\tau$$

$$+ \left[\frac{\eta_7 t^{\kappa-2}}{(1-\eta_7)\Gamma(\kappa-1)} + \frac{\eta_6 \eta_7 \sigma t^{\kappa-3}}{(1-\eta_6)(1-\eta_7)\Gamma(\kappa-2)} + \frac{\eta_5(1+\eta_6)\eta_7 \sigma^2 t^{\kappa-4}}{2(1-\eta_5)(1-\eta_6)(1-\eta_7)\Gamma(\kappa-3)} \right]$$

$$\times \int_0^\sigma (\sigma-\tau) \chi(\tau) d\tau + \left[\frac{\eta_8 t^{\kappa-1}}{(1-\eta_8)\Gamma(\kappa)} + \frac{\eta_7 \eta_8 \sigma t^{\kappa-2}}{(1-\eta_7)(1-\eta_8)\Gamma(\kappa-1)} \right.$$

$$\left. + \frac{\eta_6(1+\eta_7)\eta_8 \sigma^2 t^{\kappa-3}}{2(1-\eta_6)(1-\eta_7)(1-\eta_8)\Gamma(\kappa-2)} + \frac{\eta_5((1+\eta_6)(1+\eta_7) + \eta_6 + \eta_7)\eta_8 \sigma^3 t^{\kappa-4}}{6(1-\eta_5)(1-\eta_6)(1-\eta_7)(1-\eta_8)\Gamma(\kappa-3)} \right] \int_0^\sigma \chi(\tau) d\tau.$$

Using Banach contraction theorem in the following, we prove the uniqueness of solution of system (1).

Theorem 1. *Let the functions $\chi_1, \chi_2 : \mathfrak{J} \times \mathcal{R} \times \mathcal{R} \to \mathcal{R}$ are continuous and satisfy the hypothesis:*
H_1: *For every $t \in \mathfrak{J}$ and $u, v, Y, X, \bar{u}, \bar{v}, \bar{Y}, \bar{X} : \mathfrak{J} \to \mathcal{R}$, there are $\mathcal{L}_{\chi_1}, \mathcal{L}_{\chi_2}, \overline{\mathcal{L}}_{\chi_1}, \overline{\mathcal{L}}_{\chi_2}$, such that*

$$|\chi_1(t, u(t), Y(t)) - \chi_1(t, \bar{u}(t), \bar{Y}(t))| \leq \mathcal{L}_{\chi_1}|u(t) - \bar{u}(t)| + \overline{\mathcal{L}}_{\chi_1}|Y(t) - \bar{Y}(t)|,$$

$$|\chi_2(t, v(t), X(t)) - \chi_2(t, \bar{v}(t), \bar{X}(t))| \leq \mathcal{L}_{\chi_2}|v(t) - \bar{v}(t)| + \overline{\mathcal{L}}_{\chi_2}|X(t) - \bar{X}(t)|.$$

In addition, suppose that

$$\frac{\mathfrak{Q}_\alpha \mathcal{L}_{\chi_1}(1 - \overline{\mathcal{L}}_{\chi_2}) + \mathfrak{Q}_\kappa \mathcal{L}_{\chi_2}(1 - \overline{\mathcal{L}}_{\chi_1})}{(1 - \overline{\mathcal{L}}_{\chi_2})(1 - \overline{\mathcal{L}}_{\chi_1})} < 1,$$

where $\mathfrak{Q}_\alpha$ and $\mathfrak{Q}_\kappa$ are defined by Equations (6) and (7), respectively. Furthermore, $0 \leq \overline{\mathcal{L}}_{\chi_1}, \overline{\mathcal{L}}_{\chi_2} < 1$ (through out the paper). Then, the solution of system (1) is unique.

Proof. Consider $\sup_{t \in \mathfrak{J}} \chi_1(t, 0, 0) = \Phi^* < \infty$ and $\sup_{t \in \mathfrak{J}} \chi_2(t, 0, 0) = \Psi^* < \infty$, such that

$$r \geq \frac{2 \mathfrak{Q}_\alpha \Phi^*(1 - \overline{\mathcal{L}}_{\chi_2}) + 2 \mathfrak{Q}_\kappa \Psi^*(1 - \overline{\mathcal{L}}_{\chi_1})}{2(1 - \overline{\mathcal{L}}_{\chi_1})(1 - \overline{\mathcal{L}}_{\chi_2}) - \mathfrak{Q}_\alpha \mathcal{L}_{\chi_1} - \mathfrak{Q}_\kappa \mathcal{L}_{\chi_2}}.$$

We show that $F(\mathcal{B}_r) \subset \mathcal{B}_r$, where

$$\mathcal{B}_r = \left\{ (v, u) \in S : \|(v, u)\|_S \leq r, \ \|v\| \leq \frac{r}{2}, \ \|u\| \leq \frac{r}{2} \right\}.$$

For $(v, u) \in \mathcal{B}_r$, we have

$$t^{4-\alpha}|F_\alpha(v)(t)|$$
$$\leq \frac{t^{4-\alpha}}{\Gamma(\alpha)} \int_0^t (t-\tau)^{\alpha-1}(|\chi_1(\tau,u(\tau),Y(\tau)) - \chi_1(\tau,0,0)| + |\chi_1(\tau,0,0)|)d\tau + \left|\frac{\eta_1}{6(1-\eta_1)\Gamma(\alpha-3)}\right|$$
$$\times \int_0^\sigma (\sigma-\tau)^3(|\chi_1(\tau,u(\tau),Y(\tau)) - \chi_1(\tau,0,0)| + |\chi_1(\tau,0,0)|)d\tau + \left|\frac{\eta_2 t}{2(1-\eta_2)\Gamma(\alpha-2)}\right|$$
$$+ \frac{\eta_1\eta_2\sigma}{2(1-\eta_1)(1-\eta_2)\Gamma(\alpha-3)} \left|\int_0^T (\sigma-\tau)^2(|\chi_1(\tau,u(\tau),V(\tau)) - \chi_1(\tau,0,0)| + |\chi_1(\tau,0,0)|)d\tau \right.$$
$$+ \left|\frac{\eta_3 t^2}{(1-\eta_3)\Gamma(\alpha-1)} + \frac{\eta_2\eta_3 t\sigma}{(1-\eta_2)(1-\eta_3)\Gamma(\alpha-2)} + \frac{\eta_1(1+\eta_2)\eta_3\sigma^2}{2(1-\eta_1)(1-\eta_2)(1-\eta_3)\Gamma(\alpha-3)}\right|$$
$$\times \int_0^\sigma (\sigma-\tau)(|\chi_1(\tau,u(\tau),V(\tau)) - \chi_1(\tau,0,0)| + |\chi_1(\tau,0,0)|)d\tau + \left|\frac{\eta_3\eta_4\sigma t^2}{(1-\eta_3)(1-\eta_4)\Gamma(\alpha-1)}\right|$$
$$+ \frac{\eta_4 t^3}{(1-\eta_4)\Gamma(\alpha)} + \frac{\eta_1((1+\eta_2)(1+\eta_3) + \eta_2 + \eta_3)\eta_4\sigma^3}{6(1-\eta_1)(1-\eta_2)(1-\eta_3)(1-\eta_4)\Gamma(\alpha-3)}$$
$$+ \frac{\eta_2(1+\eta_3)\eta_4\sigma^2 t}{2(1-\eta_2)(1-\eta_3)(1-\eta_4)\Gamma(\alpha-2)} \left|\int_0^\sigma (|\chi_1(\tau,u(\tau),V(\tau)) - \chi_1(\tau,0,0)| + |\chi_1(\tau,0,0)|)d\tau\right.. \tag{9}$$

Consider
$$|v(t)| \leq |\chi_1(t,u(t),V(t)) - \chi_1(t,0,0)| + |\chi_1(t,0,0)|$$
$$\leq |\chi_1(t,0,0)| + \mathcal{L}_{\chi_1}|u(t)| + \overline{\mathcal{L}}_{\chi_1}|v(t)|$$
$$\leq \frac{|\chi_1(t,0,0)| + \mathcal{L}_{\chi_1}|u(t)|}{1-\overline{\mathcal{L}}_{\chi_1}}. \tag{10}$$

Substituting (10) in (9), we get

$$\|F_\alpha(v)\|$$
$$\leq \left[\frac{\sigma^4}{\Gamma(\alpha+1)} + \left|\frac{\eta_1\sigma^4}{24(1-\eta_1)\Gamma(\alpha-3)}\right| + \left|\frac{\eta_2(1-\eta_1)\sigma^4 + \eta_1\eta_2\sigma^4(\alpha-3)}{6(1-\eta_1)(1-\eta_2)\Gamma(\alpha-2)}\right|\right.$$
$$+ \left|\frac{\eta_3(1-\eta_2)\sigma^4 + \eta_2\eta_3\sigma^4(\alpha-2)}{2(1-\eta_2)(1-\eta_3)\Gamma(\alpha-1)}\right| + \left|\frac{\eta_1(1+\eta_2)\eta_3\sigma^4}{2(1-\eta_1)(1-\eta_2)(1-\eta_3)\Gamma(\alpha-3)}\right|$$
$$+ \left|\frac{(1-\eta_3)\eta_4\sigma^4 + \eta_3\eta_4\sigma^4(\alpha-1)}{(1-\eta_3)(1-\eta_4)\Gamma(\alpha)}\right| + \left|\frac{\eta_2(1+\eta_3)\eta_4\sigma^4}{2(1-\eta_2)(1-\eta_3)(1-\eta_4)\Gamma(\alpha-2)}\right|$$
$$+ \left|\frac{\eta_1((1+\eta_2)(1+\eta_3) + \eta_2 + \eta_3)\eta_4\sigma^4}{6(1-\eta_1)(1-\eta_2)(1-\eta_3)(1-\eta_4)\Gamma(\alpha-3)}\right|\right] \frac{2\Phi^* + \mathcal{L}_{\chi_1}r}{2(1-\overline{\mathcal{L}}_{\chi_1})}.$$

Therefore,
$$\|F_\alpha(v)\| \leq \mathcal{Q}_\alpha \frac{2\Phi^* + \mathcal{L}_{\chi_1}r}{2(1-\overline{\mathcal{L}}_{\chi_1})}. \tag{11}$$

On the same way, we can write
$$\|F_\kappa(u)\| \leq \mathcal{Q}_\kappa \frac{2\Psi^* + \mathcal{L}_{\chi_2}r}{2(1-\overline{\mathcal{L}}_{\chi_2})}. \tag{12}$$

Inequalities (11) and (12) combined give
$$\|F(v,u)\|_S \leq r.$$

For any $t \in \mathfrak{J}$, and $(v_1, u_1), (v_2, u_2) \in S$, we get

$t^{4-\alpha}|F_\alpha(v_1)(t) - F_\alpha(v_2)(t)|$

$\leq \dfrac{t^{4-\alpha}}{\Gamma(\alpha)} \int_0^t (t-\tau)^{\alpha-1}|\chi_1(\tau, u_1(\tau), Y_1(\tau)) - \chi_1(\tau, u_2(\tau), Y_2(\tau))|d\tau + \left|\dfrac{\eta_1}{6(1-\eta_1)\Gamma(\alpha-3)}\right|$

$\times \int_0^\sigma (\sigma-\tau)^3|\chi_1(\tau, u_1(\tau), Y_1(\tau)) - \chi_1(\tau, u_2(\tau), Y_2(\tau))|d\tau + \left|\dfrac{\eta_2 t}{2(1-\eta_2)\Gamma(\alpha-2)}\right|$

$+ \dfrac{\eta_1 \eta_2 \sigma}{2(1-\eta_1)(1-\eta_2)\Gamma(\alpha-3)}\left|\int_0^\sigma (\sigma-\tau)^2|\chi_1(\tau, u_1(\tau), Y_1(\tau)) - \chi_1(\tau, u_2(\tau), Y_2(\tau))|d\tau\right.$

$+ \left|\dfrac{\eta_3 t^2}{(1-\eta_3)\Gamma(\alpha-1)} + \dfrac{\eta_2 \eta_3 t\sigma}{(1-\eta_2)(1-\eta_3)\Gamma(\alpha-2)} + \dfrac{\eta_1(1+\eta_2)\eta_3\sigma^2}{2(1-\eta_1)(1-\eta_2)(1-c_0)\Gamma(\alpha-3)}\right|$

$\times \int_0^\sigma (\sigma-\tau)|\chi_1(\tau, u_1(\tau), Y_1(\tau)) - \chi_1(\tau, u_2(\tau), Y_2(\tau))|d\tau + \left|\dfrac{\eta_3\eta_4\sigma t^2}{(1-\eta_3)(1-\eta_4)\Gamma(\alpha-1)}\right.$

$+ \dfrac{\eta_4 t^3}{(1-\eta_4)\Gamma(\alpha)} + \dfrac{\eta_1((1+\eta_2)(1+\eta_3)+\eta_2+\eta_3)\eta_4\sigma^3}{6(1-\eta_1)(1-\eta_2)(1-\eta_3)(1-\eta_4)\Gamma(\alpha-3)}$

$+ \dfrac{\eta_2(1+\eta_3)\eta_4\sigma^2 t}{2(1-\eta_2)(1-\eta_3)(1-\eta_4)\Gamma(\alpha-2)}\left|\int_0^\sigma |\chi_1(\tau, u_1(\tau), Y_1(\tau)) - \chi_1(\tau, u_2(\tau), Y_2(\tau))|d\tau\right.$

$\leq \left[\dfrac{\sigma^4}{\Gamma(\alpha+1)} + \left|\dfrac{\eta_1\sigma^4}{24(1-\eta_1)\Gamma(\alpha-3)}\right| + \left|\dfrac{\eta_2(1-\eta_1)\sigma^4 + \eta_1\eta_2\sigma^4(\alpha-3)}{6(1-\eta_1)(1-\eta_2)\Gamma(\alpha-2)}\right|\right.$

$+ \left|\dfrac{\eta_3(1-\eta_2)\sigma^4 + \eta_2\eta_3\sigma^4(\alpha-2)}{2(1-\eta_2)(1-\eta_3)\Gamma(\alpha-1)}\right| + \left|\dfrac{\eta_1(1+\eta_2)\eta_3\sigma^4}{2(1-\eta_1)(1-\eta_2)(1-\eta_3)\Gamma(\alpha-3)}\right|$

$+ \left|\dfrac{(1-\eta_3)\eta_4\sigma^4 + \eta_3\eta_4\sigma^4(\alpha-1)}{(1-\eta_3)(1-\eta_4)\Gamma(\alpha)}\right| + \left|\dfrac{\eta_2(1+\eta_3)\eta_4\sigma^4}{2(1-\eta_2)(1-\eta_3)(1-\eta_4)\Gamma(\alpha-2)}\right|$

$+ \left|\dfrac{\eta_1((1+\eta_2)(1+\eta_3)+\eta_2+\eta_3)\eta_4\sigma^4}{6(1-\eta_1)(1-\eta_2)(1-\eta_3)(1-\eta_4)\Gamma(\alpha-3)}\right|\right] \dfrac{\mathcal{L}_{\chi_1}}{1-\overline{\mathcal{L}}_{\chi_1}}\|u_1 - u_2\|$

and thus we get

$$\|F_\alpha(v_1) - F_\alpha(v_2)\| \leq \dfrac{\mathcal{Q}_\alpha \mathcal{L}_{\chi_1}}{1-\overline{\mathcal{L}}_{\chi_1}}\|u_1 - u_2\|. \tag{13}$$

Similarly,

$$\|F_\kappa(u_1) - F_\kappa(u_2)\| \leq \dfrac{\mathcal{Q}_\kappa \mathcal{L}_{\chi_2}}{1-\overline{\mathcal{L}}_{\chi_2}}\|v_1 - v_2\|. \tag{14}$$

From the inequalities (13) and (14), we get that

$$\|F(v_1, u_1) - F(v_2, u_2)\|_S \leq \dfrac{\mathcal{Q}_\alpha \mathcal{L}_{\chi_1}(1-\overline{\mathcal{L}}_{\chi_2}) + \mathcal{Q}_\kappa \mathcal{L}_{\chi_2}(1-\overline{\mathcal{L}}_{\chi_1})}{(1-\overline{\mathcal{L}}_{\chi_2})(1-\overline{\mathcal{L}}_{\chi_1})}\|(v_1, u_1) - (v_2, u_2)\|_S.$$

Therefore, F is a contraction operator. Therefore, by Banach's fixed point theorem, F has a unique fixed point, so the solution of the problem (1) is unique. □

The next result is based on the following Leray–Schauder alternative theorem.

Theorem 2. *[46] Let $F: S \to S$ be an operator which is completely continuous (i.e., a map that restricted to any bounded set in S is compact). Suppose*

$$\mathcal{B}(F) = \{v \in S : v = \lambda F(v), \lambda \in [0,1]\}.$$

Then, either the operator F has at least one fixed point or the set $\mathcal{B}(F)$ is unbounded.

Theorem 3. Suppose the functions $\chi_1, \chi_2 : \mathfrak{J} \times \mathcal{R} \times \mathcal{R} \to \mathcal{R}$ are continuous and satisfy the following hypothesis:

H$_2$: For every $t \in \mathfrak{J}$ and $u, v : \mathfrak{J} \to \mathcal{R}$, there are $\phi_i (i = 1, 2, 3) : \mathfrak{J} \to \mathcal{R}^+$, such that

$$|\chi_1(t, u(t), Y(t))| \leq \phi_1(t) + \phi_2(t)|u(t)| + \phi_3(t)|Y(t)|.$$

Similarly, for every $t \in \mathfrak{J}$ and $v, X : \mathfrak{J} \to \mathcal{R}$, there are $\varphi_i (i = 1, 2, 3) : \mathfrak{J} \to \mathcal{R}^+$, such that

$$|\chi_2(t, v(t), X(t))| \leq \varphi_1(t) + \varphi_2(t)|u(t)| + \varphi_3(t)|X(t)|,$$

with $\sup_{t \in \mathfrak{J}} \phi_i(t) = \phi_i^*$, $\sup_{t \in \mathfrak{J}} \varphi_i(t) = \varphi_i^* (i = 1, 2, 3)$.

In addition, it is assumed that

$$\mathcal{Q}_0 = \max\left\{\frac{\mathcal{Q}_\kappa \varphi_2^*}{1 - \varphi_3^*}, \frac{\mathcal{Q}_\alpha \phi_2^*}{1 - \phi_3^*}\right\} < 1 \text{ and } 0 \leq \phi_3^*, \varphi_3^* < 1. \tag{15}$$

Then, the system (1) has at least one solution.

Proof. First, we prove that F is completely continuous. In view of continuity of χ_1, χ_2, the operator F is also continuous. For any $(v, u) \in \mathcal{B}_r$, we have

$$\begin{aligned}
& t^{4-\alpha}|F_\alpha(v)(t)| \\
& \leq \frac{t^{4-\alpha}}{\Gamma(\alpha)} \int_0^t (t-\tau)^{\alpha-1}|Y(\tau)|d\tau + \left|\frac{\eta_1}{6(1-\eta_1)\Gamma(\alpha-3)}\right|\int_0^\sigma (\sigma-\tau)^3 |Y(\tau)|d\tau + \left|\frac{\eta_2 t}{2(1-\eta_2)\Gamma(\alpha-2)}\right| \\
& + \frac{\eta_1 \eta_2 \sigma}{2(1-\eta_1)(1-\eta_2)\Gamma(\alpha-3)}\left|\int_0^\sigma (\sigma-\tau)^2 |Y(\tau)|d\tau + \left|\frac{\eta_3 t^2}{(1-\eta_3)\Gamma(\alpha-1)}\right|\right. \\
& + \frac{\eta_2 \eta_3 t \sigma}{(1-\eta_2)(1-\eta_3)\Gamma(\alpha-2)} + \frac{\eta_1(1+\eta_2)\eta_3 \sigma^2}{2(1-\eta_1)(1-\eta_2)(1-\eta_3)\Gamma(\alpha-3)}\left|\int_0^\sigma (\sigma-\tau)|Y(\tau)|d\tau\right. \\
& + \left|\frac{\eta_4 t^3}{(1-\eta_4)\Gamma(\alpha)} + \frac{\eta_3 \eta_4 \sigma t^2}{(1-\eta_3)(1-\eta_4)\Gamma(\alpha-1)} + \frac{\eta_2(1+\eta_3)\eta_4 \sigma^2 t}{2(1-\eta_2)(1-\eta_3)(1-\eta_4)\Gamma(\alpha-2)}\right. \\
& + \frac{\eta_1((1+\eta_2)(1+\eta_3) + \eta_2 + \eta_3)\eta_4 \sigma^3}{6(1-\eta_1)(1-\eta_2)(1-\eta_3)(1-\eta_4)\Gamma(\alpha-3)}\left|\int_0^\sigma |Y(\tau)|d\tau.\right.
\end{aligned} \tag{16}$$

Now by **H$_2$**, we have

$$\begin{aligned}
|Y(t)| & = |\chi_1(t, u(t), Y(t))| \\
& \leq \phi_1(t) + \phi_2(t)|u(t)| + \phi_3(t)|Y(t)| \\
& \leq \frac{\phi_1(t) + \phi_2(t)|u(t)|}{1 - \phi_3(t)}.
\end{aligned}$$

Therefore, (16) implies

$$\begin{aligned}
\|F_\alpha(v)\| & \leq \left[\frac{\sigma^4}{\Gamma(\alpha+1)} + \left|\frac{\eta_1 \sigma^4}{24(1-\eta_1)\Gamma(\alpha-3)}\right| + \left|\frac{\eta_2(1-\eta_1)\sigma^4 + \eta_1 \eta_2 \sigma^4(\alpha-3)}{6(1-\eta_1)(1-\eta_2)\Gamma(\alpha-2)}\right|\right. \\
& + \left|\frac{\eta_3(1-\eta_2)\sigma^4 + \eta_2 \eta_3 \sigma^4(\alpha-2)}{2(1-\eta_2)(1-\eta_3)\Gamma(\alpha-1)}\right| + \left|\frac{\eta_1(1+\eta_2)\eta_3 \sigma^4}{2(1-\eta_1)(1-\eta_2)(1-\eta_3)\Gamma(\alpha-3)}\right| \\
& + \left|\frac{(1-\eta_3)\eta_4 \sigma^4 + \eta_3 \eta_4 \sigma^4(\alpha-1)}{(1-\eta_3)(1-\eta_4)\Gamma(\alpha)}\right| + \left|\frac{\eta_2(1+\eta_3)\eta_4 \sigma^4}{2(1-\eta_2)(1-\eta_3)(1-\eta_4)\Gamma(\alpha-2)}\right| \\
& + \left.\left|\frac{\eta_1((1+\eta_2)(1+\eta_3) + \eta_2 + \eta_3)\eta_4 \sigma^4}{6(1-\eta_1)(1-\eta_2)(1-\eta_3)(1-\eta_4)\Gamma(\alpha-3)}\right|\right]\frac{2\phi_1^* + \phi_2^* r}{2(1-\phi_3^*)},
\end{aligned} \tag{17}$$

which implies that

$$\|F_\alpha(v)\| \leq \mathcal{Q}_\alpha \frac{2\phi_1^* + \phi_2^* r}{2(1-\phi_3^*)}. \tag{18}$$

Similarly, we get

$$\|F_\kappa(u)\| \leq \mathcal{Q}_\kappa \frac{2\varphi_1^* + \varphi_2^* r}{2(1-\varphi_3^*)}. \tag{19}$$

Thus, it follows from the inequalities (18) and (19) that F is uniformly bounded. Now, we prove that F is equicontinuous. Let $0 \leq t_2 \leq t_1 \leq t$. Then, we have

$$\left| t_1^{4-\alpha} F_\alpha(v)(t_1) - t_2^{4-\alpha} F_\alpha(v)(t_2) \right| =$$
$$= \Bigg| \frac{1}{\Gamma(\alpha)} \int_0^{t_1} \left[t_1^{4-\alpha}(t_1-\tau)^{\alpha-1} - t_2^{4-\alpha}(t_2-\tau)^{\alpha-1} \right] v(\tau) d\tau - \frac{1}{\Gamma(\alpha)} \int_{t_1}^{t_2} t_2^{4-\alpha}(t_2-\tau)^{\alpha-1} Y(\tau) d\tau$$
$$+ \left[\frac{\eta_4(t_1^3 - t_2^3)}{(1-\eta_4)\Gamma(\alpha)} + \frac{\eta_3 \eta_4 \sigma(t_1^2 - t_2^2)}{(1-\eta_3)(1-\eta_4)\Gamma(\alpha-1)} + \frac{\eta_2(1+\eta_3)\eta_4 \sigma^2(t_1-t_2)}{2(1-\eta_2)(1-\eta_3)(1-\eta_4)\Gamma(\alpha-2)} \right] \int_0^\sigma Y(\tau) d\tau$$
$$+ \left[\frac{\eta_3(t_1^2 - t_2^2)}{(1-\eta_3)\Gamma(\alpha-1)} + \frac{\eta_2 \eta_3 \sigma(t_1 - t_2)}{(1-\eta_2)(1-\eta_3)\Gamma(\alpha-2)} \right] \int_0^\sigma (\sigma-\tau) Y(\tau) d\tau$$
$$+ \frac{\eta_2(t_1 - t_2)}{2(1-\eta_2)\Gamma(\alpha-2)} \int_0^\sigma (\sigma-\tau)^2 Y(\tau) d\tau \Bigg|.$$

Therefore, we get

$$\left| t_1^{4-\alpha} F_\alpha(v)(t_1) - t_2^{4-\alpha} F_\alpha(v)(t_2) \right|$$
$$\leq \Bigg[\Bigg| \frac{1}{\Gamma(\alpha)} \int_0^{t_1} \left[t_1^{4-\alpha}(t_1-\tau)^{\alpha-1} - t_2^{4-\alpha}(t_2-\tau)^{\alpha-1} \right] d\tau - \frac{1}{\Gamma(\alpha)} \int_{t_1}^{t_2} t_2^{4-\alpha}(t_2-\tau)^{\alpha-1} d\tau \Bigg|$$
$$+ \Bigg| \frac{\eta_4(t_1^3 - t_2^3)}{(1-\eta_4)\Gamma(\alpha)} + \frac{\eta_3 \eta_4 \sigma^2(t_1^2 - t_2^2)}{(1-\eta_3)(1-\eta_4)\Gamma(\alpha-1)} + \frac{\eta_2(1+\eta_3)\eta_4 \sigma^3(t_1-t_2)}{2(1-\eta_2)(1-\eta_3)(1-\eta_4)\Gamma(\alpha-2)} \Bigg|$$
$$+ \Bigg| \frac{\eta_3 \sigma^2(t_1^2 - t_2^2)}{2(1-\eta_3)\Gamma(\alpha-1)} + \frac{\eta_2 \eta_3 \sigma^3(t_1-t_2)}{2(1-\eta_2)(1-\eta_3)\Gamma(\alpha-2)} \Bigg|$$
$$+ \frac{\eta_2 \sigma^3(t_1-t_2)}{6(1-\eta_2)\Gamma(\alpha-2)} \Bigg] \Bigg| \frac{\phi_1^* + \phi_2^* |u|}{1-\phi_3^*} \longrightarrow 0 \text{ as } t_1 \longrightarrow t_2.$$

Similarly

$$\left| t_1^{4-\kappa} F_\kappa(u)(t_1) - t_2^{4-\kappa} F_\kappa(u)(t_2) \right|$$
$$\leq \Bigg[\Bigg| \frac{1}{\Gamma(\kappa)} \int_0^{t_1} \left[t_1^{4-\kappa}(t_1-\tau)^{\kappa-1} - t_2^{4-\kappa}(t_2-\tau)^{\kappa-1} \right] d\tau - \frac{1}{\Gamma(\kappa)} \int_{t_1}^{t_2} t_2^{4-\kappa}(t_2-\tau)^{\kappa-1} d\tau \Bigg|$$
$$+ \Bigg| \frac{\eta_4 \sigma(t_1^3 - t_2^3)}{(1-\eta_4)\Gamma(\kappa)} + \frac{\eta_3 \eta_4 \sigma^2(t_1^2 - t_2^2)}{(1-\eta_3)(1-\eta_4)\Gamma(\kappa-1)} + \frac{\eta_2(1+\eta_3)\eta_4 \sigma^3(t_1-t_2)}{2(1-\eta_2)(1-\eta_3)(1-\eta_4)\Gamma(\kappa-2)} \Bigg|$$
$$+ \Bigg| \frac{\eta_3 \sigma^2(t_1^2 - t_2^2)}{2(1-\eta_3)\Gamma(\kappa-1)} + \frac{\eta_2 \eta_3 \sigma^3(t_1-t_2)}{2(1-\eta_2)(1-\eta_3)\Gamma(\kappa-2)} \Bigg|$$
$$+ \frac{\eta_2 \sigma^3(t_1-t_2)}{6(1-\eta_2)\Gamma(\kappa-2)} \Bigg] \Bigg| \frac{\varphi_1^* + \varphi_2^* |v|}{1-\varphi_3^*} \longrightarrow 0 \text{ as } t_1 \longrightarrow t_2.$$

Therefore, F(v, u) is equicontinuous. Thus, we proved that the operator F(v, u) is continuous, uniformly bounded, and equicontinuous, concluding that F(v, u) is completely continuous. Now, by using Arzela–Ascoli theorem, the operator F(v, u) is compact.

Finally, we are going to check that $\mathcal{B} = \{(v,u) \in S | (v,u) = \lambda F(v,u),\ \lambda \in [0,1]\}$ is bounded. Suppose $(v,u) \in \mathcal{B}$, then $(v,u) = \lambda F(v,u)$. For $t \in \mathfrak{J}$, we have

$$v(t) = \lambda F_\alpha(v)(t), \quad u(t) = \lambda F_\kappa(u)(t).$$

Then,

$$\begin{aligned}
&t^{4-\alpha}|v(t)| \\
&\leq \Big[\frac{\sigma^4}{\Gamma(\alpha+1)} + \Big|\frac{\eta_1 \sigma^4}{24(1-\eta_1)\Gamma(\alpha-3)}\Big| + \Big|\frac{\eta_2(1-\eta_1)\sigma^4 + \eta_1\eta_2\sigma^4(\alpha-3)}{6(1-\eta_1)(1-\eta_2)\Gamma(\alpha-2)}\Big| \\
&\quad + \Big|\frac{\eta_3(1-\eta_2)\sigma^4 + \eta_2\eta_3\sigma^4(\alpha-2)}{2(1-\eta_2)(1-\eta_3)\Gamma(\alpha-1)}\Big| + \Big|\frac{\eta_1(1+\eta_2)\eta_3\sigma^4}{2(1-\eta_1)(1-\eta_2)(1-\eta_3)\Gamma(\alpha-3)}\Big| \\
&\quad + \Big|\frac{(1-\eta_3)\eta_4\sigma^4 + \eta_3\eta_4\sigma^4(\alpha-1)}{(1-\eta_3)(1-\eta_4)\Gamma(\alpha)}\Big| + \Big|\frac{\eta_2(1+\eta_3)\eta_4\sigma^4}{2(1-\eta_2)(1-\eta_3)(1-\eta_4)\Gamma(\alpha-2)}\Big| \\
&\quad + \Big|\frac{\eta_1((1+\eta_2)(1+\eta_3) + \eta_2 + \eta_3)\eta_4\sigma^4}{6(1-\eta_1)(1-\eta_2)(1-\eta_3)(1-\eta_4)\Gamma(\alpha-3)}\Big|\Big] \frac{\phi_1(t) + \phi_2(t)|u(t)|}{1-\phi_3(t)}
\end{aligned} \quad (20)$$

and

$$\begin{aligned}
&t^{4-\kappa}|u(t)| \\
&\leq \Big[\frac{\sigma^4}{\Gamma(\kappa+1)} + \Big|\frac{\eta_5 \sigma^4}{24(1-\eta_5)\Gamma(\kappa-3)}\Big| + \Big|\frac{\eta_6(1-\eta_5)\sigma^4 + \eta_5\eta_6\sigma^4(\kappa-3)}{6(1-\eta_5)(1-\eta_6)\Gamma(\kappa-2)}\Big| \\
&\quad + \Big|\frac{\eta_7(1-\eta_6)\sigma^4 + \eta_6\eta_7\sigma^4(\kappa-2)}{2(1-\eta_6)(1-\eta_7)\Gamma(\kappa-1)}\Big| + \Big|\frac{\eta_5(1+\eta_6)\eta_7\sigma^4}{2(1-\eta_5)(1-\eta_6)(1-\eta_7)\Gamma(\kappa-3)}\Big| \\
&\quad + \Big|\frac{(1-\eta_7)\eta_8\sigma^4 + \eta_7\eta_8\sigma^4(\kappa-1)}{(1-\eta_7)(1-\eta_8)\Gamma(\kappa)}\Big| + \Big|\frac{\eta_6(1+\eta_7)\eta_8\sigma^4}{2(1-\eta_6)(1-\eta_7)(1-\eta_8)\Gamma(\kappa-2)}\Big| \\
&\quad + \Big|\frac{\eta_5((1+\eta_6)(1+\eta_7) + \eta_6 + \eta_7)\eta_8\sigma^4}{6(1-\eta_5)(1-\eta_6)(1-\eta_7)(1-\eta_8)\Gamma(\kappa-3)}\Big|\Big] \frac{\varphi_1(t) + \varphi_2(t)|v(t)|}{1-\varphi_3(t)}.
\end{aligned} \quad (21)$$

Therefore, from (20) and (21), we have

$$\|v\| \leq \mathcal{Q}_\alpha \frac{\phi_1^* + \phi_2^* \|u\|}{1 - \phi_3^*}$$

and

$$\|u\| \leq \mathcal{Q}_\kappa \frac{\varphi_1^* + \varphi_2^* \|v\|}{1 - \varphi_3^*},$$

which imply that

$$\|v\| + \|u\| = \frac{\mathcal{Q}_\alpha \phi_1^*}{1 - \phi_3^*} + \frac{\mathcal{Q}_\kappa \varphi_1^*}{1 - \varphi_3^*} + \frac{\mathcal{Q}_\kappa \varphi_2^* \|v\|}{1 - \varphi_3^*} + \frac{\mathcal{Q}_\alpha \phi_2^* \|u\|}{1 - \phi_3^*}.$$

Consequently, we get

$$\|(v,u)\|_S \leq \frac{\mathcal{Q}_\alpha \phi_1^* + \mathcal{Q}_\kappa \varphi_1^*}{(1-\phi_3^*)(1-\varphi_3^*)(1-\mathcal{Q}_0)},$$

for any $t \in \mathfrak{J}$, where $\mathcal{Q}_0$ is defined by (15), which infer that $\mathcal{B}$ is bounded. Therefore, by Theorem 2, F has at least one fixed point. Thus, the system (1) has at least one solution. □

4. Stability Results

Let us recall some definitions related to HU stabilities:

Suppose the functions $\Theta_\alpha, \Theta_\kappa : \mathfrak{J} \to \mathcal{R}^+$ are nondecreasing and $\epsilon_\alpha, \epsilon_\kappa > 0$. Consider the inequalities given below.

$$\begin{cases} |\mathfrak{D}^\alpha v(t) - \chi_1(t, u(t), \mathfrak{D}^\alpha v(t))| \leq \epsilon_\alpha, \ t \in \mathfrak{J}, \\ |\mathfrak{D}^\kappa u(t) - \chi_2(t, v(t), \mathfrak{D}^\kappa u(t))| \leq \epsilon_\kappa, \ t \in \mathfrak{J}, \end{cases} \quad (22)$$

$$\begin{cases} |\mathfrak{D}^\alpha v(t) - \chi_1(t, u(t), \mathfrak{D}^\alpha v(t))| \leq \Theta_\alpha(t)\epsilon_\alpha, \ t \in \mathfrak{J}, \\ |\mathfrak{D}^\kappa u(t) - \chi_2(t, v(t), \mathfrak{D}^\kappa u(t))| \leq \Theta_\kappa(t)\epsilon_\kappa, \ t \in \mathfrak{J}, \end{cases} \quad (23)$$

$$\begin{cases} |\mathfrak{D}^\alpha v(t) - \chi_1(t, u(t), \mathfrak{D}^\alpha v(t))| \leq \Theta_\alpha(t), \ t \in \mathfrak{J}, \\ |\mathfrak{D}^\kappa u(t) - \chi_2(t, v(t), \mathfrak{D}^\kappa u(t))| \leq \Theta_\kappa(t), \ t \in \mathfrak{J}. \end{cases} \quad (24)$$

Definition 3. *[47] System (1) is HU stable, if there are $\mathbf{C}_{\alpha,\kappa} = \max(\mathbf{C}_\alpha, \mathbf{C}_\kappa) > 0$ such that for some $\epsilon = \max(\epsilon_\alpha, \epsilon_\kappa) > 0$ and for each solution $(v, u) \in S$ of the inequality (22). There is a solution $(w, \zeta) \in S$ with*

$$\|(v, u)(t) - (w, \zeta)(t)\| \leq \mathbf{C}_{\alpha,\kappa}\epsilon, \ t \in \mathfrak{J}. \quad (25)$$

Definition 4. *[47] System (1) is generalized HU stable, if there is $\Phi_{\alpha,\kappa} \in \mathbb{C}(\mathcal{R}^+, \mathcal{R}^+)$ with $\Phi_{\alpha,\kappa}(0) = 0$, such that for each solution $(v, u) \in S$ of (22), there is a solution $(w, \zeta) \in S$ of problem (1), which satisfies*

$$\|(v, u)(t) - (w, \zeta)(t)\| \leq \Phi_{\alpha,\kappa}(\epsilon), \ t \in \mathfrak{J}. \quad (26)$$

Definition 5. *[47] System (1) is HU–Rassias stable with respect to $\Theta_{\alpha,\kappa} = \max(\Theta_\alpha, \Theta_\kappa) \in \mathbb{C}(\mathfrak{J}, \mathcal{R})$, if there are constants $\mathbf{C}_{\Theta_\alpha, \Theta_\kappa} = \max(\mathbf{C}_{\Theta_\alpha}, \mathbf{C}_{\Theta_\kappa}) > 0$ such that for some $\epsilon = (\epsilon_\alpha, \epsilon_\kappa) > 0$ and for each solution $(v, u) \in S$ of the inequality (23). There is a solution $(w, \zeta) \in S$ with*

$$\|(v, u)(t) - (w, \zeta)(t)\| \leq \mathbf{C}_{\Theta_\alpha, \Theta_\kappa}\Theta_{\alpha,\kappa}(t)\epsilon, \ t \in \mathfrak{J}. \quad (27)$$

Definition 6. *[47] System (1) is generalized HU–Rassias stable with respect to $\Theta_{\alpha,\kappa} = \max(\Theta_\alpha, \Theta_\kappa) \in \mathbb{C}(\mathfrak{J}, \mathcal{R})$, if there is constant $\mathbf{C}_{\Theta_\alpha, \Theta_\kappa} = \max(\mathbf{C}_{\Theta_\alpha}, \mathbf{C}_{\Theta_\kappa}) > 0$, such that for each solution $(v, u) \in S$ of the inequality (24). There is a solution $(w, \zeta) \in S$ of (1), which satisfies*

$$\|(v, u)(t) - (w, \zeta)(t)\| \leq \mathbf{C}_{\Theta_\alpha, \Theta_\kappa}\Theta_{\alpha,\kappa}(t), \ t \in \mathfrak{J}. \quad (28)$$

Remark 4. *We say that $(v, u) \in S$ is a solution of the inequality (22), if there are $\Psi_{\chi_1}, \Psi_{\chi_2} \in \mathbb{C}(\mathfrak{J}, \mathcal{R})$, which depends on v, u, respectively, such that*

(A_1) $|\Psi_{\chi_1}(t)| \leq \epsilon_\alpha, \ |\Psi_{\chi_2}(t)| \leq \epsilon_\kappa, \ t \in \mathfrak{J}$;

(A_2)

$$\begin{cases} \mathfrak{D}^\alpha v(t) = \chi_1(t, u(t), \mathfrak{D}^\alpha v(t)) + \Psi_{\chi_1}(t), \ t \in \mathfrak{J}, \\ \mathfrak{D}^\kappa u(t) = \chi_2(t, v(t), \mathfrak{D}^\kappa u(t)) + \Psi_{\chi_2}(t), \ t \in \mathfrak{J}. \end{cases}$$

Lemma 3. *Let $(v, u) \in S$ be the solution of inequality (22), then we have*

$$\begin{cases} \|v - m_1\| \leq \mathcal{Q}_\alpha \epsilon_\alpha, \ t \in \mathfrak{J}, \\ \|u - m_2\| \leq \mathcal{Q}_\kappa \epsilon_\kappa, \ t \in \mathfrak{J}. \end{cases}$$

Proof. By (A_2) of Remark 4 and for $t \in \mathfrak{J}$, we have

$$\begin{cases} \mathfrak{D}^\alpha v(t) = \chi_1(t, u(t), \mathfrak{D}^\alpha v(t)) + \Psi_{\chi_1}(t), \\ \mathfrak{D}^\kappa u(t) = \chi_2(t, v(t), \mathfrak{D}^\kappa u(t)) + \Psi_{\chi_2}(t), \\ \mathfrak{D}^{\alpha-4} v(0) = \eta_1 \mathfrak{D}^{\alpha-4} v(\sigma), \quad \mathfrak{D}^{\alpha-3} v(0) = \eta_2 \mathfrak{D}^{\alpha-3} v(\sigma), \\ \mathfrak{D}^{\alpha-2} v(0) = \eta_3 \mathfrak{D}^{\alpha-2} v(\sigma), \quad \mathfrak{D}^{\alpha-1} v(0) = \eta_4 \mathfrak{D}^{\alpha-1} v(\sigma), \\ \mathfrak{D}^{\kappa-4} u(0) = \eta_5 \mathfrak{D}^{\kappa-4} u(\sigma), \quad \mathfrak{D}^{\kappa-3} u(0) = \eta_6 \mathfrak{D}^{\kappa-3} u(\sigma) \\ \mathfrak{D}^{\kappa-2} u(0) = \eta_7 \mathfrak{D}^{\kappa-2} u(\sigma), \quad \mathfrak{D}^{\kappa-1} u(0) = \eta_8 \mathfrak{D}^{\kappa-1} u(\sigma). \end{cases} \quad (29)$$

By Lemma 1, the solution of (29) can be written as

$$\begin{cases} v(t) = \dfrac{1}{\Gamma(\alpha)} \displaystyle\int_0^t (t-\tau)^{\alpha-1} [\chi_1(\tau, u(\tau), \mathfrak{D}^\alpha v(\tau)) + \Psi_{\chi_1}(\tau)] d\tau + \dfrac{\eta_1 t^{\alpha-4}}{6(1-\eta_1)\Gamma(\alpha-3)} \\ \times \displaystyle\int_0^\sigma (\sigma-\tau)^3 [\chi_1(\tau, u(\tau), \mathfrak{D}^\alpha v(\tau)) + \Psi_{\chi_1}(\tau)] d\tau + \left[\dfrac{\eta_2 t^{\alpha-3}}{2(1-\eta_2)\Gamma(\alpha-2)} + \dfrac{\eta_1 \eta_2 \sigma t^{\alpha-4}}{2(1-\eta_1)(1-\eta_2)\Gamma(\alpha-3)} \right] \\ \times \displaystyle\int_0^\sigma (\sigma-\tau)^2 [\chi_1(\tau, u(\tau), \mathfrak{D}^\alpha v(\tau)) + \Psi_{\chi_1}(\tau)] d\tau + \left[\dfrac{\eta_3 t^{\alpha-2}}{(1-\eta_3)\Gamma(\alpha-1)} + \dfrac{\eta_2 \eta_3 \sigma t^{\alpha-3}}{(1-\eta_2)(1-\eta_3)\Gamma(\alpha-2)} \right. \\ + \dfrac{\eta_1(1+\eta_2)\eta_3 \sigma^2 t^{\alpha-4}}{2(1-\eta_1)(1-\eta_2)(1-\eta_3)\Gamma(\alpha-3)} \Bigg] \displaystyle\int_0^\sigma (\sigma-\tau) [\chi_1(\tau, u(\tau), \mathfrak{D}^\alpha v(\tau)) + \Psi_{\chi_1}(\tau)] d\tau \\ + \left[\dfrac{\eta_4 t^{\alpha-1}}{(1-\eta_4)\Gamma(\alpha)} + \dfrac{\eta_3 \eta_4 \sigma t^{\alpha-2}}{(1-\eta_3)(1-\eta_4)\Gamma(\alpha-1)} + \dfrac{\eta_2(1+\eta_3)\eta_4 \sigma^2 t^{\alpha-3}}{2(1-\eta_2)(1-\eta_3)(1-\eta_4)\Gamma(\alpha-2)} \right. \\ + \dfrac{\eta_1((1+\eta_2)(1+\eta_3)+\eta_2+\eta_3)\eta_4 \sigma^3 t^{\alpha-4}}{6(1-\eta_1)(1-\eta_2)(1-\eta_3)(1-\eta_4)\Gamma(\alpha-3)} \Bigg] \displaystyle\int_0^\sigma [\chi_1(\tau, u(\tau), \mathfrak{D}^\alpha v(\tau)) + \Psi_{\chi_1}(\tau)] d\tau, \\ u(t) = \dfrac{1}{\Gamma(\kappa)} \displaystyle\int_0^t (t-\tau)^{\kappa-1} [\chi_2(\tau, v(\tau), \mathfrak{D}^\kappa u(\tau)) + \Psi_{\chi_2}(\tau)] d\tau + \dfrac{\eta_5 t^{\kappa-4}}{6(1-\eta_5)\Gamma(\kappa-3)} \\ \times \displaystyle\int_0^\sigma (\sigma-\tau)^3 [\chi_2(\tau, v(\tau), \mathfrak{D}^\kappa u(\tau)) + \Psi_{\chi_2}(\tau)] d\tau + \left[\dfrac{\eta_6 t^{\kappa-3}}{2(1-\eta_6)\Gamma(\kappa-2)} + \dfrac{\eta_5 \eta_6 \sigma t^{\kappa-4}}{2(1-\eta_5)(1-\eta_6)\Gamma(\kappa-3)} \right] \\ \times \displaystyle\int_0^\sigma (\sigma-\tau)^2 [\chi_2(\tau, v(\tau), \mathfrak{D}^\kappa u(\tau)) + \Psi_{\chi_2}(\tau)] d\tau + \left[\dfrac{\eta_7 t^{\kappa-2}}{(1-\eta_7)\Gamma(\kappa-1)} + \dfrac{\eta_6 \eta_7 \sigma t^{\kappa-3}}{(1-\eta_6)(1-\eta_7)\Gamma(\kappa-2)} \right. \\ + \dfrac{\eta_5(1+\eta_6)\eta_7 \sigma^2 t^{\kappa-4}}{2(1-\eta_5)(1-\eta_6)(1-\eta_7)\Gamma(\kappa-3)} \Bigg] \displaystyle\int_0^\sigma (\sigma-\tau) [\chi_2(\tau, v(\tau), \mathfrak{D}^\kappa u(\tau)) + \Psi_{\chi_2}(\tau)] d\tau \\ + \left[\dfrac{\eta_8 t^{\kappa-1}}{(1-\eta_8)\Gamma(\kappa)} + \dfrac{\eta_7 \eta_8 \sigma t^{\kappa-2}}{(1-\eta_7)(1-\eta_8)\Gamma(\kappa-1)} + \dfrac{\eta_6(1+\eta_7)\eta_8 \sigma^2 t^{\kappa-3}}{2(1-\eta_6)(1-\eta_7)(1-\eta_8)\Gamma(\kappa-2)} \right. \\ + \dfrac{\eta_5((1+\eta_6)(1+\eta_7)+\eta_6+\eta_7)\eta_8 \sigma^3 t^{\kappa-4}}{6(1-\eta_5)(1-\eta_6)(1-\eta_7)(1-\eta_8)\Gamma(\kappa-3)} \Bigg] \displaystyle\int_0^\sigma [\chi_2(\tau, v(\tau), \mathfrak{D}^\kappa u(\tau)) + \Psi_{\chi_2}(\tau)] d\tau. \end{cases} \quad (30)$$

From first equation of (30), we have

$$t^{4-\alpha}|v(t) - m_1(t)| \leq \frac{t^{4-\alpha}}{\Gamma(\alpha)} \int_0^t (t-\tau)^{\alpha-1} |\Psi_{\chi_1}(\tau)| d\tau$$
$$+ \left| \frac{\eta_1}{6(1-\eta_1)\Gamma(\alpha-3)} \right| \int_0^\sigma (\sigma-\tau)^3 |\Psi_{\chi_1}(\tau)| d\tau$$
$$+ \left| \frac{\eta_2 t}{2(1-\eta_2)\Gamma(\alpha-2)} + \frac{\eta_1 \eta_2 \sigma}{2(1-\eta_1)(1-\eta_2)\Gamma(\alpha-3)} \right| \int_0^\sigma (\sigma-\tau)^2 |\Psi_{\chi_1}(\tau)| d\tau$$
$$+ \left| \frac{\eta_3 t^2}{(1-\eta_3)\Gamma(\alpha-1)} + \frac{\eta_2 \eta_3 t \sigma}{(1-\eta_2)(1-\eta_3)\Gamma(\alpha-2)} \right.$$
$$\left. + \frac{\eta_1(1+\eta_2)\eta_3 \sigma^2}{2(1-\eta_1)(1-\eta_2)(1-\eta_3)\Gamma(\alpha-3)} \right| \int_0^\sigma (\sigma-\tau) |\Psi_{\chi_1}(\tau)| d\tau + \left| \frac{\eta_4 t^3}{(1-\eta_4)\Gamma(\alpha)} \right.$$
$$+ \frac{\eta_3 \eta_4 \sigma t^2}{(1-\eta_3)(1-\eta_4)\Gamma(\alpha-1)} + \frac{\eta_2(1+\eta_3)\eta_4 \sigma^2 t}{2(1-\eta_2)(1-\eta_3)(1-\eta_4)\Gamma(\alpha-2)}$$
$$+ \left. \frac{\eta_1((1+\eta_2)(1+\eta_3) + \eta_2 + \eta_3)\eta_4 \sigma^3}{6(1-\eta_1)(1-\eta_2)(1-\eta_3)(1-\eta_4)\Gamma(\alpha-3)} \right| \int_0^\sigma |\Psi_{\chi_1}(\tau)| d\tau. \qquad (31)$$

where $m_1(t)$ are those terms which are free of Ψ_{χ_1}. Using (6) and (A_1) of Remark 4, (31) becomes

$$\|v - m_1\| \leq \mathcal{Q}_\alpha \epsilon_\alpha.$$

Similarly for second equation of (30), we obtain

$$\|u - m_2\| \leq \mathcal{Q}_\kappa \epsilon_\kappa.$$

□

4.1. Method (I)

Theorem 4. *If hypothesis* $\mathbf{H}_1$ *and*

$$\Lambda = 1 - \frac{\mathcal{Q}_\alpha \mathcal{Q}_\kappa \mathcal{L}_{\chi_1} \mathcal{L}_{\chi_2}}{(1 - \mathcal{Q}_\alpha \overline{\mathcal{L}}_{\chi_1})(1 - \mathcal{Q}_\kappa \overline{\mathcal{L}}_{\chi_2})} > 0 \qquad (32)$$

hold, with $0 \leq \mathcal{Q}_\alpha \overline{\mathcal{L}}_{\chi_1}, \mathcal{Q}_\kappa \overline{\mathcal{L}}_{\chi_2} < 1$. *Then system* (1) *is HU stable.*

Proof. Let $(v,u) \in S$ be the solution of (22) and $(w,\zeta) \in S$ be the solution of following system:

$$\begin{cases} \mathfrak{D}^\alpha w(t) - \chi_1(t, \zeta(t), \mathfrak{D}^\alpha w(t)) = 0, \ t \in \mathfrak{J}, \\ \mathfrak{D}^\kappa \zeta(t) - \chi_2(t, w(t), \mathfrak{D}^\kappa \zeta(t)) = 0, \ t \in \mathfrak{J}, \\ \mathfrak{D}^{\alpha-4} w(0) = \eta_1 \mathfrak{D}^{\alpha-4} w(\sigma), \ \mathfrak{D}^{\alpha-3} w(0) = \eta_2 \mathfrak{D}^{\alpha-3} w(\sigma), \\ \mathfrak{D}^{\alpha-2} w(0) = \eta_3 \mathfrak{D}^{\alpha-2} w(\sigma), \ \mathfrak{D}^{\alpha-1} w(0) = \eta_4 \mathfrak{D}^{\alpha-1} w(\sigma), \\ \mathfrak{D}^{\kappa-4} \zeta(0) = \eta_5 \mathfrak{D}^{\kappa-4} \zeta(\sigma), \ \mathfrak{D}^{\kappa-3} \zeta(0) = \eta_6 \mathfrak{D}^{\kappa-3} \zeta(\sigma), \\ \mathfrak{D}^{\kappa-2} \zeta(0) = \eta_7 \mathfrak{D}^{\kappa-2} \zeta(\sigma), \ \mathfrak{D}^{\kappa-1} w(0) = \eta_8 \mathfrak{D}^{\kappa-1} \zeta(\sigma). \end{cases} \qquad (33)$$

Then in view of Lemma 1, for $t \in \mathfrak{J}$ the solution of (33) is given by:

$$\begin{cases}
w(t) = \dfrac{1}{\Gamma(\alpha)} \displaystyle\int_0^t (t-\tau)^{\alpha-1} \chi_1(\tau,\zeta(\tau),\mathfrak{D}^\alpha w(\tau)) d\tau + \dfrac{\eta_1 t^{\alpha-4}}{6(1-\eta_1)\Gamma(\alpha-3)} \\
\quad \times \displaystyle\int_0^\sigma (\sigma-\tau)^3 \chi_1(\tau,\zeta(\tau),\mathfrak{D}^\alpha w(\tau)) d\tau + \left[\dfrac{\eta_2 t^{\alpha-3}}{2(1-\eta_2)\Gamma(\alpha-2)} + \dfrac{\eta_1 \eta_2 \sigma t^{\alpha-4}}{2(1-\eta_1)(1-\eta_2)\Gamma(\alpha-3)}\right] \\
\quad \times \displaystyle\int_0^\sigma (\sigma-\tau)^2 \chi_1(\tau,\zeta(\tau),\mathfrak{D}^\alpha w(\tau)) d\tau + \left[\dfrac{\eta_3 t^{\alpha-2}}{(1-\eta_3)\Gamma(\alpha-1)} + \dfrac{\eta_2 \eta_3 \sigma t^{\alpha-3}}{(1-\eta_2)(1-\eta_3)\Gamma(\alpha-2)}\right. \\
\quad \left.+ \dfrac{\eta_1(1+\eta_2)\eta_3 \sigma^2 t^{\alpha-4}}{2(1-\eta_1)(1-\eta_2)(1-\eta_3)\Gamma(\alpha-3)}\right] \displaystyle\int_0^\sigma (\sigma-\tau)\chi_1(\tau,\zeta(\tau),\mathfrak{D}^\alpha w(\tau)) d\tau \\
\quad + \left[\dfrac{\eta_4 t^{\alpha-1}}{(1-\eta_4)\Gamma(\alpha)} + \dfrac{\eta_3 \eta_4 \sigma t^{\alpha-2}}{(1-\eta_3)(1-\eta_4)\Gamma(\alpha-1)} + \dfrac{\eta_2(1+\eta_3)\eta_4 \sigma^2 t^{\alpha-3}}{2(1-\eta_2)(1-\eta_3)(1-\eta_4)\Gamma(\alpha-2)}\right. \\
\quad \left.+ \dfrac{\eta_1((1+\eta_2)(1+\eta_3)+\eta_2+\eta_3)\eta_4 \sigma^3 t^{\alpha-4}}{6(1-\eta_1)(1-\eta_2)(1-\eta_3)(1-\eta_4)\Gamma(\alpha-3)}\right] \displaystyle\int_0^\sigma \chi_1(\tau,\zeta(\tau),\mathfrak{D}^\alpha w(\tau)) d\tau, \\[4pt]
\zeta(t) = \dfrac{1}{\Gamma(\kappa)} \displaystyle\int_0^t (t-\tau)^{\kappa-1} \chi_2(\tau,w(\tau),\mathfrak{D}^\kappa \zeta(\tau)) d\tau + \dfrac{\eta_5 t^{\kappa-4}}{6(1-\eta_5)\Gamma(\kappa-3)} \\
\quad \times \displaystyle\int_0^\sigma (\sigma-\tau)^3 \chi_2(\tau,w(\tau),\mathfrak{D}^\kappa \zeta(\tau)) d\tau + \left[\dfrac{\eta_6 t^{\kappa-3}}{2(1-\eta_6)\Gamma(\kappa-2)} + \dfrac{\eta_5 \eta_6 \sigma t^{\kappa-4}}{2(1-\eta_5)(1-\eta_6)\Gamma(\kappa-3)}\right] \\
\quad \times \displaystyle\int_0^\sigma (\sigma-\tau)^2 \chi_2(\tau,w(\tau),\mathfrak{D}^\kappa \zeta(\tau)) d\tau + \left[\dfrac{\eta_7 t^{\kappa-2}}{(1-\eta_7)\Gamma(\kappa-1)} + \dfrac{\eta_6 \eta_7 \sigma t^{\kappa-3}}{(1-\eta_6)(1-\eta_7)\Gamma(\kappa-2)}\right. \\
\quad \left.+ \dfrac{\eta_5(1+\eta_6)\eta_7 \sigma^2 t^{\kappa-4}}{2(1-\eta_5)(1-\eta_6)(1-\eta_7)\Gamma(\kappa-3)}\right] \displaystyle\int_0^\sigma (\sigma-\tau)\chi_2(\tau,w(\tau),\mathfrak{D}^\kappa \zeta(\tau)) d\tau \\
\quad + \left[\dfrac{\eta_8 t^{\kappa-1}}{(1-\eta_8)\Gamma(\kappa)} + \dfrac{\eta_7 \eta_8 \sigma t^{\kappa-2}}{(1-\eta_7)(1-\eta_8)\Gamma(\kappa-1)} + \dfrac{\eta_6(1+\eta_7)\eta_8 \sigma^2 t^{\kappa-3}}{2(1-\eta_6)(1-\eta_7)(1-\eta_8)\Gamma(\kappa-2)}\right. \\
\quad \left.+ \dfrac{\eta_5((1+\eta_6)(1+\eta_7)+\eta_6+\eta_7)\eta_8 \sigma^3 t^{\kappa-4}}{6(1-\eta_5)(1-\eta_6)(1-\eta_7)(1-\eta_8)\Gamma(\kappa-3)}\right] \displaystyle\int_0^\sigma \chi_2(\tau,w(\tau),\mathfrak{D}^\kappa \zeta(\tau)) d\tau.
\end{cases} \quad (34)$$

Consider

$$t^{4-\alpha}|v(t)-w(t)| \leq t^{4-\alpha}|v(t)-m_1(t)| + t^{4-\alpha}|m_1(t)-w(t)|. \qquad (35)$$

Applying Lemma 3 in (35), we get

$$t^{4-\alpha}|v(t)-w(t)| \leq \mathcal{Q}_\alpha \epsilon_\alpha$$
$$+ \frac{t^{4-\alpha}}{\Gamma(\alpha)} \int_0^t (t-\tau)^{\alpha-1} \left|\chi_1(\tau,u(\tau),\mathfrak{D}^\alpha v(\tau)) - \chi_1(\tau,\zeta(\tau),\mathfrak{D}^\alpha w(\tau))\right| d\tau + \left|\frac{\eta_1}{6(1-\eta_1)\Gamma(\alpha-3)}\right|$$
$$\times \int_0^\sigma (\sigma-\tau)^3 \left|\chi_1(\tau,u(\tau),\mathfrak{D}^\alpha v(\tau)) - \chi_1(\tau,\zeta(\tau),\mathfrak{D}^\alpha w(\tau))\right| d\tau + \left|\frac{\eta_2 t}{2(1-\eta_2)\Gamma(\alpha-2)}\right.$$
$$+ \frac{\eta_1 \eta_2 \sigma}{2(1-\eta_1)(1-\eta_2)\Gamma(\alpha-3)} \left| \int_0^\sigma (\sigma-\tau)^2 \left|\chi_1(\tau,u(\tau),\mathfrak{D}^\alpha v(\tau)) - \chi_1(\tau,\zeta(\tau),\mathfrak{D}^\alpha w(\tau))\right| d\tau \right.$$
$$+ \left| \frac{\eta_3 t^2}{(1-\eta_3)\Gamma(\alpha-1)} + \frac{\eta_2 \eta_3 t \sigma}{(1-\eta_2)(1-\eta_3)\Gamma(\alpha-2)} + \frac{\eta_1(1+\eta_2)\eta_3 \sigma^2}{2(1-\eta_1)(1-\eta_2)(1-\eta_3)\Gamma(\alpha-3)} \right|$$
$$\times \int_0^\sigma (\sigma-\tau) \left|\chi_1(\tau,u(\tau),\mathfrak{D}^\alpha v(\tau)) - \chi_1(\tau,\zeta(\tau),\mathfrak{D}^\alpha w(\tau))\right| d\tau + \left|\frac{\eta_4 t^3}{(1-\eta_4)\Gamma(\alpha)}\right.$$
$$+ \frac{\eta_3 \eta_4 \sigma t^2}{(1-\eta_3)(1-\eta_4)\Gamma(\alpha-1)} + \frac{\eta_2(1+\eta_3)\eta_4 \sigma^2 t}{2(1-\eta_2)(1-\eta_3)(1-\eta_4)\Gamma(\alpha-2)}$$
$$+ \frac{\eta_1((1+\eta_2)(1+\eta_3)+\eta_2+\eta_3)\eta_4 \sigma^3}{6(1-\eta_1)(1-\eta_2)(1-\eta_3)(1-\eta_4)\Gamma(\alpha-3)} \Bigg|$$
$$\times \int_0^\sigma \left|\chi_1(\tau,u(\tau),\mathfrak{D}^\alpha v(\tau)) - \chi_1(\tau,\zeta(\tau),\mathfrak{D}^\alpha w(\tau))\right| d\tau$$
$$\leq \mathcal{Q}_\alpha \epsilon_\alpha + \Bigg[\frac{\sigma^4}{\Gamma(\alpha+1)} + \left|\frac{\eta_1 \sigma^4}{24(1-\eta_1)\Gamma(\alpha-3)}\right| + \left|\frac{\eta_2(1-\eta_1)\sigma^4 + \eta_1\eta_2\sigma^4(\alpha-3)}{6(1-\eta_1)(1-\eta_2)\Gamma(\alpha-2)}\right|$$
$$+ \left|\frac{\eta_3(1-\eta_2)\sigma^4 + \eta_2\eta_3\sigma^4(\alpha-2)}{2(1-\eta_2)(1-\eta_3)\Gamma(\alpha-1)}\right| + \left|\frac{\eta_1(1+\eta_2)\eta_3\sigma^4}{2(1-\eta_1)(1-\eta_2)(1-\eta_3)\Gamma(\alpha-3)}\right|$$
$$+ \left|\frac{(1-\eta_3)\eta_4\sigma^4 + \eta_3\eta_4\sigma^4(\alpha-1)}{(1-\eta_3)(1-\eta_4)\Gamma(\alpha)}\right| + \left|\frac{\eta_2(1+\eta_3)\eta_4\sigma^4}{2(1-\eta_2)(1-\eta_3)(1-\eta_4)\Gamma(\alpha-2)}\right| \quad (36)$$
$$+ \left|\frac{\eta_1((1+\eta_2)(1+\eta_3)+\eta_2+\eta_3)\eta_4\sigma^4}{6(1-\eta_1)(1-\eta_2)(1-\eta_3)(1-\eta_4)\Gamma(\alpha-3)}\right|\Bigg] (\mathcal{L}_{\chi_1}\|u-\zeta\| + \overline{\mathcal{L}}_{\chi_1}\|\mathfrak{D}^\alpha v - \mathfrak{D}^\alpha w\|).$$

Using **H**$_1$ of Theorem 1 and (6) in (36), we have

$$\|v-w\| \leq \frac{\mathcal{Q}_\alpha \epsilon_\alpha}{1-\mathcal{Q}_\alpha \overline{\mathcal{L}}_{\chi_1}} + \frac{\mathcal{Q}_\alpha \mathcal{L}_{\chi_1}}{1-\mathcal{Q}_\alpha \overline{\mathcal{L}}_{\chi_1}} \|u-\zeta\|. \quad (37)$$

Similarly, we can get

$$\|u-\zeta\| \leq \frac{\mathcal{Q}_\kappa \epsilon_\kappa}{1-\mathcal{Q}_\kappa \overline{\mathcal{L}}_{\chi_2}} + \frac{\mathcal{Q}_\kappa \mathcal{L}_{\chi_2}}{1-\mathcal{Q}_\kappa \overline{\mathcal{L}}_{\chi_2}} \|v-w\|. \quad (38)$$

We write (37) and (38) as

$$\|v-w\| - \frac{\mathcal{Q}_\alpha \mathcal{L}_{\chi_1}}{1-\mathcal{Q}_\alpha \overline{\mathcal{L}}_{\chi_1}} \|u-\zeta\| \leq \frac{\mathcal{Q}_\alpha \epsilon_\alpha}{1-\mathcal{Q}_\alpha \overline{\mathcal{L}}_{\chi_1}},$$

$$\|u-\zeta\| - \frac{\mathcal{Q}_\kappa \mathcal{L}_{\chi_2}}{1-\mathcal{Q}_\kappa \overline{\mathcal{L}}_{\chi_2}} \|v-w\| \leq \frac{\mathcal{Q}_\kappa \epsilon_\kappa}{1-\mathcal{Q}_\kappa \overline{\mathcal{L}}_{\chi_2}},$$

$$\begin{bmatrix} 1 & -\frac{\mathcal{Q}_\alpha \mathcal{L}_{\chi_1}}{1-\mathcal{Q}_\alpha \overline{\mathcal{L}}_{\chi_1}} \\ -\frac{\mathcal{Q}_\kappa \mathcal{L}_{\chi_2}}{1-\mathcal{Q}_\kappa \overline{\mathcal{L}}_{\chi_2}} & 1 \end{bmatrix} \begin{bmatrix} \|v-w\| \\ \|u-\zeta\| \end{bmatrix} \leq \begin{bmatrix} \frac{\mathcal{Q}_\alpha \epsilon_\alpha}{1-\mathcal{Q}_\alpha \overline{\mathcal{L}}_{\chi_1}} \\ \frac{\mathcal{Q}_\kappa \epsilon_\kappa}{1-\mathcal{Q}_\kappa \overline{\mathcal{L}}_{\chi_2}} \end{bmatrix}.$$

From the above, we get

$$\begin{bmatrix} \|v-w\| \\ \|u-\zeta\| \end{bmatrix} \leq \begin{bmatrix} \frac{1}{\Lambda} & \frac{\mathcal{Q}_\alpha \mathcal{L}_{\chi_1}}{\Lambda(1-\mathcal{Q}_\alpha \overline{\mathcal{L}}_{\chi_1})} \\ \frac{\mathcal{Q}_\kappa \mathcal{L}_{\chi_2}}{\Lambda(1-\mathcal{Q}_\kappa \overline{\mathcal{L}}_{\chi_2})} & \frac{1}{\Lambda} \end{bmatrix} \begin{bmatrix} \frac{\mathcal{Q}_\alpha \epsilon_\alpha}{1-\mathcal{Q}_\alpha \overline{\mathcal{L}}_{\chi_1}} \\ \frac{\mathcal{Q}_\kappa \epsilon_\kappa}{1-\mathcal{Q}_\kappa \overline{\mathcal{L}}_{\chi_2}} \end{bmatrix},$$

where

$$\Lambda = 1 - \frac{\mathcal{Q}_\alpha \mathcal{Q}_\kappa \mathcal{L}_{\chi_1} \mathcal{L}_{\chi_2}}{(1-\mathcal{Q}_\alpha \overline{\mathcal{L}}_{\chi_1})(1-\mathcal{Q}_\kappa \overline{\mathcal{L}}_{\chi_2})} > 0.$$

Further simplification gives

$$\|v-w\| \leq \frac{\mathcal{Q}_\alpha \epsilon_\alpha}{\Lambda(1-\mathcal{Q}_\alpha \overline{\mathcal{L}}_{\chi_1})} + \frac{\mathcal{Q}_\alpha \mathcal{Q}_\kappa \mathcal{L}_{\chi_1} \epsilon_\kappa}{\Lambda(1-\mathcal{Q}_\alpha \overline{\mathcal{L}}_{\chi_1})(1-\mathcal{Q}_\kappa \overline{\mathcal{L}}_{\chi_2})},$$

$$\|u-\zeta\| \leq \frac{\mathcal{Q}_\kappa \epsilon_\kappa}{\Lambda(1-\mathcal{Q}_\kappa \overline{\mathcal{L}}_{\chi_2})} + \frac{\mathcal{Q}_\alpha \mathcal{Q}_\kappa \mathcal{L}_{\chi_2} \epsilon_\alpha}{\Lambda(1-\mathcal{Q}_\alpha \overline{\mathcal{L}}_{\chi_1})(1-\mathcal{Q}_\kappa \overline{\mathcal{L}}_{\chi_2})},$$

from which we have

$$\|v-w\| + \|u-\zeta\| \leq \frac{\mathcal{Q}_\alpha \epsilon_\alpha}{\Lambda(1-\mathcal{Q}_\alpha \overline{\mathcal{L}}_{\chi_1})} + \frac{\mathcal{Q}_\kappa \epsilon_\kappa}{\Lambda(1-\mathcal{Q}_\kappa \overline{\mathcal{L}}_{\chi_2})} + \frac{\mathcal{Q}_\alpha \mathcal{Q}_\kappa \mathcal{L}_{\chi_1} \epsilon_\kappa}{\Lambda(1-\mathcal{Q}_\alpha \overline{\mathcal{L}}_{\chi_1})(1-\mathcal{Q}_\kappa \overline{\mathcal{L}}_{\chi_2})} + \frac{\mathcal{Q}_\alpha \mathcal{Q}_\kappa \mathcal{L}_{\chi_2} \epsilon_\alpha}{\Lambda(1-\mathcal{Q}_\alpha \overline{\mathcal{L}}_{\chi_1})(1-\mathcal{Q}_\kappa \overline{\mathcal{L}}_{\chi_2})}. \tag{39}$$

Let $\epsilon = \max\{\epsilon_\alpha, \epsilon_\kappa\}$, then from (39) we have

$$\|(v,u)-(w,\zeta)\|_S \leq C_{\alpha,\kappa} \epsilon, \tag{40}$$

where

$$C_{\alpha,\kappa} = \frac{\mathcal{Q}_\alpha}{\Lambda(1-\mathcal{Q}_\alpha \overline{\mathcal{L}}_{\chi_1})} + \frac{\mathcal{Q}_\kappa}{\Lambda(1-\mathcal{Q}_\kappa \overline{\mathcal{L}}_{\chi_2})} + \frac{\mathcal{Q}_\alpha \mathcal{Q}_\kappa \mathcal{L}_{\chi_1}}{\Lambda(1-\mathcal{Q}_\alpha \overline{\mathcal{L}}_{\chi_1})(1-\mathcal{Q}_\kappa \overline{\mathcal{L}}_{\chi_2})} + \frac{\mathcal{Q}_\alpha \mathcal{Q}_\kappa \mathcal{L}_{\chi_2}}{\Lambda(1-\mathcal{Q}_\alpha \overline{\mathcal{L}}_{\chi_1})(1-\mathcal{Q}_\kappa \overline{\mathcal{L}}_{\chi_2})}.$$

□

Remark 5. *By setting $\Phi_{\alpha,\kappa}(\epsilon) = C_{\alpha,\kappa} \epsilon$, $\Phi_{\alpha,\kappa}(0) = 0$ in (40), then by Definition 4 the problem (1) is generalized HU stable.*

H$_3$: Let functions $\Theta_\alpha, \Theta_\kappa : \mathfrak{J} \to \mathcal{R}^+$ be nondecreasing. Then, there are $\zeta_{\Theta_\alpha}, \zeta_{\Theta_\kappa} > 0$, such that for every $t \in \mathfrak{J}$, the inequalities

$$\mathfrak{J}^\alpha \Theta_\alpha(t) \leq \zeta_{\Theta_\alpha} \Theta_\alpha(t) \quad \text{and} \quad \mathfrak{J}^\kappa \Theta_\kappa(t) \leq \zeta_{\Theta_\kappa} \Theta_\kappa(t)$$

holds.

Remark 6. *Lemma 3 and Theorem 4 gives that the system (1) is HU–Rassias and generalized HU–Rassias stable, if $\epsilon_\alpha = \Theta_\alpha(t)\epsilon_\alpha$ and $\epsilon_\kappa = \Theta_\kappa(t)\epsilon_\kappa$ with **H$_3$** and $\Lambda > 0$.*

4.2. Method (II)

Theorem 5. *Under the hypothesis **H$_1$** and if $\Lambda^* = 1 - \left[\frac{\mathcal{Q}_\kappa \mathcal{L}_{\chi_2}}{1-\mathcal{Q}_\kappa \overline{\mathcal{L}}_{\chi_2}} + \frac{\mathcal{Q}_\alpha \mathcal{L}_{\chi_1}}{1-\mathcal{Q}_\alpha \overline{\mathcal{L}}_{\chi_1}}\right] > 0$. Then system (1) is HU stable.*

Proof. From inequality (37) and (38), we have

$$\|v-w\| + \|u-\zeta\|$$
$$\leq \frac{\mathcal{Q}_\alpha \epsilon_\alpha}{1-\mathcal{Q}_\alpha \overline{\mathcal{L}}_{\chi_1}} + \frac{\mathcal{Q}_\kappa \epsilon_\kappa}{1-\mathcal{Q}_\kappa \overline{\mathcal{L}}_{\chi_2}} + \frac{\mathcal{Q}_\kappa \mathcal{L}_{\chi_2}}{1-\mathcal{Q}_\kappa \overline{\mathcal{L}}_{\chi_2}}\|v-w\| + \frac{\mathcal{Q}_\alpha \mathcal{L}_{\chi_1}}{1-\mathcal{Q}_\alpha \overline{\mathcal{L}}_{\chi_1}}\|u-\zeta\|. \tag{41}$$

Let $\max\{\epsilon_\alpha, \epsilon_\kappa\} = \epsilon$, then from (41) we obtain

$$\|(v,u) - (w,\zeta)\|_S \leq \mathbf{C}_{\alpha,\kappa}\epsilon, \tag{42}$$

where

$$\mathbf{C}_{\alpha,\kappa} = \left[\frac{\mathcal{Q}_\alpha}{\Lambda^*(1-\mathcal{Q}_\alpha \overline{\mathcal{L}}_{\chi_1})} + \frac{\mathcal{Q}_\kappa}{\Lambda^*(1-\mathcal{Q}_\kappa \overline{\mathcal{L}}_{\chi_2})}\right].$$

□

Remark 7. *With the help of Remark 5, we can obtain the generalized HU stability of system (1).*

Remark 8. *Lemma 3 and Theorem 5 gives that the system (1) is HU–Rassias and generalized HU–Rassias stable, if $\epsilon_\alpha = \Theta_\alpha(t)\epsilon_\alpha$ and $\epsilon_\kappa = \Theta_\kappa(t)\epsilon_\kappa$ with $\mathbf{H}_3$ and $\Lambda^* > 0$.*

Remark 9. *The results of coupled systems of fourth-order nonlinear FDEs gives the results of fourth-order nonlinear system of ODEs (If $\alpha, \kappa = 4$) with anti-periodic and initial conditions, if $\eta_i = -1$ ($i = 1, 2, \ldots, 8$) and $\eta_i = 0$ ($i = 1, 2, \ldots, 8$) respectively.*

5. Example

Example 1. *Consider the following coupled system of FDEs:*

$$\begin{cases} \mathfrak{D}^\alpha v(t) - \left[\frac{1}{4(t+2)^2}\frac{|\mathfrak{D}^\alpha v(t)|}{1+|\mathfrak{D}^\alpha v(t)|} + \frac{1}{16}\sin^2 u(t)\right] = 0, \ t \in [0,1], \\ \mathfrak{D}^\kappa u(t) - \left[\frac{1}{32\pi}\sin(2\pi v(t)) + \frac{|\mathfrak{D}^\kappa u(t)|}{16(1+|\mathfrak{D}^\kappa u(t)|)} + \frac{1}{2}\right] = 0, \ t \in [0,1], \\ \mathfrak{D}^{\alpha-4}v(0) = \eta_1 \mathfrak{D}^{\alpha-4}v(\sigma), \ \mathfrak{D}^{\alpha-3}v(0) = \eta_2 \mathfrak{D}^{\alpha-3}v(\sigma), \\ \mathfrak{D}^{\alpha-2}v(0) = \eta_3 \mathfrak{D}^{\alpha-2}v(\sigma), \ \mathfrak{D}^{\alpha-1}v(0) = \eta_4 \mathfrak{D}^{\alpha-1}v(\sigma), \\ \mathfrak{D}^{\kappa-4}u(0) = \eta_5 \mathfrak{D}^{\kappa-4}u(\sigma), \ \mathfrak{D}^{\kappa-3}u(0) = \eta_6 \mathfrak{D}^{\kappa-3}u(\sigma), \\ \mathfrak{D}^{\kappa-2}u(0) = \eta_7 \mathfrak{D}^{\kappa-2}u(\sigma), \ \mathfrak{D}^{\kappa-1}u(0) = \eta_8 \mathfrak{D}^{\kappa-1}u(\sigma). \end{cases} \tag{43}$$

From system (43), we can see $\alpha = \kappa = \frac{10}{3}$, $\sigma = 1$, $\eta_1 = \eta_5 = \frac{1}{2}$, $\eta_2 = \eta_6 = \frac{1}{3}$, $\eta_3 = \eta_7 = -1$ and $\eta_4 = \eta_8 = -1$. Moreover, we have

$$|\chi_1(t, u_1(t), \mathfrak{D}^\alpha v_1(t)) - \chi_1(t, u_2(t), \mathfrak{D}^\alpha v_2(t))| \leq \frac{1}{16}|u_1(t) - u_2(t)| + \frac{1}{16}|\mathfrak{D}^\alpha v_1(t) - \mathfrak{D}^\alpha v_2(t)|,$$

$$|\chi_2(t, v_1(t), \mathfrak{D}^\kappa u_1(t)) - \chi_2(t, v_2(t), \mathfrak{D}^\kappa u_2(t))| \leq \frac{1}{16}|v_1(t) - v_2(t)| + \frac{1}{16}|\mathfrak{D}^\kappa u_1(t) - \mathfrak{D}^\kappa u_2(t)|.$$

Therefore, we get $\mathcal{L}_{\chi_1} = \overline{\mathcal{L}}_{\chi_1} = \mathcal{L}_{\chi_2} = \overline{\mathcal{L}}_{\chi_2} = \frac{1}{16}$. Therefore,

$$\frac{\mathcal{Q}_\alpha \mathcal{L}_{\chi_1}(1-\overline{\mathcal{L}}_{\chi_2}) + \mathcal{Q}_\kappa \mathcal{L}_{\chi_2}(1-\overline{\mathcal{L}}_{\chi_1})}{(1-\overline{\mathcal{L}}_{\chi_2})(1-\overline{\mathcal{L}}_{\chi_1})} \approx 0.75141 < 1,$$

Thus, solution of (43) is unique. Moreover, system (43) is HU, generalized HU, HU–Rassias and generalized HU–Rassias stable by two different approaches under the conditions of Theorem 4 and Theorem 5, i.e., $\Lambda > 0$ and $\Lambda^* > 0$.

6. Conclusions

This paper concluded that the solution of coupled implicit FDEs (1) is unique and exists by using the Banach contraction theorem and Leray–Schauder fixed point theorem. Under some assumptions, the aforesaid coupled system has at least one solution. Besides this, the considered coupled system is HU, generalized HU, HU–Rassias and generalized HU–Rassias stable. An example is presented to illustrate our obtained results. The proposed system (1) gives the following well-known system of ODEs, which has wide applications in applied sciences [5]

- $\eta_i = -1$ ($i = 1, 2, \ldots, 8$) and $\alpha, \kappa = 4$, then we get fourth-order ODEs system with anti-periodic boundary conditions.
- $\eta_i = 0$ ($i = 1, 2, \ldots, 8$) and $\alpha, \kappa = 4$, then we get fourth-order ODEs system with initial conditions.

Author Contributions: Conceptualization, U.R., A.Z., Z.A., I.-L.P., S.R., S.E.; investigation, U.R., A.Z., Z.A., I.-L.P., S.R., S.E.; writing—original draft preparation, U.R., A.Z., Z.A., I.-L.P., S.R., S.E.; writing—review and editing, U.R., A.Z., Z.A., I.-L.P., S.R., S.E. All authors have read and agreed to the published version of the manuscript.

Funding: Not applicable.

Institutional Review Board Statement: Not applicable

Informed Consent Statement: Not applicable.

Data Availability Statement: Not applicable.

Acknowledgments: The fifth author was supported by Azarbaijan Shahid Madani University.

Conflicts of Interest: The authors declare no conflict of interest.

Sample Availability: Data sharing not applicable to this article as no datasets were generated or analyzed during the current study.

References

1. Kilbas, A.A.; Srivastava, H.M.; Trujillo, J.J. Theory and Application of Fractional Differential Equation. In *North-Holl and Mathematics Studies*; Elsevier: Amsterdam, The Netherlands, 2006; Volume 204.
2. Vintagre, B.M.; Podlybni, I.; Hernandez, A.; Feliu, V. Some approximations of fractional order operators used in control theory and applications. *Fract. Calc. Appl. Anal.* **2000**, *3*, 231–248.
3. Tarasov, V.E. *Fractional Dynamics: Application of Fractional Calculus to Dynamics of Particles, Fields and Media*; Springer: Berlin/Heidelberg, Germany; Higher Education Press: Beijing, China, 2010.
4. Oldham, K.B. Fractional differential equations in electrochemistry. *Adv. Eng. Softw.* **2010**, *41*, 9–12. [CrossRef]
5. Rihan, F.A. Numerical Modeling of Fractional Order Biological Systems. *Abs. Appl. Anal.* **2013**. [CrossRef]
6. Sabatier, J.; Agrawal, O.P.; Machado, J.A.T. *Advances in Fractional Calculus*; Springer: Dordrecht, The Netherlands, 2007.
7. Deimling, K. *Nonlinear Functional Analysis*; Springer: New York, NY, USA, 1985.
8. Khan, A.; Syam, M.I.; Zada, A.; Khan, H. Stability analysis of nonlinear fractional differential equations with Caputo and Riemann-Liouville derivatives. *Eur. Phys. J. Plus* **2018**, *133*, 264. [CrossRef]
9. Riaz, U.; Zada, A.; Ali, Z.; Cui, Y.; Xu, J. Analysis of coupled systems of implicit impulsive fractional differential equations involving Hadamard derivatives. *Adv. Differ. Eq.* **2019**, *226*, 1–27. [CrossRef]
10. Rizwan, R.; Zada, A.; Wang, X. Stability analysis of non linear implicit fractional Langevin equation with noninstantaneous impulses. *Adv. Differ. Eq.* **2019**, *2019*, 85. [CrossRef]
11. Zada, A.; Ali, S. Stability Analysis of multi-point boundary value problem for sequential fractional differential equations with noninstantaneous impulses. *Int. J. Nonlinear Sci. Numer. Simul.* **2018**, *19*, 763–774. [CrossRef]
12. Ahmad, B.; Nieto, J.J. Existence results for a coupled system of nonlinear fractional differential equations with three-point boundary conditions. *Comput. Math. Appl.* **2009**, *58*, 1838–1843. [CrossRef]
13. Bai, C.; Fang, J. The existence of a positive solution for a singular coupled system of nonlinear fractional differential equations. *Appl. Math. Comput.* **2004**, *150*, 611–621. [CrossRef]
14. Chen, Y.; An, H. Numerical solutions of coupled Burgers equations with time and space fractional derivatives. *Appl. Math. Comput.* **2008**, *200*, 87–95. [CrossRef]
15. Agarwal, R.P.; Ahmad, B.; Alsaedi, A. Fractional-order differential equations with anti-periodic boundary conditions: A survey. *Bound. Value Probl.* **2017**, *2017*, 173. [CrossRef]

16. Ahmad, B.; Ntouyas, S.K. Fractional differential inclusions with fractional separated boundary conditions. *Fract. Calc. Appl. Anal.* **2012**, *15*, 362–382. [CrossRef]
17. Benchohra, M.; Hamani, S.; Ntouyas, S.K. Boundary value problems for differential equations with fractional order and nonlocal conditions. *Nonlinear Anal.* **2009**, *71*, 2391–2396. [CrossRef]
18. Goodrich, C. Existence and uniqueness of solutions to a fractional difference equation with nonlocal conditions. *Comput. Math. Appl.* **2011**, *61*, 191–202. [CrossRef]
19. Ahmad, M.; Jiang, J.; Zada, A.; Shah, S.O.; Xu, J. Analysis of coupled system of implicit fractional differential equations involving Katugampola-Caputo fractional derivative. *Complexity* **2020**. [CrossRef]
20. Ahmad, M.; Zada, A.; Wang, X. Existence, uniqueness and stability of implicit switched coupled fractional differential equations of Ψ-hilfer type. *Int. J. Nonlinear Sci. Numer. Simul.* **2019**, *21*, 327–337. [CrossRef]
21. Riaz, U.; Zada, A.; Ali, Z.; Cui, Y.; Xu, J. Analysis of nonlinear coupled systems of impulsive fractional differential equations with Hadamard derivatives. *Math. Probl. Eng.* **2019**, *2019*, 1–20. [CrossRef]
22. Zada, A.; Ali, S.; Li, Y. Ulam–type stability for a class of implicit fractional differential equations with non–instantaneous integral impulses and boundary condition. *Adv. Differ. Eq.* **2017**, *2017*, 1–26. [CrossRef]
23. Zada, A.; Ali, W.; Park, C. Ulam's type stability of higher order nonlinear delay differential equations via integral inequality of Grönwall–Bellman–Bihari's type. *Appl. Math. Comput.* **2019**, *350*, 60–65. [CrossRef]
24. Zada, A.; Mashal, A. Stability analysis of nth order nonlinear impulsive differential equations in Quasi–Banach space. *Numer. Func. Anal. Opt.* **2019**, *41*, 294–321. [CrossRef]
25. Zhou, H.; Alzabut, J.; Yang, L. On fractional Langevin differential equations with anti-periodic boundary conditions. *Eur. Phys. J. Spec. Top.* **2017**, *226*, 3577–3590. [CrossRef]
26. Zada, A.; Riaz, U.; Khan, F. Hyers–Ulam stability of impulsive integral equations. *Boll. Unione Mat. Ital.* **2019**, *12*, 453–467. [CrossRef]
27. Ulam, S.M. *A Collection of the Mathematical Problems*; Interscience: New York, NY, USA, 1960.
28. Hyers, D.H. On the stability of the linear functional equation. *Proc. Natl. Acad. Sci. USA* **1941**, *27*, 222–224. [CrossRef]
29. Alqifiary, Q.; Jung, S. Laplace transform and generalized Hyers–Ulam stability of linear differential equations. *Electron. J. Differ. Eq.* **2014**, *2014*, 1–11.
30. Rezaei, H.; Jung, S.; Rassias, T. Laplace transform and Hyers–Ulam stability of linear differential equations. *J. Math. Anal. Appl.* **2013**, *403*, 244–251. [CrossRef]
31. Wang, C.; Xu, T. Hyers–Ulam stability of fractional linear differential equations involving Caputo fractional derivatives. *Appl. Math.* **2015**, *60*, 383–393. [CrossRef]
32. Shen, Y.; Chen, W. Laplace transform mathod for the Ulam stability of linear fractional differential equations with constant coefficients. *Mediterr. J. Math.* **2017**, *60*, 1–25.
33. Liu, K.; Fečkan, M.; O'Regan, D.; Wang, J. Hyers–Ulam stability and existence of solutions for differential equations with Caputo–Fabrizio fractional derivative. *Mathematics* **2019**, *7*, 333. [CrossRef]
34. Liu, K.; Wang, J.; Zhou, Y.; O'Regan, D. Hyers–Ulam stability and existence of solutions for fractional differential equations with Mittag–Leffler kernel. *Chaos. Solitons Fractals* **2020**, *132*, 1–8. [CrossRef]
35. Fu, Y.; Yao, H. The solution of nonlinear fourth-order differential equation with integral boundary conditions. *J. Funct. Spaces* **2014**, *2014*, 8. [CrossRef]
36. Malek, A.; Beidokhti, R.S. Numerical solution for high order differential equations using a hybrid neural net-work-optimization method. *Appl. Math. Comput.* **2006**, *183*, 260–271. [CrossRef]
37. Craig, R.R.; Kurdila, A.J. *Fundamentals of Structural Dynamics*; John Wiley & Sons: Hoboken, NJ, USA, 2006.
38. Krajcinovic, D. Sandwich beam analysis. *J. Appl. Mech.* **1972**, *39*, 773–778. [CrossRef]
39. Aftabizadeh, A.R. Existence and uniqueness theorems for fourth-order boundary value problems. *J. Math. Anal. Appl.* **1986**, *116*, 415–426. [CrossRef]
40. Peno, M.A.D.; Manasevich, R.F. Existence for fourth-order boundary value problem under a two parameter nonresonance condition. *Proc. Am. Math. Soc.* **1991**, *112*, 81–86. [CrossRef]
41. Usmani, A. A uniqueness theorem for boundary value problem. *Proc. Am. Math. Soc.* **1979**, *77*, 327–335. [CrossRef]
42. Yao, Q. Existence of solutions and positive solutions to a fourth-order two-point BVP with second derivative. *J. Zhejiang Univ. SCI* **2004**, *5*, 353–357. [CrossRef]
43. Chen, H.L. Antiperiodic wavelets. *J. Comput. Math.* **1996**, *14*, 32–39.
44. Shao, J. Anti-periodic solutions for shunting inhibitory cellular neural networks with timevarying delays. *Phys. Lett. A* **2008**, *372*, 5011–5016. [CrossRef]
45. Shah, K.; Tunç, C. Existence theory and stability analysis to a system of boundary value problem *J. Taibah Univ. Sci.* **2017**, *11*, 1330–1342. [CrossRef]
46. Granas, A.; Dugundji, J. *Fixed Point Theory*; Springer: New York, NY, USA, 2005.
47. Rus, I.A. Ulam stabilities of ordinary differential equations in a Banach space. *Carpathian J. Math.* **2010**, *26*, 103–107.

Article

Stability Analysis and Optimal Control of a Fractional Order Synthetic Drugs Transmission Model

Meghadri Das [1], Guruprasad Samanta [1] and Manuel De la Sen [2,*]

[1] Department of Mathematics, Indian Institute of Engineering Science and Technology, Shibpur, Howrah 711103, India; dasmeghadri@gmail.com (M.D.); g_p_samanta@yahoo.co.uk or gpsamanta@math.iiests.ac.in (G.S.)
[2] Institute of Research and Development of Processes, University of the Basque Country, 48940 Leioa, Spain
* Correspondence: manuel.delasen@ehu.eus

Abstract: In this work, a fractional-order synthetic drugs transmission model with psychological addicts has been proposed along with psychological treatment. The effects of synthetic drugs are deadly and sometimes even violent. We have studied the local and global stability of the model with different criterion. The existence and uniqueness criterion along with positivity and boundedness of the solutions have also been established. The local and global stabilities are decided by the basic reproduction number R_0. We have also analyzed the sensitivity of parameters. An optimal control problem has been formulated by controlling psychological addiction and analyzed by the help of Pontryagin maximum principle. These results are verified by numerical simulations.

Keywords: Caputo fractional differential equation; synthetic drugs; stability; optimal control

Citation: Das, M.; Samanta, G.P.; De la Sen, M. Stability Analysis and Optimal Control of a Fractional Order Synthetic Drugs Transmission Model. *Mathematics* **2021**, *9*, 703. https://doi.org/10.3390/math9070703

Academic Editor: Ioannis Dassios

Received: 20 February 2021
Accepted: 19 March 2021
Published: 24 March 2021

Publisher's Note: MDPI stays neutral with regard to jurisdictional claims in published maps and institutional affiliations.

Copyright: © 2021 by the authors. Licensee MDPI, Basel, Switzerland. This article is an open access article distributed under the terms and conditions of the Creative Commons Attribution (CC BY) license (https://creativecommons.org/licenses/by/4.0/).

1. Introduction

Synthetic drugs, also referred to as designer or club drugs, are chemically created in a lab to mimic another group of drugs such as marijuana, cocaine, or morphine. There are more than 200 to 300 identified synthetic drug compounds and many of them are cocaine, methamphetamine, and marijuana compounds [1,2]. The effects of synthetic drugs are anxiety, aggressive behavior, paranoia, seizures, loss of consciousness, nausea, vomiting, and even coma or death [3]. Synthetic drugs are powerful, and when mixed with unknown chemical compounds are extremely dangerous and can cause overdose very quickly. If an overdose has occurred, immediate medical care is required. More lately, new designer drugs have emerged with vigorous addictive potentials such as synthetic cathinones ("Bath Salts"), also labeled as Bliss, Vanilla Sky, and Ivory Wave. These synthetic drugs stimulate the central nervous system by inhibiting the retake of norepinephrine and dopamine, leading to serious adverse effects on the Central Nervous System (CNS) or even death [1]. Moreover, many infectious diseases such as hepatitis and AIDS can easily infect drug users due to the rampant use of shared needles [4,5]. Drugs like amphetamine are mostly used in specific regions like Goa and Ahmedabad in India. A recent study shows that drug use in India continues to grow rapidly, and more disturbingly, heroin has replaced the natural opioids (opium and poppy husk). An epidemiological study from Punjab has been revealed that the use of other synthetic drugs and cocaine has also increased significantly [6]. Most synthetic drugs are manufactured in an illegal laboratory, and there are no safety measures used in the manufacture of synthetic drugs. When an addicted person attempts to quit, he/she may experience very uncomfortable withdrawal symptoms which can lower their resolve to maintain abstinence and otherwise complicate early recovery. Professional detoxification programs are needed for synthetic drug addicts to withdraw safely from synthetic drugs. Behavioral therapies and counseling are effective tools for changing negative behavior and thought patterns that may help for improving the mental help they need.

Ma et al. [7] have developed different forms of heroin epidemic models to study the transmission of heroin epidemics. Sharomi and Gumel [8] have formulated different smoking models for giving up smoking. Similarly, mathematical modeling can be also used to describe the spread of synthetic drugs. Nyabadza et al. [9] have studied the methamphetamine transmission model in South Africa. Liu et al. [10] have formulated a synthetic drug transmission model with treatment and studied global stability and backward bifurcation of the model. Saha and Samanta [11] have also studied the stability of a synthetic drug transmission model with optimal control. There are many works that have been performed on fractional-order epidemiological systems because a fractional-order system has memory effect [12]. Fractional calculus is often utilized for the generalization of their order, where fractional order is replaced with integer order [13]. During a systematic study, it has been noted that the integer order model may be a special case of fractional order model wherever the solution of fractional order system must converge to the solution of integer order system as the order approaches one [14]. There are so many fields where fractional order systems are more suitable than integer order systems. Phenomena that are connected with memory and affected by hereditary cannot be expressed by integer order system [15]. It is observed that the data collected from real-life phenomena fit better with the fractional-order system. Diethelm [16] has compared the numerical solutions of fractional-order system and integer order system, and concluded that the fractional order system gives more relevant interpretation than integer order system. There are many systems [17–22] that have been studied recently in fractional order framework. In epidemiology, the Ebola virus model has been studied in Caputo differential equation system in 2015 [23]. Agarwal [24] first studied optimal control problem in fractional order system in 2004. In 2018, Kheiri and Jafari [25] have also worked on fractional order optimal control for HIV/AIDS.

Motivation and Brief Overview

There are some relevant advantages of Caputo fractional differentiations and differential equations.

- Fractional derivatives provide an excellent instrument for the description of memory and hereditary properties of various systems and processes. Fractional-order differential equations accumulate the entire information of the function in weighted form.
- In fractional-order modeling, we have an additional parameter (order of the derivative) which is useful for numerical simulations. In that regard, there are some systems which are stable (unstable) for some parameter values near their equilibrium points can be destabilized (stabilized) by controlling the order of the derivative.
- The Caputo derivative is very useful when dealing with real-world problem because it allows traditional initial and boundary conditions to be included in the formulation of the problem, and in addition the derivative of a constant is zero which does not happen in the Riemann–Liouville fractional derivative.

Motivated by the aforementioned works and the advantages of Caputo fractional-order differential equations, a model of fractional synthetic drug transmission with psychological drug addicts has been formulated in this work using Caputo fractional-order differential equations (Section 2). In this work, we have analyzed the drug transmission model in the fractional-order framework, and the effect of the psychological treatment of the awareness campaign has also been studied by formulating fractional-order optimal control problem.

This work is presented in two different parts. In the first part (Section 3), we first carried out a basic analysis, such as existence, oneness, non-negativity, and the limit of solutions of the proposed system of equations. Dynamical behaviors of the different equilibrium points are established in the same section. Though our main aim is to study the system in fractional-order framework, a fractional-order control problem has also framed in Section 4 to study the control effect of treatment on psychological addict class which may enhance our research.

In the beginning of our work, we recall some basic definitions and theories of fractional-order differential equations (Section 3) followed by calculating equilibrium points (Section 3.1). Next, we also discuss whether the solution of the proposed system is unique (Section 3.2). We have also discussed the boundedness and feasible condition of the solutions of the system (Section 3.3). Transfer dynamics has also been discussed with the help of the reproduction number in the next section (Section 3.5). We also study sensitivity analysis (Section 3.4) of the model with local and global stability of equilibrium points (both disease-free and endemic) systematically (Sections 3.6). Then, we present our system as an optimal control problem with psychological treatment as control variable and derived optimal conditions (Section 4). Finally, numerical simulations are performed (Section 5), followed by some conclusions of the whole work (Section 6).

2. Model Formulation

We have formulated a fractional-order synthetic drugs transmission model with psychological addicts by taking susceptible (S), psychological addicts (P_1), physiological addicts (P_2), and treatment class as four compartments.

$$\begin{aligned}
{}_{t_0}^{C}D_t^{\varepsilon}x(t) &= A^{\varepsilon} - \delta^{\varepsilon}x - \beta_1{}^{\varepsilon}xy - \beta_2{}^{\varepsilon}xz, x(t_0) = x_0 > 0, \\
{}_{t_0}^{C}D_t^{\varepsilon}y(t) &= \beta_1{}^{\varepsilon}xy + \beta_2{}^{\varepsilon}xz - (k^{\varepsilon} + \delta^{\varepsilon} + \phi^{\varepsilon})y, y(t_0) = y_0 > 0, \\
{}_{t_0}^{C}D_t^{\varepsilon}z(t) &= k^{\varepsilon}y + \gamma^{\varepsilon}r - \xi^{\varepsilon}z - \delta^{\varepsilon}z, z(t_0) = z_0 > 0, \\
{}_{t_0}^{C}D_t^{\varepsilon}r(t) &= \phi^{\varepsilon}y + \xi^{\varepsilon}z - \gamma^{\varepsilon}r - \delta^{\varepsilon}r, r(t_0) = r_0 > 0,
\end{aligned} \quad (1)$$

where $0 < \varepsilon < 1$, is the order of derivative and ${}_{t_0}^{C}D_t^{\varepsilon}$ is notation due to Caputo fractional derivative, and $t_0 = 0$ is the initial time. Here, $x(t)$, $y(t)$, $z(t)$, and $r(t)$ represent the respective size of susceptible population, psychologically addicted population, physiological addicted population, and the class of addicts in treatment, respectively. From a survey on synthetic drugs, it is evident that a large number of the young population are in the susceptible class, which is roughly equivalent to the recruitment rate A of susceptible class and which is assumed to be constant [26]. After contact with an addict, the susceptible addict will first pass into the class of psychological addict, while after taking many drugs, the psychological addict will become the physiological addict. Broadly speaking, a susceptible addict is more likely to initiate drug abuse when he/she has contact with a physiological addict compared to a psychological addict. We denote the corresponding contact rates are $\beta_1{}^{\varepsilon}$ and $\beta_2{}^{\varepsilon}$. Once psychological and physiological addicts accept treatment and rehabilitation, they will enter into treatment compartment. The treatment rates are denoted by ϕ^{ε} and ξ^{ε}, respectively. In addition, some drug users in treatment may escape and reenter physiologically addicted compartment with rate γ^{ε}. The parameters k^{ε} and δ^{ε} are the escalation rate from psychological addicts to physiological addicts and natural death rate, respectively. All parameters $A^{\varepsilon}, \gamma^{\varepsilon}, \delta^{\varepsilon}, \beta_1{}^{\varepsilon}, \beta_2{}^{\varepsilon}, \phi^{\varepsilon}, \xi^{\varepsilon}, k^{\varepsilon}$ are assumed to be positive constants (briefly described in Table 1). Schematic diagram of system (3) is mentioned in Figure 1.

It is observed that the time dimension of system (1) is correct because both sides of the equations of system (1) have dimension $(time)^{-\varepsilon}$ [27]. Next, let us consider $t_0 = 0$ and omit the superscript ε to all parameters and redefine system (1) as

$$^C_0D^\varepsilon_t x(t) = A - \delta x - \beta_1 xy - \beta_2 xz, x(0) = x_0 > 0,$$

$$^C_0D^\varepsilon_t y(t) = \beta_1 xy + \beta_2 xz - (k + \delta + \phi)y, y(0) = y_0 > 0,$$

$$^C_0D^\varepsilon_t z(t) = ky + \gamma r - \xi z - \delta z, z(0) = z_0 > 0,$$

$$^C_0D^\varepsilon_t r(t) = \phi y + \xi z - \gamma r - \delta r, r(0) = r_0 > 0,$$

(2)

We have considered $N(t)$ to be the total human population and so $N(t) = x(t) + y(t) + z(t) + r(t)$. In the first phase, a susceptible individual becomes a psychological addict after they come in contact with a drug addict. However, after becomes accustomed to the persistent presence and influence of the drug, the individual is likely to become a physiological addict. A psychological or physiological addict will enter into the treatment compartment at the time of taking treatment and rehabilitation. It is shown in Section 3.3 that the number of total human population is bounded above and let $N = \inf_{t \in [0,\infty)} \{M \in R_+ : N(t) \leq M\}$. Therefore, we can assume that the total population $N(t)$ is constant (N) for large time scale ($t \to \infty$). Let us scale the state variables with respect to the total population N:

$$S(t) = \frac{x(t)}{N}, P_1(t) = \frac{y(t)}{N}, P_2(t) = \frac{z(t)}{N}, R(t) = \frac{r(t)}{N}, \Lambda = \frac{A}{N}.$$

Therefore, system (2) becomes

$$^C_0D^\varepsilon_t S(t) = \Lambda - \delta S - \beta_1 SP_1 - \beta_2 SP_2, S(0) = S_0 > 0,$$

$$^C_0D^\varepsilon_t P_1(t) = \beta_1 SP_1 + \beta_2 SP_2 - (k + \delta + \phi)P_1, P_1(0) = P_{1,0} > 0,$$

$$^C_0D^\varepsilon_t P_2(t) = kP_1 + \gamma R - \xi P_2 - \delta P_2, P_2(0) = P_{2,0} > 0,$$

$$^C_0D^\varepsilon_t R(t) = \phi P_1 + \xi P_2 - \gamma R - \delta R, R(0) = R_0 > 0.$$

(3)

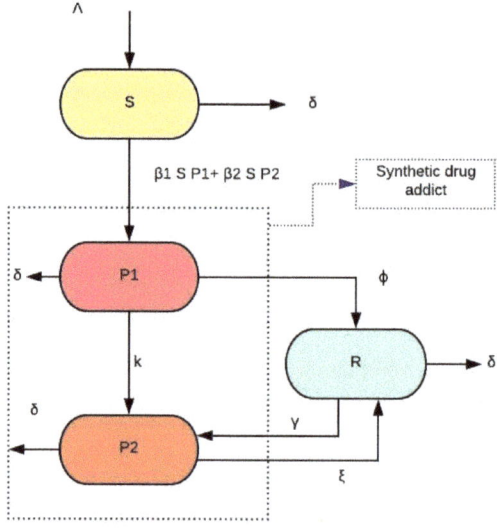

Figure 1. Schematic diagram of system (3).

Table 1. Parameters of system (3).

Parameters	Description
Λ	Rate of recruitment of S
β_1	Contact rates of psychological addicts
β_2	Contact rates of physiological addicts
δ	Natural death rate of human population
k	Proportion of psychological addicts who become physiological drug addicts by taking drugs in a regular basis, i.e., escalation rate from psychological to physiological addicts.
ϕ, ζ	Per capita pharmaceutical treatment rates for psychological and physiological addicts respectively.
γ	Rate at which some drug users in treatment may escape and re-enter the physiological addict state, i.e., relapse rate.

3. Preliminaries

Definition 1 ([28]). *The Caputo fractional derivative with order $\varepsilon > 0$ for a function $g \in C^n([t_0, \infty+), \mathbb{R})$ is denoted and defined as*

$$_{t_0}^{C}D_t^{\varepsilon} g(t) = \begin{cases} \dfrac{1}{\Gamma(n-\varepsilon)} \displaystyle\int_{t_0}^{t} \dfrac{g^{(n)}(s)}{(t-s)^{\varepsilon-n+1}} ds, \varepsilon \in (n-1, n), n \in \mathbb{N} \\ \dfrac{d^n}{dt^n} g(t), \varepsilon = n. \end{cases}$$

where $\Gamma(\cdot)$ is the Gamma function, $t \geq t_0$ and n is a natural number. In particular, for $\varepsilon \in (0,1)$:

$$_{t_0}^{C}D_t^{\varepsilon} g(t) = \frac{1}{\Gamma(1-\varepsilon)} \int_{t_0}^{t} \frac{g'(s)}{(t-s)^{\varepsilon}} ds$$

Lemma 1. *(Generalized Mean Value Theorem) [29] Let $0 < \varepsilon \leq 1$, $\psi(t) \in C[a,b]$ and if $_{0}^{C}D_t^{\varepsilon}\psi(t)$ is continuous in $(a,b]$, then*

$$\psi(x) = \psi(a) + \frac{1}{\Gamma(\varepsilon)} (x-a)^{\varepsilon} \cdot {}_{0}^{C}D_t^{\varepsilon}\psi(\zeta)$$

where $0 \leq \zeta \leq x, \forall x \in (a,b]$.

Remark 1. *If $_{0}^{C}D_t^{\varepsilon}\psi(t) \geq 0 (_{0}^{C}D_t^{\varepsilon}\psi(t) \leq 0), t \in (a,b)$, then $\psi(t)$ is a non-decreasing (non-increasing) function for $t \in [a,b]$.*

Definition 2 ([13]). *One-parametric and two-parametric Mittag–Leffler functions are described as follows:*

$$E_{\varepsilon}(w) = \sum_{k=0}^{\infty} \frac{w^k}{\Gamma(\varepsilon k + 1)} \text{ and } E_{\varepsilon_1, \varepsilon_2}(w) = \sum_{k=0}^{\infty} \frac{w^k}{\Gamma(\varepsilon_1 k + \varepsilon_2)}, \text{ where } \varepsilon, \varepsilon_1, \varepsilon_2 \in \mathbb{R}_+.$$

Theorem 1 ([30]). *Let $\varepsilon > 0, n - 1 < \varepsilon < n, n \in \mathbb{N}$. Assume that $g(t)$ is continuously differentiable functions up to order $(n-1)$ on $[t_0, \infty)$ and n^{th} derivative of $g(t)$ exists with exponential order. If ${}^C_{t_0}D_t^\varepsilon g(t)$ is piecewise continuous on $[t_0, \infty)$, then*

$$\mathscr{L}\left\{{}^C_{t_0}D_t^\varepsilon g(t)\right\} = s^\alpha F(s) - \sum_{j=0}^{n-1} s^{\alpha-j-1} g^j(t_0),$$

where $F(s) = \mathscr{L}\{g(t)\}$ denotes the Laplace transform of $g(t)$.

Theorem 2 ([31]). *Let $\mathbb{C}$ be the complex plane. For any $\varepsilon_1, \varepsilon_2 \in \mathbb{R}_+$ and $M \in \mathbb{C}$, then*

$$\mathscr{L}\left\{t^{\varepsilon_2-1} E_{\varepsilon_1,\varepsilon_2}(Mt^{\varepsilon_1})\right\} = \frac{s^{\varepsilon_1-\varepsilon_2}}{(s^{\varepsilon_1} - M)},$$

for $\mathscr{R}(s) > \|M\|^{\frac{1}{\varepsilon_1}}$, where $\mathscr{R}(s)$ represents the real part of the complex number s, and $E_{\varepsilon_1,\varepsilon_2}$ is the Mittag–Leffler function.

Theorem 3 ([28]). *Consider the following fractional-order system:*

$${}^C_{t_0}D_t^\varepsilon X(t) = \Psi(X), X_{t_0} = (x^1_{t_0}, x^2_{t_0}, ..., x^n_{t_0}), x^i_{t_0} > 0, i = 1, 2, .., n$$

with $0 < \varepsilon < 1$, $X(t) = (x^1(t), x^2(t), ..., x^n(t))$ and $\Psi(X) : [t_0, \infty) \to \mathbb{R}^{n \times n}$. The equilibrium points of this system are evaluated by solving the following system of equations: $\Psi(X) = 0$. These equilibrium points are locally asymptotically stable iff each eigenvalue λ_i of the Jacobian matrix $J(X) = \frac{\partial(\Psi_1, \Psi_2, ..., \Psi_n)}{\partial(x^1, x^2, ..., x^n)}$ calculated at the equilibrium points satisfy $|\arg(\lambda_i)| > \frac{\varepsilon\pi}{2}$.

3.1. Equilibria of System (3)

The equilibria of system (3) can be obtained by solving the system:

$$\Lambda - \delta S^* - \beta_1 S^* P_1^* - \beta_2 S^* P_2^* = 0$$

$$\beta_1 S^* P_1^* + \beta_2 S^* P_2^* - (k + \delta + \phi) P_1^* = 0 \qquad (4)$$

$$k P_1^* + \gamma R^* - \xi P_2^* - \delta P_2^* = 0$$

$$\phi P_1^* + \xi P_2^* - \gamma R^* - \delta R^* = 0$$

System (3) has two types of equilibrium points:
1. Drug-free equilibrium $E_0(\frac{\Lambda}{\delta}, 0, 0, 0)$
2. Drug-addiction equilibrium $E_1(S^*, P_1^*, P_2^*, R^*)$, where

$$S^* = \frac{(k+\delta+\phi) P_1^*}{\beta_1 P_1^* + \beta_2 P_2^*}$$

$$P_1^* = \frac{\Lambda \beta_1 \delta(\gamma+\delta+\xi) + \Lambda \beta_2 (k\delta + k\gamma + \phi\gamma) - \delta^2(k+\delta+\phi)(\gamma+\delta+\xi)}{(k+\delta+\phi)[\beta_1(\gamma+\delta+\xi) + \beta_2(k\delta + k\gamma + \phi\gamma)]} \qquad (5)$$

$$P_2^* = \frac{(k\delta + k\gamma + \phi\gamma) P_1^*}{\delta(\gamma+\delta+\xi)}$$

$$R^* = \frac{\xi P_2^* + \phi P_1^*}{\delta + \gamma}.$$

For drug-addiction equilibrium E_1 to exist in feasible region $\mathbb{R}^4_+$, it is necessary and sufficient that $\Lambda\beta_1\delta(\gamma+\delta+\xi) + \Lambda\beta_2(k\delta+k\gamma+\phi\gamma) \geq \delta^2(k+\delta+\phi)(\gamma+\delta+\xi)$

3.2. Existence and Uniqueness

Lemma 2 ([32]). *Consider the system:*

$$^C_{t_0}D^\varepsilon_t x(t) = g(t,x), t_0 > 0 \quad (6)$$

with initial condition $x(t_0) = x_{t_0}$, where $\varepsilon \in (0,1]$, $g : [t_0, \infty) \times \Omega \to \mathbb{R}^n, \Omega \subseteq \mathbb{R}^n$, if local Lipschitz condition is satisfied by $g(t,x)$ with respect to x, then there exists a solution of (6) on $[t_0, \infty) \times \Omega$ which is unique.

To study the existence and uniqueness of system (3), let us consider the region $\Omega \times [t_0, \gamma]$, where $\Omega = \{(S, P_1, P_2, R) \in \mathbb{R}^4 : \max(|S|, |P_1|, |P_2|, |R|) \leq M\}$ and $\gamma < +\infty$. Denote $X = (S, P_1, P_2, R)$ and $\overline{X} = (\bar{S}, \bar{P}_1, \bar{P}_2, \bar{R})$. Consider a mapping $L(X) = (L_1(X), L_2(X), L_3(X), L_4(X))$, where

$$L_1(X) = \Lambda - \delta S - \beta_1 S P_1 - \beta_2 S P_2$$

$$L_2(X) = \beta_1 S P_1 + \beta_2 S P_2 - (k+\delta+\phi)P_1$$

$$L_3(X) = kP_1 + \gamma R - \xi P_2 - \delta P_2$$

$$L_4(X) = \phi P_1 + \xi P_2 - \gamma R - \delta R$$

For any $X, \overline{X} \in \Omega$:

$$\|L(X) - L(\overline{X})\|$$
$$= |L_1(X) - L_1(\overline{X})| + |L_2(X) - L_2(\overline{X})| + |L_3(X) - L_3(\overline{X})| + |L_4(X) - L_4(\overline{X})|$$
$$= |\Lambda - \delta S - \beta_1 S P_1 - \beta_2 S P_2 - \Lambda + \delta \bar{S} + \beta_1 \bar{S} \bar{P}_1 + \beta_2 \bar{S} \bar{P}_2|$$
$$+ |\beta_1 S P_1 + \beta_2 S P_2 - (k+\delta+\phi)P_1 - \beta_1 \bar{S} \bar{P}_1 - \beta_2 \bar{S} \bar{P}_2 + (k+\delta+\phi)\bar{P}_1|$$
$$+ |kP_1 + \gamma R - \xi P_2 - \delta P_2 - k\bar{P}_1 - \gamma \bar{R} + \xi \bar{P}_2 + \delta \bar{P}_2|$$
$$+ |\phi P_1 + \xi P_2 - \gamma R - \delta R - \phi \bar{P}_1 - \xi \bar{P}_2 + \gamma \bar{R} + \delta \bar{R}|$$
$$\leq \delta|S - \bar{S}| + 2\beta_1|SP_1 - \bar{S}\bar{P}_1| + 2\beta_2|SP_2 - \bar{S}\bar{P}_2|$$
$$+ (\delta + 2\phi + 2k)|P_1 - \bar{P}_1| + (\delta + 2\xi)|P_2 - \bar{P}_2| + (2\gamma + \delta)|R - \bar{R}|$$
$$\leq (\delta + 2\beta_1 M + 2\beta_2 M)|S - \bar{S}| + (2\beta_1 M + 2k + 2\phi + \delta)|P_1 - \bar{P}_1|$$
$$+ (2\beta_2 M + 2\xi + \delta)|P_2 - \bar{P}_2| + (2\gamma + \delta)|R - \bar{R}|$$
$$\leq H_1|S - \bar{S}| + H_2|P_1 - \bar{P}_1| + H_3|P_2 - \bar{P}_2| + H_4|R - \bar{R}|$$
$$\leq H\|X - \overline{X}\|, \text{ where } H = \max\{H_1, H_2, H_3, H_4\},$$

and
$$H_1 = (\delta + 2\beta_1 M + 2\beta_2 M)$$
$$H_2 = (2\beta_1 M + 2k + 2\phi + \delta)$$
$$H_3 = (2\beta_2 M + 2\xi + \delta)$$
$$H_4 = (2\gamma + \delta)$$

Therefore, $L(X)$ satisfies Lipschitz's condition with respect to X. Therefore, Lemma 2 confirms that there exists a unique solution $X(t)$ of system (3) with initial condition $X(0) = (S_0, P_{1,0}, P_{2,0}, R_0)$. The following theorem is the consequence of this result.

Theorem 4. *There exists a unique solution $X(t) \in \Omega$ of system (3) for all $t \geq 0$ with initial condition $X(0) = (S_0, P_{1,0}, P_{2,0}, R_0) \in \Omega$.*

3.3. Non-Negativity and Boundedness

In this section, we have established the criterion for feasibility of the solution of system (3). Suppose $\mathbb{R}_+$ stands for the set of all non-negative real numbers and $\Gamma_+ = \left\{ (S, P_1, P_2, R) \in \mathbb{R}_+^4 \right\}$ represents the first quadrant.

Theorem 5. (Non-negativity): *The solutions $X(t) = (S, P_1, P_2, R)$ of system (3) remain in Γ_+ if $X(0) = (S_0, P_{1,0}, P_{2,0}, R_0) \in \Gamma_+$.*

Proof.
$$_{t_0}^{C}D_t^\varepsilon S(t)\big|_{S(t)=0} = \Lambda > 0 \tag{7}$$
$$_{0}^{C}D_t^\varepsilon P_1(t)\big|_{P_1(t)=0} = \beta S P_2 \tag{8}$$
$$_{0}^{C}D_t^\varepsilon P_2(t)\big|_{P_2(t)=0} = k P_1 + \gamma R \tag{9}$$
$$_{0}^{C}D_t^\varepsilon R(t)\big|_{R(t)=0} = \xi P_2 + \phi P_1 \tag{10}$$

From (7), we have
$$_{t_0}^{C}D_t^\varepsilon S(t)\big|_{S(t)=0} = \Lambda > 0.$$

From Lemma 1, we can say $S(t)$ is increasing in a neighborhood of time t where $S(t) = 0$ and $S(t)$ cannot cross the axis $S(t) = 0$. Therefore, $S(t) > 0$ for all $t \geq 0$. Now, we claim that the solution $P_1(t)$ starts from Γ_+ and remains non-negative. If not, then there exists τ_1 such that $P_1(t)$ crosses $P_1(t) = 0$ axis at $t = \tau_1$ for the first time and the following conditions hold:
$$\begin{cases} P_1(t) > 0, \text{ for } 0 \leq t < \tau_1, \\ P_1(\tau_1) = 0, \\ P_1(\tau_1^+) < 0. \end{cases}$$

From (8), we have $_{0}^{C}D_t^\varepsilon P_1(t)\big|_{P_1(\tau_1)=0} = \beta_2 S(\tau_1) P_2(\tau_1)$. Now, we have two cases

Case 1: If $P_2(\tau_1) \geq 0$ then by the Remark 1 of Lemma 1, we can say that $P_1(t)$ is non-decreasing in a neighborhood of $t = \tau_1$ and which concludes $P_1(\tau_1^+) = 0$. Therefore, we have arrived at a contradiction.

Case 2: If $P_2(\tau_1) < 0$, then there exists a τ_2 such that $0 < \tau_2 < \tau_1$ with
$$\begin{cases} P_2(t) > 0, \text{ for } 0 \leq t < \tau_2, \\ P_2(\tau_2) = 0, \\ P_2(\tau_2^+) < 0. \end{cases}$$

From (9), we have

$$\,^C_0D^\varepsilon_t P_2(t)\big|_{P_2(\tau_2)=0} = kP_1(\tau_2) + \gamma R(\tau_2)$$

Now we have two sub-cases.

Sub-case 1: If $kP_1(\tau_2) + \gamma R(\tau_2) \geq 0$, then $P_2(\tau_2^+) \not< 0$ and it contradicts our assumption.

Sub-case 2: If $kP_1(\tau_2) + \gamma R(\tau_2) < 0$, then $P_1(\tau_2) > 0$ as $0 < \tau_2 < \tau_1$ and $R(\tau_2)$ must be negative. In this case, we can find a τ_3 such that $0 < \tau_3 < \tau_2 < \tau_1$ with

$$\begin{cases} R(t) > 0, \text{ for } 0 \leq t < \tau_3, \\ R(\tau_3) = 0, \\ R(\tau_3^+) < 0. \end{cases}$$

From (10), we have

$$\,^C_0D^\varepsilon_t R(t)\big|_{R(\tau_3)=0} = \xi P_2(\tau_3) + \phi P_1(\tau_3) > 0$$

which contradicts our assumption that $R(\tau_3^+) < 0$. Therefore, we have $P_1(t) \geq 0$, $\forall t \in [0, \infty)$.

Again from (9), we have $\,^C_0D^\varepsilon_t P_2(t)\big|_{P_2(t)=0} = kP_1 + \gamma R$. If $R(t) > 0$ then $P_2(t)$ is non-decreasing (remark of Lemma 1) and $P_2(t) > 0, t \in [0, \infty)$. If possible, let $R(t)$ crosses $R(t) = 0$ axis for the first time at $t = t_1$. Then, we have

$$\begin{cases} R(t) > 0, \text{ for } 0 \leq t < t_1, \\ R(t_1) = 0, \\ R(t_1^+) < 0. \end{cases}$$

From (10), we have

$$\,^C_0D^\varepsilon_t R(t)\big|_{R(t_1)=0} = \xi P_2(t_1) + \phi P_1(t_1) > 0$$

and this opposes our assumption $R(t_1^+) < 0$. Hence $P_2(t) > 0, t \in [0, \infty)$. Again from (10), it is evident that $\,^C_0D^\varepsilon_t R(t)\big|_{R(t)=0} = \xi P_2 + \phi P_1 > 0$ and assures that $R(t) > 0$ and also $P_2(t) > 0$, $t \in [0, \infty)$.

Thus, all solutions of system (3) (and thus system (2)) starting in Γ_+ are confined in the region Γ_+. □

Theorem 6. (Boundedness): Solutions $X(t) = (x, y, z, r)$ of system (2) are uniformly bounded.

Proof. From the first equation of (2), it is noted that

$$\,^C_0D^\varepsilon_t x(t) \leq A - \delta x$$

Taking Laplace transforms on both sides, we have

$$s^\varepsilon \mathscr{L}\{x(t)\} - s^{\varepsilon-1}x(0) + \delta \mathscr{L}\{x(t)\} \leq \frac{A}{s}, \text{ where } \mathscr{L}\{\cdot\} \text{ is the Laplace transform operator}$$

$$\Rightarrow \mathscr{L}\{x(t)\} \leq A \frac{s^{\varepsilon-(1+\varepsilon)}}{s^\varepsilon + \delta} + x(0)\frac{s^{\varepsilon-1}}{s^\varepsilon + \delta}$$

Taking inverse Laplace transforms (using Theorem 2),

$$x(t) \leq x(0)E_{\varepsilon,1}(-\delta t^\varepsilon) + At^\varepsilon E_{\varepsilon,\varepsilon+1}(-\delta t^\varepsilon) \tag{11}$$

$$\therefore x(t) \leq M_1[E_{\varepsilon,1}(-\delta t^\varepsilon) + \delta t^\varepsilon E_{\varepsilon,\varepsilon+1}(-\delta t^\varepsilon)] = \frac{M_1}{\Gamma(1)} = M_1,$$

where $M_1 = \max\left\{\frac{A}{\delta}, x(0)\right\}$ and, as it is from the properties of Mittag–Leffler function [33],

$$E_{\alpha,\beta}(z) = zE_{\alpha,\alpha+\beta}(z) + \frac{1}{\Gamma(\beta)}$$

In this case
$$E_{\varepsilon,1}(-\delta t^\varepsilon) = (-\delta t^\varepsilon)E_{\varepsilon,\varepsilon+1}(-\delta t^\varepsilon) + \frac{1}{\Gamma(1)} \quad (12)$$

Let $N(t) = x(t) + y(t) + z(t) + r(t)$ represent the total population, then

$$\begin{aligned}{}_0^C D_t^\varepsilon N(t) &= {}_0^C D_t^\varepsilon x(t) + {}_0^C D_t^\varepsilon y(t) + {}_0^C D_t^\varepsilon z(t) + {}_0^C D_t^\varepsilon r(t) \\ &= A - \{\delta x(t) + \delta y(t) + \delta z(t) + \delta r(t)\} \\ &= A - \delta N(t).\end{aligned}$$

Therefore,
$${}_0^C D_t^\varepsilon N(t) + \delta N(t) = A$$

Applying Laplace transformation, we have (using Theorem 1):

$$s^\varepsilon F(s) - s^{\varepsilon-1}N(0) + \delta F(s) = \frac{A}{s}, \text{ where } F(s) = \mathscr{L}\{N(t)\}$$

$$\Rightarrow F(s) = A\frac{s^{-1}}{s^\varepsilon + \delta} + \frac{N(0)s^{\varepsilon-1}}{s^\varepsilon + \delta} = \frac{s^{\varepsilon-1}N(0)}{s^\varepsilon + \delta} + \frac{As^{\varepsilon-(1+\varepsilon)}}{s^\varepsilon + \delta}$$

Taking inverse Laplace transforms (using Theorem 2),

$$N(t) = N(0)E_{\varepsilon,1}(-\delta t^\varepsilon) + At^\varepsilon E_{\varepsilon,\varepsilon+1}(-\delta t^\varepsilon) \quad (13)$$

From (12) and (13), we get

$$N(t) \leq M_2[E_{\varepsilon,1}(-\delta t^\varepsilon) + \delta t^\varepsilon E_{\varepsilon,\varepsilon+1}(-\delta t^\varepsilon)] = \frac{M_2}{\Gamma(1)} = M_2,$$

where $M_2 = \max\left\{\frac{A}{\delta}, N(0)\right\}$

Thus, $x(t), N(t)$ are bounded and thus (using Theorem 5) the solutions $X(t) = (x(t), y(t), z(t), r(t))$ are bounded uniformly in $\{(x(t), y(t), z(t), r(t)) | x + y + z + r \leq M_2; x \leq M_1\}$ for $t \in [0, \infty)$. □

3.4. Reproduction Number and Sensitivity Analysis

The basic reproduction number is defined as the number of new addicted individuals produced by a single addicted individual during infectious period when contacted into susceptible compartment ($R_0 = 2$ means a person who has the synthetic drug addiction will transmit it to an average of 2 other people). Reproduction number R_0 of system (3) for $\varepsilon = 1$ can be calculated as the maximum eigenvalue of the next generation matrix FV^{-1} computed at the drug-free equilibrium [34]. Here,

$$F = \begin{bmatrix} \beta_1\frac{\Lambda}{\delta} & \beta_2\frac{\Lambda}{\delta} \\ 0 & 0 \end{bmatrix}; V = \begin{bmatrix} \delta + \phi + k & 0 \\ -k & \delta + \xi \end{bmatrix} \quad (14)$$

Thus, we get

$$R_0 = \frac{\Lambda[\beta_1(\xi+\delta)+k\beta_2]}{\delta(\xi+\delta)(\delta+\phi+k)} = \frac{\beta_1(\xi+\delta)\Lambda}{\delta(\xi+\delta)(\delta+\phi+k)} + \frac{k\beta_2\Lambda}{\delta(\xi+\delta)(\delta+\phi+k)} \quad (15)$$

The first part is due to the psychologically addicted people and the second part is due to the physiological addicted people.

The drug–addiction equilibrium $E_1(S^*, P_1^*, P_2^*, R^*)$ of system (3) can be rewritten as

$$S^* = \frac{(k+\delta+\phi)P_1^*}{\beta_1 P_1^* + \beta_2 P_2^*}$$

$$P_1^* = \frac{B_0(R_0-1) + B_1}{B_2}, \text{ where}$$

$$B_0 = [\delta^2(k+\delta+\phi)(\delta+\xi) + \frac{\gamma}{\delta+\xi}]$$

$$B_1 = \frac{\gamma}{\delta+\xi}[\Lambda\beta_2 k\xi + \Lambda\beta_2\phi(\delta+\xi)] \quad (16)$$

$$B_2 = (k+\delta+\phi)[\beta_1\delta(\gamma+\delta+\xi) + \beta_2(k\gamma+k\delta+\phi\gamma)]$$

$$P_2^* = \frac{(k\delta + k\gamma + \phi\gamma)P_1^*}{\delta(\gamma+\delta+\xi)}$$

$$R^* = \frac{\xi P_2^* + \phi P_1^*}{\delta+\gamma}$$

Therefore, if $R_0 > 1$, the drug–addict equilibrium E_1 exists.

The basic reproduction number (R_0) of system (3) relies upon seven parameters: per capita contact rates β_1, β_2, rate of recruitment Λ (of S), escalation rate from psychological to physiological addicts (k), per capita treatment rates for psychological and physiological addicts respectively (ϕ, ξ), and natural death rate (δ). Among these parameters, we cannot control the parameters Λ, k, and δ. Therefore, the basic reproduction number (R_0) mainly depends on $\xi, \phi, \beta_1, \beta_2$ and the value of $R_0 = 0.0266$ according to Table 2. To examine the sensitivity of R_0 to any parameter (say, θ), normalized forward sensitivity index with respect to each parameter has been computed as [11,34]

$$\chi_\theta = \frac{\partial R_0}{\partial \theta}\frac{\theta}{R_0}$$

The sensitivity index may depend on some system parameters but also can be constant or independent of some parameters. These values are very important to estimate the sensitivity of parameters, which should be done cautiously, as a small perturbation in a parameter causes relevant quantitative changes. Merely, the estimation of a parameter with a lower sensitivity index does not demand caution, because a small perturbation in that parameter causes small changes. In this context, we have examined the sensitivity of R_0 to the parameters β_1, β_2, ϕ, and ξ, normalized forward sensitivity index with respect to Table 3.

$$\frac{\partial R_0}{\partial \phi} = -\frac{\Lambda[\beta_1(\xi+\delta)+k\beta_2]}{\delta(\delta+\xi)(k+\delta+\phi)^2}$$

$$\chi_\phi = \frac{\phi}{R_0}\frac{\partial R_0}{\partial \phi} = -\frac{\phi}{k+\delta+\phi}$$

$$\frac{\partial R_0}{\partial \zeta} = -\frac{\Lambda k \beta_2}{\delta(\delta+\zeta)^2(k+\delta+\phi)}$$

$$\chi_\zeta = \frac{\zeta}{R_0}\frac{\partial R_0}{\partial \zeta} = -\frac{k\beta_2\zeta}{(\delta+\zeta)[\beta_1(\zeta+\delta)+k\beta_2]}$$

$$\frac{\partial R_0}{\partial \beta_1} = \frac{\Lambda}{\delta(k+\delta+\phi)}$$

$$\chi_{\beta_1} = \frac{\beta_1}{R_0}\frac{\partial R_0}{\partial \beta_1} = \frac{\beta_1(\delta+\zeta)}{[\beta_1(\zeta+\delta)+k\beta_2]}$$

$$\frac{\partial R_0}{\partial \beta_2} = \frac{\Lambda k}{\delta(k+\delta+\phi)((\delta+\zeta))}$$

$$\chi_{\beta_2} = \frac{\beta_2}{R_0}\frac{\partial R_0}{\partial \beta_2} = \frac{k\beta_2}{[\beta_1(\zeta+\delta)+k\beta_2]}$$

If $\beta_1 = b\beta$; $\beta_2 = \beta$, where b is a nonzero real number, then

$$\frac{\partial R_0}{\partial \beta} = \frac{\Lambda[b(\zeta+\delta)+k]}{\delta(\zeta+\delta)(\delta+\phi+k)}$$

$$\chi_\beta = \frac{\beta}{R_0}\frac{\partial R_0}{\partial \beta} = \frac{\beta}{\frac{\beta\Lambda[b(\zeta+\delta)+k]}{\delta(\zeta+\delta)(\delta+\phi+k)}} \frac{\Lambda[b(\zeta+\delta)+k]}{\delta(\zeta+\delta)(\delta+\phi+k)} = 1$$

Here, $\chi_{\beta_1}, \chi_{\beta_2}, \chi_\zeta, \chi_\phi$ are the sensitivity indexes correspond to the respective parameters $\beta_1, \beta_2, \zeta, \phi$. Therefore, it is clear that the basic reproduction number (R_0) is most sensitive to changes in β ($\chi_\beta = 1$), where $\beta_1 = b\beta$; $\beta_2 = \beta$ and b is a nonzero real number, probability of transmission from susceptible to drug addicts (both psychological and physiological).

Table 2. Sensitivity indices of different parameters of system (3) corresponding to Table 3.

Parameters	Sensitivity Index
ϕ	-0.6154
ζ	-0.0593
β_1	0.9259
β_2	0.0741

Table 3. Parameter values used in system (3) when $E_0 = (1,0,0,0)$ and $R_0 = 0.3151$.

Parameters	Λ	β_1	β_2	δ	k	ϕ	ζ	γ	ε
Values	0.02	0.01	0.001	0.02	0.1	0.2	0.1	0.1	0.95
Reference	[35]	[35]	[35]	[36]	[36]	[36]	[36]	[35]	Assumed

If β_1, β_2 increases, R_0 also increases, whereas R_0 decreases when ϕ, ζ increases, or vice versa. However, the increase in ϕ, i.e., the treatment rate for psychological addicts, cannot help as much as the treatment rate for physiological addicts ζ. In this way, it is smarter to concentrate either β_1, β_2 (the contact rates) and ϕ, treatment rate for mental addicts. It is also noticeable that R_0 is more sensitive to β_1 rather than β_2 according Table 2.

3.5. Local Stability

To analyze the local stability of disease free and endemic equilibrium points, we need the following.

Definition 3 ([37]). *The discriminant $\nabla(f)$ of a polynomial $f(x) = x^n + \alpha_1 x^{n-1} + \alpha_2 x^{n-2} + \ldots + \alpha_n$ is defined by*

$$\nabla(f) = (-1)^{\frac{n(n-1)}{2}} |S_n(f, f')|.$$

Where $S_n(f, g)$ is the Sylvester matrix of $f(x)$ and $g(x)$ of order $(n+l) \times (n+l)$ and $g(x) = x^l + \beta_1 x^{l-1} + \beta_2 x^{l-2} + \ldots + \beta_l$.

For $n = 3$, we have $f(x) = x^3 + \alpha_1 x^2 + \alpha_2 x + \alpha_3$ and $f'(x) = 3x^2 + 2\alpha_1 x + \alpha_2$.

$$|S_3(f,f')| = \begin{vmatrix} 1 & \alpha_1 & \alpha_2 & \alpha_3 & 0 \\ 0 & 1 & \alpha_1 & \alpha_2 & \alpha_3 \\ 3 & 2\alpha_1 & \alpha_2 & 0 & 0 \\ 0 & 3 & 2\alpha_1 & \alpha_2 & 0 \\ 0 & 0 & 3 & 2\alpha_1 & \alpha_2 \end{vmatrix} = -18\alpha_1\alpha_2\alpha_3 - (\alpha_1\alpha_2)^2 + 4\alpha_1^3\alpha_3 + 4\alpha_2^3 + 27\alpha_3^2$$

Therefore, $\nabla(f) = -|S_3(f,f')| = 18\alpha_1\alpha_2\alpha_3 + (\alpha_1\alpha_2)^2 - 4\alpha_1^3\alpha_3 - 4\alpha_2^3 - 27\alpha_3^2$

Lemma 3. *(Routh–Hurwitz conditions for fractional calculus) [38]: If $\nabla(P)$ is the discriminant of the characteristic equation $P(\lambda) = \lambda^n + a_1 \lambda^{n-1} + a_2 \lambda^{n-2} + \ldots + a_n$ of Jacobian matrix of system (1) evaluated at equilibrium point, then for $n = 3$ the system is asymptotically stable if any of the following conditions hold:*

1. $\nabla(P) > 0, a_1 > 0, a_3 > 0$ and $a_1 a_2 > a_3$
2. $\nabla(P) < 0, a_1 \geq 0, a_2 \geq 0, a_3 > 0$ and $\alpha < \frac{2}{3}$
3. $\nabla(P) < 0, a_1 > 0, a_2 > 0, a_1 a_2 = a_3$ and $\alpha \in (0,1)$.

To study the local stability of the system (3), we need to compute Jacobian matrices at the equilibrium points E_0 and E_1. At the drug-free equilibrium point E_0:

$$J\left\{\left(\frac{\Lambda}{\delta}, 0, 0, 0\right)\right\} = \begin{bmatrix} -\delta & -\beta_1\frac{\Lambda}{\delta} & -\beta_2\frac{\Lambda}{\delta} & 0 \\ 0 & \beta_1\frac{\Lambda}{\delta} - (k+\delta+\phi) & \beta_2\frac{\Lambda}{\delta} & 0 \\ 0 & k & -(\xi+\delta) & \gamma \\ 0 & \phi & \xi & -(\gamma+\delta) \end{bmatrix}$$

The eigenvalues of the system are $\lambda_1 = -\delta$, and the other three eigenvalues can be found from the equation $Q(\lambda) \equiv \lambda^3 + c_1\lambda^2 + c_2\lambda + c_3 = 0$, where

$$c_1 = -(K_1 + K_5 + K_3)$$

$$c_2 = K_1K_5 + K_1K_9 + K_5K_9 - K_2K_4 - K_3K_7 - K_6K_8$$

$$c_3 = -K_1K_5K_9 + K_1K_6K_8 + K_2K_4K_9 - K_2K_6K_7 - K_3K_4K_8 + K_3K_7K_5$$

$$K_1 = \beta_1 \frac{\Lambda}{\delta} - (k + \delta + \phi)$$

$$K_2 = \beta_2 \frac{\Lambda}{\delta}$$

$$K_3 = 0$$
$$K_4 = k$$
$$K_5 = -(\xi + \delta)$$
$$K_6 = \gamma$$
$$K_7 = \phi$$
$$K_8 = \xi$$
$$K_9 = -(\gamma + \delta)$$
(17)

Suppose $\nabla(Q) = 18c_1c_2c_3 + (c_1c_2)^2 - 4c_1^2c_3 - cc_2^2 - 27c_3^2$, then by the Routh–Harwitz conditions for the fractional differential equation, the endemic equilibrium point E_0 is locally asymptotically stable if any of the following conditions hold:

1. $\nabla(Q) > 0, c_1 > 0, c_3 > 0$ and $c_1c_2 > c_3$
2. $\nabla(Q) < 0, c_1 \geq 0, c_2 \geq 0, c_3 > 0$ and $\varepsilon < \frac{2}{3}$
3. $\nabla(Q) < 0, c_1 > 0, c_2 > 0, c_1c_2 = c_3$ and $\varepsilon \in (0,1)$

Jacobian matrix at $E_1(S^*, P_1^*, P_2^*, R^*)$ is given by

$$J(E_1) = \begin{bmatrix} -\delta - \beta_1 P_1^* - \beta_2 P_2^* & -\beta_1 P_1^* S^* & -\beta_2 P_2^* S^* & 0 \\ \beta_1 P_1^* + \beta_2 P_2^* & \beta_1 S^* - (k + \delta + \phi) & \beta_2 S^* & 0 \\ 0 & k & -(\xi + \delta) & \gamma \\ 0 & \phi & \xi & -(\gamma + \delta) \end{bmatrix}$$

Characteristic equation of this matrix is $P(\lambda) \equiv \lambda^3 + a_1\lambda^2 + a_2\lambda + a_3 = 0$, where

$$a_1 = \frac{e_{23}e_{32} + e_{12}e_{22} - e_{22}e_{33} - e_{22}e_{44} - e_{11}e_{12}}{e_{22}}$$

$$a_2 = [e_{11}e_{22}e_{33} + e_{11}e_{22}e_{44} - e_{11}e_{23}e_{32} + e_{22}e_{33}e_{44} - e_{22}e_{34}e_{43} - e_{23}e_{32}e_{44} \\ + e_{34}e_{23}e_{42} - e_{22}e_{12}e_{33} - e_{22}e_{12}e_{44} + e_{32}e_{13}e_{21}]/e_{22}$$
(18)

$$a_3 = [e_{11}e_{22}e_{34}e_{43} - e_{11}e_{22}e_{33}e_{44} + e_{11}e_{23}e_{32}e_{44} - e_{11}e_{23}e_{34}e_{44} + e_{12}e_{21}e_{33}e_{44} \\ - e_{12}e_{21}e_{34}e_{43} - e_{21}e_{13}e_{32}e_{44}]/e_{22}$$

and $e_{ij}, i,j = 1,2,3,4$ are as follows:

$$\begin{aligned}
e_{11} &= -\delta - \beta_1 P_1^* - \beta_2 P_2^* \\
e_{12} &= -\beta_1 P_1^* S^* \\
e_{13} &= -\beta_2 P_2^* \\
e_{14} &= 0 \\
e_{21} &= \beta_1 P_1^* + \beta_2 P_2^* \\
e_{22} &= \beta_1 S^* - (k + \delta + \phi) \\
e_{23} &= \beta_2 S^* \\
e_{24} &= 0 \\
e_{31} &= 0 \\
e_{32} &= k \\
e_{33} &= -(\xi + \delta) \\
e_{34} &= \gamma \\
e_{41} &= 0 \\
e_{42} &= \phi \\
e_{43} &= \xi \\
e_{44} &= -(\gamma + \delta)
\end{aligned} \qquad (19)$$

Therefore, $\lambda_i, i = 1, 2, 3$, can be found from this equation. Suppose $\nabla(P) = 18 a_1 a_2 a_3 + (a_1 a_2)^2 - 4 a_1^2 a_3 - 4 a_2^3 - 27 a_3^2$, then by the Routh–Hurwitz conditions for fractional differential equations, the endemic equilibrium point E_1 is locally asymptotically stable if any of the following conditions hold:

1. $\nabla(P) > 0, a_1 > 0, a_3 > 0$ and $a_1 a_2 > a_3$
2. $\nabla(P) < 0, a_1 \geq 0, a_2 \geq 0, a_3 > 0$ and $\varepsilon < \frac{2}{3}$
3. $\nabla(P) < 0, a_1 > 0, a_2 > 0, a_1 a_2 = a_3$ and $\varepsilon \in (0, 1)$

The following theorems are the consequence of these discussions.

Theorem 7. *The drug-free equilibrium E_0 of system (2) is locally asymptotically stable if any of the following conditions holds with (17):*

1. $\nabla(Q) > 0, c_1 > 0, c_3 > 0$ and $c_1 c_2 > c_3$
2. $\nabla(Q) < 0, c_1 \geq 0, c_2 \geq 0, c_3 > 0$ and $\varepsilon < \frac{2}{3}$
3. $\nabla(Q) < 0, c_1 > 0, c_2 > 0, c_1 c_2 = c_3$ and $\varepsilon \in (0, 1)$.
   Here $\nabla(Q) = 18 c_1 c_2 c_3 + (c_1 c_2)^2 - 4 c_1^2 c_3 - c c_2^3 - 27 c_3^2$.

Theorem 8. *The endemic equilibrium E_1 of system (2) is locally asymptotically stable if any of the following conditions holds with (18) and (19):*

1. $\nabla(P) > 0, a_1 > 0, a_3 > 0$ and $a_1 a_2 > a_3$
2. $\nabla(P) < 0, a_1 \geq 0, a_2 \geq 0, a_3 > 0$ and $\varepsilon < \frac{2}{3}$
3. $\nabla(P) < 0, a_1 > 0, a_2 > 0, a_1 a_2 = a_3$ and $\varepsilon \in (0, 1)$.
   Here, $\nabla(P) = 18 a_1 a_2 a_3 + (a_1 a_2)^2 - 4 a_1^2 a_3 - 4 a_2^3 - 27 a_3^2$.

3.6. Global Asymptotic Stability

We need following useful lemmas about Lyapunov direct method related with global stability of the equilibrium points in fractional order models.

Lemma 4 ([32]). *Suppose $u(t) \in \mathbb{R}_+$ be a continuous and differentiable function. Then, for any moment of time $t > 0$, ${}_0^C D_t^\varepsilon \left[u(t) - u^* - u^* \ln \frac{u(t)}{u^*} \right] \leq \left(1 - \frac{u^*}{u(t)} \right) {}_0^C D_t^\varepsilon u(t), u^* \in \mathbb{R}_+$, $\forall \varepsilon \in (0, 1)$.*

Lemma 5. *(Uniform Asymptotic Stability Theorem) [39]:*
Consider the non-autonomous system

$${}_0^C D_t^\varepsilon x(t) = f(t, x), \quad x \in \Omega \subseteq \mathbb{R}^n \qquad (20)$$

Let x^* be an equilibrium point of the system ($x^* \in \Omega \subseteq \mathbb{R}^n$) and $\Phi(t, x(t)) : [0, \infty) \times \Omega \to \mathbb{R}$ be a continuously differentiable function such that

$$ {}_0^C D_t^\varepsilon \Phi(t, x(t)) \leq -\Theta_3(x), $$

$$ \Theta_1(x) \leq \Phi(t, x(t)) \leq \Theta_2(x), \forall \varepsilon \in (0, 1), \forall x(t) \in \Omega $$

where Θ_i, $i = 1, 2, 3$, are continuous positive definite functions on Ω. Then, the equilibrium point x^* of system (20) is globally asymptotically stable.

Theorem 9. *If* $1 > \dfrac{[k\gamma\xi + \gamma\phi(\xi + \delta)]\Lambda\beta_2}{\delta^2(k + \phi + \delta)(\xi + \delta + \gamma)(\xi + \delta)}$, *then the disease-free equilibrium* E_0 *of system (3) is globally asymptotically stable when*

$$ R_0 \leq 1 - \frac{[k\gamma\xi + \gamma\phi(\xi + \delta)]\Lambda\beta_2}{\delta^2(k + \phi + \delta)(\xi + \delta + \gamma)(\xi + \delta)}. $$

Proof. We have considered a positive definite function:

$$ L = \frac{1}{M}P_1 + \frac{\beta_2(\gamma + \delta)}{\delta(\xi + \delta + \gamma)}P_2 + \frac{\beta_2\gamma}{\delta(\xi + \delta + \gamma)}R, \text{ where } M = \frac{\Lambda}{\delta}. $$

Clearly, $L \geq 0$ and $L = 0$ only when $P_1 = 0$, $P_2 = 0$ and $R = 0$.

Taking the ε order Caputo derivative ${}_0^C D_t^\varepsilon$ of L along the solution of system (3), we have (for large time t)

$$ {}_0^C D_t^\varepsilon L = \frac{1}{M} {}_0^C D_t^\varepsilon P_1 + \frac{\beta_2(\gamma + \delta)}{\delta(\xi + \delta + \gamma)} {}_0^C D_t^\varepsilon P_2 + \frac{\beta_2\gamma}{\delta(\xi + \delta + \gamma)} {}_0^C D_t^\varepsilon R $$

$$ = \frac{1}{M}[\beta_1 S P_1 + \beta_2 S P_2 - k P_1 - (\delta + \phi)P_1] + \frac{\beta_2(\gamma + \delta)}{\delta(\xi + \delta + \gamma)}[k P_1 + \gamma R - \xi P_2 - \delta P_2] $$

$$ + \frac{\beta_2 \gamma}{\delta(\xi + \delta + \gamma)}[\phi P_1 + \xi P_2 - \gamma R - \delta R] $$

$$ \leq \frac{1}{M}\beta_1 M P_1 - \frac{1}{M}(k + \delta + \phi)P_1 + \frac{\beta_2(\gamma + \delta)}{\delta(\xi + \delta + \gamma)} k P_1 + \frac{\beta_2 \gamma \phi}{\delta(\xi + \delta + \gamma)} P_1 $$

$$ = \left[\frac{\delta R_0}{\Lambda}(k + \delta + \phi) - \frac{\beta_2 k}{\xi + \delta} + \frac{\beta_2 k(\gamma + \delta) + \beta_2 \gamma \phi}{\delta(\delta + \xi + \gamma)} - \frac{(k + \delta + \phi)}{M}\right] P_1 $$

$$ = \frac{\delta(k + \delta + \phi)}{\Lambda}[R_0 - L_0]P_1, $$

where

$$ L_0 = 1 + \frac{\Lambda \beta_2 k}{\delta(\xi + \delta)(k + \phi + \delta)} - \frac{\Lambda}{\delta^2}\frac{\beta_2 k(\gamma + \delta) + \beta_2 \gamma \phi}{(k + \phi + \delta)(\xi + \delta + \gamma)} $$

$$ = 1 - \frac{[k\gamma\xi + \gamma\phi(\xi + \delta)]\Lambda \beta_2}{\delta^2(k + \phi + \delta)(\xi + \delta + \gamma)(\xi + \delta)} \leq 1 $$

Therefore, ${}_0^C D_t^\varepsilon L \leq 0$ if $R_0 \leq L_0$. Therefore, using Lemma 5:

$$ \lim_{t \to \infty} P_1(t) = \lim_{t \to \infty} P_2(t) = \lim_{t \to \infty} R(t) = 0. $$

Thus, in the limit $S(t)$ is given by the solutions of ${}_0^C D_t^\varepsilon S(t) = \Lambda - \delta S$. As $S(0) > 0$, the theorem follows. □

Theorem 10. *If $R_0 > 1$, then the endemic equilibrium $E_1(S^*, P_1^*, P_2^*, R^*)$ of system (3) is globally asymptotically stable.*

Proof. Consider a positive definite function:

$$V = \left(S - S^* - S^* \ln \frac{S}{S^*}\right) + \left(P_1 - P_1^* - P_1^* \ln \frac{P_1}{P_1^*}\right) \\ + \frac{\beta_2(\gamma + \delta)}{\delta(\xi + \delta + \gamma)}\left(P_2 - P_2^* - P_2^* \ln \frac{P_2}{P_2^*}\right) + \frac{\beta_2 \gamma}{\delta(\xi + \delta + \gamma)}\left(R - R^* - R^* \ln \frac{R}{R^*}\right) \quad (21)$$

It is observed that $V \geq 0$ and $V = 0$ only at E_1. Taking the ε order Caputo derivative ${}_0^C D_t^\varepsilon$ of V and using Lemma 4, we have

$$ {}_0^C D_t^\varepsilon(V) \leq \left(1 - \frac{S^*}{S}\right){}_0^C D_t^\varepsilon S + \left(1 - \frac{P_1^*}{P_1}\right){}_0^C D_t^\varepsilon P_1 \\ + \frac{\beta_2(\gamma + \delta)}{\delta(\xi + \delta + \gamma)}\left(1 - \frac{P_2^*}{P_2}\right){}_0^C D_t^\varepsilon P_2 + \frac{\beta_2 \gamma}{\delta(\xi + \delta + \gamma)}\left(1 - \frac{R^*}{R}\right){}_0^C D_t^\varepsilon R \quad (22)$$

From the steady-state of equilibrium point (4), we have

$$\Lambda = \delta S^* + \beta_1 S^* P_1^* + \beta_2 S^* P_2^*$$

$$\frac{\beta_1 S^* P_1^* + \beta_2 S^* P_2^*}{P_1^*} = (k + \delta + \phi)$$

$$\frac{k P_1^* + \gamma R^*}{P_2^*} = (\xi + \delta) \quad (23)$$

$$\frac{\phi P_1^* + \xi P_2^*}{R^*} = (\gamma + \delta)$$

Let $a = \dfrac{S}{S^*}, b = \dfrac{P_1}{P_1^*}, c = \dfrac{P_2}{P_2^*}, d = \dfrac{R}{R^*}$.

From (22) and (23), we have

$$\begin{aligned}
{}^C_0 D^\varepsilon_t(V) &\leq \frac{(S-S^*)}{S}\left[-\delta(S-S^*) - \beta_1(P_1 S - P_1^* S^*) - \beta_2(P_2 S - P_2^* S^*)\right]\\
&\left(1 - \frac{P_1^*}{P_1}\right)\left[\beta_1 S P_1 + \beta_2 S P_2 - (\beta_1 S^* + \beta_2 S^* P_2^*)\frac{P_1}{P_1^*}\right]\\
&+ \frac{\beta_2(\gamma+\delta)}{\delta(\delta+\xi+\gamma)}\left(1 - \frac{P_2^*}{P_2}\right)\left[k P_1 + \gamma R - P_2 \frac{k P_1^* + \gamma R^*}{P_2^*}\right]\\
&+ \frac{\beta_2 \gamma}{\delta(\delta+\xi+\gamma)}\left(1 - \frac{R^*}{R}\right)\left[\phi P_1 + \xi P_2 - \frac{\phi P_1^* + \xi P_2^*}{R^*}\right]\\
&= -\frac{\delta}{S}(S - S^*)^2 + \beta_1 P_1^* S^*\left[(1-ab)\left(1 - \frac{1}{a}\right) + \left(1 - \frac{1}{b}\right)ab - b\left(1 - \frac{1}{b}\right)\right]\\
&+ \beta_2 P_2^* S^*\left[(1-ac)\left(1 - \frac{1}{a}\right) + \left(1 - \frac{1}{b}\right)ac - b\left(1 - \frac{1}{b}\right)\right]\\
&\frac{\beta_2(\gamma+\delta)}{\delta(\xi+\delta+\gamma)} k P_1^*\left(1 - \frac{1}{c}\right)(b - c) + \frac{\beta_2(\gamma+\delta)}{\delta(\xi+\delta+\gamma)}\gamma R^*\left(1 - \frac{1}{c}\right)(d - c)\\
&+ \frac{\beta_2 \gamma}{\delta(\xi+\delta+\gamma)}\phi P_1^*\left(1 - \frac{1}{d}\right)(b - d) + \frac{\beta_2 \gamma}{\delta(\xi+\delta+\gamma)}\xi P_2^*\left(1 - \frac{1}{d}\right)(c - d)\\
&= -\frac{\delta}{S}(S - S^*)^2 + \beta_1 P_1^* S^*\left(2 - \frac{1}{a} - a\right)\\
&+ \left[\beta_2 \frac{(k\gamma + k\delta + \phi\gamma)}{\delta(\gamma+\delta+\xi)} P_1^*\right]\left(2 - \frac{1}{a} + c - \frac{ac}{b} - b\right)
\end{aligned}$$

Using $P_2^* = \frac{(k\gamma + k\delta + \phi\gamma)}{\delta(\gamma+\delta+\xi)} P_1^*$

$$+ \frac{\beta_2(\gamma+\delta)}{\delta(\xi+\delta+\gamma)} k P_1^*\left(b - c - \frac{b}{c} + 1\right) + \frac{\beta_2 \gamma}{\delta(\xi+\delta+\gamma)}(\phi P_1^* + \xi P_2^*)\left(d - c - \frac{d}{c} + 1\right)$$

Using $R^*(\delta+\gamma) = (\phi P_1^* + \xi P_2^*)$

$$+ \frac{\beta_2 \gamma}{\delta(\xi+\delta+\gamma)}\phi P_1^*\left(b - d - \frac{b}{d} + 1\right) + \frac{\beta_2 \gamma}{\delta(\xi+\delta+\gamma)}\xi P_2^*\left(c - d - \frac{c}{d} + 1\right)$$

$$= -\frac{\delta}{S}(S-S^*)^2 + \beta_1 P_1^* S^* \left(2 - \frac{1}{a} - a\right)$$

$$+ \frac{\beta_2(\gamma+\delta)}{\delta(\xi+\delta+\gamma)} kP_1^* \left(3 - \frac{1}{a} - \frac{ac}{b} - \frac{b}{c}\right) \tag{24}$$

$$+ \frac{\beta_2 \phi \gamma}{\delta(\xi+\delta+\gamma)} P_1^* \left(4 - \frac{1}{a} - \frac{ac}{b} - \frac{d}{c} - \frac{b}{d}\right)$$

Using the inequality A.M. $\geq$ G.M., we have $2 - \frac{1}{a} - a \leq 0; 3 - \frac{1}{a} - \frac{ac}{b} - \frac{b}{c} \leq 0; 4 - \frac{1}{a} - \frac{ac}{b} - \frac{d}{c} - \frac{b}{d} \leq 0$. From relation (24) it is clear that ${}_0^C D_t^\varepsilon(V) \leq 0$ and thus ${}_0^C D_t^\varepsilon(V)$ is negative definite with respect to E_1. Thus E_1 is globally asymptotically stable by Lemma 5. □

4. Fractional Optimal Control Problem

The applications of Fractional-ordered optimal control problem (FOCP) have grown in recent decades. Agrawal has introduced the general form of FOCPs in the Riemann–Liouville sense and suggests a numerical method to solve FOCP using Lagrange multiplier technique [24]. In traditional integer-order optimal control problems, the calculus of variations is the common method. Pontryagin's principle is one of the most useful approaches to solve optimal control problem. There are several works where these methods are employed in Fractional ordered optimal control problems [25,40].

Let x be the pseudo-state vector, $u = [u^1, u^2, ..., u^m] \in U \subseteq R^m$ is the input vector, and U is the set of admissible control of the dynamical system ${}_0^C D_t^\varepsilon x = f(x, u, t), x(0) = x_0$. The system's pseudo-state is supposed to reach final condition x_f in the unknown final time $T_f < \infty$. The control $u \in U$ must be chosen for all $t \in [0, T_f]$ to minimize the objective functional J which is defined by the application and can be abstracted as

$$J = \Theta(x(T_f)) + \int_0^{T_f} F(x(t), u(t)) dt$$

The constraints on the system dynamics can be adjoined to the Lagrangian F by introducing time-varying Lagrange multiplier vector λ, whose elements are called the co-states of the system. This motivates the construction of the Hamiltonian H defined for all $t \in [0, T_f]$.

$$H(x(t), u(t), \lambda(t)) = \lambda^T(t) f(x(t), u(t)) + F(x(t), u(t)).$$

where λ^T stands for transpose of λ. Pontryagin's minimum principle states that the optimal state trajectory x^*, optimal control u^*, and corresponding Lagrange multiplier vector λ^* must minimize the Hamiltonian H so that [41]

1. $H(x^*(t), u^*(t), \lambda^*(t)) \leq H(x^*(t), u(t), \lambda^*(t))$
2. $\frac{\partial \Theta(x)}{\partial T_f}\big|_{x=x(T_f)} + H(T_f) = 0$
3. ${}_t^{RL} D_{T_f}^\varepsilon \lambda^T = \frac{\partial H}{\partial x}\big|_{x=x^*}$
4. $\frac{\partial H}{\partial u}\big|_{u=u^*} = 0$ and $\frac{\partial^2 H((x^*(t), u^*(t), \lambda^*(t)))}{\partial u^2} \leq 0$

where

$${}_t^{RL} D_T^\varepsilon f(t) = \frac{-1}{\Gamma(1-\varepsilon)} \frac{d}{d\tau} \int_t^T (\tau - t)^{-\varepsilon} f(\tau) d\tau, \forall t \in [0, T]$$

is the Right Riemann–Liouville derivative of order ε. The notation "RL" stands for Right Riemann–Liouville derivative. These four conditions are the necessary conditions, but not sufficient for optimal control.

Our point is to limit the number of synthetic drug addicts by considering the impact of "awareness program, mental directing and other preventive measures" as a control strategy. We have thought about system (3) with this control system. Empowering the mindfulness mission and advising program in a successive premise can impact conduct change among mental addicts. Mindfulness crusades keep the populace from ingesting medications as well as make them mindful about the repercussions of engrossing manufactured medications. Considering this, a treatment rate work $c\eta P_1$ has been introduced in system (3) to get system (26). Here, c speaks to the therapy rate (through directing) alongside the effect of awareness missions and η is the power of treatment. There are various costs included like analysis, drugs, and different costs when advising is given. In this way, η can be utilized as a potential instrument to create a constructive outcomes on mental addicts with $0 \leq \eta \leq 1$. Here, 0 portrays no improvement throughout the directing time frame, while 1 is speaking to full improvement. Consequently, the control force η completely depends on the exertion of the mental addicts to prevent themselves from consuming synthetic drugs.

In the following, we have focus on determining the optimal treatment via counseling with minimum cost by implementing the control. From the previous discussions, we have deduced that the acceptable set for the control variable $\eta(t)$ is

$$\Theta = \{\eta(t) | \eta(t) \in [0,1], t \in [0, T_f]\}.$$

where T_f represents the final time up to which the control policy can be implemented. It is assumed that the control functions $\eta(t)$ is measurable.

Our main objective is to minimize the given objective function J, which represents cost involved in counseling and awareness programs in time interval $[0, T_f]$, by finding optimal control η^* as follows:

$$J(\eta^*) = J(\min\{\eta(t) \in \Theta\}). \tag{25}$$

Here,

$$J(\eta) = \int_0^{T_f} \left[\omega_1 P_1(t) + \frac{\omega_2}{2}\eta^2(t)\right] dt,$$

(where $\omega_1 \neq 0, \omega_2 \neq 0$ are the cost of treatment of psychological class and cost of implementation of control strategy, respectively)

subject to

$$\begin{aligned}
{}^C_0 D^\varepsilon_t S(t) &= \Lambda - \delta S - \beta_1 S P_1 - \beta_2 S P_2, S(0) > 0, \\
{}^C_0 D^\varepsilon_t P_1(t) &= \beta_1 S P_1 + \beta_2 S P_2 - (k + \delta + \phi) P_1 - c\eta P_1, P_1(0) > 0, \\
{}^C_0 D^\varepsilon_t P_2(t) &= k P_1 + \gamma R - \xi P_2 - \delta P_2, P_2(0) > 0, \\
{}^C_0 D^\varepsilon_t R(t) &= \phi P_1 + \xi P_2 - \gamma R - \delta R + c\eta P_1, R(0) > 0,
\end{aligned} \tag{26}$$

The existence of optimal control η^* can be established in the next theorem.

Theorem 11. *Let the control function $\eta \in \Theta$ be measurable on $[0, T_f]$ with value of each of $\eta(t)$ lies in [0,1]. Then, there exist adjoint variables $\lambda_1, \lambda_2, \lambda_3, \lambda_4$ and optimal control η^* minimizing the objective function $J(\eta)$ of (26) satisfying*

$$^{RL}_tD^\varepsilon_{T_f}\lambda_1(t) = \lambda_1(\delta + \beta_1 P_1 + \beta_2 P_2) - \lambda_2(\beta_1 P_1 + \beta_2 P_2)$$

$$^{RL}_tD^\varepsilon_{T_f}\lambda_2(t) = \lambda_1\beta_1 S - \lambda_2[\beta_1 S - (k + \delta + \phi + c\eta)] - \lambda_3 k - \lambda_4(\phi + c\eta) - \omega_1$$

$$^{RL}_tD^\varepsilon_{T_f}\lambda_3(t) = \lambda_1\beta_2 S - \lambda_2\beta_2 S + \lambda_3(\xi + \delta) - \lambda_4\xi$$

$$^{RL}_tD^\varepsilon_{T_f}\lambda_4(t) = -\lambda_3\gamma + \lambda_4(\gamma + \delta)$$

with transversality conditions $\lambda_i(T_f) = 0$ ($i = 1, 2, 3, 4$) and

$$\eta^* = \max\{\min\{\bar{\eta}, 1\}, 0\}$$
$$\bar{\eta} = \frac{cP_1(t)(\lambda_2(t) - \lambda_4(t))}{\omega_2} \tag{27}$$

where S^*, P_1^*, P_2^*, R^* are the corresponding optimal state solutions of (26) associated with control variable η.

Proof. We have constructed the Hamiltonian as

$$\begin{aligned} H = &\omega_1 P_1(t) + \frac{\omega_2}{2}\eta^2(t) \\ &+ \lambda_1\{\Lambda - \delta S - \beta_1 SP_1 - \beta_2 SP_2\} \\ &+ \lambda_2\{\beta_1 SP_1 + \beta_2 SP_2 - (k + \delta + \phi)P_1 - c\eta P_1\} \\ &+ \lambda_3\{kP_1 + \gamma R - \xi P_2 - \delta P_2\} + \lambda_4\{\phi P_1 + \xi P_2 - \gamma R - \delta R + c\eta P_1\} \end{aligned} \tag{28}$$

with $(\lambda_1, \lambda_2, \lambda_3, \lambda_4)$ being the associated adjoint variables with $\lambda_i(T_f) = 0$ ($i = 1, 2, 3, 4$), which satisfy the following canonical equations:

$$\begin{aligned} ^{RL}_tD^\varepsilon_{T_f}\lambda_1(t) &= -\frac{\partial H}{\partial S} = \lambda_1(\delta + \beta_1 P_1 + \beta_2 P_2) - \lambda_2(\beta_1 P_1 + \beta_2 P_2) \\ ^{RL}_tD^\varepsilon_{T_f}\lambda_2(t) &= -\frac{\partial H}{\partial P_1} = \lambda_1\beta_1 S - \lambda_2[\beta_1 S - (k + \delta + \phi + c\eta)] - \lambda_3 k - \lambda_4(\phi + c\eta) - \omega_1 \\ ^{RL}_tD^\varepsilon_{T_f}\lambda_3(t) &= -\frac{\partial H}{\partial P_2} = \lambda_1\beta_2 S - \lambda_2\beta_2 S + \lambda_3(\xi + \delta) - \lambda_4\xi \\ ^{RL}_tD^\varepsilon_{T_f}\lambda_4(t) &= -\frac{\partial H}{\partial R} = -\lambda_3\gamma + \lambda_4(\gamma + \delta) \end{aligned} \tag{29}$$

Therefore, the problem of finding η^* that minimizes J subject to (26) is converted to minimizing the Hamiltonian with respect to the control. Then, by Pontryagin principle, we have achieved the optimal condition:

$$\frac{\partial H}{\partial \eta} = \omega_2\eta - \lambda_2 cP_1 + \lambda_4 cP_1 = 0 \tag{30}$$

which can be solved in terms of the state and adjoint variables to give

$$\bar{\eta} = \frac{cP_1(t)(\lambda_2(t) - \lambda_4(t))}{\omega_2} \tag{31}$$

For the optimal control η^*, which requires considering the constrains on the control and the sign of $\frac{\partial H}{\partial \eta}$, we have

$$\eta^* = \begin{cases} 0, & \text{if } \frac{\partial H}{\partial \eta} < 0 \\ \bar{\eta}, & \text{if } \frac{\partial H}{\partial \eta} = 0 \\ 1, & \text{if } \frac{\partial H}{\partial \eta} > 0 \end{cases} \tag{32}$$

and

$$\eta^* = \max\{\min\{\bar{\eta}, 1\}, 0\}, \text{ where } \bar{\eta} = \frac{cP_1(t)(\lambda_2(t) - \lambda_4(t))}{\omega_2}. \tag{33}$$

The optimal state can be found by substituting η^* into the system (26). □

5. Numerical Simulations

Analytical study is incomplete without numerical verification of the results. In this section, we have presented numerical simulation of system (3) and fractional order control problem (27). We have used FDE12 MatLab function which is designed on predictor–corrector scheme based on Adams–Bashforth–Moulton algorithm introduced by Roberto Garrappa [42]. Diethelm [16,43] used the predictor–corrector scheme based on Adams–Bashforth–Moulton algorithm which is used in FDE12. We have used FDE12 function directly for system (3) just like ODE45, ODE23.

We have also used iterative scheme (Euler's forward and backward) in MatLab interface to develop fractional order optimal control problem. The process is briefly described below. The optimality system constitutes a two-point boundary value problem including a set of fractional-order differential equations. The state system (26) is an initial value and the adjoint system (29) is a boundary value problem. The state system is solved by forward iteration method and the costate system is solved by backward iteration method by the following algorithm through Matlab.

State system (26) is solved using the iterative scheme below:

$$S(i) = [\Lambda - \delta S(i-1) - \beta_1 S(i-1)P_1(i-1) - \beta_2 S(i-1)P_2(i-1)]h^\varepsilon$$

$$- \sum_{j=1}^{i} c(j)S(i-j)$$

$$P_1(i) = [\beta_1 S(i-1)P_1(i-1) + \beta_2 S(i-1)P_2(i-1) - (k+\delta+\phi)P_1(i-1)$$

$$- c\eta P_1(i-1)]h^\varepsilon - \sum_{j=1}^{i} c(j)P_1(i-j)$$

$$P_2(i) = [kP_1(i-1) + \gamma R(i-1) - \xi P_2(i-1) - \delta P_2(i-1)]h^\varepsilon - \sum_{j=1}^{i} c(j)P_2(i-j)$$

$$R(i) = [\phi P_1(i-1) + \xi P_2(i-1) - \gamma R(i-1) - \delta R(i-1) + c\eta P_1(i-1)]h^\varepsilon$$

$$- \sum_{j=1}^{i} c(j)R(i-j)$$

where $c(0) = 1$ and $c(j) = (1 - \frac{1+\varepsilon}{j})c(j-1), j \geq 1$ and h^ε is the time step length. Here, $S(i)$ is the value of $S(t)$ at ith iteration. The last term of each of the above system of equations stands for memory. The adjoint system (29) is solved by backward iteration method with terminal conditions $\lambda_i(T_f) = 0, i = 1, 2, 3, 4$ using the following iterative scheme:

$$\lambda_1(i) = [\lambda_1(i-1)(\delta + \beta_1 P_1(i) + \beta_2 P_2(i)) - \lambda_2(i-1)(\beta_1 P_1(i) + \beta_2 P_2(i))]h^\varepsilon$$

$$- \sum_{j=1}^{i} c(j)\lambda_1(i-j)$$

$$\lambda_2(i) = [\lambda_1(i)\beta_1 S(i) - \lambda_2(i-1)\{\beta_1 S(i) - (k + \delta + \phi + c\eta)\} - \lambda_3(i-1)k$$

$$- \lambda_4(i-1)(\phi + c\eta) - \omega_1]h^\varepsilon - \sum_{j=1}^{i} c(j)\lambda_2(i-j)$$

$$\lambda_3(i) = [\lambda_1(i)\beta_2 S(i) - \lambda_2(i)\beta_2 S(i) + \lambda_3(i-1)(\xi + \delta) - \lambda_4(i-1)\xi]h^\varepsilon$$

$$- \sum_{j=1}^{i} c(j)\lambda_3(i-j)$$

$$\lambda_4(i) = [-\lambda_3(i)\gamma + \lambda_4(i-1)(\gamma + \delta)]h^\varepsilon - \sum_{j=1}^{i} c(j)\lambda_4(i-j)$$

The optimal control is updated by the scheme below.

$$\eta^* = \max\{\min\{\bar{\eta}, 1\}, 0\}, \text{ where } \bar{\eta} = \frac{cP_1(i)(\lambda_2(i-1) - \lambda_4(i-1))}{\omega_2}.$$

We have developed MatLab code using the above algorithm and chosen $h = 0.02$ throughout the numerical simulation. In fitting the test data of memory phenomena from different fields, it has been found that the fractional order can be physically explained as an index of memory. The higher the value of order ε, the slower the forgetting is and most of the epidemic transmission dynamics depend on memory (previous stages) [15]. The value of order of fractional derivative (ε) needs to be close to 1. Theoretically, we may study the fractional order system for any value lies between 0 to 1, but it is better to choose the value close to 1. There are some cases where we have found interesting results if we reduce the order of derivative, but for very small values of ε (less than 0.5) the MatLab code become erroneous. Therefore, we have to chose the order wisely and in our context we choose the value 0.95 (it may be any value from 0.9 to 0.99) for numerical simulation. The value of the order can be estimated by least-squares method of curve fitting with real data from field survey or by graphical study [21].

In this section, we have portrayed some time series of system (3) and variation of R_0 with respect to $\beta_1, \beta_2, \xi, \phi$. Next, we have discussed about the effect of control intervention. Figure 2 represents the situation when the drug free equilibrium $E_0 = (1,0,0,0)$ is asymptotically stable corresponds to the Table 3. Next, let us consider the following three cases:

1. $\beta_1 > \beta_2$ (Table 4)
2. $\beta_1 = \beta_2$ (Table 5)
3. $\beta_1 < \beta_2$ (Table 6)

Figure 3 depicts the time series and phase portrait of system (3) (case 1) when the drug addict equilibrium is $E_1 = (0.1254, 0.0519, 0.5429, 0.0783)$ and $R_0 = 1.6246$. Figures 4 and 5 represent the cases 2 and 3 when corresponding equilibrium points are

$$(0.0567, 0.0572, 0.5984, 0.0864), (0.051, 0.0576, 0.6081, 0.0871)$$

respectively. Figure 6 represents the variation of time series of state variables when ε varies and other parameters are fixed as in Table 5. Figures 7–10 depict the change in R_0 with respect to parameters $\beta_1, \beta_2, \phi, \xi$, respectively. Figures 2 and 3 justify Theorems 7 and 8, respectively. Figure 11 depicts the variation of time series with the control parameter η.

Now, let us consider Table 7 for simulating optimal control problem (26). We have used Forward-backward iterative scheme to solve this optimal control problem [44]. For $\eta = 0$, the drug-free equilibrium point is $E_0 = (0.83, 0, 0, 0)$ and $R_0 = 0.508$. We have considered final time $T_f = 20$ days and $t = 1$ day. Note that there are more addicted population in physiological state than in psychological state. Now, we shall discuss about the effect of control intervention. The positive weights have been considered as $\omega_1 = 1.6, \omega_2 = 10$.

Figure 11 shows the variation of time series of state variables when the control parameter η changes. Figure 12 represents the time series of state variables of optimal control problem (26). Figure 13 represents time series of optimal control variable (η^*) and optimal cost function (J^*). Figure 14 depicts the case when no control is applied. There is a significant number of psychological and physiologically addicted population present in the scenario ($\eta = 0$) which will create economic burden in terms of loss of productivity, morbidity, and mortality and in obtaining protective measures (Figure 14). It has been found from Figures 13 and 14 that if the control strategy is applied, then the number of psychologically addicts and number of addicts in treatment class decrease but the number of physiological addicts increases. The values of S, P_1, P_2, R in the without control stage after 20 days are 0.5823, 0.003934, 0.01343, and 0.023, respectively, but after applying control those values change to 0.5823, 0.003917, 0.01345, and 0.02297. Though the change is smaller in fraction, it is effective in large populated countries like India and China. In Figure 13, it has been observed that the value of optimal control is increasing between 0 to 8 days and then decreases. A certain time is required to persuade a psychologically addicted person that ingesting drugs in a frequent manner is harmful and can even cause physical damages. However, once a person starts understanding these deadly affects, it becomes easy for them to take medicines and to do the other needful to make them free of this addiction. We have performed the cost design analysis for optimal control policy mentioned in Figure 13.

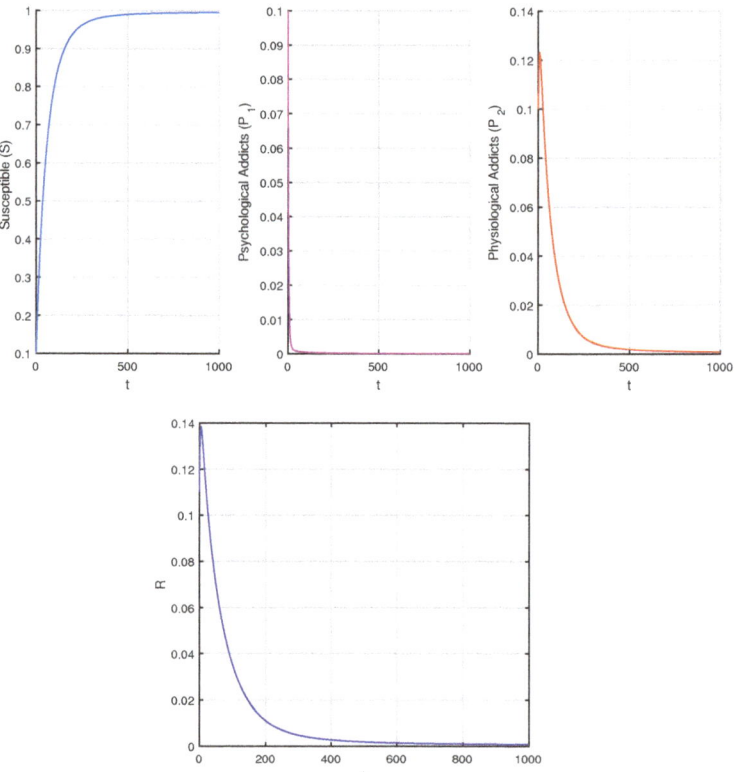

Figure 2. Time series of system (3) corresponds to Table 2 when $E_0 = (1, 0, 0, 0)$ and $R_0 = 0.3151$.

Table 4. Parametric values used in system (3) when $\beta_1 > \beta_2$, $E_1 = (0.1254, 0.0519, 0.5429, 0.0783)$ and $R_0 = 1.6246$.

Parameters	Λ	β_1	β_2	δ	k	ϕ	ζ	γ	ε
Values	0.02	0.5	0.2	0.025	0.1	0.2	0.1	0.8	0.95
Reference	[35]	[35]	[35]	[36]	[36]	[36]	[36]	[35]	Assumed

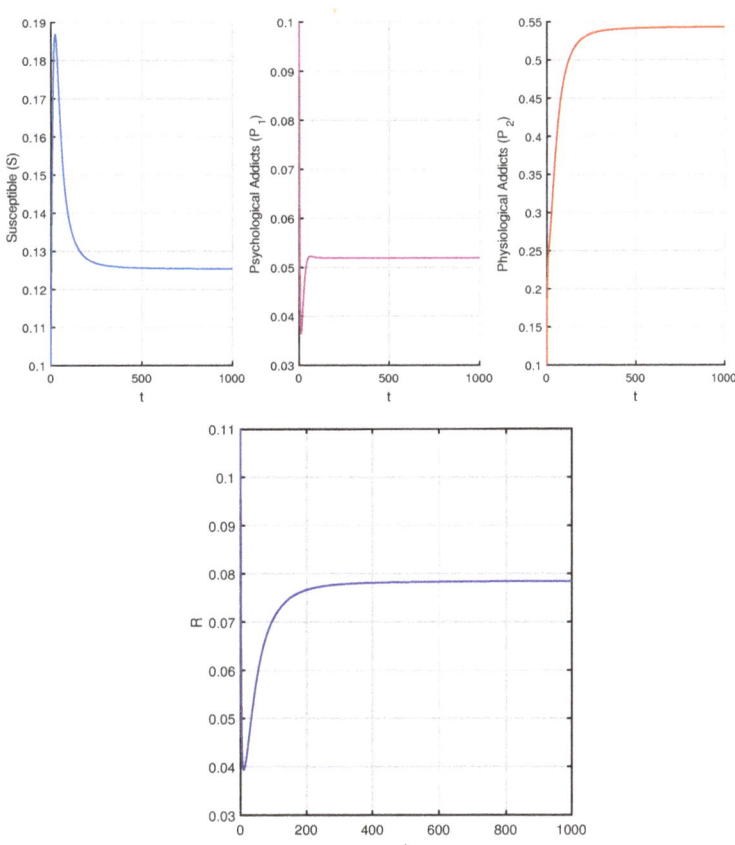

Figure 3. Time series of system (3) corresponds to Table 3 when $E_1 = (0.1254, 0.0519, 0.5429, 0.0783)$ and $R_0 = 1.6246$.

Table 5. Parametric values used in system (3) when $\beta_1 = \beta_2$, $E_1 = (0.0567, 0.0572, 0.5984, 0.0864)$ and $R_0 = 2.2154$.

Parameters	Λ	β_1	β_2	δ	k	ϕ	ζ	γ	ε
Values	0.02	0.5	0.5	0.025	0.1	0.2	0.1	0.8	0.95
Reference	[35]	[35]	[35]	[36]	[36]	[36]	[36]	[35]	Assumed

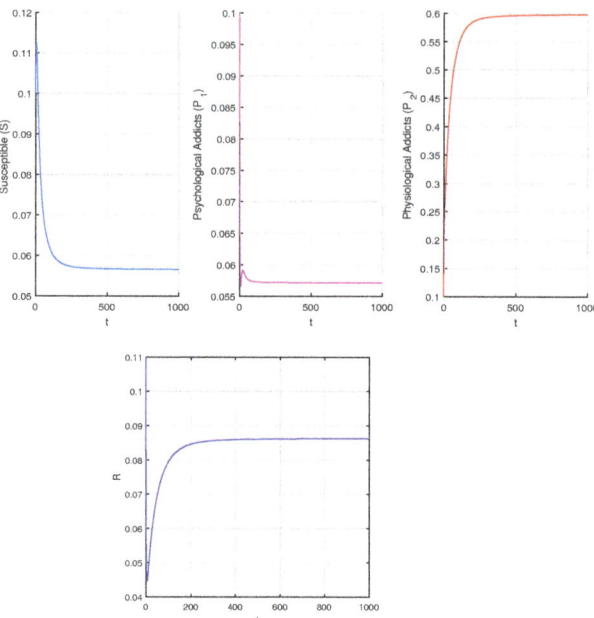

Figure 4. Time series of system (3) corresponds to Table 4 when $E_1 = (0.0567, 0.0572, 0.5984, 0.0864)$ and $R_0 = 2.2154$.

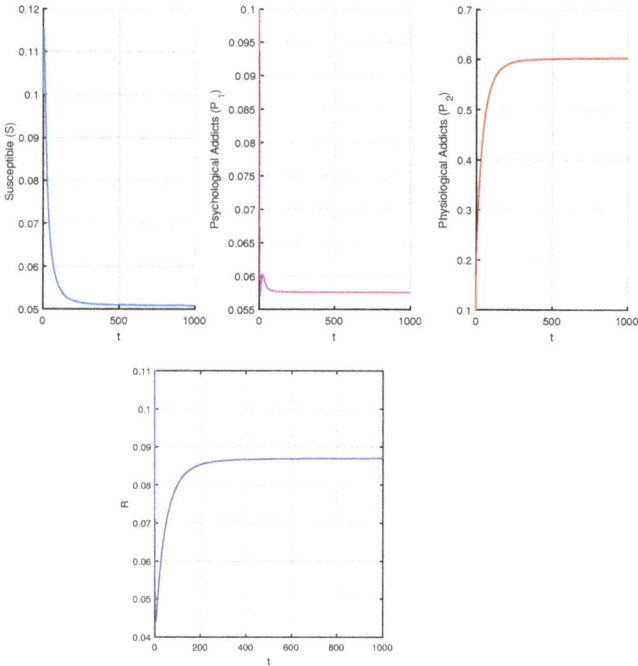

Figure 5. Time series of system (3) corresponds to Table 5 when $E_1 = (0.051, 0.0576, 0.6081, 0.0871)$ and $R_0 = 1.4277$.

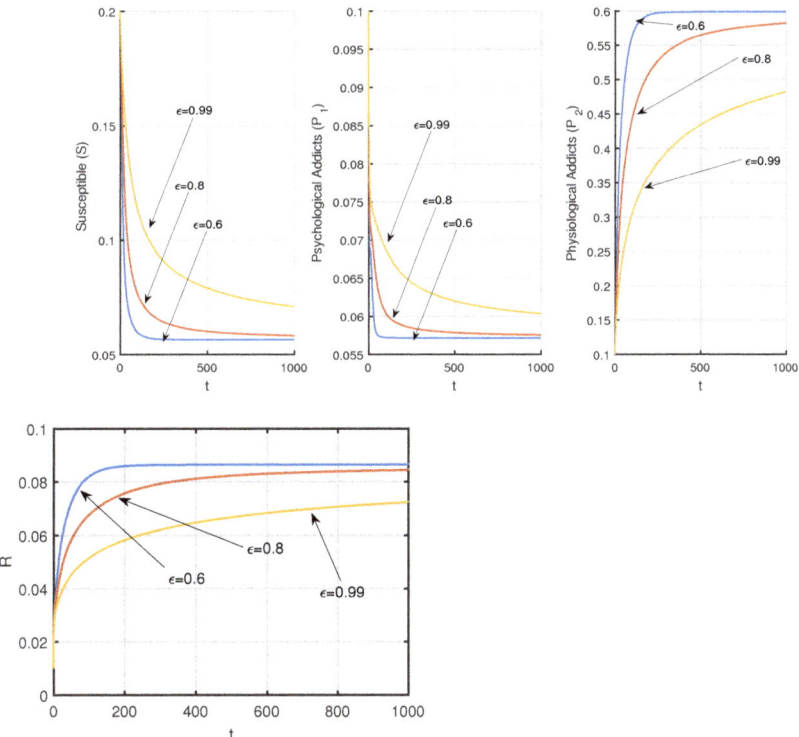

Figure 6. Variation of time series of system (3) with ε corresponds to Table 4 when $R_0 = 2.2154$.

Table 6. Parametric values used in system (3) when $\beta_1 < \beta_2$, $E_1 = (0.051, 0.0576, 0.6081, 0.0871)$ and $R_0 = 1.4277$.

Parameters	Λ	β_1	β_2	δ	k	ϕ	ζ	γ	ε
Values	0.02	0.1	0.6	0.025	0.1	0.2	0.1	0.8	0.95
Reference	[35]	[35]	[35]	[36]	[36]	[36]	[36]	[35]	Assumed

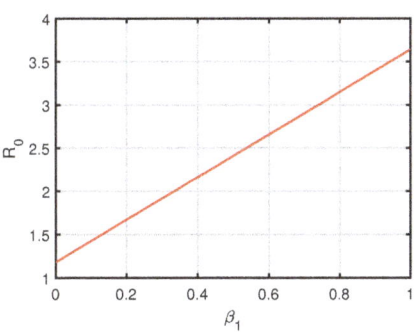

Figure 7. Variation of R_0 of system (3) with respect to β_1 while values of other parameters are taken from Table 3.

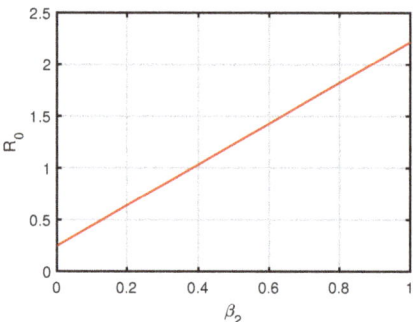

Figure 8. Variation of R_0 of system (3) with respect to β_2 while values of other parameters are taken from Table 3.

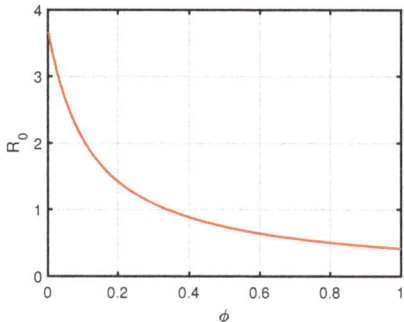

Figure 9. Variation of R_0 of system (3) with respect to ϕ while values of other parameters are taken from Table 3.

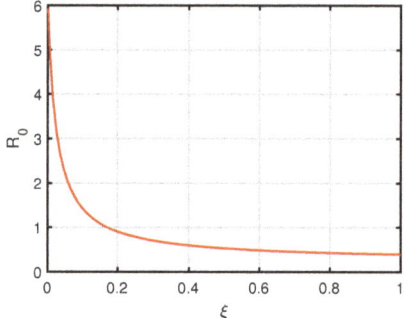

Figure 10. Variation of R_0 of system (3) with respect to ξ while values of other parameters are taken from Table 3.

Table 7. Parametric values used in system (26).

Parameters	Value	
Λ	0.1 person day^{-1}	Estimated
β_1	0.2 person^{-1} day^{-1}	[9]
β_2	0.03 person^{-1} day^{-1}	[9]
δ	0.12 person day^{-1}	Estimated
k	0.1 day^{-1}	[36]
ϕ	0.2 day^{-1}	[36]
ζ	0.1 day^{-1}	[35]
γ	0.1 day^{-1}	Estimated
c	0.15 day^{-1}	Estimated
ε	0.8–0.99	Assumed

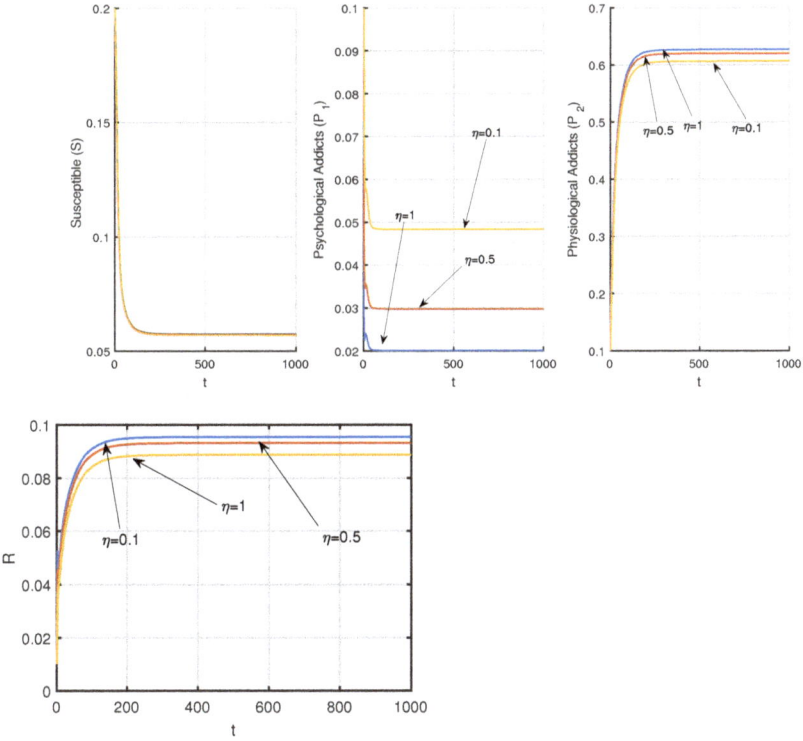

Figure 11. Variation of time series of system (26) with different control η corresponds to Table 4.

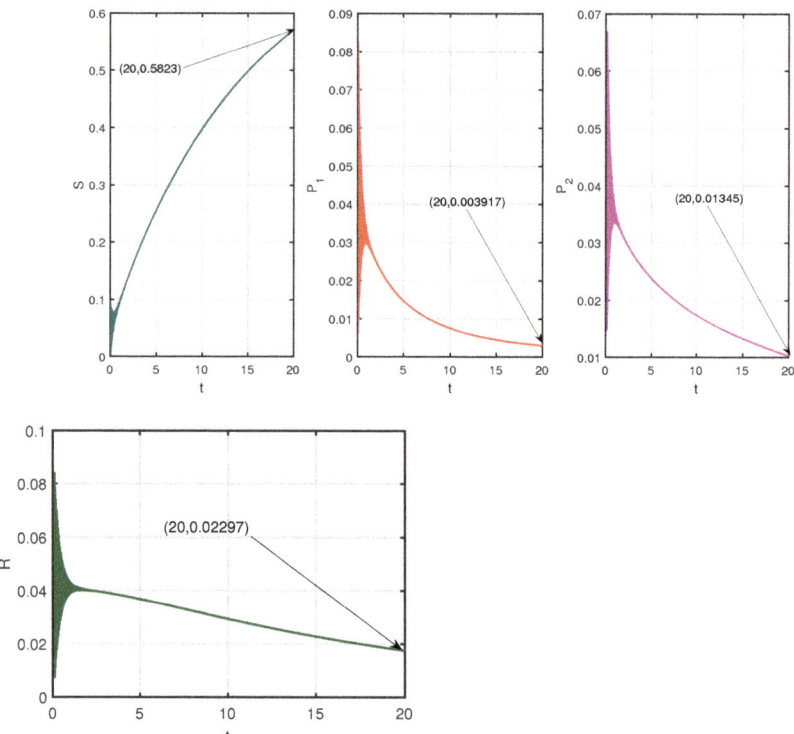

Figure 12. Time series of state variables of system (26) for Table 6 when $\varepsilon = 0.95$, $\omega_1 = 1.6, \omega_2 = 10$.

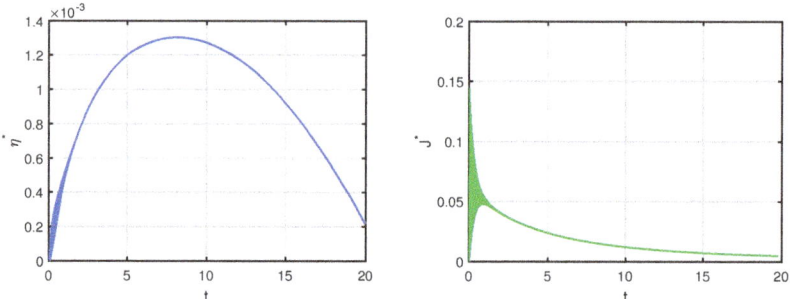

Figure 13. Time series of optimal control η^* and optimal cost J^* of system (26) for Table 6 when $\varepsilon = 0.95$, $\omega_1 = 1.6, \omega_2 = 10$.

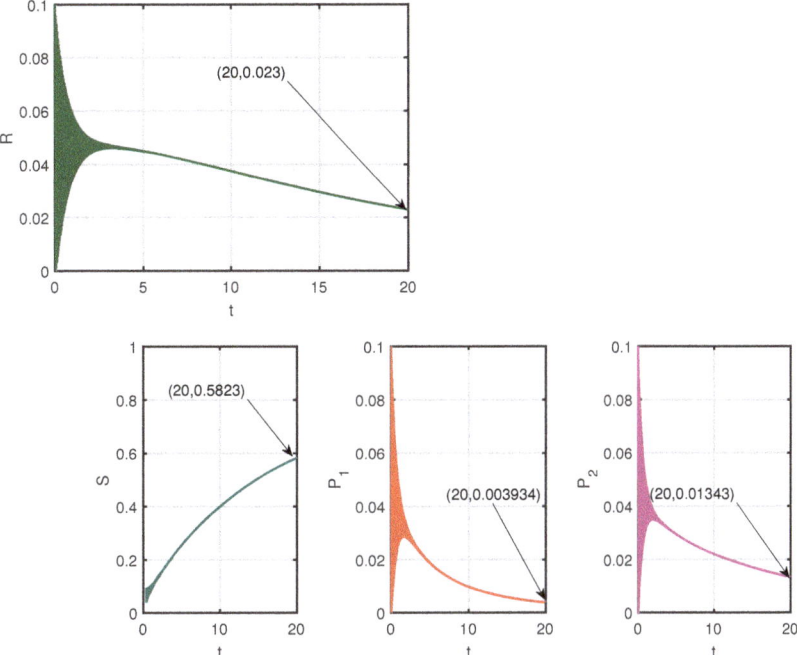

Figure 14. Time series of state variables of system (26) for Table 6 when $\varepsilon = 0.95$ and $\eta = 0$.

6. Conclusions

Fractional calculus plays an important role in dynamical processes. It gives us an extra parameter ε by which we can simulate our model properly. Here, we have studied on the fractional-order synthetic drugs transmission model with psychological addicts incorporating memory effects. We have observed that the dynamics of system (3) depends on the strength of memory effects, controlled by the order of fractional derivative ε [13].

In our work, we have framed a model in Caputo-fractional differentiation formalism where people are addicted to drugs both psychologically and physiologically. By next-generation matrix method, we have found the basic reproduction number R_0, and this R_0 gives (or, is consistent with) the local and global stability conditions of the drug-free and drug addiction equilibria. It has been observed from numerical examples that if $R_0 < 1$, the system has only drug-free equilibrium and this equilibrium is stable (Figure 2). If $R_0 > 1$, the drug addiction equilibrium persists and locally stable (Figures 3–5). By analyzing sensitivity of parameters $\beta_1, \beta_2, \xi, \phi$, we have reached the conclusion that controlling the transmission of the synthetic drugs is better than providing treatment to the addicts. Therefore, we have designed a control strategy to prevent drug transmission. From Figure 6, it has also been found that by lowering the value of fractional order, susceptible and psychological addicted populations decrease but the physiological population and population in treatment class increase.

In the next section of this work, we have discussed an optimal control problem related to the drug abuse epidemic model where we have tried to minimize the drug-addicted population along with the cost of treatment. We have reformulated our model by considering the effect of "counseling and awareness campaigns" as control variable and calculated the total cost. Analytically, we have used Pontryagin's Principle for fractional calculus to determine the value optimal control parameter [45]. The analytical results and numerical simulations are quite relevant, and by the numerical computations we can deduce certain observations that have been discussed earlier.

Nowadays, an enormous number of the populace, particularly the young population, is presented to the universe of medications because of different reasons. For guiding purposes, we hope to hone in on those populaces. As by taking a gander at them as a helpless populace, it is easier to evaluate how to best acquaint normal guiding with the mental addicts in the general public through the model. Instructive foundations and families should remind adolescents about the significance of well-being training just as the Government needs to assume some responsibility to build mindfulness among the individuals. In goodness of missions and social projects, individuals may understand the human impacts of manufactured medications and decrease interest, which could prompt a lower contact rate. The proposed model shows the effect of guiding mental addicts through mathematical re-enactments. Besides, the result of an ideal reaction because of directing can limit the cost to, and quantity of, dependent people. The approach can limit the general monetary burden. In this circumstance, we ask a legitimate control strategy which will be powerful in the feeling of the study of disease transmission and financial matters.

Author Contributions: All the authors have participate equally in all the aspects of this paper: conceptualization, methodology, investigation, formal analysis, writing—original draft preparation, writing—review and editing. All authors have read and agreed to the published version of the manuscript.

Funding: This research was funded by the Spanish Government for its support through grant RTI2018-094336-B-100 (MCIU/AEI/FEDER, UE) and to the Basque Government for its support through grant IT1207-19.

Institutional Review Board Statement: Not applicable.

Informed Consent Statement: Not applicable.

Data Availability Statement: The data used to support the findings of this study are included in the references within the article.

Acknowledgments: The authors are grateful to the anonymous referees and Nemo Guan, Special Issue Editor, for their careful reading, valuable comments, and helpful suggestions, which have helped them to improve the presentation of this work significantly. The third author (Manuel De la Sen) is grateful to the Spanish Government for its support through grant RTI2018-094336-B-100 (MCIU/AEI/FEDER, UE) and to the Basque Government for its support through grant IT1207-19.

Conflicts of Interest: The authors declare no conflict of interest.

References

1. Creagh, S.; Warden, D.; Latif, M.A.; Paydar, A. The New Classes of Synthetic Illicit Drugs Can Significantly Harm the Brain: A Neuro Imaging Perspective with Full Review of MRI Findings. *Clin. Radiol Imaging J.* **2018**, *2*, 000116. [PubMed]
2. "WHAT IS A SYNTHETIC DRUG?" Foundation for a Drug-Free World. Available online: https://www.drugfreeworld.org/drugfacts/synthetic.html (accessed on 21 March 2020).
3. The Dangers of Synthetic Drugs. Psycom, University of California, Berkeley Health and Wellness Publications. Available online: https://www.psycom.net/the-dangers-of-synthetic-drugs (accessed on 21 March 2020).
4. Garten, R.; Lai, S.; Zhang, J. Rapid transmission of hepatitis C virus among young injecting heroin users in southern China. *Int. J. Epidemiol.* **2004**, *33*, 182–188. [CrossRef] [PubMed]
5. Kapp, C. *Crystal Meth Boom Adds to South Africa's Health Challenges*; Lancet: London, UK, 2008; Volume 37, pp. 193–194.
6. Avasthi, A.; Ghosh, A. Drug misuse in India: Where do we stand & where to go from here? *Indian J. Med. Res.* **2019**, *149*, 689–692. [CrossRef]
7. Ma, M.; Liu, S.; Xiang, H.; Li, J. Dynamics of synthetic drugs transmission model with psychological addicts and general incidence rate. *Phys. A Stat. Mech. Its Appl.* **2017**, *491*. [CrossRef]
8. Sharomi, O.; Gumel, A.B. Curtailing smoking dynamics: A mathematical modeling approach. *Appl. Math. Comput.* **2008**, *195*, 475–499. [CrossRef]
9. Nyabadza, F.; Njagarah, J.B.H.; Smith, R.J. Modelling the dynamics of crystal meth ('tik') abuse in the presence of drug-supply chain in South Africa. *Bull. Math. Biol.* **2013**, *75*, 24–28. [CrossRef]
10. Liu, P.; Zhang, L.; Xing, Y. Modelling and stability of a synthetic drugs transmission model with relapse and treatment. *J. Appl. Math. Comput.* **2019**, *60*, 465–484. [CrossRef]
11. Saha, S.; Samanta, G.P. Synthetic drugs transmission: Stability analysis and optimal control. *Lett. Biomath.* **2019**. [CrossRef]

12. Mainardi, F. On some properties of the Mittag-Leffler function $E_{\alpha,1}(-t^\alpha)$, completely monotone for $t > 0$ with $0 < \alpha < 1$. *Discret. Contin. Dyn. Syst. Ser. B* **2014**, *19*, 2267–2278. [CrossRef]
13. Podlubny, I. *Fractional Differential Equations*; Academic Press: San Diego, CA, USA, 1999.
14. Teodoro, G.S.; Machado, J.T.; de Oliveira, E.C. A review of definitions of fractional derivatives and other operators. *J. Comput Phys.* **2019**, *388*, 195–208. [CrossRef]
15. Du, M.; Wang, Z.; Hu, H. Measuring memory with the order of fractional derivative. *Sci Rep.* **2013**, *3*, 3431. [CrossRef]
16. Diethelm, K. Efficient Solution of Multi-Term Fractional Differential Equations Using P(EC)mE Methods. *Computing* **2003**, *71*, 305–319. [CrossRef]
17. Das, M.; Maiti, A.; Samanta, G.P. Stability analysis of a prey-predator fractional order model incorporating prey refuge. *Ecol. Genet. Genom.* **2018**, *7–8*, 33–46. [CrossRef]
18. Das, M.; Samanta, G.P. A prey-predator fractional order model with fear effect and group defense. *Int. J. Dyn. Control* **2020**. [CrossRef]
19. Das, M.; Samanta, G.P. A delayed fractional order food chain model with fear effect and prey refuge. *Math. Comput. Simul.* **2020**, *178*, 218–245. [CrossRef]
20. Das, M.; Samanta, G.P. Optimal Control of Fractional Order COVID-19 Epidemic Spreading in Japan and India 2020. *Biophys. Rev. Lett.* **2020**, *15*, 207–236. [CrossRef]
21. Das, M.; Samanta, G.P. Stability analysis of a fractional ordered COVID-19 model. *Comput. Math. Biophys.* **2021**, *9*, 22–45. [CrossRef]
22. Das, M.; Samanta, G.P. A Fractional Order COVID-19 Epidemic Transmission Model: Stability Analysis and Optimal Control (5 June 2020). Available online: https://ssrn.com/abstract=3635938 (accessed on 20 February 2021).
23. Area, I.; Batarfi, H.; Losada, J.; Nieto, J.J.; Shammakh, W.; Torres, A. On a fractional order Ebola epidemic model. *Adv. Diff. Equat.* **2015**, *278*. [CrossRef]
24. Agarwal, O.P. A general formulation and solution scheme for fractional optimal control problems. *Nonlinear Dyn.* **2004**, *38*, 323–337. [CrossRef]
25. Kheiri, H.; Jafari, M. Optimal control of a fractional order model for the HIV/AIDS epidemic. *Int. J. Biomath.* **2018**, *11*, 1850086. [CrossRef]
26. Kelly, A.; Carvalho, M.; Teljeur, C. *Prevalence of Opiate Use in Ireland 2006: A 3-Source Capture Recapture Study*; Report Submitted to the National Advisory Committee on Drugs Sub-Committee on Prevalence; Stationery Office: Dublin, Ireland, 2010.
27. Dokoumetzidis, A.; Magin, R.; Macheras, P. A commentary on fractionalization ofmulti-compartmental models. *J. Pharmacokinet Pharmacodyn* **2010**, *37*, 203–207. 9153-5. [CrossRef] [PubMed]
28. Petras, I. *Fractional-Order Nonlinear Systems: Modeling Aanlysis and Simulation*; Higher Education Press: Beijing, China, 2011.
29. Odibat, Z.; Shawagfeh, N. Generalized Taylor's formula. *Appl. Math. Comput.* **2007**, *186*, 286–293. [CrossRef]
30. Liang, S.; Wu, R.; Chen, L. Laplace transform of fractional order differential equations. *Electron. J. Differ. Equ.* **2015**, *2015*, 1–15.
31. Kexue, L.; Jigen, P. Laplace transform and fractional differential equations. *Appl. Math. Lett.* **2011**, *24*, 2019–2023. [CrossRef]
32. Li, Y.; Chen, Y.; Podlubny, I. Stability of fractional-order nonlinear dynamic systems: Lyapunov direct method and generalized Mittag-Leffler stability. *Comput. Math. Appl.* **2010**, *59*, 1810–1821. [CrossRef]
33. Haubold, H.J.; Mathai, A.M.; Saxena, R.K. Mittag-Leffler functions and their applications. *J. Appl. Math.* **2011**, *2011*, 298628. [CrossRef]
34. Van den Driessche, P.; Watmough, J. Reproduction numbers and sub-threshold endemic equilibria for compartmental models of disease transmission. *Math. Biosci.* **2002**, *180*, 29–48. [CrossRef]
35. Gaff, H.; Schaefer, E. Optimal control applied to vaccination and treatment strategies for various epidemiological models. *Math. Biosci. Eng.* **2009**, *6*, 469–492. [PubMed]
36. Kalula, A.S.; Nyabadza, F. A theoretical model for substance abuse in the presence of treatment. *S. Afr. J. Sci.* **2011**, *108*, 96–107.
37. Gelf, I.M.; Kapranov, M.M.; Zelevinsky, A.V. *Discriminants, Resultants, and Multidimensional Determinants*; Birkhäuser: Boston, MA, USA, 1994; ISBN 978-0-8176-3660-9.
38. Ahmed, E.; El-Sayed, A.M.A.; El-Saka, H. On some Routh-Hurwitz conditions for fractional order differential equations and their applications in Lorenz, Rössler, Chua and Chen systems. *Phys. Lett. A* **2006**, *358*, 1–4. [CrossRef]
39. Delavari, H.; Baleanu, D.; Sadati, J. Stability analysis of Caputo fractional-order non linear system revisited. *Nonlinear Dyn.* **2012**, *67*, 2433–2439. [CrossRef]
40. Tabatabaei, S.S.; Yazdanpanah, M.J.; Tavazoei, M.S. Formulation and Numerical Solution for Fractional Order Time Optimal Control Problem Using Pontryagin's Minimum Principle. *IFAC-PapersOnLine* **2017**, *50*, 9224–9229. doi:10.1016/j.ifacol.2017.08.1280. [CrossRef]
41. Guo, T.L. The Necessary Conditions of Fractional Optimal Control in the Sense of Caputo. *J. Optim. Theory Appl.* **2013**, *156*, 115–126. [CrossRef]
42. Garrappa, R. On linear stability of predictor-corrector algorithms for fractional differential equations. *Internat. J. Comput. Math.* **2010**, *87*, 2281–2290. [CrossRef]
43. Diethelm, K.; Ford, N.J.; Freed, A.D. A Predictor-Corrector Approach for the Numerical Solution of Fractional Differential Equations. *Nonlinear Dyn.* **2002**, *29*, 3. [CrossRef]

44. Cao, X.; Datta, A.; Al Basir, F. Fractional-order model of the disease Psoriasis: A control based mathematical approach. *J. Syst. Sci. Complex* **2016**, *29*, 1565–1584. [CrossRef]
45. Kamocki, R. Pontryagin maximum principle for fractional ordinary optimal control problems. *Math. Methods Appl. Sci.* **2014**, *37*. [CrossRef]

MDPI
St. Alban-Anlage 66
4052 Basel
Switzerland
Tel. +41 61 683 77 34
Fax +41 61 302 89 18
www.mdpi.com

Mathematics Editorial Office
E-mail: mathematics@mdpi.com
www.mdpi.com/journal/mathematics

www.ingramcontent.com/pod-product-compliance
Lightning Source LLC
LaVergne TN
LVHW070438100526
838202LV00014B/1622